The Oldest Old

The Oldest Old

Edited by

RICHARD M. SUZMAN, PH.D.
National Institute on Aging,
National Institutes of Health

DAVID P. WILLIS, M.P.H.
Milbank Memorial Fund

KENNETH G. MANTON, PH.D.
Center for Demographic Studies
Duke University

New York   Oxford
OXFORD UNIVERSITY PRESS
1992

Oxford University Press

Oxford New York Toronto
Delhi Bombay Calcutta Madras Karachi
Kuala Lumpur Singapore Hong Kong Tokyo
Nairobi Dar es Salaam Cape Town
Melbourne Auckland

and associated companies in
Berlin Ibadan

Published by Oxford University Press, Inc.,
200 Madison Avenue, New York, New York 10016

Oxford is a registered trademark of Oxford University Press

Library of Congress Cataloging-in-Publication Data
The Oldest old / edited by Richard M. Suzman, David P. Willis,
Kenneth G. Manton.
p. cm. Includes bibliographical references.
Includes index.
ISBN 0-19-505060-6
1. Aged—Services for—United States. 2. Aged—United States—
Social conditions. 3. Social work with the aged—United States.
4. Aged—Long term care—United States. I. Suzman, Richard M.
II. Willis, David P. III. Manton, Kenneth G.
[DNLM: 1. Aged, 80 and Over. WT 100 044]
HV1461.044 1992
305.26'0973—dc20 DNLM/DLC 90-14340

9 8 7 6 5 4 3 2 1

Printed in the United States of America
on acid-free paper

Acknowledgments

In preparing this volume, the editors aimed at the highest standard of peer-reviewed papers and we are grateful to the following experts who acted as referees on the prospective chapters: John Beck, Lisa Berkman, Laurence Branch, Elaine Brody, Robert Clark, Ansley Coale, Eileen Crimmins, Thomas Espenshade, Jacob Feldman, James Fries, Alan Garber, Ernest Gruenberg, Barry Gurland, Jared Jobe, Stanislas Kasl, Sidney Katz, Lawrence Kotlikoff, Leonard Kurland, Charles Longino, Jennifer Madans, George Maddox, John McKinlay, Constance Nathanson, S. Jay Olshansky, Teresa Radebaugh, Dorothy Rice, William Satariano, William Serow, Conrad Taeuber, Sharon Tennstedt, Lois Verbrugge, Lon White, and David Wise. We are also equally grateful to Matilda White Riley, who was central to the original conceptualization of this volume, and to Mercedes Bern-Klug, Kristen Brocking, Vicki Freedman, and Elaine McMichael, without whom it could not have been brought to completion.

Contents

IV THE DYNAMICS OF BECOMING THE OLDEST OLD

V A SOCIAL PORTRAIT OF THE OLDEST OLD

VI SOCIAL AND MEDICAL POLICY TOWARD THE OLDEST OLD

Contributors

Marilyn S. Albert, Ph.D.
Department of Psychiatry
Massachusetts General Hospital
Boston, MA 02114

G. Lawrence Atkins, Ph.D.
Winthrop, Stimson, Putnam & Roberts
Washington, DC 20036

Laurel A. Beckett, Ph.D.
Department of Biostatistics
Harvard School of Public Health
Boston, MA 02115

Lisa F. Berkman, Ph.D.
Department of Epidemiology and Public
   Health
Yale University School of Medicine
New Haven, CT 06510

Robert H. Binstock, Ph.D.
School of Medicine
Case Western Reserve University
Cleveland, OH 44106

Laurence G. Branch, Ph.D.
Boston University School of Medicine
Boston, MA 02118

Marilyn J. Chown, M.P.H
Department of Biostatistics
Harvard School of Public Health,
Boston, MA 02115

Patricia L. Colsher, Ph.D.
Dept. of Preventive Medicine and
   Environmental Health
University of Iowa
Iowa City, IA 52242

Nancy R. Cook, Sc.D.
Brigham and Women's Hospital
Brookline, MA 02146

Joan C. Cornoni-Huntley, Ph.D.
National Institute on Aging, NIH
Bethesda, MD 20205

Pamela J. Doty, Ph.D.
Office of the Assistant Secretary
   for Planning and Evaluation
Department of Health and Human
   Services
Washington, DC 20201

Denis A. Evans, M.D.
Director, Center for Research on Health
   and Aging
Rush-Presbyterian–St. Luke's Medical
   Center
Chicago, IL 60612

Daniel J. Foley, M.S.
National Institute on Aging, NIH
Bethesda, MD 20205

H. Harris Funkenstein, M.D.*
Brigham and Women's Hospital, and
Harvard Medical School
Boston, MA 02115
*Deceased (May 4, 1990)

Rose C. Gibson, Ph.D.
Institute for Social Research
University of Michigan
Ann Arbor, MI 48106-1248

Evan C. Hadley, M.D.
National Institute on Aging, NIH
Bethesda, MD 20892

Tamara Harris, M.D., M.S.
National Center for Health Statistics
Department of Health and Human
   Services
Hyattsville, MD 20782

Liesi E. Hebert, Sc.D.
Channing Laboratory
Boston, MA 02115

Charles H. Hennekens, M.D.
Brigham & Women's Hospital
Brookline, MA 02146

A. Regula Herzog, Ph.D.
Institute for Social Research
University of Michigan
Ann Arbor, MI 48106-1248

James S. Jackson, Ph.D.
Institute for Social Research
University of Michigan
Ann Arbor, MI 48106-1248

Kevin G. Kinsella, M.A.
Center for International Research
U.S. Bureau of the Census
Washington, DC 20233

Frank J. Kohout, Ph.D.
CHSR
University of Iowa
Iowa City, IA 52242

Mary Grace Kovar, Dr.P.H.
National Center for Health Statistics,
Centers for Disease Control
Hyattsville, MD 20782

Kenneth G. Manton, Ph.D.
Center for Demographic Studies
Duke University
Durham, NC 27706

George C. Myers, Ph.D.
Center for Demographic Studies
Duke University
Durham, NC 27706

Samuel H. Preston, Ph.D.
Population Studies Center
University of Pennsylvania
Philadelphia, PA 19104–6298

Willard L. Rodgers, Ph.D.
Institute for Social Research
University of Michigan
Ann Arbor, MI 48106-1248

Ira Rosenwaike, Ph.D.
Graduate School of Social Work
University of Pennsylvania
Philadelphia, PA 19104-6214

Paul A. Scherr, Ph.D., D.Sc.
Division of General Medicine
University of Massachusetts Medical
  School
Worcester, MA 01655

Beth J. Soldo, Ph.D.
Department of Demography
Georgetown University
Washington, DC 20057

Robyn I. Stone, Dr.P.H.
Center for Health Affairs, Project HOPE
Chevy Chase, MD 20815

Richard M. Suzman, Ph.D.
National Institute on Aging, NIH
Bethesda, MD 20892

Cynthia M. Taeuber, M.A.
Population Division
U.S. Bureau of the Census
Washington, DC 20233

James O. Taylor, M.D.
East Boston Neighborhood Health Center
East Boston, MA 02128

Barbara Boyle Torrey, M.A.
Center for International Research
U.S. Bureau of the Census
Washington, DC 20233

Robert B. Wallace, M.D., M.Sc.
Dept. of Preventive Medicine &
  Environmental Health
University of Iowa
Iowa City, IA 52242

Richard Weindruch, Ph.D.
Department of Medicine
University of Wisconsin at Madison
Madison, WI 53706

Terrie T. Wetle, Ph.D.
Institute of Living
Hartford, CT 06106

Lon R. White, M.D., M.P.H.
National Institute on Aging NIH
Kuakini Medical Center
Honolulu, HI 96817

David P. Willis, M.P.H
Agency for Health Care Policy and Research and National Institute on Aging, NIH
(formerly Milbank Memorial Fund)

I

INTRODUCTION

1

Introducing the Oldest Old

RICHARD M. SUZMAN, KENNETH G. MANTON,
and DAVID P. WILLIS

This volume has had a long and deliberate maturation. It began, most immediately, with a session organized by Matilda White Riley and Richard Suzman for the May 1984 annual meeting of the American Association for the Advancement of Science. For the title of that session, they coined the term "oldest old," a refinement of Bernice Neugarten's earlier "old old" (see Chapter 19, this volume), to denote those aged 85 years and over. The papers presented and the ensuing discussion called attention to wide-ranging philosophical, social, economic, political, and service-related implications of the dramatic demographic changes that were then only beginning to be recognized. A selection of papers from that session was revised, expanded, and supplemented with additional papers for a special issue of the *Milbank Memorial Fund Quarterly* (63:2, 1985). The publication proved highly successful. The publicity engendered by it, including front-page *New York Times, Wall Street Journal,* and *Washington Post* news stories, boosted consciousness not only in academic and research settings, but also within the federal statistical and policy-making systems. The present editors decided to revise and update a critical selection of these articles and to add major new contributions to fill in the many gaps in the 1985 volume.

GENESIS OF THIS VOLUME

A leitmotiv permeated the 1985 presentations. The absence of adequate data allowed for only tentative and sometimes hesitant conclusions on nationally important topics and limited serious population-based research. Riley and Suzman predicted that because a concerted effort was just getting underway to collect, tabulate, and distribute significant data on the oldest old, there would be a mushrooming, albeit from a small base, of knowledge about this special population. Now, 6 years later, it is evident that there have been significant, even if still limited, gains. We no longer, for example, have to infer the dynamics of disability solely from cross-sectional data; longitudinal data on transitions in health and functional status are becoming available (see Chapters 10 and 14, this volume). The emerging availability of data on the oldest-old population has been a driving force behind analyses leading to new insights; yet the leitmotiv persists (see Chapters 9, 13, and 15, this volume).

This book has an even older genesis, however, reflecting the development of a research initiative at the National Institute on Aging (NIA). This initiative grew out of the identification of unanticipated declines in mortality and increases in the number of the very old, as demonstrated in the research of several NIA grantees, including Ira Rosenwaike, Eileen Crimmins, and Kenneth Manton. Each of these researchers observed the decline in mortality at advanced ages well before the Social Security Administration took official note. NIA set up an informal working group to pool information about this special population and to establish a research agenda to guide future activities. The activities of the working group coincided fortuitously with meetings held by the Senate Finance Committee to examine underestimates by the Social Security Administration of the growth of the very old population and how those underestimates had contributed to 1982 and 1983 crises in the Social Security Trust Fund.

The Senate Appropriations Committee recognized the significance of the rapid growth of the oldest-old population and earmarked funds in the fiscal year 1984 NIA budget for research on this group. The NIA made this initiative one of its highest priorities. The session at the American Association for the Advancement of Science and the *Milbank* publication were major activities that resulted from the initiative.

Thereafter, research interest in the newly discovered age group—85 and over—grew rapidly. The NIA working group on the development of new data bases on the oldest old continued, and can be counted as a progenitor of the Federal Interagency Forum on Aging-related Statistics, an organization of over 30 federal agencies initiated to increase coordination of federal data collection efforts. Reports from Congress, the Bureau of the Census, the National Center for Health Statistics, and other components of the Department of Health and Human Services began to provide at least limited data for the 85+ age group. Investigators and analysts in the field organized conferences and symposia, and produced companion volumes on improving the methodologies for forecasting life and active life expectancy (Manton, Singer, and Suzman), estimating the limits to human life expectancy (Johansson and Wachter) and the compression of morbidity (Rice and Haan 1991).

The significant and unprecedented methodological problems that must be overcome in order to study the oldest old successfully (see Chapters 5 to 7, this volume), coupled with a shortage of research funds, limited the number of new research projects. However, over the course of the last 6 years, a number of projects have been initiated. Some of the most significant research findings from those projects are incorporated in the chapters in this volume. Below we summarize several of the basic dimensions involved in assessing the size and nature of the oldest-old population, dimensions that tie together various chapters of the book.

SIZE OF THE POPULATION

Given current mortality levels and the increasing size of birth cohorts—especially the post–World War II baby-boom cohorts of 1946 to 1963—the oldest-old population will grow dramatically in the future. The principal question in projecting the rate of growth is, "How will mortality for the oldest old decline in the future?" The answer will determine whether the growth of the oldest-old population will be merely substantial or phenomenal.

Interestingly, although we are currently concerned with the growth of the population aged 85 and older, Chapter 2 of this volume suggests even faster relative rates of growth for both the population aged 90 and over and centenarians. The change in mortality rates at those very advanced ages, let alone for those over age 85, is hard to project even 15 to 30 years in the future. This is because we lack significant experience with such extremely elderly groups, so that the simple extrapolation methods often relied upon in making official projections break down for these groups.

This is illustrated in Figure 1–1, where we present Census Bureau (Spencer 1989) estimates of the number of oldest old in 1990 (about 3.3 million) and several projections of the size of this population in 2040.

The projections represent both the middle and high variants of the Census Bureau's official projections based on extrapolation techniques and two alternative projections based on research on health and mortality changes in the oldest old. The first, from Guralnik, Yanagishita, and Schneider (1988), assumed a continuation of recent past rates of mortality decline (about 2 percent per year). This produced large increases over even the high variant projections made by the Census Bureau (i.e., 23.5 million versus the high census variant of 17.9 million in 2040) because the Census Bureau, after determining recent rates of cause-specific mortality decline, tapered those rates to conservative "ultimate" rates of decline about 25 years in the future.

The projections by Manton, Stallard, and Singer (1992) represent extreme upper bounds to the potential growth of the oldest-old population based on data from longitudinal epidemiological studies of the dynamics of the relation of a number of known risk factors to chronic disease morbidity and mortality. These projections, although clearly making highly optimistic assumptions about future mortality reductions, serve to sensitize us to the possibility of a more rapid growth of the oldest-old population than is envisioned either by even the highest variants of official projection

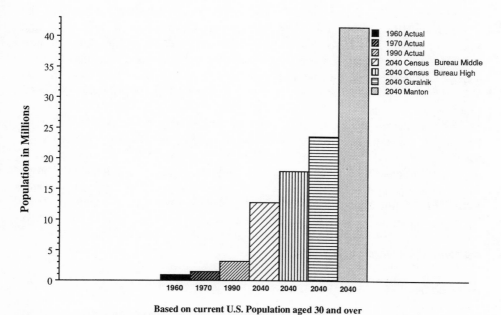

Based on current U.S. Population aged 30 and over

Figure 1–1 Forecasts of the U.S. population age 85 and over.

series or by extrapolation of current experience. Even though the assumptions about the ability of individuals to improve their health by controlling lifestyle and other risk factors are extreme, the projections make no assumptions about changes in cause-specific case mortality rates or the basic rates of aging. The possibility of changes in both types of rates has been suggested, for example, in very early trials of human growth factor and in several studies of the ability to intervene in such basic degenerative processes as osteoporosis (Johansson and Wachter 1988; Schneider and Brody 1983; Chapter 16, this volume).

The point of the extreme projections is that they envision alternative futures where basic turning points in our ability to control disease *and* degenerative changes of aging may occur. Such changes are currently speculative, so that their inclusion in official projection series may not be warranted. Nonetheless, the possibility of such changes occurring in 10 to 20 years is real, and we must begin at least to make contingency plans for them.

UNIQUENESS OF THE POPULATION

Apart from its small (but rapidly growing) size, the oldest-old population is very dissimilar to the population that (as every chapter in this volume demonstrates) has more recently passed into official old age, say, 65 to 69. The population aged 85 and over has a much greater excess of females over males than any other age group. These persons have much higher levels of morbidity and disability than those aged 65 to 69. The mix of medical conditions that afflicts them differs substantially from that of the "young old," and they are much more likely to have extensive comorbidity. They are currently much more likely to be living in institutions, less likely to be married, and are more likely to have low educational attainment. Their needs, capacities, and resources are different. They consume amounts of services, benefits, and transfers far out of proportion to their numbers. In New York City, for example, the oldest old in 1988 accounted for over 4 percent of all general hospital discharges and almost 8 percent of total patient days. One-quarter of Medicare payments to hospitals that year were on behalf of these patients (United Hospital Fund, personal communication). Indeed, because of their special needs, they receive a significant fraction of *all* federal benefits, services, and transfer payments provided to those over age 65 (see Chapter 18, this volume).

Differences within the elderly population have become so marked that it is no longer useful to treat all elderly—those aged 65 and over—as a single category, as has been done in the past (see, e.g., Moon and Sawhill [1983] on recent gains in income of the elderly in relation to those of their children). Such collapsing of some 35 or more years into a single age category, especially during a period in which restructuring of the Medicare system is being debated, is prejudicial to an understanding of the emerging facts. Even Shakespeare—although his universe of very elderly acquaintances must have been small—allocated two of the "seven ages of man" to old age and the differences within it.

HETEROGENEITY OF THE POPULATION

Even within the population aged 85 and over there is pronounced diversity. Many oldest-old people still function effectively, although others have outlived their social and financial supports and are dependent upon society for their daily living. Although nearly one-fourth of the oldest old are institutionalized (see Chapter 18, this volume), a substantial proportion report some limitation in activity or difficulty in performing personal-care activities (see Chapters 10 and 12, this volume), and significant numbers have some degree of cognitive impairment (see Chapter 13, this volume), more optimistic information is emerging. Preoccupation with disability and mortality has concealed the fact that the majority of those aged 80 and over continue to reside in the community, with most caring for themselves and living relatively independent lives (see Chapter 14, this volume). More than one-third of those aged 80 and over in the community report their health to be excellent or very good; 40 percent report no activity limitation (see Chapter 16, this volume). Of those aged 85 and over, 51 percent (47.2 percent of females and 60.1 of males) report that they can perform seven personal care activities such as bathing and dressing (activities of daily living, or ADLs) without difficulty (Dawson, Hendershot, and Fulton 1987). Somewhat smaller percentages (39.5 percent of females and 44.8 of males) also have no difficulty with six home management activities (instrumental activities of daily living, or IADLs), including managing money and shopping (Dawson, Hendershot and Fulton 1987). Furthermore, as described in Chapter 16 of this volume, a surprising proportion of those aged 80 and over are physically robust, that is, able to perform at even higher levels of functioning than represented by ADLs and IADLs. Prevailing images of all the oldest old—"mere oblivion, sans teeth, sans eyes, sans taste, sans everything" (Shakespeare, *As You Like It*)—are clearly *not* supported by the evidence.

CHANGING NATURE OF THIS POPULATION

The population of the oldest old does not have fixed limits; its members die and are replaced by oncoming cohorts, each having grown older in its own slice of historical time. Because of the interplay between societal change and the aging process, the composition and nature of the oldest-old category will continue to change rapidly. In regard to educational attainment, for example, the gap between the oldest old and the younger population is narrowing and is expected to be nearly closed in the next decade or two. The very old will be succeeded by better-educated, more recent birth cohorts. Even today, in the cohorts reaching ages 55 to 64, the proportion that has completed high school is nearly equal to that of the younger population (Taeuber 1983; Chapter 3, this volume). There are also indications that recent cohorts are more aware of their own future course of well-being and of the importance of the primary prevention of chronic disease. For example, in regard to one of the most potent health risk factors—cigarette smoking—each successive cohort of adult males in the United States is less likely than its predecessors to smoke. Even the most recent cohorts of women have begun to follow this declining pattern (Riley 1981; see also Feinleib et al. 1970; Harris 1983). It is also clear that successive cohorts will differ markedly in diet, exercise, standard of living, medical care, and experience with chronic versus acute diseases.

Furthermore (as discussed in Chapters 10, 14, 15, 17, and 18, this volume), the interwoven factors of marital status, fertility, kinship status, race, and living arrangements are important determinants of income, formal care received, and usage of long-term care by the oldest old. However, changes in the family occasioned by

increases in longevity, changing birth and divorce rates, and the increasing participation of mature women in the labor force all presage major changes for the status
and care of the oldest old (see Riley 1981). These changes are almost universal.
Even in Japan—where Respect for Elders Day continues to be celebrated after 300
years (Lock 1984; Palmore and Maeda 1985), where less than 2 percent of the elderly
live in some kind of institution (Daisaku 1980), and where 9 out of 10 of the physically and cognitively impaired elderly are cared for solely by family members (Campbell 1984)—newer cohorts are experiencing old age in different ways (Lock 1984;
Ohnuki-Tierney 1984; Samuma 1978). The possibility of dramatic changes in Japanese society is evidenced by the unprecedented levels of life expectancy observed in
Japan: 75.8 years for males and 81.9 years for females (World Health Organization
1989). These values approach or surpass the *absolute* limits of life expectancy assumed in national economic studies of the impact of aging reported in 1982 (i.e.,
77.3 years for males, to be achieved in 1998; 81.7 years for females, to be achieved
in 2000; Ogawa 1982). Thus, the estimates of the impact of aging on the Japanese
economy and culture identified in those detailed studies have, in only 8 years, become obsolete.

One can only speculate on the precise number, direction, pace, and synergistic
effects of such social and demographic changes for future cohorts in the U.S. population. It is even more difficult to estimate how these matters will be exacerbated or
modified by changes in the technological and legal milieus. Recent passage of the
Americans with Disabilities Act is a timely case in point. When the act is fully
implemented, both present and future cohorts of the oldest old will be affected. Early
disability-related retirement from the work force, with its attendant consequences for
physical, psychosocial, and economic well-being as one ages, may become a less
frequent occurrence. And those who are disabled, at whatever age, are less likely to
be isolated because of transportation and architectural barriers.

HOW HEALTHY WILL THEY BE?

Perhaps the most critical question for the future is, "How healthy will the oldest old
be?" How is the postponement of mortality in successive cohorts related to the morbidity of the survivors (see Chapter 10, this volume)? To what extent is there a
tendency simply to sustain life in those disabled older people who, under earlier
circumstances, would have been winnowed from the cohort through death (see the
discussion of Gruenberg 1977; see also Feldman 1983; Riley and Bond 1983)?

Much turns on this question of the health status of the future oldest old. A striking example relates to the structure of a future national long-term-care system, one
of the central national policy issues of our day. In fiscal terms, the potential costs of
meeting future needs for long-term care are staggering. The order of magnitude of
these costs will be materially affected by both the pace at which mortality rates at
older ages fall and the relative trends in disability-free and disabled life expectancy
at older ages. How these forces have played out over the last two decades is the
subject of active research. Because of the dynamic nature of disability and its relation
to mortality, new time-weighted concepts of health and functioning are required. One
such concept, active life expectancy, is traceable to earlier work done at the National

Center for Health Statistics on developing time-weighted measures of health (e.g., Sullivan 1971). More recently, such measures have been used to assess changes in functioning among the elderly (e.g., Nihon University 1982; Robine et al. 1989; Wilkins and Adams 1983). Most recently, active life-expectancy measures have been used to characterize the health and functioning of the oldest-old population, although, given the rapid changes in health at that advanced age, the high rate of comorbidity, and the complex and dynamic nature of disability, considerable methodological research on the way such measures are constructed, and the nature of the data needed to estimate them, is required.

The concept of active life expectancy has been used to evaluate functional status at advanced ages because of the high correlation of functional status and mortality. Early efforts to apply active life expectancy concepts were subject to methodological limitations in that disability was viewed as a discrete state with a clearly defined threshold and always progressive (e.g., Katz et al. 1983). For example, Chapter 13 in this volume shows that an important component of disability among the oldest old is due to cognitive impairment—a component of disability not directly represented in the study by Katz et al.

Manton and Soldo, in Chapter 10 of this volume, show that disability is a graded concept that involves *multiple* physical as well as cognitive dimensions and that, in addition to representing the health and functional status of the population, active life-expectancy concepts are important in estimating the need for long-term care.

To contrast old and new measures of functional ability in the oldest old, we present two figures. In Figure 1–2 the growth of persons in three broad functional states—institutionalized, chronically disabled community residents, and those with no serious chronic disability—is presented.

The proportions of the elderly population needing institutional and home care are increasing because of the relatively more rapid growth of the oldest-old population. It is important to remember, though, that institutionalization is not so much a decision determined by medical necessity as it is a social accommodation. These figures, however, only represent the problems cross-sectionally and without accommodating individual age-dependent dynamics.

The dynamics of disability influence not only the number of persons requiring long-term-care services but also the intensity, duration, and types of services needed (e.g., Densen 1987). There are large numbers of disabled elderly persons who will be able to be maintained in the community—possibly with less expensive assistive devices than with continuing personal care. This may be critical as the availability of informal caregivers decreases in the future due to smaller family sizes and as female labor-force participation increases. Also of importance, especially for designing private long-term-care products, is the ''turnover'' of disabled persons; recent data suggest that the average duration of disability may be less than is typically assumed (e.g., Manton et al. 1990). This is an important factor in designing private insurance eligibility and benefits and in designing data collection for the oldest old. Such dynamics are represented in Figure 1–3, where we present the number of years that can be expected to be lived in several impaired, institutional, and active states—both at age 65 and at age 85.

The figure presents estimates for a cohort where disability and mortality interact over time. One can see that, for both males and females, the proportion of the re-

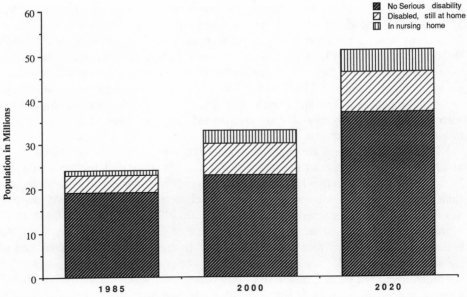

Figure 1–2 Disability among older people: projections for the population aged 65 and older. (Source: Data from Manton, Stallard, and Woodbury 1991.)

maining life expectancy in institutional residence or in a disabled state increases significantly from age 65 to 85. It is also clear, however, that a large proportion of the remaining life expectancy at age 85 is projected to be spent in an active state.

Perhaps among the most exciting results to date of research on the oldest old is the finding that disability changes in both directions; in other words, there is a high rate of functional improvement that compensates, in part, for the high incidence of disability (see Chapter 16, this volume). An important task of future research on the oldest old will be to identify the risk factors for both the prevention and amelioration of functional impairment among the oldest old. Significant epidemiological evidence is emerging on what some of these risk factors are for certain important disabling conditions (e.g., osteoporosis, non-Alzheimer's dementia, osteoarthritis, chronic heart failure). This research needs to be extended and more trials undertaken of interventions focused specifically on the oldest old. It is no longer feasible for health and social policy to accept disability as an inevitable, permanent, or residual state *at any age*.

The ability to prevent or reduce disability at advanced ages will play a prominent role in our future ability to cope with the growth of the oldest-old population. This raises the issue of whether the "compression of morbidity" concept advanced by many authors can be practically implemented at the population level. Some investigators suggest that early evidence indicates an addition to disabled states (Gruenberg 1977; Wilkins and Adams 1983); others note contrary trends (Fries 1983). Recent findings from the 1989 third wave of the National Long Term Care Survey (NLTCS) suggest that the weight of current evidence has shifted toward the side of guarded optimism (Manton, Corder, and Stallard 1992). Most notably, the rate of disablement for those over age 65 is declining. The 65 and over population grew 14.7 percent

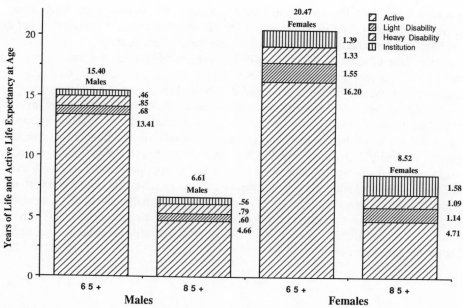

Figure 1–3 United States active and disabled life expectancy estimates. (Source: National Long-term Care Survey 1982/1984, Medicare Files 1982–86)

between 1982 and 1989, but the proportion of the 65 and over population that had chronic disability, or were institutionalized, increased only 9.3 percent, just 63 percent as fast. Moreover, the reductions in the rate of disablement were significant at all ages above 65 and were proportionately greatest above age 85.

There is also considerable debate on the future direction of life expectancy at extreme ages (Olshansky, Carnes, and Cassel 1990). After a static period from 1981 to 1988, mortality rates above age 85 have begun to fall sharply (Manton 1992). The recently discovered decline in disability may presage even greater future declines in mortality. As noted earlier, small increases in life expectancy at advanced ages lead to very large increases in the size of this population. A number of investigators (e.g., Lee and Carter 1990; Ahlburg and Vaupel 1990; Manton, Stallard, and Singer 1992) project that the growth of the oldest-old population may exceed even the most extreme federal projections. Major national policy issues—especially the structure and financing of the Social Security and Medicare systems, and the magnitude of long-term-care needs—will be affected.

INTERNATIONAL COMPARISONS

Although the oldest old have often been ignored in the rest of the world, as in the United States, their number and projected growth rate are causing their visibility to increase. If the oldest old are defined as those aged 80 and over, this age group constitutes 14 percent of the world's older population—19 percent in developed and 11 percent in developing societies (see Chapter 4, this volume). Nine countries (in order of magnitude, the United States, China, the Soviet Union, India, Japan, West Germany, France, the United Kingdom, and Italy) had more than 1 million octagenarians in 1985, with 18 countries expected to exceed this number by 2025 (see Chapter 2, this volume). The rapid growth of the oldest-old population is not restricted to the United States and is the fastest-growing portion of the elderly population in many countries (see Chapter 4, this volume). The authors of this chapter note, however, that by the year 2005, the United States will have the highest percentage of octagenarians of any country (today it is exceeded only by France and West Germany).

Escalating demands for health services caused by the growth of the oldest involve both long-term-care and acute-care health services (see Chapter 11, this volume). Cross-national comparisons of health service use in relation to aging can help distinguish "malleable" from "nonmalleable" factors for health policy. Such research may also help resolve policy dilemmas such as the appropriate balance of institutional and noninstitutional long-term-care services and the relative role of government and family support systems. In Chapter 11, Doty's cross-national analyses of the relationship between increasing age and the use of hospitals, physician services, and nursing homes show significant variation, with some industrialized countries having much higher use rates than others.

IMPLICATIONS FOR DATA AND RESEARCH

Regardless of the directions of future change, the pace of current change is so rapid that there is good reason to argue that the time between the decennial censuses is much too long to capture the changing characteristics of the oldest old and that interstitial surveys are essential. For example, life expectancy at age 85 is currently 5 to 6 years (National Center for Health Statistics 1990), so that two entire cohorts of the oldest old can experience significant health changes and substantial mortality between censuses. It is also clear that different morbid processes proceed at very different rates, with some being rapidly progressive. Surveys—our principal source of data on the population—must be designed to sample events at shorter temporal intervals; this is even more critical at advanced than at younger ages (see Chapter 5, this volume). Paralleling the need for more frequent and more focused surveys is the requirement for better sampling procedures and more sensitive survey instruments. In Chapter 15 of this volume, Gibson and Jackson examine the special problems of obtaining sufficient numbers of racial or ethnic minorities in surveys of the oldest old at *any* periodicity. For any cohort, their "slice of historical time" will have generated markedly different life courses and health states. Once they are adequately represented in survey samples, new techniques and instruments will be required to capture the health and social dynamics among those aged 85 and over (see Chapters 6, 7, 12, and 13, this volume).

There is good reason to argue also that chronological age in itself, although once a useful proxy indicator of characteristics and functioning, is becoming an increasingly imperfect measure that can trap us in dysfunctional metaphors and stereotypes (see Chapter 19, this volume). It is likely that in the future, as successive cohorts age in different ways—physiologically and socially—the definition of the oldest old will more appropriately be advanced to be those over age 90 (or even 100). Thus, perhaps the most optimistic outcome of the considerable research that has begun is that, in the future, chronological age will cease to be one of the socially defined categories used to limit individual potentials—even at the most advanced ages.

REFERENCES

Ahlburg, D.A. and J.W. Vaupel. 1990. Alternative Projections of the U.S. Population. *Demography* 27:639–52.

Campbell, R. 1984. Nursing Homes and Long-Term Care in Japan. *Pacific Affairs* 57:78–89.

Dawson, D., G. Hendershot, and J. Fulton. 1987. Aging in the Eighties: Functional Limitations of Individuals Age 65 Years and Over. Advance Data No. 33, National Center for Health Statistics.

Densen, P.M. 1987. The Elderly and the Health Care System: Another Perspective. *Milbank Quarterly* 65:614–38.

Feldman, J.J. 1983. Work Ability of the Aged Under Conditions of Improving Mortality. *Milbank Memorial Fund Quarterly* 61:430–44.

Feinleib, M., R.J. Garrison, L. Stollones, W.B. Kannel, W.P. Castelli, and P.M. McNamara. 1970. A Comparison of Blood Pressure, Total Cholesterol and Cigarette Smoking in Parents in 1950 and Their Children in 1970. *American Journal of Epidemiology* 110:291–303.

Fries, J.F. 1983. The Compression of Morbidity. *Milbank Memorial Fund Quarterly* 61:397–419.

Gruenberg, E.M. 1977. The Failures of Success. *Milbank Memorial Fund Quarterly* 55:3–24.

Guralnik, J.M., M. Yanagishita, and E.L. Schneider. 1988. Projecting the Older Population of the United States: Lessons from the Past and Prospects for the Future. *The Milbank Quarterly* 66:283–308.

Harris, J.E. 1983. Cigarette Smoking and Successive Birth Cohorts of Men and Women in the United States during 1900–80. *Journal of the National Cancer Institute* 71:473–79.

Johansson, R.S., K. Wachter. (Organizers). 1988. *Aging and Dying: The Biological Foundations of Human Longevity.* Workshop on Estimating an Upper Limit to Human Life Expectancy, sponsored by the National Institute on Aging, University of California at Berkeley, April 28.

Katz, S., L.G. Branch, M.H. Branson, J.A. Papsidero, J.C. Beck, and D.S. Greer. 1983. Active Life Expectancy. *New England Journal of Medicine* 309:1218–23.

Lee, R.D. and L. Carter. 1990. Modeling and Forecasting U.S. Mortality. Paper presented at the Population Association of America, Toronto, May 4.

Lock, M.M. 1984. East Asian Medicine and Health Care for the Japanese Elderly. *Pacific Affairs* 57:65–73.

Maeda, D. 1980. Japan. In: *International Handbook on Aging,* E. Palmore, ed., 253–270. Westport, Conn: Greenwood Press.

Manton, K.G. 1991. The Dynamics of Population Aging: Demography and Policy Analysis. *Milbank Quarterly* 69:309–338.

Manton, K.G., L.S. Corder, and E. Stallard. 1992. Health and Functional Changes in the U.S. Elderly Population 1982 to 1989: Evidence from the National Long Term Care Survey. *Journal of the American Medical Association,* in review.

Manton, K.G., and E. Stallard. 1992. Incorporating Risk Factors into the Projections of the Size and Health Status of the U.S. Elderly Population. In *Forecasting the Health of the Old,* eds. K. G. Manton, B. Singer, and R. M. Suzman. New York: Springer-Verlag.

Manton, K.G., E. Stallard, and B.H. Singer. 1992. Projecting the Future Size and Health Status of the U.S. Elderly Population. *International Journal of Forecasting,* in review.

Manton, K.G., E. Stallard, and M.A. Woodbury. 1991. A Multivariate Event History Model Based upon Fuzzy States: Estimation from Longitudinal Surveys with Informative Non-response. *Journal of Official Statistics (Stockholm, Sweden).*

Moon, M., and I.V. Sawhill. 1983. Family Incomes: Gainers and Losers. In *The Reagan Record,* eds. J.L. Palmer and I.V. Sawhill, 317–44. 1990. Cambridge, Mass., Ballinger.

National Center for Health Statistics. 1990. *Vital Statistics of the United States, 1987,* Vol. II, Sec. 6, Life Tables. DHHS pub. no. (PHS) 90-1104. Hyattsville, Md.: Public Health Service.

Nihon University. 1982. *Population Aging in Japan: Problems and Policy Issues in the 21st Century,* ed. T. Kuroda. International Conference on an Aging Society: Strategies for 21st Century Japan, Nihon University, November 24–27. Tokyo: Nihon University Population Research Institute.

Ogawa, N. 1982. Japan's Limits to Growth and Welfare. In *Population Aging in Japan: Problems and Policy Issues in 21st Century,* ed. T. Kuroda, 3- to 3-28. International Symposium on an Aging Society: Strategies for 21st Century Japan, November 24–27. Tokyo: Nihon University. Population Research Institute.

Ohnuki-Tierney, E. 1984. *Illness and Culture in Contemporary Japan.* New York: Cambridge University Press.

Olshansky, S.J., B.A. Carnes, and C. Cassel. 1990. In Search of Methuse: Estimating the Upper Limits to Human Longevity. *Science* 250:634–640.

Palmore, E.G., and D. Maeda. 1985. *The Honorable Elders Revisited.* Durham, N.C.: Duke University Press.

Preston, S.H. 1992. Demographic Change in the United States, 1970–2050. In *Forecasting the Health of Elderly Populations,* eds. K.G. Manton, B.H. Singer, and R.M. Suzman. New York: Springer-Verlag.

Rice, D.P., and M. Haan. (Eds.). 1991. Compression of Morbidity: Proceedings of the Conference Held March 18–20, 1990, Monterey, California. *Journal of Aging and Health* (Special Issue).

Riley, M.W. 1981. Health Behavior of Older People: Toward a New Paradigm. In *Health, Behavior, and Aging,* eds. D.L. Parron, R. Soloman, and J. Rodin 25–39. Institute of Medicine Interim Report No. 5. Washington: National Academy Press.

Riley, M.W., and K. Bond. 1983. Beyond Ageism: Postponing the Onset of Disability. In *Aging and Society: Selected Reviews of Recent Research,* eds., M.W. Riley, B.B. Hess, and K. Bond, 243–252. Hillsdale, N.J.: Erlbaum.

Robine, J.M., M. Labbe, M.C. Serouss, and A. Colvez. 1989. The Upper-Normandy Longitudinal Survey on Disability in the Aged, 1978–1985. *Revue d'Epidemiologie et de Sante Publique* 37(1):37–48.

Samuma, K. 1978. The Japanese Family in Relation to People's Health. *Social Science and Medicine* 12:469–78.

Schneider, E.L., and J.A. Brody. 1983. Aging, Natural Death, and the Compression of Morbidity: Another View. *New England Journal of Medicine* 309:854.

Spencer, G. 1989. Projections of the Population of the United States, by Age, Sex, and Race: 1988 to 2080. *Current Population Reports,* series P-25, no. 1018. Washington.

Sullivan, D.F. 1971. A Single Index of Mortality and Morbidity. *HSMHA Health Reports* 86:347–54.

Taeuber, C.M. 1983. America in Transition: An Aging Society. *Current Population Reports,* series P-23, no. 128, Washington.

Wilkins, R., and O. Adams. 1983. *Healthfulness of Life.* Montreal: Institute of Research on Public Policy.

World Health Organization. 1989. *World Health Statistics Annual, 1989.* Geneva.

II
THE DEMOGRAPHIC PERSPECTIVE

2

A Demographic Portrait of America's Oldest Old

CYNTHIA M. TAEUBER and IRA ROSENWAIKE

The oldest old are a small but rapidly growing group. In 1900, there were 252,000 persons aged 80 to 84 years and only 122,000 persons aged 85 years and over (Figure 2–1). In 1990 there were 3.9 million and 3.0 million, respectively. Those 85 and over represented just over 1 percent of the total population (Table 2–1). But the size of the oldest-old population is already of sufficient magnitude to have a major impact on the nation's health-care and social-service systems. Longer life expectancy has not necessarily translated into better health. It is possible that chronic, serious, and expensive health problems will increase as the population ages. Torrey estimates that the federal government spent $51 billion on the population 80 years and over in 1984 and that, under the policies of 1984, this would increase to an estimated $80 billion (in 1984 dollars) by the year 2000 (see Chapter 18, this volume).

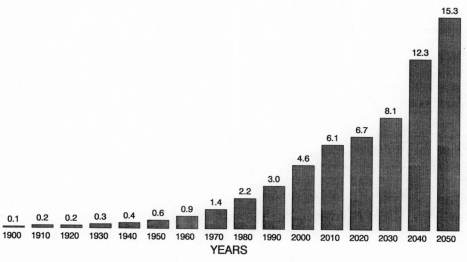

Figure 2–1 Population 85 years and over: 1900–2050, in millions. (Source: U.S. Bureau of the Census, decennial censuses for specified years; and U.S. Bureau of the Census. 1989. Projections of the Population of United States, by Age, Sex, and Race: 1988 to 2080. *Current Population Reports,* series P-25, no. 1018, middle series. Washington)

Table 2–1 Growth of the Older Population, Actual and Projected: 1900–2050 (numbers in thousands)

| | Total (all ages) | Age in years | | | | | | | | | | | |
| | | 65–74 | | 75–79 | | 80–84 | | 80+ | | 85+ | | 65+ | |
Year	N	N	%	N	%	N	%	N	%	N	%	N	%
1900	75,995	2,187	2.9	520	0.7	252	0.3	374	0.5	122	0.2	3,080	4.1
1910	91,972	2,793	3.0	667	0.7	322	0.4	489	0.5	167	0.2	3,949	4.3
1920	105,711	3,464	3.3	856	0.8	403	0.4	613	0.6	210	0.2	4,933	4.7
1930	122,775	4,721	3.8	1,106	0.9	535	0.4	807	0.7	272	0.2	6,634	5.4
1940	131,669	6,376	4.8	1,504	1.1	774	0.6	1,139	0.9	365	0.3	9,019	6.8
1950	150,697	8,415	5.6	2,128	1.4	1,149	0.8	1,726	1.1	577	0.4	12,269	8.1
1960	179,323	10,997	6.1	3,054	1.7	1,580	0.9	2,509	1.4	929	0.5	16,560	9.2
1970	203,302	12,447	6.1	3,838	1.9	2,286	1.1	3,695	1.8	1,409	0.7	19,980	9.8
1980	226,546	15,581	6.9	4,794	2.1	2,935	1.3	5,175	2.3	2,240	1.0	25,550	11.3
1990	248,710	18,045	7.3	6,103	2.5	3,909	1.6	6,930	2.8	3,021	1.2	31,079	12.5
Middle series[a]													
2000	268,266	18,243	6.8	7,282	2.7	4,735	1.8	9,357	3.5	4,622	1.7	34,882	13.0
2010	282,575	21,039	7.4	6,913	2.4	5,295	1.9	11,410	4.0	6,115	2.2	39,362	13.9
2020	294,364	30,973	10.5	8,981	3.1	5,462	1.9	12,113	4.1	6,651	2.3	52,067	17.7
2030	300,629	35,988	12.0	13,023	4.3	8,464	2.8	16,593	5.5	8,129	2.7	65,604	21.8
2040	301,807	30,808	10.2	14,260	4.7	10,790	3.6	23,041	7.6	12,251	4.1	68,109	22.6
2050	299,849	31,590	10.5	12,042	4.0	9,613	3.2	24,900	8.3	15,287	5.1	68,532	22.9

Highest series[b]

2000	278,228	18,689	6.7	7,525	2.7	4,923	1.8	9,868	3.4	4,945	1.8	36,082	13.0
2010	305,882	22,125	7.2	7,445	2.4	5,797	1.9	12,957	4.2	7,160	2.3	42,527	13.9
2020	335,022	33,170	9.9	9,983	3.0	6,266	1.9	14,854	4.4	8,588	2.6	58,007	17.3
2030	362,327	39,353	10.9	14,807	4.1	10,035	2.8	21,291	5.9	11,256	3.1	75,451	20.8
2040	388,123	34,864	9.0	16,685	4.3	13,184	3.4	31,040	8.0	17,856	4.6	82,589	21.3
2050	413,580	36,396	8.8	14,661	3.5	12,271	3.0	36,388	8.8	24,117	5.8	87,445	21.1

Lowest series[c]

2000	259,576	17,955	6.9	7,114	2.7	4,567	1.8	8,911	3.8	4,344	1.7	33,980	13.1
2010	264,193	20,360	7.7	7,570	2.9	4,911	1.9	10,232	3.9	5,321	2.0	38,162	14.1
2020	264,536	29,519	11.2	8,371	3.2	4,925	1.9	10,322	3.9	5,397	2.0	48,212	18.2
2030	258,113	33,471	13.0	11,912	4.6	7,479	2.9	13,801	5.3	6,322	2.4	59,184	22.9
2040	245,694	27,756	11.3	12,640	5.1	9,274	3.8	18,439	7.5	9,165	3.7	58,835	23.9
2050	230,158	28,262	12.3	10,337	4.5	7,918	3.4	18,629	8.1	10,711	4.7	57,228	24.9

Note: Figures for 1900 to 1950 exclude Alaska and Hawaii; figures for 1900 to 1990 are for the resident population; projections for 2000 to 2050 include armed forces overseas.

[a] Middle fertility, mortality, and immigration assumptions. Assumes an ultimate total fertility rate of 1,800, life expectancy at birth in 2050 of 76.4 years for males and 83.3 years for females and an ultimate net migration of 500,000 per year.

[b] High fertility, low mortality, and high net immigration assumptions result in high number of elderly. Assumes an ultimate total fertility rate of 2,200, life expectancy at birth in 2050 of 81.8 years for males and 88.2 years for females and an ultimate net migration of 800,000 per year.

[c] Low fertility, high mortality, and low net immigration assumptions result in lowest number of elderly. Assumes an ultimate total fertility rate of 1,500, life expectancy at birth in 2050 of 73.4 years for males and 80.5 years for females and an ultimate net migration of 300,000 per year.

Source: U.S. Bureau of the Census. 1990. Data for 1900 to 1940, 1960, and 1980 shown in 1980 Census of Population, PC80–B1, *General Population Characteristics*, tables 42 and 45. Data for 1990 from 1990 Census of Population (CPH-L-74, modified age and race counts). Data for 2000 to 2050 shown in "Projections of the Population of the United States by Age, Sex and Race: 1988 to 2080," *Current Population Reports*, P-25, no. 1018. Data for 1950 shown in "Estimates of the Population of the United States and Components of Change, by Age, Color, and Sex: 1950 to 1960," *Current Population Reports*, series P-25, no. 310. Data for 1970 from unpublished table consistent with "United States Population Estimates by Age, Race, Sex, and Hispanic Origin: 1988," series P-25, no. 1045. Washington.

The definition used here for the "oldest old" is the population aged 85 and over. The rationale for this choice is twofold. First, demographic statistics are conventionally published in 5-year categories. When an age group such as "75 plus" or "85 plus" is used, a pure age criterion is employed, with no attention to functional status. Second, more than any other age group, the population aged 85 and over most resembles the traditional image of an old age linked to frailty and dependence, illness and death. About 23 percent of this population lived in an institution in 1980; another one-fifth lived at home but needed help in taking care of their daily needs. The characteristics of this population differ markedly in many respects from those of the younger old. Hence, equation of the "oldest old" as a functional category with the population aged "85 and over" as a statistical artifact is convenient and facilitates comparisons with other published data. Selected data are also shown for the population aged 80 to 84 to facilitate comparisons with other sources that may use the age group "80 and over."

The characteristics of the oldest old differ greatly from those of the younger old, and it is important to know the nature and extent of the differences. Until recently, data on the characteristics of this important group have been almost nonexistent in official statistics except for the decennial census, which tabulated basic data for those aged 85 years and over. Because of the expected growth in the population of the extremely aged, additional tabulations showing the demographic, social, and economic characteristics of those 85 years and over were produced from the 1980 census and are presented in this chapter; the work was funded by the National Institute on Aging. Some tabulations are from the full census sample and were produced by the Bureau of the Census; other tabulations are from the 5 percent public-use microdata samples of the 1980 census and were produced by Ira Rosenwaike. Limited data were available from the 1990 census and were used where possible. These data clearly demonstrate that this fast-growing population group is heterogeneous and is distinctive from the younger old. The oldest old are heterogeneous along health and economic lines, just as other age groups are. Further, they are distinct because nearly half have serious health problems, whereas the other half are healthy enough to live independently. In short, they have carried into their very old age the inequalities and differences created previously in their life cycles, particularly through their educational and labor-market experiences as younger people.

In this chapter, we will examine the rapid growth of the oldest old population and the reasons for that growth; compare their demographic, social, and economic characteristics with those of the younger old; describe the characteristics of the centenarian population; examine the quality of census data on the oldest old; and discuss the implications of the growth and characteristics of this unique important group. Projections are from the Census Bureau's middle series unless noted otherwise.

DATA QUALITY

The reliability of data on the oldest old has long been considered a hindrance to the study of this group. Like data in general, census data are subject to both sampling and nonsampling errors. Data on the oldest old have some additional problems. It is probable that they suffer from a greater measure of error and that they are affected by biases to a greater extent than are data on the younger population. There are also variations in the proportion of persons who were not counted by the census, depending upon their race and the region of the country in which they lived. For example, coverage is better for older whites than for older blacks. There are several reasons that a count may not be accurate. Omitting persons is only one of the factors that may reduce the accuracy of the count. Another is the misreporting of age. There is evidence of substantial misreporting of age among older persons, especially for black men (Siegel and Taeuber 1982). And yet, there have been improvements in the accuracy of age reporting over the years. When census counts are compared with death records, Medicare enrollment figures, and so forth, whatever net error exists in the count of the population 85 years and over has probably been fairly small in recent years (Rosenwaike and Logue 1985).

Probably the most glaring error in the 1980 census was the count of the population 100 years and over. Although the 1980 census showed a count of 32,194, it is estimated that the actual count was closer to 15,000. About one-fourth of the error resulted from incorrect placement of young persons in the centenarian population. Research of actual census questionnaires for centenarians indicates that almost five-sixths of the unallocated centenarian population was aged 100 to 104 years. About half of the unallocated centenarians lived in group quarters, and about 10 percent were married (Spencer 1986; Spencer, Goldstein, and Taeuber 1987). Because of the compounding errors of age misreporting, and particularly the incorrect inclusion of very young people in the distribution of characteristics for centenarians, the data for this group from the 1980 census are virtually unusable without study of actual questionnaires by sworn census officials. Fortunately, however, the data for most of the group "85 years and over" are of higher quality. Although data quality is not the same as that for the younger population, findings based on the data conform to expectations in terms of demographic logic and consistency of the patterns of socioeconomic characteristics over the age span and over time.

GROWTH OF THE OLDEST OLD POPULATION

Overall, those aged 85 and over are projected to be the fastest-growing part of the older population into the next century (U.S. Bureau of the Census 1989). This is true for most other industrialized nations as well. Between the 1960 and 1990 censuses, the oldest old population increased 232 percent in the United States, compared with an increase of 89 percent for the population aged 65 years and over and 39 percent for the total population. From 1980 to 1990, the population aged 85 years and over grew by 3.8 percent annually compared with 2.2 percent for the total of those aged 65 and over and 4.6 percent for those aged 35 to 44 (the "baby boom" group born just after World War II) (U.S. Bureau of the Census 1991).

It must be pointed out, however, that although the growth rates of the oldest old seem spectacular and are important, the size of the population aged 85 years and over is relatively small. The important point is not their percentage growth but the fact that they are an increasingly large part of the elderly population; thus, individuals, families, and governments have begun to give more thought to planning for the well-being of this group. In 1900, only 4 percent of the elderly population (aged 65 years and over) was at least 85. In 1990, the oldest old were nearly 10 percent of the elderly population, and by 2000 they may be 13 percent. When the baby-boom generation begins to reach age 85 in 2031, there may be 8 million persons aged 85 and over. By 2050, there may be 15 million; they would constitute 5 percent of the nation's total population and over one-fifth of the elderly population. That is, the elderly population is itself aging as an increasing proportion reach the oldest ages.

The nation is also experiencing a steady growth in the number of people aged 100 years or more. The 1990 Census counted 35,808 centenarians (U.S. Bureau of the Census 1991). Centenarians constituted just over 1 in 10,000 persons in the total population and nearly 12 of every 10,000 elderly persons (aged 65 years and over). About 4 in 5 (78.5 percent) centenarians are women. The chances of living to age 100 have improved. For those born in 1879, the odds against living for 100 years were 400 to 1; based on the mortality rates from 1979 to 1981, persons born in 1980 had odds of 87 to 1 (Spencer, Goldstein, and Taeuber 1987).

Historically, the number of persons aged 85 and over has increased because of past high fertility levels. In addition, between 1940 and 1980, death-rate declines at the older ages were as large as or larger than those at younger ages, resulting in unprecedented numbers of persons reaching extreme old age (Fingerhut 1982). A sharp downturn in mortality from cardiovascular disease is largely responsible for declining death rates among the oldest old.

Death before the mid-sixties is relatively uncommon now. In 1980, almost 70 percent of all deaths occurred among people aged 65 or older compared with 25 percent in 1900 (Siegel 1980). Nearly one in four of those aged 65 in 1980 could expect to survive to at least age 90, compared with one in eight in 1950 (Figure 2–2). About half the women who are age 60 can expect to reach at least age 85, according to life tables of the Social Security Administration, which assume a moderate decline in mortality. For men, the probability is about one in four. A white man who was 85 in 1900 could expect to live an additional 3.8 years, compared with an additional 5.2 years under 1987 mortality conditions. For white women aged 85, it was 4.0 years in 1900 and 6.4 years in 1987 (Table 2–2). Oldest old whites in the United States, especially women, have slightly longer life expectancies than those in other developed nations. For example, in 1987 in Sweden, life expectancy at age 85 was 4.6 years for men and 5.8 years for women. For Japan, it was 5.0 and 5.9 years, respectively.

If mortality rates continue to improve throughout the age distribution more than was assumed in the U.S. Census Bureau's middle-series projections, the number and proportion of oldest old could be higher than the projections just presented. For example, if fertility and net migration were similar to what they are today, but life expectancy increased from the levels as in the middle series, projections of the population aged 85 years and over in 2050 would increase from 15.3 million to nearly 23.7 million. The oldest old would then constitute over 7 percent of the total population. The latter projections assume a total fertility rate of 1.8 children per woman, an ultimate net immigration of 500,000 per year, and life expectancy at birth in 2050 of 81.8 years for males and 88.2 years for females.

Medicare enrollment data are another source for determining the age distribution of the oldest old. Table 2–3 shows that during the periods 1970 to 1980 and 1980 to 1988, the number of persons 95 years and over increased by more than double the

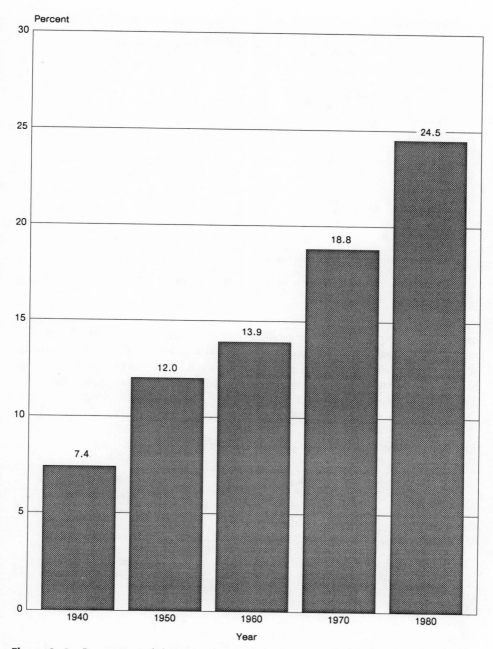

Figure 2–2 Percentage of those aged 65 expected to survive to age 90. (Source: National Center for Health Statistics)

Table 2–2   Life Expectancy at Age 85 by Sex and Race: 1900–1987

| | Average number of years of life remaining | | | |
| | Men | | Women | |
Year	White	Other races	White	Other races
1900–1902	3.8	4.0	4.1	5.1
1909–1911	3.9	4.5	4.1	5.1
1919–1921	4.1	4.5	4.2	5.2
1929–1931	4.0	4.3	4.2	5.5
1939–1941	4.0	5.1	4.3	6.4
1949–1951	4.4	5.4	4.8	6.2
1959–1961	4.3	5.1	4.7	5.4
1969–1971[a]	4.6	6.0	5.5	7.1
1979–1981[a]	5.1	5.7	6.3	7.2
1985[a]	5.1	5.9	6.4	7.0
1987[a]	5.2	5.8	6.4	6.9

[a] Deaths of nonresidents of the United States were excluded beginning in 1970.

Source: 1900–1971 from *Vital Statistics of the United States 1978*, vol. 2, sect. 5, life tables; 1979–81 from *U.S. Decennial Life Tables for 1979–81*, vol. 1, no. 1, U.S. life tables; 1987 from *Vital Statistics of the United States, 1987*, vol. 2, Mortality, pt. A, life tables.

rate of the aggregate population aged 85 years and over. Those aged 85 and over increased by nearly two-thirds in the first period and by less than one-third in the second period. Whereas the number of persons aged 90 to 94 years more than doubled between 1970 and 1988, the population aged 95 and over quadrupled during the course of this 18-year span.

Table 2–3   Persons 85 Years and Over in the Medicare Program, by Age and Sex: 1970, 1980, and 1988

| | Medicare population[a] | | | Percentage increase | |
Age and sex	1970	1980	1988	1970–1980	1980–1988
Both sexes					
85 and over	1,378,523	2,262,833	2,934,419	64.1	29.7
85–89	1,021,434	1,570,925	1,893,035	53.8	20.5
90–94	294,270	547,252	782,406	86.0	43.0
95 and over	62,819	144,656	258,977	130.3	79.0
Men					
85 and over	470,830	677,845	809,960	44.0	19.5
85–89	359,259	487,238	553,249	35.6	13.5
90–94	93,258	153,439	196,274	64.5	27.9
95 and over	18,313	37,168	60,437	103.0	62.6
Women					
85 and over	907,693	1,584,988	2,123,354	74.6	34.0
85–89	612,175	1,083,687	1,339,783	77.0	23.6
90–94	201,012	393,813	586,131	95.9	48.8
95 and over	44,506	107,488	198,540	141.5	84.7

[a] Unknown and persons 120 years and over have been excluded.

Source: Health Care Finance Administration (unpublished tabulations).

GENDER

At every age, male mortality exceeds female mortality. As a consequence, males are subject to greater attrition than females as successive cohorts age. Perhaps no feature of the oldest old is as unique as their relative number of males and females (841,000 men and 2.2 million women in 1990). At 80 years of age and over, 68 percent of the population was female in 1990 in the United States, compared with, for example, 65 percent in Japan and 46 percent in India. At ages over 85, when death rates are highest, sex ratios (the number of males per 100 females) show increasingly greater imbalances. In 1990, the sex ratio was 42 for persons aged 85 to 89 but only 27 for persons aged 95 to 99. Similarly, the centenarian population is predominantly female. By comparison, for persons aged 65 to 69 years, the sex ratio was 81. The female advantage has been expanding for decades and, by 1990, the sex ratio for persons aged 85 and older had dropped dramatically to 39 (Table 2–4). This trend should soon abate, however. Men aged 85 and over are expected to increase their numbers relative to women, so that by 2050, the sex ratio could increase to nearly 50. Nevertheless, this could mean more than 5 million more women than men aged 85 and over by the middle of the next century. Sex ratios are higher among the foreign-born oldest old because of the one-time preponderance of males among immigrants.

Another view of the extreme prevalence of women over men in the oldest ages is found in projections of males and females (Table 2–5). Only 0.7 percent of the total male population was 85 years and over compared with 1.7 percent of the female population in 1990. By 2050, 3.5 percent of the male population may be 85 or older but 6.6 percent of the total female population may be this old.

The sex ratio for blacks is increasing, just as it is for the total population. For the black population aged 85 years and over, the sex ratio is expected to increase from 42 in 1990 to 52 in 2050, compared with 39 and 50, respectively, for the total population (Table 2–5).

As men age, they suffer disproportionately from diseases that kill rather than the chronic, nonlethal diseases from which older women tend to suffer. The male/female

Table 2–4 Balance of Men and Women 85 Years and Over

Year	Sex ratio[a]	Excess of women
1930	75.4	38,000
1940	75.0	52,000
1950	69.8	109,000
1960	63.9	197,000
1970	53.3	426,000
1980	43.7	877,000
1990	38.6	1,339,000
2030	46.0	3,008,000
2050	49.9	5,115,000

[a] Sex ratio is men per 100 women 85 years and over.

Source: U.S. Bureau of the Census. Censuses of population, 1930–1980; 1991. 1990 Census of Population. Series CPH-L-74, "Modified and Actual Age, Sex, Race, and Hispanic Origin"; 1989. Projections of the Population of the United States by Age, Sex, and Race: 1988 to 2080. *Current Population Reports*, series P-25, no. 1018, middle series. Washington.

Table 2–5 Population by Age and Race: 1990–2050

Age, sex, and race	All races				Black			
	1990	2010[a]	2030[a]	2050[a]	1990	2010[a]	2030[a]	2050[a]
Both sexes								
All ages	248,710	282,575	300,629	299,849	30,483	38,833	44,596	47,146
65 years and over	31,079	39,362	65,604	68,532	2,492	3,860	7,784	9,571
85 years and over	3,021	6,115	8,129	15,287	223	478	788	1,817
Percent of persons of all ages	1.2	2.2	2.7	5.1	0.7	1.2	1.8	3.9
Percent of population aged 85 and over who are black	(X)	(X)	(X)	(X)	7.4	7.8	9.7	11.9
Males								
All ages	121,239	138,333	146,543	145,320	14,420	18,602	21,328	22,456
65 years and over	12,493	16,372	28,594	29,307	957	1,598	3,366	4,131
85 years and over	841	1,791	2,560	5,086	66	148	256	624
Percent of males of all ages	0.7	1.3	1.7	3.5	0.5	0.8	1.2	2.8
Percent of males aged 85 and over who are black	(X)	(X)	(X)	(X)	7.8	8.3	10.0	12.3
Females								
All ages	127,471	144,241	154,086	154,529	16,063	20,231	23,269	24,690
65 years and over	18,586	22,991	37,010	39,225	1,535	2,262	4,418	5,440
85 years and over	2,180	4,324	5,568	10,201	156	330	532	1,193
Percent of females of all ages	1.7	3.0	3.6	6.6	1.0	1.6	2.3	4.8
Percent of females aged 85 and over who are black	(X)	(X)	(X)	(X)	7.2	7.6	9.6	11.7
Ratio (males per 100 females)								
All ages	95.1	95.9	95.1	94.0	89.8	91.9	91.7	91.0
65 years and over	67.2	71.2	77.3	74.7	62.3	70.6	76.2	75.9
85 years and over	38.6	41.4	46.0	49.9	42.3	44.8	48.1	52.3

[a] Assumes an ultimate total fertility rate of 1,800, life expectancy at birth in 2050 of 76.4 years for males and 83.3 years for females, and an ultimate net migration of 500,000 per year. (X) Not applicable.

Source: U.S. Bureau of the Census. 1989. Projections of the Population of the United States by Age, Sex, and Race: 1988 to 2080. *Current Population Reports*, series P-25, no. 1018, middle series. Washington.

gap in life expectancy is related in varying degrees to problems among women aged 85 years and over, such as high proportions of women living alone after widowhood, earlier institutionalization than men, sharply reduced income and a disproportionately high level of poverty, a need for special support from family members or society, and other life-course changes (Siegel and Taeuber 1986). Because of these differences between men and women, issues surrounding relative expenditures for health care and research, and an emphasis on treatment more than on prevention, are a matter of debate.

RACE AND ETHNIC COMPOSITION

The oldest-old population is predominantly white. Out of a total of 3.0 million persons aged 85 or older in 1990, more than 2.8 million were white; 273,000 were black; 9,200 were American Indian, Eskimo, or Aleut; and nearly 30,000 were Asian or Pacific Islander. Over 91,000 persons of Hispanic origin (may be of any race) were 85 or older in 1990. Most centenarians were white (82 percent in 1990) (U.S. Bureau of the Census 1991).

The oldest old are more likely than other age groups to be first- and second-generation immigrants and therefore are somewhat more likely to identify with a single ancestry than is the population in general. In 1980, about 4 out of 10 persons aged 85 years and over identified their ancestry solely as English (15.9 percent), German (12.9 percent), Irish (6.1 percent), Italian (3.5 percent), Polish (2.3 percent), or French (1.7 percent). About 49,000 were Hispanic (U.S. Bureau of the Census 1983, 1986).

The black population is younger on average than the white population. But among the oldest old, the black population (especially women) is projected to grow faster than the white oldest old. Although the white population 85 years and over in 2050 is expected to be almost five times what it was in 1990, its black counterpart is expected to experience nearly an 8-fold increase (Table 2–5).

There were only 66,000 black males aged 85 or older in 1990. That is just 0.5 percent of the total black male population. But by 2050, about 3 percent of all black males may be this old. Even then, this will still be a relatively small population, about 624,000 black men. About 3.8 percent of white males are expected to be 85 or older by 2050. The oldest-old black female population is relatively small also, about 156,000 in 1990, constituting 1 percent of the total black female population. By 2050, however, oldest-old black women could number 1.2 million, representing almost 5 percent of the total black female population. White women aged 85 and over could constitute nearly 7 percent of the total white female population by 2050. The higher fertility of blacks, associated with their higher mortality under age 85, are the main factors in the difference in the proportion of the white and black populations aged 85 years and over (Siegel and Taeuber 1986).

In 1990, blacks were 7.4 percent of the total population aged 85 years and over. Their proportion of the oldest old is expected to increase gradually to 11.9 percent by 2050. Historically, blacks have accounted for a smaller share of the 85-and-over population in recent censuses than in earlier censuses. The proportional decline, however, likely reflects substantial improvement in age reporting because of improved

Table 2–6   Familial–Aged Dependency Ratios[a]

Year	All races	Black
1950	12	11
1960	15	14
1970	22	19
1980	26	20
1990	30	26
2010	50	36
2030	43	30
2050	88	67

[a]Ratio of persons 85 years and over to persons 65–69 years.

Source: U.S. Bureau of the Census. Censuses of population 1950 to 1990; U.S. Bureau of the Census. 1989. Projections of the Population of the United States by Age, Sex, and Race: 1988 to 2080. *Current Population Reports,* series P-25, no. 1018. Washington.

knowledge of actual age through the wider availability of birth certificates and increased literacy, which resulted in a diminished tendency to exaggerate age among the oldest old.

The increasing proportion of the oldest old population has implications for the magnitude of family support and care problems over time. The ratio of persons aged 85 years and over to persons aged 65 to 69 years (used as an estimate of two elderly generations, although they are not necessarily in the same families) is rising for both blacks and whites; for the total population the ratio would nearly triple from 1990 to 2050 (Table 2–6). The experience and problems of the young old in caring for the oldest old will become more and more familiar throughout society.

FOREIGN-BORN POPULATION

In 1980, the foreign born constituted 6 percent of the total U.S. population, about 8 percent of the population aged 65 to 69 years, but almost 19 percent of the 85-and-over population. The proportion of the oldest old who were born in other nations has declined considerably from the first quarter of this century, when immigrants accounted for as much as 30 percent of the population aged 85 and over. Their relative decline reflects the reduced level of immigration after World War I and the buildup of native-born cohorts of the oldest old. Even though the foreign-born elderly tend to have lower educational levels than do the native born, their income levels, even among the oldest old, are similar to those of the native born. Among both native- and foreign-born persons aged 85 and over, half had money incomes below $4,000 in 1979 and about three-fourths had incomes below $6,000 (Table 2–7).

Inability to speak English can be a particular difficulty for the oldest old. In 1980, of those foreign born who spoke a language other than English at home, about four out of five of the 7,400 oldest old who had immigrated to the United States since 1970 reported that they could not speak English at all or could not speak it well. Among the 241,000 who immigrated to the United States prior to 1970, one in three had similar difficulty with English. Among the 274,000 aged 80 to 84, about one in four had difficulty speaking English, a proportion similar to that of the younger old.

Difficulty with English is likely to be lessened if families are present to help. In

Table 2–7 Money Income in 1979 for Native- and Foreign-Born Persons 85 Years and Over with Income: 1980

Income	Native born (%)	Foreign born (%)
Total	100.0	100.0
Less than $4,000	55.7	55.5
$4,000 to $5,999	18.8	22.0
$6,000 to $9,999	13.8	13.7
$10,000 to $24,999	9.5	7.4
$25,000 or more	2.3	1.3
Total persons (N)	1,785,741	360,780

Source: U.S. Bureau of the Census, special tabulations for the National Institute on Aging from the 1980 census, table 23. Washington.

1980, there were about 69,200 oldest-old unrelated individuals (most of whom lived alone) who spoke a language other than English at home and presumably had problems with English. Three out of five oldest old spoke either German (18.4 percent), Italian (15.8 percent), Polish (9.5 percent), Spanish (10.0 percent), or French (7.5 percent). An additional 146,000 unrelated individuals aged 80 to 84 spoke a language other than English at home. Judging by the language spoken at home in 1980, of unrelated individuals aged 65 to 69, Spanish (23.5 percent) will be the dominant non-English language spoken by the oldest old by the next decade, followed by Italian (14.6 percent), Polish (11.4 percent), German (10.1 percent), and French (9.2 percent) (U.S. Bureau of the Census 1986).

The proportion of the population aged 85 and over that is foreign born varies markedly by geographic region. The northeastern states tend to have higher proportions and the southern states lower proportions in 1980. More than 30 percent of the oldest-old population were of foreign birth in Connecticut, Massachusetts, New Jersey, New York, and Rhode Island, compared with less than 2 percent of the oldest residents of Alabama, Arkansas, Georgia, Kentucky, Mississippi, and North Carolina.

MARITAL STATUS AND LIVING ARRANGEMENTS

With advancing age, patterns of marital status and living arrangements shift considerably. The general course is the same for both men and women but is much more dramatic among women. Women aged 85 years and over are likely to be widowed and living alone, whereas men are more likely to be married and living in a family setting.

Martial Status

The pronounced differences in the distribution of marital status of the older population are largely explained by the imbalances in the sex ratio. Other factors are also important, however, such as the tendency for men to marry women some years younger than themselves and the greater likelihood of remarriage for men.

The data in Table 2–8 give some sense of the fundamental life changes that older people experience as they age, especially women. About half of all men aged 85 and over were married at the time of the 1980 census, compared with about 1 of 12 women. The oldest old of both sexes were much less likely to be married than the young old. A majority (55 percent) of women aged 65 to 69 years, for example, were married, as were four out of five men of that age range. The vast majority (82 percent) or women aged 85 and over were widowed in 1980, compared with only

Table 2–8 Selected Characteristics of Persons Aged 65–69 and 85 and Over: 1970 and 1980

Selected characteristics	1970		1980	
	65–69 years	85 plus years[a]	65–69 years	85 plus years
Sex ratio (men per 100 women)	80.7	53.3	80.0	43.7
Percent currently married				
Men	80.6	42.4	83.0	48.4
Women	52.0	9.9	54.8	8.4
Percent widowed				
Men	8.8	47.0	7.3	43.8
Women	36.5	79.0	33.8	81.8
Percent living in families				
Men	83.9	60.4	85.4	58.9
Women	67.2	47.9	66.8	36.7
Percent living in households alone or with nonrelatives				
Men	13.8	24.2	12.9	24.1
Women	30.5	29.0	31.5	35.6
Percent living in institutions				
Men	1.8	14.3	1.4	16.1
Women	1.6	21.9	1.3	26.3
Education				
Percent high-school graduates	30.5	23.0	45.1	30.0
Percent with 8 + years of school	70.9	60.1	81.2	66.6
Race and nativity				
Percent black	9.0	7.6	8.8	7.1
Percent foreign born	12.8	18.6	7.8	18.6
Percent in labor force				
Men	39.0	6.8	29.2	4.2
Women	17.2	3.4	15.0	1.5
Percent below poverty level	21.6	37.1	11.6	21.3
Median income (constant 1979 dollars) in previous year				
Men	$7,160	$3,303	$8,584	$4,797
Women	$3,085	$2,319	$3,819	$3,284

[a]Data for the 85 plus population in 1970 from the public-use samples excludes centenarians since this group was seriously overstated in published sources.

Source: U.S. Bureau of the Census (1970 and 1980 censuses and public-use microdata samples).

about 85 and over were widowed in 1980, compared with only about one-third of those aged 65 to 69 years.

In other countries, about three out of four women aged 80 or older are widowed. The lowest female widowhood rates occur in Scandinavia (about 65 percent), whereas the highest occur in the Far East: China (92 percent), Japan (87 percent), and Singapore (83 percent). By comparison, for the United States, the figure was 76 percent in 1980. Worldwide, the median percentage widowed for men 80 and over is about 39 percent compared with 33 percent in the United States. In the United States, about 1 in 12 of the oldest old had never married, which is somewhat higher than has been the case for younger cohorts. Younger old men were rarely widowed (7 percent), although this status was common among oldest-old men (44 percent).

As a result of increased longevity, the oldest old are more likely to be married now than in the past. Among women aged 85 and over, however, there has been only a slight change in the most recent 30-year period: from 7.0 percent married in 1950 to 8.4 percent married in 1980. Among men, the proportion of those aged 85 and over who were married increased from one-third (33.6 percent) in 1950 to nearly half (48.4 percent) in 1980. This increase partially reflects gains in female life expectancy. The 1980 census was the first to show that more oldest-old men were married than widowed. When we look beyond the aggregate, we find that 54 percent of men aged 85 to 89 in 1980 were married, compared with 38 percent of those 90 years or older.

Gains in life expectancy have influenced the length of time spent married, divorced, and widowed; thus, the experiences of cohorts differ. Men and women who were born in the 1890s and the early part of this century were somewhat less likely to marry than are those now in their forties. Among those who marry, the turn-of-the-century birth cohort married, on average, 1 to 2 years later (about age 23 for women and 26 for men) than did the cohort of young people born from 1943 to 1950. The median age of marriage for cohorts born since 1950 is closer to that of the turn-of-the-century cohorts. Among the birth cohorts that are now aged 80 or older, about one-fifth of their marriages ended in divorce. Widowhood was, however, a more probable outcome of marriage than divorce. Women born around the turn of the century faced widowhood at younger ages than will be true of women born during the 1940s and 1950s. But once they became widows, they were also more likely to remarry than are the women of the baby-boom generation (Schoen, Urton, Woodrow, and Baj 1985).

Centenarians, especially women, are largely a widowed group. In 1980, 82 to 90 percent of centenarian women were widowed compared with 53 to 71 percent of centenarian men. Over one-fifth (20 to 37 percent) of centenarian men were married, but less than one-tenth of the women were (Spencer, Goldstein, and Taeuber 1987).

Among states, the proportion of men aged 85 years and over who were married in 1980 varied from 39 percent in Delaware to 62 percent in Idaho, but in most states, about half of the oldest-old men were married. For women, the proportion ranged from 5 percent in Delaware to 13 percent in Alaska, Arizona, and Oregon; less than 10 percent were married in the majority of the states (U.S. Bureau of the Census 1986, table 10).

Living Arrangements

Marital status variations are important in accounting for differences in living arrangements of older men and women. Because older men are also much more likely to be married than are women, they are also more likely to live in a family setting. In 1980, a majority of all men aged 85 and older (59 percent) lived in families, compared with over one-third of women (37 percent) in this age group. By contrast, two-thirds (67 percent) of all women aged 65 to 69 years lived in families, as did the overwhelming share (85 percent) of men (Table 2–8). About two-thirds of the oldest old owned or rented their residence, as did 32 to 45 percent of centenarians. Roughly half (45 to 55 percent in 1980) of the centenarians lived in group quarters, usually nursing homes. Oldest-old women were more likely to live in an institutional setting than oldest-old men (Spencer, Goldstein, and Taeuber 1987).

Elderly persons clearly prefer to live independently if possible. Health and income are major limiting factors. In 1980, almost 36 percent of all women aged 85 years and over lived alone or with nonrelatives, an increase from the 29 percent recorded in 1970. This trend toward independent living, especially among women, has been observed for the last few decades and also appears to be characteristic of many developed countries (Myers and Nathanson 1982).

Along with this trend toward independent living has been a sharp decline in the proportion of both elderly men and women who live with their children. In 1950, 32 percent of all men aged 85 years and over who lived outside of group quarters lived in a household maintained by a son, a daughter, or their child's spouse; this proportion plummeted to 9 percent in 1980; for women, it was 47 percent in 1950 and declined to 18 percent in 1980. Centenarians in households lived with their adult children more often (29 to 42 percent in 1980) (Spencer, Goldstein, and Taeuber 1987).

The trend in most developed countries is toward independent living, even among the oldest old. In Japan, for example, about 75 percent of all persons aged 65 years and over lived with their married children in 1975, down from 85 percent in 1965 (Rosenwaike and Logue 1985).

In 1980, the oldest old were more likely to live with their children in Hawaii, where some 38 percent were parents of the householder, than in any other state. Notably, the farm states (upper midwestern states) tend to have relatively low proportions of the oldest old living with their sons and daughters and relatively high proportions living alone (Longino 1986). This may be partially a result of previous high out-migration of younger people.

Institutional Population

In 1980, about 509,000 persons aged 85 years or older lived in institutional settings. Over half (276,000) were 85 to 89 years old. Of the total population 85 years of age and over, 488,000 lived in homes for the aged, 7,000 lived in mental institutions and residential treatment centers, and another 14,000 lived in other types of institutions such as homes for the mentally handicapped. Although blacks aged 85 and over constituted about 7 percent of the total oldest-old population, they were less than 4 percent of the oldest old in homes for the aged and nearly 11 percent of the oldest old in mental hospitals and residential treatment centers. There has been a remarkable increase since at least 1950 in the percentage of the oldest old residing in institutions, whereas the pattern among the younger old has remained stable (Table 2–9). It is likely that this is at least partially a result of more people living longer but with worsening health in the oldest ages.

Women are increasingly likely to live in an institutional setting as they reach the oldest ages. Table 2–8 shows that the percentage of all women aged 85 and over living in nursing homes and other long-term care facilities climbed from 22 percent in 1970 to 26 percent in 1980. During the same period, the proportion of men increased from 14 to 16 percent. In sharp contrast, since 1950, about 2 percent of all persons aged 65 to 69 years have lived in institutions.

Recent studies indicate that marital status and the availability of kin are important factors in determining the household status of elderly persons (Thomas and Wister 1984). As might be expected, the marital status of the institutionalized population aged 85 and over varies markedly from that of the noninstitutionalized. In Table 2–10, marital status for oldest-old men and women living in institutions is compared with the marital status of those living in households. Relative to oldest-old men living in the community, institutionalized men include a smaller proportion of married persons and a higher proportion who are widowed, divorced, separated, or who never married. Among oldest-old women, the differences in marital status are less striking. In both cases, more than four in five are widowed. Noninstitutionalized women were more likely to have been married than were institutionalized women, and a higher percentage of institutionalized women have never married compared with noninstitutionalized women (Table 2–10).

When type of institution is considered, in 1980 only about 4 percent of women aged 85 and over who lived in nursing homes were also married compared with 23 percent of such men; about 83 percent of the women were widowed compared with 61 percent of the men. The oldest old in mental hospitals and residential treatment centers were much more likely to have never married or to be divorced and much less likely to be widowed than those in nursing homes. This was true regardless of race or gender (Table 2–11).

Nationally, of oldest-old persons living in institutional settings, women have higher levels of education than men. Three out of five men had fewer than 8 years of education compared with half of the women; 28 percent of the men and 36 percent of the women were at least high-school graduates.

The proportion of the oldest old living in institutions ranges widely by state. The

Table 2–9 Percentage of Elderly Population in Institutions by Age: 1950 to 1980

Year	65–74 (years)	85+ (years)
1950	2.1	9.4
1960	2.2	13.8
1970	2.1	19.3
1980	1.8	23.2

Source: U.S. Bureau of the Census, decennial censuses of population.

Table 2–10 Marital Status of Persons 85 Years Old and Over, by Residential Status and Sex: 1980

Residential status	Men	Women
In households		
Total (*N*)	554,356	1,102,647
Percent	100.0	100.0
Married (includes separated)	53.3	9.8
Widowed	40.5	81.7
Divorced	1.9	2.1
Never married	4.2	6.4
In institutions		
Total (*N*)	107,638	401,280
Percent	100.0	100.0
Married (includes separated)	24.2	4.8
Widowed	60.5	82.7
Divorced	2.9	1.6
Never married	12.3	10.9

Source: U.S. Bureau of the Census. Special tabulations for the National Institute on Aging from the 1980 Census of Population, table 10 of STF 5 special tabulations.

lowest percentage in 1980 was in Florida (12 percent), whereas in seven states in the North Central region (the farm belt) the percentage is over 30 (Longino 1986). California had the highest number in 1980 (8,600 men and 38,000 women), followed by New York (7,900 men and 34,000 women) and Texas (6,100 men and 23,000 women) (U.S. Bureau of the Census 1986, table 12).

Table 2–11 Institutionalized Population 85 Years and Over for Selected Types of Institutions: 1980

	All races		Black	
Type	Men	Women	Men	Women
Institutional population	107,638	401,280	4,924	15,176
Homes for the aged				
Number	100,958	386,788	4,313	13,995
Percent	100.0	100.0	100.0	100.0
Never married	11.7	10.8	14.6	7.8
Now married (excluding separated)	23.2	4.3	20.6	4.5
Divorced/separated	3.7	1.9	6.9	4.3
Widowed	61.3	83.0	57.9	83.4
Mental hospital				
Number	2,582	4,440	303	453
Percent	100.0	100.0	100.0	100.0
Never married	28.6	18.3	35.3	14.8
Now married (excluding separated)	24.6	9.4	29.0	4.6
Divorced/separated	8.6	8.6	9.2	24.7
Widowed	38.3	63.6	26.4	55.8

Source: U.S. Bureau of the Census. Special tabulations for the National Institute on Aging from the 1980 Census of Population, table 14.

POPULATION DISTRIBUTION AND MIGRATION PATTERNS

About half (51.4 percent) of the nation's 3.1 million oldest-old population lived in just nine states in 1990: California (299,000), New York (248,000), Florida (210,000), Pennsylvania (172,000), Texas (167,000), Illinois (148,000), Ohio (138,000), Michigan (107,000), and New Jersey (96,000) (see Table 2–12 and Figure 2–3). The pattern of population redistribution among regions for the oldest old was similar to that of all age groups from 1940 to 1990. The proportion of oldest old living in the North decreased (60 percent to 50 percent), but it increased in the South (28 percent to 32 percent) and the West (12 percent to 17 percent). Such changes are a result of internal migration and differences in death rates among the regions. Many Southern and Western states increased their oldest old population by more than 40 percent in the decade of the 1980s (Figure 2–4).

Regional relocation of the elderly to the South and West has been occurring among the younger elderly since the 1960s and among the older elderly since the 1970s. Those who moved as young elderly and who have survived are now among the areas' older elderly. Some retirement areas never made provisions for services needed as people age. Analysis by Bryant and El-Attar (1984, 639) indicates that the areas of destination for elderly migrants "can anticipate making concentrated efforts in adding service facilities as demand develops."

Two percent of Iowa's population was 85 or older in 1990, the highest proportion among the states. Other farm states, such as South Dakota, Nebraska, North Dakota, and Kansas, also had relatively high proportions of oldest old (see Figure 2.5).

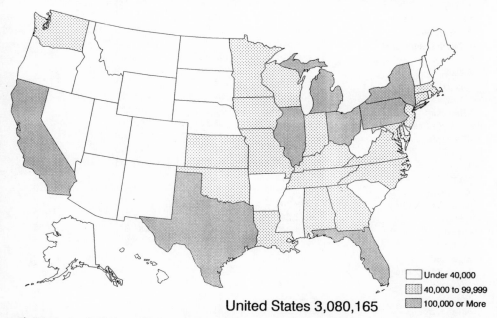

United States 3,080,165

☐	Under 40,000
▦	40,000 to 99,999
▨	100,000 or More

Figure 2–3 Total population aged 85 years and over: 1990. (Source: U.S. Bureau of the Census, 1990 Census of Population)

Table 2–12 Percent Change of U.S. Population Aged 85 Years and Over by Region, Division, and State: 1980 and 1990

Region, Division, and State	85 years and over		Change 1980–1990	Percent change 1980–1990
	1990	1980		
United States	3,080,165	2,240,067	840,098	37.5
Northeast	709,809	546,545	163,264	29.9
New England	194,253	151,371	42,882	28.3
Middle Atlantic	515,556	395,174	120,382	30.5
Midwest	839,863	649,375	190,488	29.3
East North Central	538,530	414,808	123,722	29.8
West North Central	301,333	234,567	66,766	28.5
South	992,022	663,741	328,281	49.5
South Atlantic	514,717	326,842	187,875	57.5
East South Central	186,003	134,007	51,996	38.8
West South Central	291,302	202,892	88,410	43.6
West	538,471	380,406	158,065	41.6
Mountain	132,600	86,302	46,298	53.6
Pacific	405,871	294,104	111,767	38.0
New England	194,253	151,371	42,882	28.3
Maine	18,226	14,099	4,127	29.3
Vermont	7,523	6,007	1,516	25.2
New Hampshire	13,286	9,650	3,636	37.7
Massachusetts	92.209	73,908	18,301	24.8
Rhode Island	16,016	11,978	4,038	33.7
Connecticut	46,993	35,729	11,264	31.5
Middle Atlantic	515,556	395,174	120,382	30.5
New York	248,173	192,983	55,190	28.6
New Jersey	95,547	72,231	23,316	32.3
Pennsylvania	171,836	129,960	41,876	32.2
East North Central	538,530	414,808	123,722	29.8
Ohio	138,030	108,426	29,604	27.3
Indiana	71,751	54,410	17,341	31.9
Illinois	147,549	114,682	32,867	28.7
Michigan	106,907	81,653	25,254	30.9
Wisconsin	74,293	55,637	18,656	33.5
West North Central	301,333	234,567	66,766	28.5
Minnesota	68,835	52,789	16,046	30.4
Iowa	55,255	44,940	10,315	23.0
Missouri	81,217	61,072	20,145	33.0
North Dakota	11,240	8,140	3,100	38.1
South Dakota	13,343	10,427	2,916	28.0
Nebraska	29,202	23,744	5,458	23.0
Kansas	42,241	33,455	8,786	26.3
South Atlantic	514,717	326,842	187,875	57.5
Delaware	7,142	5,269	1,873	35.5
Maryland	46,496	32,665	13,831	42.3
District of Columbia	7,847	6,385	1,462	22.9
Virginia	59,709	41,131	18,578	45.2
West Virginia	25,451	19,409	6,042	31.1
North Carolina	69,969	45,203	24,766	54.8
South Carolina	30,749	20,004	10,745	53.7
Georgia	57,244	39,434	17,810	45.2
Florida	210,110	117,342	92,768	79.1

Table 2–12   *(continued)*

Region, Division, and State	85 years and over			Percent change 1980–1990
	1990	1980	Change 1980–1990	
East South Central	186,003	134,007	51,996	38.8
Kentucky	46,367	35,036	11,331	32.3
Tennessee	58,794	41,443	17,351	41.9
Alabama	48,507	34,019	14,488	42.6
Mississippi	32,335	23,509	8,826	37.5
West South Central	291,302	202,892	88,410	43.6
Arkansas	35,216	26,354	8,862	33.6
Louisiana	43,633	30,535	13,098	42.9
Oklahoma	45,848	33,981	11,867	34.9
Texas	166,605	112,022	54,583	48.7
Mountain	132,600	86,302	46,298	53.6
Montana	10,676	8,837	1,839	20.8
Idaho	11,398	8,476	2,922	34.5
Wyoming	4,550	3,473	1,077	31.0
Colorado	32,953	24,363	8,590	35.3
New Mexico	14,232	8,783	5,449	62.0
Arizona	37,717	19,878	17,839	89.7
Utah	13,611	8,852	4,759	53.8
Nevada	7,463	3,640	3,823	105.0
Pacific	405,871	294,104	111,767	38.0
Washington	56,301	41,476	14,825	35.7
Oregon	38,815	28,431	10,384	36.5
California	299,107	218,017	81,090	37.2
Alaska	1,251	619	632	102.1
Hawaii	10,397	5,561	4,836	87.0

Source: U.S. Bureau of the Census. 1980 and 1990 Censuses of Population.

The oldest old were more likely to live in metropolitan (2,233,652 persons) than nonmetropolitan areas (846,513) in 1990. Hispanics and Asian and Pacific Islander oldest old were rarely found in nonmetropolitan areas. American Indian oldest old, however, were somewhat more likely to be found in nonmetropolitan than metropolitan areas (see Table 2–13).

The 1990 census shows America's oldest old minority population to be heavily concentrated in geographic areas popularly associated with each group: Blacks in a few large population states and the South; American Indians in the Western and Southern states; and Asians in Hawaii, California, and New York. Hispanics are concentrated in the South and in New York and California. It is particularly interesting how few oldest old minorities live anywhere else. The details of the concentrations for each group follow.

Nearly 60 percent of America's blacks aged 85 or older lived in the South in 1990. Nevertheless, compared with other minority groups, the oldest old black population was dispersed among the most states. Ninety percent lived in 20 states. Ten states had more than 10,000 blacks aged 85 or older: New York (17,973), Texas (16,564), California (12,887), Georgia (12,691), North Carolina (12,454), Alabama (11,787), Louisiana (11,413), Illinois (11,378), Florida (11,207), and Mississippi

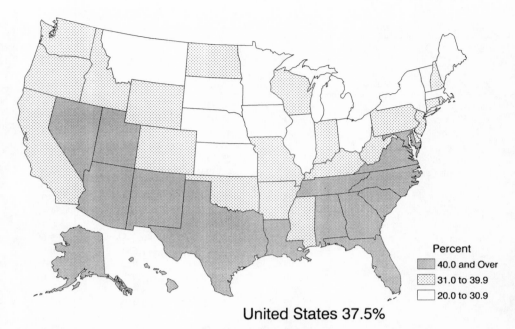

Percent

40.0 and Over

31.0 to 39.9

20.0 to 30.9

United States 37.5%

Figure 2–4 Percent change in population 85 years and over: 1980–1990. (Source: U.S. Bureau of the Census, 1990 Census of Population)

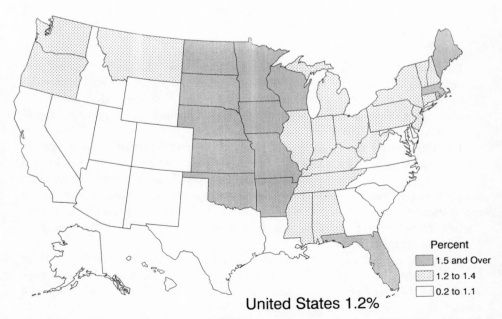

Percent

1.5 and Over

1.2 to 1.4

0.2 to 1.1

United States 1.2%

Figure 2–5 Percent of total state population 85 years and over: 1990. (Source: U.S. Bureau of the Census, 1990 Census of Population)

Table 2–13. Population of the United States for Metropolitan/Nonmetropolitan Areas by Age, Race, and Sex: 1990

Area, Race, and Sex	65–69	70–74	75–79	80–84	85 and over	80 and over
Metropolitan						
Total	7,558,466	5,892,967	4,463,816	2,855,256	2,233,652	5,088,908
Males	3,362,778	2,490,975	1,726,348	971,978	608,809	1,580,787
Females	4,195,688	3,402,012	2,737,468	1,883,278	1,624,843	3,508,121
White	6,552,823	5,188,426	3,960,211	2,559,144	2,009,481	4,568,625
Males	2,932,036	2,205,054	1,533,836	865,502	538,519	1,404,021
Females	3,620,787	2,963,372	2,426,375	1,693,642	1,470,962	3,164,604
Black	704,538	509,664	372,955	223,160	173,423	396,583
Males	297,024	201,922	136,754	74,877	50,314	125,191
Females	407,514	307,742	236,201	148,283	123,109	271,392
American Indian, Eskimo, and Aleut	21,030	13,900	9,567	5,495	3,917	9,412
Males	9,349	5,846	3,628	1,858	1,262	3,120
Females	11,681	8,054	5,939	3,637	2,655	6,292
Asian and Pacific Islander	166,601	113,880	74,272	40,233	26,820	67,053
Males	74,014	50,385	33,731	19,363	11,076	30,439
Females	92,587	63,495	40,541	20,870	15,744	36,614
Other	113,474	67,117	46,811	27,224	20,011	47,235
Males	50,355	27,768	18,399	10,378	7,638	18,016
Females	63,119	39,349	28,412	16,846	12,373	29,219
Hispanic*	388,641	254,220	188,280	114,726	83,380	198,106
Males	172,993	104,961	72,498	42,328	28,942	71,270
Females	215,648	149,259	115,782	72,398	54,438	126,836
Nonmetropolitan						
Total	2,553,269	2,101,836	1,657,553	1,078,483	846,513	1,924,996
Males	1,169,529	918,331	673,420	394,116	248,889	643,005
Females	1,383,740	1,183,505	984,133	684,367	597,624	1,281,991
White	2,346,814	1,938,138	1,524,814	993,551	778,571	1,772,122
Males	1,061,193	850,675	620,563	361,600	225,931	587,531
Females	1,265,621	1,067,463	904,251	631,951	552,640	1,184,591
Black	158,507	130,751	106,315	70,478	56,760	127,238
Males	65,918	52,777	41,786	25,782	18,278	44,060
Females	92,589	77,974	66,529	44,696	38,482	83,178
American Indian, Eskimo, and Aleut	21,680	15,370	11,585	6,621	5,288	11,909
Males	9,949	6,654	4,832	2,699	2,012	4,711
Females	11,731	8,716	6,753	3,922	3,276	7,198
Asian and Pacific Islander	11,896	8,354	5,867	3,617	2,918	6,535
Males	5,504	3,915	3,070	2,086	1,323	3,389
Females	6,392	4,439	2,797	1,551	1,595	3,146
Other	14,372	9,223	6,972	4,216	2,976	7,192
Males	6,965	4,310	3,169	1,969	1,345	3,314
Females	7,407	4,913	3,803	2,247	1,631	3,878
Hispanic*	47,616	32,552	24,985	15,699	11,184	26,883
Males	22,585	14,844	10,857	6,846	4,555	11,401
Females	25,031	17,708	14,128	8,853	6,629	15,482

*Hispanic may be of any race.

Source: U.S. Bureau of the Census. 1990 Census of Population.

(10,752). An additional 10 states had 5,000 to 10,000 oldest old blacks: Pennsylvania, Michigan, Ohio, Virginia, South Carolina, Tennessee, Maryland, New Jersey, Arkansas, and Missouri.

As might be expected, American Indians, Eskimo, and Aleut (AEI) oldest old were most likely to be found in the Western states (44 percent) and the South (35 percent), especially the western Southern states. There were only three states with more than 1,000 AEI persons aged 85 or older in 1990: Oklahoma (1,840), Arizona (1,060), and California (1,023).

Three out of four of America's oldest old Asians and Pacific Islanders lived in 1990 in California (12,722), Hawaii (7,653), or New York (2,465).

Almost 9 out of 10 oldest old of Hispanic origin (who may be of any race) lived in the following states in 1990: California (25,455), Texas (18,564), Florida (15,491), New York (10,142), New Mexico (3,753), New Jersey (2,943), Arizona (2,639), Illinois (2,207), and Colorado (2,170).

Among cities of 100,000 or more people in 1990, New York had the largest oldest old population by far (102,554), followed by Los Angeles (35,419), Chicago (30,522), and Philadelphia (22,801). For black oldest old, the largest populations were in New York (13,828), Chicago (8,174), Detroit (7,005), and Philadelphia (5,822). There were few oldest old American Indians in the major cities; the largest groups were New York City (148) and Tulsa, Oklahoma (111). Asian and Pacific Islander oldest old were concentrated only in Honolulu (3,922), Los Angeles (2,374), San Francisco (2,163), and New York City (2,112). The major cities where the oldest

Table 2–14 Percentage Distribution of Geographical Mobility of the Elderly Population between 1975 and 1980, by Age and Sex: 1980

Residence	Age (years)		
	65–69	80–84	85+
Total men			
Number	3,921,736	1,020,562	673,841
Percent	100.0	100.0	100.0
Same house	77.3	78.7	73.9
Different house, United States	22.2	21.0	25.8
Same county	11.8	13.1	16.4
Different county	10.4	7.9	9.5
Same state	4.8	4.4	5.6
Different state	5.6	3.5	3.8
Abroad	0.5	0.3	0.3
Total women			
Number	4,954,494	1,933,373	1,537,572
Percent	100.0	100.0	100.0
Same house	76.9	74.4	68.7
Different house, United States	22.5	25.3	31.1
Same county	13.0	16.1	20.0
Different county	9.5	9.3	11.1
Same state	4.6	5.2	6.6
Different state	4.9	4.0	4.5
Abroad	0.6	0.3	0.2

Source: U.S. Bureau of the Census. Special tabulations for the National Institute on Aging from the 1980 Census of Population, table 5.

old of Hispanic origin were likely to be found were New York (8,480), Los Angeles (4,365), Miami (4,254), San Antonio (3,272), and El Paso (2,055).

Older persons are much less likely than younger persons to move across state lines. Among those older people who do move across state lines, however, the rates tend to peak in the mid-sixties and again after age 85. In 1980, 22 percent of men and 23 percent of women aged 65 to 69 lived in a different house than they had in 1975, compared with 26 percent of men and 31 percent of women aged 85 and older (Table 2–14). The oldest old were much more likely than the younger old to have moved within the same county as their 1975 residence, which leads to the speculation that the moves are primarily to nursing homes or into the homes of relatives because of increased dependency due to health problems (Patrick 1980). Economic problems may be an additional reason.

SOCIOECONOMIC STATUS

Overall, there have been marked improvements in the educational and economic status of the oldest old during the last several decades. However, there are extreme differences among groups within the oldest-old population. They are heterogeneous along educational and economic lines, as are other age groups. Economic inequalities were carried into old age from activities throughout the life cycle, especially from the labor market.

Inequalities tend to grow with advancing age and are related particularly to health status and the availability of private pensions and investments that can supplement government retirement pensions and benefit programs.

The educational status of older persons has improved as better-educated cohorts have replaced less well educated ones. About 23 percent of the oldest old had at least a high-school education in 1970, increasing to 30 percent in 1980. Future generations of the oldest old will have much higher levels of educational attainment; for example, about 45 percent of those aged 65 to 69 years in 1980 had at least a high-school education (Table 2–8). Because educational level is so closely connected with economic status, health status, and functional needs over the lifetime, the oldest old are likely to be better off in these areas in the future (Blau and Duncan 1967; Feldman and Makuc 1987).

Research by Savant, Inc., and the National Association of State Units on Aging (1987) found that the functional capacity (impairment) of older persons influences their need for services (especially skilled care and in-home personal services). They used age and educational attainment to produce substate forecasts of functional capacity. Persons aged 85 years and over with fewer than 8 years of education have the highest levels of moderate or severe impairment. In 1980, the proportion of the noninstitutionalized oldest old with 8 or fewer years of education ranged from 39 percent in Maine to 74 percent in West Virginia. In the majority of states, half or more of the noninstitutionalized oldest old had such low educational attainment (Table 2–15) compared with a national average of 33 percent of the total oldest old (Table 2–8). However, we can expect to see significant improvement in the educational attainment of the oldest old in the years to come. The proportion of noninsti-

Table 2–15 Percentage of Noninstitutionalized Persons Aged 65 to 74 and 85 Years and Over with 8 or Fewer Years of Education, Ranked by State: 1980

\u200b	65–74 (years)			85+ (years)	
Rank	State	Percentage	Rank	State	Percentage
1	Kentucky	57.0	1	West Virginia	74.1
2	West Virginia	54.3	2	Kentucky	73.7
3	Louisiana	53.1	3	North Dakota	71.9
4	Tennessee	52.8	4	Hawaii	70.3
5	Georgia	52.2	5	Louisiana	69.9
6	North Carolina	51.9	6	Wisconsin	69.2
7	North Dakota	51.8	7	Arkansas	67.3
8	South Carolina	51.0	8	Tennessee	66.9
9	Alabama	49.7	9	Alabama	66.0
10	Arkansas	48.6	10	Mississippi	65.6
11	Hawaii	48.4	11	Minnesota	65.5
12	Mississippi	48.0	11	Illinois	65.5
13	Virginia	46.7	13	Missouri	65.4
14	Missouri	44.7	14	Pennsylvania	65.2
15	South Dakota	43.4	15	North Carolina	65.0
16	Rhode Island	42.8	16	New Jersey	64.4
17	Pennsylvania	42.5	17	South Dakota	63.4
18	Wisconsin	40.9	18	Oklahoma	63.2
19	Maryland	40.3	19	Georgia	63.0
20	New Jersey	40.1	20	South Carolina	62.6
21	Illinois	39.5	20	Ohio	62.1
21	Minnesota	39.5	22	Indiana	61.8
23	Texas	39.4	23	Michigan	61.4
24	Oklahoma	38.6	24	New Mexico	61.1
25	New York	38.1	25	Rhode Island	60.8
26	Connecticut	37.4	26	Maryland	60.5
27	Michigan	35.2	27	New York	59.7
27	New Mexico	35.2	28	Virginia	59.6
29	Alaska	34.3	29	Connecticut	57.9
29	Delaware	34.3	30	Iowa	57.7
31	Indiana	33.9	31	Nebraska	57.6
32	Montana	33.3	32	Kansas	57.3
33	District of Columbia	33.0	33	Montana	57.2
34	Iowa	32.9	34	Texas	56.6
35	Vermont	32.7	35	Alaska	56.1
36	Ohio	31.8	36	Delaware	53.3
37	Nebraska	31.5	37	Idaho	52.9
38	New Hampshire	30.2	38	Washington	51.9
39	Kansas	29.6	39	Wyoming	51.7
40	Maine	28.6	40	Colorado	49.8
41	Massachusetts	28.3	41	Arizona	49.4
42	Idaho	28.2	42	Oregon	48.9
43	Florida	28.0	43	Florida	48.2
44	Colorado	27.1	44	Massachusetts	48.1
45	Wyoming	26.5	45	California	47.9
46	California	26.0	46	New Hampshire	47.3
47	Oregon	25.8	47	Utah	45.3
48	Arizona	24.7	48	Nevada	45.2
49	Washington	24.1	49	District of Columbia	44.6
50	Nevada	23.8	50	Vermont	41.8
51	Utah	16.5	51	Maine	39.1

Source: U.S. Bureau of the Census. Special tabulations for the National Institute on Aging from the 1980 census, table 9.

tutionalized persons aged 65 to 74 in 1980 with fewer than 8 years of education ranged from 17 percent in Utah to 57 percent in Kentucky (Table 2–15).

In 1980, only 4 percent of oldest-old men were still in the labor force compared with 7 percent a decade earlier. About 29 percent of men aged 65 to 69 were at work or looking for work in 1980. Labor-force participation among women was about half that for men (Table 2–8).

The economic well-being of the older population has been a matter of lively debate in recent years. Statistics can be found to support almost any position, depending on whether one differentiates among various demographic groups and what concepts and data are used to determine economic status. Average income levels have improved dramatically since the 1950s for men and women of all ages. The improvements among the elderly (aged 65 years and over) have resulted from increases in Social Security benefits and a cost-of-living index to provide a cushion against inflation. Other improvements include the fact that more older persons are covered by a variety of public and private pension plans and income support programs such as Supplemental Security Income (SSI), Medicare, Medicaid, and property tax relief (Fowles 1983). During the 1950s and 1960s, coverage increased and higher average wages resulted in higher average benefits. Higher labor-force participation rates in the 1950s also resulted in more benefits in the 1980s. As a result, the elderly population as a group has shown a continuously improved economic status. But generalizations about "the elderly" are misleading because this is such a heterogeneous group. The 85-and-over population is also economically a much more heterogeneous group than was previously believed, and care should be taken not to overgeneralize about this group either. The situation for an oldest-old married couple is usually rather different from that of an 85-year-old woman living alone.

In terms of income of the population aged 85 and over, median money income for women increased in real terms from $2,300 in 1969 to $3,300 in 1979; for men, the increase was from $3,300 to $4,800 (Table 2–16). More than four out of five men (83 percent) aged 85 years and over had incomes in 1979 of less than $10,000 compared with 92 percent of women, 95 percent of black men, and 98 percent of black women (Table 2–16). These data vividly demonstrate the disparity in income levels among race–sex groups.

Variation in economic status among the oldest old is even more apparent when poverty is considered. According to the 1970 census, about 37 percent of the oldest

Table 2–16 Income in 1979 of Persons Aged 85 Years and Over, by Sex and Race: 1980

Income	All races		Black	
	Men	Women	Men	Women
With income	619,096	1,325,313	47,468	92,888
Percent with:	100.0	100.0	100.0	100.0
Less than $4,000	38.9	63.4	64.1	84.4
$4,000 to $9,999	43.7	28.2	31.0	13.9
$10,000 to $24,999	13.7	7.1	4.5	1.5
$25,000 or more	3.6	1.3	0.4	0.1

Source: U.S. Bureau of the Census. Special tabulations for the National Institute on Aging from the 1980 census, table 20.

old were poor; this fell to 21 percent in 1980. But the rate varies considerably by sex, race, and living situation. Those living alone, especially oldest-old black women, have significantly higher rates of poverty then those living in families. As shown in Figure 2–6, poverty rates in 1979 for the oldest old ranged from a low of 8 percent for women (all races) living in families to a high of 73 percent for black women living alone.

Geographically, there are considerable differences in the economic status of the oldest old. Nationally, the average income of households with a householder aged 85 and over was estimated by Longino (1986) to be $20,200 in 1985 dollars (1979 census income inflated using the December 1985 Consumer Price Index). Longino showed that, among the states, household income for the oldest old ranged in 1979 from a high of $37,800 in Hawaii (where a high proportion of oldest old lived with relatives) to a low of $12,800 in South Dakota.

In three states, Missouri, Wisconsin, and Wyoming, more than 40 percent of the oldest old were poor. By contrast, only 10 percent of this group were poor in California. In 1980 in Mississippi, a state with relatively high poverty levels among the oldest old, two-thirds of women aged 85 and over who lived alone were poor, as were over one-fifth of the oldest-old women who lived in families. California's oldest old had lower poverty rates than most states: 23 percent for those who lived alone compared with 5 percent for those living in families (U.S. Bureau of the Census 1986).

As stated earlier, much of the explanation for income differences among the oldest old lies in past labor-market activity. Income from employment makes the greatest difference in economic status, but very few persons aged 85 years and over are in the labor market. Of those who are working, most work part time and receive a relatively low income. For example, of those oldest-old men who received wages or who were self-employed in 1979, about half received less than $4,000 in 1979. The proportions of oldest-old women and blacks who received less than $4,000 for work in the marketplace were even higher.

Social Security is an important element in the income of many older people. About 72 percent of all oldest-old men, 89 percent of all women, 83 percent of black men, and 93 percent of black women received less than $4,000 in 1979 from Social Security. Ten percent of men who received public-assistance income received more than $4,000 compared with only 4 percent of black women. Of those who received income from interest, dividends, and rent, two-thirds of men received less than $4,000 from those sources. Black women were the most likely to have the lowest income levels (Table 2–17).

Even though average total income declines with age, there is evidence that the value of assets rise with age, at least through the mid-eighties. Data on asset income in the 1980 census (interest, dividends, royalties, and net rental income only) support the conclusion that the elderly, in general, tend to reduce their savings from these sources only after age 85 (Torrey and Taeuber 1986). The proportion of elderly married couples as well as unmarried men and women who received income from assets is nearly constant up to age 85, at which point there is a small decline. Because statements on receipt of property income from the census are generally biased downward, and because the elderly tend to underreport asset income more than the

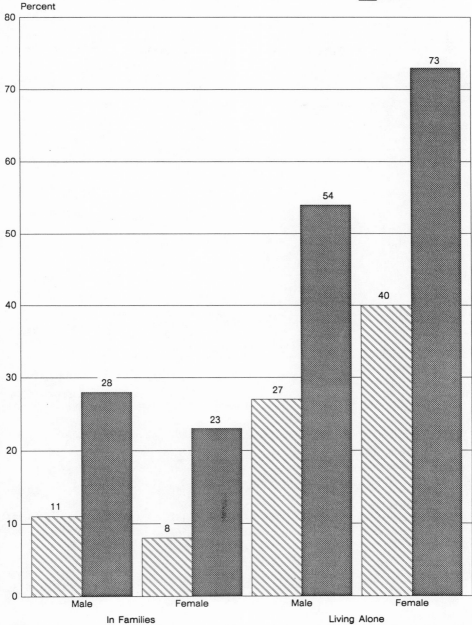

Figure 2–6 Poverty rate in 1979 for persons aged 85 and over. (Source: U.S. Bureau of the Census, special NIA tabulations from the 1980 census, table 6)

Table 2–17 Percentage of Persons Aged 85 Years and Over Receiving Less Than $4,000 from Income of Specified Types in 1979, by Race and Sex: 1980

	All races		Black	
Source of income	Men	Women	Men	Women
Wage/salary	47.5	57.6	52.5	61.3
Nonfarm self-employment	51.6	65.9	63.7	53.8
Farm self-employment	60.6	62.0	86.4	93.4
Interest/dividends	67.7	73.3	86.9	90.4
Social Security	71.5	88.7	82.5	93.0
Public assistance	90.1	95.0	94.5	96.3
All other sources	68.1	75.4	73.0	82.8

Source: Bureau of the Census. Special tabulations for National Institute on Aging from the 1980 Census, table 21A.

Table 2–18 Income in 1979 from Property, by Age and Marital Status: 1980

	Age (years)				
Marital status	65–69	70–74	75–79	80–84	85 +
Average total income (in dollars) for those who receive income					
Total	8,621	7,534	6,923	6,381	5,540
Married couples	17,458	15,018	13,676	12,810	11,723
Unmarried men[a]	8,641	7,605	7,183	6,865	6,338
Unmarried women[a]	7,023	6,462	5,996	5,536	4,803
Average income (in dollars) from property income of those who received such income[b]					
Total	3,860	4,151	4,342	4,327	4,320
Married couples	5,046	5,663	6,261	6,546	6,389
Unmarried men[a]	3,764	4,173	4,412	4,349	4,723
Unmarried women[a]	3,501	3,761	3,894	3,889	3,967
Percent of cohort receiving income from property income[b]					
Total	41	42	41	40	34
Married couples	60	60	59	58	55
Unmarried men[a]	35	35	35	37	35
Unmarried women[a]	42	42	41	39	33

[a] Includes persons who are divorced, widowed, and those who have never married, as well as those who are married but separated.

[b] The 1980 census data includes only income from interest, dividends, royalties, and net rental income. It specifically excludes lump-sum payments such as money from an inheritance or capital gains, but includes the mortgage interest received from the sale of property.

Source: B.B. Torrey, and C.M. Taeuber. 1986.

nonelderly do, the data shown in Table 2–18 are probably underestimated, and perhaps more so for the oldest old.

CONCLUSION

A growing very old population is a reality in America. Previous fertility patterns as well as dramatic improvements in life expectancy will result in a larger number and proportion of persons aged 85 years or older than the United States has ever experienced. As a nation, we will be much older in the next century, and consequently the nature of American society will be vastly different from that of today. High proportions of very old persons relative to the number of productive workers could have profound social and economic consequences. But these demographic conditions represent only one factor among many that will influence future economic prospects. The growth of the oldest-old population, however, is a virtual certainty. That knowledge allows for planning that considers the societal impact of an older age structure on all age groups, as well as for devising ways to accommodate and care for this burgeoning group.

There are major differences between today's oldest old and younger age groups. We need to be aware of the differences among age groups and of the implications of those differences as public policy for the older population is designed. As shown here, the population aged 85 years and over is demographically, socially, economically, and physically heterogeneous. Throughout we have mentioned two themes about the oldest-old population that bear repeating here: (1) the majority of this population is female, but some improvements are expected in male longevity; and (2) we can expect marked improvements in the educational attainment of this population in the future, which has implications for both health and economic status.

Beyond the personal level, there are considerable differences within the oldest-old population compared with the younger old in terms of their numbers, level of educational attainment, lifetime economic experience, and so forth, all of which have implications for their well-being.

Two major fears about old age concern health and economic status. Both catastrophic illness and illnesses of long duration are a significant threat, even to the elderly with good economic resources, because the elderly have little opportunity to replace their assets once they are depleted. Personal resources and family help that were adequate in the past may not meet the needs of tomorrow's oldest old with their greater life expectancy. The extension of life will result in ever larger numbers of economically and physically vigorous very old people along with large numbers of chronically ill, dependent persons. About half of the oldest-old population are healthy enough that they do not need significant assistance with the activities of daily life; the other half are dependent on family or society.

Under current policies, real government expenditures for the elderly can be expected to continue to grow as a result of demographic pressures. The coming demographic changes imply that either a significant share of the nation's resources will be used to maintain present social and health programs or that benefit levels will be reduced. In the past, the cost of programs for the elderly were borne mostly by the working-age population. Future changes in age structure will further increase the proportionate burden on the working-age population unless significant policy changes occur. It appears that the most likely future scenario is one in which the elderly share in the cost of their care to a greater extent than at present. As such, policy makers may begin to consider the impact of the events of youth on eventual economic status in old age. Some say that it makes economic sense over the long run to institute programs that encourage preventive health practices and improve the long-term economic prospects of the majority of young people.

Aside from the important and obvious issues of providing health care, there will be other policy decisions with potentially wide-ranging impact on the future status of the elderly. The most immediate include laws and practices affecting workers, taxpayers, and employers, as well as issues such as retirement age; leave and tax breaks for parental care; wider availability of reasonably priced day care for children so that more women can be in the labor force continuously; how a larger proportion of the population may obtain higher education or vocational training; and tax and other incentives for retirement saving, pension portability, home care, long-term care, and so on.

Once the very large baby-boom generation reaches the oldest-old ages in 2030 to 2050, America will be presented with a novel situation. We can only try to anticipate some of the problems and solutions that will ultimately evolve. To monitor adequately the dramatic changes requires a sophisticated statistical system and study of the experience of other industrialized nations. America is an aging society. If we anticipate and plan now for all age groups, individuals and families will be better able to adjust their own expectations and plan for their futures. The magnitude of the change can be foreseen to some extent and presents a challenge to adapt public policy far enough in advance to be successful.

REFERENCES

Blau, P.M., and O.D. Duncan. 1967. *The American Occupational Structure.* New York: John Wiley.

Bryant, E.S., and M. El-Attar. 1984. Migration and Redistribution of the Elderly: A Challenge to Community Services. *The Gerontologist* 24(6):634–40.

Feldman, J.J., and D. Makuc. 1987. Socioeconomic Differentials in Mortality: A Comparison of Trends in The United States with Trends in England and France. Unpublished paper presented at the International Epidemiological Association, Helsinki, Finland.

Fingerhut, L. 1982. Changes in Mortality Among the Elderly, United States, 1940–1978. *Vital and Health Statistics,* series 3, no. 22. Washington: National Center for Health Statistics.

Fowles, D. 1983. The Changing Older Population. *Aging* 339:6–11.

Longino, C.F., Jr. 1986. A State by State look at the Oldest Americans. *American Demographics* 8(11):38–42.

Myers, G.C., and C.A. Nathanson. 1982. Aging and the Family. *World Health Statistics Quarterly* 35(3/4):225–38.

Patrick, C.H. 1980. Health and Migration of the Elderly. *Research on Aging* 2(2):223–31.

Rosenwaike, I., and B. Logue. 1985. *The Extreme Aged in America: A Portrait of an Expanding Population.* Westport, Conn.: Greenwood Press.

Savant, Inc., and National Association of State Units on Aging (NASUA). 1987. *Forecasting Service Needs of the Elderly Based on Functional Capacity: An Information Resource for State and Local Decision Making*. Washington. (Unpublished.)

Schoen, R., W. Urton, K. Woodrow, and J. Baj. 1985. Marriage and Divorce in 20th Century American Cohorts. *Demography* 22(1):101–14.

Siegel, J.S. 1980. Recent and Prospective Demographic Trends for the Elderly Population and Some Implications for Health Care. *Proceedings of the Second Conference on the Epidemiology of Aging*. National Institutes of Health, pub. no. 80-969. Washington.

Siegel, J.S., and C.M. Taeuber. 1982. The 1980 Census and the Elderly: New Data Available to Planners and Practitioners. *The Gerontologist* 22(2):148–49.

Siegel, J.S., and C.M. Taeuber. 1986. Demographic Perspectives on the Long-Lived Society. *Daedalus* 115(1):87.

Spencer, G. 1986. U.S. Bureau of the Census. The Characteristics of Centenarians in the 1980 Census. Paper presented at the April meeting of the Population Association of America, San Francisco.

Spencer, G., A. Goldstein, and C.M. Taeuber. 1987. America's Centenarians: Data from the 1980 Census. U.S. Bureau of the Census. *Current Population Reports*, series P-23, no. 153. Washington.

Thomas, K., and A. Wister. 1984. Living Arrangements of Older Women: the Ethnic Dimension. *Journal of Marriage and the Family* 76:301–11.

Torrey, B.B., and C.M. Taeuber. 1986. Further Evidence for a Life Line Rather Than a Life Cycle of Assets. *The Review of Income and Wealth* 32(4):443–49.

U.S. Bureau of the Census. 1983. 1980 Census of Population, General Social and Economic Characteristics, PC80-1-C1, U.S. Summary, table 120. Washington.

———. 1986. 1980 Census of Population and Housing. Special NIA STF5 Tabulations, Washington. Available as a machine-readable computer file from The National Archives of Computerized Data on Aging, Survey Research Center, University of Michigan (Telephone: 313-764-2570).

———. 1989. Projections of the Population of the United States by Age, Sex, and Race; 1988 to 2080. *Current Population Reports*, series P-25, no. 1018. Washington.

———. 1991. 1990 Census of Population, series CPH-L-74, Modified and Actual Age, Sex, Race, and Hispanic Origin. Population Division, Washington, D.C.

3

Cohort Succession and the Future
of the Oldest Old

SAMUEL H. PRESTON

The diagonal march of birth cohorts across the grid of age and time is at once the most mundane and the most profound process known to demography. Cohorts begin the march with their own unique endowment of social and biological attributes. Along the diagonal, they experience the normal processes of development and aging; they absorb the wars, epidemics, recessions, and booms of their time; and they witness the attrition of their members in ways that transform the composition of survivors.

The lockstep progression of cohorts into new age-time blocs affords an opportunity for prediction that is rare in the social sciences. Although we have few clues about what changes will occur in per capita income over the next 20 years, or in the political climate or the fertility rate, we have a great deal of information about changes in the type of people who will occupy a particular age group. For older ages, especially, many characteristics of the pertinent cohorts have been largely determined and are directly observable. The major uncertainty is how the composition of each cohort will change as a result of selective mortality.

Chapter 2 by Taeuber and Rosenwaike and Chapter 4 by Myers, Torrey, and Kinsella provide a rich portrait of the oldest old in the United States and in other developed countries. They also note some projected changes in the size and biological attributes (age, race, and sex) of this group. They do not describe impending changes in the social characteristics of the oldest old. To fill this gap, in this chapter I will illustrate the usefulness of a cohort perspective by examining likely changes in the composition of the older population with respect to two important social characteristics: educational attainment and number of surviving children. Serow and Sly (1988) also make education and parity projections for the oldest old, but confine their attention to means and medians rather than full distributions and do not allow for differences in mortality among people with different characteristics.

EDUCATIONAL ATTAINMENT

Better-educated people tend to have lower morbidity rates, higher incomes, and greater self-sufficiency throughout the life cycle. At advanced ages, enhanced well-being is likely to occur as later and better-educated cohorts replace earlier cohorts; the need for health services and public transfers may be reduced. To demonstrate the kinds of changes that are in prospect, we have projected forward the educational distribution by cohort as recorded in the U.S. census of 1980. The assumptions used in this projection are the following:

1. Cohorts will receive no additional years of schooling after they reach age 50–54.
2. International migration beyond age 50–54 will not alter the educational distribution of cohorts.
3. Mortality differentials by educational attainment will remain as described by Kitagawa and Hauser (1973) for 1960. Among white women over age 65, mortality rates are in the ratio 1.06, .94, and .70 for persons with 0–8 years of schooling, 9–12 years of schooling, and some college, respectively. Among white men, however, these ratios are 1.01, .99, and .98, so that no adjustments for differential mortality is apparently necessary for men in this study (Kitagawa and Hauser, 1973:12). Nonwhite ratios in this study were based upon too small a sample to be reliable for the older ages, and white ratios are used for both groups in the projection. These ratios were combined with survival probabilities presented in the official U.S. life table (total female population) for 1984 (National Center for Health Statistics 1987).

The projected distribution of educational attainments among the oldest old is shown in Table 3–1. Obviously, an extraordinarily rapid upgrading of the educational distribution is in the offing, reflecting a sharp increase in enrollment among children and youth earlier in the century. Although a majority of the oldest old in 1980 did not attend high school, fewer than 20 percent will fall into this category by 2015. The progress between 1990 and 2005 will be especially rapid. The percentage of men who had attended college will rise from 13.7 percent among those aged 85 to 89 in 1980 to 31.1 percent among those aged 85 to 89 in 2015. Among women, the percentage will increase from 13.5 percent to 27.4 percent. Whereas only 31.5 percent of women aged 85 to 89 had graduated from high school in 1980, 67.1 percent will have done so by 2015.

The assumption that women with lower levels of schooling will die at a higher rate has a substantial impact on the projected educational distribution of the 85- to 89-year-old population. This effect can be illustrated by reference to the cohort aged 50 to 54 years in 1980. If there were no differences in mortality by educational level, then educational attainments in the cohort would remain distributed as they were in 1980 (see Table 3–2).

The mean years of schooling in this cohort is expected to rise as result of differential mortality by 0.3 year as it ages from 50–54 to 85–89. With effects of this size, it is instructive to examine actual cohorts to see whether they experienced changes in composition equivalent to those projected. The cohort aged 85 to 89 in 1980 did, in fact, undergo a substantial educational upgrading as it aged. Table 3–3 shows a comparison of the cohort's distribution of educational attainments in the 1940 U.S. Census, when it was 45 to 49 years of age, to its reported distribution in 1980.

The percentage of the cohort with 0 to 8 years of schooling declined by 14 percent over the 40-year period. Based upon Kitagawa and Hauser's figures, differential mortality between ages 50 to 54 and 85 to 89 was projected to reduce this percentage by 13 percent in the earlier example (i.e., from 15.8 to 13.7 percent). Thus, there is evidence that differential mortality is actually modifying cohort composition in the expected way over age and time. The percentage who had attended college increased in the cohort aged 85 to 89 in 1980 by 54 percent, which is far greater that the 19 percent increase projected to occur as a result of differential mortality. It is likely that the difference is attributable to some combination of actual college attendance and spurious inflation of stated educational achievements with age. Folger and Nam (1967) report a modest systematic net upward movement in reported educational attainments with age, which they believe reflects increasing overstatement of achievements. If this overstatement is widespread, then the upgrading of real educational compositions among the oldest old will be even faster than that shown in Table

Table 3–1 Projections of the Distribution of Educational Attainments Among the Oldest Old

Population characteristics	Percentage having completed specific years of schooling					
	0–8	High school 1–3	High school 4	College 1–3	College 4	College 5+
Males						
Population aged 85+ in 1980	63.0	11.3	12.4	6.0	4.2	3.0
Population aged 85–89 in 1980	62.1	11.6	12.5	6.2	4.3	3.2
Projected population aged 85–89 in						
1985	57.8	13.7	13.7	6.7	4.4	3.6
1990	53.4	15.2	14.9	7.2	4.8	4.4
1995	44.4	18.0	18.7	8.6	5.1	5.2
2000	37.3	18.9	24.0	9.2	5.2	5.5
2005	28.1	19.0	29.5	10.9	6.1	6.3
2010	22.5	18.5	31.1	12.1	7.8	7.9
2015	20.0	18.1	30.8	12.7	9.0	9.4
Females						
Population aged 85+ in 1980	55.3	13.4	17.7	8.1	3.9	1.5
Population aged 85–89 in 1980	54.7	13.8	17.6	8.5	3.8	1.6
Projected population aged 85–89 in						
1985	49.8	15.4	18.7	9.7	4.3	2.2
1990	44.0	17.3	19.9	10.9	5.1	2.8
1995	36.5	19.3	23.0	12.0	5.8	3.5
2000	30.1	20.7	28.3	11.9	5.4	3.6
2005	22.6	20.6	34.7	12.8	5.4	3.8
2010	16.9	19.3	38.9	15.1	5.6	4.2
2015	13.7	19.2	39.7	15.6	6.7	5.1

Sources: The projection is based upon the distribution of educational attainments in the 1980 census. Unpublished 5-year age data were supplied by Arnold Goldstein of the U.S. Census Bureau. Preparation of these data was made possible by a contract from the National Institute on Aging. Ages under 60 were taken from U.S. Bureau of the Census (1984, Table 262).

Table 3–2 Percentage of Women Aged 85 to 89 in 2015 with Various Educational Attainments

Years of schooling completed	Assuming no differential mortality by education	Assuming differential mortality by education
0–8	15.8	13.7
High school 1–3	20.0	19.2
High school 4	41.2	39.7
College 1–3	13.1	15.6
College 4	5.6	6.7
College 5+	4.3	5.1

3–1, because older cohorts would have overstated their years of schooling by more than younger cohorts in 1980.

Men also upgraded their educational attainments in the cohort aged 85 to 89 in 1980, but substantially less rapidly than did women. For example, the percentage of men attending school for less than 9 years declined by 8.8 percent between 1940 and 1980, whereas for women the decline was 13.9 percent. Kitagawa and Hauser report negligible mortality differences by education among older men, so that differential mortality may not account for the improvement. On the other hand, Rosen and Taubman (1979) report wider education differentials for older men in 1973 through 1976 than Kitagawa and Hauser found in 1960. Their sample, however, was small, and a substantial number of deaths were omitted from the record-keeping system. Clearly, better and more recent information on adult mortality differentials by major socioeconomic variables would improve our ability to forecast the circumstances of the oldest old.

Furthermore, in projecting mortality differences among groups, it is desirable to have some sense of why they arise. In the case of education, for example, do they reflect differences in economic conditions among various groups, differences in the distribution of innate endowments, or real effects of education on health-related behaviors? If they primarily reflect differences in access to material resources, then social programs such as Medicare could be expected to weaken the association between education and mortality. If they reflect differences in innate endowments, then

Table 3–3 Percentage of the Cohort Aged 85 to 89 in 1980 with Various Educational Attainments

Years of schooling completed	1940 census[a]	1980 census
0–8	63.5	54.7
High school 1–3	14.4	13.8
High school 4	13.1	17.6
College 1–3	5.6	8.5
College 4	2.7	3.8
College 5+	0.7	1.6

[a]*Source:* U.S. Bureau of the Census (1943, p. 78).

the shifting distribution of endowments among classes could be expected to alter measured differentials in predictable ways (e.g., raising the relative mortality of the most poorly educated groups and reducing the advantage of the best-educated as access to education improves). A lively debate over the importance of shifting endowments for changing social class mortality differences in Great Britain has proven inconclusive (Pamuk 1988). Illsley and Kincaid (1963) argue that selective intergenerational mobility among women has caused social class differences in perinatal mortality to widen in Great Britain. They suggest that lower-class mothers are increasingly negatively selected for such factors as height as taller women move disproportionately to higher classes. However, Wilkerson (1986) shows that such selection is incapable of accounting for more than about 10 percent of the increase in social-class differences in perinatal mortality in Aberdeen, Scotland.

Finally, if the measured differentials by education largely reflect the real effects of education on mortality, then it is reasonable to project differences among the educational groups that are basically unchanged. In regard to child-mortality differences by mother's education in developing countries, at least, evidence supports the view that the bulk of measured differentials reflects the real influence of education (United Nations 1985).

NUMBER OF OFFSPRING

A second important feature of the condition of the oldest old is their number of surviving children, who often serve as caregivers and coresidents. A Congressional Budget Office report (King 1988, 29) shows that the proportion of elderly (65+) widows living with relatives rises from 19.9 percent for women with no children to 33.1 percent for women with one child; the proportion rises monotonically to 53.1 percent for women with seven or more children.

The fertility histories of cohorts who have completed childbearing have changed rapidly in the course of the demographic booms and busts of the twentieth century. Cohort fertility variation has been much smaller than period variation (Hobcraft, Menken, and Preston 1985), but important changes have also occurred among cohorts. To project the distributions of parity (numbers of children ever born) among the oldest old, we make the same assumptions that we made in the case of educational attainment: that no childbearing will occur above age 45; that international migration will not alter the parity distribution; and that mortality differentials by parity are as recorded in the Kitagawa and Hauser (1973) study pertaining to 1960. This study is the only nationally representative study available to date that provides relative mortality ratios of women by parity. The relative mortality rates for ever-married white women aged 65 and above are shown in Table 3–4. The ratios were combined with U.S. female life tables from 1984 to project the completed parity distributions of women aged 45 to 49 in various years forward to the time that they would be ages 85 to 89. Completed parity distributions are drawn from Hauser's (1976) reconstructions from vital statistics. These are undoubtedly more accurate than reports from censuses.

Table 3–5 presents the results of these projections. It is clear that major changes in parity distributions are in prospect for the oldest old. Approximately 20 percent of

Table 3–4 Relative Mortality Rates for
Ever-married White Women
Aged 65 and Above

Number of children ever born	Age-standardized mortality ratio
0	1.00
1	0.94
2	1.02
3	0.97
4	1.01
5–6	0.97
7+	1.09

Source: Kitagawa and Hauser, 1973, p. 112.

this group will be childless through 2000, but this percentage will plummet to 10 percent by 2015 as the mothers of the baby boom move into the oldest-old category. Another 15 to 23 percent of each cohort will have had only one child through the year 2000, and often that child will not have survived. By 2015, only 12 percent of the oldest-old women will have borne only one child, and the proportion of those children who survived will have increased. The percentage with very large families will fall and then recover some of its earlier losses. Note that these tendencies have offsetting effects on mean numbers of children born; the mean completed family size is very similar for women in the youngest and the oldest cohorts shown in Table 3–5 (3.04 and 3.16, respectively; Heuser 1976), but the changing distribution of women among parities has very important implications for potential living and caring arrangements in the two cases.

It is useful to go one step further and attempt to project the number of *surviving* children among women in these cohorts. This exercise requires introducing cohort mortality rates for these women's offspring. We assume that children are born to women when they are age 27.5 and use cohort mortality rates up to 1980 prepared by Mitchell Eggers of the University of Pennsylvania by piecing together period life tables for whites. An adjustment translating white rates into total rates was based

Table 3–5 Projected Distributions of Women Aged 85 to 89 by Number of Children Ever Born, United States

Year cohort is aged 85–89	Percentage of women with specified number of children ever born							
	0	1	2	3	4	5	6	7+
1975	21.2	15.0	15.2	13.0	9.9	6.9	5.6	13.2
1980	19.5	16.9	17.3	14.1	9.9	6.3	5.0	11.0
1985	19.2	19.6	19.3	13.8	9.0	5.5	4.3	9.3
1990	19.9	22.7	20.5	13.2	8.1	5.0	3.6	7.0
1995	21.1	23.0	21.7	13.3	7.8	4.5	3.0	5.6
2000	19.7	21.6	23.4	14.7	8.2	4.5	2.8	5.1
2005	15.7	18.7	25.1	17.2	9.7	5.4	3.1	5.1
2010	11.2	16.1	25.2	19.7	11.7	6.5	3.8	5.8
2015	10.4	12.3	23.3	21.2	13.7	7.9	4.6	6.6

Source: Distributions in Heuser (1976, 124) projected forward by the procedure described in text.

upon cohort life tables up to 1968 prepared by Moriyama and Gustavus (1972). Beyond 1980, children's survival was projected forward using the official 1984 U.S. Life Tables.

We have assumed that the survival of each child born to a woman is independent of that of her other children and of her own survival. Results are not very sensitive to the assumed independence of siblings' survival, but they are somewhat sensitive to the assumption that mortality of the generations is independent. To the extent that mothers' and children's death rates are positively correlated, we will overstate the death probabilities for the children of surviving mothers.

Given the assumption of independence, the number of women aged 85 to 90 with no surviving children can be calculated as

$$F(0) + F(1) \ q(60) + F(2) \ [q(60)]^2 + \cdots$$

and the number with one surviving child as

$$F(1) \ [1 - q(60)] + 2F(2)q(60)[1 - q(60)] + 3F(3) \ [q(60)]^2[1 - q(60)] \ \cdots$$

where $F(i)$ is the number of women in the cohort with completed parity of i and $q(60)$ is the probability of survival to age 60 for the cohort born when the women were aged 27.5. Results are shown in Table 3–6.

The figures in Table 3–6 are in some respects startling. Through the year 2000, about one-quarter of women aged 85 to 89 will be childless and another one-quarter will have only one surviving child. Discussions that assume that children will accept the primary burden of caregiving for their very old parents must recognize that very large fractions of the very old have no prospects for such support. Between now and 2000, childless and one-child women will be a majority of the oldest-old women. Yet these groups have received very little attention from scholars or policy makers.

After 2000, the situation will change rapidly, and by 2015, more than two-thirds of very old women will have at least two surviving children. They will also be, as we have seen, much better educated. It would surely be misleading to assume that patterns of interaction between this group and the rest of society will be similar to those in the 1980s. The inexorable process of cohort succession ensures that their social and demographic circumstances will be very different.

Table 3–6 Projected Distributions of Women Aged 85 to 89 by Number of Surviving Children, United States

Year cohort is aged 85–89	Percentage of women with specified number of surviving children		
	0	1	2+
1980	24.0	21.0	55.0
1985	24.0	23.7	52.3
1990	25.2	26.1	48.7
1995	26.1	26.6	47.3
2000	24.3	25.8	49.9
2005	19.6	24.0	56.4
2010	14.7	21.8	63.5
2015	13.1	18.2	68.7

REFERENCES

Folger, J.K., and C.B. Nam. 1967. *Education of the American Population.* A 1960 Census Monograph. Washington: U.S. Bureau of the Census.

Heuser, R.L. 1976. *Fertility Tables for Birth Cohorts by Color.* DHEW pub. no. (HRA) 76-1152. Rockville, Md.: National Center for Health Statistics.

Hobcraft, J., J. Menken, and S. Preston. 1985. Age, Period, and Cohort Effects in Demography: A Review. In *Cohort Analysis in Social Research,* eds. W.M. Mason and S.E. Fienberg, 89–136. New York: Springer-Verlag.

Illsley, R., and J.C. Kincaid. 1963. Social Correlations of Perinatal Mortality. In *Perinatal Mortality,* eds. R. Butler and D.G. Bonham, 270–86. Edinburgh: E. & S. Livingstone.

King, M.L. 1988. *Changes in the Living Arrangements of the Elderly: 1960–2030.* Washington: Congressional Budget Office, U.S. Congress.

Kitagawa, E.M., and P.M. Hauser. 1973. *Differential Mortality in the United States: A Study in Socioeconomic Epidemiology.* Cambridge, Mass.: Harvard University Press.

Moriyama, I.M., and S.O. Gustavus. 1972. *Cohort Mortality and Survivorship: United States Death-Registration States, 1900–68.* DHEW pub. no. (HSMO) 73-1400. Rockville, Md.: National Center for Health Statistics.

National Center for Health Statistics. 1987. *Vital Statistics of the United States, 1984:* Vol. 2, *Section 6—Life Tables.* DHHS pub. no. (PHS) 87-1104. Washington.

Pamuk, E. 1988. Changing Social Class Differences in Infant Mortality: Great Britain, 1921–1981. Ph.D. diss., University of Pennsylvania, Philadelphia.

Preston, S.H. 1984. Children and the Elderly: Divergent Paths for America's Dependents. *Demography* 21(4):435–56.

Rosen, S., and P. Taubman. 1979. Changes in the Impact of Education and Income on Mortality in the U.S. In *Statistical Uses of Administrative Records and Emphasis on Mortality and Disability Research,* L. Del Bene and F. Scheuren, compilers, 61–66. Washington: U.S. Department of Health, Education, and Welfare, Office of Research and Statistics.

Serow, W., and D. Sly. 1988. Trends in the Characteristics of the Oldest Old: 1940 to 2020. *Journal of Aging Studies* 2(2):145–56.

United Nations. 1985. *Socioeconomic Differentials in Child Mortality in Developing Countries.* New York.

U.S. Bureau of the Census. 1943. *Sixteenth Census of Population: 1940. Vol. 4. Characteristics by Age.* Part 1: *United States Summary.* Washington.

———. 1984. *1980 Census of Population. Detailed Population Characteristics. United States Summary. Section A.* Washington.

Wilkerson, R.G. 1986. Socioeconomic Differences in Mortality: Interpreting the Data on Their Size and Trends. In *Class and Health: Research and Longitudinal Data,* ed. R.G. Wilkerson, 1–20. London: Tavistock.

4

The Paradox of the Oldest Old in the United States: An International Comparison

GEORGE C. MYERS, BARBARA BOYLE TORREY,
and KEVIN G. KINSELLA

The United States has a younger population age structure today than many of the world's developed countries, notably those in Western Europe, as evinced by the percentage of population 65 years of age and over. And the United States will continue to be younger in these terms than most of its counterparts well into the twenty-first century. But this simple generalization obscures an important phenomenon. The U.S. *elderly* are among the oldest of any major country; only the elderly populations of France and the Federal Republic of Germany[1] currently contain a higher proportion who are 80 years and over. By 2005, the United States will have the highest percentage of the elderly who are 80 years and over (31 percent). It is a demographic paradox that one of the younger industrial countries has such an old elderly population.

The large size of the oldest old relative to all elderly in the United States is a result of a complex interplay of demographic forces operating in the past and currently. The theoretical term "metabolism" has sometimes been used (Myers 1990) to indicate the relative size of the increments and decrements that shape the composition of the older population. The increments are determined by the initial size of birth cohorts (augmented by net migration and depleted by death) as they reach a specified age such as 65. As these elderly cohorts pass through the older ages, they are subject to further decrement from deaths until they reach a specified age, such as 80 or 85, and become defined as the oldest old. In turn, this oldest-old group is subject to mortality forces that alter its overall size. To trace these developments in the United States is a challenging task that still confronts us, but it is clear that the paradox that we have noted is due to both the relative size of cohorts that have

[1]This text was written at the time of German reunification, and combined East-West data were not yet readily available. Reunification will result in an elderly German population of nearly 12 million as of 1990. Since the population of East Germany is somewhat younger, on average, than that of West Germany, indicators such as percent elderly for the combined nation will be slightly lower than those presented here for the Federal Republic.

reached the oldest ages and mortality rates at older ages that are lower for the United States than those for other countries.

A number of publications (e.g., Hoover and Siegel 1986; Myers 1982; U.S. Bureau of the Census 1987) have focused on aging trends for the world, but concerns about the oldest old have usually been subsumed under the broader issues of aging populations in general. Until recently, the oldest old have been such a small group worldwide that they have been largely ignored, except for the even fewer centenarians who have throughout history been the subject of exotic curiosity. Today, however, as the number of oldest old grows rapidly in every country, they are requiring policy makers and family members to recognize the vulnerabilities, special needs, and long-term contributions of the oldest old to the societies that now support them.[2]

The oldest old constitute more than 14 percent of the world's elderly today—19 percent in developed countries and 11 percent in developing nations. Table 4–1, based on estimates from the United Nations and the U.S. Bureau of the Census for 31 selected countries, shows that persons aged 80 and over make up more than 3 percent of the total population in a number of industrial countries. These percentages are expected to rise significantly during the next 40 years. In many countries, the 80-and-over segment is projected to be the fastest-growing portion of the elderly population. The oldest old in the United States numbered 6.9 million as of 1990, more than in any other country of the world, and are likely to increase to more than 14 million 40 years hence.

A detailed comparison of the oldest old in 31 countries is beyond the scope both of this chapter and of the existing data. However, revealing comparisons can be drawn from a subset of these nations. This chapter compares the oldest old in the United States with their counterparts in seven other countries that represent a spectrum of the industrial world. These countries include Australia and Canada, two of the youngest developed countries; the Federal Republic of Germany, Sweden, and the United Kingdom, which are among the oldest; Japan, the emergent industrial giant; and Hungary, an Eastern European nation. Discussion focuses initially on past, present, and future growth of the oldest old, which helps to provide a perspective for the rest of the issues raised. The chapter then examines widowhood and the ratio of the oldest old to their potential caretakers over time. The life expectancy and causes of mortality of the very old also are examined, followed by a comparison of the level and sources of income of the very old in six countries. A short section on the People's Republic of China is added at the end because of the unique aging issues China faces in the future.

Many countries do not have detailed social and economic statistics on the very old because, until recently, the oldest old have not been a population group that has commanded specific attention. Therefore, this chapter is limited by the available data. For mortality statistics, data are presented for people aged 85 years and over; demographic and social statistics are given on those aged either 80 or 85 years and over; income information is available for persons aged 75 years and over.

The demographic and social statistics are primarily from national population censuses; the life expectancy and mortality statistics are from the World Health Organization; and the economic statistics are from the Luxembourg Income Study. These

---

[2] Recent publications by Suzman and Riley (1985) and Rosenwaike and Logue (1985) reflect the growing awareness of the importance of the oldest old in the United States and elsewhere.

Table 4–1 Total Population and Percentage in Elderly Age Categories, 31 Countries: 1965 to 2025

Country	1965				1985			
	Total population (in thousands)	Percentage aged 65 and over	Percentage aged 75 and over	Percentage aged 80 and over	Total population (in thousands)	Percentage aged 65 and over	Percentage aged 75 and over	Percentage aged 80 and over
United States	194,303	9.5	3.4	1.6	238,631	12.0	4.9	2.6
Western Europe								
Austria	7,255	13.3	4.5	2.0	7,502	14.1	6.5	3.0
Belgium	9,464	12.6	4.4	2.0	6,903	13.4	5.9	2.9
Denmark	4,758	11.3	4.0	1.8	5,122	14.9	6.3	3.2
France	48,758	12.1	4.5	2.1	54,621	12.4	6.2	3.2
Germany, Fed. Rep.	59,012	11.9	3.9	1.7	60,877	14.5	6.8	3.2
Greece	8,551	8.9	3.2	1.5	9,878	13.1	5.5	2.6
Italy	51,944	9.9	3.5	1.6	57,300	13.0	5.5	2.5
Luxembourg	332	11.8	3.9	1.7	363	12.7	5.2	2.3
Norway	3,723	12.0	4.2	2.0	4,142	15.5	6.4	3.2
Sweden	7,734	12.7	4.5	2.1	8,351	16.9	7.2	3.5
United Kingdom	54,520	12.0	4.3	2.0	56,125	15.1	6.3	3.1

Eastern Europe							
Bulgaria	8,201	8.4	2.6	1.0	9,071	11.3	4.3	1.8
Hungary	10,148	10.3	3.2	1.3	10,697	12.5	5.1	2.2
Poland	31,496	6.8	2.0	0.8	37,187	9.4	4.0	1.7
Other developed countries							
Australia	11,387	8.5	3.0	1.3	15,698	10.1	3.7	1.7
Canada	19,644	7.7	2.9	1.4	25,426	10.4	4.0	2.0
Japan	98,881	6.2	1.9	0.8	120,742	10.0	3.7	1.7
New Zealand	2,628	8.1	3.0	1.4	3,318	10.4	3.9	1.8
Developing countries							
Bangladesh	58,373	3.8	1.0	0.4	101,147	3.1	0.9	0.3
Brazil	84,292	3.2	0.9	0.3	135,564	4.3	1.3	0.6
China	729,191	4.4	1.3	0.4	1,059,521	5.3	1.5	0.6
Guatemala	4,568	2.7	0.8	0.3	7,963	2.9	0.9	0.4
Hong Kong	3,692	3.2	0.8	0.2	5,548	7.6	2.4	1.0
India	495,156	3.5	0.8	0.3	758,927	4.3	1.1	0.4
Indonesia	107,041	3.1	0.8	0.3	166,440	3.5	0.9	0.3
Israel	2,563	5.8	1.5	0.5	4,252	8.9	3.6	1.5
Mexico	43,500	3.4	1.1	0.5	78,996	3.5	1.3	0.6
Philippines	32,492	3.0	1.0	0.4	54,498	3.4	1.0	0.4
Singapore	1,880	2.7	0.8	0.3	2,559	5.2	1.6	0.6
Uruguay	2,693	8.4	3.0	1.4	3,012	10.7	4.0	1.9

Table 4–1 (Continued)

Country	2005 Total population (in thousands)	2005 Percentage aged 65 and over	2005 Percentage aged 75 and over	2005 Percentage aged 80 and over	2025 Total population (in thousands)	2025 Percentage aged 65 and over	2025 Percentage aged 75 and over	2025 Percentage aged 80 and over
United States	275,677	13.1	6.7	4.1	301,394	19.5	8.5	4.8
Western Europe								
Austria	7,483	15.6	6.8	3.5	7,279	19.7	8.2	4.3
Belgium	10,019	15.9	6.9	3.4	10,054	19.8	7.9	3.8
Denmark	5,034	15.8	7.2	4.0	4,690	22.2	10.1	5.0
France	57,618	14.8	6.4	3.1	58,431	19.3	7.9	3.6
Germany, Fed. Rep.	58,456	18.9	7.5	3.8	53,490	22.5	9.5	5.3
Greece	10,564	16.9	7.0	3.3	10,789	17.8	7.9	4.2
Italy	58,736	16.9	7.0	3.4	57,178	19.6	8.6	4.3
Luxembourg	355	16.1	6.3	2.8	339	21.3	8.3	4.1
Norway	4,221	14.8	7.3	4.2	4,261	20.2	8.6	4.1
Sweden	8,079	17.2	8.2	4.7	7,707	22.2	10.5	5.2
United Kingdom	56,230	15.3	6.9	3.8	55,919	18.7	8.1	4.0

Eastern Europe							
Bulgaria	9,650	15.2	6.1	2.8	10,070	16.7	7.1	3.4
Hungary	10,729	15.0	6.2	2.9	10,598	19.0	7.5	3.7
Poland	41,940	12.3	4.9	2.2	45,286	17.1	6.1	2.7
Other developed countries							
Australia	19,496	11.4	4.8	2.4	22,575	15.9	6.2	2.9
Canada	29,832	12.5	5.6	3.0	33,261	18.8	7.5	3.7
Japan	132,045	16.5	6.4	3.0	132,082	20.3	10.0	4.9
New Zealand	3,867	11.2	4.8	2.4	4,202	16.3	6.3	2.9
Developing countries							
Bangladesh	161,427	2.9	0.8	0.3	219,383	4.3	1.1	0.4
Brazil	193,603	5.8	2.1	1.0	245,809	9.3	3.2	1.5
China	1,311,247	7.7	2.6	1.1	1,475,159	12.9	4.1	1.8
Guatemala	13,971	3.8	1.3	0.6	21,668	4.9	1.7	0.8
Hong Kong	7,019	10.3	4.3	2.1	7,617	17.5	5.8	2.6
India	1,024,634	6.1	1.8	0.7	1,228,829	9.7	3.1	1.3
Indonesia	225,597	5.6	1.6	0.6	272,744	8.7	2.7	1.2
Israel	5,625	8.3	3.5	1.8	6,865	11.9	4.7	2.1
Mexico	118,876	4.6	1.6	0.8	154,085	7.7	2.6	1.2
Philippines	80,220	4.2	1.2	0.5	102,787	7.5	2.1	0.9
Singapore	3,048	8.2	2.7	1.1	3,323	17.9	5.6	2.2
Uruguay	3,475	12.1	5.0	2.5	3,875	12.3	5.0	2.7

Note: Data for China include Taiwan.

Source: U.S. Bureau of the Census, International Data Base on Aging.

statistics have been carefully compiled into an international aging database developed for the National Institute on Aging by the Center for International Research at the U.S. Bureau of the Census. Social, demographic, and economic data by 5-year age groups have been integrated not only for Western industrial countries, but also for Eastern European and developing economies. (The Appendix provides more information about the International Data Base on Aging.)

Also included in this chapter are demographic projections of future aged populations that have been prepared by the United Nations and the U.S. Bureau of the Census. Seemingly, such projections should be viewed as more reliable than most other speculations about the future (and cannot take into account the impact of events such as the reunification of Germany), for the people who will be aged in 2025 are already at least 25 years old. However, it is important to emphasize that estimates of the future elderly in 2025 are affected greatly by assumptions used to determine mortality rates. In fact, it has been found that previous projections of elderly populations have tended to underestimate mortality rate improvements and therefore to underestimate the number of older persons (Keyfitz 1981; Stoto 1983). Therefore, if there is a bias in the demographic projections discussed in this chapter, it is most likely in the direction of underestimating the size of the future elderly populations.

It is important to emphasize that all of the statistics reported in this chapter may be subject to bias in the reporting of age both in enumerations and vital statistics at these extreme ages and even in imputation procedures that have been used occasionally to adjust for nonresponse (e.g., Coale and Kisker 1986; Spencer 1986). The countries that have been selected for this analysis are deemed generally to have more reliable statistics. Nonetheless, caution must be exercised in interpreting these findings.

DEMOGRAPHIC TRENDS AMONG THE OLDEST OLD

Average Annual Growth Rates

The most common demographic measure for assessing population growth is the average annual growth rate, which translates growth over time in a continuously changing base population into a mean yearly figure. If the estimated and projected population figures for the years 1965 through 2025 are considered, then the most dramatic period of growth rates of the oldest old in a majority of developed countries has already occurred (Table 4–2). In the 20-year span beginning in 1965, the average yearly growth of the oldest old in the eight countries examined in this chapter ranged from 2.3 percent in the United Kingdom to 4.7 percent in Japan, with most countries registering a gain of approximately 3 percent per year. The past growth rate in the United States was higher than in any country except Japan. From 1985 to 2005, these average rates are expected to decline in all countries except Australia, with the yearly rates of growth in the Federal Republic of Germany, Hungary, Sweden, and the United Kingdom dropping to one-half or less of the 1965–85 rate. From 2005 to 2025, further declines are projected everywhere except in the Federal Republic of Germany.

During the period 2005 to 2025, the oldest old will actually be increasing at a

Table 4-2 Average Annual Growth Rates of the Oldest Old and Total Elderly Populations, 20-Year Periods, 1965 to 2025 (in percentages)

Country	Oldest old (aged 80 and over)			All elderly (aged 65 and over)		
	1965–85	1985–2005	2005–25	1965–85	1985–2005	2005–25
Australia	2.80	2.80	1.63	2.49	1.67	2.40
Canada	3.23	2.84	1.55	2.83	1.72	2.56
Germany, Fed. Rep.	3.38	0.66	1.24	1.12	1.13	.42
Hungary	2.96	1.31	1.13	1.20	.94	1.13
Japan	4.71	3.38	2.53	3.37	2.93	1.04
Sweden	3.06	1.27	.30	1.84	−.09	1.03
United Kingdom	2.25	1.05	.17	1.29	.09	.96
United States	3.55	3.00	1.20	2.21	1.18	2.42

Source: U.S. Bureau of the Census, International Data Base on Aging.

slower pace than the total elderly population (persons aged 65 years and older) in most of the countries examined. Outside of the Federal Republic of Germany, projected average annual growth rates for the elderly as a whole range from just under 1 percent in the United Kingdom to 2.4 percent in the United States and more than 2.5 percent in Canada.

On the basis of growth rates over the next 40 years, one might conclude that the oldest old are becoming less of a concern. In this instance, however, growth rates can be misleading. The primary reason that annual growth rates of the oldest old were relatively high in the recent past is that the absolute numbers of oldest old were relatively small, so that even modest increases in oldest-old populations may produce high growth rates. Large numerical additions to an already large population base can result in a seemingly low growth rate.

Absolute Population Increases

An alternative approach in assessing population growth of the oldest old, especially in terms of policy planning, is to examine absolute numerical changes. Table 4-3 provides estimated and projected numbers of the oldest old at four points in time, as well as the absolute and percentage increases during successive 20-year intervals. Although the rates of growth shown in Table 4-2 generally will decline from 1985 to 2005, the absolute numbers of oldest old will increase significantly in all of these countries, with several countries adding substantially more oldest-old persons in this period than was the case from 1965 to 1985. In the United States, for example, a 15 percent drop in growth rate from 1965–1985 to 1985–2005 translates into a net addition of nearly 2 million more oldest old in the latter period than occurred during 1965–1985. In Japan, the total number of persons aged 80 and over will nearly double between 1985 and 2005.

Absolute gains also will occur from 2005 to 2025 in all eight countries. Because the numbers of the oldest old will have expanded rapidly by 2005, the national percentage increases during 2005 to 2025 will generally be smaller than in preceding periods. Even so, the United States and Japan will add nearly 3.1 million and 2.6 million more oldest-old persons, respectively, to their totals as of 2005. Large gains

Table 4–3 Numbers of Oldest Old at Four Points in Time, and Absolute Growth and Percentage Increases During Successive 20-Year Periods, 1965 to 2025

Country	Total population aged 80 years and over (in thousands)				Absolute growth of population aged 80 years and over (in thousands)			Percentage increase in population aged 80 years and over		
	1965	1985	2005	2025	1965–1985	1985–2005	2005–2025	1965–1985	1985–2005	2005–2025
Australia	153	268	469	649	115	201	180	75.0	75.2	38.4
Canada	269	513	906	1,235	244	393	329	90.7	76.6	36.3
Germany, Fed. Rep.	992	1,951	2,228	2,855	959	276	628	96.7	14.2	28.2
Hungary	133	240	312	391	107	72	79	80.8	29.9	25.3
Japan	780	2,000	3,936	6,531	1,220	1,936	2,595	156.4	96.8	65.9
Sweden	160	295	381	404	135	85	23	84.6	28.9	6.1
United Kingdom	1,104	1,732	2,138	2,211	628	407	73	56.8	23.5	3.4
United States	3,046	6,198	11,289	14,348	3,152	5,091	3,059	103.5	82.1	27.1

Source: U.S. Bureau of the Census, International Data Base on Aging.

will also be recorded in Canada, the Federal Republic of Germany, Hungary, and Australia.

Oldest Old as a Percentage of All Elderly

Another useful analytic approach, which gives insight into the shifting internal composition of an elderly population, is to consider the oldest old as a percentage of the total elderly population aged 65 years and over (Figure 4–1). The oldest old constituted between 13 and 18 percent of national elderly populations in 1965 (Table 4–4). In six of the eight countries, the oldest old as a percentage of the total elderly is expected to increase from 1965 to 2005, then fall or remain constant through 2025. However, in Japan and the Federal Republic of Germany, the oldest old will continually increase as a share of all elderly persons.[3]

The proportion of the oldest old in the aged population increased rapidly in the Federal Republic of Germany and the United States from 1965 to 1985, so much so that these two nations now have the highest oldest-old proportion of total elderly in the eight countries. By 2005, the United States is expected to have the largest proportion, with more than 3 in 10 elderly being at least 80 years old. And despite a large drop in its oldest-old share of total elderly by 2025, the United States will still rank ahead of the other nations.

As is clear from Table 4–3, declines in the ratio of oldest old to total elderly after 2005 are not the result of decreasing numbers of oldest old. Rather, they reflect the more rapid growth among persons aged 65 to 79 years than among the oldest old during the period 2005 to 2025. As these persons age further, they will eventually fuel additional growth in the oldest old after 2025 in some countries, particularly those that experienced baby booms in the post–World War II era. In the United

[3]In the Federal Republic of Germany, the oldest-old share would have dipped slightly in 2005 before rising again by 2025. This would have been due to small birth cohorts 80 or so years prior to 2005 (that is, to reduced fertility in the aftermath of World War I) and to war losses.

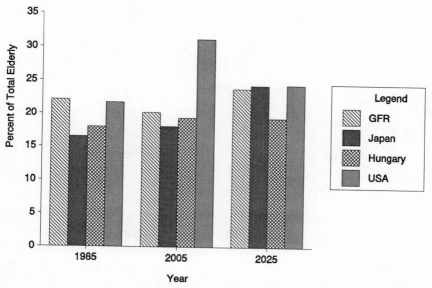

Figure 4–1 The oldest old as a percentage of total elderly in four countries, 1985 to 2025.

States, the high-fertility cohorts born from 1946 to 1960 will join the ranks of the oldest old beginning in 2020, and we may then expect to again see rising ratios of oldest old to total elderly.

Gender Composition

In terms of gender composition, populations aged 80 years and over are predominantly female and are becoming more so. Table 4–5 shows the ratio of men to women in the 80-years-and-over age bracket. During the period 1965 to 1985, each of the eight countries except Japan experienced an increase in the female proportion in this age group. The most pronounced gender imbalance is found in the United Kingdom, where in 1985 there were only 4 men for every 10 women among the

Table 4–4 Oldest Old as a Percentage of Total Elderly Population, Selected Years, 1965 to 2025

Country	1965	1985	2005	2025
Australia	15.8	16.8	21.1	18.1
Canada	17.9	19.3	24.2	19.8
Germany, Fed. Rep.	14.1	22.1	20.2	23.8
Hungary	12.7	18.0	19.4	19.4
Japan	12.6	16.5	18.1	24.3
Sweden	16.3	20.9	27.4	23.6
United Kingdom	16.9	20.5	24.8	21.2
United States	16.5	21.7	31.2	24.4

Note: Percentages refer to persons 80 years old and over divided by persons 65 years old and over.

Source: U.S. Bureau of the Census, International Data Base on Aging.

Table 4–5 Male/Female Ratio of Persons Aged 80 Years and Over, Selected Years, 1965 to 2025

Country	1965	1985	2005	2025
Australia	.56	.47	.51	.54
Canada	.83	.55	.52	.54
Germany, Fed. Rep.	.62	.42	.36	.50
Hungary	.64	.51	.42	.43
Japan	.50	.58	.52	.58
Sweden	.74	.56	.55	.57
United Kingdom	.45	.40	.45	.48
United States	.66	.47	.46	.48

Source: U.S. Bureau of the Census, International Data Base on Aging.

oldest old. In large part, past declines in the male/female ratio at age 80 years and over can be attributed to widening gender differentials in survival at older ages.

Further declines in sex ratios at ages 80 years and over are projected to continue through 2005 for most countries. These figures in the following period are expected to reverse, and in 2025 all countries will have a greater proportion of men among their oldest old than was the case 20 years earlier (Figure 4–2). Nevertheless, on average, women will still outnumber men by nearly two to one in 2025.

SOCIAL CONDITIONS OF THE OLDEST OLD

One of the major public and private concerns about the growth of the oldest-old population is how to sustain their quality of life. Relatively little is known about the

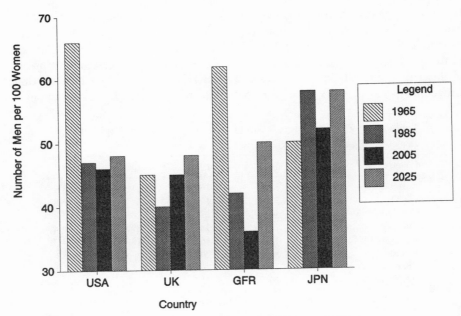

Figure 4–2 Oldest old sex ratios in four countries, 1965 to 2025.

social characteristics of this very old population, especially with respect to their living arrangements, social relations, and needed support mechanisms. Nonetheless, we can examine some sociodemographic trends in related characteristics that at least suggest basic social dimensions that will have to be addressed in the future. In this section, we consider the marital status characteristics of the oldest old, as well as caretaker ratios that relate to provision of care to this expanding population.

Marital Status

The proportion of older persons in different marital statuses at any one point in time is a function of a number of factors—the antecedent behavior of persons in cohorts reaching old age, selective survival, and marital behavior of persons currently at older ages. The last factor is of relatively minor significance in most Western societies, but the first two are of considerable importance and bear attention in the analyses that follow.

The distributions presented in Table 4–6 make it clear that the differences between men and women are considerable. Men at these later ages are much more likely to be currently married and women more frequently widowed. Women also are more apt to be single (never married) and divorced/separated. These latter differences are largely affected by marriage formation patterns in early life and, between countries, by cultural patterns. On the other hand, the married/widowed figures are mainly a result of selective survival that favor women over men. When we examine these trends for the elderly as a whole and by age groups among the elderly, it becomes evident that proportionately fewer women reach old age (say, age 65 years) in intact marriages, and at the older ages, a greater proportion become widows. By the time women reach the oldest-old age, a very high proportion are not married.

The data in Table 4–6 reveal some interesting differences among countries. Sweden has a high proportion of men and women who are single, and Japan has very low proportions single. Widowed men and women are proportionately large groups in Japan and Hungary, in contrast to other countries, although, as we note later, survival levels would suggest that whereas this should be true in Hungary, it should be less likely in Japan.

Of particular importance in this analysis is the fact that not only do we find an oldest-old population that is disproportionately female, but that these females are overwhelmingly not married compared with males. The normal supports available through the presence of spouses, even at these advanced ages, are therefore lacking for the majority of women in all countries.

Longitudinal analysis of marital status for all elderly (aged 65 years and over) have revealed that in most countries the proportion of both men and women who married is increasing; fewer are widowed over time (Myers 1986). To examine these trends over time for the oldest old, we have grouped the single, widowed, and divorced/separated together into a category termed "not married," in order to contrast it with those who are currently married. The not-married category contains persons who are more likely to require support services of one type or another.

Table 4–7 shows that the trend noted earlier for the total elderly applies only to men at the oldest-old ages. For each country, the proportion of married men increased during the period 1960 to 1980. Conversely, although the changes in propor-

Table 4–6 Percentage Distribution of Marital Status for Persons Aged 85 Years and Over, by Sex, Circa 1980

Country	Men					Women				
	Single	Married	Widowed	Divorced/ separated	Total	Single	Married	Widowed	Divorced/ separated	Total
Australia	7.3	42.0	48.3	2.3	100.0	10.7	5.8	82.0	1.4	100.0
Canada	8.7	45.5	45.1	0.7	100.0	10.3	8.5	80.9	0.3	100.0
Germany, Fed. Rep.[a]	4.5	63.0	31.1	1.4	100.0	11.4	16.0	70.2	2.3	100.0
Hungary	3.1	40.0	55.9	1.0	100.0	6.8	4.4	86.8	2.0	100.0
Japan	0.7	44.5	53.7	1.0	100.0	0.7	5.0	92.6	1.6	100.0
Sweden	11.1	37.0	49.8	2.1	100.0	19.6	6.8	70.1	3.5	100.0
United Kingdom	6.8	39.1	53.6	0.6	100.0	15.2	7.4	76.8	0.5	100.0
United States	5.6	48.4	43.8	2.1	100.0	7.9	8.4	81.8	2.0	100.0

[a]Data refer to persons 75 years of age and over.

Source: U.S. Bureau of the Census, International Data Base on Aging.

Table 4–7 Change in the Percentage of Persons Aged 85 Years and Over by Marital Category and Sex, Selected Countries, 1960 to 1980

	Married			Not married		
Country	1960	1980	Percentage change 1960–80	1960	1980	Percentage change 1960–80
Australia						
Men	34.8	42.0	7.2	65.2	58.0	−7.2
Women	8.2	5.8	−2.4	91.8	94.2	2.4
Canada						
Men	37.6	45.5	7.9	62.4	54.5	−7.9
Women	11.4	8.5	−2.9	88.6	91.5	2.9
Hungary						
Men	34.1	40.0	5.9	65.9	60.0	−5.9
Women	4.5	4.4	−0.1	95.5	95.6	0.1
United Kingdom						
Men	33.7	39.1	5.4	66.3	60.9	−5.4
Women	7.1	7.4	0.3	92.9	92.6	−0.3
United States						
Men	38.7	48.4	9.7	61.3	51.6	−9.7
Women	8.2	8.4	0.2	91.8	91.6	−0.2

Source: U.S. Bureau of the Census, International Data Base on Aging.

tion married for women are relatively small, only in the United Kingdom and the United States are they in the same direction as for men.

The proportional distributions at the oldest-old ages reveal only one aspect of the situation. The numerical growth of those married versus not married among the oldest old provides another view of the added differential burden imposed by growth of the advanced elderly. Table 4–8 indicates that both married and not-married oldest-old persons of both sexes increased in number during the period 1960 to 1980. However, much higher growth is found among not-married women. In the United Kingdom, the absolute growth of not-married women during the period was more than 12 times as high as for men. In the other countries as well, at least six times more not-married women than men were added between 1960 and 1980. In the United States, the number of not-married women 85 years and over approached 1.4 million in 1980.

Care Providers

The nature and availability of potential caregivers for the future's oldest old is a matter of great concern when anticipating the implications of an aging society. Demographic trends among various population components, elderly and nonelderly alike, will affect such issues as long-term care, home care versus institutionalization, and health-care costs, and therefore can be expected to alter society's living arrangements. These issues become extremely complex when one considers the types of caregivers who might be involved—spouses, children, other family members, younger elderly, public officials, and so forth. Each of these groups may vary both demographically in size, composition, and geographical location; and socially, in terms of

Table 4–8 Change in the Number of Persons 85 Years of Age and Over, by Marital Category and Sex, Selected Countries, 1960 to 1980

Country	Married				Not married			
			1960–80 increase				1960–80 increase	
	1960	1980	Number	Percentage	1960	1980	Number	Percentage
Australia								
Men	5,496	12,600	7,104	129.2	10,293	17,400	7,107	69.0
Women	2,381	4,400	2,019	84.8	26,659	71,400	44,741	167.8
Canada								
Men	13,913	28,965	15,052	108.2	21,931	34,670	12,739	58.1
Women	5,193	11,055	5,862	112.9	40,506	119,100	78,594	194.0
Hungary								
Men	4,200	7,800	3,600	85.7	8,100	11,700	3,600	44.4
Women	800	2,000	12,000	150.0	17,700	43,400	25,700	145.2
United Kingdom								
Men	30,417	46,582	16,165	53.1	59,757	72,659	12,902	21.6
Women	15,080	28,875	13,795	91.5	196,730	358,642	161,912	82.3
United States								
Men	129,076	323,457	194,381	150.6	204,307	344,521	140,214	68.6
Women	43,487	127,726	84,239	193.7	486,915	1,396,975	910,060	186.9

Source: U.S. Bureau of the Census, International Data Base on Aging.

availability, willingness to serve, and whether the support rendered is formal or informal.

A recent study by Stone, Cafferata, and Sangl (1986) of free home care for disabled elderly in the United States found that the average age of those providing care was 57 years, and that more than 70 percent of the care providers were women. Because more than half of the care recipients were aged 75 or over, the situation in many cases was characterized as one in which the young old were caring for the oldest old. Furthermore, the study found that daughters constituted the largest individual category of caregiver other than spouses; daughters accounted for 29 percent of all caregivers. In three-quarters of the cases, the caregiver lived with the disabled person.

Assuming that the observed correlation between advanced age and increased functional disability continues, we should ask what demographic projections portend for care of the oldest old. A first approach to better understanding of this issue is the analysis of ratios of different population groups. For this purpose, we have calculated ratios of the number of women 50 to 64 years of age to persons 80 years and older, regardless of sex. Generally speaking, the younger group of women could be expected to have parents at the oldest-old ages.

For each country the ratio declined between 1965 and 1985 (Table 4–9). The nation with the highest ratio in 1965, Japan, still had the highest level in 1985, although the ratio declined by one-third in the 20-year period. This may help explain why Japan has one of the highest proportions of aged persons residing with their children, although other cultural factors are also certainly important. The lowest ratio in 1985 is found in Sweden, but the largest decline between 1965 and 1985 actually occurred in the Federal Republic of Germany.

Table 4–9 Caretaker Ratios, 1965 to 2025

Country	Year			
	1965	1985	2005	2025
Austalia	5.2	4.1	3.6	3.3
Canada	4.4	3.5	3.1	2.5
Germany, Fed. Rep.	6.4	2.9	2.6	2.2
Hungary	7.4	4.3	3.5	2.5
Japan	8.0	5.3	3.5	2.0
Sweden	4.6	2.3	2.3	2.1
United Kingdom	4.8	2.7	2.5	2.6
United States	4.7	2.8	2.2	2.0

Note: Caretaker ratios indicate the number of women aged 50–64 per each person (both sexes combined) aged 80 and over.

Source: U.S. Bureau of the Census, International Data Base on Aging.

The ratios are expected to decline further throughout the period 1985 to 2025, but at a slower rate. These caretaker ratios serve to alert us to the fact that the potential availability of younger women for caregiving relative to the expected growth of the oldest old is decreasing, apart from factors that might constrain women from performing such caregiving tasks. In all countries, the oldest-old population is projected to increase steadily through 2025, while the younger population, 50 to 64 years, will increase mainly up to 2005, then actually decline to the year 2025 in Hungary, Japan and Sweden. This reflects, of course, the changing size of different birth cohorts—first the baby boom and then the birth-dearth groups reaching the ages in question.

Even though the caretaker ratios decline over time, the data show that there will still be at least two women aged 50 to 64 for every person 80 years and over. This translates approximately into one oldest-old person for every two married couples aged 50 to 64. Such prospects suggest that, from a societal point of view, the required level of support should not be overwhelming. At the same time, however, the living arrangements/lifestyles of many future young old could be radically altered relative to previous generations.

LIFE EXPECTANCY AND HEALTH ISSUES

Changes in Life Expectancy

According to life tables prepared in 1982, the average newborn girl can be expected to live more than 77 years and the average boy more than 70 years (Table 4–10). The exception is Hungary, where substantially lower expectations of life are noted. Data on life expectancy at birth as well as years of life remaining at age 65 indicate that Japanese of both sexes experience the highest levels of longevity.[4]

Major gains in life expectancy at birth over the period 1960 to 1980 were made

[4] It should be noted that calculation of life expectancy at the oldest old ages depends heavily on survival estimates at the extreme ages, estimates that tend to be problematic. We feel confident in presenting elderly life expectancies only for age 65.

Table 4–10   Life Expectancy at Birth and at Age 65, by Sex, 1982

| | Years of life remaining | | | |
| | At birth | | At age 65 | |
Country	Male	Female	Male	Female
Australia[a]	71.4	78.6	14.0	18.3
Canada	72.0	79.0	14.4	18.7
Germany, Fed. Rep.	70.5	77.2	13.2	17.0
Hungary	65.7	73.3	11.7	14.8
Japan	74.5	80.2	15.5	18.9
Sweden	73.5	79.5	14.6	18.5
United Kingdom				
(England and Wales)	71.3	77.2	13.1	17.1
United States	70.9	78.2	14.5	18.8

[a]Refers to 1981.

Source: Life tables prepared by the Center for Demographic Studies, Duke University, based on World Health Organization computer tape transcripts.

by all countries except Hungary (Table 4–11). Even in Hungary, life expectancies improved for females. The Japanese gains are probably unprecedented in the history of mortality transitions and, as might be surmised, their life expectancy at birth now exceeds that of any other country in the world (Myers and Manton 1987). The improvements over the period tended to favor females, thus further widening the gap in life expectation at birth between the sexes.

The relative contribution of changes in mortality above age 65 to changes in life expectancy at birth have been calculated using procedures suggested by Pollard (1982) that permit us to identify for each sex the age-specific contributions to the overall change, as well as the relative impact of changes in specific causes of death. Table 4–11 presents figures for assessing the contribution made at older ages in the 20-year

Table 4–11   Change in Life Expectancy at Birth and at Age 65, by Sex, 1960 to 1980

| | Years of change in life expectancy | | | | Change at age 65 and over as a percent of change at birth | |
| | At birth | | At age 65 | | | |
Country	Male	Female	Male	Female	Male	Female
Australia	3.1	4.2	0.9	1.9	29.3	45.7
Canada	3.4	5.1	0.8	2.6	24.9	51.4
Germany, Fed. Rep.	3.4	4.9	0.6	2.1	17.3	42.6
Hungary	−0.5	2.6	−0.5	0.7	115.4[a]	25.3
Japan	8.1	8.8	2.0	2.9	25.1	33.0
Sweden	1.6	4.1	0.5	2.4	30.3	57.7
United Kingdom						
(England and Wales)	2.5	2.6	0.5	1.2	20.4	45.6
United States	3.5	4.6	0.9	2.2	25.4	47.8

[a]Negative contribution to a total negative change.

Source: Life tables prepared by the Center for Demographic Studies, Duke University, based on World Health Organization computer tape transcripts.

period. Although there is considerable variation among these countries, the male share at age 65 and over represents roughly one-quarter and female nearly one-half of the overall change in life expectation at birth. The importance of mortality reductions at later ages has come to be recognized as an important element in assessing overall survival and likely changes in the future. It is noteworthy, however, that the large changes in overall life expectancy in Japan were *not* due, in the main, to changes at the older ages (25 percent of the male change and 33 percent of the female change, figures considerably below several other countries). This suggests that further improvements are likely in Japan as the potential for further changes comes to be focused largely on older ages.

Changes in life expectation are the result of alterations in complex disease patterns that lead to death. For the countries that we are examining, the major transition from infectious to chronic degenerative diseases was clearly completed during the period in question, 1960 to 1980. In Table 4–12 we present data for underlying cause-of-death categories that represent five major chronic disease states for older persons, an additional category for accidents, and a residual category.

Cancer was an increasingly prevalent disease during the period and made a *negative* contribution to the life-expectation improvements at birth that are reported. This

Table 4–12 Cause-Specific Contributions to Change in Life Expectancy at Birth from Changes Occurring at Age 65 Years and Over, by Sex, 1960 to 1980

	Contributions at age 65 and over							
Country	Cancer	Diabetes	Heart disease	Stroke	Cirrhosis	Accidents	Remainder	Total
Australia								
Male	−.23	—	.62	.21	.01	.06	.27	.92
Female	−.03	.04	1.06	.51	—	.09	.25	1.93
Canada								
Male	−.22	—	.78	.35	.02	.03	−.08	.84
Female	.07	.05	1.45	.78	—	.09	.16	2.60
Germany, Fed. Rep.								
Male	−.09	−.02	.09	.41	—	.06	.15	.60
Female	.19	—	.65	.85	.03	.09	.29	2.11
Hungary								
Male	−.25	.02	.14	−.09	−.05	−.09	−.17	−.54
Female	.01	−.05	.64	.11	−.01	—	.04	.66
Japan								
Male	−.05	−.01	.38	.98	.03	.03	.70	2.04
Female	.11	−.03	.59	1.36	.04	.02	.81	2.91
Sweden								
Male	−.11	−.01	−.14	.32	−.02	.04	.38	.47
Female	—	.01	.80	.71	—	.10	.76	2.39
United Kingdom								
Male	−.16	−.01	.32	.18	—	.04	.07	.50
Female	−.08	.01	.96	.48	—	.08	−.24	1.21
United States								
Male	−.21	.01	.90	.35	—	.04	−.21	.89
Female	−.02	.06	1.58	.68	—	.10	−.21	2.18

Source: Life tables prepared by the Center for Demographic Studies, Duke University, based on World Health Organization computer tape transcripts.

was true for males in all eight countries and for females in three countries. For Hungarian males, the negative cancer contribution is one of the main reasons that overall male life expectancy at birth failed to increase during the period.

Diabetes was generally not a significant factor in affecting the change in life expectancy. However, in five of the countries a slight negative impact was evident, either for males or for females. Declining heart disease mortality, however, was a very important factor in producing life expectancy gains, with an especially large impact for females. For example, over half of the total female gains in Australia, Canada, and the United States can be attributed to heart disease reductions at later ages. For males, the contributions also were proportionately large for all countries except Sweden, Japan, and the Federal Republic of Germany. A larger contribution in these three countries, for females as well as males, came instead from stroke mortality reductions. Thus, among the eight countries, there exists considerable variation as to whether reductions in either heart disease or stroke mortality played the major role in producing higher life expectancy.

Finally, we note that the contributions from changes in cirrhosis and accident mortality were not large, although they were negative for both males and females in Hungary. A more curious pattern emerges for the "remainder" of the causes of death. These reductions played a major positive role in Australia, Japan, and Sweden. In contrast, for both females and males in the United States, negative contributions were found for diseases other than those listed.

In short, examining mortality trends in this manner gives us an opportunity to assess the importance of certain diseases in producing improvements in age-specific survival rates. Generally speaking, among the causes of death that we considered, only cancer contributed negatively during the period 1960 to 1980. Cardiovascular death reductions, on the other hand, were very important in improving life expectancy, especially for females.

Survival to Advanced Ages

The probabilities of surviving to age 65 and to 85 for a child born in 1982 and experiencing the current age-specific mortality conditions are presented in Table 4–13. In addition, the table provides the probabilities of those alive at age 65 surviving for an additional 20 years. Over 80 percent of Japanese males and nearly 90 percent of Japanese females can expect to reach age 65. These values exceed those of all other countries by a considerable amount. In contrast, Hungarian males and females had slightly less than a 61 and an 80 percent probability, respectively, of reaching older ages. For the other countries, the values lie somewhere between these extreme values, but in general, three-quarters of males and over 85 percent of females survive until later life.

Roughly one out of every five males and nearly two out of every five females can expect to reach the age of 85. Japan again has the highest values and Hungary the lowest. Canada and the United States, along with Sweden, also rank highly in this regard for both males and females. By examining the probabilities of surviving between ages 65 and 85, we find that among males the Japanese have the highest percentage surviving in old age. However, U.S. and Canadian females enjoy greater longevity in this period of life than do their counterparts in Japan.

Table 4–13 Percentage of Persons Surviving to Specific Ages, by Sex, 1982

Country	Percentage of males surviving			Percentage of females surviving		
	To age 65	To age 85	From age 65 to age 85	To age 65	To age 85	From age 65 to age 85
Australia	74.7	17.6	23.6	86.4	38.4	44.5
Canada	75.1	19.6	26.1	86.3	40.0	46.3
Germany, Fed. Rep.	73.4	14.2	19.3	85.8	31.7	36.9
Hungary	60.9	8.2	13.4	79.3	21.0	26.5
Japan	80.8	23.6	29.2	89.5	41.1	45.9
Sweden	78.7	20.4	25.9	88.4	39.8	45.0
United Kingdom	75.0	14.5	19.3	84.6	32.7	38.6
United States	72.0	19.5	27.1	84.1	39.3	46.7

Note: Data in this table refer to survival probabilities of a child born in 1982 and continuing to experience age-specific mortality conditions as estimated from life tables for 1982.

Source: Life tables prepared by the Center for Demographic Studies, Duke University, based on World Health Organization computer tape transcripts.

Improvements in Survival

The chances of surviving to later ages improved during the period 1960 to 1982 for both sexes in each of the countries, with the sole exception of males in Hungary (Table 4–14). However, the degree of improvement differed markedly among the countries. The largest gains are found in Japan, with male survival to age 65 increasing 15.6 percent and female survival to age 85 increasing by nearly one-fourth. In all countries except Sweden and Hungary, the percentage increases for males surviving to age 65 exceeded the gains for females. On the other hand, the gains were greater for female survival to age 85. Even though the relative survival between ages 65 and 85 increased for males as well as females (except in Hungary), the increases were much larger for females.

Examining these trends further by country shows that relatively small gains were made in survival at later ages for males in England and Wales, the Federal Republic of Germany, and Sweden and a loss for Hungary. The downward survival trends in

Table 4–14 Change in the Percentage of Persons Surviving to Specific Ages, by Sex, 1960 to 1982

Country	Change in male survival			Change in female survival		
	To age 65	To age 85	From age 65 to age 85	To age 65	To age 85	From age 65 to age 85
Australia	7.0	5.8	6.2	5.5	13.5	13.7
Canada	6.5	5.1	5.0	5.6	13.9	13.9
Germany, Fed. Rep.	6.7	4.2	4.3	6.4	13.8	14.3
Hungary	−6.4	−2.1	−1.9	2.5	4.9	5.6
Japan	15.6	15.4	16.6	14.1	23.7	22.8
Sweden	2.5	3.8	4.2	4.8	15.9	16.5
United Kingdom	6.2	3.9	4.0	3.2	8.8	9.2
United States	8.2	7.1	7.6	5.9	14.2	14.6

Source: Life tables prepared by the Center for Demographic Studies, Duke University, based on World Health Organization computer tape transcripts.

Hungary are symptomatic of the rising male mortality at older ages that has characterized Eastern European countries in the past few decades.

Between 1960 and 1982, male survival showed gains to age 65 through reductions in mortality, changes that females for the most part had already experienced. However, survival gains at *older* ages were substantially greater for females. When considering the growth of the oldest-old populations, it is important to recognize that such growth is a function not only of who lives to experience old age (at age 65, for example) but of those who experience prolonged survival through the older ages as well. In the former category, male survival has caught up with that of females, whereas in the latter category, the gains have been experienced more fully by females. It is interesting to note that as survival to oldest-old ages reaches very high age levels, male improvements are likely to narrow the survival gap between the sexes and to raise correspondingly the sex ratios of males to females. Recent analysis of U.S. population projections clearly reveals both of these trends up to age 90.

THE INCOME OF THE VERY OLD

The very old in every country are economically vulnerable. They no longer have or choose to utilize economic options such as working full- or part-time. Even if they could work, there are few jobs available for them. Inflation in every country reduces the value of their fixed income that is not indexed. Increases in the standard of living are generally reflected in the wages of those still in the work force, whereas those no longer in the work force are left behind.

The economic realities facing the very old are described in the income estimates made by the Luxembourg Income Study (LIS). Data from national household surveys are adjusted for definitional differences of both income and housing units; they are also adjusted for the time differences. The adjusted data from these surveys have become the core of the LIS data set. Each survey covers at least 97 percent of the non-institutionalized national population. Although some ethnic groups, such as Lapps in Norway or Aleuts in the United States, have sample sizes too small to be representative, the age cohorts that are our major concern in this chapter are well represented.

The income concept, defined as disposable income (post–tax, post–transfer income), is the concept used throughout this chapter. The LIS data set contains 35 income and tax variables and 30 demographic variables. It includes all forms of cash income (earnings, property income, all cash transfers) net of direct taxes (i.e., employer and employee payroll taxes and income taxes).

The household income variables were further adjusted for differences in family size and composition. The equivalence scale employed is that used in determining the U.S. poverty line. For a more complete discussion of the development or application of this equivalence factor and its comparison to other household equivalence scales, see Smeeding, Schmaus, and Allegreza (1985). A more detailed explanation of the LIS data set is included in the Appendix.

Average Income of the Very Old Compared with the National Average Income

When the average income of older households in six LIS countries is compared with the national average income of those countries, a consistent pattern emerges (Table 4–15). Households that have a head 55 to 64 years old all have income that is higher than the national average. On average, the income of these households is 17 percent higher than the national mean. In most countries, people in this age group are still in the labor force. But by ages 65 to 74, most of them have retired, and there is an expected drop in their average household income relative to the national mean. It is important to note that, even after people retire, their household income is on average 92 percent of the national mean. This is closer to the national mean than in fact many aged think they are. But the aged measure their decline in income from the income they had before they retired rather than from the national mean.

The average household income of the 75-year-olds and older is even lower. In the six countries examined, the very old households had an average only 78 percent of the national average income Their income was 85 percent of that of the younger aged and only 67 percent of that of the 55- to 64-year age group. The sense of economic vulnerability of the very old in every country is in fact realistic; their average income is generally lower than that of any other age group in the society, and their income decline relative to their final working years is steep because of the loss of earnings. This, of course, does not take into account nonincome benefits, which may be considerable—housing, in-kind, and so forth.

Sources of Income

The shift in income sources helps explain the decline in income between the 55–64 and the 75-and-over age groups. In the younger group, earnings are the major source of income in every country but the Federal Republic of Germany and Sweden (Table

Table 4–15 Ratio of Adjusted Disposable Household Income to National Mean Income for Selected Age Groups and Countries, Circa 1980

| | Age of household head | | | | | | | |
Country	Less than 25	25–34	35–44	45–54	55–64	65–74	75 and over	Standard deviation
Canada	.87	.96	.96	1.11	1.15	.94	.81	.11
Germany, Fed. Rep.	.86	.88	.94	1.30	1.07	.85	.79	.17
Norway	.81	.96	.99	1.04	1.18	1.01	.79	.12
Sweden	.86	1.00	.98	1.12	1.17	.96	.78	.13
United Kingdom	.99	.97	.97	1.20	1.17	.76	.67	.18
United States	.77	.93	.95	1.13	1.21	.99	.84	.14
Mean	.88	.96	.96	1.13	1.17	.92	.78	—
Standard deviation	.08	.04	.02	.09	.05	.08	.08	—

Note: Disposable income is posttax and posttransfer income. The adjustment of disposable income for family size is done on an equivalence scale. For a fuller discussion, see Smeeding, Schmaus, and Allegreza (1985). The national mean equals 1.00.

Source: LIS Data File.

4–16). As earnings become a declining source of income as people age, social insurance benefits become the major source. The very old are dependent on social insurance benefits for the majority of their income in every country except the United States and Canada, where such benefits are 45 percent of total income. Welfare benefits are a very small source of income for the elderly of any age in any country. Only in Sweden and the United Kingdom do welfare benefits provide more than 2 percent of the average income of people 75 years and over. The apparent insignificance of welfare benefits to the average very old household is due to the fact that social insurance benefits for the aged in many countries incorporate welfare components, so that a minimum income can be provided to almost all aged without going through the welfare system.

Employer pensions play a more important role in the six countries than welfare benefits but a much smaller role than social insurance benefits. For the very old, employer pensions provide up to 12 percent of income (in Sweden, employer pensions are defined as part of the social insurance benefit). As households age, employer pensions become a smaller source of income in four of the five countries that have such pensions; in Germany, employer pensions provide about 12 percent of

Table 4–16 Percentage of Gross Income of Elderly Households from Various Sources, in Selected Age Groups and Countries, Circa 1980

Country and age of household head	Source of income before tax						
	Earnings	Property income	Occupational pension	Social insurance transfers	Means-tested transfers	Other income	Total
Canada							
55 years and over	56	17	6	18	2	1	100
65 to 74 years	28	22	12	35	2	1	100
75 years and over	13	30	8	45	2	2	100
Germany, Fed. Rep.							
55 years and over	43	2	8	46	1	—	100
65 to 74 years	17	2	12	67	1	—	100
75 years and over	8	4	12	75	1	—	100
Norway							
55 years and over	61	5	3	30	0	0	100
65 to 74 years	41	6	7	45	0	1	100
75 years and over	6	8	10	75	1	1	100
Sweden							
55 years and over	39	7	—	51	3	0	100
65 to 74 years	12	9	—	76	3	1	100
75 years and over	2	13	—	78	7	1	100
United Kingdom							
55 years and over	54	7	8	28	3	—	100
65 to 74 years	26	10	15	46	3	—	100
75 years and over	17	10	12	54	7	—	100
United States							
55 years and over	58	13	8	19	1	—	100
65 to 74 years	32	18	13	35	2	0	100
75 years and over	17	24	12	45	2	0	100

Source: LIS Data File.

retirees' income, regardless of age; and in Norway, these pensions actually become an increasing source of income in older households. Perhaps most revealing is that income from property is more important than employee pensions for the very old in three of six countries examined.

Low-income Elderly

The percentage of elderly households with low income (defined as less than half the median national income) increases with age (Table 4–17). This pattern is consistent with the decrease in relative disposable income shown in Table 4–15. But although persons aged 75 and over in the United States have the highest income (relative to the national average) of the six countries examined, this group also has proportionately more low-income members than that of other countries except the United Kingdom. This is because income inequality in both the 65–74 and 75-and-over age groups is considerably higher in the United States than in any other country (Smeeding, Torrey, and Rein 1986). Therefore, it is possible for high average income to coexist with a high percentage of the very old with low incomes.

THE OLDEST OLD IN THE PEOPLE'S REPUBLIC OF CHINA

Although its situation is not directly related to the main thrust of this chapter, the People's Republic of China (PRC) deserves mention here because of the magnitude of the potential population change that the PRC may face. In the world's most populous nation, the political desire to lower fertility rates quickly in the 1970s and early 1980s led to an official policy of one child per married couple. Recent popultion projections indicate that a successful implementation of this policy would result in 40 percent of the total population being 65 years or over by the middle of the next century. Further aging of this enormous elderly population could produce massive numbers of persons aged 80 and over and strain the society's capability to support and care for its oldest old.

The PRC had an estimated 6.1 million octogenarians in 1985, 65 percent of whom were women, and ranks second in total number only to the United States. By 2025, the United Nations projects this figure to rise to 26.4 million, representing an average growth rate of 3.7 percent every year during the 1985–2025 period. This projection assumes that the one-child-per-couple policy will *not* be a reality and that the total fertility rate will remain slightly under the replacement level (i.e., approximately two children per women) throughout the 40-year period.[5] The projected average age of China's elderly will increase during the period, so that the oldest old will constitute 14 percent of all elderly in 2025 versus 11 percent in 1985. If the United Nations scenario is correct, the 26.4 million Chinese oldest old would greatly outnumber those of any other country in 2025. India and the United States are expected to rank second and third, with 16.4 million and 14.3 million oldest old, respectively.

[5] The United Nations medium-variant projections as assessed in 1984 assume a decline in the total fertility rate from 2.11 in 1985–1990 to 1.91 in 1990–1995, a maintenance of this level through 2000–2005, then a return to 2.11 by 2020–2025. These projections also include the population of Taiwan.

Table 4–17 Percentage of Households with Less than One-half the National Median Income, for Selected Age Groups and Countries, Circa 1980

	Age of household head		
Country	65 years and over	65 to 74 years	75 years and over
Canada	17.2	13.7	23.9
Germany, Fed. Rep.	11.1	8.1	14.2
Norway	5.6	3.1	9.0
Sweden	0.8	0.5	1.3
United Kingdom	29.0	24.1	39.1
United States	23.9	19.8	31.7

Source: Smeeding and Torrey (1986).

A noteworthy characteristic of the oldest old in China today is their skewed marital status. More than 92 percent of all women aged 80 and over are widows, a higher percentage than in any other country investigated by the U.S. Bureau of the Census. China also exhibits the highest male rates of widowerhood for the oldest old, 59 percent. Should these abnormally high rates of widowhood continue at the same time that the number of Chinese children plummets, the traditional social support system may no longer be adequate for China's future elderly and especially the oldest old population.

CONCLUSION

The accelerated growth in the number of the oldest old in each country examined is a measure of our enormous success in providing our populations safer and healthier environments in which to grow old. Very old age is not now a potential luxury for the privileged few; it is, in fact, available to increasing numbers of the general population. Very old age, of course, is not necessarily a luxury if it is spent alone, in poor health, or poverty. And that is why the paradox of the very old population in the United States challenges our society.

The fact that the oldest old in other industrial countries are in similar social and economic situations means that the United States can learn from other countries how best to face the challenges of a very old population. We can see into our own future by observing the countries that have relatively more aged than we do. The international comparisons provide us the perspective needed to improve our programs and services to the aged that an intimate understanding of our own situation alone cannot. In observing other countries, we can see our future options. We also can begin to understand better the paradox in the United States of having both a relatively young general population and a very old elderly population.

APPENDIX: INTERNATIONAL DATA BASE ON AGING

In response to the need for reliable and internationally comparable statistics on aging, the National Institute on Aging (NIA) and the U.S. Bureau of the Census' Center for International Research (CIR) have developed a computerized data base that provides

Table 4–A Overview of LIS Datasets

Country	Dataset name	Income year	Dataset size [a]	LIS country coordinators	Population coverage [b]	Basis of household sampling frame [c]
Canada	Survey of Consumer Finances	1981	37,900	Gail Oja Roger Love	97.5 [d]	Decennial census
Germany, Fed. Rep.	Transfer Survey	1981 [e]	2,800	Richard Hausner Irene Stolz Gunther Schmaus	91.5 [f]	Electoral register on census
Israel	Family Expenditure Survey	1979	2,300	Lea Achdut Yossi Tamir	89.0 [g]	Electoral register
Norway	Norwegian Tax Files	1979	10,400	Stein Ringen Lief Korbol	98.5 [d]	Tax records
Sweden	Swedish Income Distribution Survey	1979	9,600	Peter Hedstrom Robert Erickson	98.0 [d]	Population register
United Kingdom	Family Expenditure Survey [e]	1979	6,800	Michael O'Higgins Geoffrey Stephenson	96.5 [h]	Electoral register
United States	Current Population Survey	1979	65,000	Tim Smeeding Lee Rainwater Martin Rein	97.5 [d]	Decennial census

[a] Number of actual household units surveyed.

[b] As a percentage of total national population.

[c] Sample frame indicates the overall base from which the relevant household population sample was drawn. Actual sample may be drawn on a stratified probability basis, for example, by area, age, or other bases.

[d] Excludes institutionalized and homeless populations. Also, some northern rural residents (Eskimos, Lapps, etc.) may be undersampled.

[e] The United Kingdom and German surveys collect subannual income data, which is normalized to annual income levels.

[f] Excludes foreign-born heads of households, the institutionalized, and the homeless.

[g] Excludes rural populations (those living in places with populations of 2,000 or less), the institutionalized, the homeless, people in kibbutzim, and guest workers.

[h] Excludes those not on the electoral register, the homeless, and the institutionalized.

detailed demographic and socioeconomic information about the aged in the United States and 41 other countries (Table 4–A). Additional data base funding has been provided by the U.S. Agency for International Development. The intent of this effort is twofold: to promote a better understanding of the aging process in disparate societies and concurrently, to afford researchers and policy makers in the United States a better opportunity to gain insights and formulate responses to demands generated by an aging American population.

Whereas published data often aggregate the elderly into a broad, open-ended age group (65 years and over), the NIA/CIR data base assembles census, survey, and population-projection data in 5-year age cohorts for the highest obtainable grouping. Information about these cohorts is collected from 1950 to the present and supplemented with selected projections through the year 2050. Such cohort data over time will allow researchers to go beyond mere cross-sectional comparisons to analyses of the same age cohorts in different countries.

The detailed statistics include not only the numbers of people in each cohort, but also their marital and educational status, labor force participation and occupations, mortality rates and causes of death, and other related characteristics. For certain developed countries, income comparisons of the nonaged and aged, and among the aged, are being included in the data base as information from continuing studies becomes available. This represents an important first step toward an integration of the economics and demographics of international aging.

Data base contents are reviewed for internal consistency and international comparability. Source documentation accompanies all information, and additional notation of conceptual definitions and/or data irregularities is provided where necessary. Geographical coverage includes not only the most advanced countries in the world, but also 3 Eastern European countries that have declining life expectancy and 22 developing nations with very different age profiles than the United States. Among the latter is the People's Republic of China, which contains 22 percent of the world's population and is likely to age faster than any other major country after the turn of the century.

For more details, contact

Kevin G. Kinsella
Center for International Research
U.S. Bureau of the Census
Washington, D.C. 20233
Phone: (301) 763-4221

REFERENCES

Coale, A.J., and E.E. Kisker. 1986. Mortality Crossovers: Reality or Bad Data. *Population Studies* 40:389–401.
Hoover, S.L., and J.S. Siegel. 1986. International Demographic Trends and Perspectives on Aging. *Journal of Cross-Cultural Gerontology* 1:5–30.
Keyfitz, N. 1981. The Limits of Population Forecasting. *Population and Development Review* 7:579–93.

Myers, G.C. 1982. The Aging of Populations. In *International Perspectives on Aging: Population and Policy Challenges,* eds. R.H. Binstock, W.-S. Chow, and J.H. Schulz, 1–39. New York: United Nations Fund for Population Activities.

Myers, G.C. 1986. Cross-National Patterns and Trends in Marital Status Among the Elderly. *Chaire Quetelet 86 Proceedings,* Louvain-la-Neuve, Belgium.

Myers, G.C. 1990. Demography of Aging. In *Handbook of Aging and the Social Sciences,* 3rd ed., eds. R.H. Binstock and L.K. George, 19–44. San Diego, Calif.: Academic Press.

Myers, G.C., and K.G. Manton. 1987. The Rate of Population Aging: New Views of the Epidemiologic Transitions. In *Aging: The Universal Human Experience,* eds. G.L. Maddox and E.W. Busse, 263–83. New York: Springer.

Pollard, J.H. 1982. The Expectation of Life and Its Relationship to Mortality. *The Journal of the Institute of Actuaries* 109:225–40.

Rosenwaike, I., and B. Logue. 1985. *The Extreme Aged in America: A Portrait of an Expanding Population.* Westport, Conn: Greenwood Press.

Smeeding, T., G. Schmaus, and S. Allegreza. 1985. An Introduction to LIS. Luxembourg Income Study—CEPS Working Paper No. 1, presented at the LIS Conference, July 1985.

Smeeding, T., and B.B. Torrey. 1986. An International Perspective on the Income and Poverty Status of the U.S. Aged: Lessons from the Luxembourg Income Study and the International Data Base on Aging. Luxembourg Income Study—CEPS Working Paper Series.

Smeeding, T., B.B. Torrey, and M. Rein. 1986. The Economic Status of the Young and the Old in Six Countries. Paper presented to the American Association for the Advancement of Science, Philadelphia, May.

Spencer, G. 1986. The Characteristics of Centenarians in the 1980 Census. Paper presented at the Population Association of America meetings, San Francisco, April 1986.

Stone, R., G.L. Cafferata, and J. Sangl. 1986. *Caregivers of the Frail Elderly: A National Profile.* Washington: U.S. Department of Health and Human Services.

Stoto, M.A. 1983. The Accuracy of Population Projections. *Journal of the American Statistical Association* 78:13–20.

Suzman, R., and M.W. Riley (eds.). 1985. *The Oldest Old;* special issue of the *Milbank Memorial Fund Quarterly* 63:2.

U.S. Bureau of the Census. 1987. *An Aging World.* International Population Reports, series P-95, no. 78. Washington.

III

PROBLEMS IN STUDYING
THE OLDEST OLD

5

Conceptual Issues in the Design and Analysis of Longitudinal Surveys of the Health and Functioning of the Oldest Old

KENNETH G. MANTON and RICHARD M. SUZMAN

OVERVIEW

The amount of nationally representative longitudinal data on the oldest old (i.e., the population aged 85 and over) has increased considerably over the past decade. Because of their longitudinal structure and linkage to administrative records, however, it is not easy to exploit fully the potential of these data for addressing the scientific and policy-relevant issues affecting the oldest old.

In this chapter we identify a variety of sampling, survey design, and other methodological issues affecting the use of these data sets. We draw mainly on three nationally representative longitudinal surveys specifically relevant to the oldest old: (1) the National Long Term Care Survey (NLTCS: 1982, 1984, 1989), (2) the National Health Interview Survey (NHIS) Supplement on Aging (SOA: 1984) and the Longitudinal Study of Aging (LSOA: 1986, 1988, 1990), and (3) the National Nursing Home Survey (NNHS: 1985). In discussing these issues, we focus on alternatives to designs developed initially for cross-sectional study of young and middle-aged populations and discuss strategies specific to longitudinal surveys of the oldest old.

Background

Lack of detailed data on the health and functioning of the oldest old limited research into their use of acute and long-term care and into opportunities for health interventions. Until the 1980s, few surveys or studies had sufficient numbers of the oldest old to allow more than descriptive analyses. Once the significance of the oldest old population was appreciated, however, steps were taken to remedy these limitations. For example, although not explicitly a response to the need for data on the oldest old, the National Institute on Aging (NIA) initiated its Established Populations for Epidemiological Studies of the Elderly (EPESE) program, which, in contrast to earlier epidemiological studies directed to high-risk, middle-aged populations, focused on persons aged 65 and over. These studies differed from earlier clinical studies of aging (e.g., the Baltimore Longitudinal Study of Aging; the first and second Duke longitudinal studies) by having larger sample sizes and by using sampling procedures to ensure representativeness of the community populations selected.

Of specific interest for this chapter are nationally representative surveys of longitudinally followed populations, which, as part of a conscious policy, were focused on the elderly and oldest-old populations. Our interest in these surveys is twofold. First, they have advantages in that they are both *relatively* rapid to field (as opposed to in-depth longitudinal studies; Densen 1987) and, being nationally representative, they have direct implications for the design and implementation of national health policy. Second, because longitudinal surveys of very elderly populations are a relatively new type of data collection, the surveys raise a wide range of important methodoligical issues. We will concentrate on nationally representative longitudinal surveys specifically designed to examine the health and functioning, acute and long-term-care service use, and socioeconomic status of the oldest-old population.

Policy Uses of National Longitudinal Health Surveys of the Elderly

Among the policy questions for which longitudinal surveys of the oldest old are required are health-care cost reimbursement and cost control; effects of policy changes on quality of and access to care; management of service-delivery systems; estimation and forecasting of resource needs; monitoring of short- and long-term policy effects.

Monitoring the Effects of National Health Policy Changes

Longitudinal surveys provide insight into the planning, implementation, and monitoring of acute and long-term-care health policies. If surveys are linked to Medicare (and possibly Medicaid) records, the amount and types of federally funded services provided to different population groups can be estimated for specific periods of time— as well as the quality of outcomes in terms of additional service use (e.g., rehospitalization or institutionalization), mortality, or disability. Surveys initiated before the Prospective Payment System (PPS) was introduced (e.g., the NLTCS of 1982; SOA 1984) and before the Catastrophic Care legislation in 1988 (or its repeal in 1989) contain unique *baseline* data to monitor the impact of these and other national health policy changes. Surveys begun *after* major policy changes cannot be used to assess their impact. Thus, the surveys (and linked administrative data) represent an important data resource for monitoring the extent and quality of the population impact of these (and other future) health-care program changes.

Reimbursement and Cost-containment Strategies

Changes in Medicare reimbursement of physicians and health maintenance organizations (HMOs) (Kunkel and Powell, 1981) have been considered recently and a comprehensive National Health Insurance, perhaps modeled after the Canadian system, has even been discussed. Evaluation of these and other possible policy changes requires extensive data, both for planning and development and, after implementation, for monitoring and surveillance of effects on expenditures and quality of care. To fulfill the data needs of planning, implementation, and monitoring, longitudinally followed nationally representative survey populations, linked to Medicare administrative record systems, are required to measure accurately the national effects of changes in reimbursement and service outcomes.

There is considerable interest in the public and private financing of long-term care services. Longitudinal surveys and linked health-service data can be used for long-term care design issues such as how to design private long-term-care insurance benefits and the effects of alternative designs on the affordability of the product. These issues have attracted considerable interest. Some analysts (e.g., Wiener, Hanley, Spense, and Murray, 1992) suggest that only a minority of the elderly will be able to afford private long-term-care insurance because of limited economic resources. The size of the market for private long-term-care insurance determines the scope and level of publicly financed services needed because public programs have to cover persons unable to purchase adequate private insurance. Other important reimbursement questions involve Medicaid nursing-home payment (e.g., the effect of level of payment on quality of care; the effects of constraints on nursing-home construction on the availability of institutional care, with attendant consequences for home health care), the effect of payment for institutional and community acute care on the "spend-down" process (Liu, Doty, and Manton 1990), the provision of home health services by Medicare, its substitutability for institutional care (especially for very severely impaired persons), and prospective payment systems for nursing homes to control institutional expenses.

Quality of Care Outcomes and Population Utilization Review

Recent changes in Medicare policy and reimbursement may affect the level, scope and access, and quality of care of health services for the elderly. Medicare instituted a PPS for reimbursing acute hospital stays whereby a fixed payment was made for a case assigned to one of 473 diagnosis related groups (DRGs). There has been interest in the impact of PPS both on providers (e.g., small hospitals in rural areas) and on the quality of care delivered to beneficiaries, especially beneficiaries in frail, susceptible categories like the oldest old. So far no major systemwide decrement in quality of care (measured in terms of mortality or rehospitalization risk) has been documented (Manton and Liu 1990). With continuing changes in the reimbursement system (e.g., reduction of teaching-hospital adjustments), quality surveillance, especially of service-intensive or highly vulnerable subgroups (like the oldest old), is crucial.

In addition to monitoring outcomes, utilization review at the population level is important. Utilization review (i.e., assessing the appropriateness of care delivered for the person, or for patients in an institution) is a well-known process. There is a logically similar process at the population level, where one can ascertain if shifts in service patterns (e.g., retention of oldest-old patients in institutions with lower transfer rates to hospitals) in the population are consistent with the goal of maintaining appropriate care under cost containment. Shifts in the venues where services are delivered are not prima facie evidence of inappropriate utlization, but they do require detailed evaluation. For example, a number of policies have the intended goal of reducing institutionalization: its appropriateness depends upon the characteristics of patient subgroups retained in the community.

Resource Allocation and Forecasting

Surveys can provide actuarial statistics on the health and service needs of the oldest-old population—data important for the private and public sectors to design future products and services. National longitudinal surveys have been employed not only in the design and modification of private long-term-care insurance products, but also in the design and marketing of specialized housing services for the impaired elderly and by the health-care industry for future planning of products (e.g., demand for pharmaceuticals). They are important for the Health Care Financing Administration's (HCFA) efforts to provide national health-cost benchmarks and in the actuarial analysis of program benefits; for example, the 1974–1976 Current Medicare Survey was used to estimate underwritng factors for the Adjusted Annual Per Capita Cost Index (AAPCC) (Kunkel and Powell 1981). They are important for efforts to forecast the size, survival, and active life expectancy of the oldest-old population and to conduct simulations of potential health interventions.

Management

Survey data can be used to design patient and health-system management procedures. For example, the NLTCS identified significant proportions of the impaired elderly population who require only "passive" care or can be managed with specialized equipment or housing aids. It identified behavioral problems manifest in subpopulations characterized by neurological and cognitive deficits. This information could be used in designing services to provide for care options involving housing aids and specialized equipment. Mixed strategies may be more cost effective while better preserving personal autonomy, than relying solely on personal assistance.

Implications for Sociodemographic and Biomedical Research

Acute and long-term-care policy issues have important implications for the priorities of sociodemographic and biomedical research. Any reasonable scenario of the growth of the oldest-old population projects large increases in the demand for services. Unless biomedical and sociodemographic research can help to decrease functional disability and increase social and economic autonomy at advanced ages, financing requirements, even with cost-containment policies, will increase rapidly because of population growth. Thus, high priority must be given to research on interventions to improve functional ability and "active" life expectancy (Robine and Michel 1990; chapter 16 by Suzman et al. in this volume). Longitudinal national survey data are essential in identifying national priority areas for research. Because increased survival at later ages interacts with changes in the prevalence of chronically disabling conditions, data are required to track changes in the health of very elderly persons over a significant period of time.

Longitudinal surveys of the oldest old must answer scientific questions about population health and functioning to guarantee their utility for policy design. Examples of such questions are:

1. What are the health and functional characteristics of the current oldest old and of cohorts who will be the future oldest old?
2. How rapidly do health and functional characteristics change among oldest-old individuals? What is the likelihood of improving their health and functional status?
3. What social, economic, family, and personal characteristics are associated with health and functional changes? Can they be modified to improve future health outcomes?
4. What is the pattern of acute and long-term-care services (formal and informal) used by the disabled oldest old?
5. How do those services affect the health and functioning of the oldest old?
6. How have current Medicare and Medicaid reimbursement policies (and recent changes) affected the mix of health services used by the oldest old? How have changes affected their aggregate health status?
7. What are the dynamics of impoverishment for the oldest old, and how are those related to changes in health, household composition, health-care usage, and other behaviors?
8. What sets of risk factors and behaviors can be modified to reduce the incidence and progression of chronic diseases that lead to loss of functional ability, increased service demands, and mortality.

Changes in the Availability of Data on the Oldest Old

Nationally representative longitudinal data to answer both policy and scientific questions have recently become available. In 1984 a longitudinal reinterview of the 1982 NLTCS sample was conducted—along with the screening of a new sample of persons who became 65 over the interval—to complete coverage of the elderly Medicare-eligible population in the United States. A second longitudinal reinterview was conducted in 1989; a third is planned for 1992. In 1986, a structured sample of persons 70 years of age and older drawn from the SOA in the 1984 NHIS was reinterviewed. A second reinterview of all persons aged 70 and over was conducted in 1988. A third is planned for 1990. Between 1985 and 1990, in addition to the 1985 cross-sectional survey of facility characteristics, expenses, residents, discharges, staff, and next of kin, there were three follow-up interviews with the next of kin of nursing-home residents in the 1985 NNHS to ascertain residents' mortality, institutional, and health-status changes.

The three series of national longitudinal surveys, each focusing on an important segment of the elderly and oldest-old populations, are (or will be) linked to administrative data on Medicare service utilization. Simultaneous with national survey efforts, four EPESE studies were implemented by NIA to collect descriptive information on health and functional status. Their instrumentation is sufficiently comparable to the national surveys to allow coordinated analyses and, in addition, is linked to Medicare administrative files. Thus, the three national longitudinal surveys and the community population studies represent significant elements of a data-collection system for the oldest old. They are not the only national data resources relevant for the oldest old. Although not explicitly designed to represent the oldest-old population, the Survey of Income and Program Participation (SIPP), the 1987 National Medical Expenditure Survey (NMES), the Panel Survey on Income Dynamics (PSID), the long-term-care demonstrations funded by HCFA and other federal and state agencies (e.g., the National Channeling Demonstration, the California Multipurpose Senior Services Program, the Georgia Adult Health Services program) represent significant data resources for studying the oldest old. The new National Health and Nutrition Examination Survey III may become a significant data resource as well.

The Need for Continuing and Extending Data Collection on the Oldest Old

Before these (and others; see National Institute on Aging 1989) surveys and studies were instituted, research on health and functional changes in the oldest-old population was impeded by a lack of nationally representative longitudinal survey data. The NHIS is a cross-sectional design and does not oversample the oldest-old population. Mortality data offered large numbers of oldest-old persons but did not contain the necessary covariates for many analyses. Longitudinal epidemiological (e.g., Framingham, Evans County) and clinical studies (e.g., the Baltimore Longitudinal Study on Aging, the First and Second Duke Studies on Aging) of select elderly populations did not provide national estimates of the incidence and prevalence of individual health and functional *changes*.

Although national longitudinal surveys (and associated longitudinal studies of community populations) have greatly increased the scope and volume of research on the characteristics of the oldest-old population, continuing data collection in those surveys (and possibly other types of surveys) is required to answer additional scientific and policy questions. The length of follow-up is currently 4 years for the SOA–LSOA and 7 years for the NLTCS (extended to 6 years by the 1990 LSOA and to 11 years by the 1992 NLTCS). To analyze cohort differences in health and functioning among the oldest old, a 10-year follow-up period provides both a sufficient period of observation of health changes *within* a cohort and of health transitions in overlapping age ranges *across* cohorts. Ten years is minimally sufficient for cohort studies of the oldest old because of their higher rate of morbid and disabling events and their relatively short residual life expectancy (i.e., 10 years is about double the current U.S. male and female life expectancies at age 85).

Longer-term follow-up increases the statistical power of longitudinal surveys with an oldest-old sample of a given size by the accumulation of additional person years of exposure and of health events. This is especially important for surveys like the SOA/LSOA, where the initial samples of oldest old were not large. With increases in life expectancy, oldest-old individuals will have to be followed for longer periods of time. In addition, as the size of ever-older cohorts increases with the aging of the "baby boom" cohort, and mortality continues to decline at advanced ages, surveys will have to represent even older age groups, such as those 95 and over. Continuation of existing surveys for longer follow-up, possibly with sample supplementation, is a cost-effective strategy for evaluating these extremely old groups.

The Implications of Policy and Scientific Needs for Survey Design

The considerable range of policy and scientific questions that require nationally representative longitudinal survey data on health and functioning of the oldest old makes the rationale for increasing data collection on this subpopulation compelling. The national longitudinal surveys have a broad substantive scope that can help fulfill multiple analytic tasks within targeted sample domains. The rate of change in health and functional status of persons of different ages, and in different birth cohorts with different life experiences, and the interactions of those changes with mortality can be studied. Data on health transitions and mortality are necessary to characterize the relation of active to dependent life expectancy at advanced ages, and the differences in that relation between cohorts, and to develop intervention strategies to maximize active life expectancy.

For data collection on the oldest old to be useful for studying these and other questions, the surveys must be carefully designed. Refinements of longitudinal surveys in measuring risk factors and risk-related behavior, based on the results of focused epidemiological and clinical studies, are required. Design features important for collecting data on the young old become mandatory for the oldest old (e.g., increased need for proxy response procedures and personal interviewing). Linkage of survey records to administrative records on Medicare and Medicaid expenditures is important for health-policy planning. Maintaining representativeness of the sample is more difficult for the oldest old because of the correlation of nonresponse with health characteristics. Having adequate samples of the oldest old and well-demonstrated scientific objectives relevant to the oldest old is important. Perhaps most critical, however, is the need to maintain a balance between the substantive range of the survey and its intensity of measurement. Crucial in maintaining this balance is the ability to integrate scientific and policy objectives. Survey content should *not* be solely defined by current policy. Although most congressionally proposed long-term-care benefit programs stress personal assistance, the promotion of personal autonomy through assistive devices is a promising new policy focus. Currently, many chronically disabled persons in the community rely heavily on specialized housing and assistive devices. As electronic, communication, and other technologies improve, the potential for expanding the role of assistive devices in maintaining the social autonomy of the oldest old will increase. This is only likely to happen, however, if the incentive and reimbursement structures of long-term-care policies include assistive devices as one important option. If data are not collected on the use of assistive devices, a survey could not be used in evaluating their role in long-term-care benefits.

To illustrate design concepts, we rely heavily (although not exclusively) on the 1985 NNHS, the 1984 SOA and LSOA, and the 1982 and 1984 NLTCS. We do not attempt to review even this limited group of surveys. We use them selectively to illustrate specific methodological and analytic issues arising in coordinated analyses of multiple surveys. Other surveys, such as SIPP or NMES, are used to illustrate methodological issues specific to individual survey designs.

Our focus on the three national longitudinal surveys is reasonable because of their importance for describing the oldest old. Of the three, the two National Center for Health Statistics (NCHS) surveys are best known. The 1985 NNHS is the latest in a long series of nursing-home surveys (prior nursing-home surveys were conducted in 1973 and 1977; earlier resident place surveys were conducted [National Center for Health Services 1965]). The 1984 SOA and the LSOA are derivatives of the NHIS series. Both NCHS survey series have a long tradition of monitoring the health of the U.S. population. These classic designs are now being used to respond to new challenges. Selected aspects of their design and instrumentation for describing health and health transitions will be briefly discussed in the context of studying the oldest-old population.

The history of the NLTCS is different. The survey, designed to support directly the development of long-term-care policy and programs, was originally conceived and funded by HCFA, the Office of the Assistant Secretary for Policy and Evaluation (ASPE), and the National Center for Health Services Research (NCHSR), with the most recent (1989) follow-up funded by NIA. Consequently, the survey is currently less well known in the scientific community than in the policy research community. For example, it is used in the Lewin/ICF model employed by ASPE in planning long-term-care policy (Kennell et al. 1988) and in the Brookings analyses of long-term care insurance (Rivlin and Wiener 1988; Wiener, Hanley, Spense, and Murray 1992). It has been used by NCHSR to examine different criteria for home health-care eligibility. The NLTCS was intended to be integrated with long-term-care demonstrations to make national estimates of the impact of their intervention (Gornick, Greenberg, Eggers, and Dobson 1985; Macken 1986). Thus, its content is broad enough so that coordinated analyses could be conducted with a number of different related surveys and demonstration studies of the chronically disabled population.

Restricting examination of conceptual and analytic issues to these surveys limits the discussion to the characteristics of those designs. Issues discussed in that context should, nonetheless, be partly applicable to other longitudinal surveys.

In the examination we use a conceptual model describing physical health changes and measurement as *interactive* processes. This model is described conceptually, although its implications can be mathematically formulated. Methodological issues are discussed that arise because of the correlation of the processes of data collection, both within and across survey intervals, with age-related processes of health and functional change and mortality. Without a conceptual model, it is difficult to define and organize the necessary concepts for the complex temporal phenomena we wish to describe. Elements in the design of longitudinal surveys that will be covered are initial sample coverage, size, type (e.g., list versus area probability), periodicity (i.e., how often a survey should be conducted to describe different types of health changes), richness of measures (i.e., the level of detail on substantive domains), left and right censoring (by mortality and observation design), loss to follow-up (nonresponse), use of proxy respondents, and administrative record linkage. Issues in analyzing the longitudinal surveys jointly are also discussed, such as coordination of sample domains, use of multivariate procedures to enhance measurement reliability of complex phenomena like disability, the linkage of survey data to administrative records (i.e., the mixture of fixed panel data with continuous service data), and the representation of changes in an entire system of care. These methodological issues, many of which are topics of ongoing statistical research (e.g., see Kasprzyk, Duncan, Kalton, and Singh 1989), are examined in limited detail because of their complexity.

A TWO-DIMENSIONAL MODEL FOR LONGITUDINAL DATA COLLECTION

Age-related Health Changes and Mortality: Survey Periodicity

Survey design involves balancing available resources and the types and amounts of information gathered. Paradoxically, survey design is dependent upon possessing both good models of the processes to be described and ancillary data on the behavior of those processes (i.e., estimates of transition parameters). Without prior data and theory, cost-effective data-collection strategies cannot be developed. For example, without estimates of the rate at which health events occur at different ages, it is difficult to determine the appropriate periodicity of surveys. Without quantitative models of observed and latent heterogeneity for the oldest old, and at younger ages, it is difficult to address either "left" censoring (e.g., the oldest-old population is a highly select subpopulation of any birth cohort; Riley and Bond 1983) or "right" censoring (i.e., decline in population mortality risks with age due to earlier death of high-risk persons; Vaupel and Yashin 1985).

Thus, survey design is an *evolutionary* process in which the current status of scientific knowledge shapes future design innovations. Tradeoffs must be made between the need to hold measurements and instruments constant and the need to update and modify measurements to reflect new scientific insights. Thus, surveys cannot be designed to be general purpose because defining survey content too broadly may lead to losses in the quality and utility of data forced by compromises in instrument content, sample design, and longitudinal follow-up. Questions for studying the effects of health and functioning on retirement decisions in a middle-aged population are different from those required to estimate the need for long-term-care services among the oldest old. It may be impractical to include detailed batteries of questions for both phenomena, along with necessary covariates, in a survey instrument that can be given practically in a single session to an elderly person. This forces a choice between a multiple-wave survey conducted over a period of time (e.g., 12 months) during which modules with different content are phased in and out over multiple times (increasing field costs, administrative complexity, respondent burden, and person and item nonresponse) versus multiple, independent, substantively focused surveys of specific population groups.

The design approach that maintains the integrity of the data and sample in the most practical way for management purposes, while recognizing the need to allocate restricted data collection efficiently, is the fielding of multiple focused surveys that are designed and can be analyzed in a coordinated fashion. Such "diversification" of the national "portfolio of surveys" also provides a degree of insurance against (1) having a single large survey that cannot be easily adapted to changing conditions in focused areas of interest and (2) relying too heavily, when making policy and scientific decisions, on data generated from a single sample and instrument design. In more formal terms, this suggests that one's approach to "optimal design" (i.e., analyses of how to distribute resources under overall constraints to maximize information about a phenomenon of interest) should involve optimization in multiple independent (but coordinated) survey efforts rather than a single large-scale survey effort. In effect, this suggests real limits in the returns to scale of survey design—limits that have generally not been well recognized.

In studying health and functional changes at advanced ages, there is adequate theory and ancillary data to make rational design choices for surveys. Research has identified transition parameters that must be monitored in continuing data collection. For example, confounding systematic mortality and morbidity selection in a *population* with measurements of the rate of change of *individual* health and functioning is a serious source of bias in studies of the oldest old (Lakatta 1985; Rowe 1988). In clinical studies, this confounding can be resolved by using detailed biomedical measurements to screen the population. Lakatta (1985), in a study of cardiovascular aging, screened for occult (asymptomatic) as well as manifest (symptomatic) disease. In population surveys, because detailed biomedical screening is not possible, a truly random sample of persons has to be identified as of a given time with all individuals, including nonrespondents, tracked for major health events and mortality.

Fortunately, information from longitudinal studies of aging in select populations provides us with rich prior expectations about which health and functional endpoints must be monitored and rates of change in these outcomes. The rate estimates do not have to be precise because the survey is intended to increase precision. Nonetheless, knowing that functional changes relative to hip fracture may occur in a 6- to 12-month period, those for Alzheimer's disease in a 1- to 2-year period, and for osteoporosis in a 2- to 4-year period is important in determining the periodicity of surveys.

Interaction of the Observational Period and the Rate of Health Changes

The second dimension of our model is the measurement *process* involving both sample design and instrumentation. In Figure 5–1, a model of health transitions (see World Health Organization 1984) is embedded in a model of the interviewing process to describe their age-specific interactions.

In Figure 5–1 assessment of an individual (or a homogeneous population) made at instants in time (here represented by age A at the first elevation and A' at the follow-up) provide "snapshots" of the state of the individual (or homogeneous population) at fixed times. Models of the underlying process connect the state of individuals measured at two points in time, assuming no contamination of the transitions by measurement effects during observation, or, in other words, that changes for persons measured at ages A and A', over the follow-up interval C, are not affected by changes in status during measurement.

In assessing free-living populations, the problem is complicated because (1) the population is heterogeneous and (2) measurement necessarily extends over time—the two age/time ranges marked B and B' in Figure 5–1 where C' is the *average* interval between interviews. Consequently, assumptions about the distribution of the characteristics of persons interviewed within each period B and B' are required. Changes occur during the interview periods, with the rate of change being a function of age. Further uncertainty is engendered if the processes are multidimensional, with continuously varying changes, and are capable of retrogression as well as progression (Suzman et al., Chapter 16, this volume; Manton 1988a,b). Thus, whereas death may be well demarcated in time, disability is difficult to define at a point in time because of its fluidity and complexity.

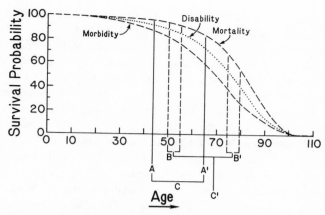

Figure 5–1 Survival probability with advancing age. A, time at first evaluation; A', time at follow-up; B, time interval over which initial evaluation is made; B', time interval over which follow-up evaluation is made; C, follow-up interval; C' average time between initial (B) and follow-up (B') assessment interval.

The shapes of the three survival curves in Figure 5–1 suggest that health events occur rapidly at advanced ages and more rapidly relative to the *residual* life expectancy of very elderly and disabled persons, that is, the event rates defined relative to their proximity to age at death. As the interview periods B and B' are moved to the right (i.e., to older ages), the number of events that occur within them (relative to the population size and length of the measurement intervals B and B') increases, raising the risk of bias in a measurement process of a fixed duration.

The interaction of the age variability of event rates with the length of the measurement interval B is affected by the length of time *between* interview periods (i.e., the ratio of B to C') because the longer the period between measurements, the greater the number of events observed (i.e., the "signal") over the follow-up period, relative to "noise" generated within measurement periods. In a longer interval C', however, because more events occur, stronger assumptions about the stability of the processes generating events are required.

With this model we can describe features of survey and sample design. For example, certain surveys (e.g,, SIPP and NMES) cover a wide range of topical areas requiring that interviews be conducted in multiple modules and spread over time. This has practical limitations. In SIPP, the health module is asked once in nine waves of interviewing; thus, despite 36 months of cohort follow-up, *changes* in individual health cannot be determined. In the 1987 NMES (as in the National Medical Care Utilization and Expenditures Survey in 1980), because multiple interviews are conducted for an individual, wave-specific nonresponse must be addressed either by complex imputation procedures or by modeling the effects of systematically missing data (Berkman, Singer, and Manton 1989). In multiple-wave surveys, the interview period B and the follow-up period C' are the same length, making transitions difficult to identify.

A second implication of the model involves the capture of "episodes" in the sample. The sample unit being an episode (rather than an "individual" or an "event") raises special design issues because the episode has a temporal dimension over which variability in the observed intensity of the phenomena may be manifest. This is illustrated in Figure 5–2.

In the figure we present a time line for components of the 1982–1992, NLTCS observational plan. The time line makes it clear that measurements are made, of different phenomena, at both fixed times (or, because it takes a period of time to complete the field work, a fixed interval) and at random times between interview periods (e.g., the date of death, specific periods of Part A or B use, recall of use of nursing homes). The sample design (or, more generally, a mixed-mode observational plan) involves measurements with different temporal characteristics, that is, time interviews during which a temporal sample on an individual health process occurs and there is continuous sampling of service episodes. This type of observational plan, though complex, is relatively common. For example, the SOA–LSOA linked to Medicare records has this general structure, as do the EPESE studies and long-term-care demonstration projects. The mixed-mode design is very resource efficient in its temporal sampling of events, but at the cost of considerable complexity in longitudinal analysis (i.e., joint analysis of fixed-time and continuous measurement). For example, the 1982 NLTCS was originally conceived as a cross-sectional survey because of resource constraints. The 1984 survey is designed longitudinally. Thus, adjustments have to be made in the sample weighting schemes (which reflect the probabilities of selection) to reconcile differences in design.

Simpler examples of temporal sampling issues emerge in other surveys. For example, the likelihood of capturing an episode like a nursing-home stay is proportional to the duration of the episode; in other words, sampling is "length biased." Length-biased sampling exists when estimating length of stay in the 1977 and 1985 NNHS. To eliminate bias from sample estimates of length of stay, analytic models that adjust for the sample selection probabilites of different-length episodes are required.

The interaction of the lengths of B and C for processes with differing rates at different ages is an important area of research for both sample design *and* instrument construction and measurement. Measurement problems in assessing disability and co-morbidity may partly be problems of cross-temporal sample design instead of instrument construction per se, although the two clearly interact. "Event histories" can be retrospectively generated from recall questions about the occurrence of events over a prior time period (Mathiowetz and Groves 1985; Moore 1988). Alternatively, the prevalence of events or episodes can be determined at multiple fixed measurement times and the rate of occurrence of episodes/events between measurements inferred from a model of the underlying processes. In the first case, the problem is viewed as one of instrument construction to improve recall. Gains from instrument redesign to improve recall may be limited for the oldest old if rates of dementia above 85 are as high as reported by Evans et al. in Chapter 13 of this volume (see also Evans et al. 1989). In the second case the problem is viewed in terms of the temporal parameters of longitudinal sample capture. Given the age dependence of the rate of events, the temporal sampling problem is even more complex because a nonstationary process (i.e., the process has age- and period-dependent rates) is being sampled. In most cases a combined sample-design instrumentation strategy will be necessary. It is important to determine how the two features of surveys interact. Focusing on one aspect (e.g., instrument construction) without consideration of the other (i.e., longitudinal sampling) is unlikely to be successful. Longitudinal sample design for elderly popu-

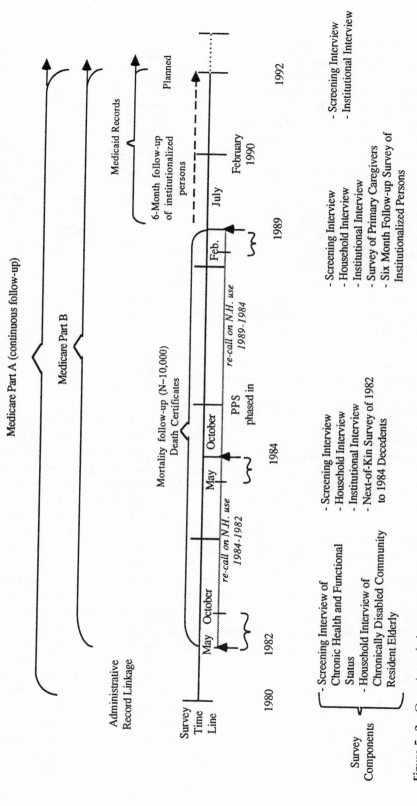

Figure 5-2 Overview of observational plan for the 1982, 1984, 1989 and 1992 NLTCS.

lations with high event rates, and the implications of those issues for describing functional and health status transitions, is an area that will require much further study (e.g., Fienberg 1989; Heckman and Robb 1989; Hoem 1985, 1989).

One implication of longitudinal sample design is that a single temporal sampling plan will probably not be efficient in describing health and functional status transitions because those transitions are driven by heterogeneous processes proceeding at very different rates. Thus, although frequent samples will describe short- and long-term transitions, once short-term transitions are characterized, the need for finely grained temporal sampling is less clear. Furthermore, there are potential nonfinancial costs of continuing a fine-grained sampling plan after adequate resolution of the short-term transitions are made. These costs involve both the increased interview burden for the respondent *and* the possibility of the contamination of measurement by a heavily intrusive observational process. Such effects are well known in public-health intervention trials, in which the nonintervention control group, due to the effects of observation (e.g., increased awareness of health), may improve as rapidly as the intervention group. The effect may be beneficial for the individual being studied, but it can confound the ability to measure accurately the natural parameters of the process in the population. Again, a diversified, multiple survey plan seems to offer the most efficient utilization of resources.

COORDINATED ANALYSES OF SAMPLE SURVEYS

Limitations of individual surveys can sometimes be addressed by coordinated analyses of multiple surveys. Coordinated analyses requires that surveys have some common instrumentation and sample domains with well-specified demographic relations. To illustrate selected sample issues arising in coordinated analyses, we will briefly discuss the NNHS, the NHIS SOA–LSOA and the NLTCS. The goal is not to review or critique the design of the surveys; these are often dictated by resource and other constraints. Rather, it is to identify limitations of specific samples that might be resolved by joint analyses. Coordination of sample features is less difficult when estimating cross-sectional characteristics than in longitudinal analyses.

The three surveys cover a recent time period over which there have been important changes in federal reimbursement of medical services for the elderly. In 1983 Medicare began the PPS. The effects of PPS appear to be greater for the oldest-old population, especially in institutions (Sager, Easterling, Kindig, and Anderson 1989). In 1988 the Catastrophic Care Act was passed, extending hospital benefits and initiating partial reimbursement for out-of-pocket payment for drugs. The act was repealed in 1989, with calls for renewed investigation of long-term-care needs. These and other policy interventions and changes in consumer and market behavior mean that significant changes in the level and interrelation of service use in the Medicare and Medicaid systems can be expected. Thus, intensive survey coverage of this period is critical for studying health changes of the oldest-old population. With the continuing evaluation of the Medicare program and its possible extension to cover long-term care, a continuation of population surveillance to aid in policy development and to monitor the effects of the changes is critical.

The temporal coverage of episodes by the three surveys can be examined in the time line in Figure 5–3. Although the three surveys are contemporaneous, their sample type and coverage are different. These differences must be considered on a survey-by-survey basis in a coordinated analysis.

NNHS: Institutional Sampling

The NNHS represents sample coverage issues raised by Gruenberg et al. (1989), since the first stage of sample selection is the institution. Three issues are (1) the definition of institutions and the existence of a sample "gap" (National Center for Health Statistics [NCHS] 1989b,1), (2) the definition of "nonresponse," and (3) the interaction of an institutional sample with the representation of characteristics of institutionalized persons.

The 1985 NNHS sampled all "types of nursing and related care homes with three or more beds set up and staffed for use by residents and routinely providing nursing and personal care services" (NCHS 1989b, 126). Facilities were required to be "freestanding" establishments "or nursing care units who maintained separate financial and employee records." The sample universe for the 1985 survey was drawn from (1) the 1982 National Master Facility Inventory (NMFI), (2) homes identified in the 1982 complement survey that were missing from the NMFI, (3) hospital-based nursing homes certified by HCFA, and (4) "data" on nursing homes opened between 1982 and June 1, 1984 (NCHS 1985, 1986, 1989b). This definition is different from that used by the Census Bureau, which is more inclusive. A list sample of Medicare-eligible persons derived from HCFA records, and using the Census Bureau definition, includes persons in "bed and care" homes—an area of interest for long-term-care policy because of the difficulty of defining their characteristics and their lack of certification. The issue of the representation of persons in residential-care facilities will become increasingly important in the future for surveys of the oldest old because the threshold of institutional care for the oldest old appears to be becoming more diffuse with continuing innovation in residential services.

The sample criteria for institutional selection and the mode of data collection have implications in calculating response rates. In the NNHS, for example, 88 percent (1,079 of 1,220 facilities) responded. Of the 12 percent not responding, 57 (4.7 percent) had gone out of business or "out of scope" since 1982 when the frame was set; 7 percent (84) refused to participate. For the 92.8 percent of "in scope" facilities "response rates" for individuals were 97 percent for residents and 95 percent for discharges. These response rates, however, are not "individual" responses because the information on the individual is gathered from a caregiver or medical record (NCHS 1989b, 128), that is, "individual" nonresponse is at the level of the institution. Overall, 90 percent of all nursing-home (within the definition used by NCHS residents and 88 percent of discharged patients in the "in scope" sample of institutions had information provided by responding facilities. Thus, the interaction of the institutional sample and the individual selected raises complicated analytic issues in combining samples to make national estimates.

In the NNHS, two "individual samples" are identified. One represents all discharges (6,014) from a facility over the previous 12 months. The "discharge" sample represents the characteristics of an "admission" cohort except that (1) entry cohorts are of different sizes, (2) period effects operate to change admission risks for

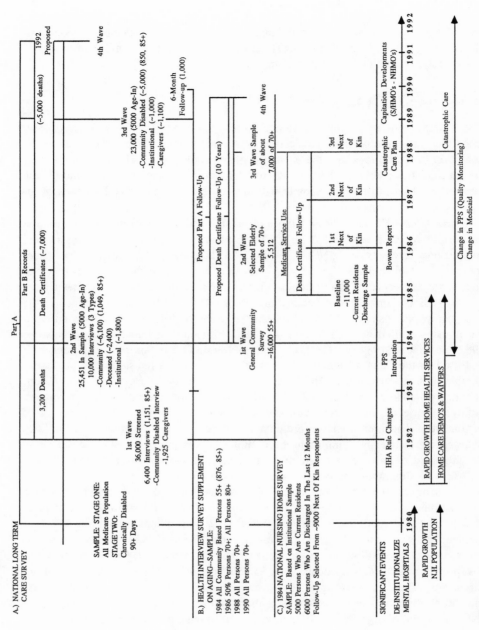

Figure 5–3 Time lines for three nationally representative longitudinal surveys.

different subpopulations over time, and (3) a person may have more than one discharge in a year. The medical content of the discharge questionnaire was reduced in 1985 in order to elicit more information on the number of episodes experienced by an individual to provide better person-based estimates of nursing-home use. This restricts the analyses that can be done jointly of the health characteristics of the 1977 and 1985 discharge samples.

The second NNHS sample (5,238) of *persons* resident in a facility on a given date is subject to "length-biased" sampling, that is, on a given date there is a higher probability of locating a long-term than a short-term resident. Length-biased sampling can be adjusted for with appropriate compartment modeling or discrete mixture techniques (Everitt 1984). Three follow-up interviews of the next of kin of nursing home residents were conducted in order to establish long-term institutional changes and vital status for the nursing-home residents identified in 1985.

SOA and LSOA: Area Probability Samples

The SOA sample is an area probability sample of individuals identified from census records. The SOA to the 1984 NHIS was given to 11,497 noninstitutionalized persons over age 65 (NCHS 1987) with 826 persons 85 and over (compared with 450 persons aged 85 and over in the 1987 NMES and 445 persons aged 85 and over in the 1984 SIPP). In 1986 a telephone survey was conducted of a 56.2 percent sample of persons aged 70 to 79 (99.5 percent of blacks aged 70 to 79) and 99.8 percent of persons aged 80 and over—5,158 persons in all (NCHS 1989a). The 1988 LSOA covered all persons aged 70 and above—7.064 persons. There was no oversampling in the 1984 SOA of disabled elderly or oldest old. Area probability samples, even with very high response rates, may allow certain types of health-service use to be underreported (NCHS 1966) and thus require special sample adjustments. In other words, random allocation of nonresponses solely on demographic factors may not eliminate bias due to health-status specific nonresponse rates (Alexander 1989). Linkage to Medicare records is limited to survey respondents who signed waivers (about 89.7 percent of respondents). In 1984, no institutionalized persons were sampled. Thus, it will take a period of time for a representative institutional population to accumulate.

Thus, care has to be taken in coordinated analyses of the NNHS and SOA–LSOA because of the difference in sample entity (institution versus individual) and the different sources (e.g., the 1982 NMFI and related sources versus census estimates) from which the samples were drawn. Such complexities can be dealt with in analyses that represent both the temporal factors in sample design and differences in sample types. However, to account for these issues in longitudinal analyses requires an explicitly model-based (rather than "finite population") statistical approach (Hoem 1989; Kalton 1989). A discussion of the inference questions raised is presented later.

NLTCS: List Sample with Two-stage Sample Capture

The 1982 NLTCS was based on a list sample of 35,018 persons aged 65 and over drawn from HCFA administrative records on Medicare-eligible persons. It is unclear precisely how the Medicare list-based frame relates to census-based frames because the latter will be influenced by undercounts and changes in the population after the date of the census; that is, persons have to be identified on an age, sex, and geographic (i.e., Primary Sampling Unit—PSU) basis. That classification will change in accuracy with time elapsed from the census date. HCFA administrative records are part of an ongoing and continuously updated management information system that does not degrade in accuracy over time as the basis for a sample frame. There will be a temporal lag for the updating of events in the file, although this will be relatively short (e.g., 6 months). The issues in comparing area probability and list samples become more complex if one considers that information from HCFA and Social Security Administration records currently is used in producing (along with the Current Population Survey) intercensal population estimates—especially at later ages (U.S. Bureau of the Census 1989).

In the NLTCS in 1982, a second-stage screen (involving 80 percent telephone screens and 20 percent personal visits) identified 6,393 persons who reported at least one impairment in activity of daily living (ADL) or instrumental activity of daily living (IADL) that had lasted (or was expected to last) 90 days or more. The 1,992 persons in institutions in 1982 at the time of the screen and 26,623 persons who were not disabled on the screen were subsequently monitored in the Medicare record system for vital status and Part A and B service use. Selected health characteristics of screen or survey nonrespondents on those records can be used to make adjustments for nonresponse.

In 1984, institutional and chronically disabled persons were automatically scheduled for reinterview (to assess functional improvements), and 5,000 persons aged 65 and 66 were added to produce cross-sectional estimates of the Medicare population. A sample of the 26,623 persons was rescreened to determine incident disability. In addition, as in 1982, rosters of family members, caregivers, and children were obtained for each sample member. An institutional survey was conducted in 1984. The design was repeated in 1989 with an additional 5,000 persons, aged 65 to 68 added to complete the cross section. Thus, the total sample size for the three surveys is approximately 45,000 persons aged 65 and over supplemented on a rolling basis to preserve the integrity of cross-sectional representation and to prevent high-mortality groups (e.g., the oldest old) from being depleted. By using a list sample, and because all disabled and institutionalized people are interviewed, board and care residents will be present in the sample.

Use of Multiple Data Sources in a Model of the National Health Care System

The three surveys can be used in *coordinated* analyses because their samples cover the entire elderly population and there is adequate common instrumentation. Such a strategy offers greater detail and precision of estimates than a single survey of similar cost. The NNHS describes the characteristics and service use of persons resident in or discharged from institutions. It does not describe noninstitutionalized persons— either frail or healthy. In 1985, there were about 2,400 persons aged 85 and over in the current resident sample (NCHS 1989b). The SOA–LSOA represents the general elderly population with, for example, 826 persons in 1984 who were 85 years of age and over. The number of persons who were 85 years of age and over in the SOA will change with time as a function of chronological aging and systematic mortality.

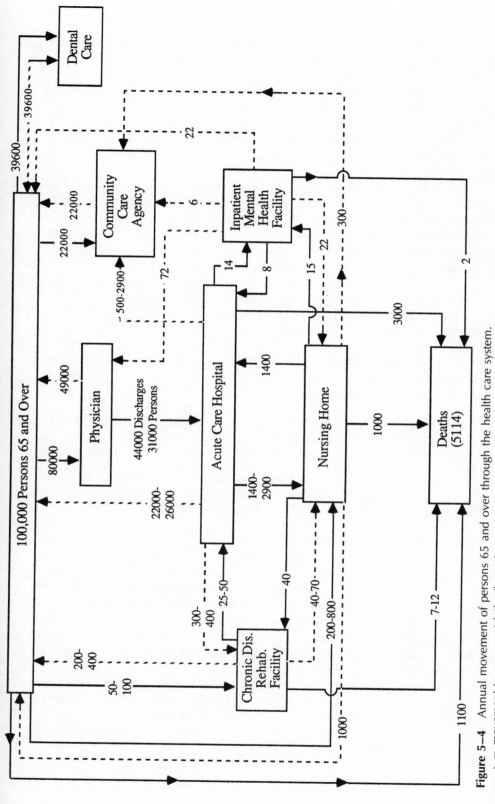

Figure 5–4 Annual movement of persons 65 and over through the health care system. $\longrightarrow$ = movement to more restrictive/intensive care setting; - - - $\longrightarrow$ = movement to less restrictive/intensive care setting. (Source: Densen 1987, 616)

The NLTCS covers the community-dwelling, disabled elderly, institutionalized persons (in 1984 and 1989) and provides rosters of all family members, children, and caregivers. There was a total of 2,555 individuals 85 years of age and over in the 1982 longitudinal subsample and 4,975 persons in 1982 and 1984 combined. Of these, 1,151 chronically disabled were interviewed in 1982 and 1,799 were interviewed (in both the community and institutional surveys) in 1984. The total number aged 85 and over in the entire 1982 sample was 3,352. The service use and mortality of all sample persons aged 85 and over are monitored on a continuing basis with the Medicare files.

Figure 5–4 presents life-table transition rates estimated from a series of NCHS surveys ([Densen 1987]; a revision used additional administrative record sources [Densen 1990]). Of 100,000 persons 65 years of age and over living in the community, 80,000 (80 percent) visited a physician during the year; of these, 49,000 remained in the community. The other 31,000 persons were sent to an acute-care hospital from which 26,000 later were discharged home and 2,900 to nursing homes. There is a directed flow of persons from less restrictive and less intensive care to more restrictive care indicated by the solid lines, and the reverse indicated by dotted lines.

The coordinated analysis of surveys to study health-service use has the advantage of not only providing nationally representative estimates, but also of being substantive and temporal in scope; in other words, it would be difficult to design and field a single data-collection effort to cover the range of services in Figure 5–4. In addition, longitudinal surveys have advantages in that their temporal sampling of events is flexible. Densen (1987, 622) notes:

> By its very nature, longitudinal research requires considerable periods of time for completion. Desirable as such research would be, it would not serve the same purpose . . . to make it possible to assess quickly and at fairly frequent intervals the shifts that take place in response to policy changes in the relations of various parts of the health care system to each other and in the way the elderly make use of the service network. In this sense, . . . the Figure . . . may be viewed as a barometer of the effects of policy changes upon the health care structure and its operation.

Figure 5–4 is extended in Figure 5–5. Administrative information on Medicare (and possibly Medicaid) use from the three longitudinal surveys produces more precise and detailed estimates than can be made from self-reports. Using longitudinal surveys linked to continuous service use records allows prospective estimates to be made along with such service outcomes as mortality or rehospitalization risks. In addition, health and service transitions not captured in the surveys may be estimated from nonsurvey data resources (e.g., the 8-year history of individual nursing-home transitions in Connecticut [Bice 1989; Gruenberg et al. 1989]; risk-factor associations from the EPESE studies) if sampling issues can be resolved.

Letters indicate the source of data used to estimate specific transitions (see legend to Figure 5–5). Transition rates are indicated by arrows, with the data sets used to estimate them indicated in parentheses and the health states represented by boxes. Letters in those boxes indicate data sources that might be used to estimate population size and volume of service use.

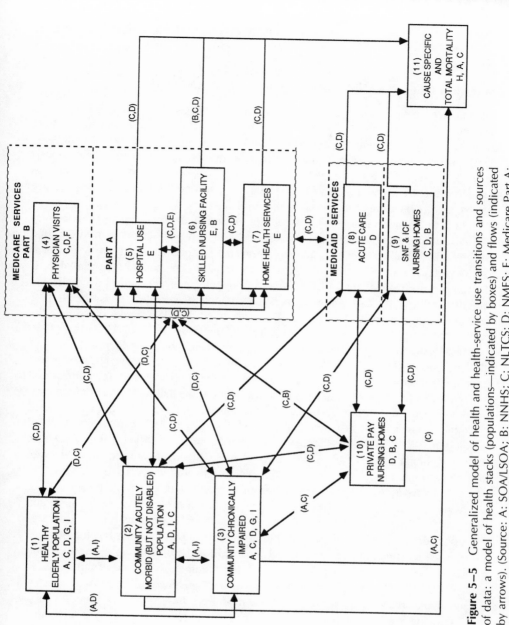

Figure 5–5 Generalized model of health and health-service use transitions and sources of data: a model of health stacks (populations—indicated by boxes) and flows (indicated by arrows). (Source: A: SOA/LSOA; B: NNHS; C: NLTCS; D: NMES; E: Medicare Part A; F: Medicare; G: SIPP; H: Vital statistics; I: Epidemiological studies and registries)

Statistical Issues: "Finite" Versus "Super" Population Models

To conduct "coordinated" analyses, we refer to the two-dimensional model of data collection in Figure 5–1. Coordinated analyses require that survey samples, time frames, and measurements be made to "match." This can be done by two strategies. One approach involves appropriate post-stratification weighting so that the composition of different reference populations can be standardized. This is most appropriate in reconstructing a population "cross-section." A second approach involves the use of "super" population models; this is appropriate for studying health transitions.

The first approach involves postweighting of population components. Community and institutional sample weights for exclusively defined populations sum to the total population for a fixed common date so long as the samples are exclusive (e.g., there is no overlap) and if estimates of changes in population composition are available. If the samples are from slightly different dates, they may be synchronized by renorming weights for a specific date using independent population estimates. Thus, the NLTCS community sample might be combined with the 1985 NNHS sample to estimate the prevalence of severe cognitive impairment by norming the 1984 NLTCS to the 1985 estimated community population. Combining the NLTCS with the SOA–LSOA population, one could exploit (1) the precision of estimates from the NLTCS in the community-disabled population and (2) the precision of estimates on the nondisabled population from the SOA–LSOA population. To ensure that the subpopulation estimates are exclusive, internal estimates of disability from the SOA–LSOA are needed to define a nondisabled subpopulation exclusive of the NLTCS chronically disabled population. When exclusive subpopulations can be defined, statistical tests based on finite population models can be conducted if the components are independent strata in global sample design with different sample designs within each subpopulation.

A second way to integrate samples from different population components is the use of models of transitions based on super-population theory (Cassel, Sarndal, and Wretman 1977). In simple terms, a "super-population" represents a theoretical stochastic model of changes in the population distribution from which all longitudinal samples are assumed drawn. The model assumed for the underlying distribution will determine both the statistical properties of the parameter estimates from different samples and the way in which those estimates are combined to form population estimates. Conceptually, the super-population model can be viewed as a general "mixing" function into which the parameters for subpopulations are fit by determining how specific samples fit into the superpopulation matrix of characteristics. This approval also allows parameter estimates to be generalized beyond the population at a fixed time.

This is conceptually different from standard "finite" population sample theory, where the population from which the sample is drawn is assumed "fixed." That is, that the stochasticity of sample estimates are assumed to result solely from the sampling process. In the super-population model, sampling is under the control of the investigator and the events in the population are stochastic. The finite population model is the conventional basis upon which variance estimates are calculated for complex cross-sectional samples and is the basis for most canned software packages for calculating those variances. However, as for any statistical model, that approach involves a set of assumptions that may, or may not, be met in a given sample. Instability in the variances calculated from that approach for survival and event analyses may result from (1) small samples in strata or PSUs, (2) small number of PSUs, or (3) very different variances for rates in different strata (e.g., between blacks and whites) (O'Brien 1981). Thus, applications of analytic software without understanding the specific assumptions of the model implemented by the software, and how appropriate those assumptions are for the specific data set, can lead to serious analytic errors (Searle 1989). Indeed, in longitudinal analyses even the determination of specific population characteristics may be affected by asynchronicity in the sampling and interviewing process. In the 1985 NNHS, if one uses age at entry to study versus current age, the estimated number of institutionalized persons aged 85 and over can vary considerably. In the 1982 and 1984 NLTCS, care must be exercised in identifying the April 1 population, and respondent, nonrespondent, and out-of-scope persons at both the time of screening and time of the effort to conduct the detailed interview. The differences in screening in 1982 and 1984 (and the "decedent" survey in 1984) makes this a complex task.

Beyond this issue of generalizability, and the operating characteristics of the finite population models in a given observational plan, there are fundamental conceptual issues implied by these different approaches to inference. For example, finite population models are used to calculate variances for certain of the EPESE sites (Cornoni-Huntley et al. 1989) for the baseline data. When one has follow-up data to analyze from the same survey, it is clear that the assumptions of the finite population model cannot be used to model transitions. These issues are well known in the statistical literature (e.g., see Fienberg 1989; Hoem 1989; Kalton 1989;) but are sometimes ignored in practice.

Measurement Issues: Instrument Construction

A second set of issues involves coordinating measurements from different surveys. This is more complex in longitudinal surveys because we must be concerned not only with the construction of instruments, and how health and function are measured, but also with how those measures are applied over time (and age). Instrumentation is easy to match at a superficial level because some variation of ADL and IADL measures is used in most surveys and because many surveys are linked to Medicare records. However, there is considerable variation in the detail and the reference period for which the functional assessments are made.

For example, in the NLTCS the ability of persons to perform a range of ADLs and IADLs was ascertained in a personal visit with respondent or proxy in terms of needs being met by (1) the use of personal care (2) special equipment, (3) standby help, or (4) no provision of care. This is useful to consider alternative policies (e.g., the use of assistive devices versus personal assistance) and to provide flexibility in conducting coordinated analyses with other surveys. To illustrate, in Table 5–1 we present ADL counts for seven different combinations of care.

There is considerable variability in the type of care received for different ADLs. For eating, much of the help received was stand-by (or passive) personal assistance (49.7 percent for persons aged 65 to 84 and 51.4 percent for persons aged 85 and over), whereas for dressing, most help received was personal assistance. Inside mo-

Table 5–1 Distribution of Persons Living in the Community with Some Type of an Impairment in One of Six Activities of Daily Living and the Types of Care Received from the 1984 NLTCS

	Activities of Daily Living											
	Eating		In/out bed		Inside mobility		Dressing		Bathing		Toileting	
	64–84	85+	64–84	85+	64–84	85+	64–84	85+	64–84	85+	64–84	85+
Personal assistance only	186 (39.8)	71 (39.2)	143 (11.3)	45 (12.0)	106 (6.0)	31 (5.5)	602 (63.2)	164 (58.4)	493 (25.2)	182 (29.8)	159 (7.6)	44 (11.8)
Personal assistance and equipment	17 (3.6)	8 (4.4)	291 (22.9)	79 (21.1)	321 (18.1)	104 (18.4)	34 (3.6)	16 (5.7)	249 (12.7)	122 (20.0)	1,268 (60.4)	56 (15.1)
Stand-by help only	232 (49.7)	93 (51.4)	183 (14.4)	58 (15.5)	161 (9.1)	46 (8.1)	179 (18.8)	60 (21.4)	212 (10.8)	50 (8.2)	212 (10.1)	77 (20.7)
Stand-by and equipment	10 (2.1)	2 (1.1)	201 (15.8)	73 (19.5)	291 (16.4)	100 (17.7)	6 (.6)	2 (.7)	209 (10.7)	43 (7.0)	119 (5.7)	46 (12.4)
Equipment only	10 (2.1)	2 (1.1)	408 (32.1)	108 (28.9)	875 (49.2)	272 (48.1)	31 (3.3)	2 (.7)	547 (28.0)	114 (18.7)	255 (12.2)	115 (30.9)
Activity of daily living not done	4 (.8)	0	31 (2.4)	6 (1.6)	20 (1.1)	11 (1.9)	78 (8.2)	30 (10.7)	214 (10.9)	88 (14.4)	64 (3.1)	26 (2.0)
Need help	8 (1.6)	5 (2.8)	13 (1.0)	5 (1.3)	3 (.1)	1 (.2)	22 (2.3)	7 (2.5)	33 (1.7)	12 (2.0)	21 (1.0)	8 (2.2)
	467	181	1,270	374	1,777	566	952	281	1,957	611	2,098	322

Note: Numbers in parentheses indicate percentages.

bility often involved equipment only, or equipment with personal assistance. Age-related differences in the use of equipment for toileting were notable.

Self-reported assessments will differ from assessments mae by institutional staff or performance measures. It is difficult to determine whether objective performance measures better represent the disability of the oldest-old population than the self-reported measures in that the latter reflect morale, self-perception, and psychiatric factors that may strongly interact with physical impairment (World Health Organization 1980) to determine a person's actual degree of disability.

The ability to match instrument elements depends upon the detail in the questions asked and the level of resolution required. The most severe levels of impairment are probably described reliably (except for nonresponse bias) in most surveys. Less disabled populations represent nuances that are more difficult to assess. The temporal aspect of measurement is also difficult because of differing lengths of follow-up and age groups. Alternative definitions of disability can produce considerable variability in estimates of the size of the disabled population. A recent study of functional status reporting among the elderly in a number of surveys in the United States examined this issue (Wiener, Hanley, Spense, and Murray 1992). In that study there was an effort to construct "comparability" between surveys of disability items. Only one version of "comparable" items was constructed (i.e., an even greater degree of "closeness" between surveys might have been obtained if alternative criteria were selected), and the issue of longitudinal changes was not explicitly addressed. Nonetheless, the results of the comparisons are useful in that comparability could be shown for a complex and dynamic phenomenon like disability across surveys of very different sample design and instrumentation. The results for the population aged 65 and above are presented in Table 5–2.

The 1982 and 1984 NLTCS and 1987 NMES were comparable (within the limits of statistical precision) using the definitions selected by the study group. SIPP and the 1984 SOA gave estimates significantly lower (for this set of time definitions) and different from one another. The estimates from the NHANES survey had to be affected because the survey did not contain persons over age 85.

In Table 5–3 comparisons of the institutional population using the 1985 NNHS, the 1987 NMES, and the 1984 NLTCS are made. The distribution of disabilities for the three institutional surveys is very similar.

Results for the 1987 NMES and the 1982 and 1984 NLTCS demonstrate that similar estimates of functional disability can be obtained from household surveys of the elderly even when the proxy response rate is high. The rate estimates for those three surveys are within the statistical precision limits of the estimates. Comparability of estimates of level of functioning was also seen in the three institutional surveys. Thus, the results suggest that functional disability can be reliably assessed in elderly populations using current survey methodology. Presumably, the estimates across surveys could have been made even more comparable if additional sample and questionnaire analytic adjustments were made. The issue of the meaningfulness of the times used (i.e., the question of validity) will depend on how well those items predict other phenomena (e.g., mortality, morbidity, service use, measures of social autonomy).

Neither table addresses the reliability of estimates of longitudinal changes. The NLTCS and the SOA–LSOA were explicitly designed to provide longitudinal estimates. The results from both surveys are encouraging in that the long-term improve-

Table 5–2 Activity of Daily Living Disabilities among the Noninstitutionalized Elderly Age 65 and Over, by Survey and Type of Activity (in thousands)

	1982 NLTCS	1984 NLTCS	1984 SOA	1984 SIPP	1987 NMES
Total aged 65 and over noninstitutionalized elderly population (millions)	25,440	26,481	26,268	26,422	27,909
One or more ADL problems	1,992 (7.8)	2,062 (7.8)	1,318 (5.0)	1,538[a] (5.8)	2,250 (8.1)
Bathing	1,609 (6.3)	1,660 (6.3)	1,211 (4.6)	1,459[a] (5.5)	1,926 (6.9)
Dressing	1,072 (4.2)	1,063 (4.0)	771 (2.9)	—[b]	1,228 (4.4)
Transferring	1,072 (4.2)	1,072 (4.0)	675 (2.6)	699 (2.6)	977 (3.5)
Toileting	857 (3.4)	880 (3.3)	619 (2.4)	n.a.[d]	670 (2.4)
Eating	624 (2.5)	618 (2.3)	183 (0.7)	—[b]	—[c]

Note: Numbers in parentheses indicate percentages.
[a] Excluded toileting.
[b] Combines bathing, dressing, eating and personal hygiene in one question.
[c] Cell size too small for reliable estimate.
[d] not asked.
Source: Wiener and Hanley (1989).

Table 5–3 Activity of Daily Living Disabilities Among the Institutionalized Elderly Age 65 and Over, by Survey and Type of Activity (in thousands)

	1985 NNHS[a]	1987 NMES[a]	1984 NLTCS
Total institutionalized elderly population (000s)	1,318	1,209	1,551
Receive help of another person with one or more ADL problems	1,207 (91.6)	1,104 (91.3)	1,416 (91.3)
Bathing	1,191 (90.4)	1,088 (90.0)	1,081 (89.0)
Dressing	1,002 (76.0)	952 (78.7)	1,092 (70.4)
Transferring	815 (61.8)	780 (64.5)	969 (62.5)
Toileting	866 (65.7)	807 (66.7)	1,021 (65.8)
Eating	502 (38.1)	422 (34.9)	659 (42.5)

Note: Numbers in parentheses indicate percentages.
[a] Current resident survey.

ment in functional status found in the NLTCS (Manton 1988a,b) was verified in the SOA–LSOA follow-up (Harris et al. 1989), results which are consistent with findings from the NIA EPESE studies (Guralnik 1989). The existence of long-term improvements in three different data sources (i.e., the NLTCS, LSOA, and EPESE) lends credence to the existence of such improvements, along with their predictive validity, that is, they predicted such "hard" outcomes as mortality. These observations raise a series of detailed research questions regarding the mechanisms (i.e., the nature of the diseases causing disability, treatment, coping strategies) by which functional status improves.

Measurement Issues: Analytic Adjustments

Measuring longitudinal changes in disability status is more difficult than making cross-sectional prevalence estimates. The measurement problem can be partly resolved if multiple questions about the objective nature of each disability are asked. In this case, multiple indicator models (appropriate to the distributional characteristics of responses) can be used. Fundamentally, a large number of objective tests (e.g., asking about the ability to perform specific functional tasks with different types of aids and personal assistance) can be used to generate an overall index of functional status, which has greater stability than any individual item because of an "averaging" process that balances false-positive and false-negative responses on individual disability items. As the number of items is increased, it can be shown that the average will converge to the true values. Such a principle is used, for example, in psychometrics to identify the dimensions of intelligence Lord and Novick 1968; Woodbury and Novick 1968).

Because of the large numbers of disability items required to produce a stable index (or a set of indices if there are multiple dimensions) and the discrete nature of those responses, multivariate statistical procedures are required for index construction. One model appropriate for discrete response data is the Grade of Membership model (Manton 1990; Manton and Woodbury 1991; NCHS 1988; Woodbury and Clive 1974; Woodbury, Clive, and Garson 1978) because it does not require strong assumptions about the distribution of responses. Additionally, instead of forcing a person to be characterized (or categorized) as a member of one homogeneous group, the person can be represented by partial membership in multiple heterogeneous groups. Groups scores are estimated so that the model parameters exactly reproduce the observed attributes of individuals (e.g., Jackson, Woodbury, and Manton 1988; Singer 1990; Woodbury, Clive, and Garson 1978). These properties are important when identifying complex health and functional profiles from data with high levels of measurement error (e.g., Berkman, Singer, and Manton 1989). They also help stabilize the averaging process described above in that the complete presence or absence of the kth type of disability is not required. They are important in coordinated analyses in that, if two surveys have sufficiently rich measures, although *not* wholly comparable, it may be possible to produce a joint analysis based on the disability *dimensions*. That is, different sets of measures may be adequate to identify very similar latent dimensions. If the latent dimensions are similar, individual scores on those dimensions may be compared. This process is logically no different from sorting through items by hand to select a most comparably worded subset of items. It is, however, statistically more efficient and open to objective evaluation. Multivariate procedures to resolve problems in the measurement domain are especially important (1) when dealing with oldest-old populations with high levels of co-morbidity and functional impairment and (2) when attempting to integrate data from surveys in which health and functional status are multidimensional but in which instrumentation, although rich, is not fully comparably on an item-specific basis.

One test of the performance of the multiple indicator approach was conducted using the 1982 and 1984 NLTCS. Twenty-seven ADL, IADL, and physical function measures were analyzed to produce six disability types (Manton, Woodbury, and Stallard 1991). To complete population coverage, a seventh profile representing in-stitutionalized persons was constructed using data from the 1985 NNHS. The profiles and scores representing the multiple health and functional status dimensions showed excellent predictive validity for Medicare service use, morbidity, long-term-care ser-vice use, and mortality (Manton, Woodbury, and Stallard 1991). The 2-year mortal-ity relative risk between the most and least disabled types was 8 to 1 for men and 10 to 1 for women—nearly double the relative risk achievable with seven ADLs. Fur-thermore, the relationship was time-variable in a way that was consistent with the pattern of medical conditions associated with the functional types; the relative risk increased as the follow-up period was shortened. Thus, multivariate procedures for averaging over a large number of objective measures of function can be empirically shown to have superior external validity on a wide range of objective variables of policy interest to individual items or summated scales.

A fundamental issue in the measurement of the health and functioning of the oldest old is the high prevalence of cognitive impairment at advanced age. This is a group for which cognitive procedures are unlikely to be helpful. Because motivation (and psychiatric disorders like depression) is important in determining the functional status of a person (especially in terms of the person's capacity for self-care), the relation of performance measures to self-reported limitations may be complex. This is why, in assessing measurements, the predictive validity of functional status for "hard" outcomes like mortality, morbidity, and service consumption is useful.

Measurement Issues: Estimates of Transitions

Unbiased estimates of health transitions and service use require that all persons in the sample be given their own sample weights—even interview nonrespondents. The use of a list sample allows all persons (nonrespondents and persons in special sample groups) to be tracked over time. Again, using the NLTCS for illustration, transitions for the disabled (those only with IADL impairments and those with one or more ADL impairments), nondisabled, and institutionalized subpopulations *and* persons who did *not* complete the survey were calculated (Manton, 1988a,b). Those analyses, consistent with results from the SOA–LSOA (see Chapter 16 in this volume by Suz-man et al.) and EPESE showed that a significant proportion of persons with func-tional impairment showed long-term (2-year) improvements in functions. Nonrespon-dents had the highest mortality rates (47.9 percent in 2 years) as well as high disability and institutional rates. Their loss from nonlist samples could produce bias in esti-mating service and health transitions (Berkman, Singer, and Manton 1989; NCHS 1966).

By using a list sample, not only can estimates of health transitions be adjusted using the characteristics of nonrespondents identified from administrative records, but the service use of the entire Medicare population can also be described. The list sample, using status at the time of the screen, can be decomposed into community nondisabled, community disabled, institutional, and nonresponse groups for which nationally representative estimates of Medicare Part A and Part B service use can be generated. For example, from administrative records, the length of stay and discharge status (adjusted for several modes of right censoring) for hospital episodes reimbursed by Part A of Medicare can be calculated for the three population groups for a 12-month period begun after the completion of interviewing. These measures can also be calculated for home health agency and SNF use and for community episodes. The total number of hospital episodes declined 10 percent between 1982 and 1984 (i.e., from 9.8 to 8.8 million), whereas the number of hospital episodes for disabled persons (and nonrespondents) was relatively stable (i.e., 3.15 versus 3.11 million discharges). The hospital admission rate from the community for nondisabled persons declined 15.1 percent; for disabled and institutional persons it declined only 2.6 and 2.1 percent, respectively (Manton, Vertrees, and Wrigley 1990). By defining the interval for assessment in this way, the problem that deaths during the early parts of 1982 and 1984 prevented the interviewing of selected groups of individuals (i.e., left censoring) was avoided. For calendar-year estimates, special sample weighting procedures are required to deal with left censoring (Manton 1990). The results from the surveys can be compared with calendar-year actuarial estimates produced by HCFA (U.S. Department of Health and Human Services 1988).

SUMMARY

Because it will be the fastest-growing age group in the U.S. population, and because it has the highest health-service requirements, the oldest-old population is extremely important for federal and state health and long-term-care policies. It is important both in the evaluation of policy (e.g., access to care; quality of care; cost reimbursement and containment; management and operation of programs; program monitoring and surveillance) and in helping to design new and improved policies and programs (e.g., how to introduce long-term-care benefits into Medicare; identification of the appropriate mix of private insurance and public long-term-care benefits; how to provide incentives for assistive devices and specialized housing services as well as for personal assistance). In order to have cohesive and efficient policy and programs, it is necessary to have appropriate data on the social and health characteristics of the oldest old, as well as on the performance and impact of programs on that population. Until the 1980s, such data, in the large part, did not exist. Recently, a number of new longitudinal studies and national longitudinal surveys with enhanced data on the oldest old have been designed and fielded. Although the situation is improved and much new research has been stimulated, much remains to be done. First, it is clear that the existing efforts should continue—both to provide longer-term data on individual changes to answer questions on the health transition of elderly cohorts and because they document conditions among the oldest old before many interventions were started. It is also clear, however, that the scope and design of surveys needs to be enhanced.

To this end, we have examined a number of conceptual issues in the design of longitudinal surveys to describe health and functional transitions and service use in the oldest-old population. A theoretical model of health transitions was presented that could be used to examine temporal parameters (e.g., age sampling, periodicity; linkage to continuous service data) of survey design and strategies for assessing functional status. The use of multivariate procedures to deal with measurement problems in describing functional status for the oldest old was discussed.

Although there is considerable recent data on the health characteristics of the oldest-old population, significant data gaps remain (e.g., the board and care population; income and assets, risk factors for disabling conditions). Furthermore, because of the wide variation in sample design and measurement, combined analysis of the surveys is difficult and requires considerable effort. Although heterogeneity of design makes coordinated analyses difficult, it is probably dangerous to make survey designs overly homogeneous: a multiplicity of surveys with different designs provides different samples and measurements of what is a very complex process. In a sense we can view multiple surveys as systematic, conscious "sampling" from a "universe" of surveys. This concept was made explicit in an analysis of how convenience and other samples of different design could be combined to make improved estimates of the prevalence of AIDS (Manton and Singer 1989). The multiplicity of diverse measures and samples increases our confidence in results that are robust to sample and instrument design. The fact that functional status has been observed to improve at advanced ages in a large proportion of cases over a lengthy period of time in at least three different studies (i.e., the NLTCS, the SOA–LSOA, and EPESE) suggests that the phenomenon is real and that extensive research of the mechanisms producing these improvements is justified. If this were observed only in one survey (or if there were only one survey to observe it in), one's confidence in the observation could not be as great. This finding by itself has tremendous policy implications, suggesting that improvements in active life expectancy is possible at advanced ages. A similar principle is operational in clinical trials where multiple clinical trials are undertaken, often with quite different designs. The multiplicity of the trials occurs because some study deficiency or new condition had to be addressed by a new design. Nonetheless, it is the accumulation of evidence from multiple (even if partly flawed) trials, rather than the results of a single trial, that is most convincing (Early Breast Cancer Trialists' Collaborative Group 1988; Mansour et al. 1989). In addition, it may only be by the accumulation of multiple trials (in our case, surveys) that adequate sample size (and statistical precision) can be achieved for certain detailed analyses. Such is the recent case where meta-analyses showed the benefits of hypertensive control for heart disease.

Correlated with the need for a multiplicity of surveys (and designs) is a need for rapid access to the data generated in those surveys. A multiplicity of analyses is also likely to produce results in which we have greater confidence but, without improved data access, such analyses (and replication of analyses) cannot be done. The question of access is both an ethical and a technical one. If data are collected with federal resources, their maximal use for the national good is mandated (NCHS 1988). The technical support required to facilitate the use of multiple surveys and data sources is considerable. An effective national statistical system must encompass the provision of adequate technical assistance and the development of appropriate analytic machinery, as well as foster data collection.

REFERENCES

Alexander, C. 1989. Sample Weights. Presented at the National Long-Term Care Survey (NLTCS) Data Users' Forum, sponsored by ASPE and Social & Scientific Systems, Bethesda, Md, January 26.

Berkman, L., B. Singer, and K.G. Manton 1989. Black/White Differences in Health Status and Mortality among the Elderly. *Demography* 26:661–78.

Bice, T.W. 1989. *Preliminary Analysis of Spend-down in Connecticut Nursing Homes.* Department of Epidemiology and Public Health, Yale University, New Haven, Ct.

Cassel, C.-M., C.-E. Sarndal, and J.H. Wretman. 1977. *Foundations of Inference in Survey Sampling* (Series in Probability and Mathematical Statistics.) New York: Wiley.

Cornoni-Huntley, J., D.B. Brock, A.M. Ostfeld, J.O. Taylor, and R.B. Wallace (Eds.). 1989. *Established Populations for Epidemiologic Studies of the Elderly: Resource Data Book.* NIH Pub. No. 86-2443, Bethesda, Md.: National Institute on Aging.

Densen, P.M. 1987. The Elderly and the Health Care System: Another perspective. *Milbank Quarterly* 65(4):614–38.

———. 1990. *The Elderly and the Health Care System: Another Perspective II.* Rockville, Md.: Agency for Health Care Policy and Research.

Early Breast Cancer Trialists' Collaborative Group: 1988. Effects of Adjuvant Tamoxifen and of Cytotoxic Therapy on Mortality in Early Breast Cancer: An Overview of 61 Randomized Trials among 28,896 Women. *New England Journal of Medicine* 319:1681–91.

Evans, D.A., H.H. Funkenstein, M.S. Albert et al. 1989. Prevalence of Alzheimer's Disease in a Community Population Higher than Previously Reported. *Journal of the American Medical Association* 262:2251–56.

Everitt, B.S. 1984. *An Introduction to Latent Variable Models.* London: Chapman and Hall.

Fienberg, S.E. 1989. Modeling Considerations: Discussion from a Modeling Perspective. In *Panel Surveys* eds. D. Kasprzyk et al., 566–74. New York: Wiley.

Gornick, M., J.N. Greenberg, P.W. Eggers and A. Dobson. 1985. Overview: Twenty Years of Medicare and Medicaid: Covered Populations, Use of Benefits and Program Expenditures. *Health Care Financing Review* (Annual Supplement): 13.

Gruenberg, L., K. Farbstein, P. Hughes-Cronwick, C. Pattee, and K. Mahoney. 1989. An Analysis of the Spend-down Patterns of Individuals Admitted to Nursing Homes in the State of Connecticut. Connecticut Partnership for Long Term Care Research Institute Discussion Paper No. 1–89. Office of Policy and Management, State of Connecticut.

Guralnik, J. 1989. Epidemiology of Physical Disability and the Associated Needs for Care. Presented at the Meetings of the Gerontological Society of America, November 18 Minneapolis.

Harris, T., M.G. Kovar, R. Suzman, J.C. Kleinman, and J.J. Feldman: 1989. Longitudinal Study of Robustness in the Oldest-old. *American Journal of Public Health* 79:698–702.

Heckman, J.J., and R. Robb, 1989. The Value of Longitudinal Data for Solving the Problems of Selection bias in Evaluating the Impact of Treatments on Outcomes. In *Panel Surveys*, eds. D. Kasprzyk et al., 512–38. New York: Wiley.

Hoem, J. 1985. Weighting, Misclassification and Other Issues in the Analysis of Survey Samples of Life Histories. In *Longitudinal Analysis of Labor Market Data*, eds. J. Heckman and B. Singer, 249–93. Cambridge: Cambridge University Press.

————. 1989. The Issue of Weights in Panel Surveys of Individual Behavior. In *Panel Surveys*, eds. D. Kasprzyk, et al., 539–59. New York: Wiley.

Jackson, D.J., M.A. Woodbury, and K.G. Manton. 1988. An Introduction to the Grade of Membership Classification Model. *Bulletin de Methodologies Sociologique* July (No. 19): 22–52.

Kalton, G. 1989. Modeling Considerations: Discussion from a Survey Sampling Perspective. In *Panel Surveys*, eds. D. Kasprzyk, et al. 575–85. New York: Wiley.

Kasprzyk, D., G. Duncan, G. Kalton, and M.P. Singh (eds.). 1989. *Panel Surveys*. New York: Wiley.

Katz, S. and C.A. Akpom 1976. A Measure of Primary Socio-biological Functions. *International Journal of Health Services* 6:493–508.

Kennell, D., J. Wiener, R. Hanley, and L. Alecxih. 1988. Nursing Home Admissions among Elderly Community Residents: Results from the 1982–84 National Long Term Care Survey. Financing of Long Term Care, Delivery Order No. 5, September. Washington: U.S. Department of Health and Human Services.

Kunkel, S.A. and C.K. Powell 1981. The Adjusted Average per Capita Cost under Risk Contract with Providers of Health Care. *Transactions of the Society of Actuaries* 33:221–30.

Lakatta, E.G. 1985. Health, Disease, and Cardiovascular Aging. In *America's Aging: Health in an Older Society*, 73–104. Washington: National Academy Press.

Liu, K., P. Doty, and K.G. Manton 1990. Medicaid Spenddown in Nursing Homes. *Gerontologist* 30:7–15.

Lord, F.M., and M.R. Novick 1968. *Statistical Theories of Mental Test Scores*. Reading, Mass.: Addison-Wesley.

Macken, C.L. 1986. A Profile of Functionally Impaired Elderly Persons Living in the Community. *Health Care Financing Review* 17(4):33.

Mansour, E.G., R. Gray, A.H. Shatila, et al. 1989. Efficacy of Adjuvant Chemotherapy in High-risk Node-negative Breast Cancer: An Intergroup Study. *New England Journal of Medicine* 320:485–90.

Manton, K.G. 1988a. A longitudinal study of functional change and mortality in the United States. *Journal of Gerontology* 43(5):153–61.

————. 1988b. Planning Long-term Care for Heterogeneous Older Populations. In *Annual Review of Gerontology and Geriatrics*, vol. 8, eds. G. Maddox and M.P. Lawton, 217–55. New York: Springer.

————. 1990. Mortality and Morbidity. In *Handbook of Aging and the Social Sciences*, 3rd ed., eds. R.H. Binstock and L.K. George New York: Academic Press.

Manton, K.G. and K. Liu. 1990. Recent changes in Service Use Patterns of Disabled Medicare Beneficiaries. *HCF Review* 11:51–66.

Manton, K.G. and B. Singer. 1989. Forecasting the Impact of the AIDS Epidemic on Elderly Populations. In *AIDS in an Aging Society: What We Need to Know* eds. M.W. Riley, M.G. Ory, and D. Zablotsky, 169–91. New York: Springer.

Manton, K.G., J.C. Vertrees and J.M. Wrigley 1990. Changes in Health Service Use and Mortality among the U.S. Elderly: 1980–86. *Journal of Aging and Health* 2:131–156.

Manton, K.G., and Woodbury, M.A. 1991. Grade of Membership Analysis in the Epidemiology of Aging. In *Methodologic Issues in the Epidemiologic Study of the Elderly*, eds. R.B. Wallace and R.F. Woolson. New York: Oxford University Press.

Manton, K.G., M.A. Woodbury, and E. Stallard 1991. Statistical and Measurement Issues in Assessing the Welfare Status of Aged Individuals and Populations. *Journal of Econometrics* 50:151–181.

Mathiowetz, N.A. and R. Groves. 1985. The Effects of Respondent Rules on Health Survey Reports. *American Journal of Public Health* 75: 639–44.

Moore, J.C. 1988. Self/Proxy Response Status and Survey Response Quality: A Review of the Literature. *Journal of Official Statistics* 4:155–72.

National Center for Health Statistics. 1965. Characteristics of Residents in Institutions for the Aged and Chronically Ill, United States, April–June 1963. *Vital and Health Statistics* series 12, no. 2, pub no. (PHS) 1000. Hyattsville, Md.

———. 1966. *Vital and Health Statistics Data Evaluation and Methods Research,* Computer Simulation of Hospital Discharges. PHS pub. no. 1000-series 2, no. 13. Hyattsville, Md.

———. 1988. Health in An Aging America: Issues on Data for Policy Analysis. *Vital and Health Statistics,* series 4, no. 25. USDHDS pub. no. (PHS) 89–1488. Hyattsville, Md.

National Center for Health Statistics, J. Fitti and M.G. Kovar 1987. The Supplement on Aging to the 1984 National Health Interview Survey. *Vital and Health Statistics,* series 1, no. 21. USDHHS pub. no. (PHS) 87–1323, Hyattsville, Md.

National Center for Health Statistics, and M. G. Kovar 1989a. National Health Interview Survey: 1988 Longitudinal Study of Aging Public Use File, Version 2, 1988 Release— Public Use Tape, January 12, Hyattsville, Md.

National Center for Health Statistics, E. Hing, E. Sekscenski, and G. Strahan. 1989b. The National Nursing Home Survey; 1985 Summary for the United States. *Vital and Health Statistics,* series 13, no. 97. USDHHS pub. no. (PHS) 89–1758. Washington.

National Center for Health Statistics, and D. Roper. 1986. Nursing and Related Care Homes as Reported from the 1982 National Master Facility Inventory Survey. *Vital and Health Statistics,* series 14, no. 32. USDHHS pub. no. (PHS) 86–1827. Washington.

National Center for Health Statistics, and A. Sirrocco. 1985. An Overview of the 1982 National Master Facility Inventory Survey of Nursing and Related Care Homes. *Advance Data from Vital and Health Statistics,* no. 111. USDHHS Pub. No. (PHS) 85–1250. Hyattsville, Md.

National Institute on Aging. 1989. The Federal Interagency Forum on Aging-Related Statistics Inventory of Data on the Oldest Old Population. Bethesda, Md.

O'Brien, K.F. 1981. Life Table Analysis for Complex Survey Data. Institute of Statistics Mimeo Series 1337, April, Chapel Hill: University of North Carolina.

Riley, M.W., and K. Bond 1983. Beyond Ageism: Postponing the Onset of Disability. In *Aging and Society: Selected Reviews of Recent Research,* eds. M.W. Riley, B.B. Hess, and K. Bond. Hillsdale, N.J.: Erlbaum.

Rivlin, A.M. and J.M. Wiener 1988. *Caring for the Disabled Elderly: Who Will Pay?* Washington: Brookings Institution.

Robine, J.M. and J.P. Michel 1990. Recommendations for International Guidelines for Comparisons of Healthy Life Expectancy. Principal working paper, REVES, March. Geneva: World Health Organization.

Rowe, J.W. 1988. Aging and Geriatric Medicine. In *Cecil, Textbook of Medicine,* eds. W.B. Wyngaarden and L.H. Smith Philadelphia: Harcourt, Brace and Jovanovich.

Sager, M., D.V. Easterling, D.A. Kindig, and O.W. Anderson. 1989. Changes in the Location of Death after Passage of Medicare's Prospective Payment System: A National Study. *New England Journal of Medicine* 320:433–39.

Searle, S.R. 1989. Statistical Computing Packages: Some Words of Caution. *The American Statistician* 43:189–90.

Singer, B. 1990. Grade of Membership Representations: Concepts and Problems. In *Festschrift for Samuel Karlin,* eds. T.W. Anderson, K.B. Athreya, and D. Inglehardt, 317–44. Orlando Fla.: Academic Press.

U.S. Bureau of the Census, Gregory Spencer. 1989. *Projections of the Population of the United States by Age, Sex, and Race: 1988 to 2080.* Current Population Reports, Series P-25, no. 1018. Washington.

U.S. Department of Health and Human Services. 1988. *Health Care Financing: Program Statistics, Medicare and Medicaid Data Book, 1988.* HCFA pub. no. 03270. Baltimore, Md.

Vaupel, J.W. and A.I. Yashin. 1985. The Deviant Dynamics of Death in Heterogeneous Populations. *Sociological Methodology 1985,* ed. N.B. Tuma, 179–211. San Francisco: Jossey-Bass.

Wiener, J.M. and R.J. Hanley 1989. *Measuring the Activities of Daily Living among the Elderly: A Guide to National Surveys.* Report to the Forum of Aging-Related Statistics by the Committee on Estimates of Activities of Daily Living in National Surveys.

Wiener, J., R. Hanley, R. D. Spense, and S. Murray. 1992. Financing and Utilization of Long-term Care for the Elderly: The Next 34 Years. In *Forecasting the Health of Elderly Populations,* eds. K.G. Manton, B.H. Singer, and R. Suzman. New York: Springer-Verlag.

Woodbury, M.A. and J. Clive. 1974. Clinical Pure Types as a Fuzzy Partition. *Journal of Cybernetics* 4:111–121.

Woodbury, M.A., J. Clive, and A. Garson. 1978. Mathematical Typology: A Grade of Membership Technique for Obtaining Disease Definition. *Computers and Biomedical Research* 11:277–98.

Woodbury, M.A., and M.R. Novick 1968. Maximizing the Validity of a Test Battery as a Function of Relative Test Lengths for a Fixed Total Testing Time. *Journal of Mathematical Psychology* 5:242–59.

World Health Organization. 1980. *International Classification of Impairments, Disabilities, and Handicaps: A Manual of Classification Relating to the Consequences of Disease.* Geneva.

————. 1984. The Uses of Epidemiology in the Study of the Elderly. Report of a WHO Scientific Group on the Epidemiology of Aging, Technical Report Series 706, Geneva.

Acknowledgments. Research reported herein was supported by NIA Grant Nos. AG 07198 and AG 07469-02 and ASPE Grant No. 87ASPE185A. Acknowledgment is made to Dr. Paul M. Densen of Harvard University, Robert Clark of the office of the Assistant Secretary for Policy and Evaluation, Dr. Jack Guralnik of the National Institute on Aging, Dr. Joshua Wiener of the Brookings Institution, Dr. Burton Singer of Yale University, and Dr. Mary Grace Kovar of the National Center for Health Statistics for reviews, opinions, and comments on this chapter. The resulting manuscript and any errors are the responsibility of the authors.

6

OBSERVATIONS ON INTERVIEW SURVEYS OF THE OLDEST OLD

ROBERT B. WALLACE, FRANK J. KOHOUT,
and PATRICIA L. COLSHER

As the number of older persons increases and they become more frequent subjects of survey and other quantitative research, investigators will face special methodological problems in obtaining credible and useful interview data. Although the problems and issues discussed here are not unique to the oldest old, they become particularly important with this group. We have not attempted to review exhaustively the issues that emerge in interviewing the oldest old. Instead,we focus on selected issues and problems that we have found particularly troublesome in our own research and that should be addressed in future studies.

The formal scientific literature contains little research on the methodological issues we raise. To be sure, several studies have contrasted various age groups with regard to factors such as the accuracy of factual information obtained in surveys (Anderson, Kasper, and Frankel 1979; Balamuth 1965; Herzog and Dielman 1985; Schuman and Presser 1981; Sudman and Bradburn 1974), response rates and refusal rates (Herzog and Rodgers 1986; Herzog, Rogers, and Kulka 1983; Thornberry and Massey 1978), and responses to telephone versus face-to-face interviews (Herzog and Rodgers 1986; Herzog, Rogers, and Kulka 1983). However, these studies generally define "old" as greater than 60 or 65 years of age and often do not separately consider the oldest-old group. Here we report observations and experiences in surveying that age group, supported by selected literature and analyses from our survey of the elderly in two rural Iowa counties, the Iowa 65+ Rural Health Study (65+ RHS) (Cornoni-Huntley et al. 1985).

THE LOCATION OF THE OLDEST OLD

An initial consideration is that 20 percent or more of persons 85 years and older live in long-term-care (LTC) institutions (National Center for Health Statistics 1984). Thus, comprehensive characterization of health status in this age group must consider institutionalized persons. Table 6–1 shows selected morbidity prevalence rates for the oldest old from our two-county household survey, contrasted with record review of the 11 long-term-care facilities therein. These data show that, not unexpectedly, mor-

Table 6–1 Prevalence of Selected Conditions in Household and LTC
Populations, Persons 85 Years of Age and Older

	Household survey (%)		LTC survey (%)	
Condition	Men	Women	Men	Women
Diabetes mellitus	10.0	8.8	23.5	4.8
Emphysema	8.3	6.6	15.4	2.6
Heart attack	15.8	12.5	9.6	7.4
Hip fracture	4.2	11.3	14.7	29.7
Functional blindness	3.9	5.8	14.7	10.6
Dependent in:				
Bathing	15.7	11.1	84.3	88.7
Eating	10.5	9.1	89.5	91.0
Toileting	10.2	11.4	79.3	82.2

bidity rates are generally higher in LTC facilities, but substantial morbidity also occurs in the community population. The relative distribution of illness will depend on
many factors, including the community's health status, the use of home care and
related support services, and the number of LTC beds available. Even above 85
years, the mean age of persons in LTC facilities is higher than in the community,
and it thus may not be analytically justified to consider them in a single category.

GAINING ACCESS TO THE ELDERLY

In conducting household interview surveys of the oldest old, particularly in the home,
gaining access to potential participants can be difficult. If there is sense-organ impairment, target participants may not be exposed to preparatory community advertis-
ing or announcements. Many persons live in guarded environments, so that approaching living quarters requires passing security provisions or personnel, often necessitating
prior arrangements and credentials. Older persons may have special fears of crime or
exploitation, diminishing their willingness to cooperate. A few of our study participants expressed concern that their responses in our federally funded health studies
might be used in some way to alter their government health benefits; additional and
direct assurances of confidentiality of individual identifying information help in this
situation. In some instances, family or other caregivers were highly protective of
potential interviewees, despite being generally sympathetic and supportive to the study
at hand. This may lead to unnecessarily higher rates of proxy interviews, which in
general is less desirable. In our experience, resorting to proxy interviews will increase response rates and the quality of information about those too ill to participate
usefully. However, this option may lead to fewer data about those who could fully
participate but are merely reticent or otherwise "too busy."

Through informants, confidants, and health professionals, we became aware that
some older persons were willing to participate in scientific research but refused because they were embarrassed by their personal appearance, a physical or functional
abnormality, or the appearance of their household. In our experience, overcoming
this personal embarrassment is extremely difficult, whether due to illness or meager
personal resources. Sometimes the embarrassment about the household's presentation

can be mitigated by arranging to hold the interview at a convenient site outside the home.

Our preliminary evidence is that it is more difficult to gain access to those with chronic physical and emotional disabilities or handicaps, including sensory deficits. In our household surveys (Cornoni-Huntley et al. 1985), response rates decreased and proxy interview rates increased with increasing age, and the 2-year mortality rate of our nonrespondents was higher than among respondents (Wallace 1985), suggesting more severe disease or disability among these nonrespondents at the time of survey. However, it is not clear that this finding is generalizable to other study settings. Reaching those who are more infirm in household surveys may be complemented and enhanced by contacting persons through health professionals and health-care agencies. However, the impact of this strategy on the representativeness of the sample and the inferences that can be drawn from it should be clearly understood.

Gaining access for surveys of LTC residents can also be challenging. One may be required to obtain administrative approval to conduct research in the facility not only from the local director or manager but also, if the facility is part of a larger company, from owners remote from the site. Because patients in nursing homes are much more likely to be ill or dysfunctional than those living in the community, it may be prudent to have permission from the next of kin or someone with legal power of attorney to approach the institutionalized subject. Considerable resistance by next of kin has been reported (Warren et al. 1986), but this has not been our experience. Because these persons may also be remote from the study site, at the very least, a longer preparatory phase is required for executing institutional surveys. Once one has gained access to potential subjects, it is crucial to have the assistance of institutional personnel in determining who is well enough on a given day to be approached for study. Many institutionalized persons will never be suitable for interview, but in others, physical or mental health status may fluctuate sufficiently so that returning at a later time may yield a successful interview. In our institutional patient survey, 41 percent of LTC patients were deemed by the nursing staff to be sufficiently healthy and cognitively intact to undergo a 20-minute interview.

Despite potential access problems, our experiences and those of other investigators indicate the feasibility of achieving acceptable and credible participation by the oldest old and by the elderly in general. Rates of 80 to 90 percent or greater can be expected with appropriate skill and preparation.

INFORMED CONSENT AND ADVERSE EFFECTS OF INTERVIEWING THE OLDEST OLD

Although the principles and ethics of research on humans are obviously relevant to all age groups, there may be special issues that are more common in the oldest old. The prevalence of dementia and cognitive impairment is highest here, and many studies include instruments that evaluate such impairment. If substantial impairment is discovered, with or without a confirmed neuropsychological diagnosis, the researcher should consider whether consent procedures can be truly informed. Whatever the nature of ethical review procedures, it seems important to develop standard practices for "expanded" consent when clear cognitive deficits are found during a study. Also, we have encountered several potential subjects who were quite willing and capable of participating in our studies, but were unwilling to sign the consent form because others had told them "never to sign anything." These persons have all been successfully interviewed using implied consent offered verbally and documented by the interviewer.

In general, interview studies are thought to be at relatively low risk of adverse events, with lapses of confidentiality being the most frequently cited potential risk. However, another important problem is provoking emotional responses in the subject, even with items that are usually not considered of high emotional content. A case history from our own experience is useful:

> We studied an 89-year-old wheelchair-bound woman with multiple health problems in her home. Interviewer notes suggested that the procedures had gone satisfactorily, but a few days later, the subject's daughter contacted the research staff to report that the subject had become severely depressed after the interview. This was attributed to the systematic and detailed cataloguing of the extent of her impairment and disability, using several function status indices and scales. We subsequently visited the participant several times, and within a month she seemed to return to her preinterview emotional condition.

Such situations may be more common than was previously appreciated, and the interviewer should be trained to anticipate them. Some mitigating dialogue *after* as well as before administration of function status items may be helpful in this regard.

INITIAL ASSESSMENT OF THE STUDY PARTICIPANT

As in acquiring informed consent, the issue of cognitive status arises in the initial assessment of an elderly subject's ability to contribute useful survey information. Standard interview techniques such as replicate items in the instrument, validation of responses, and terminal interviewer assessment of the respondent's reliability should be maintained. However, because demonstrable cognitive decline is relatively common in this age group, it may be useful to assess at the outset whether it is worthwhile to administer the entire interview. We feel that the interviewer should be trained to detect in preliminary conversation overt communicative disorders such as dysphasia or confabulation, as well as any physical discomfort or environmental distractions that may preclude a successful interview.

One additional approach to cognitive function screening is to apply brief instruments (Folstein, Folstein, and McHugh 1975; Pfeiffer 1975) that screen for major cognitive impairment, subsequently aborting the interview when certain criteria are met. One problem with these instruments is the negative response invoked in some cognitively intact participants by simple items (e.g., "Who is the president of the United States?"). To our knowledge, there has been no systematic evaluation of whether screening for cognitive status adequately discriminates among respondents for the intended purpose. Clearly, this technique's effectiveness depends on the nature of the items included and the study goals. Also, although it is not necessarily a universal problem, we have encountered some resistance to psychological testing in elderly subjects. This should be anticipated and mitigated in introductory dialogue.

Sensory impairment in study subjects should also be anticipated. It seems useful to prepare interviewers for dealing with the hearing impaired by practicing on volunteer subjects, so that they have experience in voice modulation, speaking distinctly, eliminating background environmental noise, and directly facing the subject to maximize lip reading. To the extent possible, structured questions and alternative responses should be printed, in large type, to minimize the amount of conversation necessary for data collection; this technique is useful in many circumstances for complex items. Telephone interviews should not be ruled out if the subject has suitable equipment. Interviewing the visually impaired is generally easier once the subject is comfortable, although psychometric tests that use visual stimuli or items that require the subject to select responses visually from a long or complex list may be precluded. In our experience, interviews of the visually and hearing impaired take longer, adding to the burden of the interview. Thus, the need for extending the interview or using multiple sessions should be anticipated.

There is evidence that sensory impairment may contribute to impaired cognitive performance (Jones, Victor, and Vetter 1984). Table 6–2 shows bivariate correlations between levels of reported hearing function (Cornoni-Huntley et al. 1986) and four measures of cognitive function in persons 85 years and older from the 65+ RHS. The four measures included the Pfeiffer Short Portable Mental Status Questionnaire (Pfeiffer 1975); a 20–word free recall memory test (Cornoni-Huntley et al. 1986); self-assessment of global memory function (Cornoni-Huntley et al. 1986); and a scale of self-rated memory problems (Cornoni-Huntley et al. 1986). In all instances, decreased hearing function was associated with poorer cognitive performance. However, the correlations were modest and strongest for the association between *reported* memory performance and hearing. This suggests that knowledge of hearing performance in a survey participant may be a useful response variable in assessing data quality as well as participant health status, although further evaluation is needed.

Table 6–2 Correlations between Reported Hearing Impairment and Scales of Cognitive Performance

Cognitive performance scale	Correlation coefficient for hearing
Mental Status Questionnaire Score	
Men	−.19
Women	−.02
20-Item Recall	
Men	−.19
Women	−.04
Global Self-Rated Memory	
Men	.27
Women	.16
Scale of Memory Problems	
Men	.39
Women	.31

Note: See text for references on the variables used. All signs are in the direction of decreased hearing function being associated with decreased cognitive function.

RECALL, MOTIVATION, AND RAPPORT

It is important to recognize that the type and extent of interview response bias depends on the type of information sought. Following Sudman and Bradburn (1974), we distinguish "factual" and "attitudinal" items. The former refers to information that, at least in principle, can be verified through sources other than a respondent's self-report; the latter refers to perceptions, opinions, self-judgments, and psychological states that must be obtained through respondent self-report and for which there are no truer validation criteria. We will deal first with factual and then with attitudinal information, pointing out what we believe to be the most important sources of response bias for each type.

In epidemiological research, some factual information can usually be verified against such sources as hospital or physician records, but one should not assume that these latter sources are more accurate in all respects than are self-reports. Typically, interviews are selected over truer sources of information because they are less costly or because they are the only accessible source. Yet, it is usually feasible to verify a subsample of interviews against some more veridical source, allowing researchers to estimate the extent of probable response bias and random error in their factual interview data. Because we cannot confidently extrapolate from current knowledge about response biases in younger age groups, it would seem desirable to build some form of verification into all surveys of the oldest old, at least until a reliable body of evidence is accumulated.

For factual information, perhaps the most important source of response error by the oldest old is faulty recall, hypothetically related to memory impairment. Yet, some other threats to accurate recall may be as important as memory impairment. Compared to younger subjects, the oldest old, by virtue of their longevity, may be required to recall more incidents (e.g., illness episodes, hospital stays, and physician visits) and events more remote in time (e.g., their age at first pregnancy, when they started smoking, or whether they took certain drugs at menopause).

Accurate recall also depends upon the motivation of the respondent, which in turn depends upon the salience or importance of interview information for the respondent (Sudman and Bradburn 1974). Assuming that the respondent perceives the overall interview as important and is generally motivated to provide accurate self-reports, parts of any interview are bound to touch upon topics the respondent considers unimportant, irrelevant, or even trivial. Consequently, the accuracy of such interview items may be more suspect. In our own health interviews, for example, we included items dealing with social networks and social support, which we considered important for assessing stress and stress buffering. However, many of our elderly respondents did not share our view of social factors, and only with considerable prompting could we get them to venture guesses about such things as the number of intimate friends they have or the frequency of contacts they had with friends over the past month.

Adequate pretesting should identify segments of an interview schedule that respondents consider unimportant or irrelevant, and suitable modifications of the interview protocol and interview training can be made to address these problem areas. However, it is crucial to recognize that adequate pretesting for the oldest old may be quite different from pretesting of younger respondents. It requires a good deal of prior knowledge of and sensitivity to the lifestyles, central life interests, and preoccupations of this age group. The untested suppositions and values of younger investigators may be misleading or incorrect.

For example, we typically assume that the oldest old are preoccupied with their health. Although this may be tenable, it does not follow that they are *knowledgeable* about their health, nor does it follow that they are concerned about the details of health care they have received. A spouse, caretaker, or other family member may be more knowledgable about a respondent's health and health-care experiences. Older people may delegate such details to someone who can better understand the health professional's jargon or to someone who merely provides transportation to health-care providers. If such delegation of details is as widespread as we suspect, surveys in this age group will encounter a good deal of faulty recall even with regard to severe conditions, the details of which respondents may never have committed to memory. An 85-year-old man may indeed be concerned about the heart disease a physician has just diagnosed, but he may have no interest in the technical term that specifies the diagnosis. He may not have counted the number of visits he made to the physician or be interested in learning the names of all the drugs prescribed for his condition. All he needs to know is how to comply with the physician's orders; the rest may be delegated to others, including the physician. Consequently, it may be appropriate to obtain detailed health information from a proxy, especially if it is apparent that such details have been delegated to a family caretaker. In some cases, it may be best to have the caretaker present while the respondent is interviewed; in others, it may be more appropriate to interview the caretaker/proxy in a separate session.

In contrast to interview items that probe for factual information, there is no external criterion by which we can validate items that probe for attitudinal information. Although we must still depend on the respondent's motivation, it is motivation for frank and open self-disclosure that is involved. Invoking and maintaining this motivation depends largely on the ability of the interviewer to maintain rapport. Yet, even the most skillful interviewer will fail if an interview protocol is ill suited to the respondent and, equally important, ill suited to the interviewer–respondent relationship. For example, intimate questions that are appropriate in the clinic, within a physician–patient relationship, are often totally inappropriate in an interviewer–respondent relationship, where the interviewer is not a health professional and the interview takes place in the respondent's own home.

INTERVIEW RESPONDENT BURDEN IN THE OLDEST OLD

Besides matters of content and its suitability for the interviewer–respondent relationship, perhaps the major threat to rapport with the oldest old is respondent burden, a rubric under which we subsume not only the time demands of an interview, but also the physical and emotional demands. The importance of respondent burden in interviewing the oldest old derives from both humanistic concerns and concerns for the quality of interview data.

In any health survey one can expect the length of interviews to vary considerably among respondents, with the greatest burden falling on the sickest and oldest respondents. The sickest respondents have the most to report, and the oldest respondents are usually slower to respond. Such respondents also require more interviewer assistance, in the form of probing and repeating questions and response categories. Thus, an interview designed for an average length of 1 hour could easily run 2 hours for the sickest and oldest, who are generally the least capable of withstanding the rigors of an interview.

Unfortunately, the true measure of respondent burden is not reflected in time alone; we must also consider the level of stress that interviews engender. Here again, the sickest and oldest are likely to bear the greatest burden. Little stress may be involved for healthy respondents, who can be heartened by the absence of problems a health interview addresses. The experience is much different for people who must report a long list of health problems, the absence of social support, and impaired functioning. For them, the health interview can systematically bring to painful awareness their major sources of worry, embarrassment, and despair. Questions about memory loss, incontinence, or life-threatening diseases mean little to those who are unaffected but can be devastating to those who must admit to them.

Despite all the thoughtfulness and sensitivity we can muster in interview design, and despite extensive interviewer training, we can reduce but never eliminate the emotional burden of our interviews. On the other hand, it is feasible to reduce the time burden substantially and, consequently, to minimize the physical burden our respondents must bear. This is not to say that interviews can always be shortened without sacrifice, but often we need only sacrifice items that are superfluous, redundant, or merely supplementary. Ideally, we should have multiple measures of all our key variables, but such redundancy may be self-defeating if elderly respondents are too fatigued to respond appropriately.

In recommending shorter and more streamlined interviews for the oldest old, it may seem that we are arguing against some of the most firmly established practices in health research and measurement. In most cases, health researchers make a conscious effort to measure key variables through indices and scales gleaned from the literature, and conventional wisdom demands that such measures be used as is. Any modification of standard instruments is believed to destroy them, or at least to vitiate comparability with prior research. Besides the issue of comparability, our call for shorter instruments conflicts with classical measurement theory, which teaches us that reliability increases as the number of items composing an index increases (assuming that the items are similar). We are not arguing that the problems of comparability and reliability should be ignored. On the contrary, we recognize that a good deal of research is needed to develop measures that preserve the best of standard indices while at the same time being better adapted to the oldest old.

Many of the multi-item indices and scales commonly used in epidemiologic surveys were developed in other settings and not originally designed for large-scale surveys. Typically, multi-item instruments are developed on captive populations such as hospital patients and college students, a context in which investigator authority serves to legitimate asking virtually any type or volume of questions. A similar authority relationship will rarely be established between interviewer and respondent in large-scale surveys, where respondents are interviewed in their own setting and interviewers are not physicians or psychology professors. Respondents are freer to refuse to answer any questions that are too personal, embarrassing, or impertinent when asked by an interviewer who can claim no authority over the respondent. In the case of the oldest old, respondents will nearly always be senior to the interviewers, and norms that prescribe respect for one's elders tend to place the interviewer in a subordinate role.

The popularity of widely used scales derives largely from the reliability that can be claimed for them; rarely is a scale widely adopted unless its reliability exceeds rule-of-thumb minimums of .70 or .80, as measured by such coefficients as Cronbach's alpha. Unfortunately, highly reliable multi-item indices tend to be quite long, because *ceteris paribus* the reliability of an index increases with increasing length. However, the items in an index must correlate well with one another and, in practice, this usually means that they have similar content or a common theme. Indeed, it is common to find scales in which several items are merely paraphrases of other items. (Some paraphrases are negatively worded versions of positively worded items, added to the index to reduce so-called acquiescence response bias.)

Lengthy indices, with or without extensive paraphrasing, tend to be logically redundant, and respondents may perceive them as unnecessarily repetitious. This may be only a minor annoyance to captive respondents, but in noncaptive settings, respondents are much less forbearing, more likely to express their irritation, and more likely to refuse to answer. The oldest old will generally have less motivation for forbearance and indeed have every reason to interpret repetitious questions as impertinent and demeaning. Lengthy scales risk destroying the very fragile rapport that is necessary for interviewing, and the irritation and fatigue they cause will doubtless carry over to the remainder of the interview. As the oldest old become a target population for extensive epidemiological research, much work will be needed to develop abbreviated forms of commonly used scales. By shortening a scale, we may sacrifice some reliability, but we will obtain important benefits that may outweigh reliability.

Shorter scales should be less susceptible to a potential response bias that has gone virtually unrecognized by developers of psychometric devices, which we propose to call "consistency response bias" or simply "consistency bias." Consistency bias is similar to what is usually called "social desirability bias," except that the latter term refers to a tendency to answer a given item in a socially acceptable fashion. Consistency bias, on the other hand, refers to the *relation* of items to one another; it is the tendency to keep one's responses (answers) consistent with prior responses. Like social desirability, consistency bias derives from societal norms, but the latter bias derives from norms that equate consistency with normality and equate inconsistency with illogic, eccentricity, cognitive impairment, and mental illness. Thus, once one has expressed a certain attitude, opinion, or judgment in an interview, it is unlikely that one will intentionally express contradictory or inconsistent one later on.

If indeed redundant items invoke little more than consistency bias, the reliability of a multi-item scale is, by definition, inflated not be true-score variance but by systematic error variance. Thus, whereas eliminating redundant items may not increase a scale's reliability, it may enhance its validity. Thus, besides reducing respondent burden, shorter scales may hypothetically be justified by principles of measurement.

OBSERVATIONS ON DATA QUALITY IN SURVEYS OF THE OLDEST OLD

It is apparent that obtaining high-quality data from surveys of the oldest old requires many considerations and challenges. With this in mind, we have begun to assess empirically elements of survey response quality in the elderly, with emphasis on the oldest old. In preliminary analyses, we have explored rates of missing responses ("don't knows" and refusals) and inconsistent responses in the baseline survey of the 65+ RHS (Cornoni-Huntley et al. 1986). Overall, the rates of missing responses for individual items in our population survey were gratifyingly low (< 0.2 percent). However, there were selected items where the respondent could not or would not answer. These items or item categories are shown in Table 6–3, which display the percentage of items missing across all participants. The rates of "don't knows" all increased with age in the categories shown: health history, mood, social support, function status assessment, and income. The income item had the highest rate and has been problematic in survey work. In a multivariate analysis (to be published elsewhere), the significant cross-sectional predictors of "don't know" rates in addition to age included educational attainment and both objective and subjective measures of memory function contained in the survey instrument.

Table 6–3 shows the percentage of persons refusing to answer certain items. Income was again prominent, followed by the increasing unwillingness with age to participate in an overt memory test. Refusal rates were lower but increased with age for the mood items, possibly reflecting sensitivity to queries about loneliness and depression.

The inability to answer a given item may itself have health implications. Table 6–4 shows age-specific 2-year all-cause mortality rates according to the presence or

Table 6–3 Percentage of Missing Responses within Various Item Categories

	Age group (years)		
Item category	65–74 (%)	75–84 (%)	85+ (%)
"Don't Knows"			
Health history[a]	0.2	0.3	0.4
Mood[b]	0.7	0.8	1.3
Social support[c]	1.4	2.2	4.5
Function status[d]	2.0	3.4	5.5
Annual income	7.3	10.3	12.0
Refusals			
Mood[e]	0.2	0.1	0.6
Memory problems[f]	0.1	0.3	0.7
Memory test	4.9	7.3	7.9
Annual income	7.3	8.4	9.4

[a] Nine items concerning history of heart attack, glaucoma, Parkinson's disease, arthritis, shortness of breath during sleep or with wheezing, and other respiratory complaints.

[b] Six items from a group assessing depressive symptoms.

[c] Two items assessing availability of person with whom to talk or share activities.

[d] Three items from the Rosow-Breslau function scale (Rosow and Breslau 1966)

[e] Seventeen items relating to the assessment of depressive or anxiety symptoms.

[f] Three items on global self-rated memory assessment and ability to remember phone numbers.

Table 6–4 Age-Specific 2-Year All-Cause Mortality Rates According to Presence of "Don't Know" Responses on Rosow-Breslau Function Status Items: Men

	Response			
	Complete		"Don't know"	
Age group (yrs)	N	Rate (%)	N	Rate (%)
65–74	797	4.8	29	13.8
75–84	448	12.9	24	33.3
85 +	94	21.2	7	57.1

absence of one or more "don't know" responses to any items in the Rosow-Breslau function status index (Rosow and Breslau 1966). In all age groups, a "don't know" response was associated with a higher mortality rate. This has implications for data analysis when missing responses occur, as well as for the cognitive aspects of survey design and evaluation.

Finally, Table 6–5 shows the proportion of persons who had a disparate response to at least one of two situations where nearly identical subjective mood-related items were contained in two different parts of the survey instrument. The "inconsistency rate" ranged from 25 to 30 percent but did not vary substantially with age. This approach to data reliability is well established and may have further application for the oldest old.

Thus, it appears that missing data and inconsistent response rates give some insight into the quality of data for the oldest old and suggest that some special problems may exist. There are many additional dimensions of data quality, including the validity of individual responses, that must be further explored as more experience with this age group is obtained.

CONCLUSION

There is still much to be learned about the techniques of interviewing and surveying the elderly, especially the oldest old. Obtaining high-quality information in the face of increasing illness, dysfunction, and frailty adds new challenges to the existing lore, techniques, and problems of surveying young and middle aged adults. Comprehensive reliability and validity studies are clearly needed to determine optimal methods and the scope of information that can be reliably obtained from such surveys.

Table 6–5 Percentage of Persons with at Least One Inconsistent Response-Baseline Questionnaire, Iowa 65 + RHS

	Age group (years)		
Sex	65–74 (%)	75–84 (%)	85 + (%)
Men	24.5	25.3	30.2
Women	28.6	28.5	28.0

The emerging application of cognitive function measurement to such surveys can have an informative dual role: determining the magnitude and nature of cognitive status in populations and simultaneously evaluating the quality of other information obtained.

REFERENCES

Anderson, R., J. Kasper, M. Frankel, et al. 1979. *Total Survey Error.* San Francisco: Jossey-Bass.

Balamuth, E. 1965. *Health Interview Responses Compared with Medical Records,* series 2, no. 7. Hyattsville, Md.: National Center for Health Statistics.

Cornoni-Huntley, J.C. et al. 1985. Epidemiology of Disability in the Oldest Old: Methodologic Issues and Preliminary Findings. *Milbank Memorial Fund Quarterly* 63:350.

Cornoni-Huntley, J., D.B. Brock, A.M. Ostfeld, et al. (Eds.) 1986. *Established Populations for Epidemiologic Study of the Elderly. Resource Data Book.* National Institute on Aging. DHHS pub. no. (NIH) 86-2443. Bethesda, Md.

Folstein, M.F., S.E. Folstein, and P.R. McHugh. 1975. Mini-Mental State: A Practical Method for Grading the Cognitive State of Patients for the Clinician. *Journal of Psychiatric Research* 12:189.

Herzog, A.R., and L. Dielman. 1985. Age Differences in Response Accuracy for Factual Survey Questions. *Journal of Gerontology* 40(3):350–57.

Herzog, A.R. and W.L. Rodgers. 1986. Interviewing the Elderly: Mode Comparison Using Data from a Face-to-Face Survey and a Telephone Re-Survey. Institute for Social Research, University of Michigan. (Unpublished Report.)

Herzog, A.R., W.L. Rogers, and R.A. Kulka. 1983. Interviewing Older Adults: A Comparison of Telephone and Face-to-Face Modalities. *Public Opinion Quarterly* 47:405–18.

Jones, D.A., C.R. Victor, and N.J. Vetter. 1984. Hearing difficulty and its implications for the elderly. *Journal of Epidemiology and Community Health* 38:75–78.

National Center for Health Statistics. 1984. Trends in Nursing and Related Care Homes and Hospitals. United States, Selected Years 1969–80. *Vital and Health Statistics,* series 14, no. 30. DHHS pub. no. (PHS) 84-1825. Hyattsville, Md.

Pfeiffer, E. 1975. A Short Portable Mental Status Questionnaire for the Assessment of Organic Brain Deficit in Elderly Patients. *Journal of the American Geriatric Society* 23:433.

Rosow, I., and N. Breslau. 1966. A Gutman Health Scale for the Aged. *Journal of Gerontology* 21:556–62.

Schuman, H. and S. Presser. 1981. *Questions and Answers in Attitude Surveys.* New York: Academic Press.

Sudman, S. and N.M. Bradburn. 1974. *Response Effects in Surveys.* Chicago: Aldine.

Thornberry, O.T., and J.T. Massey. 1978. Correcting for Undercoverage Bias in Random Dialed National Health Surveys. *Proceedings of the Section on Survey Research Methods, American Statistical Association,* 224–29.

Wallace, R.B. 1985. Institutionalized and Non-institutionalized Mortality Rates in a Rural Elderly Population: The Iowa 65+ Rural Health Study. Paper presented at the annual meeting of the American Public Health Association, Washington, November 19.

Warren, J.W., J. Sobal, J.H. Tenney, et al. 1986. Informed Consent by Proxy. An Issue in Research with Elderly Patients. *New England Journal of Medicine* 315:1124–28.

Acknowledgments. Supported by Contract NO1-AG-0-2106 and Grant AG 07094 from the National Institute on Aging.

7

Collecting Data About the Oldest Old: Problems and Procedures

WILLARD L. RODGERS and A. REGULA HERZOG

There is considerable speculation, and a more limited amount of supporting evidence, that some types of survey error are more likely to occur when surveying older respondents, particularly the oldest old, than when surveying younger respondents. Several reasons usually are cited for such possible errors, including health problems, sensory and cognitive impairments, and personality and motivational factors associated with age or cohort. Finally, many procedures were developed or modified in order to deal with those presumed problems. To learn more about what is known or speculated about the quality of data from the oldest old and what procedures are being used in surveys of the oldest old, we interviewed a number of investigators who have been actively involved in collecting data form this age group. (The list of investigators, developed in collaboration with the National Institute on Aging, included representatives of some of the major surveys of the aged, but was neither a systematic sample nor the universe of all survey researchers dealing with older adults. The list of investigators who reported on their experiences is included in the Appendix to this chapter.) The information from these interviews was combined with published reports to produce this chapter, which is intended as a working paper on current practices and speculations in survey research on the oldest old. However, the document is not intended as a general review of survey errors and survey procedures; good recent reviews of a more general nature are provided by Bradburn (1983) and Groves (1989).

We begin by considering various sources of error in surveys and the extent to which age differences have been reported or suspected. We then review the established age differences in cognitive and motivational factors that are thought to be implicated in potential survey errors in data on the oldest old. We conclude with an overview of current practices used in obtaining information from and about the oldest old.

SOURCES OF ERROR IN SURVEYS OF THE ELDERLY

We use a conceptualization of survey error proposed by Kish (1965) and elaborated more recently by Groves (1989). In general terms, error is defined as the deviation of a measure from the true value. More specifically, errors may be broken down into two broad components, usually labeled as "bias" and "variable error." *Variable error* is random, with an expected value of zero. Given sufficiently large sample sizes, the variable error in estimates of central tendency can be reduced to any desired level. *Bias*, on the other hand, is a systematic distortion and adds a constant factor to survey measures; it can sometimes be reduced by changing procedures but not, in general, by increasing the sample size. Two major sources of bias and variable error are usually distinguished: sampling and nonsampling errors. Within nonsampling errors, a further distinction can be made between those arising from nonresponse and those arising from responses. There are reasons to expect several types of error to be particularly frequent (or larger in magnitude) in surveys of the very old, and in some cases empirical evidence supports those expectations.

Sampling Error

One major source of sampling error is incomplete coverage by the sampling frame. If a sample design does not properly cover the target population, sample-based estimates may be biased (as well as having variable error). A potential source of bias is the fact that many sampling frames include only the population living in private households, whereas the target populations of interest—the older and the oldest-old populations—live in institutions as well as in households. Moreover, the institutionalized elderly are distinctly different from the noninstitutionalized elderly household population (Rosenwaike 1985): Among those aged 85 and older, the institutionalized are much more likely to be female, to be white, to have hearing (45 versus 25 percent) and visual impairments (43 versus 12 percent), and to require assistance in activities of daily living (ADLs) such as eating (36 versus 5 percent) and walking (78 versus 24 percent). (Wallace et al., in Chapter 6, this volume, discuss this point further.) Surveys based on household samples may therefore produce biased statistics about the entire population of the oldest old.

Another potential sampling error derives from the need for screening on age when drawing a household sample of older Americans. Because some households or persons cannot be screened for age eligibility, the total number of eligibles may never be known. This complication, plus the costs of screening, has further led to the utilization of commercially available lists that contain age information. Many of these have their own coverage problems.

Nonresponse

One source of nonsampling error is nonresponse. The resulting bias is a function of both the proportion and the distinctive characteristics of nonrespondents. Older adults seem less likely than individuals in the general population to participate in a survey (DeMaio 1980; Hawkins 1975; Herzog and Rodgers 1988a; Hoinville 1983; Lowe and McCormick 1955; Weaver, Holmes, and Glenn 1973), and somewhat less likely to grant a reinterview after a few months—although the latter finding is not entirely consistent (Herzog and Rodgers 1988a). The response rates appear particularly low among those over age 85 (Herzog and Rodgers 1988a; Wallace 1987). Several of the investigators interviewed for this report corroborate the lower response rate from their own observations. Concern about response rates among elderly persons has most recently surfaced during pilot testing for the National Health and Nutrition Examination Survey (NHANES) III: only 57 percent of 46 women aged 80 and older were successfully interviewed, and only 35 percent of these were willing to take the physical examination, compared with response rates of 86 and 76 percent for these two types of data collection from women under age 70 (unpublished table, distributed to participants in a National Center for Health Statistics [NCHS] workshop on April 26, 1988). Since then, NHANES III has been launched and preliminary response rates for interviews and physical examinations run considerably higher than in the pretest, probably in part because of procedures discussed at the workshop, such as eliciting the cooperation of local seniors groups in gaining access to selected respondents. These procedures are currently being evaluated.

In other surveys of the elderly, response rates are quite high. For example, in the National Long Term Care Survey, conducted by the Bureau of the Census for the Health Care Financing Administration (HCFA), they were 95.2 percent for persons living in households and 97.9 percent for those living in institutions, although a substantial proportion of the responses were by proxy rather than by self-report. In the three initial Established Populations for Epidemiological Studies of the Elderly (EPESE) sites, the response rates of adults 65 years of age and older ranged between 80 and 85 percent. See Chapter 6, this volume, for a discussion of gaining access to the oldest old. Finally, in the Supplement on Aging (SOA) to the 1984 National Health Interview Survey, a 93 percent response rate was obtained among adults 55 years of age and older when proxy as well as self-reports were included (Fitti and Kovar 1987). All of the studies with relatively high response rates were specifically designed to survey an older population, and it is possible that they used more appropriate procedures than general population surveys for obtaining cooperation among the elderly. However, the possibility cannot be excluded that at least part of the difference is attributable to the way the response rate was calculated: for example, whether proxy respondents were included in the numerator or whether eligibles who died or were hospitalized before they could be interviewed were included in the denominator.

Response rates might be particularly low for those in institutions because of difficulties in gaining access to some of these people, either due to resistance on the part of administrators or caregivers, or because of the requirement in some institutions to obtain consent from a responsible relative of the person. We have not been able to document researchers' concerns about these difficulties, however. The completion rate in the National Long Term Care Survey was somewhat higher for those living in institutions than for those in households, and in that study the interviewers did not encounter any particular problems in gaining access to those in institutions. Likewise, in the East Boston EPESE and the Iowa EPESE (see Chapter 6, this volume), no major problems with institutional access were encountered.

The potentially larger proportion of nonrespondents and panel dropouts among the elderly carries a potential for larger bias, depending on whether a systematic difference exists between respondents and nonrespondents/dropouts (Moser and Kalton 1972). Older panel dropouts have poorer physical health, higher rates of intellectual impairment, and lower socioeconomic status, and are less well socially integrated than are respondents (Goudy 1985; Norris 1985). Because nonrespondents have not volunteered information about themselves, generally less is known about them, but there are some suggestions that older nonrespondents are less healthy and socially involved than are respondents (Rodgers and Herzog 1987b; Wallace 1985).

Item Missing Data

Failure to answer a question can also introduce biases into statistics if those not answering the question systematically differ from those who do. Again, this source of potential bias appears to be more serious for older people who are more likely to give nonsubstantive responses consisting largely of "don't know" (DK) answers (Ferber 1966; Francis and Busch 1975; Gergen and Back 1966). The age-related increase is much larger for questions that deal with attitudes, feelings, and expectations than for those eliciting facts (Herzog and Rodgers, 1982). To gauge the bias resulting from item missing data, one needs to know whether DK respondents are systematically different from those who give substantive answers, and research suggests that DK respondents tend to be less healthy, less interested in survey content, less socially involved, less highly educated, and less likely to be male (Colsher and Wallace 1989; Ferber 1966; Francis and Busch 1975; Glenn 1969; Herzog and Rodgers, 1982).

Another source of item missing data is the use of proxies for persons considered unable to be interviewed themselves. Proxies are routinely asked factual questions, but generally *not* evaluative or attitudinal questions as, for example, about the quality of health care. Moreover, depending on the relationship of the proxy to the sampled person, the proxy may be unable to supply answers to certain factual questions. The consequence is that subjective, and some objective, information is typically missing for those with proxy interviews.

Response Accuracy

Finally, for many reasons, nonsampling errors are present in the responses of those who do participate in a survey: respondents may misunderstand questions, forget information, or misunderstand answer categories. Survey research findings on validity of substantive answers from adults are mixed, sometimes demonstrating rather large biases (Andersen et al. 1979; Cannell, Fisher, and Bakker 1965; Sudman and Bradburn 1974; U.S. Department of Justice 1981). Herzog and her colleagues found no support for the hypothesis of increased response error among older adults when examining factual survey questions that can be checked against external records (Herzog and Dielman 1985; Rodgers and Herzog 1987a). There is some evidence that the responses of older adults to attitudinal and other subjective items have more measurement error than those of younger adults, at least in part because the answers of older people are somewhat more influenced by question format and less by the substantive content of the question (Andrews and Herzog 1986; Herzog and Rodgers 1982; Kogan 1961; Rodgers et al. 1985; Wallace 1987). However, the age differences are small and not entirely consistent (Rodgers, Andrews, and Herzog, in preparation). Colsher and Wallace (1989) observed less consistency in the responses of the oldest old than in those of young-old adults and found that the inconsistencies were accounted for in part by relatively poor memory performance.

Unfortunately, most of the investigations examining response error among the elderly do not include enough respondents over age 80, or even over age 70, for reliable estimates on these groups. Therefore, the oldest old are usually combined with those over age 60 or 65, and because of their relatively small proportion they do not affect the data noticeably. Further, we suspect that even greater problems of response accuracy may be encountered among the oldest old, who tend to avoid survey participation. That is, the possible higher nonresponse bias among the elderly probably masks larger measurement-error problems.

SUGGESTED PROCEDURES FOR IMPROVING THE QUALITY OF SURVEY DATA FROM THE ELDERLY

The data obtained from the oldest old are generally believed to be of lower quality than those obtained from younger adults. There are several reasons why this may be the case. Perhaps the most obvious problem associated with old age is the deterioration of health. Cognitive impairments may prevent a sampled older person from participating in an interview. Once participation has been secured, sensory, cognitive, and physical health problems may affect performance. Personality and social differences may also explain lower-quality data from older adults. Older persons have less frequent contact with unfamiliar persons and thus may not be as willing to participate in surveys. In addition, fear of crime, associated with nonresponse in cities, is disproportionately high among older adults (Clemente and Kleiman 1976). The distinct social characteristics of the older population may also contribute to higher levels of item nonresponse and inaccurate reports. Many topics of interest to sociologists and epidemiologists, such as nutritional, employment and earnings, and life event histories, are inherently more complex for older persons because of their relatively longer lifetimes. In addition, older adults generate more missing data problems because they are more likely than younger adults to disregard standardized scale formats (Jobe and Mingay 1990). This may be a cohort effect rather than an age effect, given that today's oldest old are less educated on average and encountered fewer tests and standardized interviews during their lifetimes than younger cohorts.

Given these observations and speculations, there is fairly widespread concern about the quality of survey data on older adults, particularly the oldest old. Wallace et al. (Chapter 6, this volume) review the issues surrounding data quality with respect to the oldest old respondents. Here we focus on procedures intended to improve the quality of data for this age group. In many cases, the researchers we have surveyed have put their suggestions into practice, at least in an exploratory or experimental fashion, and offer at least tentative evaluations. It is important to understand that these suggestions are often based on nonsystematic observations and that, among the few systematic evaluations, not all have been formally published. We have included the citation wherever we were aware of published documentation.

Use of Medicare Rolls and Other Lists of Older Adults for Sampling Purposes

Because of the costs and problems associated with screening for older adults in household samples, it has become standard practice to use the HCFA list of Medicare enrollees as the sampling frame for studies of elderly populations. For example, the

National Cancer Institute does numerous epidemiologic studies using samples (e.g., case controls for known cancer victims) drawn from HCFA files; the Department of Preventive Medicine of the University of Iowa used Medicare files for drawing control cases; the NCHS had pretest samples for the NHANES III drawn in part from these files; and so did the Census Bureau for the sample for the NLTCS. The information supplied by HCFA is a list of names and addresses. Race and age of each person in the sample are also available.

The proportion of the elderly U.S. population enrolled in the Medicare program has been estimated to be 96.5 percent in 1983, a slight decline from the estimate of 97.2 percent in 1977, but it is expected to rise as federal government and nonprofit organization employees "age" into the system (Waldo and Lazenby 1984). Thus, the coverage appears to be complete. However, the accuracy of this estimate of coverage is questioned by some. For example, Medicare coverage estimated from SOA data is only 93 percent, and thus the possibility of biases due to noncoverage remains. The New Haven EPESE compared their own hospital-based data with HCFA data, and, although they found that the hospital data were more likely to be complete, the HCFA data were of adequate quality. Others suspect that in a place like Los Angeles County, with a large number of Hispanics, the population may not be covered as well as it is in other places. Poor people and illegal aliens—who tend not to be in the oldest-old age group anyway—may not be enrolled in Medicare. A study to assess the coverage of older Americans provided by the HCFA Medicare files would be extremely valuable.

Procedural problems with HCFA files were also mentioned by the investigators. For some enrollees, the address supplied is the one to which checks are to be sent, which may be a bank rather than the home address. Persons with such addresses are probably not a random set, they include enrollees who spend parts of each year in different locations, who are unable to handle their own financial affairs, and who are concerned about thievery. For some persons, the HCFA files do include more than one address: if the bank address is given for checks, they also have a home address. HCFA can draw the sample from lines with the home addresses, rather than from addresses where checks are sent.

Another problem with samples drawn from HCFA files concerns the recency of the tapes. There are several types of tape, some that are very current, some that are updated only every 6 months, and others that are updates only every 2 years. A particular problem with updates concerns deaths, which for a variety of reasons are not entered into the system promptly. Address changes seem to be entered more promptly.

Investigators with a government grant can obtain permission to draw a sample from HCFA files. The process is facilitated, however, if there is a person designated within the funding agency to serve as an intermediary between grant recipients and HCFA. In this way, HCFA can also ensure that those asking to use its files have legitimate reasons for the request. Although HCFA does not have the capacity to screen requests, it is interested in protecting the integrity and confidentiality of its data. Federal grants or contracts are preferred because such projects have been peer reviewed for scientific merit and generally have been reviewed by a human subjects review committee.

Special justification is required by HCFA if the requested sample is more than 5 percent of the enrollees in a particular area. Their concern is that if the sample is a larger proportion of the population, the research activity could interfere with their own operations in an area. On the other hand, to avoid making the request too complex, it is often easier to specify a fairly large sample from which a smaller number of persons would actually be selected for a study. Thus there may be a need to strike a balance: on the one hand, make the request as simple as possible (thus getting an overinclusive sample from which to subsample); on the other hand, keep the sample below 5 percent in any one area.

There is a requirement that those in the sample first be sent a standard letter from HCFA explaining that participation in the research is completely voluntary and that benefits will not be affected in any way by nonparticipation.

Other sampling frames may be attractive for certain subpopulations of the oldest old. For the NNHS, the sampling frame is a listing of all nursing-home facilities, which is compiled from a variety of sources, many from states that keep a list because of licensing procedures. However, once the population of interest extends beyond residents of nursing homes to residents of *any* type of institution, a sampling frame may be more difficult to achieve because there are many types of institutions and the distinction between institutions and households is not always clear. If a person lives in a unit with its own bath and kitchen, but in a context where nursing care is provided by staff members, that person would be classified as living in a household according to the criteria applied in some current studies, whereas other studies would define the same person as institutionalized.

Files of Medicaid enrollees might be used, although researchers who have attempted to use this frame have encountered serious difficulties. The MEDSTAT system, which incorporates Medicaid information, shows promise but is not yet available for all states.

Use of Multiplicity-type Sampling Procedures

Multiplicity-type sampling techniques have been proposed (Sirken 1970; Sudman and Kalton 1986) by which the oldest old may be referred to by family members who are sampled in a standard household sample. For these procedures the referring person must know the age of the older person to be sampled, and accuracy rates for knowledge of the exact age of even a close relative are not known. Although false positives can be eliminated at the point when the age is confirmed with the sampled person, false negatives cannot be as easily confirmed. One procedure to minimize false negatives is to lower the age criterion for referral; to contact the referred person for age verification; and to administer only a very brief or no interview, if the person is a true negative, but the full interview if he or she is a false negative.

This and other sampling techniques that may be applicable to drawing samples of older adults are discussed in Kalton and Anderson (1989).

Cooperation from Institutions

Because of the high proportion of the oldest old that is institutionalized, researchers must consider the cooperation of institutions in data-collection efforts. Some cooperation is essential, whether the request involves gaining access to residents to ask for their participation, obtaining information about how to contact the next of kin or other relatives of residents, recording information from records on residents, or interviewing caretakers and other employees of the institutions.

Success in eliciting the cooperation of institutions apparently is related to a variety of factors that vary from state to state, including type of institution and regulations. Concern about privacy laws seems to vary widely and to be reflected in rather idiosyncratic practices and requirements. In the follow-up study to the NNHS, where telephone interviews were sought with the next of kin of those in the original institutionalized sample, names of next of kin were eventually obtained for an estimated 80 percent of the selected persons. In some cases, the nursing homes sought permission from the next of kin before releasing their names to the study. The East Boston EPESE, which successfully collected information on nursing-home residents, was aided by the legal situation in Massachusetts: After the State Department of Public Health declares a study to be "in the public interest," institutions are not held legally responsible for information provided to that study. In the NLTCS, the participating institutions indicated that the letters requesting their cooperation would have been more effective if they had come from someone in NIH rather than from the Census Bureau, and this was planned for subsequent rounds. It was not felt that this was a major factor, however, because the institutions appeared satisfied once the sponsorship of the study was explained.

One investigator suggested that an entire set of issues has to be negotiated with institutions, issues such as confidentiality, informed consent, and access to information. The investigator suggested negotiating with the on-site manager; if this is not possible, the owner may have to be consulted.

Sponsorship and Endorsement

The sponsorship is believed to be critical in attaining a high response rate because it can confer legitimacy, credibility, and even authority on the survey. Yet there is no consensus on which sponsors are likely to be the most influential. Local sponsorship seemed to be more effective than federal sponsorship in rural Iowa. Likewise, group discussions conducted in the Questionnaire Design Laboratory at NCHS suggested that the endorsement of a study by local seniors' groups would help in making the study credible to those asked to participate. The high response rate in SOA was attributed to the fact that the Census Bureau conducted the interviews. Representatives from the Census Bureau felt that for the NLTCS the sponsorship of the NIH would have been more effective in gaining access to institutions than the Census. Other researchers suggest that endorsements be elicited from well-known older personalities or senior advocate groups. To our knowledge, no systematic data on the success of any such endorsements are available.

In other studies, such as the SOA or the New Haven EPESE, media coverage was sought at the beginning of the study. Copies of the resulting article were then provided to the interviewers, who could show it to respondents. The impression gained from this experience, which is typical of other studies, is that seeing the study mentioned in the newspaper lent it legitimacy.

Media campaigns have been suggested as a general means of familiarizing the community with the ongoing survey, although such efforts may be lost on some older persons who, because of sensory impairments, may not read the newspaper or listen to television programs.

More generally, Adrian Ostfeld (principal investigator of the New Haven EPESE) is convinced that extended prior involvement in a community is necessary to obtain a high participation rate. In the initial data collection in New Haven, the overall response was 82 percent, and even higher among poorer and black persons. For follow-up data collections, the reinterview completion rate has been on the order of 96 percent annually. A total of only 20 out of 812 respondents have been lost in the 6 years of the study. Ostfeld attributes the high participation rate to his knowledge of and investment in the senior community.

Extended Field Period

Health problems can cause nonresponse among elderly persons. Extended field periods, which can accommodate respondents who are temporarily indisposed, will eventually achieve a higher response rate than investigations that must be completed in a shorter period. More generally, experience at the University of Michigan's Survey Research Center has shown that about one-third of all initial nonrespondents agree to be interviewed when approached a few weeks or months after the initial request.

Length of the Interview

Researchers often express the opinion that interviews are disproportionately tiring for elderly respondents, resulting in relatively high nonresponse rates and in poor data quality. Quantitative substantiation of this assertion is less easy to come by. Moles (1987) reports that the length of the interview and the proportion of respondents who feel tired at the end of their interviews increases with their age. Herzog, Rodgers, and Kulka (1983) report similar and pronounced age differences for telephone interviews. Gibson and Aitkenhead (1983) corroborate the basic finding in a sample of Australians within the restricted age range of 60 years and older.

However, not all investigators agree. For example, in the New Haven EPESE, in which the face-to-face interviews averaged 70 minutes and telephone interviews averaged 8 to 9 minutes, interviewers did not cite respondent fatigue as a problem; in fact, interviewers were often asked to stay for coffee or to visit following the interview.

By keeping the interviews as short as possible, the effects of fatigue may be minimized. Alternatively, Gibson and Aitkenhead (1983) propose using an abbreviated instrument for impaired respondents or proxies. In the Iowa EPESE, visits were sometimes split into two sessions. Carp (1989) also suggests dividing the interview into two halves and conducting the parts on different days. All these methods have their shortcomings. If abbreviated interviews are administered, information on many variables will be lost. If the interviews are split into two or more sessions, the break between sessions allows respondents to refuse the completion of the interview.

Some would argue that the complexity and sequencing of many survey questions and the respondents' lack of interest, rather than the sheer length, account for the survey's tiring effect. Procedures suggested to address these problems include asking tedious and less important questions near the end and breaking up long sequences of questions with physical activities or alternative topics.

Incentives

Incentives of a financial or other nature for survey participation have a long history in survey research. Most of the available research is on financial incentives and is inconclusive (Groves 1989).

Current practice varies with respect to offering incentives to those who agree to participate in surveys. In surveys done by the Census Bureau, incentives are not ordinarily offered, but if requests are made beyond a single interview, it is more common to offer some sort of gift or payment. A similar practice is observed by the Survey Research Center at the University of Michigan.

Sometimes incentives are even offered for first-time contacts when they are particularly onerous. NHANES offers monetary compensation for completion of the home interview and the health examination (which takes about 3.5 hours and requires the respondent to go to a mobile examination center), compensation of a lesser amount for the home interview and a shortened health examination given in the home (for those unable or unwilling to travel to the examination center), but nothing for those who complete the home interview only. Although sufficiently high incentives are likely to increase the response rate somewhat, they may also raise suspicion, thereby counteracting the positive effect. Furthermore, because of their costs, financial incentives are not feasible for many surveys. A further negative effect of a reward contingent on completion of an interview is the possibility that it introduces the idea of a business exchange into the interview context, and, once this altered context is invoked, the size of the reward may be judged against a realistic hourly fee for services rendered, which may be quite high. In communal (as opposed to business) relationships, benefits are given in response to need or in order to please, rather than in return for favors received (Clark and Mills 1979; Mills and Clark 1982). In one instance, a benefit offered as a "sign of appreciation" was more effective than one offered as an "incentive" (Gould 1984).

Anecdotal evidence from Laurence Branch and from the Survey Research Center suggests that coffee mugs with the signet of the study, the sponsoring agency, or the like, given before or at the outset of the interview are good incentives. Other nonfinancial incentives include a free medical exam or health-related information and feedback, but researchers on the elderly do not agree on the effectiveness of such incentives. Some believe that a free health exam in itself is not much of an incentive to elderly respondents because most of them receive medical care that is paid for by Medicare, and those who do not have such coverage may not want an examination. Others feel that a free examination, particularly for something not covered by standard health insurance, is often appreciated. In general, researchers agree that incentives may have some marginal impact on some respondents, but that factors such as the perceived importance of the study, the sponsor of the research, the personality of the interviewer, and the burden (in terms of time and effort) placed on the respondents are much more important.

Mixed Modes of Data Collection

Surveys that use telephone and mail interviews in addition to face-to-face interviews may obtain higher response rates than surveys that rely on a single mode of data collection. Although all modes have their characteristic strengths and weaknesses, combining methods may overcome the limitations inherent in any one approach. In general, the quality of the resulting responses does not differ across modes (Bradburn, 1983; Groves and Kahn 1979), even for older respondents (Herzog and Rodgers 1988b; Herzog, Rodgers, and Kulka 1983).

Because the different modes reach and obtain interviews with somewhat different populations and vary in their relative costs, while appearing to produce data of similar quality, strategies that combine modes have proven useful in the general population. Mixed modes have increased response rates by 5 to 15 percent over those obtained with the original mode at a reduced cost (Hochstim 1967; Siemiatycki 1979). McKinlay and his colleagues (McKinlay 1988; Tennstedt and McKinlay 1987) argue that for elderly populations, mixed-mode surveys are cost effective in maximizing the response rate, minimizing nonresponse bias, and ensuring high-quality data.

However, there may be differences in the quality of data collected by different modes, or biases in data collected by one mode relative to data collected by another mode. For example, in the NHANES III, two telephone follow-up interviews will be conducted to measure 24-hour recall of food; there is considerable concern about the possibility of mode effects, but no evidence supporting or refuting such concerns.

Proxy Reporters

One way to reduce nonresponse is to seek information from another source about persons who are unwilling or unable to respond to an interviewer themselves. In existing surveys, a proxy is generally someone who knows the sampled individual well. For those living in households, the proxy is almost always someone in the same household—preferably the spouse—whereas for those in institutions it is often a caregiver or a grown son or daughter.

Proxy reporters appear to be a much more important source of information about the oldest old than about younger adults, because of substantial proportions who may be incapable of providing accurate responses to survey questions, or even participating in the interview, due to cognitive impairment or frail health. For example, in the 1984 SOA of people 55 years of age and over, 8.5 percent of all the interviews were with proxies, but for those aged 85 and older, the rate was 26.6 percent (Fitti and Kovar 1987). This increase in reliance on proxies for the oldest old parallels an increase of those having difficulty and/or receiving help with activities of daily living and those experiencing cognitive impairments (Cornoni-Huntley et al. 1986; Fitti and Kovar 1987, 22). Indeed, in the longitudinal component of the SOA, those with proxy respondents were more likely to be dead 2 years later than those who reported for themselves, suggesting that they were sick already in 1984. Likewise, Wallace estimates that 20 to 70 percent of institutional residents cannot answer survey questions, depending on the type of institution and the type of residents they serve. There was a general consensus among the polled investigators that proxy respondents must be used in research on the oldest old in order to avoid biasing the data in favor of healthy older persons.

Given that an interview with a proxy reporter may be the only way of obtaining information about frail older adults, how should the decision to choose a proxy over the selected respondent be made? Some surveys, particularly the general-population-type surveys, do not accept proxy respondents at all. Most surveys of older adults seem to permit a proxy if the sampled person is impaired but prefer to obtain the information directly from the sampled person. If the latter procedure is chosen, a set of decision rules has to be developed for determining when the sampled older person is too impaired to answer personally. In several surveys, the decision is made by the interviewers, who have been trained in observing critical incidences of impairment. In the New Haven EPESE, the interviewers review their assessment with the supervisor before proceeding to invite a proxy instead of the sampled older person. In other surveys, such as the NHANES and the Iowa EPESE, the interviewers proceed on the spot but carefully document the reasons for their decision. The National Long Term Care Channelling Demonstration Project permits a switch to proxy if the sampled respondent becomes confused or exhausted during the interview. The specific decision rule that is used involves a checkpoint at the end of each section of the interview about the status of the respondent, with the possibility of switching to the end of the interview for a few critical questions remaining there.

A formal test of cognitive impairment, like the Mental Status Questionnaire, is utilized in several surveys of the elderly. This questionnaire was originally included as a screening device; however, it is generally recognized that the validity of such a test for establishing an older person's ability to provide accurate information has not been proven. In addition, if the questionnaire is used as a screener, the interviewer has to score the respondent's answers immediately and decide how to proceed. Even with extensive interviewer training, issues of reliability emerge. As a consequence, the test results are often used after the interview to supplement observation and assess the trustworthiness of the information obtained from the respondent, rather than as a decision tool for choosing a proxy respondent.

The issue of proxy reporters rests to a large extent on the tradeoff between two sources of error: errors due to unit and item nonresponse may be reduced by seeking information from proxies, but errors due to inaccurate responding may be increased. To date both of these assumptions remain unsubstantiated. Research evaluating the quality of proxy reports is flawed because sampled persons for whom proxies are sought are different in their physical and mental health from sampled persons who can respond for themselves. Even in well-designed studies, external validation criteria are rarely available to establish which of two discrepant reports is more accurate. These and other methodological problems affecting most existing investigations of the quality of proxy responses are discussed in a recent literature review by Moore (1988).

The existing literature on proxy information in epidemiological studies suggests that its validity varies considerably, depending on the relationship of the proxy to the respondent, on the type of information sought, and on the time period involved. Household surveys typically ask a close relative, such as a spouse or an adult son or daughter, to serve as proxy, whereas in institutional settings the immediate caretaker is often sought. However, some surveys, such as the New Haven EPESE, retain the original proxy even if the sampled person moves into an institution. How often the proxy interacts with the sampled person may be important. Bassett and Magaziner (1988) have recently reported that the frequency of contact is related to the response quality of the proxy if the proxy does not live with the sampled person. It would seem logical that the choice of proxy be determined by the nature of the information sought. For example, caretakers may be more knowledegable than family members about the physical health and functional symptoms of institutionalized respondents, whereas family members may be more knowledgeable about personal and family history, economic situation, and the like. Among family members, wives have been shown to be particularly reliable proxy reporters for dietary information (Kolonel, Hirohata, and Nomura 1977), and siblings for events of childhood years (Pickle, Brown, and Blot 1983).

Regarding the type of information, it is widely assumed that proxies can be asked to report about factual information but not about feelings like satisfactions or depression, nor about cognitive performance. Recent findings (Bassett and Magaziner 1988; Rodgers 1988) suggest that properly chosen proxies can provide fairly accurate information even on such topics.

One final issue concerns the setting in which the proxy reports. Although in many surveys the proxy respondent is interviewed alone—sometimes over the telephone—in the New Haven EPESE the proxy answers the survey questions in the presence of the sampled person. This provides the unique opportunity for the sampled person and the proxy to assist each other in retrieving the requested information. We turn to the issue in a more systematic fashion in the next section.

Assistors

By standard practice, survey interviews are sought in private on the assumption that the presence, and especially the participation, of another person may influence the respondent and thereby decrease response accuracy. For example, in the National Long Term Care Channelling Demonstration Project and in the SOA, interviewers tried *not* to interview the target person and the caregiver jointly, although sometimes this proved to be unavoidable because the target person was being protected by the family and they wanted to be present. In this situation, a family member sometimes answered for the patient, which the interviewers tried to discourage by saying that they had questions for them in the caregiver interview. In other surveys the norm is deliberately violated. For example, in the NHIS an attempt is made to include the entire family in a group interview. One can speculate that when family members or caregivers are present, they sometimes remind respondents of factual information, thereby increasing accuracy, although they may also sometimes influence the respondent to give less accurate answers.

Among older respondents, one could speculate that spouses or grown children could provide assistance in interviewing the sampled older person. If they are properly instructed in their role, such assistance could potentially alleviate fears about the interview situation and facilitate communication during the interview. Such a procedure should be systematically investigated.

Characteristics of the Survey Questions

Many aspects of survey questions, including their substantive content, their length, the format of the response categories, the frame of reference, and the context, have been previously investigated. The interested reader may consult Andrews (1984), Bradburn (1983), and Sudman and Bradburn (1974).

One aspect of the response scale has received a good deal of confirmation: seven to nine response categories result in more valid responses than do two to four (Bollen and Barb 1981; Cochran 1968; Cox 1980). In the past, Lawton (1977) and other investigators have raised concerns that fewer response categories may be easier and therefore produce more valid responses among the elderly. A recent piece (Rodgers, Andrews, and Herzog, in preparation), however, demonstrates the importance of the number of response categories for those under as well as those over 60 years of age. Preliminary data from this piece support on "unfolding" format to present a relatively large number of categories to older respondents. Using this format, response categories are presented in a stepwise fashion, with major distinctions (e.g., "Do you agree or disagree?") elicited first and minor distinctions probed thereafter (e.g., if the respondent agrees, "Do you agree very much or just somewhat?").

One investigator raised a number of questions about the wording of questions. Some survey questions that were developed using younger respondents are too complex for older adults. A prime example would be the forced-choice items from the Rotter Internal-External Control Scale (Rotter 1966), which require respondents to hold in memory two highly abstract and lengthy sentences in order to decide which one applies to them. Typically, numerous repetitions of the Rotter items are required in interviews with elderly adults, and the interviewer is often still left with the impression that the response was as much determined by chance as by the content of the alternatives. Simpler wording and the presentation of single alternatives are preferable for older respondents. The avoidance of questions worded as double negatives is also advisable because they appear to be very taxing to the cognitive flexibility of older adults.

Other survey questions seem inappropriate because of disabling conditions of many elderly. For example, asking whether the respondent can walk a mile or more or could borrow a car may be difficult to answer if a respondent has not tried to walk or does not have a driver's license.

Finally, the researcher must pay careful attention to the meaning of questions at different age levels. For example, today's elderly seem to be less willing than younger age groups to draw comparisons between themselves and others as is often requested by survey questions ("Compared to others your age . . ."), because admitting that one is better than others would seem presumptuous. In addition, older adults seem less comfortable with the kinds of psychological self-descriptions that are the mainstay of scales of personality characteristics or mental health.

Characteristics of Interviewers

Speculations about the effect of the age of the interviewer abound. Moreover, response rates vary considerably by interviewer. It is less clear which interviewer characteristics account for the differences, and whether the age of the interviewer has anything to do with these differences. In general, little rigorous research is available on this topic, and we are unaware of any study investigating the age of the interviewer. Anecdotal evidence supports the notion that older interviewers might appear less threatening to older respondents. At least some of the persons in the New Haven EPESE preferred older interviewers (i.e., "gray hair" was welcome). Persons refusing to be interviewed, when recontacted, gave reasons such as that the interviewer "was so young" or that the respondent "did not think she would understand," and an offer to provide a more mature interviewer was often welcomed. No instances of the reverse pattern were encountered. In the Iowa EPESE, older interviewers were also preferred, partly because it was assumed that using interviewers of the same age group could reduce communication problems across generations. In summary, matched ages were believed to facilitate participation and to increase valid responding.

It was also noted that the interviewer's behavior and manner are particularly important to older respondents. Interviewers in the New Haven EPESE wear white jackets and carry black bags, invoking a medical focus that is appropriate for that study because a substantial number of the questions are health related.

Several investigators suggest that an advance letter introducing the survey and the interviewer should be sent. Indeed, several survey organizations include information about the interviewer in their advance letter and mention that the interviewer carries identification material to prove her legitimacy. This is generally believed to be useful and to alleviate fear of victimization and of the unknown, although again, no systematic tests seem to have been done.

Interviewer Training

Interviewers in studies of the oldest old are generally given at least some special training to acquaint them with the problems often encountered with such respondents. These procedures include, for example, the use of videotapes and role-playing exercises.

In some studies—most notably the evaluation of the National Long Term Care Channelling Demonstration Project by Mathematica Policy Research (MPR)—interviewers were sensitized to physical problems often faced by old and frail people. For example, hearing impairments were simulated with a tape, the "Unfair Hearing Test," and vision impairments were simulated by making interviewers wear glasses smeared with petroleum jelly. The results of this sensitization program have been promising, but we are not aware of any systematic evaluations, and the apparent effects of sensitization may be confounded with interviewer characteristics. MPR has also developed a videotape on interviewing the elderly, which is available and has been used elsewhere. Actors were hired to play the roles of elderly respondents.

Another issue to be addressed during training is that interviews with the elderly may be more stressful for the interviewer than those with the general population. Interviews with the elderly take longer—an observation corroborated by every survey research organization that was contacted. Older adults are more likely to digress from the topic of the question, and are less willing or able to use the standardized response categories. For these reasons, interviewing the elderly is in some respects more strenuous than interviewing younger adults (Gibson and Aitkenhead 1983). The interviewer must be more attentive to catch possible deviations from appropriate response behavior and must offer more assistance to improve response behavior. In addition, interviews with older persons raise awareness and empathy among the interviewers for problems faced by the aged. Discussion of possible sources of distress and suggestions about how to deal with it helps to minimize problems and burnout during field work.

Respondent Training

Training and intervention procedures have been used in survey research and in gerontologic research on cognitive functioning. In survey research, one set of procedures (Cannell, Miller, and Oksenberg 1981) is based on the recognition that those who are selected for an interview are often unclear about what is expected of them in the role of respondent, and that instructing them in this role improves their reporting. The procedures, which include three dimensions—commitment, instructions, and feedback—have been shown to improve reporting in face-to-face and telephone interview surveys on health and mass media use (Cannell, Oksenberg, and Converse 1977; Cannell, Miller, and Oksenberg 1981; National Center for Health Statistics 1987b).

In research on intellectual processes among older persons, considerable evidence exists to show that with proper training older adults can improve their performance in intelligence tests and other problem-solving tasks (Baltes and Willis 1982). Training procedures that appear to be successful include modeling, direct instructions, and possibly feedback (see Denney 1979). Although most training procedures for cognitive functioning consist of extensive efforts, even a minor exposure can have a beneficial effect. For example, Baltes and Willis (1982) note an improvement from pre- to posttesting of cognitive functioning that was conducted on an older control group. They suggest that this reflects a facilitative effect of the first experience with the test. Likewise, Wallace (1987) observed a decline in missing data from an earlier to a later interview among older adults (using a similar interview schedule). He interpreted the decline as the effect of the experience with the first interview.

Because today's older adults have had less experience with standardized testing and interviewing than younger cohorts, possibly they could benefit from some guidance in how to view and relate to a survey interview. Procedures such as those developed by Cannell should be investigated.

Obtaining Third-Party-Source Information

A promising means of upgrading the quality of data on the oldest old is to supplement self-reports with administrative records. The National Death Index (NDI) rapidly is gaining popularity as a means of following up respondents who are lost from a panel and may have died and as a means of confirming reports by others that the panel member has died. The NDI was created for nationwide tracking of deaths that have occurred in research populations (Rogot et al. 1983; Wentworth, Neaton, and Rasmussen 1983). Upon approval by the NDI, the NDI will match submitted names and identify the states in which the deaths occurred, the dates of the deaths, and the corresponding death-certificate numbers. Copies of the actual death certificates, including the cause of death, can then be obtained from the appropriate state offices. The matches have to be done carefully because neither research nor administrative files are perfect; generally, the more identifying information available for each person, the more successful the matching procedure.

The Medicare file compiled from data collected by HCFA, discussed above, represents a source of information on dates of hospitalizations and diagnoses. It can also be matched with research data to supplement self-report information.

The MEDSTAT files that are currently being developed will contain information on Medicaid enrollees that can be linked to research data files. The information is compiled and managed by HCFA and includes information on eligibility history, health-service utilization, expenditures, and personal information.

CONCLUSIONS

Researchers who have collected survey data on the old and the oldest old in this country have a wealth of suggestions on how these respondents, many of whom are frail or impaired, might be approached and interviewed to produce the valid information that is needed for basic research and policy discussions. Many researchers have made commonsense adjustments to the interview process and procedures to accommodate older respondents. These include the simplification of response scales by using fewer and more simply worded alternatives or by a stepwise presentation procedure, sometimes referred to as an ''unfolding'' scale. They also include the presentation of respondent booklets and other survey materials in large print. They may offer the option to read survey materials or self-administered forms to the respondent if vision problems or intellectual limitations make reading difficult. Many researchers have made modifications in the sampling and nonresponse procedures to obtain unbiased samples of the elderly. Some of these, and other suggestions discussed in this chapter, are based on rigorous research; many more derive from observations in the field and require more systematic tests. On some suggestions there is consensus, whereas on others there is wide disagreement; only systematic investigations can settle the disagreement and confirm the consensus. Throughout this chapter we noted issues that could benefit from systematic investigations.

A general theme of the discussions with investigators was that the highly structured and standardized interview format typical of most surveys may have to be relaxed for interviews with older adults. Because variations in survey and interview procedures can introduce variable error and bias into resulting data, standardized interview questions and procedures are the rule in established survey research organizations. However, the inflexibility of these methods may introduce errors of their own into surveys of the oldest old: information is lost when respondents refuse to participate in an onerous interview or decline to answer an unintelligible question, and information is erroneous when respondents guess answers or misunderstand questions. Critics have pointed out that standardized interviews violate norms of ordinary discourse, thereby introducing error; they say that interviews should follow more closely the conventions of normal discourse, which has several characteristics that distinguish it from the course of the typical survey interview (Briggs 1986; Jordan and Suchman 1987; Mishler 1986). This criticism may be particularly relevant to interviews with specific subgroups such as older respondents (as noted in the collaborations between cognitive psychologists and survey methodologists; see Jabine et al.

1984), among whom resistance to the standardized interview format has been noted by many researchers.

The sensitivity of the investigators to the special challenges of research on the oldest old demonstrated in these interviews and the wealth of suggested procedures bode well for the development of methods that produce data of high quality on the oldest subgroup of the population. A small body of systematic methodological research speaks to the scientific commitment among a small but growing body of methodological researchers. We hope that policy makers and funding agencies concerned with the oldest old will recognize the need for evaluation and potential modification of relevant research methods and will wholeheartedly support such research efforts.

Acknowledgments—This work was supported by a personal service contract from the National Institute on Aging and by Grant R01 AG0 2038-08, also from the National Institute on Aging. The authors are most grateful to their colleagues who shared their knowledge and experiences and who commented later on a draft of the chapter. If the process of reaching agreement on a written document by many authors were not so cumbersome, the names of these colleagues would be included as authors.

APPENDIX: LIST OF INVESTIGATORS INTERVIEWED

Michael Alevanjaa
National Cancer Institute

Debra Bersini
National Center for Health Statistics

Laurence Branch
Boston University

Larry Corder
Duke University

Ronald Dopkowski
Bureau of the Census

Denis A. Evans
Senior Health Project

Mary Harahan
Department of Health and Human Services

Tamara Harris
National Center for Health Statistics

Mary Grace Kovar
National Center for Health Statistics

Tom McKenna
Westat

Joseph McLaughlin
National Cancer Institute

Jennifer Madans
National Center for Health Statistics

Jay Magaziner
University of Maryland Medical School

Adrian Ostfeld
Yale University

Margaret Phillips
Mathematica Policy Research

Patricia Royston
National Center for Health Statistics

Richard Schulz
University of Pittsburgh

Judith Tanur
State University of New York

Robert Wallace
University of Iowa

REFERENCES

Andersen, R., J. Kasper, M.R. Frankel, et al. 1979. *Total Survey Error*. San Francisco: Jossey-Bass.
Andrews, F.M. 1984. Construct Validity and Error Components of Survey Measures: A Structural Modeling Approach. *Public Opinion Quarterly* 48:409–42.

Andrews, F.M., and A.R. Herzog. 1986. The Quality of Survey Data as Related to Age of Respondent. *Journal of the American Statistical Association* 81:403–10.

Baltes, P.B., and S.L. Willis. 1982. Plasticity and Enhancement of Intellectual Functioning in Old Age: Penn State's Adult Development and Enrichment Project (ADEPT). In *Aging and Cognitive Processes*, eds. F.I.M. Craik and S. Trehub. New York: Plenum.

Bassett, S.S., and J. Magaziner. 1988. The Use of Proxy Responses on Mental Health Measures for Aged, Community-dwelling Women. Paper presented at the 41st Annual Scientific Meeting of The Gerontological Society of America, San Francisco.

Bollen, K.A., and K. H. Barb. 1981. Pearson's R and Coarsely Categorized Measures. *American Sociological Review* 46:232–39.

Bradburn, N.M. 1983. Response Effects. In *Handbook of Survey Research*, eds. P.H. Rossi, J.D. Wright, and A.B. Anderson, 289–328. New York: Academic Press.

Briggs, C.L. 1986. *Learning How to Ask*. Cambridge: Cambridge University Press.

Cannell, C., G. Fisher, and T. Bakker. 1965. Reporting of Hospitalization in the Health Interview Survey. *Vital and Health Statistics*, series 2, no. 6. Hyattsville, Md.: National Center for Health Statistics.

Cannell, C.F., P.V. Miller, and L. Oksenberg. 1981. Research on Interviewing Techniques. In *Sociological Methodology*, ed. S. Leinhardt, 389–438. San Francisco: Jossey-Bass.

Cannell, C.F., L. Oksenberg, and J.M. Converse. 1977. Striving for Response Accuracy: Experiments in New Interviewing Techniques. *Journal of Marketing Research* 14:306–15.

Carp, F.M. 1989. Maximizing Data Quality in Community Studies of Older People. In *Special Research Methods for Gerontology*, eds. M.P. Lawton and A.R. Herzog, 93–122. Amityville, N.Y.: Baywood.

Clark, M.S., and J. Mills. 1979. Interpersonal Attraction in Exchange and Communal Relationships. *Journal of Personality and Social Psychology* 37:12–24.

Clemente, F., and M.B. Kleiman. 1976. Fear of Crime among the Aged. *The Gerontologist*, 16:207–10.

Cochran, W.G. 1968. The Effectiveness of Adjustment by Subclassifications in Removing Bias in Observational Studies. *Biometrics* 24:295–313.

Colsher, P.L., and R.B. Wallace. 1989. Data Quality and Age: Health and Psychobehavioral Correlates of Item Nonreponse and Inconsistent Responses. *Journal of Gerontology: Psychological Sciences* 44:P45–P52.

Cornoni-Huntley, J.C., D.B. Brock, A.M. Ostfeld, J.O. Taylor, and R.B. Wallace. 1986. *Established Populations for Epidemiologic Studies of the Elderly*. NIH pub. no. 86-2443. Bethesda, Md.: National Institute on Aging.

Corso, J.F. 1986. Sensory-perceptual Processes and Aging. *Annual Review of Gerontology and Geriatics* 7:29–35.

Cox, E.P., III. 1980. The Optimal Number of Response Alternatives for a Scale: A Review. *Journal of Marketing Research* 17:407–22.

DeMaio, T.J. 1980. Refusals: Who, Where and Why. *Public Opinion Quarterly* 44:223–33.

Denney, N.W. 1979. Problem Solving in Later Adulthood: Intervention Research. In *Lifespan Development and Behavior*, eds. P.B. Baltes and O.G. Brim, Jr. New York: Academic Press.

Ferber, R. 1966. Item Nonresponse in a Consumer Survey. *Public Opinion Quarterly* 30:399–415.

Fitti, J.E., and M.G. Kovar. 1987. The Supplement on Aging to the 1984 National Health Interview Survey. *Vital and Health Statistics*, series 1, no. 21. DHHS pub. no. (PHS) 87-1323. Hyattsville, Md. National Center for Health Statistics.

Francis, J.D., and L. Busch. 1975. What We Know about "I don't know." *Public Opinion Quarterly* 39:207–18.

Gergen, K.J., and K.W. Back. 1966. Communication in the Interview and the Disengaged Respondent. *Public Opinion Quarterly* 30:385–98.

Gibson, D.M., and W. Aitkenhead. 1983. The Elderly Respondent: Experiences from a Large-scale Survey of the Aged. *Research on Aging* 5:283–96.

Glenn, N.D. 1969. Aging, Disengagement, and Opinionation. *Public Opinion Quarterly* 33:17–33.

Goudy, W.J. 1985. Sample Attrition in Multivariate Analysis in the Retirement History Study. *Journal of Gerontology* 40:358–67.

Gould, R. 1984. Fundraising as a Communal Exchange: Donor Response and the Availability Heuristic. Proceedings of the American Psychological Association, Consumer Psychology Division, August.

Groves, R.M. 1989. *Survey Errors and Survey Costs*. New York: Wiley.

Groves, R.M., and R.L. Kahn. 1979. *Surveys by Telephone: A National Comparison with Personal Interviews*. New York: Academic Press.

Hawkins, D.F. 1975. Estimation of Nonresponse Bias. *Sociological Methods and Research* 3:461–88.

Herzog, A.R., and L. Dielman. 1985. Age Differences in Response Accuracy for Factual Survey Questions. *Journal of Gerontology* 40:350–57.

Herzog, A.R., and W.L. Rodgers. 1982. *Surveys of Older Americans: Some Methodological Investigations*. Final Report to the National Institute on Aging. Ann Arbor: Mi: Institute for Social Research.

———. 1988a. Age and Response Rates to Interview Sample Surveys. *Journal of Gerontology: Social Sciences* 43:S200–S205.

———. 1988b. Interviewing Older Adults: Mode Comparison Using Data from a Face-to-Face Survey and a Telephone Resurvey. *Public Opinion Quarterly* 52:84–99.

Herzog, A.R., W.L. Rodgers, and R.A. Kulka. 1983. Interviewing Older Adults: A Comparison of Telephone and Face-to-Face Modalities. *Public Opinion Quarterly* 47:405–18.

Hochstim, J.R. 1967. A Critical Comparison of Three Strategies of Collecting Data from Households. *Journal of the American Statistical Association* 62:976–89.

Hoinville, G. 1983. Carrying Out Surveys Among the Elderly: Some Problems of Sampling and Interviewing. *Journal of the Market Research Society* 25:223–37.

Jabine, T.B., M.L. Straf, J.M. Tanur, and R. Tourangeau (Eds.) 1984. *Cognitive Aspects of Survey Methodology: Building a Bridge between Disciplines*. Washington: National Academy Press.

Jobe, J.B., and D.J. Mingay. 1990. Cognitive Laboratory Approach to Designing Questionnaires for Surveys of the Elderly. *Public Health Reports* 105:518–24.

Jordan, B., and L. Suchman. 1987. Interactional Troubles in Survey Interviews. *Proceedings of the Section on Survey Research Methods. American Statistical Association.*

Kalton, G., and D.W. Anderson. 1989. Sampling Rare Populations. In *Special Research Methods for Gerontology*, eds. M.P. Lawton and A.R. Herzog, 7–30. Amityville, N.Y.: Baywood.

Kish, L. 1965. *Survey Sampling*. New York: Wiley.

Kogan, N. 1961. Attitudes toward Old People in an Older Sample. *Journal of Abnormal and Social Psychology* 62:616–22.

Kolonel, L.N., T. Hirohata, and A.M.Y. Nomura. 1977. Adequacy of Survey Data Collected from Substitute Respondents. *American Journal of Epidemiology* 106:476–84.

Lawton, M.P. 1977. Morale: What Are we Measuring? In *Measuring Morale*, ed. C.N. Nydegger. Washington: Gerontological Society.

Lowe, F.E., and T.C. McCormick. 1955. Some Survey Sampling Biases. *Public Opinion Quarterly* 19:303–15.

McKinlay, J. 1988. Optimal Methods for Studying Health related Behaviors of the Elderly in Household Surveys. Paper presented at the International Symposium on Data on Aging: Developing Research on Measuring Health and Health Care, National Center for Health Statistics, Bethesda, Maryland.

Mills, J., and M.S. Clark. 1982. Communal and Exchange Relationships. In *Review of Personality and Social Psychology*, vol. 3, ed. L. Wheeler, 121–44. Beverly Hills, Calif.: Sage.

Mishler, E.G. 1986. *Research Interviewing*. Cambridge, Mass.: Harvard University Press.

Moles, E.L. 1987. *Perceptions of the Interview Process*. Paper presented at the 40th Annual Scientific Meeting of The Gerontological Society of America, Washington.

Moore, J.C. 1988. Self/Proxy Response Status and Survey Response Quality: A Review of the Literature. *Journal of Official Statistics* 4:155–72.

Moser, C.A., and G. Kalton. 1972. *Survey Methods in Social Investigations*, 2nd ed. New York: Basic Books.

National Center for Health Statistics. 1987. An Experimental Comparison of Telephone and Personal Health Surveys. *Vital and Health Statistics*, series 2, no. 106. Hyattsville, Md.: National Center for Health Statistics.

Norris, F.H. 1985. Characteristics of Older Nonrespondents over Five Waves of a Panel Study. *Journal of Gerontology* 40:627–36.

Pickle, L.W., L.M. Brown, and W.J. Blot. 1983. Information Available from Surrogate Respondents in Case-control Interview Studies. *American Journal of Epidemiology* 118:99–108.

Rodgers, W.L. 1988. The Relative Validities of Self- and Proxy-reports. Part of Symposium, in J. Magaziner (Chair), *Epidemiological Surveys of Older Adults: Response Rates, Data Quality and the Use of Proxies*. Presented at the 41st Annual Scientific Meeting of the Gerontological Society of American, San Francisco, November.

Rodgers, W.L., F.M. Andrews, and A.R. Herzog. In preparation. Quality of Survey Measures: A Structural Modeling Approach.

Rodgers, W.L., & Herzog, A.R. 1987a. Interviewing Older Adults: The Accuracy of Factual Information. *Journal of Gerontology* 42:387–94.

Rodgers, W.L., and A.R. Herzog. 1987b. Measurement Error in Interviews with Elderly Respondents. In *Proceedings of the 1987 Public Health Conference on Records and Statistics*, 433–38. DHHS pub. no. (PHS) 88-1214. Hyattsville, Md.

Rodgers, W.L., A.R. Herzog, F.M. Andrews, and E. Moles. 1985. Age Differences in Survey Measures: A Multitrait–Multimethod Approach. Paper presented at the 38th Annual Scientific Meeting of the Gerontological Society of America, New Orleans, November.

Rogot, E., M. Feinleib, K.A. Ockay, et al. 1983. On the Feasibility of Linking Census Samples to the National Death Idex for Epidemiologic Studies: A Progress Report. *American Journal of Public Health* 73:1265–69.

Rosenwaike, I. 1985. *The Extreme Aged in America: A Portrait of an Expanding Population*. Westport, Conn.: Greenwood Press.

Rotter, J. 1966. Generalized Expectancies for Internal vs. External Control of Reinforcement. *Psychological Monographs* 609 (monograph).

Schulz, R., C.A. Tompkins, and M.T. Rau. 1988. A Longitudinal Study of the Psychosocial Impact of Stroke on Primary Support Persons. *Psychology and Aging* 3:131–41.

Shanas, E. 1962. *The Health of Older People*. Cambridge, Mass.: Harvard University Press.

Siemiatycki, J. 1979. A Comparison of Mail, Telephone, and Home Interview Strategies for Household Health Surveys. *American Journal of Public Health* 69:238–45.

Sirken, M.G. 1970. Household Surveys with Multiplicity. *Journal of American Statistical Association* 65:257–66.

Sudman, S., and N.M. Bradburn. 1974. *Response Effects in Surveys: A Review and Synthesis*. Chicago: Aldine.

Sudman, S., and G. Kalton. 1986. New Developments in the Sampling of Special Populations. *Annual Review of Sociology* 12:401–29.

Tennstedt, S.L., and J.B. McKinlay. 1987. Choosing the Most Appropriate Field Approach for Older Populations: The Case for Mixed-mode Surveys. In *Proceedings of the 1987 Public Health Conference on Records and Statistics*, 427–32. USDHHS pub. no. (PHS) 88-1214. Hyattsville, Md.

U.S. Department of Justice. 1981. *Issues in the Measurement of Victimization*. Bureau of Justice Statistics, NCJ-74682. Washington.

Waldo, D.R., and H.C. Lazenby. 1984. Demographic Characteristics and Health Care Use and Expenditures by the Aged in the United States: 1977–1984. *Health Care Financing Review* 6:1–29.

Wallace, R.B. 1985. Factors Associated with the Prevalence of Physical Dysfunction among the Elderly in the Community. Paper presented at the Annual Meeting of the American Public Health Association, Washington.

———. 1987. The Relationship of Cognitive Function, Health Status and Mood to Missing Data and Inconsistent Responses in an Interview Survey of the Elderly. In *Proceedings of the 1987 Public Health Conference on Records and Statistics*, 423–26. DHHS pub. no. (PHS) 88-1214. Hyattsville, Md.

Weaver, C.N., S.L. Holmes, and N.D. Glenn. 1973. Some Characteristics of Inaccessible Respondents in a Telephone Survey. *Journal of Applied Psychology* 60:260–62.

Wentworth, D.N., J.D. Neaton, and W.L. Rasmussen. 1983. An Evaluation of the Social Security Administration Master Beneficiary Record file and the National Death Index in the Ascertainment of Vital Status. *American Journal of Public Health* 73:1270–74.

8

Mortality and Life Expectancy Changes Among the Oldest Old

KENNETH G. MANTON

The mortality of the oldest-old population (those aged 85 and over) has received considerable attention because large increases in life expectancy at very advanced ages have recently occurred in both the United States and other developed countries. These increases have occurred despite the expectation that mortality at advanced ages would be static relative to that at younger ages because of its closer proximity to what has typically been viewed as the probable biological limits to the human life span.

The fact that mortality rates are declining past the age of 85 also is of considerable interest because this oldest-old population has the highest prevalence of multiple chronic diseases, the greatest prevalence of disability, and the highest per capita long-term-care needs, and has progressed furthest in terms of physiological aging changes. It is therefore important to study this population in terms of how (1) mortality interacts with the prevalence of chronic disease and functional impairments, (2) mortality changes the demand for long-term care services, and (3) intrinsic physiological processes of senescence interact with age-related disease. Such phenomena will determine how much "active" life expectancy (i.e., the number of years a person at a given age can expect to live in a functionally independent state) has increased at advanced ages as total life expectancy has increased.

Recent declines in the mortality rates of the oldest old must be interpreted in light of new scientific evidence on the preogression of physiological aging changes. This evidence suggests that our estimates of the age rate of decline in various physiological functions were too high because earlier studies of functional loss were generally conducted in representative study populations that, at advanced ages, had a high prevalence of chronic disease. Estimation of the individual's age rate of loss of physiological function was confounded with the average function loss in those populations due to the increased prevalence of chronic diseases at advanced ages. More recent studies of only healthy survivors to advanced ages suggest that physiological functions of many types either decline much more slowly than previously estimated (e.g., cardiovascular function of healthy 80-year-olds was found not to be much different than that of 30-year-olds [Lakatta 1985]), or that many types of declines were concentrated in a relatively short period just prior to death (e.g., mental function [Katzman 1985]). Important questions raised by the new evidence on mortality and rate of functional loss are: (1) how might physiological function be preserved more generally at later ages? and (2) what do strategies designed to preserve (and perhaps even retrieve) function imply for further increases in life expectancy at advanced ages? Also significant in this regard is the recent observation that traditional chronic-disease risk factors continue to be strongly related to morbidity and mortality risks at advanced ages, implying that their control at each age may also contribute to an improvement in health at later ages.

To examine the changes in mortality rates at advanced ages in terms of these questions, we will need to look at a variety of data.

First, we will examine the currently observed limits to human life expectancy both by presenting international mortality data that show the highest life expectancies currently observed and by presenting data from an international set of longitudinal studies in which a wide range of risk factors was assessed. The focus of this later analysis is to determine the potential for changing total mortality risks at advanced ages (i.e., over the age of 85).

Second, we will examine in detail the cause of death patterns in the United States among the oldest old. To do this, we analyzed multiple-cause-of-death data for the period 1968 to 1982 to determine trends in multiple and underlying cause reporting, both cross-sectionally and by cohort, for major chronic degenerative diseases. In these studies we will examine changes both in mortality rates and in multiple decrement life-table parameters that control for the mortality risks of other causes of death.

Finally, to help interpret multiple-cause mortality trends, we will examine the reliability of multiple-cause-of-death coding on death certificates. This has not been systematically done before because the multiplicity of combinations of diseases coded on death certificates makes the use of standard procedures for assessing the reliability of cause-of-death reporting problematic in this case. We resolved these problems by using a pattern-recognition procedure (Woodbury and Manton 1982) to identify patterns of conditions reported in hospital records as causing death and the association of those patterns with the combination of causes recorded on the death certificate. This analysis was performed on 3,114 deaths of decedents aged 55 and over occurring in 22 hospitals in North Carolina in 1975 to 1977.

BOUNDS ON LIFE EXPECTANCY INCREASES AT ADVANCED AGES: EVIDENCE ON MORTALITY TRAJECTORIES AT ADVANCED AGES

In evaluating possible bounds to life expectancy increases at advanced ages, one must deal with the problem that such bounds, representing intrinsic biological potential for the life span, can never be directly observed because of the variations in the organism's environment that influence the observed length of life. Consequently, the intrinsic biological life span must be inferred from a variety of different types of data in the hope of determining the intrinsic biological limits from the environmentally imposed constraints on life expectancy. One important type of information is that in international mortality patterns—specifically, the life expectancies achieved in different countries and the cause-of-death pattern determining that life expectancy.

In discussing the potential for life expectancy increases in the United States that many other countries have higher life expectancies than the United States. Table 8–1 shows the life expectancy at birth for 15 countries that presently exceeds American life expectancies for males and/or females (World Health Organization 1984, 1985).

Four countries or areas with population and vital statistics judged to be of relatively high quality by the World Health Organization have female life expectancies in excess of 80 years—Iceland (80.6), Switzerland (80.8), Japan (80.7), and Hong Kong (81.4). In Japan, a country with particularly high quality mortality data because of cultural norms about celebration of birthdays at select advanced ages (Horiuchi and Coale 1983), female life expectancy is 2.3 years greater than in the United States. The discrepancy is even greater for male life expectancy, with Japanese male life expectancy exceeding that of the United States by 3.9 years.

Life expectancy values recorded in international data are approached in specific U.S. state populations where, for the 3-year period 1979 to 1981, female life expectancy was 79.95 years for whites in North Dakota and 80.72 years for nonwhites in Hawaii (National Center for Health Statistics 1986). Similar subpopulation variation is observed in developed countries with life expectancies higher than in the United States. For example, in the Okinawan prefecture of Japan, female life expectancy in 1980 reached 81.7 years (Kuroda 1984).

Not only can one document, in contrast to earlier expectations, that many countries are approaching or surpassing life expectancies of 75 years for males and 80 years for females, but one can also show that mortality rates at advanced ages increase less rapidly with age than predicted by several well-known models of human aging and mortality. For example, the Gompertz function has been proposed by many scientists as a model for mortality changes at advanced ages (e.g., Fries 1980; Sacher

Table 8–1 Life Expectancy at Birth for the United States and 15 Countries with Values for Men and/or Women Higher than the United States

| Country | Year | Age in years | |
		Males	Females
United States	1982	70.9	78.4
Australia	1983	72.2	79.0
Canada[a]	1982	72.0	79.0
Cuba	1981	72.2	75.9
Federal Republic of Germany	1984	71.3	78.1
Finland	1983	70.2	78.5
France[a]	1981	70.9	79.1
Hong Kong	1984	75.1	81.4
Iceland	1983	73.4	80.6
Israel	1983	73.1	76.4
Japan	1984	74.8	80.7
Netherlands	1983	73.0	79.8
Norway	1983	72.8	79.8
Panama	1983	72.8	77.0
Sweden[a]	1982	73.5	79.6
Switzerland	1984	73.8	80.8

[a]Reported in World Health Organization (1984).
Source: World Health Organization (1985).

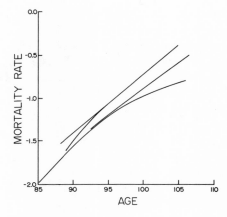

Figure 8–1 Chart B. Log of colog of graduated survival rates of females versus age (cohorts born 1872–1875). (Source: Bayo and Faber 1983)

1977). A considerable body of evidence suggests that mortality above the age of 80 rises less rapidly than predicted by the Gompertz function. This can be illustrated in three types of data for U.S. women in figure 8–1 (Bayo and Faber 1983; Wilkin 1982).

The three curves in Figure 8–1 were derived by (1) an "extinct cohort" method using only National Center for Health Statistics mortality data (2) data on the charter beneficiaries of social security (i.e., 31,557 persons aged 65 who were alive on February 1, 1940), and (3) using Medicare-only data. We see that in the regular vital statistics data there is very little increase in mortality above age 100. Although this may result from age-reporting errors in the vital statistics data, there is clearly a deviation of the observed mortality rates from the Gompertz curve above age 90 in the charter beneficiary and Medicare data—probably the most reliable U.S. data sources on mortality at advanced ages.

Similar patterns of deviation from the Gompertz function at advanced ages have been found in other developed countries. For example, in Figure 8–2 we present data on British mortality above the age of 100 (Barrett 1985).

Again, we see there is a slower increase in mortality rates than expected with the Gompertz function—indeed, there is an actual decline above age 104. The data in this figure are based upon British population registry data, which have extremely

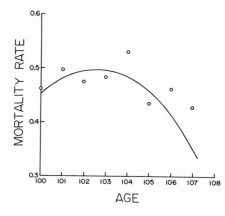

Figure 8–2 Age-specific rates of mortality for male centenarians aged 100 to 107 and fitted mortality function (smooth line). (Source: Barrett 1985)

accurate age reporting. Similar findings have been found in the United States, (Manton, Stallard, and Vaupel 1986; Wilkin 1982), Sweden (Manton, Stallard, and Vaupel 1981), France (Depoid 1973; Vincent 1951), in the study of female mortality in 12 countries (Horiuchi and Coale 1983), and in select other studies (e.g., Humphrey 1970; Perks 1932).

One plausible explanation for this slower rate of increase in mortality at advanced ages is that persons surviving to those ages have a slower rate of physiological aging change. In order to evaluate this possibility, we need to examine models of the age increase in mortality rates whose parameters can be interpreted in terms of the rate of physiological aging (or loss of physiological reserve). One such mortality model is the well-known Gompertz model (Strehler 1977). In this model the age-specific mortality rate, say μ_a, is an exponential function of age ($\alpha e^{\theta a}$), where θ is a parameter describing the rate of aging related to its impact on mortality—specifically, it is the percentage per year increase in mortality. Unfortunately, as just described, the Gompertz model does not seem to describe mortality very well at advanced ages. This may be due to the effect of the high rate of mortality selection upon frailer numbers of the population at earlier ages. To account for this, we assumed that the proportionality factor α is distributed across members of a cohort and then allowing members with high levels of frailty (i.e., large values of α) to die at earlier ages. By generalizing the Gompertz model to represent such individual differences in the level of mortality risks, the model can also represent at least part of the slower rate of aging among survivors as due to exposures that vary over cohorts.

In Table 8–2 we show estimates of the Gompertz and Weibull exponential parameters (the two most frequently cited models of the effect of physiological aging on mortality [Economos 1982]), which represent the age rate of increase in mortality for select U.S. male and female cohorts, using Medicare data.

As described, the Gompertz and Weibull exponential parameter estimates in Table 8–2 have been adjusted to represent the effect of differential survival to the same age across cohorts, that is, they have been adjusted for the effects of population heterogeneity and differentials in early mortality rates. We see that, even after the adjustment for differentials in age-specific survival probabilities, there is a significant decline in the Gompertz and Weibull rates of aging parameters (θ and m) across the birth cohorts. This suggests that the intrinsic rate of aging is significantly affected by environmental and lifestyle influences—even at very advanced ages—and that these influences or exposures have, on average, become relatively more benign for more recent birth cohorts.

The data on total mortality show that current U.S. life expectancy is lower than that of Japan, Hong Kong, and Switzerland, suggesting potential for further life expectancy gains in the United States. To understand better the disease mechanisms that produced higher life expectancies in other countries, it is useful to examine the causes that have contributed to recent gains in life expectancy at different ages. These gains are examined for Japan, the United States, Sweden, and Canada, during 1970 to 1980, in Table 8–3. This table presents (1) the number of years of life expectancy gained from reduction of a particular cause-specific mortality rate (e.g., for Canada there was a 0.27 year gain in life expectancy due to a reduction in the risk of stroke—with 0.19 years of that reduction occurring after the age of 65), and (2) the percentage change of the total gain in life expectancy in a specific age range (e.g., 27.1

Table 8–2 Estimates of Gompertz and Weibull Rate Parameters for Select U.S. Male and Female Cohorts Observed 1968–1978

Cohort/ age range in years	Gompertz θ $(\mu = \alpha e^{\theta t})$		Weibull m $(\mu = \beta t^{m-1})$	
	Males	Females	Males	Females
1902	7.34	8.22	5.77	6.58
65–75	(.10)	(.08)	(.06)	(.06)
1900	7.38	8.33	5.86	6.74
67–77	(.11)	(.09)	(.07)	(.06)
1898	7.73	8.78	6.16	7.16
69–79	(.12)	(.09)	(.08)	(.06)
1896	7.88	9.14	6.31	7.50
71–81	(.14)	(.10)	(.09)	(.07)
1894	8.20	9.52	6.58	7.84
73–83	(.15)	(.11)	(.10)	(.08)
1892	8.65	9.93	6.91	8.18
75–85	(.18)	(.13)	(.12)	(.09)
1890	9.14	10.29	7.29	8.45
77–87	(.21)	(.16)	(.14)	(.11)
1888	9.48	10.61	7.51	8.65
79–89	(.24)	(.19)	(.17)	(.14)
1886	9.81	11.08	7.69	8.93
81–91	(.28)	(.22)	(.20)	(.16)
1884	10.29	11.38	7.98	9.05
83–93	(.32)	(.26)	(.24)	(.20)

Note: Standard errors are given in parentheses.

percent of the total increase in life expectancy is due to mortality reduction after the age of 65).

Table 8–3 shows that male life expectancy gains above the age of 65 were between 22.8 and 27.1 percent of their total life expectancy gains for the United States, Canada, and Japan, between 1970 and 1980. Only in Sweden, where male life expectancy at birth increased by only a half-year was there a decline (4 percent) in male life expectancy above the age of 65. Among the three causes of death, we see that cancer was responsible for a decline in life expectancy above the age of 65 in all countries, while in three of the countries there were significant gains in life expectancy due to declines in both stroke and heart-disease mortality. The magnitude of the contributions of stroke and heart disease to life expectancy gains above the age of 65 is quite variable.

Roughly half (45.7 to 53.5 percent) of females' larger total life expectancy gains occurred above the age of 65. For females, there is relatively less of an increase in cancer mortality, while there were greater improvements in stroke and heart disease mortality. As for males, there was considerable between-country variability in the relative contributions of stroke and heart-disease mortality declines to life expectancy gains at advanced ages.

These life expectancy gains can be further studied by examining the average age

Table 8–3 Total and Cause-Specific Gains in Life Expectancy at Birth and for Broad Age Groups, 1970–1980, for Four Countries

Age (years) and country	Males					Females				
	Cancer	Heart disease	Stroke	All causes	Percent	Cancer	Heart disease	Stroke	All causes	Percent
All ages										
Canada	−0.12	1.00	0.27	2.23	100.0	0.12	1.03	0.50	2.78	100.0
U.S.	−0.04	1.54	0.40	2.99	100.0	0.05	1.54	0.66	3.13	100.0
Japan	0.04	0.30	1.44	4.14	100.0	0.27	0.33	1.42	4.27	100.0
Sweden	−0.14	−0.22	0.10	0.50	100.0	0.04	0.41	0.25	1.67	100.0
0–49										
Canada	0.04	0.10	0.02	1.15	51.1	0.10	0.02	0.03	1.02	36.9
U.S.	0.07	0.24	0.05	1.40	46.9	0.11	0.05	0.06	1.21	38.8
Japan	0.05	0.04	0.01	1.65	39.8	0.11	0.02	0.04	1.33	31.1
Sweden	0.01	0.00	0.02	0.57	114.5	0.07	−0.01	0.00	0.58	34.8
50–64										
Canada	−0.08	0.40	0.06	0.48	21.8	0.02	0.13	0.07	0.37	13.2
U.S	−0.01	0.58	0.11	0.87	29.0	−0.02	0.27	0.10	0.49	15.5
Japan	0.04	0.09	0.43	0.94	22.8	0.13	0.09	0.31	0.86	20.2
Sweden	−0.03	−0.12	0.02	−0.05	−10.5	0.01	0.05	0.05	0.20	11.7
65 +										
Canada	−0.08	0.50	0.19	0.60	27.1	0.00	0.88	0.40	1.39	49.9
U.S.	−0.10	0.72	0.24	0.72	24.1	−0.04	1.18	0.50	1.43	45.7
Japan	−0.05	0.17	0.91	1.55	22.8	0.03	0.22	1.07	2.08	48.7
Sweden	−0.12	−0.10	0.06	−0.02	− 4.0	−0.04	0.37	0.20	0.89	53.5

Source: Tabulation of World Health Organization Data Files.

at death from a given disease and the lifetime proportion of deaths expected from a given conditon in Table 8–4.

The first panel shows that the mean time to death for heart disease and cancer varies significantly over countries—although the variation is less than for total life expectancy, which is also affected by differences in the proportions of deaths due to specific conditions. The cross-country variation in the proportion of deaths due to each condition is even higher—especially for heart disease and stroke. Thus, even in countries with very high life expectancies, there is considerable variation in the structure and timing of causes of death, suggesting further potential for life expectancy increases. For example, a reduction in mortality due to cancer with its low mean time to death could significantly raise the overall life expectancy, even in Japan. Additional improvements in life expectancy could result from increases in the mean ages at death for these conditions. For example, the mean age at death from cancer in the United States for white males increased 2.66 years, from 68.45 to 71.11 between 1968 and 1982—despite a large increase in the proportion of deaths caused by cancer.

A different way to examine the potential for increases in mortality at advanced ages, especially increases to levels beyond those currently observed, is to examine the relation of risk-factor levels to mortality risks at advanced ages and then to ask what life expectancy might be achieved if the risk-factor distribution were improved.

Table 8–4   Mean Time to Death and Proportion of Deaths Expected at Birth for Three Conditions in Four Countries

Country	Data year	Males				Females			
		Cancer	Heart disease	Stroke	All causes	Cancer	Heart disease	Stroke	All causes
		Mean time to death							
Canada	1982	71.4	74.4	78.3	72.0	72.9	82.4	83.5	79.0
U.S.	1980	70.3	74.1	77.7	70.1	71.7	82.2	83.1	77.2
Japan	1982	71.7	78.3	78.4	74.5	73.3	83.7	82.8	80.2
Sweden	1982	72.2	75.8	77.9	73.5	73.0	83.0	82.6	79.5
Maximum difference		1.4	4.2	0.7	4.4	1.5	1.5	0.7	3.0
		Proportion of deaths expected × *100*							
Canada	1982	23.9	32.0	7.5	100.0	20.6	30.8	12.5	100.0
U.S.	1980	21.1	32.5	7.5	100.0	18.4	32.9	12.4	100.0
Japan	1982	23.4	9.8	22.3	100.0	16.6	11.7	27.2	100.0
Sweden	1982	19.7	38.7	8.6	100.0	19.6	33.2	13.4	100.0
Ratio		1.21	3.95	2.97		1.24	2.84	2.19	

Source: Tabulations of World Health Organization Data Files.

This type of analysis obviously requires different types of data than are used in the prior demographic analyses (i.e., data with extensive risk-factor measurements for individuals) and analytic models that can exploit those data. In the following, we will exploit a life-table model with covariates due to Woodbury and Manton (1977). This mode of analysis will be applied to three major longitudinal studies in three different countries United States, USSR, and Finland) to see how controlling risk factors at advanced ages might improve survival at those ages.

The life-table model with covariates we will apply to the longitudinal studies is different from other life-table and hazard-modeling efforts in that it represents two types of processes. First, it describes the mortality process as a function of the current value of risk factors and a Gompertz function describing mortality due to basic aging processes. The second component of the model, which is not usually represented in hazard modeling (Andersen 1986), describes change in risk factor values as a function of (1) age, (2) other risk factor values at an earlier time, and (3) stochastic error (Manton and Woodbury 1983). By modeling the process describing risk-factor change with time, we can simulate the long-term effects on survival of changing risk factor values in several ways. For example, one may modify the equations representing the age change of the risk factors so that the mean of the risk factor distributioin does not increase with age. Alternatively, the variance of the risk factor distribution may be reduced, for example, by eliminating persons with extreme risk-factor values. The separate and combined effects of both types of interventions on three different study populations in three different countries are presented in Table 8–5.

We see that eliminating both the age increase in risk factors and reducing their variance produces large increases in life expectancy at age 30, that is, male life expectancy at 30 increased between 5.3 to 16.6 years—to ages 80.1 to 87.3 years for males, with the median life expectancy being between 82 and 89 years. Part of the large difference in the effect of the interventions across the studies results from the different set of risk factors available in each study. In addition, the two studies with longer follow-up (i.e., Framingham, 20 years; the Finnish East-West Study, 25 years) have greater life expectancy changes than in the Kaunas, Lithuania study, with only 11 years' follow-up. This may be because the Kaunas population has not yet progressed to sufficiently advanced ages to manifest the full effect of the circulatory-disease risk factors.

The tables suggest that control of *known* chronic disease risk factors could produce increases in life expectancy to and beyond the limits to life expectancy increases that Fries (1980, 1983, 1984) identified as the biologically determined maximum. Other potentially controllable risk factors not yet identified could increase life expectancy even more. Furthermore, the risk-factor distribution preserved in the simulations are the values observed in each population at age 30 and probably are not optimal, that is, other risk factor values may be associated with even lower mortality risks.

Table 8–5 Life-Table Results for Males with Different Types of Risk Factor Controls from Three Longitudinal Studies

Age (years)	Age-specific life expectancies (e_x)				Proportion surviving to age x (ℓ_x)			
	Baseline observed	Control means	Control variance	Control means & variance	Baseline observed	Control means	Control variance	Control means & variance
Kaunas, Lithuania Study[a]								
30	44.84	46.73	50.98	50.11	100,000	100,000	100,000	100,000
40	35.84	37.43	41.55	40.66	97,506	98,334	98,765	98,792
50	27.54	28.67	32.60	31.65	92,353	94,643	95,983	96,089
60	20.15	20.78	24.35	23.36	82,612	86,769	90,158	90,194
70	13.94	14.12	17.12	16.14	65,848	71,325	78,673	78,063
80	9.08	8.99	11.23	10.37	41,517	46,068	58,354	56,142
90	5.61	5.55	7.02	6.34	16,294	17,717	30,019	26,463
Framingham Study[b]								
30	44.52	48.88	51.21	57.32	100,000	100,000	100,000	100,000
40	35.17	39.42	41.46	47.59	98,366	98,767	99,464	99,477
50	26.35	30.44	31.92	38.13	94,588	95,854	98,202	98,217
60	18.34	22.29	22.74	29.15	86,306	89,233	95,206	95,225
70	11.53	15.35	14.32	20.98	69,071	75,438	87,082	88,335
80	6.39	9.98	7.48	14.07	38,708	51,586	63,521	73,611
90	3.13	6.32	3.14	8.92	8,061	22,861	18,581	47,280
Finnish East-West Study[c]								
30	39.30	46.24	46.43	55.86	100,000	100,000	100,000	100,000
40	30.69	37.49	37.02	46.57	96,051	97,033	98,587	98,605
50	22.87	29.43	28.00	37.73	88,430	91,511	95,627	95,918
60	15.95	22.31	19.45	29.53	75,239	81,741	89,831	90,847
70	10.14	16.31	11.85	22.26	54,026	65,998	76,618	81,647
80	5.75	11.80	6.17	16.22	25,679	44,508	45,740	66,187
90	3.30	8.72	3.16	11.87	3,769	22,216	7,907	43,806

[a] Risk factors controlled were pulse pressure, diastolic blood pressure, quetelet index, cholesterol, glucose tolerance, and smoking. (N = 2,455; initial age range = 45–59 years; follow-up time = 11 years)
[b] Risk factors controlled were pulse pressure, diastolic blood pressure, quetelet index, cholesterol, blood sugar, hemoglobin, vital capacity index, and smoking. (N = 2,454; initial age range = 30–62 years; follow-up time = 20 years)
[c] Risk factors controlled were pulse pressure, diastolic blood pressure, quetelet index, cholesterol, vital capacity index, smoking, and pulse rate. (N = 1,711; initial age range = 40–60 years; follow-up time = 25 years)

As indicated earlier, we are interested not only in total life expectancy, and the potential for its increase, but also in the potential for increasing active life expectancy, that is, the proportion of the life span during which one can expect to be functionally independent. The changes in morbidity and mortality predicted by the interventions in the age-related change of risk-factor values may be related to the loss of function by combining those results with data on the conditions reported to cause disability among the elderly. We combined the data in two steps (Manton 1987). First, we identified disability profiles generated by the same pattern recognition model used in the multiple-cause reliability study using data on limitations in (1) Activities of Daily Living, (2) Instrumental Activities of Daily Living and (3) Activities in Daily Living 2 from the 1982 National Long-Term Care Survey. In that analysis five different disability patterns were identified: (1) a relatively healthy population; (2) a population with musculoskeletal problems; (3) a population with cardiopulmonary conditions; (4) a physically healthy group with dementia; (5) a frail extremely elderly group. Each person has a score on each of the disability profiles. These scores (g_{ik}) could be related to the different conditions by the simple age specific regression function:

$$g_{ik} = \text{Age}_i \sum_{m=1}^{12} \beta_{km} D_{im} + e_{ik}$$

where $\text{Age}_i * \beta_{km}$ is the product of the observed age of the person with the regression coefficient that applies to D_{im}, a zero-one variable indicating whether a person had 1 of 12 major conditions. This regression is presented in Table 8–6.

We see that eliminating a given condition changes a person's score on that profile by the amount in the table. Thus, eliminating dementia would reduce the prevalence of profiles 4 and 5 by 10.2 and 23.9 percent. Because the equation uses age interaction terms, the coefficients can be calculated for any age simply by substituting the appropriate value in the function. The effects of risk-factor interventions would be calculated by (1) conducting simulations using the life-table with covariate methodology (e.g., Table 8–5), and (2) using the changes in age specific disease prevalence forecast by that model in the equations in Table 8–6 to determine the change in the disability distribution.

MULTIPLE CAUSE OF DEATH TRENDS

In the prior section we examined the question of the potential for further increases in life expectancy and active life expectancy among the oldest old using a variety of data sources, for example, by examining the highest life-expectancy levels achieved globally, by examining the trajectory of the mortality function at very advanced ages, and by examining what alteration of risk-factor values might imply for life expectancy gains at advanced ages. In this section we turn to an empirical analysis of recent cause-specific mortality trends among the oldest old in the United States. In those analyses we will examine both cross-sectional and cohort trends, from 1968 to 1982, for selected major causes of death.

In Table 8–7 we present, for four race/sex groups, the change in both underlying

Table 8-6 Regression Coefficient Multiplied by Age 67, Crude Prevalence by Type (in parentheses), and Intercept

Disease	Proportion in total sample with trait	Regression coefficients				
		Type 1 "Healthy" (31.4%)	Type 2 Mobility limited (20.7%)	Type 3 Circulatory and respiratory impaired (19.3%)	Type 4 Cognitive impaired (11.4%)	Type 5 Frail with acute medical problems (17.2%)
Rheumatism	73.2	− 8.04	1.97	6.69	− 2.61	2.01
Diabetes	16.6	− 7.01	− 1.47	1.88	0.61	6.03
Cancer	6.4	− 3.62	− 0.21	− 1.74	− 0.61	6.23
Arteriosclerosis	31.4	− 6.63	− 2.41	1.21	2.68	5.16
Dementia	9.2	−15.41	−10.72	− 7.84	10.18	23.85
Heart attack	6.2	− 7.37	0.72	4.29	0.29	2.08
Hypertension	47.1	− 1.34	0.64	3.35	− 1.41	− 1.22
Stroke	6.6	−10.39	− 0.87	− 2.55	− 0.35	14.07
Bronchitis	12.9	− 5.23	− 3.28	7.34	− 1.34	2.35
Emphysema	9.9	− 1.81	− 1.76	1.27	0.01	2.28
Hip fracture	2.3	−13.67	14.74	− 5.16	− 4.76	8.84
Other fractures	5.5	− 6.50	0.88	3.75	− 2.88	4.71
Intercept (%)		47.6	21.2	10.7	12.6	7.8

cause (UC) and total mention (TM) mortality rates for three age groups for cancer, cerebrovascular disease, heart disease, diabetes mellitus, and influenza/pneumonia.

In the table we present percentage changes in average age-specific mortality rates between two 3-year periods (1968–1970 and 1980–1982). Very different UC and TM patterns emerge for the different disease groups. For example, despite large increases in cancer UC mortality rates, the ratio of UC to TM mentions changed little, that is, non-underlying cause mentions of cancer increased nearly as rapidly as the underlying cause mentions. This ratio increases with age for all four race/sex groups, that is, the relative number of cases for which cancer is not the underlying cause increases rapidly with age. For example, for white males in 1980 through 1982, the TM/UC ratio increases from 11 percent at ages 65 to 69 to 35 percent at ages 85 to 89. This increase is higher for males than females and greater for whites than blacks. This increase partly results from the types of cancer most prevalent at later ages being less lethal (e.g., prostate cancer for males). It may also be a function of (1) persons with other lethal conditions having a tumor found at death (i.e., a large proportion of persons with cancer die of other conditions at later ages), and (2) the fact that tumors may be less aggressive at advanced ages.

Cerebrovascular disease shows major declines in mortality at advanced ages, with UC mentions declining faster than total mentions producing increases in the TM/UC ratios for all race/sex groups. These ratios decline only slightly with age for whites even though the UC rate increases rapidly with age, for example, by a factor of 10 to 15. The evidence suggests that the morbidity process generating cerebrovascular disease deaths is quite stable despite decreases in the UC mention rate.

Like cerebrovascular disease, heart disease has exhibited recent major declines that contributed to life expectancy gains at advanced ages. It is interesting, however, that although UC mortality rates declined rapidly for whites, the TM rate has de-

Table 8–7. U.S. Age-Specific Mortality Rates, Underlying Cause (UC) and Total Mentions (TM), Ratio of Total Mentions to Underlying Cause and Percentage Change in Rates 1968–1970 to 1980–1982, for Four Diseases and Three Elderly Age Groups, by Race and Sex

White

		Age 65–69			Age 75–79			Age 85–89		
		UC	TM	Ratio	UC	TM	Ratio	UC	TM	Ratio
Cancer										
White males	1968–70	787.9	882.3	1.12	1381.1	1612.4	1.22	1709.5	2368.3	1.39
	1980–82	866.6	966.0	1.11	1507.6	1797.7	1.19	2167.4	2931.4	1.35
	% Change	9.99	9.49	-0.89	14.38	11.49	-2.46	26.79	23.78	-2.88
White females	1968–70	441.6	481.8	1.09	706.3	824.2	1.17	1003.1	1296.7	1.29
	1980–82	519.5	565.2	1.09	742.6	852.5	1.15	1103.3	1405.4	1.27
	% Change	17.64	17.31	a	5.14	3.43	-1.71	9.99	8.38	-1.55
Cerebrovascular disease										
White males	1968–70	309.1	504.5	1.63	1082.0	1728.1	1.60	2908.9	4445.8	1.53
	1980–82	160.2	292.5	1.83	619.7	1082.2	1.75	1815.9	3077.7	1.69
	% Change	-48.17	-42.02	12.27	-42.73	-37.38	9.38	-37.37	-30.77	10.46
White females	1968–70	205.5	330.2	1.61	851.7	1332.5	1.56	2755.1	4070.1	1.48
	1980–82	113.1	192.8	1.70	468.1	783.3	1.67	1803.4	2925.2	1.62
	% Change	-44.96	-41.61	5.59	-45.04	-41.22	7.05	-34.54	-28.13	9.46
Heart disease										
White males	1968–70	1831.5	2295.1	1.25	3942.2	5080.3	1.29	8492.5	10818.8	1.23
	1980–82	1396.2	1965.5	1.41	3177.4	4608.1	1.45	7451.0	10815.4	1.45
	% Change	-23.77	-14.36	12.80	-19.40	-9.29	12.40	-12.26	-0.03	17.89

Nonwhite

		Age 65–69			Age 75–79			Age 85–89		
		UC	TM	Ratio	UC	TM	Ratio	UC	TM	Ratio
Cancer										
Nonwhite males	1968–70	998.2	1107.3	1.11	1327.3	1565.0	1.18	1472.7	1862.3	1.26
	1980–82	1172.1	1284.9	1.10	1606.0	1842.5	1.15	2469.2	3135.0	1.27
	% Change	17.42	16.04	-0.90	21.00	17.73	-2.54	67.66	68.34	0.79
Nonwhite females	1968–70	576.2	634.6	1.10	549.9	633.4	1.15	672.5	823.6	1.22
	1980–82	549.5	604.9	1.10	686.3	785.6	1.14	1069.0	1302.1	1.22
	% Change	-4.63	-4.68	a	24.80	24.03	-0.87	58.96	58.10	a
Cerebrovascular disease										
Nonwhite males	1968–70	698.3	1070.3	1.53	1277.4	1958.3	1.53	2229.4	3343.3	1.50
	1980–82	330.6	542.0	1.64	770.8	1252.0	1.62	1663.8	2836.3	1.70
	% Change	-52.66	-47.49	7.19	-39.66	-36.07	5.88	-24.37	-15.16	13.33
Nonwhite females	1968–70	617.1	960.8	1.56	963.1	1475.4	1.53	1762.3	2618.6	1.49
	1980–82	251.6	417.0	1.66	610.1	1004.5	1.65	1565.8	2568.1	1.64
	% Change	-59.23	-56.60	6.41	-36.65	-31.92	7.84	-11.15	-1.93	10.07
Heart disease										
Nonwhite males	1968–70	1997.4	2576.2	1.29	3328.5	4315.2	1.30	5700.6	7172.3	1.26
	1980–82	1485.5	2336.1	1.57	2672.1	4181.1	1.56	6209.7	9547.5	1.54
	% Change	-25.63	-9.32	21.71	-19.72	-3.11	20.00	8.93	33.12	22.22

Note: This rotated table presents death-rate data by cause of death, race, sex, and period. Each race–sex block contains three sub-groups, each shown as two values plus a ratio. Rows are 1968–70, 1980–82, and % Change.

(section continued)

White females

Period									
1968–70	780.4	1002.4	1.28	2409.9	3076.2	1.28	6695.2	8418.2	1.26
1980–82	589.7	898.2	1.52	1795.0	2563.1	1.43	5748.7	7992.6	1.39
% Change	−24.44	−10.40	18.75	−27.38	−16.68	11.72	−14.14	−5.06	10.32

Nonwhite females

Period									
1968–70	1452.4	1887.5	1.30	2104.4	2682.3	1.27	4006.5	4969.2	1.24
1980–82	907.8	1441.8	1.59	1841.1	2774.3	1.51	4684.8	6761.4	1.44
% Change	−37.50	−23.61	22.31	−12.51	3.43	18.90	16.93	36.07	16.13

Diabetes mellitus

White males

Period									
1968–70	67.6	282.9	4.18	149.9	615.5	4.11	244.6	929.0	3.80
1980–82	48.0	227.0	4.73	110.3	514.3	4.66	198.6	862.0	4.34
% Change	−28.99	−19.76	13.16	−26.42	−16.44	13.38	−18.81	−7.21	14.21

White females

Period									
1968–70	70.3	250.4	3.56	171.1	627.7	3.67	244.2	896.9	3.67
1980–82	45.6	175.9	3.86	103.2	427.2	4.14	205.5	825.8	4.02
% Change	−35.14	−29.75	8.43	−39.68	−31.94	12.81	−15.85	−7.93	9.54

Nonwhite males

Period									
1968–70	112.4	321.4	2.86	165.9	482.4	2.91	179.5	533.5	2.97
1980–82	86.0	292.3	3.40	147.2	483.8	3.29	227.3	786.2	3.46
% Change	−23.49	−9.05	18.88	−11.27	0.29	13.06	26.63	47.37	16.50

Nonwhite females

Period									
1968–70	199.9	535.2	2.68	192.2	523.3	2.72	193.0	580.3	3.01
1980–82	125.2	369.2	2.95	170.3	548.5	3.22	301.9	887.6	2.94
% Change	−37.37	−31.02	10.07	−11.39	4.82	18.38	56.42	52.96	−2.33

Pneumonia and influenza

White males

Period									
1968–70	98.3	397.7	4.05	315.1	1166.1	3.70	971.1	3082.9	3.17
1980–82	51.2	215.5	4.21	201.2	719.7	3.58	881.6	2343.8	2.66
% Change	−47.91	−45.81	3.95	−36.15	−38.28	−3.24	−9.22	−23.97	−16.09

White females

Period									
1968–70	43.7	166.0	3.80	159.9	571.4	3.57	652.0	2048.3	3.14
1980–82	23.9	95.7	4.00	101.4	314.4	3.10	524.0	1349.9	2.58
% Change	−45.31	−42.35	5.26	−36.59	−45.03	−13.17	−19.63	−34.10	−17.83

Nonwhite males

Period									
1968–70	182.1	560.6	3.08	376.2	1137.4	3.02	686.0	1944.5	2.83
1980–82	92.3	304.1	3.30	203.7	632.7	3.11	750.5	1768.8	2.36
% Change	−49.31	−45.75	7.14	−45.85	−44.37	2.98	9.40	−10.55	−16.61

Nonwhite females

Period									
1968–70	99.9	308.7	3.09	152.1	467.3	3.07	388.3	990.5	2.55
1980–82	34.3	114.3	3.33	96.1	269.5	2.80	340.8	898.8	2.64
% Change	−65.67	−62.97	7.77	−36.82	−42.33	−8.79	−12.23	−9.26	3.53

[a]Indicates no change.

Source: Tabulations of National Mortality Data 1968–1982.

clined much less rapidly. Thus, the TM/UC ratios have increased markedly at all ages for whites. For example, among white men aged 85 to 89, there has been little decline (0.03 percent) in the rate of occurrence of heart disease reported anywhere on the death certificate—although there was a 12.3 percent decline in the underlying cause report. This again implies a much higher prevalence of multiple chronic diseases at death—an observation that our profile analyses of hospital and death certificate patterns shows is not likely to be an artifact of certification.

The pattern of changes in heart disease morbidity for nonwhites shows one significant difference from that for whites. Above age 85, there is a large increase in heart disease UC and TM mortality for both nonwhite males and females. Below age 85, the heart disease mortality decline is roughly similar to that for whites.

Diabetes differs from the first three conditions because it is not generally viewed as an acutely life-threatening condition. Rather, it operates as a risk factor that increases the risk of stroke and other circulatory disease causes of death because it seems to accelerate the rate of arteriosclerotic degeneration. The UC rates for diabetes show large declines for both race groups at most ages—probably because of declines in mortality from the circulatory disease causes of deaths with which they are associated. The major exception is for nonwhite males and females above age 85 where, for diabetes as for heart disease, mortality increased.

The rates presented here do not relate the risk of the condition to total mortality, which itself changed significantly over this period. Furthermore, we do not know the net shift in the mean time to death from these conditions. This can be estimated by calculating multiple decrement life-tables. Specifically, in multiple decrement life-tables we can calculate (1) the mean time to death from the condition (either UC or TM) in a life-table population, and (2) the proportion of deaths after a certain age that willl result from the condition (again either for the UC or TM). The mean time to death for the five conditions for 1968 and 1982 are presented in Table 8–8 for the four race/sex groups.

The mean time to death from the reported conditions increased from 2 to 16 years to UC mentions and from 2 to 11 years for TM mentions over the interval. Increases occurred even for cancer, which increased in importance as a cause of death.

The relative significance of each cause of death at ages 65 and over and at ages 85 and over is described in Table 8–9, which shows the percentage of all deaths ascribable to the condition in both UC and TM occurrences.

Cancer, heart disease, pneumonia, and cerebrovascular disease increase in importance at advanced ages, while diabetes mellitus decreases. Over time, cancer consistently increases as both UC and TM occurrences, while both stroke and pneumonia decrease. Heart disease is relatively stable in terms of its UC effect on mortality for all race/sex groups above age 85.

To determine if cohort differentials are responsible for changes in the period mortality rates, we present cohort trends for UC and TM mentions of heart diseases, diabetes mellitus, and cerebrovascular diseases for six white male cohorts in Figures 8–3 through 8–5.

In Figure 8–3 we see that there are very large declines in both UC and TM stroke mortality. This suggests that the downward trend in cerebrovascular disease mortality is likely to continue for a number of years, with stroke mortality reaching quite low

Table 8–8 Mean Time to Death and Number of Years Increase Caused by Selected Diseases, 1968 and 1982 by Underlying Cause and Total Mention Occurrences

White males / White females:

Disease	Underlying cause 1968	Underlying cause 1982	Underlying cause Increase	Total mentions 1968	Total mentions 1982	Total mentions Increase
White males						
Cancer	68.45	71.11	2.66	69.43	72.06	2.63
Heart disease	71.70	74.80	3.10	71.76	74.65	2.89
Cerebrovascular disease	76.15	78.70	2.55	75.46	78.43	2.97
Diabetes mellitus	69.83	72.48	2.65	71.35	73.59	2.24
Influenza and pneumonia	70.45	79.95	9.50	71.91	78.02	6.11
White females						
Cancer	69.28	71.61	2.33	70.34	72.69	2.35
Heart disease	79.75	82.61	2.86	79.31	81.58	2.27
Cerebrovascular disease	80.83	83.59	2.76	80.29	83.41	3.12
Diabetes mellitus	74.32	77.30	2.98	75.45	78.10	2.65
Influenza and pneumonia	77.88	85.26	7.38	78.42	83.34	4.92

Nonwhite males / Nonwhite females:

Disease	Underlying cause 1968	Underlying cause 1982	Underlying cause Increase	Total mentions 1968	Total mentions 1982	Total mentions Increase
Nonwhite males						
Cancer	66.25	69.34	3.09	66.88	70.01	3.13
Heart disease	69.23	72.74	3.51	68.70	71.92	3.22
Cerebrovascular disease	70.63	74.12	3.49	70.31	74.46	4.15
Diabetes mellitus	65.64	69.83	4.19	67.48	70.41	2.93
Influenza and pneumonia	58.98	72.83	13.85	63.33	72.65	9.32
Nonwhite females						
Cancer	66.04	70.27	4.23	66.75	71.05	4.30
Heart disease	75.71	80.23	4.52	74.69	78.65	3.96
Cerebrovascular disease	75.94	80.01	4.07	75.52	80.18	4.66
Diabetes mellitus	68.68	73.89	5.21	69.59	74.28	4.69
Influenza and pneumonia	65.72	81.66	15.94	69.65	80.46	10.81

Source: Tabulations of National Mortality Files.

Table 8–9 Percentage of Deaths Caused by Selected Diseases, 1968 and 1982, by Underlying Cause and Total Mention Occurrences

White males / White females

Disease	Underlying cause				Total mentions			
	At age 65+		At age 85+		At age 65+		At age 85+	
	1968	1982	1968	1982	1968	1982	1968	1982
White males								
Cancer	14.27	19.30	7.86	11.77	17.29	23.33	11.13	16.36
Heart disease	45.92	44.02	46.61	46.73	57.80	63.69	58.26	67.21
Cerebrovascular disease	12.40	8.15	16.49	10.74	19.13	14.23	23.79	17.87
Diabetes mellitus	1.56	1.37	1.13	1.05	6.15	6.29	4.17	4.62
Influenza and pneumonia	4.12	3.44	6.46	5.91	13.92	10.51	18.51	15.05
White females								
Cancer	11.05	14.17	5.77	7.53	13.06	16.80	7.62	10.00
Heart disease	46.51	46.62	48.29	50.74	58.14	65.57	59.45	69.33
Cerebrovascular disease	17.18	12.55	19.43	14.64	25.59	20.50	27.55	23.49
Diabetes mellitus	2.45	1.97	1.30	1.44	8.75	8.01	4.76	5.72
Influenza and pneumonia	4.31	3.47	5.96	4.85	13.16	9.49	16.41	11.98

Nonwhite males / Nonwhite females

Disease	Underlying cause				Total mentions			
	At age 65+		At age 85+		At age 65+		At age 85+	
	1968	1982	1968	1982	1968	1982	1968	1982
Nonwhite males								
Cancer	14.63	22.05	8.20	14.49	16.95	25.52	10.48	18.47
Heart disease	39.56	38.70	43.01	42.50	50.03	60.41	52.41	63.99
Cerebrovascular disease	15.06	9.72	16.41	10.46	22.75	16.27	23.56	17.72
Diabetes mellitus	1.74	1.61	1.13	1.26	5.03	6.06	3.46	4.21
Influenza and pneumonia	4.78	3.14	6.60	4.86	13.10	8.77	15.49	11.45
Nonwhite females								
Cancer	9.63	13.60	5.46	7.96	11.10	15.72	6.60	9.82
Heart disease	3.43	43.66	45.18	47.24	53.56	65.03	53.79	66.88
Cerebrovascular disease	9.41	13.20	19.95	14.04	28.92	21.56	28.54	22.71
Diabetes mellitus	3.37	3.16	1.71	2.09	8.77	9.98	4.47	6.51
Influenza and pneumonia	4.20	2.68	5.82	3.80	10.82	7.03	12.95	8.89

Source: Tabulations of National Mortality Data.

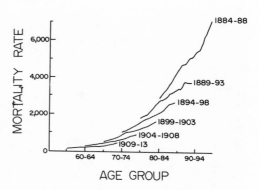

Figure 8–3a Cohort plot of six white male cohorts born 1884–1888 to 1909–1913 for total mention occurrences cerebrovascular disease.

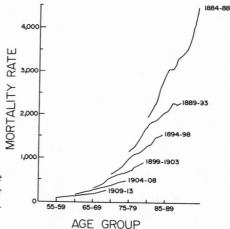

Figure 8–3b Cohort plot of six white male cohorts born 1884–1888 to 1909–1913 for underlying cause occurrences of cerebrovascular disease.

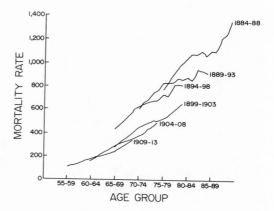

Figure 8–4a Cohort plot for six white male cohorts born 1884–1888 to 1909–1913 for total mention occurrences of diabetes mellitus.

levels. The fact that TM cerebrovascular mortality rates are also declining suggests that cohort differentials are affecting the basic disease process.

The decline for diabetes mortality are less pronounced and consistent than for stroke. For example, for UC diabetes mortality there were large declines between the 1884 to 1888 and 1889 to 1893 and 1894 to 1898 and 1899 to 1903 cohorts, whereas the differentials for other cohorts are less pronounced.

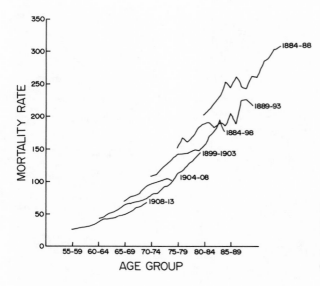

Figure 8–4b Cohort plot for six white male cohorts born 1884–1888 to 1908–1913 for underlying cause mentions of diabetes mellitus.

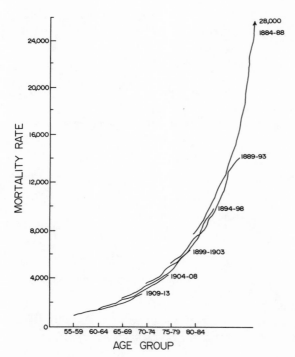

Figure 8–5a Cohort plot for six white male cohorts born 1884–1888 to 1909–1913 for total mention occurrences of heart disease.

For heart disease, there are consistent declines in UC cohort mortality that are not as clearly manifest in the TM data.

The cohort data suggest that recent life expectancy increases at advanced ages may have been determined by risk-factor exposures much earlier in life. The juxtaposition of these cause-specific cohort trends with the parameter estimates for the Gompertz and Weibull cohort models in Table 8–2 suggests that the difference in

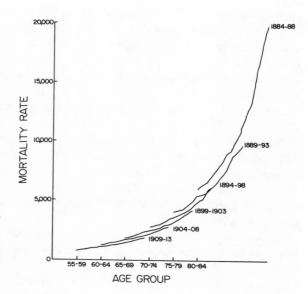

Figure 8–5b Cohort plot for six white male cohorts born 1884–1888 to 1909–1913 for underlying cause mentions of heart disease.

aging trajectories is determined by persistent exposure effects on multiple underlying disease processes, which interact more strongly at advanced age as the prevalence of multiple conditions increases, as suggested by the multiple cause data.

MULTIPLE CAUSE REPORTING AND ITS RELIABILITY

In interpreting cause-specific mortality data, we must be mindful of the quality and nature of the data. For example, it has been argued that the underlying cause of death coding of medical conditions contributing to death is an inadequate characterization of mortality at advanced ages because of the high prevalence of multiple chronic conditions at those ages. Multiple-cause-of-death data have been argued to be a more appropriate description of mortality at later ages. Although multiple-cause data are clearly more appropriate in describing the more complex medical circumstances surrounding death at advanced ages, we must also be aware of questions about the reliability and completeness of these data. Unfortunately, although numerous studies have been conducted of the reliability of underlying cause-of-death data (Manton and Stallard 1984), few studies of the reliability of multiple-cause-of-death reports on the death certificate have been made because of the difficulty in evaluating the large number of patterns of conditions using standard procedures for evaluating concordance and reliability. In this section we examine the reliability of multiple-cause-of-death coding using a multivariate pattern recognition technique.

This procedure, the Grade of Membership model (Woodbury and Manton 1982), involves the estimation of two types of coefficients from data on the pattern of conditions reported for each decedent. One type of coefficient represents the probability that each of K profiles has one of the specific diagnoses of interest. The second type of coefficient relates the person's observed set of diagnoses to each of the analytically defined profiles. Because this coefficient can vary continuously (between 0 and 1 while summing to 1 for all K types), it describes the person's observed medical state at death as a weighted combination of the conditions identified with multiple analytically defined profiles. Thus, the procedure can describe differences in complex sets of diseases recorded for an individual by predicting them as a weighted combination of a small number of base profiles representing the conditions most frequently reported with one another.

We applied this multivariate procedure to diagnostic data on 3,114 persons aged 55 and over who died in one of 22 hospitals in the state of North Carolina between 1975 and 1977. For each of these deaths, three types of diagnostic information were collected: (1) information on 32 medical conditions reported as contributing to death in hospital records; (2) the report of the same 32 conditions from any place on the medical condition fields on the death certificate; and (3) the Automated Classification of Medical Entities (ACME) determination of the underlying cause of death for the same 32 conditions.

In the analysis, the 32 conditions coded from the hospital records were used to define six basic condition profiles. The results of that analysis are presented in Table 8–10.

This table shows that cancers occur with greater frequency than would normally be expected because cancer deaths were over-sampled in order to better describe specific cancer types.

We see that each of the six profiles is well identified by specific sets of diseases. Type 1 is characterized by lung cancer, lymphoma, heart attack, pneumonia, chronic respiratory disease, venous disease, and/or cirrhosis. This pattern is more prelavent among late middle-aged (55 to 64) males. The second type is characterized by colo-rectal cancer, cancer of the breast, and cancer of female reproductive organs. It is more prevalent among late middle-aged females. The third group is characterized by leukemia, lymphoma, and associated infectious diseases (i.e., septicemia, pneumonia, bronchitis, urinary-tract infections). This group is most prevalent among persons of either sex aged 65 to 74. The fourth group is characterized by other solid tumors; pancreatic, liver, or gallbladder cancer, and prostate cancer. Its prevalence is highest among 75 to 84-year-olds. The fifth type has a condition profile similar to the first type, with lung cancer, lymphoma, pneumonia, and chronic respiratory disease. However, it has a lower frequency of multiple conditions (i.e., fewer reported infectious complications) and is more prevalent above age 85. The final type represents major circulatory disease problems (i.e., ischemic heart disease, heart attack, cerebrovascular disease, arteriosclerosis) and associated complications—pneumonia, urinary-tract infection. It is more prevalent at advanced ages.

In order to see how well these profiles related to the profiles of conditions reported on the death certificate, we calculated the probability that a person fitting exactly into one of the profiles described in Table 8–10 had that condition reported on the death certificate. These probabilities are reported in Table 8–10.

A number of small probabilities are noted in Table 8–11 that did not occur in Table 8–10. This is because the variables in Table 8–10 were used to determine the six types so that small probabilities tended to be set to zero whereas the large coefficients tended to be increased as the model maximized the accuracy of the prediction of the observed characteristics. Because the coefficients in Table 8–11 are not "optimized'' (i.e., they are generated conditionally on the profiles described in Table 8–10), the small coefficients remain.

We can see that most of the major features of the six profiles in Table 8–10 are reproduced in Table 8–11, for example, the largest coefficients in this table parallel

Table 8–10 A GOM Analysis of Conditions Recorded in Hospital Records for 3,114 Persons Aged 55+

Variable	Frequency	Profile					
		1	2	3	4	5	6
A. *Infectious diseases*							
1. Septicemia	8.0	0.0	0.0	55.5	0.0	0.0	0.0
2. Urinary-tract infection	10.1	6.7	0.0	27.1	0.0	8.7	21.2
3. Nephritis	1.4	3.8	0.0	1.9	0.8	1.1	0.0
4. Pneumonia	11.5	15.0	0.0	26.9	0.0	13.0	15.2
5. Bronchitis	5.6	0.0	0.0	40.9	0.0	0.0	0.0
6. Other infections	56.3	73.5	100.0	0.0	100.0	0.0	0.0
B. *Neoplasms*							
7. Colo-rectal cancer	6.8	0.0	53.2	0.0	0.0	0.0	0.0
8. Pancreatic, liver, gallbladder cancer	5.2	0.0	0.0	0.0	34.7	0.0	0.0
9. Lung cancer	15.2	52.7	0.0	0.0	0.0	26.8	0.0
10. Breast cancer	4.7	0.0	42.6	0.0	0.0	0.0	0.0
11. Female reproductive system cancer	3.4	0.0	28.4	0.0	0.0	0.0	0.0
12. Prostate cancer	5.1	0.0	0.0	0.0	39.7	0.0	0.0
13. Other solid tumors	36.5	0.0	100.0	0.0	100.0	0.0	0.0
14. Lymphoma	5.1	7.2	0.0	14.6	0.0	7.7	0.0
15. Leukemia	5.6	0.0	0.0	40.7	0.0	0.0	0.0
16. Benign neoplasms	0.2	0.0	1.3	0.0	0.0	0.0	0.0
17. Unspecified neoplasms	0.0	0.0	0.0	0.2	0.0	0.0	0.0
C. *Major circulatory diseases*							
18. Ischemic heart disease	23.0	0.0	0.0	0.0	0.0	0.0	100.0
19. Heart attack	29.9	46.8	0.0	0.0	0.0	0.0	100.0
20. Cerebrovascular disease	12.0	0.0	0.0	0.0	0.0	0.0	80.5
D. *Other circulatory diseases*							
21. Hypertension	4.0	0.0	0.0	0.0	0.0	0.0	28.1
22. Chronic rheumatic heart disease	0.7	0.0	0.0	0.0	0.0	0.0	4.7
23. Arteriosclereosis	6.7	0.0	0.0	0.0	0.0	0.0	47.6
24. Circulatory disease	2.9	0.0	0.0	0.0	0.0	0.0	20.4
25. Venous disease	5.5	11.4	0.0	0.0	3.3	0.0	19.7
E. *Chronic conditions*							
26. Diabetes	5.1	0.0	0.0	0.0	0.0	0.0	34.9
27. Metabolic disorders	0.8	0.0	0.0	0.0	0.0	0.0	5.6
28. Diseases of blood-forming organs	3.4	0.0	0.0	15.7	0.0	5.4	0.0
29. Influenza	0.4	1.2	0.0	0.0	0.0	0.8	0.0
30. Chronic respiratory disease	6.6	20.4	0.0	0.0	0.0	8.8	4.3
31. Digestive disease	1.4	0.0	0.0	10.7	0.0	0.0	0.0
32. Cirrhosis	1.5	8.3	0.0	0.0	0.0	0.0	0.0

Table 8–11 Medical Diagnoses Reported on the Death Certificate for 3,114 Decedents Aged 55+

Variable	Frequency	Profile					
		1	2	3	4	5	6
A. *Infectious diseases*							
1. Septicemia	5.5	7.9	0.1	27.3	0.0	1.6	0.4
2. Urinary tract infection	5.4	4.5	0.0	9.7	2.3	7.8	5.5
3. Nephritis	2.0	5.8	0.0	2.5	0.0	0.6	3.4
4. Pneumonia	11.4	19.4	0.0	20.5	0.0	14.4	11.4
5. Bronchitis	2.3	1.5	0.0	6.3	0.0	4.4	0.0
6. Other infections	2.5	4.3	0.0	7.6	0.0	2.2	0.5
B. *Neoplasms*							
7. Colo-rectal cancer	6.7	0.0	48.6	0.0	2.5	0.4	0.4
8. Pancreatic, liver, gallbladder cancer	4.7	0.0	0.4	1.1	29.7	0.6	0.0
9. Lung cancer	15.5	52.1	0.0	0.0	0.0	27.4	0.0
10. Breast cancer	4.8	0.0	41.8	0.6	0.0	0.0	0.5
11. Female reproductive system cancer	3.3	0.0	26.6	0.0	0.0	0.4	0.0
12. Prostate cancer	5.1	0.0	0.0	1.6	36.6	0.1	0.9
13. Other solid tumors	31.5	6.3	82.0	0.6	100.0	13.3	0.0
14. Lymphoma	5.6	7.9	0.0	16.2	0.0	8.0	0.0
15. Leukemia	5.6	0.0	0.0	38.7	0.0	1.3	0.0
16. Benign neoplasms	0.2	0.0	0.5	0.7	0.0	0.0	0.0
17. Unspecified neoplasms	0.3	0.5	1.3	0.2	0.2	0.1	0.0
C. *Major circulatory diseases*							
18. Ischemic heart disease	21.4	2.7	0.0	3.3	6.5	2.4	100.0
19. Heart attack	19.0	27.2	0.7	5.9	7.3	4.4	76.7
20. Cerebrovascular disease	11.7	4.4	1.1	0.5	1.9	2.0	71.3
D. *Other circulatory diseases*							
21. Hypertension	3.2	0.0	1.2	0.0	0.2	1.2	18.9
22. Chronic rheumatic heart disease	1.1	2.6	0.0	0.0	0.0	0.5	3.7
23. Arteriosclerosis	4.9	1.3	0.0	0.0	0.0	2.0	28.8
24. Circulatory disease	3.3	1.7	0.9	0.0	0.8	0.1	19.5
25. Venous disease	4.3	7.1	1.7	1.0	4.9	1.4	11.0
E. *Chronic conditions*							
26. Diabetes	5.1	1.5	0.0	0.0	1.4	2.0	28.6
27. Metabolic disorders	0.9	0.6	0.0	0.7	0.0	1.1	2.6
28. Diseases of blood-forming organs	2.4	1.3	0.0	8.1	0.0	4.0	0.3
29. Influenza	0.2	0.0	0.0	0.0	0.0	0.2	0.8
30. Chronic respiratory disease	7.3	14.9	0.0	10.4	0.0	10.0	5.2
31. Digestive disease	1.5	0.4	0.0	6.5	0.9	1.0	0.8
32. Cirrhosis	1.1	5.2	0.0	1.1	0.0	0.1	0.0

the nonzero coefficients in Table 8–10. The primary difference between Tables 8–10 and 8–11 seems to be in the size of the coefficients for certain complicating conditions. For example, 56.3 percent of the hospital records recorded some minor infection (e.g., septicemia, pneumonia, bronchitis) compared with 2.5 percent of the death certificates. Heart attack (as opposed to chronic ischemic heart disease) was also more frequently reported on the hospital record (29.9 percent) incontrast to the death certificate (19.0 percent), as was urinary-tract infection (i.e., 10.1 percent vs. 5.4 percent). By comparison, the overall level of reporting of major lethal conditions (e.g., lung cancer 15.2 percent vs. 15.5 percent; ischemic heart disease 23.0 percent vs. 21.4 percent; cerebrovascular disease 12.0 percent vs. 11.7 percent) and chronic complicating conditions (e.g., diabetes 6.6 percent vs. 7.3 percent) is similar in both types of records.

In Table 8–12 we present the probabilities that each of the 32 conditions will occur as the underlying cause of death.

The marginal frequencies in this table are generally smaller than in the two prior tables because only one condition can be reported per decedent. This table is consistent with Tables 8–10 and 8–11 in that the major lethal conditions reported for a profile in those tables emerge as the underlying causes of death. For example, 58.0 percent of deaths in profile 1 are from lung cancer and 21.0 percent and 39.9 percent of deaths for profile 3 are from leukemia and lymphoma. However, the probability of recording a chronic condition or complicating factor is much lower in this table than in Table 8–11 (e.g., diabetes 1.4 percent vs. 5.1 percent; ischemic heart disease and heart attack combined 15.6 percent vs. 40.4 percent; cerebrovascular disease 6.0 percent vs. 11.5 percent; chronic respiratory disease 1.4 percent vs. 7.3 percent).

Several conclusions can be drawn from the analysis. First, the death certificate multiple-cause reporting does a reasonable job in reproducing the multiple conditions reported in the hospital records. Second, the primary differences in the profiles have to do with complicating factors that may vary in their severity so that under-reporting of these conditions on the death certificate may result from the physician's judgment that the condition was not severe enough to have significantly contributed to death. Finally, there are major differences between the cause-of-death structure as reported in the underlying cause-of-death data versus that in either the hospital or multiple-cause-of-death data. Generally, in the underlying cause-of-death data, only major lethal conditions are reported, while many chronic disease risk factors (e.g., diabetes, hypertension) and chronic conditions (cerebrovascular disease) are not. Thus, the multiple-cause death certificate data seem to reliably describe the medical condition of older persons as recorded in hospital records and provide a better representation of the medical status of the person at death than the underlying cause-of-death data.

SUMMARY

In the United States and other developed countries, increases in the life expectancy of the elderly (65+) and oldest old (85+) have been noted. This was surprising because mortality at those advanced ages was generally due to chronic diseases that had been viewed as relatively difficult to treat and manage and because those ages were viewed as being close to the biological limits of the human life span. With these increases, a number of questions arose. One was whether the increase in overall life expectancy was accompanied by a compensating increase in "active" life expectancy, that is, the number of years that a person could expect to remain functionally independent. Second was whether the increase in life expectancy was due to the

Table 8–12 Probability of Conditions Occurring as Underlying Cause of Death for 3,114 Decedents Aged 55 +

Variable	Frequency	Profile					
		1	2	3	4	5	6
A. *Infectious disease*							
1. Septicemia	0.6	0.6	0.0	4.7	0.0	0.0	0.1
2. Urinary tract infection	0.8	0.9	0.0	2.4	0.6	0.5	1.1
3. Nephritis	0.5	1.6	0.0	1.4	0.0	0.0	0.6
4. Pneumonia	2.2	2.8	0.0	5.0	0.0	1.6	4.0
5. Bronchitis	0.6	0.0	0.0	4.2	0.0	0.4	0.8
6. Other infections	0.6	1.5	0.7	0.5	0.8	0.0	0.0
B. *Neoplasms*							
7. Colo-rectal cancer	5.7	0.0	31.5	0.0	0.9	0.0	0.0
8. Pancreatic, liver, gallbladder cancer	4.4	0.0	0.6	0.6	22.4	0.0	0.0
9. Lung cancer	14.4	58.0	0.0	0.0	0.0	47.7	0.0
10. Breast cancer	4.1	0.0	23.0	0.0	0.0	0.0	0.0
11. Female reproductive system cancer	2.8	0.0	15.9	0.0	0.0	0.0	0.0
12. Prostate cancer	3.6	0.0	0.0	1.7	18.4	0.0	0.0
13. Other solid tumors	15.8	2.5	27.5	0.0	53.9	3.6	0.0
14. Lymphoma	4.8	6.6	0.0	21.0	0.0	15.2	0.0
15. Leukemia	4.2	0.0	0.0	39.9	0.0	0.7	0.0
16. Benign neoplasms	0.0	0.0	0.1	0.2	0.0	0.0	0.0
17. Unspecified neoplasms	0.1	0.2	0.4	0.0	0.0	0.0	0.0
C. *Major circulatory diseases*							
18. Ischemic heart disease	14.3	0.0	0.2	0.0	1.8	0.7	51.4
19. Heart attack	1.3	2.6	0.0	0.0	0.0	0.0	3.3
20. Cerebrovascular disease	6.0	0.7	0.0	0.0	0.2	1.6	21.0
D. *Other circulatory diseases*							
21. Hypertension	0.6	0.0	0.0	0.0	0.0	0.8	1.7
22. Chronic rheumatic heart disease	0.6	1.8	0.0	0.0	0.0	1.3	0.6
23. Arteriosclerosis	0.6	0.0	0.0	0.0	0.0	1.0	1.8
24. Circulatory disease	1.6	1.5	0.1	0.0	0.2	0.8	4.7
25. Venous disease	0.8	1.4	0.0	0.0	0.3	1.2	1.5
E. *Chronic conditions*							
26. Diabetes	1.4	0.3	0.0	0.0	0.0	0.0	5.1
27. Metabolic disorders	0.2	0.0	0.0	0.0	0.0	1.3	0.0
28. Diseases of blood-forming organs	0.3	0.0	0.0	2.7	0.0	0.6	0.0
29. Influenza	0.1	0.0	0.0	0.0	0.0	0.0	0.4
30. Chronic respiratory disease	1.4	3.7	0.0	4.4	8.0	3.3	0.0
31. Digestive disease	0.6	0.0	0.0	4.3	0.3	0.7	0.2
32. Cirrhosis	0.6	4.0	0.0	0.0	0.3	0.0	0.0

better control of specific diseases or the net effect of all overall "slowing" of the rate of aging. Third, one would wish to determine the potential for further increases in life expectancy and, finally, the mechanisms by which such increases might occur.

In this chapter we briefly explored these questions using a wide variety of data.

Although no definitive answers were reached, a number of useful insights were produced. For example, it appeared, from longitudinal studies in three countries, that control of known risk factors could both increase life expectancy at advanced ages and increase the period of active life expectancy. It also appeared, from the study of international mortality patterns, that there remains considerable potential for future life expectancy gains at advanced ages. It also appeared that the rate of aging was reduced on a cohort-specific level by intervening in multiple interacting disease processes. These and other insights need more careful analysis in these and other data sets, which are only now becoming available.

REFERENCES

Andersen, P.K. 1986. Time-dependent Covariates and Markov Processes. In *Modern Statistical Methods in Chronic Disease Epidemiology*, eds. S.H. Moolgavkar and R.L. Prentice, 82–103. New York: Wiley.

Barrett, J.C. 1985. The Mortality of Centenarians in England and Wales. *Archives for Gerontological Geriatrics* 4:211–218.

Bayo, R.B., and J.F. Faber. 1983. Mortality Rates around Age One Hundred. *Transactions of the Society of Actuaries* 35:37–59.

Depoid, F. 1973. La Mortalité des Grand Viellards. *Population* 28:755–92.

Economos, A.C. 1982. Rate of Aging, Rate of Dying and the Mechanism of Mortality. *Archives of Gerontological Geriatrics* 1:3–27.

Fries, J.F. 1980. Aging, Natural Death, and the Compression of Morbidity. *New England Journal of Medicine* 303:130–35.

Fries, J.F. 1983. The Compression of Morbidity. *Milbank Memorial Fund Quarterly* 61:397–419.

Fries, J.F. 1984. The Compression of Morbidity: Miscellaneous Comments About a Theme. *The Gerontologist* 24:354–59.

Horiuchi, S., and A.J. Coale. 1983. Age Patterns of Mortality for Older Women: An Analysis Using the Age-specific Rate of Mortality Change with Age. Paper presented at Population Association of America Meeting, Pittsburgh, April 14–16.

Humphrey, G.T. 1970. Mortality at the Oldest Ages. *Journal of the Institute of Actuaries* 96:105–19.

Katzman, R. 1985. Age and Age-dependent disease: Cognition and Dementia. In *Health in an Older Society*, U.S. Committee on an Aging Society, 129–52. Washington: National Academy Press.

Kuroda, T. 1984. Comment. IUSSP-NIRA Seminar on Biological and Social Correlates of Mortality, November 24–27.

Lakatta, E.G. 1985. Health, Disease and Cardiovascular Aging. In *Health in an Older Society*, U.S. Committee on an Aging Society, 73–104. Washington, D.C.: National Academy Press.

Manton, K.G. 1987. The Linkage of Health Status Changes and Workability. *Comprehensive Gerontology* 1:16–24.

Manton, K.G., and E. Stallard. 1984. *Recent Trends in Mortality Analysis*. Orlando, Fla.: Academic Press.

Manton, K.G., E. Stallard, and J.W. Vaupel. 1981. Methods for Comparing the Mortality Experience of Heterogeneous Populations. *Demography* 18:389–410.

———. 1986. Alternative Models for the Heterogeneity of Morality Risks among the Aged. *Journal of the American Statistical Association* 81:635–44.

Manton, K.G., and M.A. Woodbury. 1983. A Mathematical Model of the Physiological Dynamics of Aging and Correlated Mortality Selection: II. Application to the Duke Longitudinal Study. *Journal of Gerontology* 38:406–13.

National Center for Health Statistics. 1986. *State Life Tables, Alabama-Wyoming: U.S. Decennial Life Tables for 1979–81.* Vol. 2, nos. 1–51. DHHS pub. no. (PHS) 8601151. Washington.

Perks, W. 1932. On Some Experiments in the Graduation of Mortality Statistics. *Journal of the Institute of Actuaries* 58:12–40.

Sacher, G.A. 1977. Life Table Modification and Life Prolongation. In *Handbook of the Biology of Aging,* eds. J. Birren, and C. Finch, 582–638. New York: Van Nostrand Reinhold.

Strehler, B.L. 1977. *Time, Cells, and Aging.* New York: Academic Press.

Vincent, P. 1951. La Mortalité des Viellards. *Population* 6:181–204.

Wilkin, J.C. 1982. Recent Trends in the Mortality of the Aged. *Transactions of the Society of Actuaries* 33:11–62.

Woodbury, M.A., and K.G. Manton. 1977. A Random Walk Model of Human Mortality and Aging. *Theoretical Population Biology* 11:37–48.

———. 1982. A New Procedure for Analysis of Medical Classificaiton. *Methods of Information in Medicine* 21:210–20.

World Health Organization. 1984. *Annual Statistics 1984.* Geneva.

———. 1985. *Annual Statistics 1985.* Geneva.

9

Causes of Death Among the Oldest Old

EVAN C. HADLEY

This chapter reviews recent data on causes of death among the oldest old, with particular regard to two topics: the relative incidence of specific causes of death in extreme old age and differences among specific causes of death in their rate of increase with age. Information on these points is of public health value for decisions about health services and disease prevention programs and for monitoring changes in the health of the very old. Such information is also useful for projections of future trends in morbidity and mortality as mortality rates from specific diseases of old age change over time (Brody and Schneider 1986). In addition, data on causes of death at various ages provide clues to the rates of failure of various physiological systems with advancing age. International comparisons of causes of death in very old age also can suggest genetic or environmental factors that may affect late-life mortality.

Unfortunately, the present data on causes of death among the oldest old allow only limited insights on these issues. This chapter discusses the limitations of these data, some tentative conclusions drawn from them, and some possibilities for research.

LIMITATIONS OF CAUSE-OF-DEATH DATA

The studies reviewed in this chapter consist of autopsy series, with the exception of the U.S. vital statistics data based on death certificates. In all the studies, an individual pathology was assigned as the cause of death for each subject. In the reports of Jonsson and Hallgrimsson (1983) and the National Center for Health Statistics (1987), this cause was assigned using the approach recommended by the World Health Organization (1977), in which deaths are ascribed to the underlying cause initiating the sequence of events leading to mortality. (In this chapter, "underlying cause" refers to such pathologies.) In the other studies, the criteria for assigning the cause of death were not stated in detail. However, from the causes of death listed, in most cases it appears that they employed a similar approach to that of these two studies.

Some studies also identified associated or contributory conditions at death. Jonsson and Hallgrimsson (1983) used the approach recommended by the World Health Organization (1977), in which other conditions contributing to death but not directly related to the underlying cause are listed. (In this chapter, "contributory cause" refers to such conditions.) In the other studies the criteria for listing these conditions were not stated.

The cause-of-death data have significant limitations, as the following three sections will demonstrate.

Autopsy-based Data

Autopsies provide much information unavailable antemortem. However, most autopsy studies of the very old to date have presented very limited clinical correlates of their findings. Often their data are confined to anatomic diagnoses whose clinical significance is often uncertain. An additional limitation is the nonrandom selection of cases for autopsy. Many of the studies have been based on hospital series and are hence questionably representative of the general population. Over 20 percent of the U.S. population over 85 years of age are in nursing homes (National Center for Health Statistics, 1987), whose patients are underrepresented in autopsy series (Mortimer 1985). Among hospital deaths there is probably a bias toward interesting or puzzling cases in selecting cases for autopsy.

A particularly significant problem in interpreting autopsy studies on the oldest old is the long time interval over which the deaths occurred. Because of the small number of autopsies per year in this age range at most of the centers conducting these studies, some have included deaths over a period of more than 10 years. Cohort effects and secular changes may confound the interpretation of pooled data on deaths over such a long interval.

Vital Statistics Data

Vital statistics mortality data have significant advantages over the available autopsy data in that they are based on much larger and more representative populations. In addition, because vital statistics have been collected over many years, they permit analyses that can distinguish between cohort, secular, and aging effects on the proportion of deaths due to specific diseases. However, the information available from death-certificate data is limited by the low frequency of autopsies, particularly among the oldest old. A comprehensive study of autopsies in New Jersey during 1979–1980 found that autopsies were performed on only 6.3 percent of men and 4.5 percent of women dying between the ages of 80 and 89 (Ahronheim, Bernholc, and Clark 1983). This was the lowest rate for any age cohort of adults on this study.

The lack of autopsies may be especially detrimental to the accuracy of cause-of-death data on the oldest old because the rate of discrepancy between the clinical and postmortem diagnosis may be particularly high in this age range. A prospective British study found that discrepancies among major International Classification of Disease (ICD) categories (e.g., infective, neoplastic, etc.) between the clinically diagnosed cause of death and the postmortem determination increased from 39 percent in persons dying at ages 65–74 to 53 percent in patients dying over the age of 75 (Cameron and McGoogan 1981). A similar increase with age in the rate of discrepancies was seen in a Swedish study (Britton 1974). Even these high rates may be underestimates because they do not include discrepancies within the major ICD categories (which may be very significant). A recent U.S. study also found that a large proportion of postmortem diagnoses (not confined to causes of death) among subjects over 80 were not made clinically, although the proportion of missed diagnoses in this age range was only modestly higher than for subjects aged 30 through 79. This study did not report the proportions of "false-positive" clinical diagnoses not confirmed at autopsy (Battle et al. 1987).

For some diseases, rates of clinical under- and overdiagnoses may be approximately equal, but it appears that cerebrovascular diseases may be overestimated by clinical diagnoses, whereas diseases of the digestive tract may be underestimated (Cameron and McGoogan 1981). Other studies have found that acute myocardial infarction, Alzheimer's disease, active tuberculosis, pulmonary embolism, and bronchopneumonia tend to be underdiagnosed clinically (Battle et al. 1987; Bobrowitz 1982; Rossman, Rodstein, and Bornstein 1974). Clinical over- and underdiagnoses limit the value of death-certificate data even when they are approximately equal: although they may yield realistic estimates of the frequency of these causes of death, they impair studies of the relationships between antemortem risk factors and death from various causes.

Because autopsy series may have a higher proportion of "difficult" cases than the overall population represented in vital statistics, extrapolating directly from the results of the studies I have cited may overstate the inaccuracy of the vital statistics cause-of-death data. Even discounting for this, however, it would appear that the lack of autopsy information contributes significantly to error rates.

Single– and Multiple–Cause-of-Death Data

The limitations of ascribing a single pathology as the cause of death, and the value of using a multiple-cause approach, have been well described (Israel, Rosenberg, and Curtin 1986; Manton, Chapter 8 in this volume). This is particularly true in extreme old age, when multiple pathologies are very common. Many chronic conditions that contribute to mortality are assigned as the underlying cause of death in a low proportion of death certificates. Indeed, because in some cases certain chronic conditions are not reported on the death certificate at all (Tokuhata, Miller, Digon, and Hariman 1975) even multiple-cause data may underestimate the contribution to mortality of conditions such as diabetes, osteoporosis, Alzheimer's disease, and others.

SPECIFIC CAUSES OF DEATH IN EXTREME OLD AGE

Data from recent autopsy-based studies of persons over the age of 80 appear in Table 9–1. (The study by Jonsson and Hallgrimsson [1983] included a comparison group of young-old subjects. Data on these are also presented in Table 9–1.) National U.S. data based on death certificates also appear for comparison. To facilitate comparisons among the studies, deaths were grouped into the categories shown. Not all studies reported ICD classifications. In these cases, causes were categorized according to ICD-9 criteria (U.S. Department of Health and Human Services 1980) as well as possible from the information reported in the studies.

To allow comparisons of the relative contribution of different causes of death to total mortality, the deaths in each category have been recalculated as a percentage of

Table 9–1 Causes of Death in Older Age Groups (percentage of total deaths)

				DIAGNOSES (ICD codes)								
Study	Age	N and Gender	Population	CV[a] (390–429) (440–448)	MI[b] (410)	CA (140–208)	NEUR[c] (290) (320–359) (430–438)	RESP (460–519)	PNEU[b] (480–486)	DIG (520–579)	UNK	Other
Howell 1965	80–89	156 M 199 F	England	37	3	20	7	15	10	14	0	7
Lockett and Stemmerman 1971	90	25 M 11 F	Hawaii (Japanese immigrants)	31	17	25	3	28	28	11	0	3 (Sepsis 3)[g]
Ishii and Sternby 1978	100	7 M 16 F	Sweden	22	4	9	0	52	48	0	4	13 (Suicide 9)
Ishii et al. 1980	80–89	2,643 M	Japan	≥16[f]	7	24	≥8[f]	≥20[f]	15	≥4[f]	N.D.	N.D.
	80–89	2,077 F		≥17[f]	6	21	≥11[f]	≥15[f]	13	≥4[f]	N.D.	N.D.
	90–99	149 M		≥16[f]	7	17	≥11[f]	≥25[f]	18	≥6[f]	N.D.	N.D.
	90–99	225 F		≥22[f]	8	11	≥13	≥17[f]	15	≥4[f]	N.D.	N.D.
Kohn 1982	85–	85 M 115 F	U.S.	24	N.D.	12	4	16	9	N.D.	26	17 (Trauma 9, infections other than pneumonia 8)

Study	Age	N	Country	CV	MI	CA	NEUR	RESP	PNEU	DIG	UNK	Other
Jonsson and Hall-grimsson 1983	60–70[e]	35 M	Iceland	34	N.D.	37	11	3	N.D.	6	0	9 (Accidents 3)[g]
	60–70[e]	65 F		35	N.D.	29	18	2	N.D.	6	0	10 (Urogenital 3, accidents 5)[g]
	90–	35 M		20	N.D.	17	11	26	N.D.	3	0	22 (Urogenital 11, accidents 11)[g]
	90–	65 F		14	N.D.	29	26	8	N.D.	8	0	14 (Urogenital 6, accidents 8)[g]
Waller and Roberts 1983	90–	11 M / 29 F	U.S.	53	25	18	10	5	0	8	3	5 (Fractures 5)
Tanaka 1984	100–	4 M / 16 F	Japan	10	5	5	5	50	50	5	10	15
NCHS[d] 1987	65–74	279,378 M	U.S.	43	18	29	7	9	2	3	1[h]	8 (Accidents and adverse effects 2)[g]
	65–74	197,192 F		39	15	30	9	7	2	4	1[h]	11 (Accidents and adverse effects 2)[g]
	75–84	270,437 M		45	16	22	10	11	4	3	1[h]	8 (Accidents and adverse effects 2)[g]
	75–84	280,475 F		47	15	18	13	7	3	3	1[h]	12 (Accidents and adverse effects 2)[g]
	85–	136,799 M		49	12	13	12	10	6	3	1[h]	12 (Accidents and adverse effects 2)[g]
	85–	262,667 F		54	11	9	15	8	5	3	1[h]	10 (Accidents and adverse effects 2)[g]

CV: Cardiovascular; MI: myocardial infarction; CA: cancer; NEUR: neurologic; RESP: respiratory; PNEU: pneumonia; DIG: digestive tract; UNK: unknown. N.D.: No data presented. Totals may exceed 100 percent due to rounding.

a Does not include cerebrovascular disease.

b Myocardial infarction and pneumonia are subsets of cardiovascular and respiratory diseases, respectively.

c Includes cerebrovascular disease.

d National Center for Health Statistics.

e Includes a small unspecified proportion of subjects slightly under age 60.

f The "≥" indicator reflects the fact that not all causes of death in this category were listed in this series.

g First figure lists total deaths from other causes. Selected diseases within this group are listed in parentheses.

h Coded as "symptoms, signs, and other ill-defined conditions."

total deaths in the age cohort under consideration. Where possible, the proportion of deaths caused by each disease category was calculated separately for men and for women. Because of the sharp age-related rise in overall mortality rates, a decline with increasing age in the proportion of total deaths due to a particular cause does not imply a decline with age in the incidence per unit of population of deaths due to that cause. Indeed, for each of the causes of death discussed in this chapter, the death rate per thousand increases with age, although the proportion of deaths caused by some of them declines.

Five countries are represented in the studies. The data provide some insights into international differences on patterns of morbidity associated with extreme old age. However, inferences from these differences are limited by the fact that they may also be related to different practices in assigning diagnoses and causes of death.

Several important morbid conditioins that almost certainly contribute to mortality, such as Alzheimer's disease and osteoporosis, are notably missing in the causes of death reported in these studies. This is probably due to the tendency, discussed earlier, to refrain from reporting certain chronic diseases as underlying causes of death.

Cardiovascular Diseases

Although all studies indicate that cardiovascular diseases are an important cause of death throughout extreme old age, the two autopsy studies that compare different older age groups found apparently different trends. Data from the study of Ishii, Hosoda, and Maeda (1980), comparing subjects aged 80 through 89 with those aged 90 through 99, suggest that in Japan the proportion of deaths from cardiovascular disease did not increase with age among men, but did increase in women. An Icelandic study that compared a group who died between the ages of 60 and 70 with a group who died over the age of 90 found that in the older age group, the percentage of cardiovascular deaths was markedly lower for both men and women (Jonsson and Hallgrimsson 1983).

There are no U.S. autopsy-based data comparing death rates of the oldest old with other ages. The two U.S. autopsy studies present widely discrepant percentages of cardiovascular deaths: 24 percent (Kohn 1982) and 53 percent (Waller and Roberts 1983). The former figure may have been lowered by the investigator's skepticism about the possibility of attributing a single cause of death in very old people—26 percent of deaths in this series (far higher than in any other) were deemed to be from unknown causes. Many of these may have been termed cardiovascular deaths by others. Waller and Roberts's figure of 53 percent is roughly consistent with U.S. death-certificate data (National Center for Health Statistics 1987), but markedly higher than any other autopsy series, including those from Western Europe. This study was primarily focused on cardiac pathology. Whether this may have contributed to a disproportionate number of cardiovascular deaths in the series is unknown. The U.S. death-certificate data show a rise in the proportion of cardiovascular deaths throughout the later years of life, with more than half the deaths over the age of 85 attributed to cardiovascular causes.

Among the specific diseases contributing to cardiovascular mortality in extreme old age, only myocardial infarction was reported in enough studies to allow comparisons. The studies vary widely in the proportion of cardiovascular deaths attributed to this cause, from over half (Lockett and Stemmerman 1971) to less than 10 percent (Howell 1965). The higher end of this range is comparable to the proportion found in younger age groups in the United States (National Center for Health Statistics 1987), while the lower end is far below it. Only one American autopsy study reported on acute myocardial infarctions (AMIs) as a cause of death: Waller and Roberts (1983), in a study of 40 subjects dying at age 90 or older, attributed one-fourth of all deaths and almost one-half of cardiovascular deaths to this cause. This is in marked contrast to national U.S. death-certificate data on older persons indicating that the older the age group, the lower the proportion of deaths from AMI (ICD code 410). Less than 12 percent of deaths in persons over age 85 was attributed to this cause (National Center for Health Statistics 1987).

Death-certificate data may underestimate the contribution of AMIs to mortality in the oldest old because the proportion of AMIs with "atypical" clinical presentations increases with advancing age (Bayer, Chadha, Farag, and Pathy 1986). However, it also seems likely that the higher contribution of cardiovascular diseases to mortality in the older age cohorts is due to causes other than acute myocardial infarction. In particular, cumulative damage from ischemic heart disease is implicated with increasing frequency the older the age group: in the U.S. vital statistics, among persons over 85 years old, deaths due to "old myocardial infarction and chronic ischemic heart disease" (ICD codes 412 and 414) comprised 19 percent of all deaths in men, and 22 percent of all deaths in women, compared with 12 and 10 percent, respectively, among persons aged 65 to 74 (National Center for Health Statistics 1987). The terminal processes reported under this diagnostic category are not specified further. It is presumed that congestive heart failure is a major component, but it is possible that this category, and other cardiovascular diagnostic categories such as atherosclerosis, are being used as "wastebasket" terms to describe deaths for which a single cause is difficult to ascribe.

Cancer

The most striking impression from the cancer mortality data on older persons is that, within this group, the older the cohort, the smaller the proportion of deaths due to malignancies, even though age-specific mortality rates from all cancers combined and from most individual major cancers of adult life increase throughout the latter part of the life span. (The main exception is mortality from lung cancer, which declines in the oldest age cohorts.) The U.S. death-certificate data (National Center for Health Statistics 1987) and the autopsy-based studies comparing different age groups in Japan (Ishii, Hosada, and Maeda 1980) and Iceland (Jonsson and Hallgrimsson 1983) show this in all age and sex groups, with the exception of Icelandic women, among whom the share of deaths attributed to cancer was equal in the young old and old old. In addition, the two autopsy studies of centenarians (Ishii and Sternby 1978; Tanaka 1984) found a very low proportion of deaths due to cancer.

However, cancer mortality data confined to deaths in which cancer was the underlying cause may underrepresent the full contribution of cancers to mortality in very advanced age. Many malignancies not deemed to be the underlying cause of death in advanced age may nevertheless contribute to it. This is suggested by an autopsy study that listed contributory causes of death as well as underlying causes and found that cancers contributed to death in 13 percent of persons over the age of 90, in addition to being the underlying cause in 25 percent. In a comparison group of sexagenarians, cancers were a contributory cause of death in 5 percent of subjects and an underlying cause in 32 percent (Jonsson and Hallgrimsson 1983). Thus the total proportion of deaths in which cancers were either an underlying or a contributory cause of death was approximately equal in the two age groups.

Malignancies of the digestive tract, primarily gastric, esophageal, and colorectal, are the most frequent cause of cancer deaths in the oldest old, exceeding deaths from malignancies of any other organ system in all series reporting on specific malignancies (Howell 1965; Ishii et al. 1980; Jonsson and Hallgrimsson 1983; Lockett and Stemmerman 1971; National Center for Health Statistics 1987), and accounting for approximately half the cancer deaths. Breast cancer was relatively infrequent as the cause of death in the British, Japanese, and Hawaiian Japanese autopsy series, but ranked second after digestive-tract malignancies in autopsied Icelandic women over 90 and in U.S. vital statistics data for women over 85. There was a considerable variability in the proportion of deaths due to prostate cancer. The U.S. vital statistics (National Center for Health Statistics 1987), as well as U.S. cancer surveillance data (Horm, Asire, Young, and Pollack 1985) indicate that this malignancy has the fastest proportional increase with age in mortality rates in the later years of life and is the leading single type of cancer mortality in men over age 85.

Neurological Diseases

Alzheimer's disease and related dementias of later life, which contribute to mortality, are marked by their absence from cause-of-death tables. Cerebrovascular disease accounts for the vast majority of the deaths assigned to this category in the studies reviewed, with the exception of that of Jonsson and Hallgrimsson (1983), in which half the neurologically related deaths were ascribed to other factors. There is a great variation among studies in the proportion of total deaths due to cerebrovascular disease. Taking into account the variability among the smaller studies, which one would expect to see on the basis of chance alone, it seems likely that in most populations cerebrovascular disease accounts for between 5 and 20 percent of deaths among persons over age 80, and that the proportion increases with advancing age throughout later life (Ishii, Hosoda, and Maeda 1980; Jonsson and Hallgrimsson 1983; National Center for Health Statistics 1987). It is not clear which, if any, of these figures include dementias, such as multi-infarct dementias, which are related to cerebrovascular disease.

Respiratory Diseases

Although autopsy-based and vital statistics data both suggest an increasing frequency of deaths from respiratory diseases throughout the later years of life, with at least 5 percent of deaths over the age of 85 due to respiratory diseases (Table 9–1), there are noteworthy discrepancies among the studies. The autopsy-based studies tend to attribute a greater share of all deaths (and of respiratory disease-related deaths) to pneumonia than the U.S. vital statistics, in which deaths attributed to chronic obstructive pulmonary disease are also prominent. It is not clear how much this is due to population differences, discovery of clinically important but undetected pneumonias at autopsy, or differences in the interpretation of the clinical significance of the pneumonias.

The cause of the pneumonias is also unclear. It is likely that the incidence of fatal infectious pneumonias increases in successively older age cohorts. However, it is also plausible that a very large share of these pneumonia-caused deaths are from aspiration pneumonias, many in cognitively impaired or obtunded patients. Indeed, it is possible that a very large share of deaths ultimately due to dementias are classified in this category.

In addition to their role as an underlying cause of mortality, respiratory-tract disorders appear to be an important life-threatening complication of diseases contributing to mortality among the oldest old. For example, pulmonary embolism has been reported to be a common life-threatening condition that is often missed clinically in older persons (Taubman and Silverstone 1986). Although only one study (Howell 1965) found pulmonary embolism to be a frequent cause of death among the oldest old, an autopsy series that distinguished between underlying and intervening causes of death (the latter consisting of complications of the underlying causes) found pulmonary embolism to be an intervening cause in 11 percent of sexagenarians and 13 percent of nonagenarians (Jonsson and Hallgrimsson 1983). This suggests that the clinical importance of pulmonary embolism may be understated by data based on underlying cause of death alone.

The role of respiratory-tract infections may be similarly understated if their contribution as an intervening cause of death is not noted: Jonsson and Hallgrimsson found respiratory-tract infections to be an intervening cause of death in 36 percent of the sexagenerarians and 52 percent of the nonagenarians, whereas respiratory diseases were listed as an underlying cause in only 2 percent and 14 percent of these groups, respectively.

Diseases of the Digestive Tract

As with respiratory diseases, there is wide variation among the autopsy-based studies in the share of deaths attributed to diseases of the digestive tract (Table 9–1). American death-certificate data show a lower proportion of deaths due to digestive diseases than almost any of the autopsy studies. This may in part be due to clinical underdiagnosis of digestive-tract diseases antemortem (Cameron and McGoogan 1981).

The specific diseases contributing to this category varied from study to study. Intestinal obstruction was prominent in Howell's series (1965). Gastric ulcer and duodenal ulcer were also common in this series and in that of Ishii et al. (1980). Infectious and/or inflammatory diseases (colitis, cholangitis, pancreatitis) accounted for the deaths in this category observed by Lockett and Stemmerman (1971).

The studies do not yield a clear picture of the relationship of age within the older population to the relative frequency of digestive disease-related deaths. The two age-stratified autopsy studies show no clear trend (Ishii et al. 1980; Jonsson and Hallgrimsson 1983), whereas the U.S. vital statistics suggest that the proportion of these deaths remains relatively constant from age 65 on (National Center for Health Statistics 1987).

Unknown Causes of Death

Despite the report of Kohn (1982) (Table 9–1) that a cause of death could not be found in over one-fourth of autopsies of persons over 85 years of age, all the other studies were able to assign causes to almost all deaths (Table 9–1).

Other Causes of Death

In almost all groups studied, the preceding causes of death account for over 80 percent of the deaths. In only two series did infections other than pneumonia comprise 3 percent or more of causes of death (Kohn 1982; Lockett and Stemmerman 1971). Trauma was quite common in several series (Table 9.1). It is likely that fractures, particularly of the hip, were prominent in this category. Urogenital disorders were common only in the series of Jonsson and Hallgrimsson (1983). Only two reports can be applied to the issue of whether other causes become more or less prominent with advancing age among older persons: Jonsson and Hallgrimsson (1983) found them to be considerably more prominent in nonagenarians compared to a young-old group, whereas U.S. vital statistics show no essential differences among the older age cohorts (National Center for Health Statistics 1987).

CONCLUSIONS

Despite the limitations of the data, some patterns among the major causes of mortality among the oldest old may be discerned.

Cardiovascular Diseases

The differences in the proportion of deaths attributed to cardiovascular disease among very old populations with a variety of genetic, environmental, and lifestyle factors indicate that even at very advanced ages, such factors influence the impact of cardiovascular disease. On the other hand, in all studies, cardiovascular diseases were a major cause of death among the oldest old. This indicates that the progression of cardiovascular pathologies is only partially mitigated by these factors.

The ratio of deaths from chronic ischemic heart disease compared with deaths from acute myocardial infarction is much higher in the oldest old than in the young old, at least in the United States (National Center for Health Statistics 1987). This suggests that continued major decreases in mortality from cardiovascular disease could stem from progress in the treatment of chronic heart disease, as well as progress in prevention and treatment of coronary atherosclerosis and myocardial infarction.

Cancer

The decline in advanced age in the proportion of deaths due to cancer has been noted (Brody and Schneider 1986). This decline is somewhat less dramatic if one includes deaths in which cancer was a contributory cause, as well as those in which it was an underlying cause (Jonsson and Hallgrimsson 1983). The contributory role of malignancies to deaths in very old age may be underestimated in vital statistics data (even when multiple-cause analyses are conducted) because clinical records probably significantly understate the prevalence of malignancies among very old persons. Autopsy studies have revealed an increase with age in the proportion of malignancies detected only after death. Berg, Hajdu, and Foote (1974) found that the percentage of men in whom previously undiagnosed cancer was found at autopsy increased from 9.4 at ages 70 through 79 to 16.5 at ages 80 and above. In women the percentage increased from 4.8 to 7.4 in these age groups. Suen, Lau, and Yermakov (1974) found that the percentage of cancers at autopsy that were clinically undetected rose from 29.4 in persons aged 76 through 85 to 36.2 in those aged 86 and above. Malignancies that were frequently undetected clinically included major contributors to cancer mortality in this age range, such as lung, colorectal, and gastric cancers. Many of these may have contributed to mortality through such effects as inhibition of immune function or morbid weight loss.

Despite the preceding considerations, the weight of the evidence suggests a decline in very advanced age in the contribution of cancers to mortality. Several factors may contribute to this phenomenon. Tumors have been noted to progress more slowly at older ages (Ershler 1986). Also, the higher incidence in younger cohorts of some malignancies, such as lung cancer, may be due to the fact that their exposure to certain carcinogens (e.g., tobacco smoke) is higher than that of the oldest old. As these younger cohorts age, the age of peak incidence of such cancers may increase. This would contribute to future increases in the proportion of deaths among the oldest old due to cancer. The high proportion of undetected cancers in very old age also has implications for projections of future death rates in this age range because it implies that cancer prevalence estimates may be too low among the oldest old. This could lead to an underestimate of future cancer deaths in projections of the effects of reductions in deaths from other causes. The extent to which this effect occurs depends on such factors as the growth rates and metastatic properties of these silent tumors.

Other Diseases

Of the three remaining major disease categories, there is good evidence that, compared with younger groups, a higher proportion of deaths among the oldest old are related to neurologic diseases, particularly cerebrovascular disease, and respiratory diseases, particularly pneumonia. This age difference may be understated in the present mortality data, which do not fully reflect the contributions to mortality of chronic diseases, including many neurological diseases, and of intervening complications of other diseases, among which pneumonias are especially prominent. The share of deaths due to diseases of the digestive tract among the oldest old appears to be roughly the same as in the young old.

Methodological Issues

Many of the most important questions about causes of mortality in the oldest old require an approach that addresses the complex interactions of diseases and the sequences of morbid events they produce. The analytic techniques discussed by Manton in Chapter 8 make this possible.

There are two important general issues to which these approaches could be applied. One is the contribution to mortality of numerous chronic diseases such as diabetes and osteoporosis which are rarely cited as underlying causes of death. Because they do play a role in the causal sequence leading to death, estimates of their contributions would be very valuable. The second is the role of intervening events secondary to the underlying cause. The pattern of these complications of illness differs in the very old from that in younger patients. Analyses to elucidate which of these developments are particularly life-threatening would be very useful.

When applying multiple-cause approaches to these issues, questions such as the following could be addressed: What chronic conditions are associated with fatal pulmonary embolism? How frequently is pneumonia a fatal event in cancer patients? What are the most common terminal events in deaths following hip fracture? What chronic diseases predispose to nutritional deficiencies that contribute to mortality?

However, the value of sophisticated analyses of multiple factors in mortality is limited by the extent and quality of the basic data. Autopsy-based studies on representative populations would remedy some of the gaps in the vital statistics. Further refinement of the criteria and practice by which chronic diseases are reported on death certificates would help to clarify the contribution of such conditions to mortality.

However, many questions about the processes that lead to death among the oldest old require clinicopathological correlations that are not possible with autopsy or vital statistics data alone. These could be accomplished through retrospective or prospective studies. The latter would provide the opportunity to collect standardized data on patients before as well as during their terminal episode of illness.

Such studies would contribute crucial basic knowledge of the pathology of aging and its role in mortality. For example, for some causes of death, such as cardiovascular and cerebrovascular diseases, which appear to become increasingly predominant in extreme old age, it is not clear how much the increase is due to the progression of pathologies from middle age, the development of new pathologies, or greater vulnerability to pathology of a given severity. Such studies could also address an important issue raised by Kohn (1982): many of the pathological findings implicated in the deaths of very old people are not severe enough to cause death in a younger person and hence should not in themselves be termed the causes of death. It is quite possible that there are other factors in extreme old age that, although they are not currently recognized diseases, critically affect survival from recognized diseases, and hence may be equally good or better candidates for causes of death than some of the currently listed major causes of mortality in this age range. Because of the short remaining life expectancy of the very old, relatively short-term prospective studies could monitor the physiological findings and clinical events of the last years of life and compare them with autopsy data. These studies could add much to our understanding of the interacting processes that contribute to our final common pathway.

Acknowledgments—I would like to thank Dr. Richard Havlik of the National Institute on Aging (NIA) for valuable advice regarding the U.S. Vital Statistics data; Karen Patrias of the National Library of Medicine and Joanna Badinelli of the NIA for critical bibliographic assistance; Dr. David Lavrin of NIA for expertise in the preparation of Table 9–1; and Peggy Shaw of NIA for manuscript preparation.

REFERENCES

Ahronheim, J.D., A.S. Bernholc, and M.A. Clark. 1983. Age Trends in Autopsy Rates. Striking Decline in Late Life. *Journal of the American Medical Association* 250:1182–86.

Battle, R.M., D. Pathak, C.G. Humble, C.R. Key, P.R. Vanatta, R.B. Hill and R.E. Anderson. 1987. Factors Influencing Discrepancies between Premortem and Postmortem Diagnoses. *Journal of the American Medical Association* 258:339–44.

Bayer, A.J., J.S. Chadha, R.R. Farag, and J. Pathy. 1986. Changing Presentation of Myocardial Infarction with Increasing Old Age. *Journal of the American Geriatrics Society* 34:263–66.

Berg, J.W., S.I. Hajdu, and F.W. Foote. 1971. The Prevalence of Latent Cancers in Cancer Patients. *Archives of Pathology* 91:183–86.

Bobrowitz, I.D. 1982. Active Tuberculosis Undiagnosed Until Autopsy. *American Journal of Medicine* 72:650–58.

Britton, M. 1974. Diagnostic Errors Discovered at Autopsy. *Acta Medica Scandinavica* 1962:203–10.

Brody, J.A., and E.L. Schneider. 1986. Diseases and Disorders of Aging: An Hypothesis. *Journal of Chronic Diseases* 30:871–76.

Cameron, H.M., and E. McGoogan. 1981. A Prospective Study of 1152 Hospital Autopsies: I. Inaccuracies in Death Certification. *Journal of Pathology* 133:273–83.

Ershler, W.B. 1986. Why Tumors Grow More Slowly in Old People. *Journal of the National Cancer Institute* 77:837–39.

Horm, J., A.J. Asire, J.L. Young, and E.S. Pollack (eds.). 1985. *SEER Program: Cancer Incidence and Mortality in the United States 1973–81.* U.S. Department of Health and Human Services. NIH pub. no. 85-1837. Washington.

Howell, T.H. 1965. Causes of Death in Octogenarians: A Comparison between General Hospital and Geriatric Unit. *Gerontologia Clinica* 7:193–201.

Ishii, T., Y. Hosoda, and K. Maeda. 1980. Cause of Death in the Extreme Aged—A Pathologic Survey of 5106 Elderly Persons 80 Years Old and Over. *Age and Ageing* 9:81–89.

Ishii, T., and N.H. Sternby. 1978. Pathology of Centenarians. III. Osseous System, Malignant Lesions, and Causes of Death. *Journal of the American Geriatrics Society* 26:529–33.

Israel, R.A., H.M. Rosenberg, and L.R. Curtin, 1986. Analytical Potential for Multiple Cause-of-Death Data. *American Journal of Epidemiology* 124:161–79.

Jonsson, A., and J. Hallgrimsson. 1983. Comparative Disease Patterns in the Elderly and the Very Old: A Retrospective Autopsy Study. *Age and Ageing* 12:111–17.

Kohn, R.R. 1982. Cause of Death in Very Old People. *Journal of the American Medical Association* 247:2793–97.

Lockett, L.J. and G.N. Stemmermann. 1971. A Necropsy Study of Nonagenarian Hawaii Japanese. *Journal of Chronic Diseases* 24:433–52.

Mortimer, A. 1985. Perspectives on the Status of the Autopsy. Discussion paper prepared for the U.S. National Academy of Sciences Institute of Medicine Ad Hoc Advisory Committee on Autopsy Policy. (Unpublished.)

National Center for Health Statistics. 1987. *Vital Statistics of the United States, 1984. Vol. 2—Mortality, Part A.* DHHS pub. No. (PHS) 87-1122. Hyattsville, Md.

National Center for Health Statistics, E. Hing. 1987. Use of Nursing Homes by the Elderly: Preliminary Data from the 1985 National Nursing Holme Survey. Advance data from *Vital and Health Statistics,* 135. DHHS pub. no. (PHS) 87-1250.

Rossman, I., M. Rodstein, and A. Bornstein. 1974. Undiagnosed Disease in an Aging Population. *Archives of Internal Medicine* 133:366–69.

Suen, K.C., L.L. Lau, and V. Yermakov. 1974. Cancer and Old Age: An Autopsy Study of 3,535 Patients Over 65 Years Old. *Cancer* 33:1164–68.

Tanaka, Y. (ed). 1984. *Pathology of the Extremely Aged.* Vol. 1—Centenarians. Tokyo: Ishiyaku EuroAmerica.

Taubman, L.B., and F.A. Silverstone. 1986. Autopsy Proven Pulmonary Embolism among the Institutionalized Elderly. *Journal of the American Geriatrics Society* 34:752–56.

Tokuhata G.K., W. Miller, E. Digon, and T. Hartman. 1975. Diabetes Mellitus: An Underestimated Public Health Problem. *Journal of Chronic Diseases* 28:23–35.

U.S. Department of Health and Human Services. 1980. *The International Classification of Diseases: Clinical Modification,* 9th rev. DHHS pub. no. (PHS) 80-1260.

Waller, B.F., and W.C. Roberts. 1983. Cardiovascular Disease in the Very Elderly: Analysis of Necropsy Patients Aged 90 Years or Over. *American Journal of Cardiology* 51:403–21.

World Health Organization. 1977. *International Classification of Diseases. Manual of the International Statistical Classification of Diseases, Injuries, and Causes of Death,* vol. 1, 9th rev. Geneva: World Health Organization.

IV
THE DYNAMICS OF BECOMING
THE OLDEST OLD

10

Disability and Mortality Among the Oldest Old: Implications for Current and Future Health and Long-term-Care Service Needs

KENNETH G. MANTON and BETH J. SOLDO

The aging of the U.S. population has wide-ranging implications for both social and health policy, some aspects of which are well understood and documented. For example, the elderly population is projected to grow to 36.3 million by the year 2000 and to 67.3 million by 2040. We can anticipate many of the changes produced by this growth (Myers, Manton, and Bacellar 1986), such as increases in the proportion of the gross national product devoted to health care. This share grew from 5.3 percent in 1960 to 9.5 percent in 1980 and is projected to reach 12.0 percent by 1990 (Freeland and Schendler 1983a; Rice 1980; Rice and Feldman 1983).

Other aspects of aging trends in the United States are, however, historically unique and are neither well understood nor documented. Four historically unique aspects of current aging trends are (1) the rapid growth of the oldest old (aged 85 and older) population, (2) increases in life expectancy at advanced ages, (3) the predominance of women at advanced ages, and (4) reduction in the age-specific mortality rates of certain major chronic degenerative diseases (e.g., stroke, ischemic heart disease). These historically unique elements of current population aging suggest a need to examine the dynamics of health changes in the oldest old, for their number is projected to increase rapidly (to 5.4 million in 2000; to 13.3 million in 2040) and to become a significant proportion of the total population (4.0 percent by 2040). The improvement in survival at advanced ages suggests that changes in health and the natural history of disease processes may be occurring concurrently.

In assessing health changes at later ages, it is important to employ concepts of health and disease general enough to describe newly emerging patterns. Given the highly selected nature of survivors to extreme old age, it is also important to distinguish between changes in the mechanisms of aging and morbidity at the individual level and the pattern of morbidity and mortality rates expressed at the population level. For example, while the age-specific risk of certain types of cancer may increase throughout life, there may be a tendency for the age trajectory of population mortality rates to flatten, or even decline, at advanced ages due to systematic removal by mortality at relatively young ages of high-risk persons (e.g., heavy smokers). Thus we cannot simply infer the age dependence of morbidity processes for individuals from population rates.

In the following, individual health changes at advanced ages are assessed using a broad range of vital statistic, epidemiological, and longitudinal study data. A general model of health changes based upon cohort and life-course perspectives is presented. This model is used to describe the relation of morbidity, disability, and mortality and the changes of those relations over age. Because no single U.S. data source on the oldest old contains detailed and nationally representative time series information on all three types of health outcomes, the model combines information from a number of studies, each of which is limited in scope, quality, or size.

We also examine the implications of changes in the health of the oldest old for social and health policy. The current public policy concern with the increase in the number of the oldest old is motivated, in part, by the expected impact of this trend on levels of federal expenditures, particularly for chronic-care health services (Fox and Clauser 1980; Freeland and Schendler 1981; Vladeck and Firman 1983). One way to understand these trends is to relate the dynamics of demographic aging to age-specific rates of use for various health services. Assuming no change in either morbidity or service use rates and only gradual declines in rates of old-age mortality, by 2040 there would be a fivefold increase in the number of very old nursing-home residents and the functionally dependent in the community (Manton and Liu 1984a; New York State Office for the Aging 1983; Rice and Feldman 1983). In absolute numbers this translates into an increase of 2.6 to 13.3 million elderly aged 85 and over (Social Security Administration 1981), of whom 4 million would require personal care assistance in the community and, without constraints on nursing-home bed construction, 2.7 million would be in nursing homes. In order to meet the demand for services, the production of long-term-care services (LTC) would have to increase from 6.9 million to 19.8 million daily units of LTC services between 1982 and 2040 (Manton and Liu 1984a).

If current programs are maintained, a major share of the costs incurred in meeting the future health-care needs if the old and the oldest old will be borne by the public sector. Government programs (Medicare, Medicaid, and those of the Veterans Administration) today provide two-thirds of the $120 billion spent for the health care of those aged 65 and over. Nearly 75 percent of the government's 1984 outlay of $80.5 billion was for inpatient care for the elderly—$48.0 billion for hospital care and $12.2 billion for nursing home care (Waldo and Lazenby 1984). The costs of inpatient services have been the fastest growing of any of the national health-care cost categories (Freeland and Schendler 1983b).

Between 1977 and 1984 the costs of health care for the elderly tripled, with their relative share of the gross national product increasing from 2.3 to 3.3 percent (Waldo and Lazenby 1984). Historically, only a small share of the total increases has been attributed directly to growth in the size of the older age groups. Waldo and Lazenby (1984), for example, note that total health-care spending by the elderly grew at an annual rate of 15.6 percent from 1977 to 1984, while that segment of the population aged 65 and over grew only 2.3 percent per annum.

In the future, population aging may have even more effect on health care expenditures than that projected from the absolute growth in the elderly population because dramatic reductions in old age mortality (National Center for Health Statistics 1984) may produce increases in the duration and prevalence of chronic disease morbidity at older ages (Golini and Egidi 1984; Manton and Liu 1984b; Verbrugge 1984).

In addition, health care system changes (e.g., in the coverage and eligibility restrictions of third-party payers) may alter the demand for specific kinds of health-care services, particularly the mix of LTC services. Thus, we extend the model of morbidity, disability, and mortality linkage to include patterns of health service utilization. This formulation provides a framework for discussing changes in the structure and coverage of various health care programs.

A MODEL OF HEALTH CHANGES AT ADVANCED AGES

There is considerable debate over the implications of recent mortality changes for the aggregate health characteristics of the elderly population (e.g., Brody 1983, 1984; Feldman 1982; Fries 1980, 1983; Manton 1982, 1983). To focus this debate, a common conceptual framework to describe health changes at later ages is needed. A model, developed at a World Health Organization (WHO) Scientific Group meeting on the Epidemiology of Aging in January 1983 (WHO 1984) may serve this purpose. The model is constructed from life-table survival curves that describe the change in the proportion of a cohort that can expect to survive to a given age without morbidity, disability, or mortality.

In Figure 10–1 the horizontal axis represents age and the vertical axis describes the probability (expressed as a percentage) of surviving to a given age without suffering one of the health events. The spatial relation of the three curves can be used to interpret changes in the health burden on society of age-related morbidity and disability. Specifically, the areas in the figure are defined by a product of age (time) and the *average* probability of being in a given health state. Consequently, the areas describe the number of person-years the cohort or life-table population occupies specific health states. Area A represents the number of person-years spend free of disease, area B represents the number of person-years spent with chronic disease but unimpaired, and area C represents the number of person-years spent disabled. Areas A and B combined represent productive or active life expectancy.

This model is presented as a conceptual device representing aging and health changes at advanced ages. The model uses the information-organizing power of mathematics to describe complex aging processes.

Figure 10–1 The mortality (observed), morbidity (hypothetical), and disability (hypothetical) survival curves for U.S. females in 1980. (Source: World Health Organization 1984)

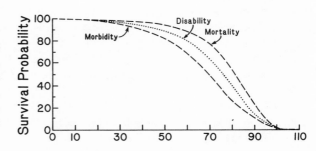

The utility of the model can be assessed by its range of uses. It can be operation-alized in various ways for different types of evidence and questions. For example, it can be used to portray the mortality risks of a cohort. If cohort data are unavailable, period mortality rates can be used to construct a hypothetical life-table. Useful infor-mation can be derived from such a life table, such as the life expectancy at birth that would obtain under the mortality rates for a given period.

We consider three uses of the model: (1) as a conceptual framework to relate different theories of aging-related health changes, (2) as a measure of population health status, and (3) as an actuarial tool for describing the need at the population level for specific types of health services. First, the model is used to examine six different perspectives on health changes at advanced ages.

Strehler (1975), and more recently Walford (1983), have suggested that research into the aging process may identify interventions that could increase the human life span by 25 years or more. Strehler (1975) suggested that such a breakthrough could occur within 35 years, that is by 2010. In discussing health changes produced by such life span extension, Strehler argued that because interventions would be made into the physiological processes determining the age at onset of disease and disabil-ity, the same amount of time would be spent in terminal decline (i.e., the size of area A would increase, but the sizes of areas B and C would be fixed). Consequently, only the productive or active life span would be lengthened. This implies a fixed relation between the curves, with a 25-year shift along the age axis.

In discussing recent trends in health changes in the United States, Gruenberg (1977) and Kramer (1981) suggest that, despite significant increases in life expec-tancy, there is little evidence of changes in the age at onset of morbidity and disabil-ity. Thus, while the morbidity and disability curves in Figure 10–1 remain relatively fixed (i.e., area A unchanged), the mortality curve would be shifted to the right, increasing the number of person-years expected in morbid and disabled states (i.e., areas B and C). These authors suggest that this results from an imbalance between expenditures on disease prevention versus the clinical management of disease.

Fries (1980, 1983) argued for the possibility of the "compression of morbidity" by appropriate lifestyle interventions. Specifically, he suggested that we are rapidly approaching the point in the United States where the survival curve would become "rectangularized," that is, where most persons would survive to the end of their biologically endowed life span and die of "natural death." He suggests that, al-though the mortality curve has become nearly fixed, it is possible, with appropriate interventions, to move the morbidity and disability curves toward the mortality curve, that is, that the age at onset of morbidity and disability would converge toward a relatively fixed age at death. This would compress areas B and C and significantly reduce the number of person-years spent in health-impaired states.

Feldman (1982), in a report for the commission restructuring Social Security, advised caution in changing the entitlement age of the system. The proposed in-creases in entitlement age (i.e., to age 67 by the year 2000) were accepted on the argument that there were age-specific improvements in health status parallel to recent increases in life expectancy at age 65. He proposes a simple model of health state transitions, such as those that must underlie the survival curves in Figure 10–1, which he used to illustrate how life expectancy could have increased, yet with a net increase in the prevalence of chronic morbidity and disability. He argues that the available time-series data are currently inadequate to answer the question of whether health status has truly improved.

Schneider and Guralnik (1988) reviewed a number of recent health surveys and epidemiological studies that showed little evidence of compression of morbidity, that is, reduction of areas B and C. They also showed that the mortality curve at advanced ages was not yet manifesting signs of rectangularization and that significant proportions of U.S. women were already surviving beyond what Fries (1980) has postulated as an "ideal" survival curve (i.e., a life expectancy of 85 years with a standard deviation of ages at death of 4 to 5 years).

Golini and Egidi (1984) simulated the effects on population health status of disease incidence, disease duration, and case fatality. They used a simple one-disease model, and experience representative of Italian morbidity and mortality at advanced ages, to examine the impact on survival, population structure, and disease prevalence of different health interventions. Thus, they were examining the health transitions that would produce a particular age configuration of morbidity, disability, and mortality curves. They found that reasonable changes in case fatality rates and disease duration tended to dominate any likely changes in disease incidence. That is, a 1-year increase in disease duration for a disease like cancer with initially a 2-year average survival increased disease prevalence by 50 percent. They suggested that it would be unreasonable to postulate a decrease in incidence of 50 percent. Consequently they projected, as inevitable, increases in the prevalence of chronic degenerative diseases in developed aging societies.

Riley and Bond (1983) found both a high degree of individual variability in rates of aging changes and maintenance of certain physiological functions, even to the eighth decade of life (Lakatta 1985). These findings suggest that many of the physiological changes associated with aging can be identified with age-related pathological changes and are not directly tied to intrinsic aging processes. This suggests that (1) the three health outcomes are interrelated, (2) changes or interventions at one level will have feedback to other health outcomes (i.e., improvement in morbidity or slowing the rate of progression of chronic disease will have an impact on mortality), and (3) there is greater potential for specific interventions in select dimensions of age-related health changes than have heretofore been recognized (e.g., World Health Organization 1982). This suggests that all three curves can be moved and that, for example, an appropriate allocation of resources can compress the morbid and disabled period, but not with an absolutely fixed mortality curve. Manton (1982) described this interdependence as a dynamic equilibrium of morbidity and mortality—an equilibrium that is played out on multiple interacting dimensions of physiological aging changes. These last perspectives (and Schneider and Guralnik 1988), which reflect the recent scientific evidence on aging processes and health changes at advanced age, suggest that, although Figure 10–1 is a useful conceptual model, its empirical application must consider two further factors.

One factor is the heterogeneity of aging rates and health changes in the extremely elderly population. Riley (1981) recognizes this in terms of cohort differences (i.e., the life-course experience of a cohort is an important determinant of rates of health change at later ages) and the observation that the extreme elderly population is composed of highly selected cohort survivors. It also suggest caution in discriminating between health changes for the individual and the aggregate implications of those changes at the population level. For example, individuals with specific chronic diseases may have those diseases better controlled with a net improvement of life quality; this, however, may lead to increased age-specific prevalence rates due to improved survival and possibly to greater aggregate demands for health services.

A second factor is that the scientific evidence shows that aging changes at advanced ages are multidimensional and that the different dimensions have different trajectories. For example, although certain cardiac output parameters show little degradation with age in the absence of explicit disease (Lakatta 1985), other physiological functions such as renal function show linear declines. Also, many manifestations of aging at advanced ages represent a gradual accumulation of aging changes and not an acceleration of aging processes at advanced ages. To determine the effect of specific interventions, the systematic feedback between interventions for specific organ systems must be examined to determine its effect on the rate of accumulation of aging changes.

As a consequence of these two factors, empirical application of the survival curve model in Figure 10–1 requires analytic procedures that recognize (1) the effects of population heterogeneity and mortality selection on aggregate health changes and (2) the multidimensionality of aging processes at advanced ages. Such procedures have been developed and applied both to cause specific mortality data (e.g., Manton and Stallard 1984) and to community epidemiological data (e.g., Manton, Stallard, and Woodbury 1986). From those analyses, empirical estimates of the transition rates between the various health states in Figure 10–1 can be made. By understanding the health state transitions, one can determine how a population changes health status over time and age (Feldman 1982). This is important in understanding the physiological mechanisms generating those changes, identifying factors affecting the transitions between health states, and projecting the future health status of the population at different ages and for different times (e.g., Manton 1987a; Manton and Liu 1984b; Manton, Stallard, and Tolley 1983).

A second use of the survival curve model is as a measure or index of health status in elderly populations that summarizes the cross-sectional relation of morbidity, disability, and mortality. This is illustrated in Figures 10–2 and 10–3 for Japanese males and females in 1979 and for changes in Canadian males and females from 1951 through 1978.

The curves for Japan were constructed from life tables and several surveys describing the level of medical-care utilization and disease prevalence. Several dimensions of health can be described. First, a cross-sectional comparison of sex differentials in mortality, morbidity, and health-service utilization was made. From Figure 10–2, this suggested a pattern similar to that observed in the United States, that is, women survive longer, report more chronic conditions and use more health services (Verbrugge 1984). Second, cross-temporal comparisons within sex from 1965 to 1979 showed consistent improvement in survival but little improvement in either disease prevalence or degree of medical care received on an age-specific basis. This implied that the number of person-years spent in the morbid and disabled states (areas B and C in Figure 10–1) increased more rapidly than those spent free of disease (area A).

The Canadian figure shows that of 6.0 years gain in life expectancy between 1951 and 1978, overall, nearly 4.7 years were in an activity-limited state. The findings

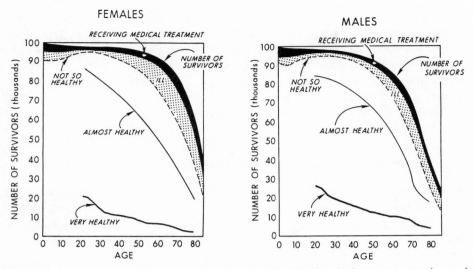

Figure 10–2 Quality of life as seen from state of health first draft, Japanese males and females. (Source: Koizumi 1982)

seem consistent with those discussed for the United States by Schneider and Guralnik (1988).

A third use of the survival curve model is as a device to weight actuarial calculations, not only for changes in life expectancy but also for changes in the portion of life expectancy spent in health states with different health-service needs. Similar models and concepts have been used to describe changes in the proportion of increases in life expectancy that are expected to be spent in "productive man-years" (Sanders 1964) or Quality Adjusted Life Years (QALY) (Shepard and Zeckhauser 1977). QALY involves assigning weights to different disability states in terms of their relation to full functioning or death. The QALY was used, for example, as a measure of health outcomes in reviewing the impact of pneumococcal vaccine (Office of Technology

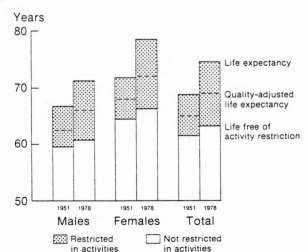

Figure 10–3 Health expectancy at birth by sex, Canada, 1951 and 1978. (Source: Wilkins and Adams 1983)

Assessment 1979). Recently, Katz (e.g., Katz et al. 1983) has been developing and evaluating the use of "active life expectancy" measures as a tool for describing the relative change of functional status and life expectancy at advanced ages. Wilkins and Adams (1983) applied a similar concept in an assessment of health status in the elderly population in Canada. We focus on the implications of the model for the development of models of the *processes* of health changes at later ages rather than for the development of indexes or specific measures.

MORTALITY AND SURVIVAL: RECENT TRENDS

We have described a conceptual model of health status changes at advanced ages and discussed three different uses of that model. In this and following sections, we will discuss the vital statistics and epidemiological evidence on individual components of that model, that is, morbidity, disability, and mortality. Mortality data will be examined first.

Total Mortality Changes at Advanced Ages: The Age-at-Death Distribution

The first model element we examined is the survival curve. There has been debate about whether the survival curve has become increasingly rectangular in recent years. The answer to that question is yes if we examine the entire curve from birth. However, we know that the chronic disease processes that cause most deaths at later ages are different from the causes of infant and childhood mortality and accidental mortality at early ages. Indeed, the apparent rectangularization of the survival curve seems more a function of mortality rates at early ages, having reached low levels relative to the mortality rates among the elderly, than of the mortality changes observed at advanced ages. At advanced ages there is evidence that the upper age bound to survival has increased significantly (~8 years) from 1900 to 1980 (Social Security Administration 1982). Thus, for mortality changes at advanced ages, the evidence on the impact of rectangularization is very different. To illustrate, consider Table 10–1.

In Table 10–1 the means and standard deviations are presented for all deaths occurring in the United States in persons over 60 years of age for several years. Rectangularization, if operational, ought to be manifest in a decreasing standard deviation in the age at death because of the truncation of the age at death distribution by a fixed upper bound to life span (Fries 1980). This reduction should be greatest for those who are closest to the bound, that is, those who die at advanced ages. We see that not only has the mean age at death past age 60 increased, but so has the standard deviation (Myers and Manton 1984).

Fries (1984) suggests that using a fixed age to make this comparison is inappropriate because of the shift of the distribution to more advanced ages. Table 10–2 presents the changes in the age at death distribution for all deaths occurring above the age that delineates a specified proportion of the deaths.

For the last 75 percent of deaths there is a 0.4- and a 0.7-year decline in the standard deviation for males and females, respectively. This decline has, however, been accompanied by increases of 2.2 and 3.6 years in the mean age at death. The

Table 10–1 Means and Standard Deviation of Ages of Death at Ages 60 Years and Over by Sex, United States, 1962–1979

Year	Male Mean age	Male S.D.	Female Mean age	Female S.D.	Total Mean age	Total S.D.	Number	Deaths at all ages (%)
1962	74.1	8.5	76.8	8.9	75.3	8.8	1,209,810	68.9
1967	74.2	8.6	77.2	8.9	75.6	8.8	1,298,800	70.2
1971	74.4	8.7	77.6	9.1	75.9	9.0	1,373,889	71.2
1975	74.5	8.8	78.0	9.2	76.2	9.2	1,387,422	73.2
1979	74.9	8.9	78.6	9.4	76.7	9.4	1,436,416	75.0

Source: National Center for Health Statistics Mortality Data Tapes.

size of the decline in the standard deviation of the age at death decreases as we move further into the tail of distribution, presumably closer to a fixed upper bound. For males, the standard deviation decreases only negligibly after the 66.6 percentile while, for females, the decrease is negligible for the last 25 percent of deaths. Because we would expect the most advanced ages of death to be most affected by a fixed upper bound on life span, this suggests that, up to 1979, the effects of rectangularization had been minimal at the ages where one would expect to see it most in evidence.

The change in the mean age at death for the different groups in Table 10–2 suggests that the 25 percent of all deaths occurring in the United States at the latest ages (nearly 500,000 of the total 2 million deaths in 1979) had a mean age of 84.3 for males and 89.0 for females. This represents an increase of 2.0 years for males and 2.7 years for females over the corresponding 1962 values. Thus, not only has the standard deviation been constant at advanced ages, but the distribution has shifted significantly upward.

An alternative way to examine rectangularization is to take Fries' (1980) parameters describing the "ideal" survival curve and plot that curve against (1) the observed female survival curve for 1980 and (2) the hypothetical male-survival curve

Table 10–2 Means and Standard Deviations of Ages of Death Following Various Percentile Points of Death by Sex, United States, 1962 and 1979

Year	Percentile	Male Mean age	Male S.D.	Female Mean age	Female S.D.	Total Mean age	Total S.D.
1962	75.0	71.6	10.0	76.2	9.3	73.6	9.8
	66.6	73.6	8.7	78.0	8.0	75.6	8.6
	50.0	77.1	6.9	81.3	6.2	79.1	6.7
	33.3	80.5	5.6	84.5	4.9	82.3	5.4
	25.0	82.3	5.0	86.3	4.2	84.8	4.5
1979	75.0	73.8	9.6	79.8	8.6	76.4	9.6
	66.6	75.3	8.7	81.3	7.7	78.2	8.5
	50.0	79.0	6.9	84.7	5.8	81.8	6.6
	33.3	82.4	5.5	87.8	4.5	85.1	5.2
	25.0	84.3	4.9	89.0	4.1	86.8	4.5

Source: National Center for Health Statistics Mortality Data Tapes.

derived from controlling risk-factor changes in the Framingham male cohort (see Figure 10–4).

Both the 1980 female (labeled A) and the optimized male survival curves (labeled C) show much higher survival to advanced ages that Fries' curve (labeled B) (e.g., Manton 1988; Schneider and Guralnik 1988). This is a result of mortality rising much less rapidly than predicted by the Gompertz function at advanced ages. As discussed in Chapter 7 of this volume, the generalized Gompertz and Weibull models with heterogeneity produce a significantly better fit to mortality data at advanced ages.

In Chapter 7 of this volume, mortality trends of both underlying and multiple-cause mortality for major causes of death for the period 1968 to 1982 are described. Hence, we will not reproduce that analysis here except to summarize the mortality trend. In Chapter 8, the limitations of cause-of-death data are described in detail.

Although there were clear trends in the relative significance of the major causes of death after age 85, the mix of causes of death at age 85 was relatively stable from 1968 to 1982. An important change affecting all causes was an increase of at least 2 to 3 years in the mean age at death for most major causes of death. Furthermore, it is notable that several of the conditions for which we have identified major risk factors at earlier ages (e.g., cancer, stroke) remain important at advanced ages, at least suggesting the possibility of further mortality reduction at advanced ages through risk factor intervention. Also important in interpreting mortality patterns was the potential significance of dependent competing risks. That is, for several diseases, mortality rates appeared to have declined because of an association with another chronic condition whose mortality rate had declined (Hachinski 1984). Given the

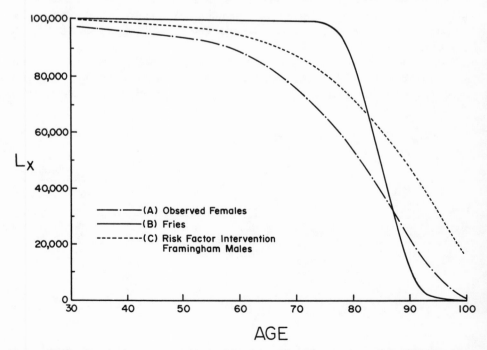

Figure 10–4 Survival curve as proposed by Fries (B) and as estimated for U.S. women observed in 1980 (A) and for Framingham men with risk factor intervention (C).

high prevalence of multiple chronic conditions at advanced ages, such cause dependency is potentially a very important factor in mortality changes.

Certain important morbid states are not reflected in the mortality statistics, notably, for the oldest-old population, Alzheimer's disease. In Chapter 13 of this volume, Evans et al. estimate that over 1 million persons aged 85 and over have clinically diagnosed Alzheimer's disease. By 2000, the number of oldest-old persons affected is projected to be between 2 and 2.5 million; by 2020 the projection is 2.5 to 4.2 million.

MORBIDITY AT ADVANCED AGES

Cross-sectional Patterns

Health "status" is distinct from the "need" for health-care services (Kovar 1980). The former concept refers to self- or physician-appraisal of physical and mental well-being, whereas the latter describes the diagnostic, treatment, rehabilitative, or compensatory regime for supporting or restoring well-being once compromised. Although health status and health-care need are linked as cause and effect, empirically relating one to the other is difficult because both are multidimensional.

Two general approaches that establish the health care requirements of a population may be considered. Note that neither of these specifically operationalize need. Rather, need is inferred from either the patterns of service use or the behavioral consequences of ill health, that is, disability.

The first strategy identifies the medical needs of a population with the distribution and mix of disease states within the population. The most common chronic diseases of the elderly are shown in Table 10–3.

These diseases are a heterogeneous collection of pathologies, ranging from only mildly uncomfortable conditions (e.g., chronic sinusitis), associated with minimal health-care needs, the life-threatening chronic degenerative diseases (e.g., malignant neoplasms and cerebrovascular diseases), associated with extensive inpatient care needs. In the year preceding the death of older (age 65 and over) patients, malignant neoplasms of diseases of the heart and circulatory system account for 84 percent of hospital episodes (Lubitz and Prihoda 1984). These three chronic conditions, together with diseases of the nervous system and sense organs, also account for more than one-third of elderly persons' visits to physicians' offices (National Center for Health Statistics 1980b). The data in Table 10–3 also indicate that the major chronic degenerative diseases convey substantial age-related risks of disability. For both men and women, the six chronic degenerative diseases included in Table 10–4 are consistently associated with higher rates of activity limitations for those aged 75 years of age and over than for younger age groups. The disability impact of cerebrovascular disease is particularly striking. At age 75 and over, 87 percent of males and 61 percent of females with this type of disease are restricted in their usual activity.

The disease-specific approach is frequently viewed as less appropriate for the elderly, in whom multiple chronic diseases interact with each other and with age-related physiological changes in determining health-care needs (Besdine 1984; Minaker and Rowe 1985). The disease-specific basis of assessing health-care needs,

Table 10–3 Top 15 Chronic Conditions Affecting Persons 65 Years of Age and Over: Number of Persons Affected and Rate per 1,000 Persons, by Age: 1981 (numbers in thousands)

Chronic condition	No. of persons affected		Rate per 1,000 persons		
	All ages	65+	<45	45–64	65+
Arthritis	27,283	11,548	47.7	246.5	264.7
Hypertensive disease	25,524	9,407	54.2	243.7	378.6
Hearing impairments	18,666	7,051	43.8	142.9	283.8
Heart conditions	17,186	6,883	37.9	122.7	277.0
Chronic sinusitis	31,036	4,562	158.4	177.5	183.6
Visual impairments	9,084	3,395	27.4	55.2	136.6
Orthopedic impairments	18,417	3,186	90.5	117.5	128.2
Arteriosclerosis	3,398	2,410	.5	21.3	97.0
Diabetes	5,500	2,073	8.6	56.9	83.4
Varicose veins	6,130	2,067	19.0	50.1	83.2
Hemorrhoids	8,848	1,637	43.7	66.6	65.9
Frequent constipation	3,599	1,472	9.2	22.4	59.2
Diseases of urinary system	5,689	1,395	25.8	31.7	56.1
Hay fever	17,874	1,290	100.2	77.5	51.9
Corns and callosities	4,290	1,290	14.0	35.8	51.9
Hernia of abdominal cavity	3,698	1,220	8.9	33.1	49.1

Source: National Center for Health Statistics. Data reported in the U.S. Senate, Select Committee on Aging, 1984, *Aging America: Trends and Projections*. Washington. (Unpublished.)

Table 10–4 Prevalence of Selected Chronic Diseases and of Condition-related Disabilities, by Age and Sex: United States, 1980

Sex, condition, and age	No. of persons with condition[a] (000s)	Percentage with condition	Percentage with condition who are limited
Male			
Malignant neoplasm			
55–64	418	4.20	30.79[b]
65–74	501	7.72	54.48
75+	269	8.96	72.02
Cerebrovascular disease			
55–64	206	2.07	79.82
65–74	331	5.10	87.15
75+	291	9.66	86.86
Hypertensive disease			
55–64	2,448	24.55	27.02
65–74	1,945	29.99	55.88
75+	846	28.18	72.24
Ischemic heart disease			
55–64	675	6.77	49.06
65–74	456	7.03	68.23
75+	351	11.68	76.40
Diseases of the upper respiratory tract			
55–64	1,781	17.86	22.13
65–74	1,114	17.18	41.83
75+	446	14.84	61.35

Sex, condition, and age	No. of persons with condition[a] (000s)	Percentage with condition	Percentage with condition who are limited
Other respiratory diseases			
55–64	2,585	25.93	23.22
65–74	1,626	25.07	58.89
75+	719	23.92	68.54
Female			
Malignant neoplasm			
55–64	495	4.43	13.57[b]
65–74	353	4.06	44.51
75+	353	6.67	52.95
Cerebrovascular disease			
55–64	224	2.00	62.01[b]
65–74	335	3.86	63.65
75+	375	7.09	60.86
Hypertensive disease			
55–64	3,400	30.81	16.53
65–74	3,560	41.01	31.19
75+	2,284	43.10	39.83
Ischemic heart disease			
55–64	390	3.49	35.95[b]
65–74	455	5.24	46.80
75+	343	6.47	55.13
Diseases of the upper respiratory tract			
55–64	2,848	25.51	9.87
65–74	1,926	22.14	24.82
75+	1,013	19.12	41.62
Other respiratory diseases			
55–64	3,217	28.81	14.47
65–74	2,254	25.97	34.81
75+	1,126	21.26	39.87

[a] Population weighted estimates.

[b] Relative standard error equals or exceeds 30 percent of estimate.

Source: Preliminary estimates from 1980 National Medical Care Expenditure Survey prepared by the Research Triangle Institute at the request of the Health Care Financing Administration.

however, is explicit in WHO's (1980) morbidity model and in the design of the Medicare's Prospective Payment System (PPS) for hospital services. Under this system, hospital reimbursements per case are tied to 470 "homogeneous" diagnosis-related groups (DRGs), adjusted for patient age and facility location (Grimaldi and Micheletti 1983).

Employing a model that explicitly recognizes the relationship of chronic degenerative disease to the need for health services is important for forecasting. Physical health status changes can be projected more reliably than functional disability distributions using epidemiological data, relations, and disease etiology. Functional disability forecasts may be improved by first forecasting physical health changes and then determining what those distributions imply for the level and mix of functional disabilities and service needs in the population. This approach calls for the adaptation of the standard medical/epidemiological model (World Health Organization 1983). Examples of such forecasting are provided in Manton (1987b).

Table 10–5 Percentage of the Persons 65 Years of Age and Over Living in the Community with Functional Dependencies, by Age and Sex: 1982

Age and sex	Only IADL limited[a]	Type of dependency			
		ADL score[b]			
		1–2	3–4	5–6	Total
65–74	4.5	4.2	1.8	2.1	12.6
Male	4.2	3.4	1.7	2.4	11.7
Female	4.8	4.7	1.9	1.9	13.3
75–84	7.9	9.0	3.6	4.5	25.0
Male	7.1	6.5	2.5	4.6	20.9
Female	8.5	10.3	4.3	4.4	27.6
85+	10.2	17.4	7.8	10.4	45.8
Male	9.9	15.7	7.7	7.5	40.8
Female	10.3	18.2	7.9	11.8	48.2
Total 65+	6.0	6.6	2.8	3.5	18.9
Male	5.4	5.1	2.3	3.3	16.0
Female	6.4	7.7	3.2	3.6	20.9

[a] Needs assistance with the instrumental activities of daily living (IADL): managing money, shopping, light housework, meal preparation, making a phone call, and taking medication.

[b] ADL score is the sum of the number of ADLs with which respondent requires assistance.

Source: Tabulations from the 1982 Long-term Care Survey prepared by the Center for Demographic Studies, Duke University.

The second strategy for establishing health care requirements reflects a multidimensional functional understanding of health and the need for specific personal and supportive care services. Measures of functional dependency summarize the behavioral consequences of disease in terms of capacities to perform basic activities of daily living (ADL) (Katz 1983). Deficient capacities are viewed as relating directly to the need for assistance, usually from another person, in carrying out such basic functions as eating, bathing, and dressing. As shown in Table 10–5, community residents aged 85 and over have very high rates of functional dependency. Nearly one-half of all these extremely aged are functionally limited in some way, and 1 in 10 are extremely limited in self-care capacity. In addition, nearly 30 percent of all nursing-home residents aged 85 and over are dependent in all four of the ADLs measured in the National Nursing Home Survey (National Center for Health Statistics 1981).

Physiological Changes with Age Over Time

Longitudinal studies permit a more exact characterization of physiological aging and mortality changes within elderly individuals. One type of longitudinal study examines risk factors associated with specific chronic diseases (e.g., Framingham, Evans County). A second type describes individual aging changes. A classic study of the second type is the Duke Longitudinal Study of Aging (1955 to 1976), which involves the application of an extremely broad range of physiological, clinical, and psychological instruments to a relatively small ($N = 267$) but extremely elderly (mean age at study entry was 71.3 years) population 11 times over a 21-year period. The purpose of the study was to describe normal aging changes and to discriminate between those changes and changes due to explicit age-related pathology (Palmore 1970, 1974).

In analyzing these data, we employed a multivariate analytic strategy called "Grade of Membership" (GoM) analysis. The GoM analysis identifies subpopulations that have similar physiological characteristics, demographic attributes, and responses to physical measurements as they relate to morbidity (Clive, Woodbury, and Siegler 1983; Woodbury and Manton 1982). The subpopulations are described by two types of parameters. The first represents the probabilities that persons in a given subpopulation have a particular attribute or quality. The probabilities for each of five subpopulations defined in this way are presented in Table 10–6. These five states can be examined to determine if they describe the trajectory of aging changes in individuals. The second type of parameter represents how well individuals are described by each of the typical characteristics of the analytically identified subpopulations. Hence they represent individual differences not captured by the multivariate descriptions of the subpopulations. In the current analysis, we were less interested in the population distribution over these states than in the description of the aging trajectories implied by the distribution of attributes within each subpopulation. Hence we did not discuss the individual level parameters since, for our current purposes, their function is to ensure that the subpopulation definitions were not confounded with distributional artifacts.

In Table 10–6, the variables (e.g., pulse pressure), and the response intervals (e.g., pulse pressure less than 50) are described on the left, the proportions of the sample with specific attributes are described in column 2, and the next five columns describe the proportions of persons in each subgroup that can be expected to have a particular attribute. We can see that the first four groups are roughly ordered in terms of decreasing health, with the fifth group having manifest morbid changes. We also see that not only are there consistent patterns in terms of physical attributes, but that the last two groups have significantly poorer intellectual performance.

Given these groups defined on physical health and intellectual function, it is important to assess their characteristics in terms of age, survival time, and social status. Because these three sets of variables were *not* used to form the groups, they represent information that is independent of the group definitions. The first four groups are ordered in terms of an increasing average age (i.e., 75.0, 75.6, 79.3, 83.2 for groups 1 to 4). The last group has the lowest expected age (74.8). The first four groups appear to describe the gradual physiological decline with age for the same set of persons followed over the course of the study. The fifth group consists of persons who entered the study physiologically impaired. Although the fourth group is the oldest (83.2), it has fewer explicit pathological changes than the fifth (and youngest) group. The fifth group has the shortest expected survival time. Thus, it appears to be an initially morbid group who died out of the study population fairly rapidly. Both the oldest group and the young, physically impaired group are of lower socioeconomic status and proportionately more likely to be black.

These patterns confirm at the individual level two types of mortality selection processes found in aggregate-level data (Manton, Stallard, and Vaupel 1986). Specifically, the existence of a relatively young, morbid subgroup that dies out rapidly is consistent with models that describe mortality patterns at advanced ages (85 and over) as a result of the rapid mortality selection. Impairment may be either intrinsic (e.g., genetic) or acquired. Both types of impairment will produce the same population mortality patterns if acquired risks are permanent and mortality is analyzed after

Table 10–6 The Probability of Five Subgroups (defined using the GoM methodology) of Having Specific Physiological Characteristics, Duke Longitudinal Study of Aging

Variable	Sample proportion	Subgroups				
		1	2	3	4	5
Pulse pressure						
<50	13.5	32.4	0.0	0.0	0.0	30.3
50–60	17.3	42.7	0.0	0.0	14.2	18.4
61–70	18.1	22.2	20.6	10.0	39.8	0.0
71–80	18.7	0.0	79.4	0.0	0.0	51.4
81–90	12.3	2.7	0.0	22.0	45.9	0.0
90+	20.1	0.0	0.0	68.0	0.0	0.0
Diastolic blood pressure						
<86	13.4	41.4	0.0	0.0	0.0	0.0
86–95	61.0	58.6	100.0	0	100.0	0.0
96–105	20.8	0.0	0.0	100.0	0.0	55.0
116+	4.9	0.0	0.0	0.0	0.0	45.0
Infarction (EKG)	14.2	0.0	0.0	0.0	0.0	100.0
Injury (EKG)	2.2	0.0	0.0	0.0	0.0	100.0
Ischemia (EKG)	24.3	0.0	0.0	0.0	0.0	100.0
Arteriosclerotic etiology	48.6	0.0	0.0	100.0	0.0	100.0
Hypertensive etiology	29.4	0.0	0.0	100.0	0.0	100.0
Rheumatic etiology	6.8	0.0	0.0	100.0	0.0	0.0
Cholesterol						
<206	24.6	0.0	69.2	0.0	80.4	0.0
206–255	41.0	60.2	30.8	39.6	19.6	31.0
256–305	27.0	21.9	0.0	44.0	0.0	61.0
306+	7.4	8.0	0.0	16.5	0.0	7.1
Hematocrit						
<40	25.3	0.0	0.0	55.7	65.9	0.0
40–41	19.9	37.2	0.0	25.0	0.0	40.1
42–45	38.6	43.9	54.6	19.4	34.1	42.0
46+	16.1	18.9	45.4	0.0	0.0	17.0
Arteriosclerotic retinopathy						
None	16.2	0.0	99.9	0.0	0.0	0.0
Grade 1	52.7	99.7	0.0	99.9	0.0	0.0
Grade 2	28.6	0.0	0.0	0.0	94.2	89.0
Grade 3	2.5	0.0	0.0	0.0	5.7	10.0
Grade 4	0.1	0.3	0.1	0.1	0.1	0.0
Hypertensive retinopathy						
None	62.5	68.2	100.0	55.6	53.7	0.0
Grade 1	26.3	31.8	0.0	44.4	46.3	0.0
Grade 2	9.7	0.0	0.0	0.0	0.0	89.0
Grade 3	1.5	0.0	0.0	0.0	0.0	11.0
Overall cardiovascular functional status						
No disease	54.6	100.0	100.0	0.0	0.0	0.0
Definite disease not limiting	28.0	0.0	0.0	69.3	0.0	51.2
Moderate to severe disease	17.4	0.0	0.0	30.7	100.0	48.8
Tobacco use	25.3	0.0	100.0	0.0	100.0	0.0
Sugar						
Absent	96.5	100.0	96.3	91.8	96.5	96.1
Trace	0.6	0.0	1.2	0.0	0.0	3.9
1+	1.0	0.0	2.5	0.0	3.5	0.0
2+ more	1.9	0.0	0.0	8.2	0.0	0.0

Variable	Sample proportion	Subgroups				
		1	2	3	4	5
Albumin						
Absent	87.7	100.0	92.4	100.0	100.0	23.0
Trace	10.5	0.0	0.0	0.0	0.0	77.0
1+	1.2	0.0	7.6	0.0	0.0	0.0
2+ more	0.6	0.0	0.0	0.0	0.0	0.0
Subjective health						
Very poor	2.9	0.0	0.0	0.0	0.0	31.1
Poor	7.3	0.0	0.0	0.0	37.1	0.0
Fair for my age	3.7	0.0	0.0	7.0	12.4	0.0
Fair	20.2	1.1	21.5	0.0	50.6	56.9
Good	28.0	31.4	36.6	56.0	0.0	0.0
Good for my age	18.1	36.3	0.0	37.0	0.0	0.0
Excellent	10.8	31.2	0.0	0.0	0.0	12.0
Excellent for my age	9.0	0.0	42.0	0.0	0.0	0.0
Verbal scaled scores						
<31	11.4	0.0	0.0	0.0	25.1	100.0
31–50	29.6	0.0	0.0	0.0	74.9	0.0
51–70	29.5	0.0	100.0	0.0	0.0	0.0
71–90	25.3	79.8	0.0	100.0	0.0	0.0
91+	4.2	20.2	0.0	0.0	0.0	0.0
Performance scaled scores						
<26	41.2	0.0	0.0	0.0	100.0	100.0
26–40	41.0	42.1	100.0	64.3	0.0	0.0
41–55	16.5	52.1	0.0	35.8	0.0	0.0
56–70	1.4	5.8	0.0	0.0	0.0	0.0
Height (inches)						
<60	9.4	0.0	0.0	45.2	7.7	0.0
60–62	25.3	0.0	0.0	0.0	92.3	0.0
63–65	27.3	61.0	0.0	54.8	0.0	34.0
66–68	22.1	39.0	24.3	0.0	0.0	66.0
69+	16.0	0.0	75.7	0.0	0.0	0.0
Obesity						
2	5.3	0.0	0.0	0.0	0.0	37.9
3	67.2	77.0	55.7	80.4	100.0	0.0
4	23.7	23.0	44.3	8.3	0.0	51.1
5	3.8	0.0	0.0	11.3	0.0	10.0

Source: Duke Longitudinal Study Data Files.

the age of initial impairment. This is consistent with the concept that the population aged 85 years and over is a highly selected group of survivors with special attributes (Riley and Bond 1983). The fact that both the oldest and the youngest, most morbid groups have high proportions of blacks is consistent with explanations of black–white mortality crossovers or convergences (Manton 1980) as due to adverse mortality selection of socioeconomically deprived persons—an observation also made in the Evans County (Wing et al. 1985) and Charleston Heart (Manton, Stallard, and Wing 1991) studies.

A similar type of analysis was conducted on four surveys of persons aged 65 and over conducted in Malaysia, the Philippines, the republic of Korea, and Fiji (Manton,

Myers, and Andrews 1987). The subgroups identified are presented in Table 10–7. Five groups explained the variation on the health measures.

The first group was primarily visually impaired. The second group was functionally intact and healthy but used alcohol and tobacco products. The third group had a broad range of acute medical problems and reported large amounts of hospital use. The fourth group had instrumental activities of daily life (IADL) impairments, while the frail elderly comprised the fifth group.

The sociodemographic characteristics of these groups are presented in Table 10–8.

We see that being male is associated with consumption of alcohol and tobacco products (subgroup 2) and with acute morbidity (subgroup 3). It is interesting to note that subgroup 3, with the greatest morbidity, is the youngest group, consistent with our results from the Duke Longitudinal Study population. Subgroups 4 and 5, who are both very elderly, seem to reflect the healthy and frail extreme elderly subgroups found in the analysis of the Duke community population. Thus, the basic patterns of change of disability and morbidity seem to be found even in these less developed societies.

We have found similar results in several other national surveys and community study populations. Using GoM we usually found a subgroup among the extreme elderly (i.e., mean age over 80) who were healthy and unimpaired and a frail extreme elderly group with multiple chronic diseases (i.e., diabetes, hypertension, dementia, arteriosclerosis) and severe functional impairments. We also tended to find a young subpopulation (mean age in the mid-seventies) with severe acute illness and high rates of service use who had short survival. The presence of this last group possibly explains why mortality curves at advanced ages deviate from the Gompertz curve. This is because of their systematic early selection by mortality.

Table 10–7 The Probability of Five Subgroups (Defined Using the GoM Methodology) of Having Specific Physiological Characteristics, Malaysia, The Republic of Korea, Philippines, and Fiji Disability Study

Variable	Sample proportion	Subgroups				
		1	2	3	4	5
Medical conditions						
Infections/parasitic disease	3.9	0.0	0.0	51.2	0.0	0.0
Cancer	0.3	0.0	0.0	4.0	0.0	0.0
Diabetes	3.7	0.0	0.0	49.0	0.0	0.0
Disease of blood and blood-forming organs	0.5	0.0	0.0	6.8	0.0	0.0
Disease of eye	3.2	0.0	0.0	42.8	0.0	0.0
Hypertension	12.0	0.0	0.0	100.0	0.0	0.0
Cerebrovascular disease	0.9	0.0	0.0	0.0	0.0	12.6
Atherosclerosis	0.5	0.0	0.0	6.4	0.0	0.0
Pneumonia/influenza	1.1	0.0	0.0	14.9	0.0	0.0
Bronchitis	4.0	0.0	0.0	51.6	0.0	0.0
Stomach disease	3.3	0.0	0.0	44.0	0.0	0.0
Rheumatism	15.5	0.0	0.0	100.0	0.0	0.0
Hip fracture	0.4	0.0	0.7	0.0	1.4	0.0
Other	27.7	0.0	0.0	100.0	0.0	0.0

Variable	Sample proportion	Subgroups				
		1	2	3	4	5
Does patient use:						
Cane	7.5	0.0	0.0	0.0	30.7	28.2
Walker	3.4	0.0	0.0	0.0	0.0	41.6
Wheelchair	0.3	0.0	0.0	0.0	0.0	4.1
Leg brace	0.6	0.0	0.0	0.0	0.0	7.9
Back brace	0.3	0.0	0.0	2.7	0.0	0.9
Pacemaker	1.3	0.0	3.4	0.0	0.0	4.9
Glasses	49.8	77.8	0.0	100.0	0.0	52.9
Artificial limb	0.5	0.0	0.0	0.0	0.0	6.9
Hearing aid	0.4	0.0	0.0	0.0	0.0	5.2
Colostomy bag	0.2	0.2	0.0	0.0	0.0	1.0
Catheter	1.7	0.0	4.3	0.0	0.0	7.4
Other	5.1	8.7	0.0	0.0	9.7	0.0
Does person have trouble:						
IADL limitations						
Telephoning	39.0	0.0	0.0	0.0	100.0	100.0
Traveling	33.7	0.0	0.0	0.0	100.0	100.0
Shopping	29.3	0.0	0.0	0.0	100.0	100.0
Preparing meals	17.4	0.0	0.0	0.0	100.0	100.0
Managing money	20.3	0.0	0.0	0.0	100.0	100.0
ADL limitations						
Eating	3.1	0.0	0.0	0.0	0.0	62.3
Dressing	4.1	0.0	0.0	0.0	0.0	100.0
Grooming	4.6	0.0	0.0	0.0	0.0	100.0
Walking	10.5	0.0	0.0	0.0	0.0	100.0
Bathing	6.8	0.0	0.0	0.0	0.0	100.0
Hearing	19.6	0.0	0.0	0.0	0.0	93.1
Seeing	63.6	100.0	0.0	100.0	100.0	84.5
Walking distance of 3 m	23.6	0.0	0.0	0.0	100.0	100.0
Bedfast	6.0	0.0	0.0	0.0	0.0	100.0
Number of incontinent episodes (bowel/bladder)/week						
None	92.0	100.0	100.0	100.0	100.0	23.8
1 or 2	5.2	0.0	0.0	0.0	0.0	48.9
2+	2.9	0.0	0.0	0.0	0.0	27.3
Does person use:						
Tobacco products	40.0	0.0	100.0	0.0	0.0	16.2
Alcohol	29.4	0.0	100.0	0.0	0.0	20.0
Number of sick days in last month						
None	86.4	100.0	92.7	0.0	100.0	34.0
1–3	3.9	0.0	7.3	30.0	0.0	4.1
4–7	2.9	0.0	0.0	70.0	0.0	0.0
8–29	3.6	0.0	0.0	0.0	0.0	38.7
29+	2.1	0.0	0.0	0.0	0.0	23.2
Number of days hospitalized in last month						
None	95.9	100.0	100.0	70.2	100.0	70.0
1–7	2.6	0.0	0.0	29.8	0.0	10.4
7+	1.5	0.0	0.0	0.0	0.0	19.7
Person in nursing home last month	0.9	0.0	0.0	0.0	0.0	12.1

Source: Malaysia, The Republic of Korea, Philippines and Fiji Disability Study.

Table 10–8 Sociodemographic Variables, Grade of Membership Analysis of Malaysia, The Republic of Korea, Philippines, and Fiji Disability Survey

		Subgroups				
Variable	Proportion	1	2	3	4	5
Sex						
Male	41.8	32.3	67.4	79.3	4.9	51.1
Female	58.2	67.7	32.6	20.7	95.1	48.9
Marital status						
Married	58.5	63.4	70.7	88.3	20.5	44.2
Not married	41.5	36.6	29.3	11.7	79.5	55.8
Living arrangement						
Alone	4.4	5.6	4.6	0.0	5.4	0.0
With spouse	53.7	58.0	63.8	93.4	16.1	39.0
With children	82.5	81.6	77.4	90.5	86.3	88.4
With other relatives or friends	11.3	6.8	8.3	40.5	12.0	14.8
With paid helpers	1.9	1.6	0.0	11.8	0.6	2.9
Age						
60–64	26.6	35.4	28.9	46.6	1.0	6.2
65–74	46.6	49.6	55.1	52.0	33.3	23.7
75–84	22.8	14.3	15.1	2.3	53.6	51.4
85+	4.0	0.7	1.0	0.0	12.1	18.8
Years of education completed						
None	48.4	47.0	46.3	0.0	83.6	60.0
1–3	15.0	9.5	16.9	36.6	10.1	13.4
4–6	22.6	28.3	24.3	25.7	6.4	20.8
7–12	12.0	12.9	10.5	34.2	0.0	4.3
12+	1.9	2.3	2.0	3.5	0.0	1.6
Employment status						
Full-time worker	12.8	18.1	20.6	2.4	0.0	0.0
Part-time worker	6.1	7.9	8.8	0.0	3.2	0.0
Unemployed	81.2	74.0	70.6	97.6	96.8	100.0
Who helps you when you are ill?						
No one	13.7	15.0	12.2	9.3	8.9	27.6
Spouse	24.9	28.9	26.4	52.6	3.6	12.3
Child	54.1	51.1	57.8	11.9	77.7	53.9
Relative	6.5	3.5	3.1	26.2	9.2	6.2
Other	0.8	1.4	0.6	0.0	0.6	0.0
Country of residence						
Malaysia	28.2	54.6	3.7	0.4	61.2	6.5
Philippines	23.4	23.7	2.8	64.6	8.7	2.4
The Republic of Korea	27.7	17.7	64.7	0.0	0.9	72.4
Fiji Islands	20.7	3.8	28.8	34.9	29.3	18.7

Source: Malaysia, The Republic of Korea, Republic of the Philippines and Fiji Disability Study.

DISABILITY

Disability in the Life-Table Models

The final component of the conceptual model is disability. In Figure 10–1 we assumed that disability results from the progression of chronic degenerative disease. This concept of a process is explicit in WHOs model of impairments, disabilities, and handicaps (WHO 1980), the origin of which can be found in Susser (1973). In contrast, the standard medical-epidemiological model represents impairments as the result of pathological changes in the organism's physiology. Disabilities represent functional limitations in the organism's ability to perform basic self-care and other functions (e.g., eating, bathing, toileting), whereas handicaps are defects in the ability to perform certain social functions. In this analysis we will assume that disabilities can be measured by Katz's ADL and IADL system (Katz and Akpom, 1976); detailed later in this chapter.

The 1982 and 1984 NLTCS surveys provide detailed information on disability in the noninstitutional population. For a description of the design of this longitudinal survey, see Chapter 5 of this volume. These data provide the basis for estimating transition probabilities. Although we have data on 2,555 persons over age 85, some of the rate estimates presented will be variable, particularly for subgroups of the 85-and-over population. Such estimates and projections should be interpreted with caution.

From the survey, a scale was constructed to represent degree of disability. Because the ADL limitations are based upon a sociobiological model of development (Katz and Akpom, 1976), they can be viewed as hierarchically ordered and may be summed into a simple scale ranging from 1 (least disabled) to 6 (most disabled). We grouped the ADL score into three groups (i.e., one or two limitations; three or four limitations; five or six limitations). Persons with IADL limitations but no ADL limitation were put into a separate category. To understand the pattern of increase of functional limitation with age we present, in Figure 10–5 separately for males and females, age-specific disability levels adjusted to reflect the proportion expected to survive to age x based upon the period life tables prepared for 1980 by Social Security Actuaries.

The graph in Figure 10–5 shows that both the prevalence of disability to all levels and the rates of institutionalization are lower at most ages for men than for women. For example, of persons who survive to age 90, 63 percent of the men either report disability or are in nursing homes compared to 71 percent for women. The increased prevalence of disability among women up to age 90 is correlated with the greater survival of women. The growth of the risk of disability with age is clearly illustrated, with 24 percent of men and 35 percent of women who are either in institutions or have three or more ADL limitations by ages 85 to 89. It should be noted, however, that the proportion of the community population of women over age 85 who report disability does not increase, but actually drops from 38 percent at ages 85 through 89, to 34 percent at age 90 and older. However, if one adds in the proportion of women in nursing homes at these ages, the proportion reporting disability increases.

Thus the apparent stability of disability rates in the community at later ages is due to mortality and institutionalization of highly disabled persons. As a consequence of the selection process, noninstitutional female survivors to ages 90 and over are a very special subpopulation who do not experience degenerative processes at the same rates experienced by persons who died at younger ages. It is interesting to speculate whether, for younger cohorts for whom higher proportions can expect to survive to advanced ages, the increasing heterogeneity at advanced ages will cause the prevalence of disability in the community or increase the proportion of the population who is institutionalized. In this regard it is interesting to note that, while female survival at advanced ages increased, the proportion of the population over age 85 in nursing

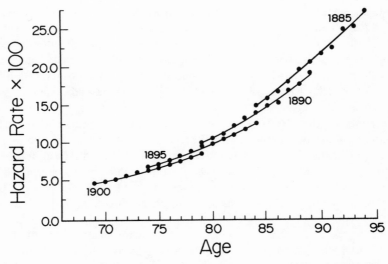

Figure 10–5   The fit of the generalized (i.e., gamma mixed) Weibull hazard function to cohort Medicare population and mortality data. Mortality rates for the male birth cohorts of 1885, 1895, 1895, and 1900 are plotted as are the predicted values (continuous lines) from the model.

homes decreased substantially (i.e., by 15 percent from 253.7 to 216.4) between 1973 and 1977.

To further examine the question of mortality selection we present, in table 10–9, the transition proportions of the NLTCS population between 1982 and 1984.

In this table we present the transitions for both the total population and three age groups. For both the total and age-specific populations, the mortality probability increases with the level of disability. The 5 to 6 ADL group has nearly the same mortality as institutionalized persons. The risk of institutionalization also increases with the level of disability up to 3 to 4 ADLs, where it stabilizes. There are also large proportions of persons with better functional status in 1984 than in 1982, especially for persons aged 65 to 74, but even for persons aged 85 and over. This indicates that there is a significant probability that even chronic disability among the oldest old may improve.

Disability and Morbidity

We can also examine the linkage of mortality and disability using the NLTCS. In Table 10–10, we present the distribution of conditions reported by ADL status and age.

Major lethal conditions like heart disease and cancer cause little chronic disability because of their short survival times. In contrast, conditions like hip fracture, arthritis, and dementia cause the most disability. The amount of disability they produce

Table 10–9 Transition Proportions by Age Group, National Long-term Care Survey, 1982 and 1984

Status and age (years) in 1982	Nondisabled	Status in 1984				Institutionalized	Deceased
		IADL only	1–2 ADLs	3–4 ADLs	5–6 ADLs		
Nondisabled							
65+	79.1	4.6	3.2	1.1	1.0	1.9	9.2
65–74	86.0	3.6	1.9	0.8	0.6	0.7	6.3
75–84	70.1	6.2	4.9	1.4	1.5	3.1	12.8
85+	42.3	7.5	9.3	2.8	3.2	9.7	25.2
IADL only							
65+	11.6	39.1	19.4	4.8	4.1	5.7	15.3
65–74	16.4	45.3	16.4	3.7	3.3	3.1	11.7
75–84	9.4	34.8	21.2	5.7	4.4	7.5	17.1
85+	1.7	30.2	24.1	6.0	6.0	9.5	22.4
1–2 ADLs							
65+	6.5	13.8	33.2	12.2	6.3	7.6	20.6
65–74	8.8	17.5	35.7	12.1	5.3	4.6	16.0
75–84	5.6	13.4	33.5	11.4	5.2	7.7	23.2
85+	3.7	7.6	27.7	13.7	10.1	13.2	24.0
3–4 ADLs							
65+	4.1	4.0	16.8	22.1	19.2	10.0	23.9
65–74	6.7	5.4	22.7	25.7	16.0	4.2	19.3
75–84	2.7	3.5	16.5	20.9	20.0	12.1	24.4
85+	2.1	2.1	7.4	17.9	23.2	16.3	31.1
5–6 ADLs							
65+	3.2	4.5	7.4	8.5	29.9	9.8	36.8
65–74	5.2	6.9	8.8	9.6	31.1	7.2	31.1
75–84	2.9	4.4	7.0	8.6	30.5	10.7	35.9
85+	0.4	0.9	5.7	6.6	26.9	12.3	47.1
Institutionalized							
65+	2.5	1.1	1.0	1.1	1.1	52.9	40.5
65–74	4.4	1.9	1.9	2.2	1.4	58.4	29.9
75–84	3.1	1.4	1.4	0.9	1.2	54.4	37.6
85+	1.1	0.4	0.1	0.7	0.7	48.8	48.1

Source: 1982 and 1984 National Long-term Care Surveys.

increases with age. Thus, instead of recent reduction in circulatory disease mortality at advanced ages causing large increases in disability because disabled persons are differentially saved, it appears that the recent mortality reductions and disability merely increased the exposure time for the disability processes to operate. This is consistent with the view of the aging process as multidimensional and mandates extensive research to establish the risk factors for the specific diseases that produce the most disability.

Projections of Disability in the Community

In Table 10–11 we present projections of the noninstitutionalized disabled population. The projections are of the numbers of persons, specific to marital status, age, and sex, at the four disability levels from 1980 to 2040—the year by which the post–

Table 10–10 Age-specific Conditional Probabilities of Having a Specific Medical Condition for Persons with a Given Disability Level (number of persons in thousands)

Condition and age	Number of persons with condition				
	IADL only	1–2 ADLs	3–4 ADLs	5–6 ADLs	Total
Age 65–74					
Cancer	39.3	36.3	16.1	33.8	125.5
	(5.6)	(5.7)	(5.8)	(10.4)	(6.4)
Diabetes	50.0	70.2	29.2	49.4	198.8
	(7.2)	(10.9)	(10.5)	(15.2)	(10.2)
Dementia	30.5	20.2	3.7	9.6	63.9
	(4.4)	(3.1)	(1.3)	(3.0)	(3.3)
Emphysema and bronchitis	65.5	44.8	22.9	36.8	140.0
	(9.4)	(7.0)	(8.2)	(11.3)	(8.7)
Ischemic heart disease	50.1	33.0	10.9	23.0	117.1
	(7.2)	(5.1)	(3.9)	(7.1)	(6.0)
Hypertension	99.9	87.2	46.3	36.8	270.2
	(14.3)	(13.6)	(16.6)	(11.3)	(13.9)
Arteriosclerosis	207.6	179.2	105.4	166.9	659.0
	(29.7)	(27.9)	(37.8)	(51.4)	(33.8)
Arthritis	213.6	292.2	122.0	90.6	718.4
	(30.5)	(45.5)	(43.7)	(27.9)	(36.9)
Cerebrovascular disease	183.5	170.0	94.7	150.3	598.5
	(26.2)	(26.4)	(33.9)	(46.3)	(30.7)
Hip and other fractures	168.6	216.0	91.0	98.2	572.9
	(24.1)	(33.6)	(32.3)	(30.2)	(29.4)
Total number of persons (in thousands)	700.0	643.0	270.0	325.0	1948.0
Age 75–84					
Cancer	25.5	24.9	6.5	23.8	80.7
	(4.4)	(3.8)	(2.5)	(7.3)	(4.4)
Diabetes	37.0	45.4	17.9	36.6	136.8
	(6.4)	(6.9)	(6.8)	(11.2)	(7.5)
Dementia	81.6	89.6	21.8	53.5	246.5
	(14.4)	(13.7)	(8.3)	(16.4)	(13.5)
Emphysema and bronchitis	25.1	31.3	9.8	17.9	84.12
	(4.3)	(4.8)	(3.7)	(5.5)	(4.6)
Ischemic heart disease	27.3	26.8	13.9	22.0	90.0
	(4.7)	(4.1)	(5.3)	(6.7)	(4.9)
Hypertension	67.3	57.4	22.1	28.7	175.4
	(11.7)	(8.8)	(8.4)	(8.8)	(9.6)
Arteriosclerosis	173.0	206.0	160.0	202.2	687.3
	(30.0)	(31.5)	(40.2)	(62.0)	(37.7)
Arthritis	187.1	272.7	126.0	106.5	692.3
	(32.4)	(41.7)	(47.7)	(32.7)	(38.0)
Cerebrovascular disease	152.9	174.5	91.0	151.8	570.3
	(26.5)	(26.7)	(34.5)	(46.6)	(31.3)
Hip and other fractures	95.4	163.3	81.7	58.5	398.9
	(16.5)	(25.0)	(31.0)	(18.0)	(21.9)

	Number of persons with condition				
Condition and age	IADL only	1–2 ADLs	3–4 ADLs	5–6 ADLs	Total
Total number of persons (in thousands)	577.0	654.0	264.0	326.0	1821.0
Age 85 +					
Cancer	1.5 (0.8)	7.8 (2.3)	1.6 (1.1)	6.0 (3.0)	17.0 (1.9)
Diabetes	4.0 (2.1)	10.4 (3.1)	5.0 (3.3)	9.6 (4.8)	29.0 (3.3)
Dementia	78.8 (40.4)	98.5 (29.5)	44.6 (29.5)	82.7 (41.3)	304.4 (34.6)
Emphysema and bronchitis	3.7 (1.9)	4.9 (1.5)	4.1 (2.7)	1.64 (0.8)	14.3 (1.6)
Ischemic heart disease	6.4 (3.3)	10.4 (3.1)	3.0 (2.0)	9.0 (4.5)	28.8 (3.3)
Hypertension	17.1 (8.7)	29.4 (8.8)	11.3 (7.5)	17.3 (8.6)	75.1 (8.5)
Arteriosclerosis	47.6 (24.4)	96.5 (28.9)	49.2 (32.6)	103.1 (51.6)	296.4 (33.7)
Arthritis	45.1 (23.1)	133.1 (39.9)	63.6 (42.1)	65.1 (32.6)	307.0 (34.9)
Cerebrovascular disease	36.6 (18.8)	79.2 (23.7)	37.4 (24.8)	84.2 (42.1)	237.4 (27.0)
Hip and other fractures	23.6 (12.1)	67.1 (20.1)	37.6 (24.9)	32.5 (16.2)	160.8 (18.3)
Total number of persons (in thousands)	195.0	334.0	151.0	200.0	880.0

[a]Numbers in parentheses indicate conditional probability.

Source: 1982 National Long-term Care Survey.

World War II baby boom cohort reaches age 85. These projections hold constant age, sex, marital status, and disability specific rates (estimated from the NLTCS) and apply them to Social Security population projections.

In the year 2000 we can expect 2.4, 1.0, 1.3, and 2.0 million persons at ADL levels 1 to 2, 3 to 4, 5 to 6, and with an IADL limitation only. By the year 2040 these numbers increase dramatically to 13.1 million persons in the community with at least an IADL limitation (4.6 million with three or more ADL limitations). These projections are based on the assumption that the current rate of institutionalization can be maintained. If it cannot, due to nursing-home-bed constraints, even higher numbers of noninstitutionalized elderly can be expected.

These projections describe the potential population in need of LTC services. They clearly show that the greatest growth will be among unmarried females 75 years of age and over. Interestingly, married males represent a larger population than do married females.

In some ways these projections are a "worst case" scenario because we have assumed that age-specific disability rates remained constant. In effect this assumes

Table 10–11 Projections of the Noninstitutionalized Long-term Care Population and the Institutionalized Population by Age, Sex, Marital Status, and Disability Level, 1980–2040 (numbers in thousands)

Age and year	Noninstitutionalized disability level						Noninstitutionalized disability level					
	IADL	1–2 ADL	3–4 ADL	5–6 ADL	Nursing home	Total[a]	IADL	1–2 ADL	3–4 ADL	5–6 ADL	Nursing home	Total[a]
	Married Males						*Married Females*					
Age 65–74												
1980	217	167	79	136	22	622	143	170	76	85	20	492
2000	256	197	94	161	25	733	175	207	93	104	25	604
2040	399	308	146	250	40	1,143	288	343	153	171	41	996
Age 75–84												
1980	133	114	49	89	39	424	76	73	47	52	29	310
2000	230	198	84	154	67	733	150	145	94	102	58	549
2040	452	389	165	303	131	1,440	310	299	193	211	120	1,133
Age 85 +												
1980	19	46	28	25	24	142	11	14	9	12	14	60
2000	42	98	60	53	51	304	20	24	16	21	24	106
2040	112	263	162	143	137	808	57	68	46	59	68	298
	Unmarried Males						*Unmarried Females*					
Age 65–74												
1980	59	56	30	20	65	230	260	231	86	75	118	771
2000	79	74	39	27	86	305	277	247	92	80	126	822
2040	153	144	76	52	167	592	413	368	137	119	188	292
Age 75–84												
1980	53	65	16	30	90	254	283	365	138	137	339	1,261
2000	82	101	25	47	139	393	416	536	202	201	498	1,853
2040	194	239	59	111	331	933	755	972	367	364	903	3,361
Age 85 +												
1980	39	47	18	19	77	201	111	204	85	130	407	937
2000	67	80	31	33	132	343	253	463	193	294	924	2,127
2040	176	212	82	87	347	904	585	1,069	445	680	2,133	4,912

[a]Totals may reflect rounding errors.

that changes in the morbidity and disability curves in Figure 10–1 are unrelated to changes in the mortality curve. We also evaluate the implications of varying this assumption—for example, of assuming that the projected improvement in life expectancy is a result of improvement in underlying health. If recent reductions in stroke mortality (e.g., after 1972) are a result of reduced incidence due to improved control of hypertension, then this should also lead to a reduction of stroke-related disability in addition to the decrease in stroke mortality. The effect of a strong linkage between mortality reductions and disability rates is portrayed separately for men and women over age 85 in Figure 10–6.

In Figures 10–6 and 10–7, we have assumed that disability rates were reduced, on an age- and sex-specific basis, proportional to the projected mortality rate declines utilized in the Social Security Administration projections (SSA 1981). These projec-

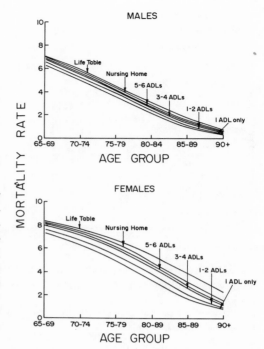

Figure 10–6 Age-specific disability levels adjusted to reflect proportion expected to survive to age *x* based on Social Security Administration period life tables. (Source: NNHS Data Tapes. 1982. U.S. Census Bureau, *Current Population Reports* P25, no. 917, table 2; NLTCS Data Tapes. 1982. SSA Office of the Actuary. *Life-Tables for the U.S. 1900–2059.* Actuarial report no. 87, SSA pub. no. 11–115).

tions show large declines in the disabled population, that is, 17 and 23 percent reduction for men and women aged 85 and over in 2000, and 27 and 34 percent reductions in male and female disability rates in 2040. This translates, for example, into reductions of 318,000; 237,000; 519,000; and 289,000 persons aged 85 and over at disability levels 5 to 6, 3 to 4, 1 to 2, and IADL-only limitations. Thus, if the morbidity and disability curves move jointly with the survival curve, there would be much smaller increases in the disabled population. A more probable scenario is that some improvement in health at advanced ages will occur, but without a perfect correlation between changes in the different curves. This suggests that the projections under the two scenarios (i.e., constant rates vs. linked morbidity, disability, and

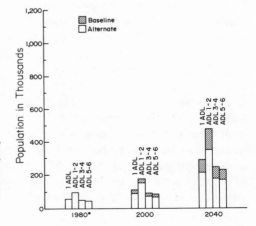

Figure 10–7a Baseline and alternate projections for men aged 85+ in years 1980, 2000, and 2040 (population in thousands). Baseline and alternate figures for 1980 are the same. (Source: National Long-term Care Survey)

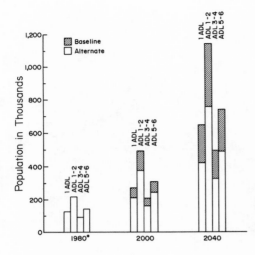

Figure 10–7b Baseline and alternate projections for women aged 85 + in years 1980, 2000, and 2040 (population in thousands). Baseline and alternate figures for 1980 are the same. (Source: National Long-term Care Survey)

mortality) represent upper and lower bounds on the likely future numbers of community-based elderly disabled—and hence bounds on the total need for LTC services.

Identification of Subgroups in the Elderly Community-based Disabled Population

Thus far, we have focused primarily on the quantitative growth of the U.S. LTC population. A different type of analysis, providing insights into the qualitative dimensions of this population, was performed by applying the GoM analysis to the 1982 NLTCS. In particular, the GoM methodology was used to identify subgroups based upon sociodemographic factors and functional limitations. The purpose of the GoM analysis of the NLTCS was different from that of our analysis of the Duke Longitudinal Study. For the Duke study, we were interested in identifying trajectories as age changes in multivariate physiological states. In the NLTCS study, we identify subpopulations who represent different target populations in order to evaluate the effect of policy options on the required service mix. The result of the GoM analysis of the NLTCS is presented in Table 10–12.

In Table 10–12 there are 33 sociodemographic and functional limitation measures. Column 2 lists the probability of a particular attribute being found in the sample. The final four columns show the probability of a particular attribute being found in the four subgroups identified by the analysis. The four subgroups are clearly distinguished by the patterns of association among attributes. Subgroup 1 is relatively young (mean age, about 73), consisting of generally intact couples with relatively few functional limitations. Subgroup 4, in contrast, is seriously disabled and relatively young (mean age, 78). This group has a greater than average chance of being married—probably because such a disabled group would be unlikely to remain non-institutionalized unless the spouse is present. The most interesting groups are the second and third, who are both likely to be female and unmarried. The second subgroup is extremely elderly (mean age, 86) and relatively free of ADL limitations. They suffer from several IADL limitations (e.g., managing money, taking medication) but possess basic mobility (e.g., climbing stairs). This combination suggests significant

Table 10–12 Sociodemographic and Functional Limitation Response Profiles, GoM Analysis of the National Long-term Care Survey, 1982

Internal variables	Sample proportion	Subgroups			
		1	2	3	4
A. Sociodemographic					
1. Sex					
Men	34.1	63.6	27.2	0.0	47.1
Women	65.9	36.4	72.8	100.0	52.9
2. Age					
65–69	18.9	34.4	0.0	14.6	19.2
70–74	21.7	30.3	0.0	30.7	21.1
75–79	21.9	26.2	5.4	31.4	21.7
80–84	18.6	9.2	31.0	23.3	15.3
85–89	12.7	0.0	45.9	0.0	12.2
90+	6.2	0.0	17.7	0.0	10.6
3. Marital status					
Married	41.4	77.8	0.0	0.0	65.2
Not married	58.6	22.2	100.0	100.0	34.8
4. Education					
Never attended school	5.5	0.0	22.6	0.0	6.8
Grades 1 through 8	21.6	13.2	41.0	21.1	18.8
Junior high school	33.2	29.8	16.4	49.5	31.1
Senior high school	27.8	38.5	14.9	22.2	29.7
College	10.2	15.4	5.0	6.5	11.3
Graduate school	1.7	3.1	0.1	0.7	2.3
5. Employed ≥ 30 hours/week (binary)	1.4	4.3	0.0	0.0	0.0
6. Income					
≤ $4,999	18.5	0.0	0.0	56.7	6.1
$5,000–$6,999	14.5	17.5	12.4	17.1	8.0
$7,000–$9,999	16.1	22.1	6.7	10.4	22.2
$10,000–$14,999	15.1	29.1	0.0	0.0	27.1
$15,000–$29,999	12.5	15.1	19.0	0.0	21.2
$30,000+	4.4	2.8	14.8	0.0	5.1
Refused to answer	5.9	6.1	8.9	5.4	4.1
Do not know	13.0	7.3	38.2	10.4	6.2
B. Functional status					
IADL or ADL respondent needs help with (individual binary variables):					
7. Eating	7.3	0.0	0.0	0.0	39.2
8. Getting into/out of bed	29.6	0.0	0.0	24.7	100.0
9. Getting around indoors	44.2	9.2	0.0	63.6	100.0
10. Dressing	22.9	0.0	0.0	0.0	100.0
11. Bathing	47.4	10.1	34.7	47.6	100.0
12. Getting to or using toilet	22.9	0.0	0.0	0.0	100.0
13. Bedfast	1.2	0.0	0.0	0.0	5.6
14. Did not get around inside at all	1.8	0.0	0.0	0.0	8.5
15. Wheelchair fast	3.6	0.0	0.0	0.0	17.3
16. Doing heavy work	82.9	49.0	100.0	100.0	100.0
17. Doing light work	27.8	0.0	0.0	0.0	100.0
18. Doing laundry	51.3	0.0	50.6	50.6	100.0
19. Preparing meals	37.0	0.0	0.0	0.0	100.0
20. Shopping for groceries	69.1	0.0	100.0	100.0	100.0
21. Getting around outside	68.6	26.6	61.8	100.0	100.0

Table 10–12   (*Continued*)

Internal variables	Sample proportion	Subgroups			
		1	2	3	4
22. Going places outside of walking distance	63.6	0.0	100.0	100.0	100.0
23. Managing money	31.2	0.0	100.0	0.0	81.9
24. Taking medicine	27.5	0.0	71.4	0.0	100.0
25. Making phone calls	20.6	0.0	64.6	0.0	65.2
26. Difficulty climbing stairs					
No difficulty	12.6	32.1	27.4	0.0	0.0
Some difficulty	28.8	67.9	72.6	0.0	0.0
Very difficult	34.2	0.0	0.0	80.6	13.2
Unable at all	24.4	0.0	0.0	19.4	86.8
27. Difficulty bending for socks					
No difficulty	37.0	76.9	77.5	0.0	0.0
Some difficulty	30.4	23.1	22.5	54.7	8.4
Very difficult	20.8	0.0	0.0	45.3	31.0
Unable at all	11.8	0.0	0.0	0.0	60.6
28. Difficulty lifting and holding 10-lb package					
No difficulty	22.3	66.5	26.0	0.0	0.0
Some difficulty	17.7	33.5	52.2	5.7	0.0
Very difficult	18.3	0.0	21.8	42.6	0.0
Unable at all	41.7	0.0	0.0	51.7	100.0
29. Difficulty reaching above head					
No difficulty	49.4	100.0	100.0	0.0	0.0
Some difficulty	22.9	0.0	0.0	55.0	26.2
Very difficult	17.0	0.0	0.0	34.3	32.4
Unable at all	10.7	0.0	0.0	10.7	41.4
30. Difficulty brushing or combing hair					
No difficulty	66.6	100.0	100.0	15.8	0.0
Some difficulty	18.3	0.0	0.0	64.3	30.1
Very difficult	8.5	0.0	0.0	19.9	27.5
Unable at all	6.6	0.0	0.0	0.0	42.4
31. Difficulty washing hair					
No difficulty	49.0	100.0	95.1	0.0	0.0
Some difficulty	16.1	0.0	4.9	59.6	0.0
Very difficult	11.4	0.0	0.0	40.4	3.8
Unable at all	23.5	0.0	0.0	0.0	96.2
32. Difficulty grasping and handling small objects					
No difficulty	63.0	100.0	100.0	20.4	32.8
Some difficulty	20.2	0.0	0.0	55.6	19.7
Very difficult	12.6	0.0	0.0	23.9	27.4
Unable at all	4.2	0.0	0.0	0.0	20.1
33. Can see well enough to read news-print with glasses	70.7	100.0	0.0	100.0	53.3

Source: Analysis of National Long-term Care Survey.

cognitive impairment relatively independent of serious physical impairment. In contrast, the third group is younger (mean age, 76), has more ADL limitations, and is more restricted in physical morbidity. Although more limited physically, this group has no IADL impairments. The relative independence of physical and cognitive impairment in these two groups suggests different policy options with respect to providing LTC services. Specifically, it would appear that the physical limitations of the younger third group could be compensated for by appliances and special equipment, while the cognitive impairments of the second group would seem more likely to require personal-care assistance.

The probability distribution of medical conditions for each were examined and are reported in Table 10–13.

There is a strong association between the patterns of medical conditions reported and the degree and nature of disability. For example, the least disabled population reports few of the most serious medical problems. In contrast the fourth, most disabled population is also clearly the most morbid group, with high reported rates of paralysis, heart attack, diabetes, cancer, stroke, and dementia. This group is probably rapidly selected out by mortality and, if mortality improvements were concentrated among the highly debilitated, the age-specific prevalence of this group would be expected to increase. The extreme elderly group (mean age, 86) reports a low prevalence of certain major diseases but a high prevalence of conditions associated with advanced age—arteriosclerosis, glaucoma and, most important, dementia. The low prevalence of diabetes may be a result of selective processes. The third group, consistent with its high level of disability, reports significant rates of diabetes and circulatory disease but no dementia and low levels of stroke. Thus, the health-status profiles of these four subpopulations seem consistent with their levels and types of reported disability and, although based only on cross-sectional data, seem to imply the operation of mortality selection.

The Institutional Population

Any assessment of disability in the population must include a study of health characteristics of the nursing-home population. In fact, a number of health-policy issues may be considered in terms of the probability of exchange between different subpopulations in the community and institutions. Here we use GoM to identify subgroups in the older institutionalized population.

Separate analyses for Medicare and non-Medicare recipients were conducted on the 1977 NNHS (Manton, Liu, and Cornelius 1985). Five subpopulations were found in both groups that could be identified with major diagnoses. Diagnosis was a better discriminator of subtypes within the shorter-stay Medicare population. In the non-Medicare population, groups with similar sets of diagnoses were found except for the emergence of a group whose primary limitation was in terms of mental illness and retardation.

The groups that were identified appeared to relate to certain subpopulations in the community population. For example, there existed, in both the Medicare and non-Medicare populations, a "cancer" subpopulation with short lengths of stay and high mortality. In comparison, the fourth group consisted of highly morbid, potentially

Table 10–13 Association of Response Profiles with Medical Conditions, GoM Analysis of the National Long-term Care Survey

Internal variables	Sample proportion	Subgroups			
		1	2	3	4
Subjective health index					
Excellent	10.5	18.8	23.7	0.3	2.4
Good	30.0	43.7	50.2	18.8	10.3
Fair	33.8	30.6	26.0	51.9	19.9
Poor	25.7	6.9	0.1	29.0	67.4
Medical condition					
Rheumatism or arthritis	73.2	65.2	46.3	97.9	69.1
Paralysis	9.8	4.9	0.0	4.0	33.6
Permanent numbness or stiffness	25.3	16.7	0.1	36.0	43.1
Multiple sclerosis	0.5	0.2	0.0	0.2	1.6
Cerebral palsy	0.5	0.5	0.4	0.0	1.1
Epilepsy	1.0	0.1	0.4	0.9	2.8
Parkinson's disease	3.3	0.7	3.1	3.2	7.7
Glaucoma	8.8	3.7	20.4	7.1	9.7
Diabetes	17.3	11.8	9.7	24.2	22.7
Cancer	6.2	4.0	2.5	5.7	13.1
Frequent constipation	33.8	19.6	20.4	46.6	48.0
Frequent trouble sleeping	42.0	29.4	22.7	61.6	50.2
Frequent severe headache	17.9	8.5	7.7	30.8	23.5
Obesity or overweight	23.3	29.7	0.0	37.6	15.2
Arteriosclerosis or hardening of arteries	33.4	18.1	42.4	30.9	53.0
Mental retardation	2.0	0.0	4.1	0.0	6.1
Dementia	10.1	0.3	23.9	0.0	31.3
Medical conditions experienced in last 12 months					
Heart attack	6.8	3.6	0.0	11.4	10.8
Other heart problems	30.0	19.6	16.2	44.6	36.9
Hypertension	47.7	46.0	20.6	67.2	46.0
Stroke	7.2	2.6	5.4	2.9	21.2
Circulatory trouble in arms or legs	55.0	37.8	27.0	76.7	72.2
Pneumonia	5.9	3.3	4.6	6.7	9.8
Bronchitis	12.7	12.7	0.6	18.4	14.9
Flu	17.2	13.9	9.2	26.4	16.2
Emphysema	10.9	14.9	2.3	10.0	12.5
Asthma	7.1	5.8	0.4	12.2	7.8
Broken hip	2.5	0.9	0.0	3.1	6.3
Other broken bones	5.6	3.0	0.0	9.3	9.1

Source: Analysis of National Long-term Care Survey.

terminal persons in the community population. We also found stroke and hip fracture acute-care groups and several groups identified by circulatory problems, multiple chronic diseases, and dementia.

In this chapter the focus is on the oldest old—a group that was over 21 percent institutionalized in the 1977 survey. Consequently, GoM analysis was conducted of the population aged 85 years and over in 1,618 cases randomly drawn from the three surveys of institutionalized persons (1969, 1973, 1977). We found that there was heterogeneity even in the institutionalized population aged 85 and over. In Table 10–

14 we present the probabilities of having each of certain select characteristics for three analytically determined subgroups.

The three groups were defined on 15 variables (age, sex, marital status, medical condition, primary diagnosis, and functional limitation). The first group is very elderly (27 percent over age 94), female, and unmarried. The second group is intermediate in age, but also tended to be female and unmarried. The third group is young (i.e., and 85 to 89), and was more likely to be male and married. The three groups were very different in terms of health characteristics and level of care. The oldest group had dementia, stroke, and hardening of the arteries, required intensive nursing care, and was most prevalent in the more recent surveys. The intermediate group had a wide range of conditions, required lower levels of care, and was most prevalent in

Table 10–14 Probability of Having Each of Certain Select Characteristics for Three Analytically Determined Subgroups, GoM Analysis of Nursing Home Surveys of 1969, 1973, and 1977

Variables	Sample proportion	Subgroups 1	2	3
Age				
85–89	59.0	37.1	59.4	100.0
90–94	30.3	36.5	40.6	0.0
95+	10.8	26.4	0.0	0.0
Primary diagnosis				
Dementia	15.8	43.7	0.0	0.0
Heart attack	7.2	0.0	19.9	0.0
Stroke	6.2	17.2	0.0	0.0
Hardening of arteries	26.2	38.5	0.0	44.4
Circulatory	10.7	0.0	29.5	0.0
Accident	5.3	0.0	14.6	0.0
Mental	2.4	0.0	0.0	8.6
Musculatory	6.6	0.0	18.3	0.0
Endocrine	4.3	0.0	0.0	15.7
Respiratory	1.6	0.0	4.4	0.0
Neoplasm	2.5	0.0	6.8	0.0
Nervous	2.4	0.0	0.0	8.6
Digestive	1.5	0.0	4.1	0.0
Infection	0.3	0.0	0.4	0.4
Genitourinary	1.2	0.0	0.0	4.2
Skin	0.5	0.0	1.0	0.3
Blood	0.6	0.6	1.1	0.0
Other	4.9	0.0	0.0	17.8
Level of care				
Intensive	45.2	75.9	22.1	31.1
Other intensive	38.7	20.7	51.2	48.6
Personal	14.7	3.4	24.2	18.5
Neither	1.4	0.0	2.5	1.9
Year of survey				
1969	30.9	22.0	48.2	14.8
1973	32.0	37.0	36.2	16.0
1977	37.1	41.1	15.5	69.2

Source: National Center for Health Statistics data tapes on the Institutionalized Population for 1969, 1973, 1977.

early surveys. The third group is interesting in that it is a predominantly male group found primarily in the most recent survey. This suggests significant changes in the extreme elderly nursing-home population with the further aging of the female population and the recent emergence of an extreme elderly male group.

MORBIDITY, DISABILITY, AND HEALTH SERVICE USE

Although chronic disease morbidity is most likely to be associated with functional disability among the oldest old, the correlation between age and either morbidity or disability is not sufficiently strong to warrant the use of the age group 85 and over as a proxy for service need in a population. This is particularly true for those aged 85 and over today. For these cohorts, the process of selective survivorship may have already claimed persons most vulnerable to the chronic degenerative diseases that are associated with the highest levels of service need. Population-based need assessment strategies also are not fully adequate for identifying those with intensive service needs or suggesting future changes in the size or age distribution of this subgroup. These concerns are even more important once the implications of individual variability in rates of aging are recognized and incorporated into program designs (Riley and Bond 1983). The "targeting" of limited health care resources to those most in need also is becoming an increasingly important public concern as the eligibility criteria for program participation are reviewed for their cost-containment potential. Previous efforts have not been successful, however, in using a single dimension (e.g., functional disability) to identify specific targeting subgroups, for example, those for whom home-care services could prevent or delay nursing-home admission (Weissert 1981). Rather, it is clear that targeting requires identifying groups that manifest a consistent pattern of both need and service use.

Longitudinal panel data provide even further evidence of concentrated service use of very few elderly, even in the oldest age group: Over a five-year period, only 4 percent of those 85 and over accounted for nearly one-third of all acute hospitals days and 9 percent accounted for 57 percent of all acute and chronic care days consumed by this age group (Roos, Shapiro, and Roos 1984).

Table 10–15 shows the probability distribution of selected service use variables for each of the four NLTCS subgroups described earlier. Column 2 shows the marginal proportion of each health service use variable for the full sample; the other columns show the probability of persons in each of the four groups just described having each service use characteristic. In general, the health service profile of each group is appropriate to the group's health status/need profile described earlier.

Persons in group 1, the least functionally dependent of the four, are light consumers of health care services. Of the four groups, group 1 members are the least likely to have been placed in a nursing home or to be on a waiting list for one. These individuals are most likely to depend on a single person, usually a spouse, to provide minimal informal assistance. In contrast, group 4, the most disabled, exhibits patterns suggesting intensive use of hospital and nursing-home facilities and paid home-care attendants. This group also has intensive use of informal-care services and requires assistance from more than one person to sustain them in the community.

While the service utilization profiles of the two extreme groups are predictable

Table 10–15 The Probability of Four Analytically Defined Subgroups Having Specific Service Utilization Characteristics,[a] GoM Analysis of National Long-term Care Survey

Service use characteristics	Marginal proportion	Group			
		1 Minimal ADL or IADL dependency	2 Substantial IADL dependency	3 ADL + mobility limited	4 Extreme ADL dependency
Living in community for older persons	8.6	7.2	8.6	15.2	1.9
Patient in nursing home at any time	7.2	2.4	8.4	6.1	15.3
On waiting list to go to nursing home	0.9	0.4	2.1	0.3	1.6
Patient in hospital overnight in last 12 months	36.4	27.4	19.2	40.4	57.6
Helpers (individual binary variables)					
Spouse	35.1	64.5	0.0	0.0	60.8
Offspring	44.6	10.9	81.8	57.9	48.7
Other relative	31.4	6.0	59.8	43.8	30.6
Friend	11.8	2.3	17.4	23.1	6.8
Other, unpaid	29.0	12.9	24.7	32.2	52.6
Paid helper	25.3	11.8	19.5	29.5	44.9
Number of helpers					
None	5.0	15.5	0.0	0.0	0.0
One	37.8	64.8	22.0	29.6	22.0
Two	28.2	15.6	36.1	35.6	30.9
Three	15.7	3.3	22.4	21.2	21.2
Four+	13.3	0.7	19.5	13.6	25.9
Total number of days per week helpers provide some assistance					
None	11.7	29.8	0.7	6.4	0.0
1–5	21.4	27.8	1.3	46.1	0.2
6–7	33.6	36.4	36.9	29.4	32.2
8–12	17.4	3.7	31.5	12.4	31.5
13+	15.9	2.3	29.6	5.4	36.1

[a] Subgroups defined through Grade of Membership Analysis using 33 sociodemographic and health characteristics. All variables shown in the table, however, were external to the analysis.

Source: Analysis of the 1982 National Long-term Care Survey.

from their disability profiles, differences in service use are perhaps of most interest for groups 2 and 3. Group 2 is distinguished by IADL dependencies, sensory impairments, and cognitive impairment. Although persons in group 4 are far more likely to manifest the extreme functional disability usually associated with nursing-home placement, the risk of admission is actually greater in group 2. An analysis of other group characteristics suggests that the nursing-home risk of persons in group 2 may be largely a function of deficiencies in their informal support network, whereas the risk for group 4 is more directly related to their care needs. In support of this interpretation, note that persons in group 2 are uniformly unmarried women of advanced age (over half are aged 85 and over). In the absence of spousal care providers, persons in group 2 are disproportionately dependent on offspring and other relatives for substantial daily assistance. Unlike the situation of those in group 4, the burden of informal caregiving is less likely to be offset by paid home-care service providers. This finding suggests that restricting home care services under Medicare or Medicaid to those with advanced ADL dependencies will screen out a group of individuals whose nursing-home admissions may be effectively deterred through the introduction of intensive community services.

Group 3 is distinguished primarily in terms of mobility restrictions. Although unlikely to be wait-listed for a nursing home, persons in group 3 are more likely than those in the second group to have experienced at least one hospital admissions in the preceding 12 months. In addition, the probability of living in a structured community for the elderly is greatest in group 3, although even in this group the probability is not large. Perhaps because of their residential patterns, these mobility-restricted persons are more dependent on friends and neighbors for assistance than those in any other group. In spite of this, individuals in group 3 are still likely to receive assistance from offspring and other relatives. The service-utilization profile that emerges for this group is one of moderately intensive care needs met by multiple helpers. Their profile also suggests the feasibility of using special equipment or appliances or modifying the built environment (e.g., removal of interior thresholds) as compensation strategies.

Thus, the four homogeneous need-based groups appear to be internally consistent in terms of health services utilization. For assessing the health and service requirements of older populations, the analysis also calls into question the use of observed or projected age distributions to indicate the volume of demand for health care services. Of the four groups, only the second IADL-dependent group was very elderly (i.e., mean age, 86). Our results also highlight the importance of the qualitative aspects of aging, particularly, living arrangements and the availability of informal care providers, in relating health status to the need for long-term personal-care services. In the next section we consider in more detail how these qualitative factors condition the current demand for both formal LTC and nursing-home services and how those factors may shape the future demand for both types of formal LTC services.

QUALITATIVE ASPECTS OF AGING AND THE DEMAND FOR LTC SERVICES

At low levels of functional dependence, the need for assistance is most likely to be satisfied in a community setting through the informal caregiving of family, friends, and neighbors (Cantor 1979). At moderate levels of dependency, the introduction of formal care providers (e.g., home health aides) may be necessary to augment the caregiving capacity of the informal support network. At advanced levels of need, the benefits of a nursing-home admission may offset the preference for continued community residence.

Because such generalizations provide little guidance for health-care planning, considerable effort has been devoted to pinpointing precisely where along the need continuum these transitions occur. Most research has focused on predicting nursing-home admission; only recently has attention turned to predicting use of formal services in the community.

Predicting Institutionalization

Numerous investigators have attempted to predict nursing-home admission at older ages. Branch and Jette (1982) concluded from a review of relevant research that no one set of variables consistently differentiated nursing-home residents from disabled community elderly. Neither age nor need (whether measured in terms of functional disability or medical condition), although statistically significant in most studies, uniformly correlated with LTC setting. Data compiled by the 1980 Task Force on Long-Term Care show that even among those aged 85 and over with substantial ADL needs, there is at lest one community resident for every five comparably disabled nursing-home residents (Department of Health and Human Services 1981).

A majority of studies (including Branch and Jette's, as well as more recent research by Weissert and Scanlon [1983]) identify as predictors of institutionalization the absence of a viable informal support network and factors that undermine the caregiver's capacity or commitment to noninstitutional care. Among these latter factors are incontinence, need for nearly constant supervision, and the presence of cognitive impairments and/or behavioral problems (Smyer 1980).

For the oldest old, the effects of these conditions are compounded by the fact that their caregivers, even if adult children, are themselves likely to be elderly and experiencing some restriction in activity. This is particularly significant for the oldest old women (the majority of whom are widowed) because they are considerably more dependent on offspring for caregiving than are men of comparable age and disability or younger, equally frail, women. One in three caregivers to women aged 85 and over is an adult child who contributes nearly half of all the supporting service days consumed by community-based ADL-dependent women in this age group.

Predicting Use of Community Services
Conditioning Effect of Informal Providers

Future demographic factors (e.g., changes in family size and composition, changes in probability of survival of spouse) and policy will affect the actual level or type of LTC services available. However, it is useful to examine the nature and mix of services currently received by persons at different disability levels and ages (Manton and Liu 1984a). In Table 10–16 we present the total number of excess hours spent per week in providing informal care by different classes of caregivers for different disability levels for the population aged 85 and over.

The sources of informal care are quite different by sex and marital status. Men are more dependent on their spouses for informal care. Women receive more care from offspring and relatives. The importance of the spouse as a source of care decreases with age, reflecting the decreasing likelihood of both members of a couple surviving to advanced age. With age, the likelihood of formal-care services increases—as it does with increasing disability.

The involvement of informal caregivers, however, minimizes the demand for for-

Table 10–16 Projections of Total Excess Hours Per Week (in thousands) Spent in Providing Informal Care for Disabled Elderly Age 85+, by Disability Level, Sex, and Marital Status

Source of help and year	IADL	1–2 ADL	3–4 ADL	5–6 ADL	Total[a]	IADL	1–2 ADL	3–4 ADL	5–6 ADL	Total[a]
			Married Males					*Married Females*		
Spouse										
1980	377	991	705	630	2,703	117	183	227	141	668
2000	808	2,124	1,513	1,351	5,796	207	323	401	250	1,180
2040	2,176	5,719	4,072	3,636	15,603	581	908	1,127	702	3,318
Offspring										
1980	34	232	189	354	809	163	104	83	236	586
2000	73	497	405	760	1,736	287	184	147	416	1,034
2040	197	1,339	1,091	2,046	4,673	808	517	413	1,170	2,908
Relative										
1980	36	94	93	53	277	28	103	57	157	345
2000	78	203	199	114	594	49	182	100	277	609
2040	210	545	536	308	1,599	139	513	282	780	1,714
Nonrelative										
1980	29	88	64	60	241	27	27	42	61	157
2000	63	189	137	129	517	48	48	73	108	278
2040	169	509	368	347	1,393	135	135	206	304	781
			Unmarried Males					*Unmarried Females*		
Offspring										
1980	482	573	370	226	1,651	1,317	2,425	1,341	2,837	7,921
2000	819	973	629	385	2,805	2,990	5,508	3,045	6,443	17,986
2040	2,161	2,569	1,660	1,016	7,406	6,906	12,719	7,033	14,881	41,539
Relative										
1980	384	338	203	202	1,128	592	1,383	745	1,383	4,103
2000	653	575	346	343	1,917	1,344	3,140	1,692	3,140	9,316
2040	1,724	1,518	912	905	5,060	3,103	7,253	3,909	7,251	21,516
Nonrelative										
1980	95	217	86	203	601	247	718	397	881	2,242
2000	162	368	146	344	1,021	560	1,630	901	2,000	5,090
2040	427	973	386	909	2,695	1,293	3,764	2,081	4,619	11,756

[a]Totals may reflect rounding errors.

Source: National Long-term Care Survey and NORC Survey of Caregivers.

mal, or paid, services in the community. Estimated probabilities of formal service receipt, by level of need, for disabled community-based persons aged 65 and over are shown in Table 10–17. These probabilities were calculated from a logistic regression of the Home Care Supplement to the 1979 NHIS. The regression included multiple indicators of need as well as "enabling" and "predisposing" indicators. Age was not statistically significant independent of the need variables. The coefficient for receipt of informal care, however, was the largest of any of the 12 variables included in the analysis. Receipt of informal services decreased the logged odds of formal service provision by 3.3; the next largest coefficient, for medical needs, was 1.5.

Table 10–17 Probability of Formal Service Receipt by Type of Living Arrangement and Need, for Women 65 Years of Age and Over with Informal Supports[a]

Type of need	Probability of formal service receipt			
	Living alone	Living with nonrelative	Living with spouse	Living with other relative
IADL need only	.17	.31	.08	.04
ADL need only	.27	.44	.14	.08
Medical need only	.31	.50	.17	.09
ADL and IADL need	.44	.62	.26	.14
ADL and medical need	.63	.79	.43	.27
ADL, IADL, and medical needs	.78	.61	.44	.44
All types of needs and incontinence problems	.84	.92	.71	.54
All types of need and supervision problems	.86	.93	.74	.58
All types of need and incontinence and supervision problems	.90	.95	.81	.68

[a]Logistic function (probability $(P) = 1/1 + e^{-xb}$) evaluated for modal group: white, ever-married women residing in central cities with annual family incomes of $5,000–$9,999 (in 1978 dollars) who did not participate in Medicaid in 12 months preceding interview.

Source: Analysis of the Home Care Supplement to the 1979 National Health Interview Survey reported in Soldo, B.J. 1985. In-home Services for the Dependent Elderly: Determinants of Current Use and Implications for Future Demand. *Research on Aging* 7:281–304.

Estimates are shown only for white, ever-married women with modal income, residence, and Medicaid status.

The probabilities in Table 10–17 confirm that the more complex the service need, the more likely is the receipt of formal services. Compared to either ADL or IADL needs, medical care needs are more likely to stimulate the use of formal services. Perhaps of most interest for forecasting the service requirements of a population are differences in the service use probabilities across different types of households. At any level of need, the probability of formal service is lowest for those elderly who live with either spouses or with other relatives.

The data in Table 10–17 appear to provide strong support for the differential tolerance on threshold hypothesis advanced by Cantor (1981). For those living with nonrelatives, formal service use is more likely to occur once ADL and IADL needs combine; for those living alone, this threshold is defined as the point at which ADL and medical needs are present. Frail women cared for by their spouses, however, do not cross this threshold until incontinence problems add to the care demands associated with IAD, ADL, and medical needs. The threshold for those cared for by other relatives (most likely adult children) is postponed further still and does not occur until both supervision and incontinence problems are present independent of IADL, ADL, and medical needs.

Two competing interpretations are tenable for the higher tolerance of nonspouse family caregivers. Because spouses of dependent elderly are themselves often elderly, they may require assistance from community services at lower levels of disability than younger, and presumably more vigorous, kin caregivers. The second interpretation posits that formal services are less likely to be introduced into the homes of nonspouse careproviders simply because these relatives are more likely to have opted for an earlier institutional placement.

These findings also suggest that the volume of demand for formal services in the community will be influenced by the distribution of the disabled elderly across different types of living arrangements. A number of factors must be considered: change in intergenerational attitudes, increasing incidence of divorce, and male–female differences in old-age mortality. Projected increases in the number of elderly women living alone (Glick 1979) imply that increases in the demand for community long-term-care services may far outpace the growth of even the disabled portion of the population aged 85 and over.

Costs of Community Services

One subgroup of particular interest are the 1.1 million persons reporting that they received some formal care. This group is likely to increase in size because of (a) the increased survival of the extreme elderly, (b) the possible decrease of informal care resources with changing family patterns and (c) possible future constraints or institutionalization causing more severely disabled persons to remain in the community. Of the 1.1 million persons who reported receiving some formal care in the 1982 NLTCS, we know that 605,000 reported providing some portion of the expenditure for formal care from their own resources. These persons reported spending $99.2 million per month on such services. Of the 605,000 about 465,000, or 77 percent, report paying for all of their formal care. This group reports paying $65.5 million monthly, or $141 per person, for care. In Table 10–18, reported expenditures are disaggregated by age and disability level.

Table 10–18 Monthly Out-of-Pocket Expenditures on LTC Services for Disabled Persons Who Pay for All of Their Care

Variable	Number of persons (000s)	Average expenditures (dollars)
Age		
65–74	167	108
75–84	198	142
85+	100	193
Total	465	
Disability level		
IADL Only	134	82
1–2 ADLs	181	70
3–4 ADLs	71	111
5–6 ADLs	79	429
Age 85+		
IADL Only	20	65
1–2 ADLs	34	66
3–4 ADLs	19	163
5–6 ADLs	27	466

Source: National Long-term Care Survey.

Monthly out-of-pocket expenses reported for persons who use formal care increased from $108 for persons aged 65 through 74 to $193 for persons aged 85 and over. Much of this increase is due to the higher disability levels of the population over age 85. Monthly expenses increased from $82 to $429 with disability level. Nonetheless, for persons aged 85 and over at the highest and next-to-highest disability levels, expenses are greater than for the average for all ages combined. If similar levels of expenditures were to be maintained (in constant 1980 dollars), this would imply roughly $107 million in out-of-pocket expenditures for formal care in 2000 (+172 percent over 1980) and $222 million in 2040 (+356 percent over 1980), with 41 percent of those expenditures being made for persons 85 and over in 2000 and 48 percent in 2040.

At face value, these findings provide empirical support for the position that publicly subsidized LTC services could be reoriented away from their current institutional basis without incurring the costs of inappropriate service use. Aside from the obvious measurement problems (e.g., inferring volume of service used or demanded from simple service receipt), other considerations militate against drawing a definite conclusion. Price-demand elasticities, for example, may be very sensitive to level of need. LTC needs, by definition, generate enduring service demands. Thus, cross-sectional data are inadequate for identifying the long-range implications of a national LTC policy emphasizing community alternatives.

Model of Service Substitution

Luce, Liu, and Manton (1984) proposed a general framework for research on LTC issues, the evaluation of interrelated health-policy initiatives, and models that project the need for LTC services. This framework lends itself to formulation of a number of basic policy issues, but perhaps the most general concerns the substitution of one type of service for another. Policies that implicitly or explicitly promote service substitution ultimately affect the quality, cost, and efficiency of care in a variety of ways.

A current expression of the service substitution issue focuses on the question: Will increased public financing of home-care services diminish private-sector efforts (Greene 1983)? The risk of widespread transference of health-care responsibilities from the informal sector is considerable, if only because of the increased labor-force participation of women (the traditional caregivers to the elderly) and the implications of four-generation families for the age and vitality of potential caregivers (Treas 1977).

Before the issue of service substitution is examined, it is necessary to determine the age-specific prevalence of the functional limitations that determine the need for specific services. Earlier, survival curves of functional limitations estimated from data on the noninstitutionalized disabled population in 1982 were presented. As with other definitions of health-status change, there is a natural aging imperative underlying such functional transitions. Further analysis also indicated considerable heterogeneity in the trajectory of age-related declines in disability and shows that different diseases could generate similar age patterns of functional limitations.

In Figure 10–8, the basic survival curve model (Figure 10–1) is extended to include hypothetical age-specific probabilities of various LTC service configurations and the transition from one level of service to the next. In this figure, age is shown on the horizontal axis. The probability (expressed as a percentage) of a member of the initial, hypothetical birth cohort surviving to a given age without experiencing a critical health event or health-service transition is shown on the vertical axis. The partitioned area (A–F) under the mortality curve corresponds to estimates of person-years spent in a particular state. For example, the area marked F represents, for the cohort, the number of institutionalized person-years. Areas D, E, and F together provide time-weighted estimates of the long-term care service requirements of a population.

In Figure 10–7, a hypothetical sequence of LTC service providers is assumed. Initially, and at lower levels of need, caregiving is the responsibility of the informal support network. Either as a time- or need-dependent function, the efforts of family and friends are augmented by services from the community formal support network—an augmentation most likely to occur at advanced levels of functional need or when medical care needs (e.g., physical therapy or regular injections) require professional expertise. Ultimately, LTC needs are satisfied only in institutional settings.

Proposals now being considered are intended to alter the risk of specific service use patterns at age *x* by shifting up the curve representing the risk of institutionalization and thereby increasing the number of disabled person-years spent in the community (areas D + E). One important issue is how this time would be partitioned between reliance solely on the family and on a mix of informal and formal providers.

Figure 10–7 clarifies that the service-substitution question is not one of short-run transference of effort (which is probably inevitable), but rather one of long-run service utilization patterns. If Medicare or Medicaid changes were to reduce price and supply barriers to formal services, the curve for the combined service use would probably shift downward. Formal providers would be introduced into informal caregiving arrangements at lower levels of disability. The consequence of this would be expressed in the relative positions of the other service use curves. If, for example, the curve for the risk of institutionalization were unaltered by new service options,

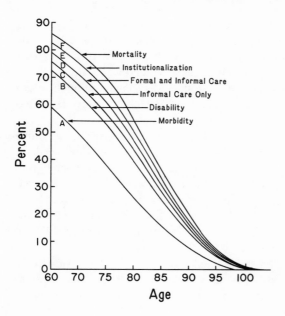

Figure 10–8 The observed mortality and hypothetical morbidity, disability, and long-term-care service use survival curves for U.S. women, 1980.

the objective of cost containment through reduced rates of nursing-home placement could be defeated. If, on the other hand, the institutionalization curve were displaced upward, short-run service substitution would ultimately serve the long-range objectives of public policy. Increases in life expectancy, however, might leave untouched the average duration of nursing-home stay even while the average age at admission increases.

Our intent in this chapter is not to forecast the substitution effects of alternative program options, but simply to illustrate some different service delivery scenarios. In particular, applying the survival curve concept to the substitution issue demonstrates that simple prevalence rates of service use, and changes therein, are inadequate for decision making. Both the costs and benefits of various service substitutions are best estimated in terms of their effects on person-years of use. The model also identifies the service implications of increases in the size of the disabled population as life expectancy increases (particularly at the advanced ages) and the interaction of changes in health status and life expectancy.

The model further illustrates the implications of increase in the absolute or relative number of disabled in the community. As the population ages, the disabled will not only be older and possibly require more service, but informal care providers also are more likely to be elderly themselves. Such changes are likely to affect family life (Brody 1984) because the probability of young-elderly (aged 65–69) women having at least one surviving parent aged 85 or over will more than double over the next 60 years (see Table 10–19). As they begin their own retirement and enter the empty-nest stage in the family life cycle, a substantial number of women in their late sixties are likely to confront the stressful caregiving demands of at least one parent *or* parent-in-law aged 85 and over.

Projecting Use—Implications of Mortality, Morbidity, and Disability Trends/Linkages

Future patterns of community LTC service use will be shaped not only by changes in LTC reimbursement policies and the availability of informal care providers, but

Table 10–19 Probability of Surviving Parents at Ages 65–69 by Birth Cohort: Women Only

Birth cohort	Forecast year[a]	Probability of surviving parents			
		Father alive	Mother alive	Either alive	Average expected probability of surviving parents
1921–25	1990	.026	.140	.154	.166
1926–30	1995	.034	.174	.197	.207
1931–35	2000	.039	.196	.222	.235
1936–40	2005	.048	.225	.257	.279
1941–45	2010	.054	.234	.269	.288
1946–50	2015	.060	.243	.281	.303

[a] Year in which birth cohort will be 65–69 years of age.

Source: D.A. Wolfe. 1983. Kinship and the Living Arrangements of Older Americans. Final report submitted to the National Institute of Child Health and Human Development. Contract No. NO1-HD-12183. Washington: Urban Institute.

also by the functional disability manifest by the oldest old in the future. Earlier, we presented projections of functional dependency by age, sex, marital status, and type of caregiver. These projections—expressed in terms of extra hours of work engendered by caregiving—indicated substantial increases in the volume of informal service consumption for women aged 85 and over.

These projections are summarized for offspring helpers to women aged 85 and over in Table 10–20. Although these alternative projections show increases over time in the volume of offspring-provided care hours, the rate of increase is slowed. Between 2020 and 2040, when the large baby-boom cohorts will begin turning 85, the rate of increase under the constant rate assumption is 67.1 percent, in contrast to 53.6 percent under the declining mortality assumption. Perhaps more important, the total volume of offspring care services projected under assumed mortality declines (27.4 million hours per week) is 61.8 percent of that required by women aged 85 and over if morbidity remains constant (44.4 million care hours per week).

These two sets of caregiving projections likely represent upper and lower limits in the volume of offspring services needed to sustain women of extreme age in the

Table 10–20 Aggregate Number of Offspring Helper Hours per Week[a] for Women, 85 Years of Age and Over: Estimate 1980 and Projections, 1990–2040, Under Alternative Assumptions, by Level of Functional Dependency (numbers in thousands)

Year and morbidity assumptions	Only IADL limited[b]	ADL score[c]			Total[d]	Percentage increase[e]
		1–2	3–4	5–6		
Estimate						
1980	1,480	2,529	1,424	3,073	8,506	—
Projections[f]						
1990						
Constant	2,132	3,728	2,087	4,477	12,425	46.1
Declining	1,739	3,048	1,706	3,656	10,149	19.3
2000						
Constant	3,278	5,691	3,192	6,859	19,020	53.1
Declining	2,395	4,175	2,339	5,022	13,932	37.3
2020						
Constant	4,584	7,962	4,465	9,595	26,606	39.9
Declining	3,074	5,362	3,004	6,447	17,887	28.4
2040						
Constant	7,714	13,236	7,446	16,050	44,447	67.1
Declining	4,752	8,202	4,607	9,916	27,477	53.6

[a] Total number of caregiving service hours provided by offspring for women 85 years of age and over.

[b] Needs assistance with IADLs: managing money, shopping, light housework, meal preparation, making a phone call, or taking medication.

[c] Sum of the number of ADLs with which respondent required assistance.

[d] Totals may reflect rounding error.

[e] Percentage increase in total number of offspring helper hours per week over last projection data shown, by morbidity assumptions.

[f] Projection labeled "constant" assume 1980 age-, sex-specific rates of IADL and ADL limitations prevail; projections labeled "declining" assume reductions in age-, sex-specific rates of IADL and ADL limitations proportionate to mortality declines forecast by the Social Security Administration. Both sets of projections assume projected mortality rate declines (Social Security Administration 1981).

Source: Analysis of the 1982 National Long-term Care Survey and the NORC Survey of Caregivers.

community. These projections, however, assume continued rates of offspring care-giving—an assumption that may prove unrealistic unless offspring caregivers, pri-marily daughters, have access to a variety of home-care services (Horowitz and Shin-delman 1983).

IMPLICATIONS FOR HEALTH-CARE DELIVERY SYSTEMS

The projected progress in controlling the rate of chronic disease progression and reduction in the severity of the chronic degenerative diseases implies increases in the number of productive, nondisabled years of life, but also difficult tradeoffs between social and individual benefits. By postponing age at death, the period of intense service need may be postponed until later in the life cycle, when fewer financial and/ or family resources may be available to ameliorate the public costs of LTC. In order to illustrate the effects of these changes, two aspects of the health-care delivery sys-tem organizations are examined.

Vertical and Horizontal Integration

The dynamics of health status and life expectancy changes have particular signifi-cance for the organization of long-term care reimbursement systems. The vertical integration of health services seems inevitable either as an explicit policy objective (e.g., the Long-Term Care Channelling Demonstrations) or as a consequence of the DRGs' effect on discharge planning (Brody and Magel 1983). Whether a person remains in an acute care facility, is transferred to a nursing home, or is sent home with a specific service package will be governed, to some degree, by the relative benefits of different reimbursement policies for each type of service option. Clearly, this calls for careful coordination of reimbursement policies across service types. The need for various health care services is governed, however, by the health status tran-sitions described in our life-table model. Thus, reimbursement policies also must take the imperatives of health status change into account.

The near inevitability of chronic morbidity and disability at advanced age means that there will be a natural evolution of the mix of services required by an aging population. This evolution must be factored into the design of health care policies if we are to avoid creating major disincentives to providers to serve select subgroups of the oldest-old population.

The survival curve model can also be used to determine long-range planning for HMOs. If it is true that there are major medical expenses associated with terminal illness, then an HMO with a healthy population is likely to experience heavy levels of disbursement as their population progresses to advanced ages. Thus, though a HMO can help promote health and prevent disease, it will remain at risk to high expenditures as large proportions of its population survive to advanced ages where mortality risks eventually rise. This is illustrated in Table 10–21, where, using na-tional cost figures, age-specific differences in costs are presented for two U.S. coun-ties (Davis County, Utah and Benton County, Washington).

The Washington county has significantly higher costs through age 77, whereas the Utah county has a greater life expectancy and consequently higher medical ex-

Table 10–21   Annual Per Capita Costs Due to the Mortality Process Assuming Cause-Specific Mortality Costs as Estimated by Lubitz and Prihoda (1983)[a]

Age (1-year intervals)	Benton County, Washington (dollars)	Davis County, Utah (dollars)	Ratio Benton/Davis
70	319	312	1.02
71	374	331	1.13
72	438	347	1.26
73	502	363	1.38
74	550	381	1.44
75	576	405	1.42
76	563	437	1.29
77	526	470	1.12
78	478	514	0.93
79	452	559	0.81

[a]Lubitz, J.E., and R. Prihoda. 1983. Use and Costs of Medicare Services in the Last Year of Life. In *Health, United States*, 1983. DHHS pub. no. (PHS) 84-1232. Washington.

Source: Tolley, H.D., and K.G. Manton. 1984. Assessing Health Care Costs in the Elderly, table 8. *Transactions of the Society of Actuaries* 36:579–603.

penditures at more advanced ages (age 78 or higher). The implication of this different age pattern of costs is significant. First, it suggests that the fiscal viability of an HMO will be strongly determined by the age structure of its population and the interaction of that structure with its mortality risk structure (i.e., its age- and cause-specific mortality rates). Second, even for the Utah county, a population exhibiting many of the healthy lifestyle practices promoted as preventive strategies, there will eventually be a period of high fiscal risk when the mortality rates for that population start to increase at advanced ages (Tolley and Manton 1984).

CONCLUSION

A distinctive feature of the current process of population aging is the reduction of mortality at advanced ages, which is leading to rapid growth of the population aged 85 and over—the population group with the highest per capita service needs. If the projections produced by the Social Security Administration (SSA 1982) are correct, and there are 5.4 million persons over age 85 in 2000 and more than 13 million persons over age 85 in 2040, then policy responses that do not take into account qualitative dimensions may be misdirected. Current policy does not yet adequately reflect these qualitative factors. Presently we lack adequate concepts and models of the health changes that will be associated with increases in life expectancy at advanced ages. For example, Omran's (1971) theory of the "epidemiological transition" did not envisage a stage in which chronic disease would decrease in importance. The possibility of life expectancy increases at very advanced ages was not represented in most demographic and actuarial projections until 1981 (e.g., Social Security Administration 1981).

Developing strategies to allow policy makers to respond to the qualitative dimensions of population aging requires two elements. The first is a broad conceptual framework to relate basic health and survival changes. Such a framework is presented in Figure 10–1. This framework is necessary to organize the multiple interacting processes describing health changes at advanced ages into a coherent and readily comprehensible model. With such a conceptual model, we can apply the information-organizing capacity of mathematics to analyses of a wide range of types of information and for different questions. The range of mathematical tools that will be required to operationalize the model in different contexts will be broad. In some cases, actual cohort survival can be described, while in other cases, only the experience of a cross section is available. The mathematical tools may be even more detailed than the model presented representing individual differences in risk or a more complete set of health state transitions where disability and mortality may be reversed at the individual level. Nonetheless, all of these models can be developed from the basic concepts of the age correlation of morbidity, disability, and mortality described in Figure 10–1.

The second element is a comprehensive review of a broad range of data on the interrelation of morbidity, disability, and mortality changes at advanced ages. Naturally, one probable conclusion of any such review will be that our current knowledge of the health changes among the oldest old is seriously and systematically deficient. However, by *systematically* identifying gaps in our knowledge, we can begin to develop a map for needed research initiatives. A requirement of such a review is that disciplinary boundaries be bridged so that a broad consensual view of the phenomena is forged.

Our review of data and models suggests principles for further research and policy development. First, morbidity, disability, and mortality are generated by a multidimensional physiological process operating at the level of the individual organisms. Second, there is wide variability in the parameters of this process and greater possibility for intervention than was previously thought. Because of the linkage of morbidity, mortality, and disability in an individual-level process, intervention must be evaluated with respect to feedback in the system. Third, the relevant history of the process relating morbidity, disability, and mortality extends over the full life of an individual. Thus, life course and cohort perspectives are important in policy development. Fourth, the extreme elderly are a highly selected group of survivors. Finally, current stereotypes of degenerative health changes at advanced ages are inaccurate and must be changed.

With these and other insights, policy and planning to meet the health and social needs of the elderly can be improved in a number of areas. First, a better understanding of the age dependency of the transition between health status at advanced ages can improve our forecasts of life expectancy change (Manton 1983) and changes in disease and disability prevalence (Manton 1987b; Manton and Liu 1984b). It may also define new areas of needed research (e.g., identifying the risk factors for disability at advanced ages). Second, a better understanding of the heterogeneity of the extreme elderly population and the qualitative aspects of their health status may help define new, more effective policy responses. This was illustrated in analyses of the NLTCS, where cognitive and physical impairments were found to occur independently and to be predictors of differential needs for service (i.e., special equipment seemed more useful for the younger, physically disabled group while personal assistance was more likely to be necessary for the older, cognitive impaired group). Third, the insights gained from such studies appear promising for the development of PPS for different types of health services. For example, the analysis of the NLTCS suggested that reimbursement classifications for LTC services must be multidimensional, going beyond simple functional classification to include mitigating socioeconomic and housing factors as well as medical status (Luce et al. 1984). This preliminary study of the changing health characteristics of the extreme elderly suggests the need for intensive review of the concepts and evidence upon which we now base current and future policies.

Acknowledgments—The research reported in this report was supported by NIA Grant Nos. AG01159, AG07198, and AG07469; and HCFA Grant No. 18 P-97710/04-4.

REFERENCES

Besdine, R.W. 1984. Functional Assessment in the Elderly: Relationship Between Function and Diagnosis. Paper presented at the Fifth Annual Invitational Symposium on the Elderly and Their Health, Department of Epidemiology and Preventive Medicine, University of Maryland School of Medicine, Baltimore, Md, October 9.

Branch, L.G., and A.M. Jette. 1982. A Prospective Study of Long-Term Care Institutionalization among the Aged. *American Journal of Public Health* 72:1373–79.

Brody, J.A. 1983. Testimony Before the Subcommittee on Savings, Pensions, and Investment Policy of the Committees on Finance, U.S. Senate, July 15. Senate Hearing document no. 98-359. Washington.

———. 1984. The Best of Times/The Worst of Times: Aging and Dependency in the 21st Century. In *Ethical Dimensions of Geriatric Care: Value Conflicts of the 21st Century*, ed. S.F. Spicker, 3–22. Dordrecht, Holland: D. Reidel.

Brody, S.J., and J.S. Magel. 1983. DRG—The Second Revolution in Health Care for the Elderly. Paper presented at the Annual Meeting of the American Public Health Association, Dallas, Tex.

Cantor, M.E. 1979. Neighbors and Friends: An Overlooked Resource in the Informal Support System. *Research on Aging* 1:434–63.

———. 1981. Factors Associated with Strain Among Family, Friends and Neighbors Caring for the Frail Elderly. Paper presented at the Annual Scientific Meeting of the Gerontological Society of America, Toronto, Canada.

Clive, J., M.A. Woodbury, and I.C. Siegler. 1983. Fuzzy and Crisp Set-Theoretical-Based Classification of Health and Disease. *Journal of Medical Systems* 7:317–32.

Department of Health and Human Services, Office of the Assistant Secretary for Planning and Evaluation. 1981. Working Papers in Long-Term Care. Prepared for the 1980 Undersecretary's Task Force on Long-Term Care. Washington.

Feldman, J.J. 1982. Work Ability of the Aged under Conditions of Improving Mortality. Statement before the National Commission on Social Security Reform. Washington, June 21.

Fox, P.D., and S.B. Clauser. 1980. Trends in Nursing Home Expenditures: Implications for Aging Policy. *Health Care Financing Review* 2:65–70.

Freeland, M.S., and C.E. Schendler. 1981. National Health Expenditures: Short-term Outlook and Long-Term Projection. *Health Care Financing Review* 2:97–138.

———. 1983a. National Health Expenditure Growth in the 1980's: An Aging Population, New Technologies, and Increasing Competition. *Health Care Financing Review* 4:1–58.

———. 1983b. Health Spending in the 1980's: Integration of Clinical Practice Patterns with Management. *Health Care Financing Review* 5:1–68.

Fries, J.F. 1980. Aging, Natural Death, and the Compression of Morbidity. *New England Journal of Medicine* 303:130–35.

———. 1983. The Compression of Morbidity. *Milbank Memorial Fund Quarterly/Health and Society* 61:397–419.

———. 1984. The Compression of Morbidity: Miscellaneous Comments About a Theme. *Gerontologist* 24:354–59.

Glick, P.C. 1979. The Future Marital Status and Living Arrangements of the Elderly. *Gerontologist* 19:301–09.

Golini, A., and V. Egidi. 1984. Effect of Morbidity Changes on Mortality and Population Size and Structure. In *Methodologies Collection and Analysis of Data,* eds. J. Vallin, J.H. Pollard, and L. Heligman, 405–48. Leige, Belgium: International Union for the Scientific Study of Population.

Greene, V.L. 1983. Substitution Between Formally and Informally Provided Care for the Impaired Elderly in the Community. *Medical Care* 21:609–19.

Grimaldi, P.L., and J.A. Micheletti. 1983. *DRG's: Medicare's Prospective Payment Plan.* Chicago: Pluribus.

Gruenberg, E.M. 1977. The Failures of Success. *Milbank Memorial Fund Quarterly/Health and Society* 55:3–24.

Hachinski, V. 1984. Decreased Incidence and Mortality of Stroke. *Stroke* 15:376–378.

Hartunian, N.F., C.N. Smart, and M.S. Thompson. 1981. *The Incidence and Economic Costs of Major Health Impairments.* Lexington, Mass.: D.C. Heath.

Horowitz, A., and L.W. Shindelman. 1983. Social and Economic Incentives for Family Caregivers. *Health Care Financing Review* 5:25–33.

Katz, S. 1983. Assessing Self-maintenance: Activities of Daily Living Mobility and Instrumental Activities of Daily Living. *Journal of the American Geriatrics Society* 31:721–27.

Katz, S., and C.A. Akpom. 1976. A Measure of Primary Sociobiological Functions. *International Journal of Health Services* 6:493–508.

Katz, S., L.G. Branch, M.H. Branson, J.A. Papsidero, J.C. Beck, and D.S. Greer. 1983. Active Life Expectancy. *The New England Journal of Medicine* 309:1218–23.

Koizumi, A. 1982. Toward a Healthy Life in the 21st Century. In *Population Aging in Japan. Problems and Policy Issues in the 21st Century,* ed. T. Kuroda. Tokyo: Nihon University.

Kovar, M.G. 1980. Morbidity and Health Care Utilization. In *Proceedings of the Second Conference on the Epidemiology of Aging,* eds. S.G. Haynes and N. Feinleib, 317–328. NIH Pub. no. 80-969. Bethesda, Md.: National Institutes of Health.

Kramer, M. 1981. The Increasing Prevalence of Mental Disorders: Implications for the Future. Paper presented at National Conference on the Elderly Deinstitutionalized Patient in the Community, Arlington, Va., May 28.

Kuller, L.H., A. Bolker, M. Saslaw, et al. 1969. Nationwide Cerebrovascular Disease Mortality Study. *American Journal of Epidemiology* 90:536–78.

Kunkel, S.A., and C.K. Powell. 1981. The Adjusted Average Per Capita Cost Under Risk Contracts with Providers of Health Care. *Transactions of the Society of Actuaries* 23:221–230.

Lakatta, E.G. 1985. Health, Disease, and Cardiovascular Aging. In *Health in An Older Society,* U.S. Committee on Aging, Institute of Medicine, and National Research Council, 73–104. Washington: National Academy Press.

Lubitz, J., and R. Prihoda. 1983. Use and Costs of Medicare Services in the Last Years of Life. In *Health, United States, 1983.* DHHS pub. no. (PHS) 84-1232. Washington.

———. 1984. Use and Costs of Medicare Services in the Last 2 Years of Life. *Health Care Financing Review* 5:117–31.

Luce, B.R., K. Liu, and K.G. Manton. 1984. Estimating the Long-Term Care Population and

Its Use of Services. In *Long Term Care and Social Security*, 34–58, International Society Security Association Studies and Research, no. 21, Geneva.

Manton, K.G. 1980. Sex and Race Specific Mortality Differentials in Multiple Cause of Death Data. *Gerontologist* 20:480–93.

————. 1982. Changing Concepts of Morbidity and Mortality in the Elderly Population. *Milbank Memorial Fund Quarterly/Health and Society* 60:183–244.

————. 1983. Forecasting Life Expectancy. Testimony before the Subcommittee on Savings, Pensions, and Investment Policy of the Committee on Finance, United States Senate, July 15. Senate Hearing document no. 98-359. Washington.

————. 1987a. Forecasting Health Status Changes in the Aging U.S. Population: Assessment of the Current Status and Some Proposals. In *Climatic Change* 11:179–210.

————. 1987b. The Linkage of Health Status Changes and Workability. *Comprehensive Gerontology* 1:16–24.

Manton, K.G. 1988. Response to Papers by Fries and Schneider & Guralnik. *Gerontologica Perspecta* 1:23–29.

Manton, K.G., and T. Hausner. 1987. A Multidimensional Approach to Case Mix for Home Health Services. *Health Care Financing Review* 8:37–54.

Manton, K.G., and K. Liu. 1984a. The Future Growth of the Long-Term Care Population: Projections Based on the 1977 National Nursing Home Survey and the 1982 Long-Term Care Survey. Paper presented at the Third National Leadership Conference on Long-Term Care Issues. Washington.

————. 1984b. Projecting Chronic Disease Prevalence. *Medical Care* 22:511–26.

Manton, K.G., K. Liu, and E. Cornelius. 1985. An Analysis of the Heterogeneity of U.S. Nursing Home Patients. *Journal of Gerontology* 40:34–46.

Manton, K.G., G.C. Myers, and G. Andrews. 1987. Morbidity and Disability Patterns in Four Developing Nations: Their Implications for Social and Economic Integration of the Elderly. *Journal of Cross Cultural Gerontology* 2:115–29.

Manton, K.G. and E. Stallard. 1984. *Recent Trends in Mortality Analysis*. Orlando, Fla.: Academic Press.

Manton, K.G., E. Stallard, J.P. Creason, and W.B. Riggan. 1985. U.S. Cancer Mortality 1950–1978. A Strategy for Analyzing Spatial and Temporal Patterns. *Environmental Health Perspectives* 60:369–80.

Manton, K.G., E. Stallard, and H.D. Tolley. 1983. The Economic Impact of Health Policy Interventions. *Risk Analysis* 3:265–75.

Manton, K.G., E. Stallard, and J.W. Vaupel. 1986. Alternative Models for the Heterogeneity of Mortality Risks Among the Aged. *Journal of the American Statistical Association* 81:635–44.

Manton, K.G., E. Stallard, and S. Wing. 1991. Analyses of Black and White Differentials in the Age Trajectory of Mortality in Two Closed Cohort Studies. *Statistics in Medicine* 10:1043–59.

Manton, K.G., E. Stallard, and M.A. Woodbury. 1986. Chronic Disease Evolution and Human Aging: A General Model for Assessing the Impact of Chronic Disease in Human Populations. *Mathematical Modelling* 7:1155–71.

Minaker, K.L., and J.L. Rowe. 1985. Health and Disease Among the Oldest Old: A Clinical Perspective. *Milbank Memorial Fund Quarterly/Health and Society* 63:324–49.

Myers, G.C. and K.G. Manton. 1984. Compression of Mortality: Myth or Reality? *Gerontologist* 24:346–53.

Myers, G.C., K.G. Manton, and H. Bacellar. 1986. Sociodemographic Aspects of Future Unpaid Productive Roles. In *America's Aging: Productive Roles in an Older Society*, U.S. Committee on an Aging Society, Institute of Medicine, and National Research Council, 110-48. Washington: National Academy Press.

National Center for Health Statistics. 1978. *Health: United States, 1976–1977*. DHHS pub. no. (HRA) 77-1232. Hyattsville, Md.

―――. 1980b. The National Ambulatory Medical Care Survey, 1977 Summary. *Vital and Health Statistics*, series 13, no. 44. Rockville, Md.

―――. 1981. *Characteristics of Nursing Home Residents, Health Status, and Care Received: The National Nursing Home Survey, 1977*. DHHS pub. no. 81-1712. Hyattsville, Md.

―――. 1984. Changes in Mortality Among the Elderly: United States 1970–78, Supplement to 1980. *Vital and Health Statistics, Series 3*, No. 22a. Rockville, Md.

New York State Office for the Aging. 1983. Family Caregiving and the Elderly. Albany, N.Y.: Office for the Aging.

Office of Technology Assessment. 1979. *A Review of Selected Federal Vaccine and Immunization Policies*. Washington.

Omran, A.R. 1971. The Epidemiologic Transition: A Theory of the Epidemiology of Population Change. *Milbank Memorial Fund Quarterly/Health and Society* 49:509–38.

Palmore, E., ed. 1970. *Normal Aging: Reports from the Duke Longitudinal Study 1955–1969*. Durham, N.C.: Duke University Press.

―――. 1974. *Normal Aging II: Reports from the Duke Longitudinal Studies 1970–1973*. Durham, N.C.: Duke University Press.

Rice, D.P. 1980. Impact and Implications of the Changing Age Structure on Health Status and Use of Health Care. Paper presented at the Federal Statistics Users' Conference, Washington, May 12.

Rice, D.P., and J.J. Feldman. 1983. Living Longer in the United States: Demographic Changes and Health Needs of the Elderly. *Milbank Memorial Fund Quarterly/Health and Society* 61:362–96.

Riley, M.W. 1981. Health Behavior of Older People: Toward a New Paradigm. In *Health Behaviors and Aging*, eds. D.L. Parron, F. Soloman, and J. Rodin, 25–39. Institute of Medicine Interim Report no. 5. Washington: National Academy Press.

Riley, M.W., and K. Bond. 1983. Beyond Ageism: Postponing the Onset of Disability. In *Aging in Society: Selected Reviews of Recent Research*, eds. M.W. Riley, B.B. Hess, and K. Bond, 243–52. Hillsdale, N.J.: Lawrence Erlbaum.

Roos, N., E. Shapiro, and L.L. Roos. 1984. Aging and the Demand for Health Services: Which Aged and Whose Demand? *Gerontologist* 214:31–36.

Sanders, B.S. 1964. Measuring Community Health Levels. *American Journal of Public Health* 54:1063–1070.

Schneider, E.L., and J.M. Guralnik. 1988. The Compression of Morbidity: A Dream Which May Come True Someday! *Gerontologica Perspecta* 1:8–13.

Shepard, D., and R. Zeckhauser. 1977. Interventions in Mixed Populations: Concepts and Applications. Discussion Paper Series, JFK School of Government, Harvard University, no. 49D. (Machine Copy.)

Singer, R.B., and L. Levinson. 1976. *Medical Risks: Patterns of Mortality Survival*. Lexington, Mass.: Lexington Books.

Smyer, M.A. 1980. The Differential Use of Services by Impaired Elderly. *Journal of Gerontology* 35:249–55.

Social Security Administration. 1981. *Social Security Area Population Projections, Actuarial Study no. 85*. SSA pub. no. 11-11532. Washington.

―――. 1982. *Life Table for the United States: 1900–2050, Actuarial Study no. 87*. SSA pub. no. 11-11534. Washington.

Spiegelman, M. 1969. *Introduction to Demography*. Cambridge, Mass.: Harvard University Press.

Strehler, B.L. 1975. Implications of Aging Research for Society. *Proceedings* (58th Annual Meeting of the Federation of American Societies for Experimental Biology) 34:5–8.

Susser, M.W. 1973. *Causal Thinking in the Health Sciences*. London: Oxford University Press.

Tolley, H.D., and K.G. Manton. 1984. Assessing Health Care Costs in the Elderly. *Transactions of the Society of Actuaries* 36:579–603.

Treas, J. 1977. Family Support Systems for the Aged: Some Social and Demographic Considerations. *Gerontologist* 17:486–91.

U.S. Bureau of the Census. 1984. *Current Population Reports,* series P-23, no. 138. Washington.

Verbrugge, L.M. 1984. Longer Life But Worsening Health? Trends in Health and Mortality of Middle-Aged and Older Persons. *Milbank Memorial Fund Quarterly/Health and Society* 62:475–519.

Vladeck, B.C., and J.P. Firman. 1983. The Aging of the Population and Health Services. *The Annals* (Health Care Policy in America) 468:132–48.

Waldo, D.R., and H.C. Lazenby. 1984. Demographic Characteristics and Health Care Use and Expenditures by the Aged in the United States: 1977–1984. *Health Care Financing Review* 6:1–49.

Walford, R. 1983. Testimony Before the Subcommittee on Savings, Pensions, and Investment Policy of the Committee on Finance, U.S. Senate, July 15. Senate Hearing document no. 98-359. Washington.

Weissert, W. 1981. Long-Term Care: Current Policy and Directions for the 80's. Paper presented at the 1981 White Conference on Aging, Committee on Long-term Care. Washington.

Weissert, W., and W. Scanlon. 1983. Determinants of Institutionalization of the Aged. Working Paper no. 1466-21 (Rev.). Washington: Urban Institute.

Wilkins, R., and O. Adams. 1983. *Healthfulness of Life*. Montreal: Institute for Research on Public Policy.

Wing, S., K.G. Manton, E. Stallard, C. Hames, and H.A. Tryoler. 1985. The Black/White Mortality Crossover: Investigation in a Community Based Cohort. *Journal of Gerontology* 40:78–84.

Woodbury, M.A., and K.G. Manton. 1982. A New Procedure for Analysis of Medical Classification. *Methods of Information in Medicine* 21:210–220.

World Health Organization. 1980. *International Classification of Impairments, Disability, and Handicaps: A Manual of Classification Relating to the Consequences of Disease*. Geneva.

———. 1983. *Report of the Scientific Group for TRS: Uses of Epidemiology in the Care of the Elderly*. Geneva.

———. 1984. *The Uses of Epidemiology in the Study of the Elderly: Report of a WHO Scientific Group on the Epidemiology of Aging*. Technical Report Series 706. Geneva.

World Health Organization. Regional Office for Europe. 1982. *Epidemiological Studies on Social and Medical Conditions of the Elderly: Report on a Survey*. Copenhagen.

11

The Oldest Old and the Use of Institutional Long-term Care from an International Perspective

PAMELA J. DOTY

Health policy makers in the world's advanced industrial nations are only just beginning to realize the implications of population growth among the oldest old in terms of increased demand for certain types of health services and associated increases in national health expenditures (Ray et al. 1987). This chapter addresses the relation between advancing age and use of health services—particularly long-term care services—from an international perspective. The principal value of cross-national comparisons of health services use in relation to aging is to bring into clearer focus the relative role of "malleable" versus "nonmalleable" variables in shaping health policy. By examining the experience of other countries, policy makers can more readily understand the interplay between the factors that they can control and the elements that are so deeply rooted in biology, history, and social structure as to constitute predetermined imperatives that leave little room for maneuvering.

That health policy makers have an interest in cross-national comparisons of aging and health-services use is evidenced by comparative studies of long-term-care policy commissioned by the International Social Security Association (Doty 1986b), the World Health Organization (Wright 1986), the Organization for Economic Cooperation and Development (Mooney 1987, and other work in progress), and the European Community (Illsley 1988). These studies indicate that among the major policy questions related to long-term care of current concern to health policy makers in advanced industrial countries are the following: How should long-term care services be financed? How much should government versus the consumer—or some other private third party such as the family or insurance—be expected to pay? What is the appropriate balance between institutional and noninstitutional long-term-care services? To what extent can the family be expected, or perhaps encouraged, to continue to meet most of the long-term-care service needs of the elderly outside of institutions, or will government be required to take increasing responsibility to pay for formal home-care services?

In this chapter, I will look at how demographic forces are shaping the environment of long-term-care policy making. My purpose is to try to determine the degree to which the demographic imperatives of an aging elderly population are likely to dictate the answers to the preceding policy questions. I seek also to gauge the possibilities for health policy makers to exercise their political "free will" in shaping their countries' response to the challenges posed by the health-services needs of the growing numbers of their citizens who are living on into advanced old age.

Although this chapter does not hesitate to draw inferences from international comparative data concerning the degrees of freedom available to policy makers in long-term care, these should be considered hypotheses in need of further testing rather than definitive conclusions. International comparative work in long-term care is a relatively new field in large part because individual countries have only recently begun to accumulate sufficient data—of sufficiently reliable quality—to conduct their own policy research, let alone comparative analyses.

AGE IN RELATION TO USE AND COST OF HEALTH SERVICES

Although the long-term-care needs of the oldest old constitute the principal focus of this chapter, long-term care must be put in context, that is, to understand that the rising demand for long-term-care services brought about by growth in the older cohorts of the elderly population is just one feature of the association between advanced age and increased health-services use. Thus, the pressure on health-care financing systems created by the increased use of long-term-care services by the oldest old is in addition to the increased pressure brought about by this age group's greater use of acute health-care services as well.

Advancing age has been found to be associated with higher use rates and higher costs of health services generally in the United States, France, the Federal Republic of Germany, Great Britain, the Netherlands, and Finland (Sandier 1987). Dutch planning authorities, for example, calculated health expenditures by age group as of 1981 to be 2,710 guilders per capita among persons aged 65 to 79, compared with 7,020 guilders per capita among persons aged 80 and older (Netherlands, Social and Cultural Planning Office 1984). It is likely that this very sizable per capita health-expenditure differential between the younger and older elderly cohorts reflects the fact that the Netherlands is—apart from some Canadian provinces—the only major Western industrial nation to cover most nursing-home costs under national health insurance.

Even in countries where government coverage of nursing-home and other long-term-care services is much more limited, however, age-related increases in hospital use rates and associated costs per hospital stay emerge as quite pronounced. In the United States, for example, in calendar year 1981, the use rate of inpatient hospital care by Medicare enrollees aged 85 and older was 82 percent greater than that of enrollees aged 65 to 69 (335.7 per 1,000 enrollees aged 85 and older compared with 184.7 per 1,000 enrollees aged 65 to 69) (U.S. Health Care Financing Administration 1984). In France, the use rate for hospital services in 1981 among the cohort aged 85 and older was 217 percent greater than that of the elderly aged 60 to 69 (326 per 1,000 aged 85 and older compared with 103 per 1,000 aged 60 to 69) (Caisse Nationale de l'Assurance Maladie des Travailleurs Salaries [CNAMTS] 1983).

Hospital costs increase with age, both because of the increased frequency of hospital use at older ages, and because of greater service intensity, as measured by higher average costs per hospital stay. Medicare hospital costs per enrollee averaged $667 among those aged 65 to 69 compared with $1,321 among those aged 85 and older. Medicare reimbursements per hospital stay averaged $1,997 among the cohort aged 65 to 69 compared with $2,253 among those aged 85 and older (U.S. Health Care Financing Administration 1984). In France in 1981, average annual hospital expenditures per person aged 85 and older were 8,361 francs compared with 2,394 francs per person among those aged 60 to 69. Average expenditures per hospital stay were 18,623 francs for those aged 85 and older compared with 15,855 francs among those aged 60 to 69. In France, however, the peak average annual expenditures for hospital stays was experienced by the cohort aged 70 to 79 (22,662) (CNAMTS 1983).

Patterns of physician services use show a similar but less marked tendency to increase with advancing age in the United States, though not in France. The differential use rate for physician services in the United States for the cohort aged 85 and older compared with the cohort aged 65 to 69 in 1981 was 28 percent (757.5 per 1,000 Medicare enrollees aged 85 and older. 588.8 per enrollees aged 65 to 69) (U.S. Health Care Financing Administration 1984). Use rates for generalist physician services in France among those aged 85 and older in 1981 are quite similar to those of physician-services use in the United States (787 per 1,000 aged 85 and older). The difference is that in France the younger elderly also use generalist physician services at these same comparatively high rates. Per capita expenditures for physician services increase with advancing age in both countries, however.

In the United States, these higher costs appears to be due more to higher frequency of physician-services use, whereas in France they appear to be due more to higher intensity—that is, higher costs per visit. Average 3-month expenditures per person for generalist physician services in France in 1980 to 1981 were 111.3 francs for persons aged 80 and older compared with 86.2 francs per person for persons aged 66 to 79. For all physicians, including both generalists and specialists, 3-month per-capita expenditures averaged 168.2 francs for persons aged 80 and older compared with 143.6 francs for persons aged 65 to 79 (Mizrahi and Mizrahi 1985b). A more detailed examination of per capita physician expenditures in both France and the United States reveals, however, that per capita expenditures reach a peak among the cohort aged 80 to 84 and begin to decline again after the age of 85 (Mizrahi and Mizrahi 1985b; U.S. Health Care Financing Administration 1984).

AGE IN RELATION TO NURSING-HOME USE

Advancing age is very strongly associated with increased use of long-term-care services, especially institutional long-term-care services. In the United States, according to the 1985 National Nursing Home Survey, approximately 1.3 percent of the population aged 65 to 74 resided in nursing homes; this increased to 5.8 percent among those aged 75 to 84 and reached 22 percent among those aged 85 and older (Hing 1987). In Canada, the comparable percentages have been estimated to be 2.4 percent of those aged 65 to 74, 10.6 percent of those aged 75 to 84, and 31 percent of those aged 85 and older (Kane and Kane 1985). In France, a 1982 study calculated that the institutionalization rate among the elderly increases from 4.1 percent among those aged 66 to 70, to 7.3 percent among those aged 71 to 75, to 13.8 percent among those aged 76 to 80, to 28 percent among those aged 81 to 85, to 48.7 percent among those aged 86 to 90, to 75.6 percent among those aged 91 to 95, to virtually universal institutionalization above age 96 (CNAMTS 1984). In the Netherlands, the rate of institutionalization of the elderly in 1980 was 8.1 percent for the population as a whole aged over 65, but this averaged age-specific rates that ranged from a low of 0.6 percent among those aged 65 to 69 to a high of 41.2 percent among those aged 90 and older (Sandier 1987). A comparative study of long-term-care institutional use rates in the three Scandinavian countries of Norway, Denmark, and Sweden found rates of 2.4 to 2.5 percent among those aged 65 to 79 in all three countries and rates ranging from 20.5 to 24.6 percent for those aged 80 and older (Daatland 1985). In Switzerland, 4.5 percent of the elderly aged 65 to 79 were reported to be in institutions as of 1980, compared with 20.1 percent of those aged 80 and older (Jurg Siegenthaler, American University, Washington, personal communication 1985). In Israel, age-specific use rates of long-term-care institutions have been calculated to be 2.1 percent among the group aged 65 to 69, 4 percent for persons aged 70 to 74, 8.2 percent for the group aged 75 to 79, 13.6 percent for the group aged 80 to 84, and 20.6 percent among those aged 85 and older (Habib, Kop, and Shmueli 1985).

These sharply rising institutionalization rates with advancing age reflect in part the strong association between age and increased functional disability (Mizrahi and Mizrahi 1985a; Weissert 1985). According to U.S. data, only 2.6 percent of persons aged 65 to 74 need assistance with personal care, compared with 31.6 percent of those aged 85 and older (U.S. Health Care Financing Administration 1981). Nevertheless, U.S. data also indicate that, whereas 24 percent of the elderly aged 65 to 84 with personal-care dependencies (i.e., need for assistance with basic activities of daily living, such as bathing, dressing, eating, toileting, and transferring from bed to chair) are in nursing homes, 61 percent of the elderly aged 85 and older with personal-care dependencies are institutionalized (U.S. Department of Health and Human Services 1986).

Advancing age is also associated with a greater risk of developing Alzheimer's disease and related dementias. The prevalence of severe dementia rises from 1 percent among the group aged 65 to 74, to 7 percent among those aged 75 to 84, to 25 percent among persons aged 85 and older (U.S. Congress, Office of Technology Assessment 1987). Mental incapacity has been found to be a statistically significant predictor of nursing-home use versus continued community residence (Weissert and Scanlon 1982).

A comparison of the characteristics of the elderly in long-term-care institutions in the United States, France, and the Netherlands found that from 44 to 56 percent of the residents of medically oriented long-term-care facilities either had mental disorders as their primary diagnosis or were characterized as suffering from mental confusion (Doty 1986b). Recent data from the 1985 National Nursing Home Survey (Hing 1987) suggest that senile dementia and/or disorientation or memory impairment may have become even more prevalent among U.S. nursing-home residents over the eight-year period since the 1977 National Nursing Home Survey (U.S. National Center for Health Statistics 1979). In 1985, 62.6 percent of nursing-home residents were found to have disorientation or memory impairment and 47 percent had been diagnosed as having senile dementia or organic brain syndrome.

Increased likelihood of nursing-home placement at advanced ages also reflects, in part, the loss of informal support through death of the spouse, a trend that particularly affects older women due to the greater gains in longevity experienced by older women compared with older men in the advanced industrialized nations. According to the U.S. 1985 National Nursing Home Survey, higher percentages of the younger elderly in institutions are still married, have never married, or are divorced or separated compared with the institutionalized elderly aged 85 and older who, in contrast, are more likely to be widowed (Hing 1987). Childlessness, however, was found to be more prevalent among the younger elderly in nursing homes; 69 percent of those aged 85 and older in nursing homes had living children compared with only 50 percent of the institutionalized elderly aged 65 to 74. The fact that those aged 85 and older are more likely to have children who themselves are senior citizens may partially explain these relatively greater percentages of nursing-home residents in the oldest-old cohort with living children. It is also possible that the children of persons who enter nursing homes at older ages have already spent a number of years providing care informally and have exhausted their capacity to go on providing such care. One cannot help but raise the question, however, of whether it is perhaps not also more socially acceptable to place one's parents in a nursing home once they have attained advanced old age.

This speculation about the social acceptability of institutionalization with advancing age is raised, in part, because major studies of the factors that predict nursing-home placement versus continued residence in the community have repeatedly found that age is a statistically significant predictor of nursing-home entry independent of functional disability, mental status, social supports, or income (Cohen et al. 1986; Weissert and Scanlon 1982). It is particularly interesting to observe that for large numbers of U.S. elderly aged 85 and older who enter nursing homes, poverty is clearly not a factor in the initial decision to seek institutional placement. Indeed, the 1985 National Nursing Home Survey found that nursing-home residents aged 85 and older were more likely to have themselves or family members as their primary source of payment upon entry compared with younger elderly residents, who were more likely to have Medicaid as their primary payment source. Although, generally speaking, it is clearly dependency rather than negative societal attitudes toward old age that explains institutionalization, the exceptionally high rates of nursing-home use by those aged 85 and older—use rates that are not fully explained by functional dependency and loss of social supports—point to the possibility that some form of ageism may play a role in the increased likelihood of institutionalization at advanced ages. Anecdotal evidence offered by social workers active in hospital discharge planning and case management of community-based long-term-care services suggests that if ageism is indeed a factor, it is not an age prejudice causing family members to want to dump the very elderly in institutions to be rid of them. Rather, it appears that family members may be more anxious about the safety of elderly persons at advanced ages living alone or even being home alone for lengthy periods. The family may be less willing to permit those aged 85 and older to run the risks perceived to be associated with being alone in an unsupervised setting. One interesting potential question for cross-national research is whether such protective attitudes toward the very old— assuming that they do exist and are a factor in institutional placement—vary from country to country.

MALLEABLE VERSUS NONMALLEABLE VARIABLES: DEFINING THE RANGE OF POLICY OPTIONS

Policy makers in most advanced industrial countries, according to a questionnaire survey that I conducted for the International Social Security Association (Doty 1986b), consider excessive use of long-term-care institutions to be a major policy concern. This concern reflects not only budget-conscious desires by officials to curb the high costs associated with institutionalization, but also their more idealistic desire to enhance the quality of life of the disabled elderly by meeting their care needs in less restrictive environments.

We have seen that increased use of health services, particularly the use of institutional long-term care, is strongly associated with advancing age in every country for which data are available. Because every country has nursing homes or their equivalent and because their use rates rise steeply with age, it seems clear that policy options in long-term care are constrained to some extent by the sociobiological determinants of need for nursing-home care. Nevertheless, within each age cohort, some countries show strikingly higher use rates than others, suggesting that there is a range within which institutional use patterns are not fully determined by demographic factors such as age and age-associated health and social status. In the following section, we will explore the relative roles of demographic imperatives versus health-policy choices with respect to cross-national differences in institutionalization rates.

COMPARATIVE CROSS-NATIONAL INSTITUTIONALIZATION RATES

As part of a cross-national study of long-term-care policy in 18 countries for the International Social Security Association (Doty 1986b), I attempted to estimate the pure effects of age/sex population structure differences (that is, older and more heavily female populations) on institutionalization rates by projecting the institutional use rate of the elderly aged 65 and over for each country if its age/sex-specific institutional use rates were the same as those in the United States (as measured by the 1977 National Nursing Home Survey, U.S. National Center for Health Statistics 1979). The 18 countries whose institutionalization rates are compared are selected from the 27 countries included in the survey sample that responded to a questionnaire sent out under the auspices of the International Social Security Association. For purposes of consistency, United Nations population figures were employed to make the projections. These projections, in effect, adjust elderly institutional-use rates for cross-national differences in the age structure of the elderly population (i.e., relative proportion of the population aged 65 and over in the age cohorts 65 to 69, 70 to 79, and 80 and older) and differences in male versus female longevity. By comparing the projected rates against the actual institutionalization rates in each country, one can begin to get a rough idea of the degree to which differences in institutional use are due to demographic imperatives versus cultural and political factors that are potentially more amenable to deliberate policy changes.

Projected and actual use rates are reported here both separately and in total for two types of long-term-care institutions. Long-term-care institutions for the elderly in most countries can be roughly categorized as either "medically oriented" or "nonmedically oriented." The former include long-stay geriatric wards in hospitals, psychiatric facilities serving the elderly with dementia, and nursing homes; the latter include the types of facilities that, in the United States, go by such varying names as "homes for the aged," "rest homes," "domiciliary care facilities," "personal-care homes," and "board and care homes." In other countries, these nonmedically oriented facilities go by even more varied names—such as "local authority homes" (Great Britain), "hostels" (Australia), and "hospices" (France). In principle, the difference between medically and nonmedically oriented long-term-care institutions is that the former have trained medical or nursing personnel on staff, whereas the latter do not. In many countries, nonmedically oriented institutions are supposed to cater to the so-called fit or independent elderly or elderly who are frail but still able to attend to their own personal-care needs. In practice, the distinction between medically and nonmedically oriented facilities often is unclear. Many ostensibly nonmedical institutions actually are nursing homes in all but name. Sometimes this is because elderly persons who enter while still fit are allowed to remain after they have become disabled and over time become a majority of the residents. In other cases, the politics of bureaucracy are at issue; for example, social services authorities may wish to emphasize the social as opposed to the medical dimension of care by calling facilities they operate something other than nursing homes. In other cases, even though a deliberate policy has been undertaken to "medicalize" what were formerly nonmedical facilities, the facility continues to be called by its traditional name. This is the case in Belgium, for example, where a policy is underway to medicalize rest homes and to close or convert geriatric long-stay hospital beds. In sum, although there are major variations among countries in the use rates of nonmedical as well as medical institutions, and these variations highlight some of the possibilities for policy choice, it is well to bear in mind in examining the comparative use rates discussed here that, in reality, there is often somewhat less to the distinction between medically and nonmedically oriented long-term-care facilities than the facility names suggest.

Table 11–1 displays the age/sex-specific, medically oriented institutional (i.e., nursing home) use rates employed to make the projections that are derived from the 1977 National Nursing Home Survey. Age/sex-specific use rates for nonmedical institutional facilities in the United States are not available. In principle, these nonmedically oriented long-term care facilities are also covered in the National Nursing Home Survey as long as they have more than two beds. Many experts believe, however, that such facilities were undersampled in the 1977 National Nursing Home Survey. Accordingly, estimates of the use rate of nonmedically oriented long-term-care institutions in the United States have been derived from special studies (Sherwood, Mor, and Gutkin 1981; and Stone 1984), and the projections are based on the ratio of nonmedical to medical facility use (0.27).

The use of U.S. age/sex-specific institutionalization rates as the comparative standard should not be interpreted as having normative significance. U.S. rates were employed because they were readily available. Nevertheless, it is fortuitous for purposes of estimating the impact of demographic factors on institutional use rates that U.S. age/sex-specific institutionalization rates are among the lowest of the industrialized nations.

Table 11–1 Constant Prevalence Rates Utilized in Projections
(rate per 1,000 population)

Residential status	Sex	65–69	70–79	80+
			Age group	
Institutionalized elderly	Male	8.73920	24.17599	96.22000
	Female	10.49900	35.37000	175.72000
Noninstitutionalized elderly				
IADL needs only[a]	Male	40.23100	51.04800	70.85500
	Female	39.30600	57.75500	82.61000
1 or 2 ADLs[b]	Male	26.97099	44.65700	103.57500
	Female	41.32201	61.42999	121.80701
3 or 4 ADLs	Male	14.75200	18.99899	41.80600
	Female	16.05099	25.96201	51.88000
5 or 6 ADLS	Male	8.73920	24.17599	96.22000
	Female	10.49900	35.37000	175.72000

[a] IADL = instrumental activities of daily living (e.g., shopping, meal preparation, laundry, chores).
[b] ADL = activities of daily living (e.g., bathing, dressing, eating, toileting, mobility).
Source: Prevalence rates for these age/sex categories were calculated by Kenneth G. Manton and Michael Carney of the Duke University Center for Demographic Studies, Durham, N.C., from the 1977 National Nursing Home Survey (for the institutional rates) and the 1982 Long-term Care Survey (for rates of functional disability among the noninstitutionalized elderly). Both surveys were conducted by the Department of Health and Human Services.

Table 11–2, which records the cross-national projected institutional use rates based on U.S. age/sex-specific institutional rates compared with actual use rates, indicates that the differences in use rates that would be anticipated due to certain countries having older, more female elderly populations are considerably less than the variations in actual use rates. In the early 1980s, only France and the Netherlands would be expected to have higher use rates of long-term-care facilities based on population characteristics alone—although the differences (0.3 percent in the case of France) are minor. Only Costa Rica, Israel, and Japan would be expected to have more than negligibly lower institutional use rates based on elderly population characteristics. However, by 1985, (see the comparison in Table 11–3 of 1980 vs. 1985 projected

Table 11–2 Comparison of Projected Use Rates versus Actual Institutional Use Rates: 1980

Countries	Projected rate in percent			Actual rate in percent		
	Total	Medical facilities	Nonmedical facilities	Total	Medical facilities	Nonmedical facilities
United States	5.7	4.5	1.2	5.7	4.5	1.2
Argentina[a]						
1984	5.0	3.9	1.1	<0.1	N/A	N/A
Australia[b]						
1981	5.3	4.2	1.1	6.4	4.9	1.5
Belgium[c]						
1981–1983	5.7	4.5	1.2	6.3	2.6	3.7
Canada[d]	5.3	4.2	1.1	8.7	7.1	1.6
Costa Rica[e]						
1980	4.7	3.7	1.0	1.5–2.0	N/A	1.5–2.0
Denmark[f]	5.7	4.5	1.2	7.0	N/A	N/A

Countries	Projected rate in percent			Actual rate in percent		
	Total	Medical facilities	Nonmedical facilities	Total	Medical facilities	Nonmedical facilities
France[g]						
1982	6.1	4.8	1.3	6.3	5.3	1.0
Federal Republic of Germany[h]						
1980	5.5	4.3	1.2	3.6–4.5	1.2–3.6	0.9–2.4
Greece[i]						
1982	5.4	4.2	1.1	0.5	N/A	0.5
Israel[j]						
1981	4.4	3.5	0.9	4.0	1.4	2.6
Japan[k]						
1981	4.9	3.9	1.0	3.9	3.1	0.8
Netherlands[l]						
1982–1983	5.8	4.6	1.2	10.9	2.9	8.0
New Zealand[m]						
1982–1983	5.2	4.1	1.1	6.3–6.7	2.4–2.8	3.9
Spain[n]						
1982	5.3	4.2	1.1	2.0	N/A	2.0
Sweden[o]						
1980	5.7	4.5	1.2	8.7–10.5	4.8	4.1–5.9
Switzerland[p]						
1982	5.7	4.5	1.2	7.8–9.0	2.8	5.0–7.2
Turkey[q]						
1984	4.2	3.3	0.9	<0.2	N/A	N/A

Notes: N/A is not available. ISSA is International Social Security Association.

[a] Calculated from bed supply figures given in the ISSA questionnaire reply provided by the National Insurance Institute.

[b] Cameron, R.J.: Australia's Aged Population, 1982. Catalog No. 41090:0. Australian Bureau of Statistics, July 1982.

[c] Calculated from figures given in the ISSA questionnaire reply provided by the National Sickness and Invalidity Insurance Institute.

[d] The figures for medical facilities are from the ISSA questionnaire reply provided by the Department of National Health and Welfare. The figures for nonmedical facilities are based on: Schwenger, C.W.: 1976 Canada Census. Paper presented at the Final Plenary Session of the National Conference on Aging. Ottawa. Oct. 1983. Paper cited in: U.S. Senate, Special Committee on Aging: *Long-Term Care in Western Europe and Canada: Implications for the United States.* Washington, July 1984.

[e] Calculated from figures given in: Costa Rican National Report for the U.N. World Assembly on Aging, Vienna, Austria, 1982 and Costa Rica, Oficina de Planificación Nacional y Política Económica, División de Planificación Global: *Lineamientos para una Politica Gerontológíca en Costa Rica.* San José, Costa Ríca, Aug. 1980.

[f] Calculated from figures given in the ISSA questionnaire reply provided by the National Social Security Office.

[g] Based on figures from the French National Report for the U.N. World Assembly on Aging, Vienna, Austria, 1982.

[h] Based on figures from the National Report for the Federal Republic of Germany for the U.N. World Assembly on Aging, Vienna, Austria, 1982.

[i] Based on figures from the Greek National Report of the U.N. World Assembly on Aging, Vienna, Austria, 1982.

[j] Calculated from figures given in the ISSA questionnaire reply provided by the National Insurance Institute.

[k] Ikegami, N.: Institutionalized and the noninstitutionalized elderly. *Social Science Medicine* 16:2003, 1982. Cited in Campbell, R.: Nursing homes and long-term care in Japan. *Pacific Affairs,* 57(1):82, Spring 1984.

[l] Calculated from figures given in the ISSA questionnaire reply provided by the Council of Sickness Funds.

[m] Calculated from figures given in the ISSA questionnaire reply provided by the Department of Social Welfare and the Department of Health and in the New Zealand National Report for the U.N. World Assembly on Aging, Vienna, Austria, 1982.

[n] Calculated from figures given in the ISSA questionnaire reply provided by the National Institute for Social Services.

[o] Calculated from figures given in the ISSA questionnaire reply provided by the National Board of Health and Welfare.

[p] Based on figures from the Swiss National Report for U.N. World Assembly on Aging, Vienna, Austria, 1982.

[q] Calculated from bed supply figures given in: Council of Europe/Conseil de l'Europe: Colloque sur la Protection Sociale des Personnes Trés Agées—Alternatives à l'Hospitalisation, Sept. 1985, Rapport Établi par la Délégation de la Turquie, Strasbourg, France, June 1985. Also personal communication: Marsel Heïsel, Assistant Professor of Social Work, Rutgers University, New Jersey, United States, based on research in nursing homes in Turkey.

use rates) somewhat greater differences begin to appear, with Belgium, France, the Federal Republic of Germany, and Switzerland showing increases in projected use rates of long-term institutions more than slightly above U.S. rates due to population aging and greater proportions of elderly females.

In sum, when actual use rates are compared with the projected rates, it appears that population characteristics—at least age and sex alone—explain only a small amount of the variance. Population characteristics alone would suggest quite similar use rates for the United States, the Netherlands, and Sweden, yet both these latter countries use institutional services at almost twice the rate of the United States. In the Netherlands, however, use of medical institutions is one-third less than the U.S. rate, while the use rate of nonmedical institutions is six and one-half times greater. The Swedish use rate of medical institutions is quite similar to the U.S. use rate of such facilities, but the Swedish use rate of nonmedical facilities is four to five times as great as the U.S. rate. In contrast, the use rate of all long-term-care institutions in the Federal Republic of Germany, especially medical facilities, is considerably less than that of the United States—at least 20 percent less and perhaps as much as one-third less. (It is important to note, however, that various sources indicate that there is a significant amount of use of hospital beds by elderly long-stay patients. Unlike

Table 11–3 Cross-National Projected Institutional Use Rates for Elderly Aged 65 and Over in Medically Oriented Long-term Care Facilities (based on U.S. age/sex specific nursing home use rates)

Country	Rate	
	1980	1985
United States	4.5	4.4
Argentina	3.9	4.1
Australia	4.2	4.2
Belgium	4.5	5.0
Canada	4.2	4.2
Costa Rica	3.7	3.8
Denmark	4.5	4.7
France	4.8	5.5
Federal Republic of Germany	4.3	5.1
Greece	4.2	4.6
Israel	3.5	3.9
Japan	3.9	4.1
Netherlands	4.6	4.7
New Zealand	4.1	4.2
Spain	4.2	4.4
Sweden	4.5	4.7
Switzerland	4.5	4.9
Turkey	3.3	3.7

Source: These rates were calculated by the author with assistance from K.G. Manton and M. Carney of the Duke University Center for Demographic Studies, Durham, N.C., using U.S. age/sex-specific institutional use rates from the 1977 National Nursing Home Survey and United Nations population statistics.

the case of Japan, however, we were unable to quantify such hospital use sufficiently to include it in the medical institutional use rate.)

It is striking that the use rates of long-term-care facilities in Costa Rica, Spain, and especially in Argentina, Greece, and Turkey, are considerably lower than the rate in the United States. Although population characteristics alone would make Costa Rica's actual use rate appear 20 percent lower were it actually the same as the U.S. rate, it is, in fact, less than one-half the U.S. rate. Very little of the differences in institutional use rates among the United States, Greece, and Spain appear to be attributable to population characteristics, however.

RATES OF FAMILY CAREGIVING

To what can we attribute such variations in institutional use rates? The lower institutional use rates characteristic of Japan and the less industrialized countries almost certainly reflect higher levels of family caregiving. Research indicates that reliance on family caregiving remains high in the Western industrialized countries (Conference des Ministres Europeens Charges des Affaires Familiales 1983; Dooghe 1984; Doty 1986a; Kendig and Rowland 1983; Macken 1986; Morginstin and Shamai 1984; Oldiges 1984; Stone, Cafferata, and Sangl 1986). These studies, carried out in the United States, the Federal Republic of Germany, Australia, Belgium, Israel, and Sweden, indicate that approximately 60 to 80 percent of all long-term care provided to the elderly disabled living in the community is provided by family members rather than by paid professionals. As Elaine Brody (1985) has noted in writing about the "myth of abandonment" of the elderly by their adult children in modern industrial societies, the level of family care-giving is much higher than commonly supposed.

However, even though rates of family caregiving in the Western advanced industrialized countries are high, they are nevertheless almost certainly lower than those of Japan, the less industrialized countries of Europe, and the developing countries. Cultural norms probably account for some of the difference, but it is likely that a greater share is explained by factors affecting the availability of family caregivers. Thus, contrary to prevailing beliefs about Japanese versus U.S. cultural norms, a comparative study of willingness of family to provide care for elderly family members in the two countries found little difference in the sense of "filial obligation" on the part of Japanese and Americans (Maeda and Sussman 1980). According to further work by Maeda (1982), actual differences in levels of family caregiving between Japan and the United States reflected higher rates of marriage and fertility in Japan, which meant that Japanese elderly had more relatives available to provide care informally at home.

Interpreting Maeda's findings more broadly would suggest that in the advanced industrialized societies, larger percentages of never-married, divorced, and childless elderly and lower average numbers of children translate into fewer available family members to provide long-term care informally at home. If this hypothesis is correct— that the higher rates of family caregiving in less-industrialized countries are primarily due to greater availability rather than greater willingness of family to provide care— then deliberate social policy efforts to support, maintain, or promote family caregiving are unlikely to have much overall effect on preventing increases in institutional use rates. Such policies may lighten the burden on existing family caregivers, but will not change the decisions made in early adulthood about marriage, divorce, and how many children to have, which ultimately determine the availability of family caregivers for the elderly.

INSTITUTIONAL BED SUPPLY POLICIES

On the other hand, certain factors that probably explain the higher rates of institutional use in some advanced industrial countries versus others are more open to deliberate policy influence. Availability of institutional beds and the policies that determine bed availability are a major example.

Studies conducted in both the United States (Weissert and Scanlon 1982) and Australia (Howe and Preston 1985) of intranational variations in institutionalization rates have found that such regional differences are explained more by availability of bed supply than by demographic factors associated with need for long-term care. In the United States, for example, in the nine states and the District of Columbia with the lowest nursing-home bed to elderly population ratios in the nation (fewer than 44 beds per 1,000 elderly aged 65 and older), only 53.9 percent of the unmarried elderly aged 75 and older needing assistance with toileting and eating were in nursing homes, compared with 92.1 percent of elderly who had the same characteristics in the ten states with the highest nursing-home bed to elderly population ratios (those with more than 85 beds per 1,000 elderly) (U.S. General Accounting Office 1983). Note that the states with the highest bed-to-population ratios had roughly twice as many beds per 1,000 elderly as the states with the lowest bed-to-population ratios; yet, nursing homes in both the high- and low-ratio states were operating at full occupancy rates. This suggests that there is a considerable amount of elasticity in the market demand for nursing home care. It would also seem to indicate a sizable variation in the definition of "need" for nursing-home care as it is applied by state health-planning agencies. Nursing-home bed supply is regulated (in all but a handful of recently deregulated states) according to laws that require would-be builders to obtain a "certificate of need," based on an official determination that there is, in fact, unmet need for institutional care in the area where the builder wishes to build a new or expand an existing facility.

Since the late 1970s, new nursing-home bed construction in the United States has not kept pace with the growth rate of the population aged 85 and older, who are the greatest users of nursing home care (U.S. General Accounting Office 1983; unpublished Health Care Financing Administration statistics). This may explain why nursing-home use rates did not increase between 1977 and 1985 while higher levels of disability were found among nursing-home residents in the 1985 compared with the 1977 and 1974 National Nursing Home Surveys. Indeed, it would appear from these findings that "inappropriate" placement in nursing homes of elderly who are not sufficiently sick or disabled to require nursing-home care is no longer the problem it was thought to be in the mid-1970s. Indeed, since at least 1980, experts have been debating, without coming to a clear consensus, whether there is a surplus or a shortage of nursing-home beds (U.S. Department of Health and Human Services, Office of the Assistant Secretary for Planning and Evaluation 1981). Either way, U.S. experience seems to indicate that regulation of long-term-care institutional bed supply can be a powerful policy tool for controlling institutional use rates, but a tool whose application may not allow for sufficient fine-tuning to avoid access problems affecting some geographic areas or certain population subgroups.

The Netherlands, according to its 1982 report to the World Assembly on Aging, has recognized the importance of bed-supply policy on elderly institutionalization rates. Dutch authorities would like to lower institutionalization rates but they have discovered, as have a number of individual states in the United States, that once a condition of "overbedding" has developed, it is difficult and time-consuming to reverse, especially by applying limits on new construction alone.

Perhaps the easiest way to implement a policy of lowering institutional bed-to-population ratios rapidly is by singling out a particular category of facilities to be phased out. Thus, nonmedically oriented homes for the aged, which traditionally served frail but independent or only slightly disabled elderly, can be phased out and replaced with service flats, as is being done in Sweden. Use of mental hospitals for the elderly with dementia can be phased out in preference to nursing homes, as was done in the United States during the late 1960s and early 1970s, based on current thinking among both mental-health and geriatric-care professionals that held mental hospitals to be inappropriate treatment sites for such patients. Unlike the United States, which tends to mix dementia patients together with the physically disabled but mentally intact, the Netherlands has established separate facilities for "psychiatric" and "somatic" nursing-home patients. Finally, as exemplified by Belgium, hospital-based long-term care may be phased out as representing an overly expensive and excessively medicalized model of long-term care. Even where it is necessary to replace many of the phased-out beds with new beds in facilities considered more appropriate (e.g., free-standing nursing homes), it may still be possible to effect an overall decrease in the institutional bed-supply ratio. There is evidence that these trends are, in fact, underway in several European countries, particularly the trend to close old-fashioned homes for the aged in countries that have had relatively high use rates for nonmedical residential facilities (Doty 1986b).

EFFECTS OF FINANCING POLICY

Differences in financing policies may appear to influence institutional use rates. More generous public financing of institutional long-term care, such that out-of-pocket payments by the elderly resident are limited, appears to be associated with higher use rates. In the United States, the greater likelihood of nursing home use by the poor and upper-income elderly as compared to the middle-income elderly (Weissert and Scanlon 1982), suggests the deterrent effect of Medicaid spend-down requirements on use of nursing homes by the middle-income elderly who run the risk of exhausting their income and savings in paying for nursing home care. Although it is often claimed that U.S. financing policy is "institutionally biased," these findings on the relation of income to nursing home use, as well as the implications of cross-national comparisons of institutional use rates in relation to financing policies, suggest otherwise. The United States and Germany—countries that, by and large, withhold public sub-

sidy altogether unless or until an individual has no ability to pay privately for care—
have lower institutional use rates than countries such as the Netherlands (which pays
for nursing-home care under national health insurance), Canada (which also pays for
nursing-home care under national health insurance but requires individuals to forfeit
their Social Security payments as "user fees"), and Sweden and Denmark (which
require individuals to apply their Social Security payments and a portion of private
income toward their nursing-home care but ensure that a certain percentage of private
income and assets [including the home] is protected [Doty 1986b]). If this association
between more generous public financing and higher national nursing-home use rates
holds up in further research, it would imply that the "price" of lower overall institutionalization rates is paid by those elderly who do enter institutions in the form of
very high rates of private cost sharing.

PUBLICLY FUNDED HOME AND COMMUNITY-BASED CARE

Finally, most of the advanced industrial countries report attempts to reduce institutionalization rates among the elderly by pursuing policies that would make publicly
funded home and community-based alternatives more widely available (Doty 1986b).
Well-controlled evaluations of such policies are not readily available, except for the
United States. The U.S. experience has been disappointing in that most experiments
broadening the availability of publicly funded home and community-based care have
not yielded statistically significant reductions in nursing home use (Berkeley Planning
Associates 1984; Kemper et al. 1986). The few exceptions in which some decreased
nursing-home use was achieved involved programs tied rather narrowly to hospital
discharge and nursing-home preadmission screening rather than programs where publicly funded services were targeted more broadly to the disabled elderly still residing
in the community who had not sought nursing-home care. These broader-based programs, including those that identified support for family caregivers as a major goal,
tended to supplement rather than substitute for nursing-home care. Such programs
provide additional publicly funded home and community-based care to elderly whose
informal supports are already sufficient to maintain them in the community. The
evaluation findings indicate that, even though it rarely prevents institutionalization,
the additional government help is appreciated by both the elderly and their family
caregivers and enhances their sense of subjective well-being (Kemper et al. 1986).

One reason why the U.S. experience with home and community-based alternative
programs has not had much success in reducing nursing-home use may be that U.S.
nursing-home use rates are, as we have seen, already low by comparison with most
other advanced industrial countries. Countries like Sweden, which claim to have
achieved significant reductions in institutional use rates during the 1970s in part via
promoting home and community-based care (Daatland 1985), may have been able to
achieve such results because they started from—and indeed still have—higher rates
of long-term-care institutional use than the United States. In any case, there is no
clear cross-national association between relatively generous government financing for
home and community-based care and lower rates of institutionalization (Doty 1986b).
In Scandinavia, the Netherlands, and Canada, as in the United States, publicly funded
home and community-based care appears to serve a different population from those

imminently at risk of institutionalization and, as such, is primarily a supplement rather than an alternative to nursing-home care. Moreover, European countries as well as the United States are largely unwilling to finance home-care alternatives that would cost more than institutional care (Comité Europeen de la Santé 1985; Ennuyer 1983).

CONCLUSION

In sum, use of health services, particularly institutional long-term care, has been found to be strongly related to advancing age in the United States and a number of other industrialized countries, including Canada, France, the Netherlands, the Scandinavian countries, Switzerland, and Israel. Differences in overall institutional use rates of those aged 65 and older in these countries—which range from 4 to 11 percent—cannot, for the most part, be explained by differences in population age/sex structure (i.e., older and more heavily female populations in some countries as compared to others). Policy variables appear to bear more responsibility than demographic imperatives in producing these differential institutional-use rates. Although too little comparative international policy research has been conducted to permit definitive conclusions, this analysis suggests that institutional bed supply and financing policies are probably the main policy sources of the differences that presently exist in institutionalization rates of the elderly among the Western industrialized countries. In contrast, policies promoting greater availability of home and community-based care or support for family caregivers, appear not to play much of a role in explaining existing cross-national differences in institutionalization rates of the elderly.

Note. The views expressed in this chapter do not represent official views of the Department of Health and Human Services.

REFERENCES

Berkeley Planning Associates. 1984. *Evaluation of Coordinated Community-oriented Long-term Care Demonstration Projects.* Prepared under contract no. 500-80-0073 for the U.S. Health Care Financing Administration. Berkeley, Calif.

Brody, E. 1985. Parent Care as a Normative Family Stress. *Gerontologist* 25:19–25.

Caisse Nationale de l'Assurance Maladie des Travailleurs Salaries. 1983. *La Consommation en Soins de Santé des Personnes de Plus de 60 Ans en 1981.* Carnets Statistiques no. 6 (Decembre).

———. 1984. *Les Personnes Agées dans les Etablissements de Soins et d'Hebergement.* Paris.

Cohen, M.A., E. Tell, and S.S. Wallack. 1986. Client-related Risk Factors of Nursing Home Entry among Elderly Adults. *Journal of Gerontology* 41:785–92.

Comité Europeen de la Santé. 1985. *Organisation des Soins Medicaux et Infirmiers à Domicile pour les Personnes Agées.* Strasbourg. Council of Europe.

Conference des Ministres Européens Chargés des Affaires Familiales. 1983. *Le Role des Personnes Agées dans la Famille, dans la Perspective de la Société des Années 80: Synthèse.* Eighteenth session. Strasbourg, July 25.

Daatland, S.O. 1985. Care of the Aged in the Nordic Countries: Trends and Policies the Last

Two Decades. Paper presented at the 13th International Congress of Gerontology, New York, July 12–17.

Dooghe, G. 1984. *Relational and Assistance Pattern between the Elderly and their Children.* Brussels: Ministerie van de Vlaamse Gemeenschap.

Doty, P. 1986a. Family Care of the Elderly: The Role of Public Policy. *Milbank Quarterly* 64(1):34–75.

―――. 1986b. Long-term Care for the Elderly Provided within the Framework of Health Care Schemes. Report of the Permanent Committee on Medical Care and Sickness Insurance, U.S. Health Care Financing Administration. Paper presented at the 22nd General Assembly of the International Social Security Association, Montreal, September 2–12.

Ennuyer, B. 1983. Les Enjeux du Maintien a Domicile. Gerontologie et Société no. 25. *Cahiers de la Fondation Nationale de Gerontologie* 22–33.

Habib, J., Y. Kop, and A. Shmueli. 1985. Patterns of Institutionalization of the Elderly in Israel. No. D-121-85. Jerusalem: Joint (J.D.C.) Israel Brookdale Institute of Gerontology and Adult Human Development in Israel.

Hing, E. 1987. Use of Nursing Homes by the Elderly: Preliminary Data from the 1985 National Nursing Home Survey. In *Advance Data from Vital and Health Statistics,* 135. DHHS pub. no. (PHS) 87-1250. Hyattsville, Md.: National Center for Health Statistics.

Howe, A.L., and G.A.N. Preston. 1985. Handicap in the Australian Aged Population. Part 2: Interstate Variations in Handicap in Relation to Nursing Home Provision. *Journal of the Australian Population Association* 2(1):68–78.

Illsley, R. 1988. *Age Care Research Europe.* Bath, England: Committee on Medical Research of the European Economic Commission.

Kane, R.L., and R.A. Kane. 1985. *A Will and a Way: What the United States Can Learn from Canada about Caring for the Elderly.* New York: Columbia University Press.

Kendig, H.L., and D.T. Rowland. 1983. Family Support of the Australian Aged: A Comparison with the United States. *Gerontologist* 23(6):643–49.

Kemper, P., R. Brown, G. Cariagno, et al. 1986. *The Evaluation of the National Long-term Care Demonstration: Final Report.* U.S. DHHS contract no. HHS-100-80-0157. Princeton, N.J.: Mathematica Policy Research.

Macken, C.L. 1986. A Profile of Functionally Disabled Elderly Persons Living in the Community. *Health Care Financing Review* 7(4):33–49.

Maeda, D. 1982. The Cultural Forces Encouraging and Supporting Caregivers in Japan. Paper presented at the 12th International Congress of Gerontology, Hamburg, Federal Republic of Germany, July 12–17.

Maeda, D., and M.B. Sussman. 1980. Japan–U.S. Cross-cultural Study on the Knowledge of Aging, the Attitude toward Old People and the Sense of Responsibility for Aged Parents. *Japanese Journal of Gerontology* 12:29–40.

Mizrahi, A. and A. Mizrahi. 1985a. Indicateurs de Morbidité et Facteurs Socio-demographiques. Paris: Centre de Recherche D'Etude et De Documentation en Economie de la Santé.

―――. 1985b. L'Évolution des Consommations Medicales des Personnes Agées. *Futuribles* 69:103–118.

Mooney, G. 1987. Long-term Care of the Elderly: Some Economic Perspectives. Paper presented for the Working Party on Social Policy, Organization for Economic Co-operation and Development, Paris. (Unpublished.)

Morginstin, B., and N. Shamai. 1984. Planning Long-term Care Insurance in Israel. In *Long-term Care and Social Security, Studies and Research* 21:59–79. Geneva: International Social Security Administration.

Netherlands, Social and Cultural Planning Office. 1984. (Cited in Sandier 1987).

Oldiges, F.J. 1984. Long-term Care of the Elderly and Disabled in the Federal Republic of Germany. In *Long-term Care and Social Security, Studies and Research* 21:106–16. Geneva: International Social Security Association.

Ray, W., C. Federspiel, D. Baugh, and S. Dobbs. 1987. Impact of Growing Numbers of the Very Old on Medicaid Expenditures for Nursing Homes: A Multi-state, Population-based Analysis. *American Journal of Public Health* 77(6):699–703.

Sandier, S. 1987. *Le Vieillissement de la Population en Europe et le Cout des Soins Medicaux*. Paris: Centre de Recherche D'Etude et de Documentation en Economie de la Santé.

Sherwood, S., V. Mor, and C.E. Gutkin. 1981. *Domiciliary Care Clients and the Facilities in Which They Reside*. Boston: Hebrew Rehabilitation Center for the Aged.

Stone, R. 1984. Board and Care Housing: The State Role. In *Long-term Care of the Elderly: Public Policy Issues*, vol. 157 ed. C. Harrington, et al. 177–95. Beverly Hills: Sage.

Stone, R., G. Cafferata, and J. Sangl. 1986. Caregivers of the Frail Elderly: A National Profile. *Gerontologist* 27(5):616–26.

U.S. Congress, Office of Technology Assessment. 1987. *Losing a Million Minds: Confronting the Tragedy of Alzheimer's Disease and Other Dementias*. OTA-BA-323. Washington.

U.S. Department of Health and Human Services. 1986. *Report to the Secretary on Private Financing of Long-term Care for the Elderly*. Washington: Technical Work Group on Private Financing of Long-term Care for the Elderly, Public Health Service.

U.S. Department of Health and Human Services, Office of the Assistant Secretary for Planning and Evaluation. 1981. *Working Papers on Long-term Care, Prepared for the 1980 Undersecretary's Task Force on Long-term Care*. Washington.

U.S. General Accounting Office. 1983. *Medicaid and Nursing Home Care: Cost Increases and the Need for Services Are Creating Problems for the States and the Elderly*. Washington.

U.S. Health Care Financing Administration. 1981. *Long-term Care: Background and Future Directions*. HCFA pub. no. 81-20047. Washington.

———. 1984. *The Medicare and Medicaid Data Book*. Department of Health and Human Services: Baltimore.

U.S. National Center for Health Statistics. 1979. *The National Nursing Home Survey: 1977 Summary for the United States*. DHEW Pub. no. (PHS) 79-1794. Hyattsville, Md.

Weissert, W. 1985. Estimating the Long-term Care Population: Prevalence Rates and Selected Characteristics. *Health Care Financing Review* 6(4):83–91.

Weissert, W., and W. Scanlon. 1982. *Determinants of Nursing Home Use*. Washington: Urban Institute.

Wright, K.G. 1986. *Economic Aspects of Strategies for the Health Care of the Elderly: A Report Prepared for the European Office of the World Health Organization*. York, England: Centre for Health Economics, University of York.

12

Epidemiology of Disability in the Oldest Old

JOAN C. CORNONI-HUNTLEY, DANIEL J. FOLEY, LON R. WHITE,
RICHARD M. SUZMAN, LISA F. BERKMAN, DENIS A. EVANS,
ROBERT B. WALLACE, AND LAURENCE G. BRANCH

The rapid growth of the U.S. population 65 years of age and older has been frequently noted. Less well known is that, among this elderly group, the proportion of persons 85 years and older has grown at an unprecedented rate, increasing 165 percent from 1960 to 1982 (Taeuber 1983). In addition, we know the least about existing health problems and impairments for this group; few studies are available that include representative samples of persons aged 85 years and older from which estimates of prevalence and incidence of illness and disability might be derived.

The level of physical, sensory, and cognitive functioning often determines whether the very old live comfortably and independently in the community. An association between independent living and the type and severity of limitations is intuitively apparent; however, the threshold for independent living varies and is not clearly understood. We lack knowledge of the interacting factors that influence the health and needs of elderly persons in their own physical and social environments. We must better understand the needs for help for the elderly from individuals or from community-based services, and the needs for institutional care. Gender, cultural, geographic, and even cohort differences must be studied.

The purpose of this chapter is to describe the major prospective studies that have been developed by the National Institute of Aging to provide information on health conditions and impairments of persons aged 65 years and older with representation of persons aged 85 years and older. Using these survey data, we will present prevalence information on physical, sensory, and mental disabilities among the oldest old and their younger elderly peers. These data illustrate the limitations of cross-sectional studies of the oldest old and emphasize the value of prospective studies for this age group.

DEVELOPMENT OF NEW SOURCES OF DATA: ESTABLISHED POPULATIONS FOR EPIDEMIOLOGIC STUDIES OF THE ELDERLY (EPESE)

Recognizing the need for data to describe the normal aging process, and the development of chronic disease and impairments in the oldest segment of this country's population, the National Institute on Aging developed a project titled "The Establishment of Populations for Epidemiologic Studies for the Elderly" (EPESE) (Cornoni-Huntley et al. 1991). This project consists of four prospective studies of community-based elderly populations. The goals are to identify predictors of mortality, hospitalization, and placement in long-term-care facilities and to study risk factors for common chronic diseases and for disability in this age group. It is anticipated that the information from this research will result in new strategies for the prevention of illness and impairments and will suggest ways to maintain the elderly person's function and independence in the community for as long as possible.

EPESE Study Populations

The four populations under investigation are in East Boston, Massachusetts; Iowa and Washington counties, Iowa; New Haven, Connecticut; and five counties of Piedmont, North Carolina. The studies are coordinated, with common design and methodology, and they also have unique investigator-initiated components.

East Boston, Massachusetts

The East Boston study population consists of all persons living in that community who were 65 years of age and older as of January 1, 1982, as well as persons who reached age 65 during the course of the study. East Boston residents are largely low-middle-income, working-class people of Italian-American background. At the initial enumeration, there were 4,485 persons aged 65 and older residing in the community. A response rate of 84 percent yielded a study population of 3,812. Among these individuals were 296 persons 85 years of age or older when they were enrolled (Table 12–1).

Iowa and Washington Counties, Iowa

The Iowa study population consists of all elderly residents of two counties in east central Iowa. The counties contain approximately 4,600 residents aged 65 years and older. There was an 80 percent response rate yielding 3,673 participants. The majority of the target population is classified as rural. One hundred percent of the Iowa County population and 67 percent of Washington County are farm or rural nonfarm dwellers. The remaining 33 percent of the Washington County population reside in a town of approximately 6,000 residents. There were 361 participants in the two counties aged 85 and older at the time of the baseline survey (Table 12–2).

Table 12–1   East Boston, Massachusetts, Study Population by Age and Sex

	Males		Females		Total	
Age	N	%	N	%	N	%
65–69	571	39.2	851	36.4	1,429	37.5
70–74	397	27.3	628	26.6	1,025	26.9
75–79	252	17.3	425	18.0	677	17.8
80–84	123	8.5	262	11.1	385	10.1
85+	112	7.7	184	7.8	296	7.8
Total	1,455	100.0	2,357	100.0	3,812	100.0

Table 12–2   Washington and Iowa Counties, Iowa Study Population by Age and Sex

	Males		Females		Total	
Age	N	%	N	%	N	%
65–69	428	30.2	560	24.8	988	26.9
70–74	398	28.1	588	26.1	986	26.8
75–79	307	21.7	508	22.5	815	22.2
80–84	164	11.6	359	15.9	523	14.2
85+	120	8.5	241	10.7	361	9.8
Total	1,417	100.0	2,256	100.0	3,673	100.0

New Haven, Connecticut

The New Haven study population is a stratified random sample of 3,420 persons aged 65 years and older representing the more than 18,000 elderly New Haven residents. The elderly in New Haven live, for the most part, in three types of housing: (1) public elderly housing, which is age- and income-restricted; (2) private elderly housing, which is age-restricted; and (3) houses and private apartments. The sampling frame includes a sample drawn from each of these three types of housing arrangements. Sampling weights have been assigned to respondents to adjust for deficient sampling response and coverage rates; the weighted data represent the older population of New Haven.

The response rate was 82 percent, yielding 2,811 participants, of whom 274 were aged 85 and older. New Haven is a racially mixed community of primarily middle- and low-income residents (Table 12–3). In all of the accompanying tables, the percentages and numbers presented for the New Haven study are population projections, calculated using sampling weights.

Five Counties in North Carolina

The North Carolina study population is a three-stage sample of noninstitutionalized persons 65 years of age or older residing in Durham, Vance, Franklin, Granville, and Warren counties. This study was initiated 4 years after the other three locations. The specific goal of this study is to provide information on the health of black elderly persons. There is a high representation of nonwhite, primarily black persons, in these counties.

Table 12–3   New Haven, Connecticut, Population Estimates by Age and Sex

	Males		Females		Total[a]	
Age	N	%	N	%	N	%
65–69	2,017	36.2	3,013	30.6	5,030	32.6
70–74	1,500	26.9	2,522	25,6	4,022	26.1
75–79	985	17.7	2,139	21.7	3,124	20.3
80–84	611	11.0	1,262	12.8	1,873	12.2
85+	461	8.3	906	9.2	1,367	8.9
Total	5,574	100.0	9,842	100.0	15,416	100.0

[a] Does not include individuals for whom age is unknown (N = 16).

[b] Numbers and percentages are population estimates, projected from sample data.

The sample size is 4,165 persons, of whom 51 percent are black elderly. A total of 325 persons were aged 85 years and older at the time of the baseline survey. Prevalence data from the North Carolina location were not available at the time that this chapter was prepared.

In summary, there are 1,256 persons aged 85 years and older participating in the four EPESE studies. Prevalence data on the 931 persons aged 85 years and older, who participated in the studies at East Boston, New Haven, and the two counties in Iowa beginning in 1980 are presented in this chapter.

EPESE Study Design

The EPESE is a prospective study. Participants in the baseline survey have been followed for 6 years. The baseline survey established the populations for further observation and estimation of the incidence of chronic conditions, including cardio-vascular disease, diabetes, and respiratory problems. Data on physical functioning, the ability to perform daily activities, as well as vision and hearing impairments were obtained. A mental status questionnaire was administered to evaluate cognitive functioning (Pfeiffer 1975). This initial survey was a household interview and included blood pressure measurements taken by interviewers trained in standardized techniques.

The major study endpoints are chronic disease mortality, hospitalization, admission to nursing homes or other long-term care facilities, and development of physical and cognitive disability. Total and cause-specific mortality information is determined using death certificates from state sources. Causes of death are defined by a single nosologist to maintain standard criteria. Hospitalization experience will be determined using Health Care Financing Administration (HCFA) records supplemented by local sources. Information on admissions to nursing homes and other long-term-care facilities and on the development of disabilities is assessed by self-reports to standardized questions at annual interviews. Proxy information is obtained if the participant cannot supply the necessary data.

All participants are contacted annually within 2 weeks of the anniversary of the baseline interview. The first two recontacts and the fourth and fifth recontacts are brief telephone interviews, during which information is obtained on changes in household composition, health status, physical functioning, and episodes of illness, hospitalization, or institutionalization. The third and sixth recontacts with participants are interviews in the household, obtaining information similar to that acquired in the baseline interviews. Repeated contacts with participants will provide not only information on new episodes of illness, hospitalization, and nursing home admission, but also insight into the progression of certain chronic conditions, disabilities, and the occurrence of major life changes.

Physical Disability

Assessing an individual's physical functioning represents only one dimension of a comprehensive functional assessment, which must also touch upon the social, emotional, and mental well-being, particularly among older individuals (William 1983).

The extent of physical disability may be defined by quantifying limitations in mobility and in the activities of daily living. Rosow and Breslau (1966) have developed and tested a "functional health scale" for measuring disability which scores subjects on six questions with "yes" or "no" answers, valued 1 or 0. The full scale includes questions about a bothersome illness, physical condition, or health problem; heavy work around the house; climbing stairs; going out to a movie, to church, to a meeting, or to visit friends; walking half a mile; and whether an individual is limited in any activity. Possible scale scores range from 0 (very disabled) to 6 (no disability).

Nagi (1976) examined disability among non-institutionalized adults by asking about the degree of difficulty in performing certain activities including walking, standing for long periods, stooping, bending or kneeling, reading, climbing stairs, and lifting or carrying weights of about 10 pounds. Katz et al. (1963) have developed and validated a scale for measuring the ability to perform activities of daily living (ADL). The original ADLs were defined as bathing, dressing, using the toilet, transferring from bed to chair, continence, and eating.

Branch and colleagues used portions of the Rosow and Breslau functional health scale, measures of physical performance adapted from the work by Nagi, and a modification of the ADL by Katz in the Massachusetts Health Care Panel Study (Branch et al. 1984) and in the Framingham Disability Study (FDS) (Jette and Branch 1981). The FDS was conducted between 1976 and 1978 and consisted of interviews with more than 2,600 persons between 55 and 84 years of age who were participants in the Epidemiological Study of Heart Disease in Framingham, Massachusetts (Dawber, Meadows, and Moore 1951).

The EPESE used 14 items, derived from the FDS, to construct three indices of physical disability. Three items measure functional mobility, four items measure specific physical activities, and seven items measure ADL:

Functional Mobility
  1. Heavy housework
  2. Climbing stairs
  3. Walking half a mile

Physical Activities
  4. Pushing large objects
  5. Stooping, crouching, or kneeling
  6. Reaching above shoulder level
  7. Writing or fingering or handling small objects

Activities of Daily Living
  8. Walking
  9. Bathing
 10. Grooming
 11. Dressing
 12. Eating
 13. Getting from a bed to a chair
 14. Using the toilet

Figures 12–1 through 12–3 present prevalence rates of various levels of disability for each of the three communities. The dark shade in each of the bars represents the most disabled according to each of the indices. The functional mobility scale results

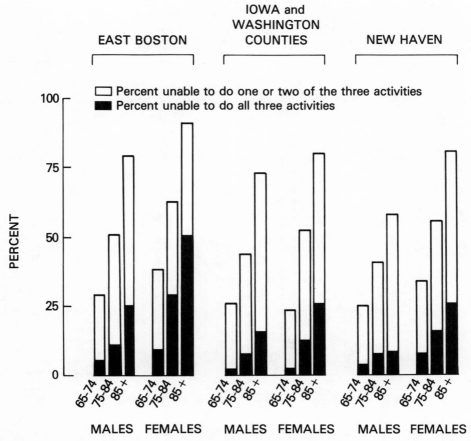

Figure 12–1   Prevalence of limitations in functional mobility according to age, sex, and study population.

are shown in Figure 12–1. The proportion unable to perform at least one of the activities was progressively greater for both sexes for each older age group. For example, among the Iowa subjects, 24 percent of the women aged 65 to 74 years reported an inability to perform at least one of the activities, whereas among those aged 85 years and older, 80 percent were unable to perform at least one activity.

Figure 12–2 presents the prevalence rates for the physical activities scale. A large proportion of the oldest old reported difficulty in performing at least one of the physical activities, with rates ranging from 35 percent for New Haven men to 83 percent for East Boston women. The proportion in each age and sex group reporting difficulty in all four activities was considerably lower. Only in the oldest East Boston women did more than 10 percent of subjects report difficulty in all four activities. None of the oldest males in the Iowa study population reported difficulty in all four activities.

Figure 12–3 presents the age- and sex-specific prevalence rates of a need for assistance in at least one of the activities of daily living. In general, the proportion of people requiring assistance doubled in each successive age group for each sex.

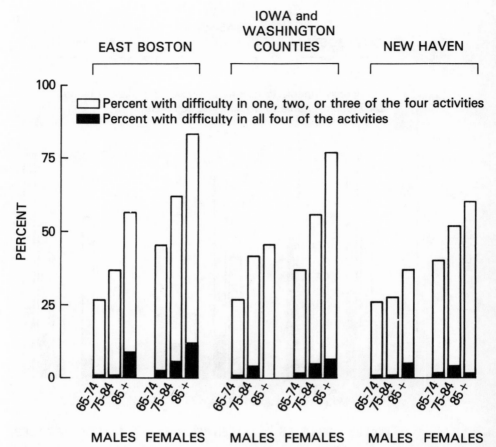

Figure 12–2 Prevalence of limitations in activities according to age, sex, and study population.

For example, among the East Boston men, the prevalence was 9 percent for those aged 65 to 74 years, 17 percent for those aged 75 to 84 years, and 36 percent for those aged 85 years and older.

Vision and Hearing Problems

Changes with increasing age in both the structure and function of various tissues and organs have been well documented. With respect to the sensory organs, diminished vision and hearing are among the most obvious problems and often contribute to a loss of independence. An appearance of cognitive loss, physical inactivity, or social withdrawal may occur with the loss of vision or hearing.

Rates from the Supplement on Impairments of the 1977 NHIS show a decrease with age in the proportion of older persons wearing eyeglasses or contact lenses but an increase in the use of hearing aids with age. Among persons aged 65 to 74 years, 94 percent wore eyeglasses, decreasing to 92 percent for those aged 75 to 84 years and 91 percent among those aged 85 years and older. The use of a hearing aid

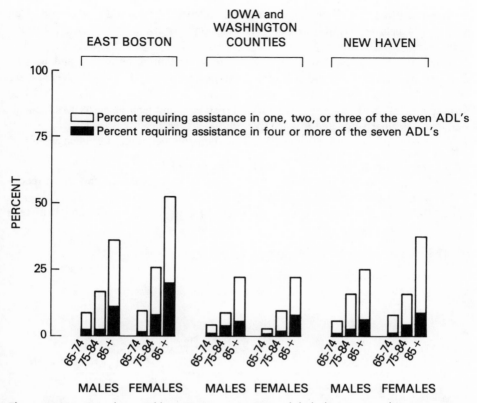

Figure 12–3 Prevalence of limitations in activities of daily living according to age, sex, and study population.

increased from 4 percent in those aged 65 to 74 years to 7 percent among those aged 75 to 84 years and 13 percent for those aged 85 years and older.

Rates for impaired vision and hearing increased sharply with age. Among those aged 65 to 74 years, 2 percent could not read ordinary newspaper print, 3 percent could not recognize a friend across the street, and 6 percent were unable to hear and understand a normal voice spoken in a quiet room. The rates for those aged 75 to 84 years were 7 percent unable to read newsprint, 8 percent unable to recognize a friend across a street, and 14 percent unable to hear and understand a normal voice. Among those aged 85 years and older, the rates were 18 percent, 19 percent, and 30 percent, respectively.

More recent figures from the Supplement on Aging to the 1984 NHIS reported similar trends with age. For persons aged 65 to 74 years, 4 percent were unable to read ordinary newspaper print, 4 percent could not recognize a friend across the street, and 4 percent were unable to hear and understand a normal voice. Among persons aged 75 to 84 years, 8 percent were unable to read ordinary newspaper print, 10 percent could not recognize a friend across the street, and 8 percent were unable to hear and understand a normal voice. Rates for the oldest old were 22 percent, 28 percent, 19 percent, respectively. The age-specific estimates for an inability to hear a normal voice were lower than those reported in 1977 resulting from a change in the question. In 1977 the ability to hear a normal voice was asked of a person when not using a hearing aid and in 1984 the question was asked when using a hearing aid.

The EPESE baseline survey included similar questions on vision and hearing from the National Health and Nutrition Examination Survey I (NHANES I) and the 1977 NHIS (Feller 1981; NCHS 1978). Vision was assessed in terms of ability to read newsprint and recognize a person at a distance, and hearing in terms of understanding a normal voice and a voice over the telephone.

The specific items asked of all EPESE participants pertaining to vision were:

1. Do you wear eyeglasses, contact lenses, or both?
2. When wearing (eyeglasses/contact lenses) can you SEE well enough to recognize a friend across the street?
3. When wearing (eyeglasses/contact lenses) can you SEE well enough to read ordinary newspaper print?

The specific items pertaining to hearing were:

1. Have you ever worn a hearing aid?
   a. How often do you usually wear a hearing aid, these days?

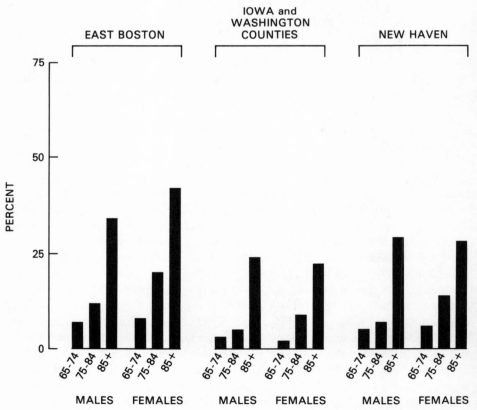

Figure 12–4 Prevalence of vision problems according to age, sex, and study population.

2. (With/without a hearing aid) can you usually hear and understand what a person says without seeing his face if that person talks in a normal voice to you in a quiet room?

Figures 12–4 and 12–5 illustrate the fact that vision and hearing problems represent a major disability for older persons, in particular the oldest old. In Figure 12–4, a vision problem is defined as the inability to read ordinary newspaper print, and in Figure 12–5, a hearing problem is defined as the inability to hear a normal voice. As in the national survey data, the rates for hearing problems among males are higher than females in most age groups (Figure 12–5). The high national rates for both these impairments in persons aged 85 years and older are replicated among the participants at each of the EPESE locations.

Distant and near visual functioning falls sharply after age 85 years. Approximately one quarter of the oldest old cannot recognize a friend across a street. The rates for the inability to read a newspaper are even higher. Both of these rates were slightly higher for women than for men in most age groups.

Although there is an increase with age in the percentage of persons having hearing aids, few EPESE participants wear hearing aids. A higher percentage of the

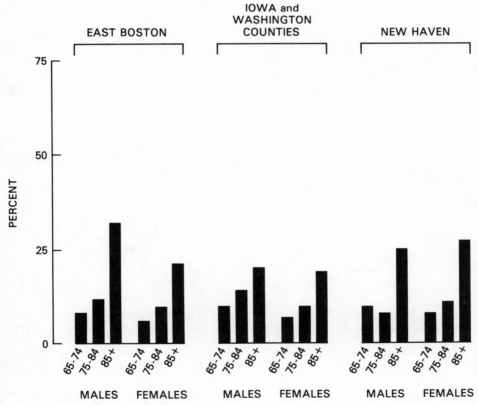

Figure 12–5   Prevalence of hearing problems according to age, sex, and study population.

oldest old in Iowa report having a hearing aid and using it than in East Boston and New Haven.

As seen with vision impairments, hearing ability falls sharply for the oldest old. For the three EPESE locations the rates for not being able to hear a normal voice are two to three times higher among those aged 85 and older than for those aged 75 to 84.

Cognitive Disability

While physical and sensory disability is usually identified by asking a subject what he or she can or cannot do (with or without assistance), cognitive disability is assessed with a test such as a mental status questionnaire (MSQ). The MSQ score then serves as an indicator of the level and quality of cognitive functioning at the time of testing.

The MSQ administered to EPESE participants was derived from Pfeiffere's (1975) "short portable mental status questionnaire," in turn based on an earlier instrument described by Kahn, Goldfarb, Pollack, and Peck (1960). It consisted of nine questions:

1. What is the date today?
2. What day of the week is it?
3. How old are you?
4. When were you born?
5. Who is the president of the United States?
6. Who was president just before him?
7. Subtract 3 from 20, and keep subtracting 3 from each new number all the way down.
8. What is your telephone number (or street address)?
9. What was your mother's maiden name?

Each item was scored as 0 (correct) or 1 ("don't know," refusal, or incorrect answer), giving a possible range of 0 (all correct) through 9 (none correct).

Percentage distributions of MSQ scores (the number of errors) for the EPESE

Table 12–4 Percent Distribution of MSQ Scores for EPESE Participants Aged 85 Years and Older

	MSQ Score (Number of Errors in Percent)										
	0	1	2	3	4	5	6	7	8	9	N
East Boston											
Men	10.1%	18.0%	13.5%	22.5%	14.6%	9.0%	4.5%	3.4%	2.2%	2.2%	89
Women	4.3	15.9	18.1	11.6	15.9	8.7	8.0	9.4	5.8	2.2	138
Iowa											
Men	37.2	31.4	18.6	4.7	3.5	2.3	1.2	1.2	0	0	86
Women	33.0	26.1	17.6	8.5	9.6	3.2	1.6	0.5	0	0	188
New Haven											
Men	16.5	23.5	24.4	12.8	11.4	4.9	3.6	0.5	0	2.0	439[a]
Women	20.6	18.4	23.0	11.2	10.3	7.8	6.5	0.8	0.9	0.5	757[a]

[a] These are estimated numbers projected using sampling weights.

participants aged 85 and older are shown in Table 12–4. Four or more errors were made by a substantial proportion of both men and women, with prevalence rates ranging from 8.2 percent (Iowa males) to 50 percent (East Boston female subjects). The performance of subjects grouped according to education, age, and study site is presented in Figure 12–6. The prevalence of high MSQ scores was greatest among the oldest old, with the exception of Iowa's lowest education group (fewer than 8 years of school completed). In general, high scores were associated with lower educational attainment. Among subjects of similar age and education, high MSQ scores were most prevalent in the East Boston population and least prevalent in Iowa.

DISCUSSION

For many years, epidemiological and demographic data were reported with aggregation of persons aged 65 and older. Although information is now being published for older age groups, we still have very few data resources for the oldest old. It is now apparent that even within the oldest groups we should not ignore age-specific variation related to chronic disease, disability, health care utilization, and economic and community health issues.

Analysis of available data sources is currently contributing to a much better understanding of the health status of the elderly. Interpretation of these data, however,

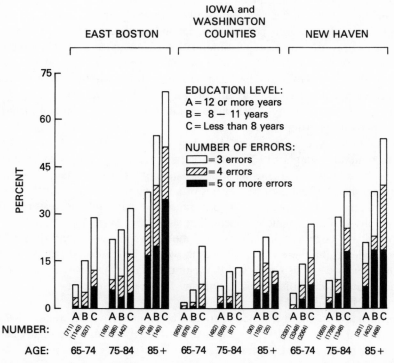

Figure 12–6 Prevalence of high MSQ scores according to age, education, and study population.

requires critical consideration of the study design, sampling, and analytic methodology. The disadvantages of certain approaches are more pronounced in the very old, because certain biases are much more relevant in this group.

The limitations in inferring causality from observations made in cross-sectional studies have been well described. Some of these issues seem particularly applicable to the study of older populations. With cross-sectional designs, interpretations are limited by the definition of the sampling frame and possibly the biases of selective survival, nonresponse, and selective recall.

The problem of selective recall may be especially important in the elderly. Health events are likely to be more frequent and therefore to be confused with one another. Memory difficulties experienced by many persons in their later years may account for a large part of nonreporting of events. In addition, the recall of certain events may be selectively enhanced or triggered by an associated experience.

Elderly nonrespondents (persons who are sampled but decline to participate) may have health characteristics that are different from those of study participants, and these differences may be systematic with regard to age, sex, socioeconomic status, marital status, or other factors. Furthermore, the influence of these factors may differ qualitatively and quantitatively between communities. These considerations serve to emphasize the importance of striving for a high response rate. It is important to obtain as much information as possible on the nonrespondents.

Selective survival results in the elderly being a subset of persons from a larger cohort existing at a previous time. One should be cautious in drawing conclusions from a cross-sectional study of an elderly population because persons with certain characteristics may have been systematically removed from the cohort.

Because institutionalized persons account for a substantial portion of the oldest old, samples drawn from the noninstitutionalized community are likely to be nonrepresentative of the total elderly. This may lead to underestimation of rates of disability and disease because the most dependent persons will have been selectively excluded from the sampling frame. Poor health or disability may lead to the elderly person moving out of a community. Such changes influence enumeration and identification of individuals in the sampling frame.

The preliminary cross-sectional data just presented, drawn from the three National Institute on Aging's EPESE, must be interpreted with full consideration of the problems just described. Inclusion in the sampling frames and participation in the study imply that the health characteristics of study participants may differ from those of nonparticipants. The prevalence figures presented may well underestimate the true extent of physical and cognitive functioning at all three sites.

Physical and cognitive disabilities were most common among the EPESE's oldest old and tended to be more prevalent among women as compared with men at every age. Differences were also observed between the study populations, with both physical and cognitive disabilities generally being least prevalent in Iowa and most common in East Boston.

The meaning of the differences between communities is uncertain. In the Iowa counties, families are smaller, geographically more separated, more highly educated, and more affluent. In East Boston, large families often live in a single dwelling, or family members live close to one another in the neighborhood. The lesser affluence of East Boston may make it more difficult for an elderly person to move to a retirement community or other living situation especially suited for a partially disabled or partially dependent elderly person. It would be reasonable to expect dependent or disabled elderly to remain in the East Boston community substantially longer than might be necessary or possible in the Iowa counties. The situation in New Haven is much more difficult to understand because that study population is more heterogeneous with regard to race, housing type, and socioeconomic status. Because the EPESE data reported here are cross-sectional, and because biases that influence prevalence estimates vary systematically and substantially among communities, caution should be used when comparing the three communities with regard to risks for developing disease and disability.

CONCLUSION

Both the review of the available data sources and the results presented in this chapter point to the value and need for prospective designs in epidemiologic studies of the oldest old. Although prospective studies are certainly more costly and time consuming, these disadvantages are outweighed by the pertinent results that can be produced. The data presented here, generated from the EPESE baseline interviews, exemplify both the value and limitations of using prevalence rates to describe the health and disability of residents of different communities. Even though the period of longitudinal observation for the EPESE is 6 years, the health endpoints of new disease, disability, and death are occurring at sufficiently high rates that it will soon be possible to evaluate a number of risk factors for these events. Information now being generated by these and similar prospective studies will provide an improved knowledge base for understanding the needs and health-care utilization patterns of the oldest old in the United States.

REFERENCES

Branch, L.G., and A.M. Jette. 1981. The Framingham Disability Study: I. Social Disability Among the Aging. *American Journal of Public Health* 71:1202–10.

Branch, L.G., S. Katz, K. Knielmann, and J.A. Papsidero. 1984. A Prospective Study of Functional Status among Community Elders. *American Journal of Public Health* 74:266–68.

Cornoni-Huntley, J.C., D.G. Blazer, M.E. Lafferty, D.S. Everett, D.B. Brock, M.E. Farmer, J.V. Cruz, C. Service, and C.L. Phillips (eds.). 1990. *Established Populations for Epidemiologic Studies of the Elderly, Vol. II: Resource Data Book.* NIH pub. no. 90-495. Bethesda, Md.: National Institute on Aging.

Cornoni-Huntley, J.C., D.B. Brock, A.M. Ostfeld, J.O. Taylor, R.B. Wallace, and M.E. Lafferty (eds.). 1986. *Established Populations for Epidemiologic Studies of the Elderly, Vol. I: Resource Data Book.* NIH pub. no. 86-2443. Bethesda, Md.: National Institute on Aging.

Dawber, T.R., G.F. Meadows, and F.E. Moore. 1951. Epidemiological Approaches to Heart Disease: The Framingham Study. *American Journal of Public Health* 41:279–86.

Feller, B.A. 1981. Prevalence of Selected Impairments. *Vital and Health Statistics*, series 10, no. 134. Washington.

Havlik, R.J. 1986. Aging in the Eighties, Impaired Senses for Sound and Light in Persons Age 65 Years and Over. *Advance Data* no. 125, September 19. Hyattsville, Md.: National Center for Health Statistics.

Hing, E. 1981. Characteristics of Nursing Home Residents, Health Status, and Care Received. *Vital and Health Statistics,* series 13, no. 43. Hyattsville, Md.: National Center for Health Statistics.

Jette, A.M., and L.G. Branch. 1981. The Framingham Disability Study: II. Physical Disability Among the Aging. *American Journal of Public Health* 71:1211–16.

Kahn, R.L., A.I. Goldfarb, M. Pollack, and A. Peck. 1960. Brief Objective Measures for the Determination of Mental Status in the Aged. *American Journal of Psychiatry* 117:326–28.

Katz, S., A. Ford, R. Moskowitz, B. Jackson, and M. Jaffe. 1963. Studies of Illness in the Aged. *Journal of the American Medical Association* 185:914–19.

Nagi, S.Z. 1976. An Epidemiology of Disability among Adults in the United States. *Milbank Memorial Fund Quarterly/Health and Society* 54(4):439–68.

National Center for Health Statistics. 1978. Plan and Operation of the NHANES I Augmentation Survey of Adults 25-74 Years. *Vital and Health Statistics,* series 1, no. 14. Hyattsville, Md.

———. 1986. Unpublished data from the 1977 NHIS and the 1984 NHIS Supplement on Aging.

Pfieffer, E. 1975. A Short Portable Mental Status Questionnaire for the Assessment of Organic Brain Deficit in Elderly Patients. *Journal of the American Geriatrics Society* 23:433–41.

Rosow, I., and N. Breslau. 1966. A Guttman Health Scale for the Aged. *Journal of Gerontology* 21:557.

Taeuber, C.M. 1983. America in Transition: An Aging Society. *Current Population Reports,* series P-23, no. 128. Washington.

Williams, T.F. 1983. Comprehensive Functional Assessment: An Overview. *Journal of the American Geriatrics Society* 31 (November):640.

13

The Impact of Alzheimer's Disease in the United States Population

DENIS A. EVANS, PAUL A. SCHERR, NANCY R. COOK,
MARILYN S. ALBERT, H. HARRIS FUNKENSTEIN,*
LAUREL A. BECKETT, LIESI E. HEBERT, TERRIE T. WETLE,
LAURENCE G. BRANCH, MARILYN J. CHOWN,
CHARLES H. HENNEKENS, and JAMES O. TAYLOR

Awareness of Alzheimer's disease as a major public health problem has increased strikingly among clinicians, researchers, policy makers and the general public over the past several years. As described by Alzheimer (1907), this term was used only for dementia arising in middle age. Such "presenile" dementia exhibits characteristic neuropathological findings, including neuritic plaques and neurofibrillary tangles. The term "Alzheimer's disease" is now applied, as well, to the much more common primary degenerative dementia occurring in later life, previously referred to as "senile dementia," because of apparent clinical and neuropathological (Tomlinson, Blessed, and Roth 1970) similarities regardless of age of onset. Many conditions other than Alzheimer's disease cause dementia among older persons, including certain strokes, Parkinson's disease, deficiency of vitamin B_{12}, and a wide range of uncommon conditions. Most population studies, however, suggest that the majority of moderate to severe cognitive impairment in older age groups is due to Alzheimer's disease, at least by clinical (rather than pathological) criteria for the disease. Regardless of age of onset, Alzheimer's disease is often devastating for affected individuals and their families. In terms of the total number of persons affected, however, Alzheimer's disease is predominantly a problem of the oldest old, that is, those aged 85 and older. The occurrence of Alzheimer's disease is strongly associated with increasing age among those 65 years of age and older. With increasing life expectancy in developed countries, the impact of Alzheimer's disease will continue to increase.

Despite ongoing research efforts and consequent substantial increases in knowledge, many fundamental questions have not yet been answered. The etiology of the disease is unknown. Genetic, toxic, infectious, and degenerative influences are being studied (Katzman 1986). Like many other common chronic diseases, Alzheimer's

---

*Deceased, May 4, 1990.

disease likely has multiple risk factors. Further, the possibility that Alzheimer's disease itself may be a heterogeneous category has received increasing attention. The extent, if any, to which Alzheimer's disease, in mild or early cases, may form a continuum with normal cognitive functioning is uncertain. Several other common chronic diseases, most notably chronic obstructive lung disease and hypertension, appear to have no abrupt separation from normality.

At present, we do not have optimal means to estimate the number of individuals affected by Alzheimer's disease now or in the future. There are few studies of cognitive impairment in large, noninstitutionalized populations in either the United States or other countries, and still fewer studies that attempt differential diagnosis of the conditions responsible for the impairment. Most population-based studies (Copeland et al. 1987; Essen-Moller 1956; Gilmore 1974; Gurland et al. 1983; Hobson and Pemberton 1955; Kay et al. 1985; Kramer et al. 1985; Myers et al. 1984; Park and Ha 1988; Parsons 1965; Pfeiffer 1975; Robins et al. 1984; McAuley, and Arling 1983; Staff of the Mental Health Research Unit 1960) have investigated cognitive impairment or dementia in general, without reference to specific underlying diagnoses. Fewer studies of noninstitutionalized populations (Broe et al. 1976; Folstein et al. 1985; Kay, Beamish, and Roth 1964; Molsa, Marttila, and Rinne 1982; Pfeffer, Afifi, and Chance 1987; Sayetta 1986; Schoenberg, Anderson, and Haerer 1985; Schoenberg, Kokmen, and Okazaki 1987; Shibayama, Kasahara, and Kobayashi 1986; Sulkava et al. 1985) provide clinical diagnoses of conditions causing dementia, such as Alzheimer's disease. The sample sizes of some studies are small, especially for the oldest age groups. All of the studies in noninstitutionalized populations noted above have been concerned with prevalent disease. There have been no large-scale community-based studies of incident Alzheimer's disease. Studies of incident disease may lead to improved understanding of both the risk factors for Alzheimer's disease and its course. Both are difficult to investigate in studies of prevalent disease.

In addition, it has been difficult to project the results of existing population-based studies to national populations. Pfeffer et al. (1987) applied age-specific prevalence rates of clinically diagnosed Alzheimer's disease from a middle-class retirement community in southern California to the 1980 U.S. Census age distribution of whites age 65 and over. The prevalence estimate for the U.S. population was 11.2 percent. The U.S. Congress, Office of Technology Assessment (1987), has provided estimates of 1.4 million persons with "severe dementia" in the United States in 1980, 2.4 million in 2000, 3.3 million in 2020, and 7.3 million in 2040. These last estimates, however, were not based directly on the results of a single population-based study.

The availability of data on disease prevalence from a large cohort of individuals from a defined U.S. community provided us the opportunity to estimate the prevalence of Alzheimer's disease in 1980 and to project future prevalence rates through the year 2050 for the U.S. population 65 years of age and older.

METHODS

The Community Study

East Boston, Massachusetts, is a geographically defined community of approximately 32,000 persons. This urban, working-class community has many persons of Italian descent. Educational attainment in East Boston is low compared with other Boston neighborhoods and with the U.S. population as a whole. One of four centers of the National Institute on Aging Established Populations for Epidemiologic Studies of the Elderly (EPESE) project (Cornoni-Huntley et al. 1986) is located in the community.

These community studies employed a two-stage design. In the first stage, brief performance tests of certain areas of cognitive function were administered to all participating community residents 65 years of age and older in their homes (Scherr et al. 1988). The tests included immediate and delayed recall of a three-sentence story. Participants were divided into groups according to their memory test performance, and individuals were selected for the second-stage clinical evaluation for dementing illness from all levels of performance, with the largest proportion sampled from the poor-performance group. The second-stage clinical evaluation included neuropsychological testing, neurological examination, brief psychiatric evaluation, laboratory evaluation, brief review of the medical history, and interview of a significant other individual for each participant. All prescription and over-the-counter medications used during the previous 2 weeks were inspected and identified. Structured instruments were used and examiners were blinded to performance on the population survey's cognitive testing.

Of the 4,485 eligible residents in the community, 3,623 had memory testing; 188 persons did not, usually because they participated through proxy respondents. Of 714 persons sampled for clinical evaluation from those participating in the population survey, 54 died prior to being invited to undergo clinical evaluation; 467 (70.8 percent of the surviving eligible individuals) were evaluated, and 193 declined evaluation.

Disease Classification

From the results of the clinical evaluation, each individual was classified in two ways: first, according to the presence and severity of any cognitive impairment, and, second, according to the condition responsible for the impairment, with each of a series of diagnoses, including Alzheimer's disease, rated as absent, possible, or probable. The probable category corresponds to the probable Alzheimer's disease category of the criteria developed by the joint working group of the National Institute of Neurological and Communicative Disorders and Stroke and the Alzheimer's disease and Related Disorders Association (NINCDS-ADRDA criteria) (McKhann et al. 1984). The NINCDS-ADRDA criteria consider absence of other diagnoses of dementing illness in determining the probability of Alzheimer's disease. This restriction, although useful in clinical practice, results in underestimation of disease prevalence in a population, as the presence of one disease leading to dementia does not exclude the occurrence of another. Therefore, for the estimates presented here, we calculated Alzheimer's disease prevalence, omitting the NINCDS-ADRDA restriction that any other diseases possibly accounting for dementia be absent for the diagnosis of probable Alzheimer's disease. The difference in estimated prevalence of Alzheimer's disease if the restriction is applied or omitted was small in the East Boston population. If the restriction was omitted, the estimated prevalence of Alzheimer's disease among those 65 years of age and older in the East Boston community was 11.6 percent; if it was applied, the estimate fell to 10.3 percent (Evans et al. 1989).

Estimates of the Prevalence of Alzheimer's Disease for the U.S. Population

The prevalence estimates of Alzheimer's disease for the U.S. population were obtained by a three-step process. In the first step, the results for the sample undergoing clinical evaluation were summarized using a logistic model. The second step consisted of projecting these results to the East Boston population, and the third step consisted of projecting the East Boston results to the U.S. population, both present and future.

At the first step, the observed proportions with Alzheimer's disease in the sample of 467 persons undergoing clinical evaluation were determined for subgroups stratified by 5-year age group, sex, level of education, and screening memory test performance. Because some of these groups in the sample were small, a logistic regression model was used to smooth the observed proportions and to provide estimates of the effects of age (as a linear term), sex, education, and screening memory performance on disease prevalence. At the second step, the East Boston population was divided into subgroups by age (65–69, 70–74, 75–79, 80–84, 85–89, 90+), sex, years of formal education (0–7, 8, 9–11, 12+), and memory test group. The disease prevalence in each subgroup of the East Boston population was then estimated using the smoothed prevalences, obtained by applying the logistic regression coefficients from the first step to the subgroup characteristics (sex, education group, memory test group, and mean age) (Beckett, Scherr, and Evans submitted). The covariance of the subgroup estimates was obtained using the logistic regression covariance matrix (Bishop, Fienberg, and Holland 1975). The memory-group strata were then combined to give age, sex-, and education-specific prevalence for East Boston with an estimated covariance matrix.

In the third step, community prevalence estimates within each subgroup were applied to the distribution of age, sex, and education groups for the U.S. population in 1980. U.S. Bureau of the Census population figures were used for the U.S. population in 1980 by age, sex, and years of formal education (Miller 1983). Standard error estimates were obtained using the covariance estimates for the prevalence in East Boston, and 95 percent confidence intervals were derived. Steps one, two, and three were also repeated, omitting adjustment for level of education but adjusting for age and sex.

The community prevalence estimates from East Boston were also applied to U.S. population projections by age and sex from 1990 to 2050 according to decade in order to assess the potential public-health impact in future years. In applying the East Boston estimates to future population projections, there are two sources of uncertainty: possible errors in the prevalence estimates in East Boston and possible errors in the U.S. population projections. To approximate the combined impact of these two sources of error, the confidence intervals from the East Boston prevalence estimates were applied to three series of population projections: the U.S. Bureau of the Census high, middle, and low series (Spencer 1984). These series vary with respect to assumptions regarding fertility, mortality, and net immigration. The mortality assumptions in all three series reflect revised mortality rates for those 95 years of age and older (Faber 1982).

East Boston residents 65 years of age and older have fewer years of formal education than the national average for this age group. Unpublished preliminary data from our studies suggest that the rate of clinically diagnosed Alzheimer's disease may be higher among those with lower educational attainment. At this time, the interpretation of an association between education and rates of Alzheimer's disease in cross-sectional data is uncertain (Berkman 1986; Kittner et al. 1986). The estimates of Alzheimer's disease prevalence for the U.S. population presented here are adjusted for the difference in level of formal education between the East Boston and U.S. populations. In addition, overall estimates without adjustment for education, which are higher, are also given. For the years 1990 through 2050, the distributions for education were calculated under the assumption that there was no differential mortality with respect to education. Thus, the percent distribution of years of education for those aged 65 to 74 in 1980 would be the same as the percent distribution for those aged 75 to 84 in 1990.

RESULTS

Estimates of Alzheimer's Disease Prevalence for the U.S. Population in 1980

The estimated prevalence of probable Alzheimer's disease for age, sex, and educational strata of the East Boston population 65 years of age and older, given in Table 13–1, were applied to the 1980 U.S. population. The estimated number of persons 65 years of age or older in the U.S. population with probable Alzheimer's disease in 1980 was 2.88 million (95 percent confidence interval: 2.17–3.59 million). This is 11.3 percent (8.5–14.1) of the persons in this age group.

Within the group 65 years of age and older, the proportion of individuals with Alzheimer's disease rises sharply with increasing age. Among those 65 to 74 years of age, 3.9 percent (1.7–6.1) were estimated to have probable Alzheimer's disease.

Table 13–1 Estimated Prevalence of Probable Alzheimer's Disease by Age, Sex, and Education Strata for Persons 65 Years of Age and Older Residing in East Boston, Massachusetts, 1982

| | | Percentage of persons with probable Alzheimer's disease in each stratum | | | |
| | | Years of formal education | | | |
Age group	Sex	0–7	8	9–11	12+
65–69	Women	5.4	3.2	3.2	1.4
	Men	4.9	3.2	3.4	1.5
70–74	Women	8.6	6.1	6.9	2.6
	Men	7.7	5.5	6.3	2.7
75–79	Women	22.6	10.3	13.7	4.8
	Men	18.7	10.8	12.4	9.6
80–84	Women	30.7	23.5	23.3	14.5
	Men	33.8	20.6	20.4	13.5
85–89	Women	52.4	40.8	48.1	34.2
	Men	51.0	15.3	21.0	27.0
90+	Women	64.7	83.8	72.3	41.9
	Men	73.0	68.2	36.9	79.7

For those 75 to 84 years of age, this prevalence rises to 16.4 percent (12.0–20.6), and, among those aged 85 years and over, to 47.55 percent (37.7–57.4). In terms of the absolute number of affected individuals in the U.S. population in 1980, however, the highest number was from the 75- to 84-year-old age group. Among those 65 to 74 years old, there were 0.61 million (0.26–0.96) persons with Alzheimer's disease, compared with 1.25 million (0.92–1.58) persons 65 to 74 years old and 1.02 million (0.81–1.24) persons 85 years old and over.

Projections of Alzheimer's Disease Prevalence for the U.S. Population from 1990 to 2050

The results of applying the age-, sex-, and education-specific estimates of disease prevalence to projections of the U.S. population in the older age groups suggest that the prevalence of Alzheimer's disease will grow substantially. The projected rate of growth varies somewhat according to whether the high, middle, or low series projections are used, but the increase in the number of individuals affected by Alzheimer's disease is large with any of the three series. In the year 2050, the number of persons in the U.S. population 65 years of age and older affected by Alzheimer's disease is estimated to be 7.50 million (4.39–10.6) using the low series projections, 10.3 million (6.16–14.4) using the middle series, and 14.3 million (8.77–19.8) using the high series. These projections for the high, middle, and low series are shown in Table 13–2 and Figure 13–1. The limits indicated in parentheses for these and other future projections are not 95 percent confidence limits in the usual sense. Rather, they are limits calculated by applying the upper and lower confidence limits for the cross-sectional community estimates to the census projections at a given date. Thus, they do not take forecasting error into account. As discussed above, a better approximation of both sources of uncertainty in the projections comes from considering these limits together with the three U.S. Bureau of the Census series of population estimates.

Projections of Alzheimer's Disease Prevalence by Age Group

Inspection of projections from 1990 to 2050 by age group (Figure 13–2 and Table 13–2) shows that increases in the oldest age groups will account for most of the projected increase in the prevalence of Alzheimer's disease over this period. Using the middle-series census projections, for example, the number of persons with Alzheimer's disease in the 65- to 74-year age group rises only moderately, from 0.61 million (0.26–0.96) in 1980 to 0.74 million (0.13–1.34) in 2050. In contrast, the number of affected individuals 85 years of age and over rises almost sevenfold, from 1.02 million (0.81–1.24) in 1980 to 7.07 million (4.46–9.67) in 2050.

Estimates Unadjusted for Educational Attainment

If the adjustment for education is not performed, the resulting estimates of Alzheimer's disease prevalence are substantially higher. Figure 13–3 gives prevalence estimates without adjustment for education for the U.S. population from 1980 to 2050. In 1980, the unadjusted estimate of the number of persons aged 65 and older with

Table 13–2 Estimated Number (in millions) of Persons in the U.S. Population with Clinically Diagnosed Alzheimer's Disease from 1980 through 2050 by Age Groups Using Three Different U.S. Census Population Projections

Year	U.S. census projection series	65–74	75–84	85+	Total (age 65 and over)
1980		0.61	1.25	1.02	2.88
		(0.25–0.96)[a]	(0.92–1.58)	(0.81–1.24)	(2.17–3.59)
	High	0.59	1.59	1.62	3.80
		(0.22–0.96)[b]	(1.12–2.05)	(1.28–1.97)	(2.85–4.76)
1990	Middle	0.59	1.57	1.59	3.75
		(0.22–0.95)	(1.12–2.03)	(1.25–1.93)	(2.80–4.70)
	Low	0.58	1.55	1.53	3.67
		(0.22–0.95)	(1.10–2.01)	(1.20–1.86)	(2.74–4.60)
	High	0.55	1.71	2.55	4.82
		(0.19–0.92)	(1.10–2.33)	(1.95–3.16)	(3.49–6.15)
2000	Middle	0.54	1.65	2.32	4.51
		(0.18–0.90)	(1.06–2.24)	(1.76–2.87)	(3.25–5.77)
	Low	0.53	1.59	2.07	4.19
		(0.18–0.88)	(1.02–2.16)	(1.58–2.57)	(3.00–5.38)
	High	0.56	1.71	3.57	5.84
		(0.14–0.98)	(1.01–2.40)	(2.56–4.59)	(4.00–7.68)
2010	Middle	0.54	1.61	2.98	5.12
		(0.14–0.94)	(0.96–2.25)	(2.12–3.83)	(3.48–6.76)
	Low	0.51	1.48	2.46	4.46
		(0.13–0.90)	(0.88–2.09)	(1.75–3.17)	(2.99–5.93)
	High	0.77	1.84	4.17	6.78
		(0.14–1.40)	(0.95–2.72)	(2.87–5.47)	(4.34–9.22)
2020	Middle	0.73	1.68	3.22	5.62
		(0.13–1.33)	(0.87–2.48)	(2.20–4.23)	(3.52–7.72)
	Low	0.69	1.53	2.46	4.68
		(0.12–1.26)	(0.79–2.26)	(1.68–3.24)	(2.86–6.50)
	High	0.93	2.67	5.07	8.68
		(0.17–1.69)	(1.23–4.11)	(3.33–6.82)	(5.17–12.2)
2030	Middle	0.86	2.40	3.73	6.99
		(0.16–1.56)	(1.11–3.68)	(2.43–5.03)	(4.05–9.92)
	Low	0.80	2.14	2.74	5.69
		(0.15–1.46)	(0.99–3.30)	(1.78–3.71)	(3.20–8.18)
	High	0.82	3.27	7.72	11.8
		(0.15–1.48)	(1.52–5.02)	(4.87–10.6)	(7.02–16.6)
2040	Middle	0.74	2.84	5.49	9.07
		(0.14–1.33)	(1.32–4.37)	(3.44–7.55)	(5.28–12.9)
	Low	0.67	2.49	3.92	7.08
		(0.12–1.22)	(1.16–3.83)	(2.43–5.40)	(4.02–10.1)
	High	0.84	2.92	10.5	14.3
		(0.15–1.53)	(1.36–4.47)	(6.72–14.4)	(8.77–19.8)
2050	Middle	0.74	2.46	7.06	10.2
		(0.13–1.34)	(1.15–3.77)	(4.46–9.67)	(6.16–14.4)
	Low	0.66	2.09	4.74	6.50
		(0.12–1.20)	(0.98–3.21)	(2.96–6.52)	(4.39–10.6)

[a] For 1980 estimates, numbers in parentheses are 95 percent confidence limits.

[b] The limits indicated in parentheses for this and other future projections are not confidence limits in the usual sense. Rather, they are limits calculated by applying the upper and lower confidence limits for the cross-sectional community estimates to the census projections at a given date. Thus, they do not take forecasting error into acount. See text.

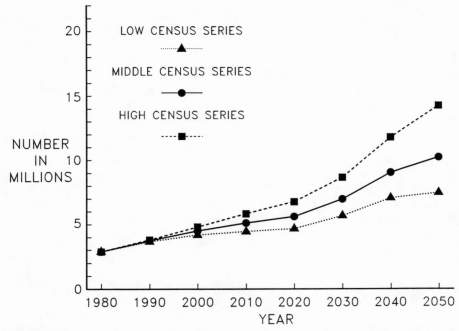

Figure 13–1 Projected number of persons over age 65 with probable Alzheimer's disease in the U.S. population from 1980 through 2050 using low, middle, and high U.S. census projections of population growth. Disease prevalence data from studies in East Boston, Massachusetts, adjusted for years of education.

Alzheimer's disease was 3.44 million (2.71–4.71), in contrast to the education-adjusted estimate of 2.88 million. By 2050, this difference between the adjusted and unadjusted estimates widens. Using the middle-census series projections, in this year the estimated number of affected persons without adjustment for education is 15.4 million (13.1–17.8), compared with the adjusted estimate of 10.3 million.

DISCUSSION

We estimate the prevalence of Alzheimer's disease in the U.S. population in 1980 to have been 2.88 million people, or 11.3 percent of those 65 years of age and older. The public-health impact of Alzheimer's disease will increase strongly in the future as rapid growth of the oldest age groups of the population continues.

Strengths and Limitations of the Estimates

Any estimates of Alzheimer's disease prevalence must be interpreted with some caution. Although there is a reasonable consensus (McKhann et al. 1984) about the concepts forming the clinical diagnosis of Alzheimer's disease, the translation of these concepts into specific operational criteria is not a matter of secure agreement (Henderson and Jorm 1987; Kay et al. 1985). This is especially true with regard to

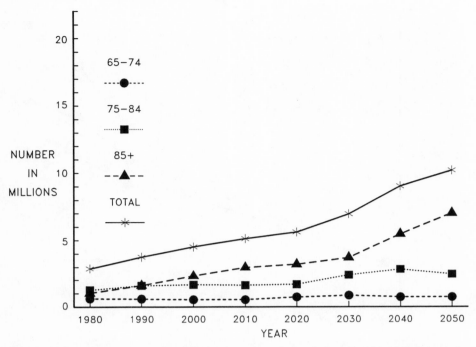

Figure 13–2 Projected number of persons over age 65 with probable Alzheimer's disease in the U.S population from 1980 through 2050 by three age subgroups, using U.S. census middle projection of population growth. Disease prevalence data from studies in East Boston, Massachusetts, adjusted for years of education.

the type and severity of cognitive impairment thought to be characteristic of the disease. Therefore, criteria used in different studies will range along a spectrum, and prevalence estimates from these studies will vary substantially according to the placement of cut points along this diagnostic continuum. This variation especially affects studies in community populations in which mild disease that is difficult to separate from normal may be expected to predominate.

Estimates of Alzheimer's disease prevalence used here are based on uniform, structured clinical evaluations by blinded examiners of individuals sampled from a defined community population. These evaluations permitted clinical diagnosis of various conditions responsible for cognitive impairment in this population. Conditions responsible for dementia other than Alzheimer's disease were relatively uncommon in this population (Evans et al. 1989), and the confidence limits about population prevalence estimates for them are large. Therefore, we have not attempted to estimate the prevalence of these other dementing conditions in the U.S. population. For estimation of Alzheimer's disease, the sample size is relatively large and includes a substantial number of individuals 85 years of age and older, the age group for which disease prevalence is highest. The clinical criteria for Alzheimer's disease correspond to NINCDS-ADRDA criteria (McKhann et al. 1984). For the purpose of estimating disease prevalence in the population, the NINCDS-ADRDA restriction that the presence of a coexisting diagnosis of another dementing illness removes a person from

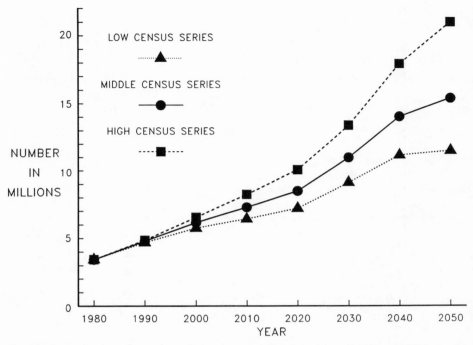

Figure 13–3 Projected number of persons over age 65 with probable Alzheimer's disease in the U.S. population from 1980 through 2050 using low, middle, and high U.S. census projections of population growth. Disease prevalence data, from studies in East Boston, Massachusetts, omitting adjustment for years of education.

the probable Alzheimer's disease category was not used. (See the discussion of disease classification above and Evans et al. 1989.) The ability to assign clinical diagnosis, inclusion of a relatively large number of persons aged 85 and over, use of structured, uniform procedures, and selection of subjects from all strata of performance on a population screening test are unusual compared with most existing population studies. Each of these features increases the validity of the estimates from the study.

Our estimate of Alzheimer's disease prevalence is in close agreement with the 11.2 percent reported by Pfeffer et al. (1987) from a study using different methods. Our estimate is substantially higher than those from some other population-based studies, however, and is also higher than the estimate of 1.4 million affected persons in the 1980 U.S. population provided by the U.S. Congress, Office of Technology Assessment (OTA) (1987). Three reasons account, at least in part, for these differences. First, and most important, the OTA estimate and some earlier studies (Molsa, Marttila, and Rinne 1982; Schoenberg, Anderson, and Haerer 1985) were intentionally restricted to severe disease, where the present study includes the full range of behaviorally manifest disease present in the community.

This restriction substantially reduces estimates of disease prevalence. For example, of those with probable Alzheimer's disease in the East Boston study, 26 percent had severe cognitive impairment, 51 percent moderate impairment, and 23 percent mild impairment. Second, some previous community-based studies have confined selection of subjects for clinical evaluation to those who scored poorly on population screening instruments. This, again, leads to substantial underestimates of disease prevalence in the population because the large group of individuals passing the screening tests will include a number of persons with disease. Third, some previous studies (Kokmen et al. 1989) were based on records of those coming to medical attention for dementia and having the diagnosis entered in the record, but the proportion of individuals whose dementia is formally recognized and diagnosed during routine delivery of medical care is unknown and, perhaps, small. The East Boston study, on the other hand, was based on a sample of persons from a total community survey examined by a single research team.

Prevalence estimates from a cross-sectional study such as ours tend to exclude cases with a rapidly progressive course because of their selective removal from the community by death or institutionalization. Further, our study was restricted to non-institutionalized individuals. Rates of Alzheimer's disease among institutionalized persons are almost certainly higher. Preliminary data (Hing 1987) from the 1985 U.S. National Nursing Home Survey suggest that 47 percent of nursing-home residents 65 years of age and older were diagnosed as having "senile dementia or chronic organic brain syndrome." Rovner et al. (1986) found that 28 of 50 residents of a U.S. intermediate-care nursing home met DSM III criteria (American Psychiatric Association 1980) for primary degenerative dementia. Thus, despite the fact that our estimates are higher than some previous ones, to the extent that they are affected by these limitations, they may well understate the full impact of the disease.

Estimates of the future impact of Alzheimer's disease are determined more by factors other than the current overall prevalence estimate. The rate of projected growth in the prevalence of Alzheimer's disease depends strongly on the current age distribution of the disease and the projected rate of growth of the oldest population age groups. Therefore, both of these factors deserve close examination.

With regard to the age distribution of disease in the community population, the high proportion of individuals meeting criteria for probable Alzheimer's disease in the group 85 years of age and over has a strong influence on projections of disease prevalence for the total population. An excess of mildly impaired individuals in the oldest age groups relative to the younger groups would raise the possibility that the increase in disease prevalence with age was overestimated. Therefore, we examined age-specific estimates of severe, moderate, and mild cognitive impairment in the community population without considering the condition responsible for the impairment. For severe cognitive impairment, the prevalence was 0.3 percent (0–0.9) in the 65- to 74-year-old group, 5.6 percent (1.9–9.2) in the 75- to 84-year-old group, and 19.6 percent (11.1–28.1) in the group 85 years of age and older. For moderate cognitive impairment, the prevalence for the three age groups was 4.6 percent (0.8–8.5), 14.3 percent (9.5–19.1), and 31.3 percent (21.3–41.4). For mild cognitive impairment, the prevalence for the three age groups was 14.3 percent (7.6–21.0), 27.0 percent (20.0–33.9), and 28.6 percent (18.9–38.2) (Figure 13–4). Thus, the increase in the prevalence of cognitive impairment with age is most strikingly seen with severe and moderate impairment. Any estimate of the point prevalence of Alzheimer's disease is strongly dependent on disease criteria and how they are implemented. These data suggest, however, that if more restrictive cut points were used

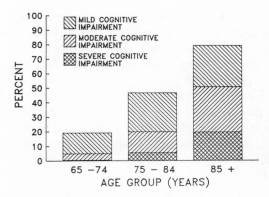

Figure 13–4 Prevalence of severe, moderate, and mild cognitive impairment according to age group, among persons 65 years of age and older in East Boston, Massachusetts.

for disease according to severity of impairment, the prevalence rates for any one age group would change, but the striking increase in disease prevalence with age would remain.

Some projections of population changes suggest that future growth of the oldest age groups of the population may substantially exceed the U.S. Bureau of the Census projections used here because of greater reductions in mortality (Manton 1982; Vaupel and Gowan 1986). The estimated increase in the prevalence of Alzheimer's disease in the U.S. population is largely a consequence of projected increases in size of the oldest age groups, especially those aged 85 years and older. Therefore, if increases in these age groups were to exceed Census Bureau estimates substantially, the projected prevalence of Alzheimer's disease would be higher. There have been few previous projections of future prevalence of Alzheimer's disease with which to compare our results. The estimate by the U.S. Congress, OTA (1987), is substantially lower, reflecting the restriction of the OTA estimates to severe dementia.

A substantial limitation of our estimates is that no single community, including the one that we studied, is likely to be representative of the total U.S. population. Moreover, risk factors for Alzheimer's disease are largely unknown, so that comparison of a community's characteristics with those of the U.S. population is not useful. Because level of formal education may be a risk factor for Alzheimer's disease, prevalence estimates are presented adjusted for this potentially confounding variable. The adjustment for difference in average level of education between the study community and the U.S. population affects the estimated current prevalence of disease. The projected future estimates of Alzheimer's disease prevalence are also adjusted for anticipated changes in educational attainment in the U.S. population. This adjustment has a major effect on estimates of disease prevalence in the future because of the strong trend toward greater educational attainment among older persons (Siegel and Davidson 1984; Taeuber 1983). If this adjustment is not performed, substantially higher estimates of future disease prevalence are obtained, as may be seen by comparing Figures 13–1 and 13–3. The assumption in making these projections presented here, that there is no differential mortality by education, is in accord with recent U.S. Bureau of the Census estimates (Siegel and Davidson 1984) but may not be completely correct (Kitagawa and Hauser 1973). If lower educational attainment is associated with higher mortality, projected future educational levels in the oldest age groups of the U.S. population may be higher than those used here, and the projected overall prevalence of Alzheimer's disease may be correspondingly overestimated.

In the projections, age is modeled using the mean age of each subgroup in the East Boston community in 1982. It seems very likely, however, that the mean age of the oldest age groups of the U.S. population will increase substantially. If the prevalence of Alzheimer's disease continues to rise with increasing age within the oldest age groups, the projected prevalence of Alzheimer's disease will be underestimated. Finally, although the study providing data for these estimates is large compared with previous investigations, the confidence limits about many of our current prevalence estimates are wide. An additional source of uncertainty in applying these estimates to future projections is possible error in U.S. population projections. Although we have approximated the combined impact of these two sources of error by applying the confidence intervals from the East Boston prevalence estimates to three series of U.S. Bureau of the Census population projections, this may understate the uncertainty, especially because, as noted above, it is possible that Bureau of the Census projections underestimate growth of the oldest age groups.

Implications

Despite their limitations, these estimates indicate the overall present and future magnitude of the problem. Statements by institutional bodies (Council on Scientific Affairs, American Medical Association 1986; Royal College of Physicians of London 1980; U.S. Congress, OTA 1987) and by individuals (Brody 1982; Plum 1979; Weiler 1987) suggest that both the rapidly growing seriousness of Alzheimer's disease as a public health issue and the need for vigorous action are now widely appreciated. The estimates presented here suggest several areas in which action will be necessary.

An increase in the number and size of studies in large noninstitutionalized populations, particularly studies able to provide accurate estimates of disease incidence, would aid planning. The increase in the prevalence of Alzheimer's disease will place substantially increased demands on the delivery of long-term care services to older persons in the United States and other developed countries experiencing similar demographic changes. Much of the information necessary for planning to deal with this development is not presently available. Medical care costs are only one component of the economic impact of Alzheimer's disease. Currently available estimates of the costs of Alzheimer's disease vary widely. This variation arises, at least in part, from substantial limitations in the data used to calculate these estimates. Hay and Ernst (1987), using an estimate of 1.5 million cases of Alzheimer's disease in the U.S. population in 1983 (substantially lower than our estimate), calculated a total net annual cost to society from the disease of approximately $30 billion. Huang, Cartwright, and Hu (1988), using an estimate of 3.66 million cases of Alzheimer's disease in the U.S. population in 1985 (somewhat higher than our 1990 estimate based on the middle-census series), calculated direct and indirect costs of the disease at $88 billion.

Those with Alzheimer's disease are at increased risk of institutionalization, but we have little ability to quantify this risk for community-dwelling persons. Similarly, we know little of the disease features that determine the need for long-term care, or of the role of noninstitutional forms of long-term care in this disease. On a more general level, there are few studies of predictors of use of institutional or other long-term-care services in community populations. The factors that enable some individuals with severe impairments of physical or cognitive function to remain in their homes while others, with similar levels of function, are placed in nursing homes or other institutions are not identified. The increasing severity of Alzheimer's disease as a public health problem, combined with this lengthy list of unknowns, raise the question of whether the current level of support for relevant health-care services research in the United States is adequate.

As with other common chronic diseases, an ultimate goal of research concerning Alzheimer's disease is prevention of the condition. At present, the etiologic factors remain undetermined, but it is essential that this long-term goal not be obscured. The formulation and testing of hypotheses regarding the etiology of Alzheimer's disease must have a very high priority. Support for Alzheimer's disease research has been growing at an accelerating pace over the last several years. The rapidly increasing magnitude of the problem outlined here suggests that even greater emphasis on both basic and applied research is necessary.

Acknowledgments—Supported by a cooperative agreement (AG-06789) and contracts (NO1-AG-1-2106, NO1-AG-0-2107) with the National Institute on Aging. The authors thank the residents of East Boston and the staff of the East Boston Neighborhood Health Center for their cooperation and support and Dr. Kenneth Manton for his review of the manuscript and valuable advice.

REFERENCES

Alzheimer, A. 1907. Uber eine Eigenartige Erkraukung der Hirwrinde. *Allg Z Psychiat* 1907; 64:146–148.

American Psychiatric Association. 1980. *Diagnostic and Statistical Manual of Mental Disorders.* 3rd ed. Washington: American Psychiatric Association.

Beckett, L.A., P.A. Scherr, and D.A. Evans. Population Prevalence Estimates from Complex Samples. (Submitted.)

Berkman, L.F. 1986. The Association between Educational Attainment and Mental Status Examinations: Of Etiologic Significance for Senile Dementias or Not? *Journal of Chronic Diseases* 39:171–74.

Bishop, Y.M., S.E. Fienberg, and P.W. Holland. 1975. Discrete Multivariate Analysis: Theory and Practice. Cambridge, Mass.: MIT Press.

Brody, J.A. 1982. An Epidemiologist Views Senile Dementia—Facts and Fragments. *American Journal of Epidemiology* 115:155–62.

Broe, G.A., A.J. Akhtar, G.R. Andrews, F.I. Caird, A.J. Bilmore, and W.J. McLennan. 1976. Neurological Disorders in the Elderly at Home. *Journal of Neurology, Neurosurgery and Psychiatry* 39:362–66.

Copeland, J.R.M., M.E. Dewey, N. Wood, R. Searle, I.A. Davidson, and C. McWilliam. 1987. Range of Mental Illness among the Elderly in the Community; Prevalence in Liverpool Using the GMS-AGECAT Package. *British Journal of Psychiatry* 150:815–23.

Cornoni-Huntley, J., D.B. Brock, A.M. Ostfeld, J.O. Taylor, and R.B. Wallace (Eds.) 1986. *Established Populations for Epidemiologic Studies of the Elderly Resource Data Book.* Washington.

Council on Scientific Affairs, American Medical Association. 1986. Dementia. *Journal of the American Medical Association* 256:2234–38.

Essen-Möller, E., H. Laisson, C.E. Uddenberg, and G. White. 1956. Individual Traits and Morbidity in a Swedish Rural Population. *Acta Psychiatrica Neurologica Scandinavica* Supplementum 100:1–160.

Evans, D.A., H.H. Funkenstein, M.S. Albert, P.A. Scherr, N.R. Cook, M.J. Chown, L.E. Hebert, C.H. Hennekens, J.O. Taylor. 1989. Prevalence of Alzheimer's Disease in a Community Population Higher than Previously Reported. *Journal of the American Medical Association* 262:2251–56.

Faber, J.F. 1982. *Life Tables for the United States: 1990–2050.* Actuarial study no. 87. Washington: Security Administration, Office of the Actuary.

Folstein, M., J.C. Anthony, I. Parhad, B. Duffy, and E.M. Gruenberg. 1985. The Meaning of Cognitive Impairment in the Elderly. *Journal of the American Geriatrics Society* 33:228–35.

Gilmore, A.J.J. 1974. Community Surveys and Mental Health. In *Geriatric Medicine,* ed. W.F. Anderson and T.G. Judge, 77–93. New York: Academic Press.

Gurland, B., J. Copeland, J. Kuriansky, M. Kelleher, L. Sharpe, and L.L. Dean. 1983. *The Mind and Mood of Aging: Mental Health Problems of the Community Elderly in New York and London.* New York: Haworth Press.

Hay, J.W. and R.L. Ernst. 1987. The Economic Costs of Alzheimer's Disease. *American Journal of Public Health* 77:1169–75.

Henderson, A.S. and A.F. Jorm. 1987. Is Case-Ascertainment of Alzheimer's Disease in Field Surveys Practicable? *Psychological Medicine* 17:549–55.

Hing, E. 1987. Use of Nursing Homes by the Elderly: Preliminary Data from the 1985 National Nursing Home Survey. In *Advance Data from Vital and Health Statistics,* no. 135. OHHS publ no. (PHS) 89–1758. Hyattsville, Md.

Hobson, W., and J. Pemberton. 1955. The Health of the Elderly at Home. London: Churchill.

Huang, L.F., W.S. Cartwright, and T.W. Hu. 1988. The Economic Costs of Senile Dementia in the United States, 1985. *Public Health Reports* 103:3–7.

Katzman, R. 1986. Alzheimer's Disease. *New England Journal of Medicine* 314:964–73.

Kay, D.W.K., P. Beamish and M. Roth. 1964. Old Age Mental Disorders in Newcastle upon Tyne. Part I. A Study of Prevalence. *British Journal of Psychiatry* 120:146–58.

Kay, D.W.K., A.S. Henderson, R. Scott, J. Wilson, D. Rickwood, and D.A. Grayson. 1985. Dementia and Depression Among the Elderly Living in the Hobart Community; The Effect of Diagnostic Criteria on the Prevalence Rates. *Psychological Medicine* 15:771–88.

Kitagawa, E.M. and P.M. Hauser. 1973. *Differential Mortality in the United States: A Study in Socioeconomic Epidemiology.* Cambridge, Mass. Harvard University Press.

Kittner, S.J., L.R. White, M.E. Farmer, M. Wolz, E. Kaplan, E. Moes, J.A. Brody, and M. Feinleib. 1986. Methodological Issues in Screening for Dementia: The Problem of Education Adjustment. *Journal of Chronic Diseases* 39:163–70.

Kokmen, E., C.M. Beard, K.P. Offord, and L.T. Kurland. 1989. Prevalence of Medically-Diagnosed Dementia in a Defined United States Population: Rochester, Minnesota, January 1, 1975. *Neurology* 39:773–76.

Kramer, M., P.S. German, J.C. Anthony, M. Von Korf, and E.A. Skinner. 1985. Patterns of Mental Disorder among the Elderly Residents of Eastern Baltimore. *Journal of the American Geriatric Society* 33:236–45.

Manton, K.G. 1982. Changing Concepts of Morbidity and Mortality in the Elderly Population. *Milbank Memorial Fund Quarterly Health and Society* 60:183–244.

McKhann, G., D. Drachman, M. Folstein, R. Katzman, D. Price, and E.M. Stadlan. 1984.

Clinical Diagnosis of Alzheimer's Disease: Report of the NINCDS-ADRDA Work Group under the Auspices of Department of Health and Human Services Task Force on Alzheimer's Disease. *Neurology* 34:939–44.

Miller, L. 1983. Estimates of the Population of the United States by Age, Sex and Race: 1980 to 1982. *Current Population Reports,* series P-25, no. 929. Washington: U.S. Bureau of the Census.

Molsa, P.K., R.J. Marttila and U.K. Rinne. 1982. Epidemiology of Dementia in a Finnish Population. *Acta Neurologica Scandinavica* 65:541–42.

Myers, J.K., M.M. Weissman, G.L. Tischler, C.E. Holzer, P.J. Leaf, H. Orvaschel, J.C. Anthony, J.H. Boyd, J.D. Burke, M. Kramer, and R. Stolzman. 1984. Six-Month Prevalence of Psychiatric Disorders in Three Communities, 1980 to 1982. *Archives of General Psychiatry* 41:959–67.

Park, J.H. and J.C. Ha. 1988. Cognitive Impairment Among the Elderly in a Korean Rural Community. *Acta Psychiatrica Scandinavica* 77:52–57.

Parsons, P.L. 1965. Mental Health of Swansea's Old Folk. *British Journal of Preventive and Social Medicine* 19:43–47.

Pfeffer, R.I., A.A. Afifi, and J.M. Chance. 1987. Prevalence of Alzheimer's Disease in a Retirement Community. *American Journal of Epidemiology* 125:420–36.

Pfeiffer, E. 1975. A Short Portable Mental Status Questionnaire for the Assessment of Organic Brain Deficit in Elderly Patients. 1975. *Journal of the American Geriatric Society* 23:433–41.

Plum, F. 1979. Dementia: An Approaching Epidemic. *Nature* 279:372–73.

Robins, L.N., J.E. Helzer, M.M. Weissman, H. Orvaschel, E. Gruenberg, J.D. Burke, and D.A. Regier. 1984. Lifetime Prevalence of Specific Psychiatric Disorders in Three Sites. *Archives of General Psychiatry* 41:949–58.

Romaniuk, M., W.J. McAuley, and G. Arling. 1983. An Examination of the Prevalence of Mental Disorders Among the Elderly in the Community. *Journal of Abnormal Psychology* 92:458–67.

Rovner, B.W., S. Kafonek, L. Filipp, M.J. Lucas, and M.F. Folstein. 1986. Prevalence of Mental Illness in a Community Nursing Home. *American Journal of Psychiatry* 143:1446–49.

Royal College of Physicians of London, Committee on Geriatrics. 1980. Organic Mental Impairment in the Elderly. Implications for Research, Education and the Provisions of Services. *Journal of the Royal College of Physicians of London* 15:141–67.

Sayetta, R.B. 1986. Rates of Senile Dementia-Alzheimer's Type in the Baltimore Longitudinal Study. *Journal of Chronic Diseases* 39:271–86.

Scherr, P.A., M.S. Albert, H.H. Funkenstein, N.R. Cook, C.H. Hennekens, L.G. Branch, L.R. White, J.O. Taylor, and D.A. Evans. 1988. Correlates of Cognitive Function in an Elderly Community Population. *American Journal of Epidemiology* 128:1084–1101.

Schoenberg, B.S., D.W. Anderson, and A.F. Haerer. 1985. Severe dementia: Prevalence and Clinical Features in a Biracial US Population. *Archives of Neurology* 42:740–43.

Schoenberg, B.S., E. Kokmen, and H. Okazaki. 1987. Alzheimer's Disease and Other Dementing Illnesses in a Defined United States Population; Incidence Rates and Clinical Features. *Annals of Neurology* 22:724–29.

Shibayama, H., Y. Kasahara, and H. Kobayashi. 1986. Prevalence of Dementia in a Japanese Elderly Population. *Acta Psychiatrica Scandinavica* 74:144–51.

Siegel, J.S., and M. Davidson. 1984. Demographic and Socioeconomic Aspects of Aging in the United States. *Special Studies,* series P-23, no. 138. Washington: U.S. Bureau of the Census.

Spencer, G. 1984. Projections of the Population of the United States by Age, Sex, and Race:

1983 to 2080. *Current Population Reports,* series P-25, no. 952. Washington: U.S. Bureau of the Census.

Staff of the Mental Health Research Unit. 1960. A Mental Health Survey of Older People III. *Psychiatric Quarterly* 34(suppl., part 1):34–75.

Sulkava, R., J. Wikstrom, A. Aromaa, R. Raitasalo, V. Lehtinen, K. Lahtela, and J. Palo. 1985. Prevalence of Severe Dementia in Finland. *Neurology* 35:1025–29.

Taeuber, C.M. 1983. America in Transition: An Aging Society. *Current Population Reports,* series P-23, no. 128. Washington: U.S. Bureau of the Census.

Tomlinson, B.L., G. Blessed, and M. Roth. 1970. Observations on the Brains of Demented Old People. *Journal of the Neurological Sciences* 11:205–42.

U.S. Congress, Office of Technology Assessment. 1987. *Losing a Million Minds: Confronting the Tragedy of Alzheimer's Disease and Other Dementias* (OTA-BA-323) Washington.

Vaupel, J.W., and A.E. Gowan. 1986. Passage to Methuselah: Some Demographic Consequences of Continued Progress Against Mortality. *American Journal of Public Health* 76:430–33.

Weiler, P.G. 1987. The Public Health Impact of Alzheimer's Disease. *American Journal of Public Health* 17:1157–58.

V

A SOCIAL PORTRAIT OF THE OLDEST OLD

14

The Social Environment of the Very Old

MARY GRACE KOVAR and ROBYN I. STONE

The preoccupation with institutionalization, disability, and death conceals the fact that the majority of very old people continue to live in households in the community. They are survivors; they have not only outlived their expected number of years of life, they have also outlived their expected number of *active* years. Besides residing in the community, most of them care for themselves, see and talk with family and friends, and go about their daily business with relative independence.

In 1975, John Cassel presented the Wade Hampton Frost Lecture at a meeting of the American Public Health Association. In that address, published the following year as "The Contribution of the Social Environment to Host Resistance" (Cassel 1976), he charted a course for social epidemiology.

These social factors are not etiologically specific for any one disease, at least as presently classified, although the psychosocial processes enhance or reduce susceptibility to disease. Furthermore, susceptibility is not a function of any particular stressor. Therefore, it is necessary to consider the ability to function in general rather than a particular disease, and it is necessary to consider the social environment in general rather than any specific stressor.

He argued that the classical view of disease resulting from new exposure to pathological agents may have provided a satisfactory basis for inferences when most diseases were the result of overwhelming pathology and virulence. However, this perspective was not sufficient in our technologically developed society. Most of the pathological agents are ubiquitous in our environment—everyone who lives long enough is exposed to them; the social factors are what make people more or less resistant to these agents.

Lawton (1982, 1985) and Lawton and Nahemow (1973) have proposed a social environment model of person–environment fit that considers the physical, cognitive, and social characteristics of the individual and the environmental factors that influence the well-being of older people. The purpose of this chapter is to describe the social environment of the oldest old in an effort to understand the context within which these people are able to continue residing in the community. This overview focuses on key elements of the social environment of people 80 years and over, including housing characteristics; residential patterns and living arrangements; social contacts with family, friends, and neighbors; and use of community services.

Although we recognize that the social environment of the oldest old is a web of structural, environmental, and individual factors, this chapter does not examine all of these complex interrelationships. We describe the social environment of the people in general, although we do make comparisons by selected subgroups, such as gender and disability, to highlight several characteristics. Further, although research indicates that the "young old" are generally better off than the "old old" (Commonwealth Fund Commission 1987; Crystal 1982), we have not attempted to make comparisons between age groups. Finally, we want to emphasize that the limitations of our cross-sectional data preclude our examining causal relationships. We hope, however, that this descriptive information will provide a background for future research that will include multivariate and causal analyses.

In the next section we describe the data used for our profile of the social environment of people aged 80 and over, followed by a brief review of the life history of this cohort. We then present data on major components of the social environment of the oldest old and conclude with a summary of our observations and some general comments concerning future research.

DATA SOURCES

The source of the original data in this chapter was a supplement to the National Health Interview Survey, the National Center for Health Statistics' large continuing survey of the health of the civilian noninstitutionalized population of the United States. In 1984 a special questionnaire was added to obtain information about older people. This supplemental questionnaire, the Supplement on Aging (SOA), was designed to obtain information about interactions with family and organizations, use of community services, housing, retirement status, physical functioning, chronic conditions, and other health-related and social information about middle-aged and older people.

A total of 2,095 people interviewed for the SOA were aged 80 or over. They provided the information for this chapter. Most of them, 83 percent, described their own lives; they answered all of the questions for and about themselves. Those who did not were likely to be very old, aged 90 or older, or to be people who received help with activities of daily living. Someone else, almost always a family member living with the older person, provided the information about these people. Except for the data on opinions about oneself and one's future (questions that were asked only of people who answered all the questions for themselves), data about all sample members, whether they answered for themselves or not, are included in this chapter to give the most complete picture possible of this extremely important and varied group of older Americans. To do otherwise would bias the picture of older Americans, because people who answered for themselves, even among the people aged 80 and over, were younger and healthier than the total sample.

Both the National Health Interview Survey and the 1984 Supplement on Aging have been described in detail, and the questionnaires have been published (Fitti and Kovar 1987; Kovar and Poe 1985). All data in the chapter are national estimates based on the sample. They are subject to sampling error. This is a point-in-time study. Conditions at the time the people were interviewed could have existed for a long time or could have resulted from a recent change. Conversely, the conditions could have changed soon after the interview. The relationships and associations discussed in this chapter should not be interpreted as causal.

LIFE HISTORY

There were 4.8 million Americans aged 80 or above who were living in communities outside nursing homes or other institutions in 1984. Most of them were in their early eighties; 2.9 million were aged 80 through 84, 1.3 million were aged 85 through 89, and half a million were 90 or older. Two-thirds were women, and 46 percent were widowed, white, and women.

A brief overview of the life history of these people helps to show the diseases and stresses to which their cohort has been subject and to set the context for their present lives. Most of them were born in the very late 1890s or early 1900s, and their present status reflects the events of the twentieth century. They were certainly exposed to disease early in life. The death rate for children under 1 year of age was 162 per 1,000 people, and the expectation of life in the United States was 47 years in 1900 (Linder and Grove 1947; U.S. Bureau of Census 1975). During their early years, death rates from childhood diseases, diptheria, and tuberculosis were high. They were subject to the influenza pandemic that followed World War I. The magnitude of that pandemic can be seen from the death rates; in October 1918 the crude death rate was 44 deaths per 1,000 people, in contrast to 14 in September of that year and 12 in October the year before (Linder and Grove 1947).

People born at that time, and women in particular, are part of a cohort that may be unusually vulnerable to being left unprotected in their old age. In the United States, there are only two major sources of support when one grows old. One is family support and the other is earned by work. Women born early in the twentieth century are at unusual risk of lacking either source of support.

Women born in the early 1900s had fewer children than the cohorts that preceded or followed them (Heuser 1976). They were born into large families, but war and the Great Depression coincided with their childbearing years. Birth rates were extremely low during the Depression (Heuser 1976; Linder and Grove 1947), and the Depression was followed by World War II, which caused the temporary absence of many men. By the time the men returned home, it was late for the women of this generation to bear children. Moreover, infant mortality rates were still relatively high. Therefore, as we shall see, many of the oldest old may not have many children to provide family support.

Many of these women did have work experience, particularly during the war, but most (see Chapter 2, this volume) left the labor force when the war ended and they earned no pensions. Among those women who did bear children, many experienced an M-shaped pattern of labor-force history, with the highest employment rates before and after childbearing. Childbearing, in turn, was likely to be associated with interrupted or delayed careers. Women who entered the labor force late or who were intermittently employed were apt to earn less retirement income because these employment patterns decrease one's opportunity to achieve pension vesting rights and ensures lower wages upon which retirement income is based (Clark 1980; O'Rand and Henretta 1982).

Many men also had interrupted careers. About 4.7 million of them served in the armed forces in World War I, and casualty rates were high; 117,000 died in combat, and 204,000 others were wounded (U.S. Bureau of the Census 1975). Some men in this cohort also served in World War II. Many were unemployed during the Depression; in 1932 about 13 million people—25 percent of the civilian labor force—were unemployed. The suicide rate, a documented measure of stress, reached its peak in the United States at 17.4 suicides per 100,000 people in 1932 (Linder and Grove 1947). The peak for insurance policy holders, who represented urban wage-earning classes, had occurred a year earlier in 1931 (Dublin 1963).

Those people aged 80 and older who were living in the community in the 1980s had survived major diseases and stresses. There may be much that we can learn from them.

THE SOCIAL ENVIRONMENT OF THE OLDEST OLD

The basic profile of people aged 80 years and over has been described (see Chapter 2, this volume). They are likely to be widowed, white, and female, with relatively low levels of formal education and little income. Such a description, however, is insufficient for recognizing their demographic heterogeneity. In fact, 29 percent of the people aged 80 and over were married and living with a spouse in 1984. One-third were men. Sixteen percent had formal education beyond high school. Of those who provided income data, 75 percent were living above the poverty level; 21 percent had incomes of $20,000 or more in 1983. The majority perceived their health as good and received no help with personal care, although many received assistance with household chores and outside activities. Thus, the oldest old are a heterogeneous group and many, despite their age, are doing reasonably well and view themselves as doing well.

Living Arrangements

The living arrangements and the marital status of the oldest old are major components of their social environment. In 1984, 2.2 million people aged 80 years or older, 45 percent of the oldest old who were living in the community, were living alone (Tables 14–1 and 14–2). Those living alone were likely to be women, a phenomenon that is attributable, in large part, to the fact that three-quarters of the women were widowed compared with only one-third of the men. Fewer men survive to their 65th or 80th birthday, and even at older ages, a man's life expectancy is shorter than a woman's (NCHS 1986a). Regardless of whether or not they were living alone, the women were likely to be widowed and to have been widows for a long time; 43 percent of the widowed women had been without a spouse for 20 years or more.

In addition, women tend to marry men older than themselves, thus increasing their likelihood of being widowed. Furthermore, marriage or remarriage in later life is relatively infrequent, particularly for older women; 9 percent of the men who were married, in contrast to 4 percent of the women, had been married for less than 15 years. Data from the marriage registration system show clearly that men are more likely than women to marry at older ages; men who have had their 65th birthday are

Table 14–1   With Whom People Live

Family information	Population (thousands)	Percentage of population
One-person family	2,261	46.8
Alone	2,170	45.0
Nonrelative	91	1.9
Two-person family	1,842	38.2
Spouse	1,250	25.9
Other relative	592	12.3
One generation	148	3.1
Two generation	444	9.2
Three- or more person family	723	15.0
One generation	29	0.6
Two generation	405	8.4
Three generation	289	6.0
Total	4,825	100.0

Source: National Center for Health Statistics, National Health Interview Survey, 1984 Supplement on Aging.

nine times as likely to remarry as their female age peers—19 percent versus 2 percent (NCHS 1986b).

Another 38 percent of the people aged 80 and over lived in two-person families; the majority were married couples. Only 15 percent were living with families of three or more persons. Contrary to the belief that the oldest old are likely to reside in multigenerational households, only 6 percent were living in households with three or more generations.

Shared living arrangements have been found to be largely a function of the poor health status of elderly people (Bishop 1986; Soldo and Manton 1984; Tissue and McCoy 1981). We also found this to be true. Fifty-two percent of the people who were living with someone other than, or in addition to, a spouse were doing so because they had a health problem (Tables 14–3 and 14–4). People living with someone other than or in addition to a spouse were also more likely to have spent time in bed during the previous year because of illness.

Among people aged 80 and above, difficulty with one or more of the seven activities of daily living (ADLs), especially walking, was fairly common (Table 14–5). Difficulty with one or more of the six instrumental activities of daily living (IADLs), especially doing heavy housework, was even more common (Table 14–6). However, about half of the people had no difficulty with any of the 13 activities (Table 14–7). We also found that a larger proportion of those living with others than those living alone had difficulty and received help with one or more activities.

Table 14–2   Generations in the House

Number of generations	Population (thousands)	Percentage
One	3,686	76.4
Two	851	17.6
Three or more	289	6.0
Total	4,825	100.0

Source: National Center for Health Statistics, National Health Interview Survey, 1984 Supplement on Aging.

Table 14-3   Reasons People Live with Someone Else

Reason	Total population (percentage)	Living with others[a] (percentage)
Health	14.7	52.3
Share expenses	10.4	36.9
Both	6.4	22.8

Note: The total population represented in this table is 4,825,000 persons. The number of elderly persons living with others is 1,353,000 persons.

[a] Living with someone other than or in addition to a spouse.

Source: National Center for Health Statistics, National Health Interview Survey, 1984 Supplement on Aging.

Table 14-4   Reasons People Live with Someone Else

Family information	Health (percentage of population)	To share expenses (percentage of population)
One-person family		
Alone	—	—
Nonrelative	42.6	11.7
Two-person family		
Spouse	—	—
Other relative	39.5	37.3
One generation	31.0	49.8
Two generation	42.3	33.2
Three-or-more-person family	60.3	37.0
One generation	40.2	39.6
Two generation	57.8	32.6
Three generation	65.8	43.1
Total	14.7	10.4

Source: National Center for Health Statistics, National Health Interview Survey, 1984 Supplement on Aging.

Table 14-5   People with Difficulty and Receiving Help with Activities of Daily Living

ADLs	With difficulty (percentage)	Receiving help (percentage)
One or more ADLs	40.1	22.2
Walking	33.3	10.7
Getting outside	22.5	14.2
Bathing or showering	21.2	14.9
Getting in or out of bed or chair	15.1	6.3
Dressing	12.4	9.1
Using toilet	10.3	5.5
Eating	3.6	2.2

Source: National Center for Health Statistics, National Health Interview Survey, 1984 Supplement on Aging.

Table 14-6 People with Difficulty and Receiving Help with Instrumental Activities of Daily Living and People Who Do Not Do the Activity

IADLs	With difficulty (percentage)	Receiving help (percentage)	Does not do[a] (percentage)
One or more IADLs	46.0	40.7	—
Heavy housework	39.4	34.2	14.8
Shopping personal	27.3	26.1	5.1
Preparing meals	17.5	15.1	7.6
Light housework	16.6	14.8	6.2
Managing money	14.4	13.8	4.2
Using telephone	11.6	7.6	1.5

[a]People who did not do the activity; the reason was not a health or physical problem.

Source: National Center for Health Statistics, National Health Interview Survey, 1984 Supplement on Aging.

Older people also may live with family or friends because they do not have the financial resources to live alone. In fact, 37 percent of those aged 80 and over living with people other than a spouse in 1984 did so because they needed to share expenses—40 percent of the women and 27 percent of the men. Approximately 23 percent gave both health and expenses as reasons for co-residence.

Where People Live

Residential location and housing characteristics also are important components of the social environment of the oldest old. In support of the conventional wisdom that many elderly people live in the Sunbelt, one-third of the very old people resided in the South in 1984, 28 percent lived in the North Central states, a little more than one-fifth resided in the Northeast, and 18 percent resided in the West.

Most of the people aged 80 years and over lived in houses or apartments. Seven percent resided in retirement communities. People living alone were more likely than those sharing households to be living in retirement communities; they were also three times as likely as those living with others to be renters rather than owners.

Table 14-7 Prevalence of Difficulty and Help with Activities of Daily Living and Instrumental Activities of Daily Living

Difficulty and help status	Total	Living Alone (percentage)	Living With others (percentage)
Difficulty with:			
ADLs	40.1	37.6	42.1
IADLs only	12.4	12.5	12.4
Neither	47.5	49.9	45.5
Help with:			
ADLs	22.2	14.2	28.8
IADLs only	21.0	23.6	18.9
Neither	56.8	62.3	52.4

Note: The total population represented in this table is 4,825,000 persons. The number of persons who live alone is 2,170,000; the number living with others is 2,655,000.

Source: National Center for Health Statistics, National Health Interview Survey, 1984 Supplement on Aging.

A small but significant number of the people lived in trailers, although not necessarily in trailer parks.

Some studies indicate that remaining in place is by far the most significant decision on residence made by older people (Lawton 1982, 1985; Struyk and Katsura 1987; Tillson 1989). The oldest old have certainly not been a very mobile population. Approximately 47 percent of the people aged 80 and over living in the community had resided in precisely the same house or apartment for 20 years or more; 11 percent had not moved in 50 years; a few still lived where they had lived since they were born.

Because of elderly persons' limited mobility, visual difficulties, and the likelihood of falling, physical characteristics of their housing are critical to their ability to continue living in the community. About four-fifths of the people aged 80 and over resided in dwellings with one or more steps to the outside. However, they were likely to live on one floor. Fifty-five percent lived entirely on one floor and another 34 percent had their bedroom, bathroom, and kitchen on the same level. Thus, 89 percent had the three essential rooms on the same floor, even though only 42 percent said that they needed a one-level residence because of a health or physical problem. In contrast, three-quarters of those who said that they needed a walk-in shower did not have one.

Having one-floor housing with no steps to the outside and walk-in showers is important because of the frequency of falls among these very old people; 31 percent had fallen within the past 12 months—some more than once. That may be an underestimate. Campbell, Borrie, and Spears (1989), who closely monitored the people in their study, found that 39.6 percent of the women and 28.4 percent of the men fell at least once.

Falls are important because of the relationship between falls, fractures, and institutionalization. Falls are especially likely to lead to fractures when one is very old. Fractures, especially broken hips, are a leading cause of hospitalization and long hospital stays among very old women (Havlik, Liu, and Kovar 1987). Older women who break hips are also at increased risk of institutionalization and of death (Evans, Prudham, and Wandless 1979; Jensen and Tondevold 1979).

Family and Frequency of Contacts with Children

There is a persistent myth that the oldest old, particularly those who live alone, are lonely and socially isolated. Although this myth, like others, has some basis in reality, the data show that most of the very old people are not socially isolated. They also show that the desire for more social contacts is not limited to those living alone.

During the past decade, prospective cohort studies have explored the social environment hypothesis originally articulated by Cassel. These studies have confirmed the beneficial effects of various forms of social support on global mental health (Williams, Ware, and Donald 1981), incidence of depressive symptoms (Gore 1978; Schaefer, Coyne, and Lazarus 1981); psychological distress (Holahan and Moos 1981; Turner 1981), physical symptoms (Gore 1978); and all causes of mortality (Berkman and Syme 1979; Blazer 1982). It is assumed that very elderly people with weak social contacts and support will be at higher risk for physical and mental-health problems.

Table 14–8   Whether People Have Living Children and Siblings

Children and siblings status	Total	Living	
		Alone	With others
Children			
None	23.2	28.4	19.0
Sons only	16.8	19.2	14.8
Daughters only	17.3	16.6	17.9
Both	42.7	35.9	48.3
Siblings			
None	35.8	37.1	34.8
Brothers only	12.1	13.0	11.4
Sisters only	26.1	26.3	25.9
Both	26.0	23.7	27.9
Children and siblings			
Neither	9.0	11.7	6.8
Children only	26.8	25.4	27.9
Siblings only	14.2	16.7	12.2
Both	50.0	46.2	53.1

Note: The total population represented in this table is 4,825,000 persons. The number of persons living alone is 2,170,000; the number living with others is 2,655,000.

Source: National Center for Health Statistics, National Health Interview Survey, 1984 Supplement on Aging.

The concept of social support is complex and has been defined in many ways, such as in terms of the individual's perceptions, the type of support provided, and the effect of the supportive exchange (Antonucci 1985). Social networks are vehicles through which social support is distributed or exchanged.

The data from the SOA provide some insights into the social networks of the oldest old. They reveal that most of the people aged 80 and over who were living in the community in 1984 had living children or siblings and that half had both (Table 14–8). People with children tended to have frequent contact with them. Most saw a child at least once a week (Table 14–9); they talked with their children by telephone even more frequently than they saw them; and about half either saw or talked with a child daily.

Our data reveal that most of the people aged 80 and older who were living in the

Table 14–9   Frequency with which People with Children Have Contact with at Least One Child

Frequency of contact	Type of contact		
	In person (percentage)	By phone (percentage)	Either (percentage)
Daily	27.7	38.4	49.1
2–6 times per week	39.5	37.4	35.7
1–3 times per month	14.1	12.0	9.8
1–11 times per year	15.4	3.1	3.2
Less than yearly	2.0	6.3	1.1
No information	2.2	2.8	1.3

Note: The population is 2,721,000 people with children.

Source: National Center for Health Statistics, National Health Interview Survey, 1984 Supplement on Aging.

community did have family and few are socially isolated. Most had living children or siblings, and half of them had both (Table 14–8). The 2.2 million people aged 80 and over who were living alone were less likely to have children than those living with someone else; 28 percent had no living children, and 12 percent had neither children nor siblings. However, 37 percent had daily contact with a child. Further, of those who had at least one child, almost three-quarters had a child who could be at their home within an hour; 30 percent had a child who could be there within 10 minutes.

The frequency with which the people living alone had contact with their children further vitiates the myth of social isolation. People with children tended to live near them, to see them, and to talk with them by telephone frequently. Most saw a child at least once a week (Table 14–9). They talked with children by telephone even more frequently, and about half either saw or talked with a child daily.

Of the 1.6 million people living alone who had at least one child, almost three-quarters had a child who could be at their home within an hour; 30 percent had a child who could be there within 10 minutes. Twenty-nine percent saw a child daily, and another 41 percent saw a child at least once a week, usually more than once. The frequency of telephone contact was even higher than that of personal contact; 42 percent talked with a child daily, and another 35 percent talked with a child one or more times a week. When personal and telephone conversations are both considered, 52 percent of those with children had daily contact with a child.

Recent Social Contacts

Although children are a primary source of social support, other relatives, friends, and neighbors also are potentially important components of the network. However, the potential cannot be realized unless the older person has contact with such people. Most of the people aged 80 and over had had recent contact; 95 percent had had contact with friends, neighbors or relatives, either in person or by telephone within 2 weeks (Table 14–10).

The data in Table 14–10 also reinforce the importance of the telephone in maintaining social contacts, especially for people living alone. Of the 2.2 million people aged 80 and over who lived alone, 98 percent had visited with or talked on the telephone with friends, family, or neighbors during the previous two weeks; 92 per-

Table 14–10 Recent Social Contacts

		Living	
Type of contact	Total (percentage)	Alone (percentage)	With others (percentage)
Seen friends, neighbors, or relatives within 2 weeks	87.1	89.8	84.9
Talked with friends, neighbors, or relatives within 2 weeks	86.8	91.9	82.6
Seen or talked with friends, neighbors, or relatives within 2 weeks	95.4	97.7	93.5

Source: National Center for Health Statistics, National Health Interview Survey, 1984 Supplement on Aging.

cent had talked with them on the telephone; 90 percent had visited with them. About 84 percent had both met and talked on the telephone with people; only 2 percent had done neither.

These very old people also participated in institutionalized social activities. For example, 43 percent (48 percent of those living alone) had gone to a church or temple within the 2 weeks prior to the interview; about 18 percent (22 percent of those living alone) had attended a movie or a sports event.

People who answered the questions about themselves were asked a few more questions about their social activities. Three-quarters felt that their present level of social activity was adequate; however, one-quarter desired more activity. About 10 percent of these people had done some volunteer work during the past year. Answers to these questions suggest that people living alone do not feel more isolated than those living with others. Both groups were equally likely to feel that their present level of social activity was adequate or to want more social activity, and people living alone were more likely to have done volunteer work during the year (13 percent vs. 9 percent).

In general, people who had one form of social contact were likely to have several forms of interaction. That is, individuals who had visited with family were also more likely to have seen friends and neighbors than those who had no contact with kin. Similarly, people who had talked on the phone with one were likely to have talked with others. People who had attended a movie or sports-event activity were more likely to have gone to a church or temple. There were relatively few individuals who did not have many social contacts and who did appear to be true social isolates. However, the majority of the oldest old did engage in multiple social interactions.

Use of Community Services

During the past decade, policy makers and researchers have focused on the role of community services in enhancing the capacity of elderly people to live independently. These encompass both community-based services (for example, senior-citizen centers, adult day-care centers, and special transportation programs for the elderly), and in-home services (such as homemaker services, home health aides, visiting nurses, home-delivered meals, and telephone call-check services).

We found that 30 percent of the people aged 80 and over had used one or more of these services within a year (Table 14–11). About 16 percent had used a senior center and 10 percent had eaten meals there. In addition, 8 percent had used special transportation for the elderly in the past year, and 8 percent had used one or more home-nursing services.

The community-based services do seem to be enhancing the social environment of the oldest old, especially those who live alone, who are more likely to use such services than those living with others. For example, one-fifth of the former had used a senior center, compared with 11 percent of those sharing households. Similarly, a higher proportion of those living alone had eaten meals at the senior center, or had used special transportation for the elderly, than those living with others.

The in-home services provide a different kind of support. People who had difficulty with one or more ADLs were more likely to use in-home services than those with no functional impairment. Among those living alone, individuals having diffi-

Table 14–11   Use of Community Services During the Year

		Living	
Services used	Total (percentage)	Alone (percentage)	With others (percentage)
One or more services	30.2	39.7	22.4
Senior center	15.7	21.1	11.4
Meals in senior center	9.7	14.1	6.2
Special transportation	7.8	12.5	3.9
Home nursing services	7.5	7.6	7.5

Note: The total population represented in this table is 4,825,000. The number of persons living alone is 2,170,000; the number living with others is 2,655,000.

Source: National Center for Health Statistics, National Health Interview Survey, 1984 Supplement on Aging.

culty with one or more ADLs were almost three times as likely as those with no difficulty to have used home nursing services during the year. The disparity was even greater among the oldest old living with others; functionally impaired people who were sharing households were seven times as likely as those with no difficulty to have used one or more home nursing services.

The use of senior centers by those living alone did not vary by level of functional impairment; approximately one-fifth of those with no difficulty and those with difficulty with one or more ADLs had used senior centers during the year. Among those living with others, however, individuals who were not disabled were more likely to have visited a senior center.

Health Insurance and Health Concerns

The majority of the people felt that they had someone to care for them if they became ill for a few days or a few weeks (Table 14–12). People living with others, some of whom were already receiving care and help from household members, were more likely than those living alone to feel that they had someone to take care of them. The difference was especially large when the time period was a few weeks rather than a few days; about 30 percent of the people living alone, in contrast to 10 percent of those living with others, had no one to care for them if they became ill for a few weeks. Having children reduced the difference, but it remained large.

Almost all had health insurance as one means of taking care of themselves. Medicare coverage was almost universal; 97 percent had Medicare coverage in 1984, with 93 percent indicating that they also subscribed to Medicare Part B. Sixty-three percent also had private insurance for hospital care and 60 percent for care from a physician. Only 35 percent had no private insurance for either hospital or physician care. Only about 2 percent had neither Medicare nor private insurance. Care under Medicaid was rare; only 7 percent had received care that was covered by Medicaid during the previous year and only 5 percent had a current Medicaid card.

The people who answered the questions for themselves were asked specifically about their concerns and their sense of control of their health. Although such people were less likely to be very ill or very old than people who did not answer for themselves, the answers reveal a high degree of self-sufficiency among many of the oldest old. The majority (53 percent) felt that they were taking excellent or very good care

Table 14–12 People Who Say They Have Someone to Care for Them If They Become Sick

| | | For a few | |
	Population (thousands)	Days (percentage)	Weeks (percentage)
Living arrangements			
Living:			
Alone	2,170	83.1	70.1
Who have children	1,555	87.2	75.3
With others	2,655	94.7	90.0
Total	4,825	89.5	81.1

Source: National Center for Health Statistics, National Health Interview Survey, 1984 Supplement on Aging.

of their own health, and another 35 percent said that they were taking good care of themselves. Twenty-eight percent felt that they had a great deal of control over their future health. Over three-quarters felt that their health status was the same or better than it was 1 year ago. Forty-six percent had not worried at all about their health during the previous year, although 9 percent had worried a great deal.

TWO YEARS LATER

People who were aged 70 and over when they participated in the SOA in 1984 are being followed through the Longitudinal Study of Aging (LSOA), which is designed to explore changes on functional status and living arrangements. The LSOA, a collaborative project of the National Institute on Aging and the National Center for Health Statistics, will take 10 years to complete (Kovar and Fitti 1987). By that time, people who were in their seventies when the study began will be in their eighties— they will be the oldest old. Eventually the LSOA will provide more information about the paths people follow as they become old and the dynamics of social change than we have now. Even the information from the first two years is adding to our knowledge.

We are learning more about the dynamic nature of changes. The data from the LSOA confirm data from other studies (Branch and Jette 1982). People who had been living alone were more likely than people who had been living with others to be in a nursing home two years later (Kovar 1988). However, older people who were living with others because of health problems were even more likely to be in a nursing home than those living alone. The best predictor of being in a nursing home was not age; it was dependency at the beginning of the study. People who were receiving help with one or more ADLs or who were living with other people because of their health were more likely to have died or to be in a nursing home by 1986 than those who were not dependent (Kovar 1987; Kovar and Harris 1987).

Of the people living alone who were receiving help with one or more ADLs in 1984, 16 percent were in nursing homes 2 years later, in contrast to 2 percent of those who had no difficulty with either ADLs or IADLs. When the analysis was restricted to those people who were not receiving help with any ADLs, people living alone who had had contact with friends or neighbors or who had attended a religious or social event within 2 weeks of the 1984 interview were more likely to be still in the community than those who had not had such social contacts (Kovar 1988).

Although much of the public-health interest has been in predicting institutionalization, one of the more important findings from the LSOA is the stability of the living arrangements of most older people. Eighty-five percent of the people who were 70 and over in 1984 were living in the community 2 years later. Some people who had been living alone were living with others 2 years later, and some who had been living with others, especially those who had been living with someone other than a spouse, were living alone. However, the majority had the same living arrangements in 1986 that they had had in 1984. Of the people who had been living alone, 78 percent were still living alone 2 years later; of the people who had been living with others, 75 percent were still living with others (Kovar 1988). People aged 80 and over were less likely than those who were 70 through 79 to be still in the community. Nevertheless, three-quarters of the oldest old were still in the community 2 years later (Kovar 1987).

There were changes in directions that were perhaps unanticipated. Some older people who had been receiving help with an ADL had no difficulty with the ADL 2 years later. Some of those who had been living alone were now living with others because they had married. Some of those who had been living with others were living alone because they did not like the person with whom they had lived. The people who had moved were asked why they had moved. Their reasons covered a wide range: Poor health or the health of a spouse, and the wish or need to be near children or other family members were common answers, but a desire for smaller or more convenient housing, an opportunity for a better house or apartment, lower golf fees, and better climate were also cited. One response was "To spend summers in Maine and winters in Florida."

DISCUSSION

Despite the extensive body of literature that has emerged in the field of social gerontology, few studies have focused exclusively on the oldest old living in the community. In this chapter, we have described the social environment of those individuals who are 80 years and over and who live at home either alone or with others. Although the myth of social isolation and frailty continues to prevail, data from the 1984 SOA suggest that the majority of the oldest old are doing reasonably well. Almost half of them live alone and most of them engage in several forms of social interaction. Many have lived in the same residence for years and appear to enjoy living near, but not necessarily with, children. A large proportion of those who lived with children did so because of their health.

Empirical evidence supports anecdotal reports that elderly individuals want to remain independent as long as possible (Schorr 1980; Troll 1971). Unmarried older people prefer to live separately but in close proximity to relatives: what Rosenmayr (1977) has called "intimacy at a distance." Many of the people who have had an 80th birthday and who remain in the community seem to have achieved this goal. Those who lived near their children saw and talked with them often. Among those living alone who had children, there was a strong and statistically significant association between the time it took the nearest child to get to the parent and the frequency of seeing one or more children, talking with a child on the telephone, or both.

Lindheim and Syme (1983) have argued that the uncritical continuation of many current health, housing, and city-planning policies is inappropriate because these policies do not take into account the evidence linking social and spatial conditions to health and disease. People need to be connected to their biological and cultural heritage.

Many of the people did seem to have those connections. They had lived in the same place for a long time. Many who had moved had settled into retirement communities where peers and services were available. If married, they had been married for a long time. They lived near children if they had them.

Community services appeared to be fulfilling the need for social contacts and mobility for some people. Those who lived alone were more likely to have used senior centers and transportation for the elderly than people living with others. People who had difficulty with ADLs were more likely than those who did not to use in-home services.

The success of these very old people in coping should not conceal the difficulties and the probable fragility of the oldest old, particularly those who live alone. They may be subject to more change than data from a single survey or census reveal. Consider, for example, changes in living arrangements. Noelker and Poulshock (1982) argued that the proportion of elders ever residing in an intergenerational household has been undocumented and underestimated because a one-time survey does not count all the people who live in such a household at some time. Beck and Beck (1984), who used longitudinal data, found that of the men who were aged 45 through 49 and who remained married for the subsequent decade, 6.1 percent of the white men and 9.5 percent of the black men had parents in the household in 1966, but 10.9 of the white men and 12.7 percent of the black men had parents in the household at some time during the subsequent 10 years. Because virtually all of these men were heads of households, the data give an estimate of the incidence of parents moving in with middle-aged married children.

Many very elderly people, particularly women, have little money income and survive solely or primarily on Social Security benefits. Most people are covered by Medicare, and many have private health insurance to help pay for their medical care, but premiums need to be paid and insurance seldom covers expenses for long-term care. Most own their own homes, but taxes still need to be paid. Many live in houses or apartments that are old and that may require extensive maintenance.

The historical past of the cohort that is now 80 and over is reflected in their present. A relatively high proportion have no living children. Many, especially the women, have low retirement incomes. Men may fare better; 19 percent of the men are veterans (11 percent of World War I) and may be eligible for care under veterans' benefits.

We have tried to show a profile of people who were old in the mid-1980s. One can speculate about future cohorts, but there is no single answer; each future cohort will reflect its own experience just as this one does. People reaching old age in the future will have more formal education. Whether they will be better educated in how to live to a successful old age is not known. The generations that came of age after World War II had more children (Heuser 1976). Also, because infant and childhood mortality rates were lower, more of their children survived. However, because they were born into small families, they will have fewer siblings. The women will have had higher levels of labor-force participation, but it will be many years before women's retirement income equals that of men. A higher proportion of women will have married, but a higher proportion will have divorced, and men entering second marriages are likely to marry women younger than themselves. A very high proportion of the men in some cohorts will be veterans; 16.4 million people were in the armed forces in World War II and 5.8 million in the Korean War (U.S. Bureau of Census 1975).

We can learn a great deal from these successful survivors, but projecting their experience to future cohorts could be misleading.

REFERENCES

Antonucci, T.C. 1985. Personal Characteristics, Social Support and Social Behavior. In *Handbook of Aging and the Social Sciences*. eds. R.H. Binstock and E. Shanas, 94–128. New York: Van Nostrand Reinhold.

Beck, S.H. and R.W. Beck. 1984. The Formation of Extended Households during Middle Age. *Journal of Marriage and the Family* 46:277–87.

Berkman, L.F., and S.L. Syme. 1979. Social Networks, Host Resistance, and Mortality: A Nine Year Follow-up Study of Alameda County Residents. *American Journal of Epidemiology* 109:186–204.

Bishop, C.E. 1986. Living Arrangement Choices of Elderly Singles: Effects of Income and Disability. *Health Care Financing Review* 7(3):65–73.

Blazer, D.G. 1982. Social Support and Mortality in an Elderly Community Population. *American Journal of Epidemiology* 115:684–94.

Branch, L.G., and A.M. Jette. 1982. A prospective study of long-term institutionalization among the aged. *American Journal of Public Health* 72(12):1373–79.

Campbell, A.J., M.J. Borrie, and G.F. Spears. 1989. Risk Factors for Falls in a Community-Based Prospective Study of People 70 Years and Older. *The Journals of Gerontology: Medical Sciences* 44(4):M112–17.

Cassel, J. 1976. The Contribution of the Social Environment to Host Resistance. *American Journal of Epidemiology* 104:107–23.

Clark, R.L. 1980. *Retirement Policy in an Aging Society*. Durham, N.C.: Duke University Press.

Commonwealth Fund Commission on Elderly People Living Alone. 1987. *Old, Alone and Poor*. Report of the Commonwealth Fund Commission on Elderly People Living Alone. Technical Analysis by ICF Inc., Baltimore.

Crystal, S. 1982. *America's Old Age Crisis: Public Policy in the Two Worlds of Aging*. New York: Basic Books.

Dublin, L.I. 1963. *Suicide: A Sociological and Statistical Study*. New York: Ronald Press.

Evans, J.G., D. Prudham, and I. Wandless. 1979. A Prospective Study of Fractured Proximal Femur: Factors Predisposing to Survival. *Age and Ageing* 8:246–50.

Fitti, J., and M.G. Kovar. 1987. The Supplement on Aging to the 1984 National Health Interview Survey. *Vital and Health Statistics* series 1, no. 21. DHHS pub. no. (PHS)87-1323. Hyattsville, Md.: National Center for Health Statistics.

Gore, S. 1978. The Effect of Social Support in Moderating the Health Consequences of Unemployment. *Journal of Health and Social Behavior* 19:157–65.

Havlik, R., B. Liu, and M. G. Kovar. 1987. Health Statistics of Older Persons, United States, 1986. *Vital and Health Statistics* series 3, no. 25. DHHS pub. no. (PHS)87-1409. Hyattsville, Md.: National Center for Health Statistics.

Heuser, R.L. 1976. *Fertility tables for birth cohorts by color: United States, 1917–73.* DHEW pub. no. (HRA)76-1152. Hyattsville, Md.: National Center for Health Statistics.

Hing, E. 1981. Characteristics of Nursing Home Residents, Health Status, and Care Received. *Vital and Health Statistics* series 13, no. 51. DHHS pub. no. (PHS)81-1712. Hyattsville, Md.: National Center for Health Statistics.

Hing, E., E. Sekscenski, and G. Strahan. 1989. The National Nursing Home Survey: 1985 Summary for the United States. *Vital and Health Statistics* series 13, no. 97. Hyattsville, Md.: National Center for Health Statistics.

Holahan, C.J., and R.H. Moos. 1981. Social Support and Psychological Distress: A Longitudinal Analysis. *Journal of Abnormal Psychology* 49:365–70.

Jensen, J.S. and E. Tondevold. 1979. Mortality after Hip Fractures. *Acta Orthopedica Scandinavia* 50:161–67.

Kovar, M.G. 1987. The Longitudinal Study of Aging: Some Estimates of Change Among Older Americans. *Proceedings of the 1987 Public Health Conference on Records and Statistics.* Hyattsville, Md.: National Center for Health Statistics.

———. 1988. Aging in the Eighties. People Living Alone—Two Years Later. *Advance Data from Vital and Health Statistics,* no. 149. Hyattsville, Md.: National Center for Health Statistics.

Kovar, M.G., and J.E. Fitti. 1987. A Multi-Mode Longitudinal Study: The Longitudinal Study of Aging. *Proceedings of the Survey Research Section,* American Statistical Association.

Kovar, M.G., and T. Harris. 1987. Who Will Care for Older People? *Proceedings of the Social Statistics Section,* American Statistical Association.

Kovar, M.G., and G.S. Poe. 1985. National Health Interview Survey Design, 1973–84, and Procedures, 1975–83. *Vital and Health Statistics,* series 1, no. 18. DHHS pub. no. (PHS)85-1320. Hyattsville, Md.: National Center for Health Statistics.

Lawton, M.P. 1982. Competence, Environmental Press, and the Adaptation of Older People. In *Aging and the Environment: Theoretical Approaches,* eds. M.P. Lawton, P.G. Windley, and T.O. Byerts, 33–59. New York: Springer.

———. 1985. Housing and Living Environments of Older People. In *Handbook of Aging and the Social Sciences,* eds. R.H. Binstock and E. Shanas, 450–78. New York: Van Nostrand Reinhold.

Lawton, M.P. and L. Nahemow. 1973. Ecology and the Aging Process. In *Psychology of Adult Development and Aging,* eds. C. Eisdorfer and M.P. Lawton. Washington: American Psychological Association.

Linder, F.E., and R.D. Grove. 1947. *Vital Statistics Rates in the United States, 1900–1940.* Washington: National Office of Vital Statistics, Federal Security Agency, United States Public Health Service.

Lindheim, R., and S.L. Syme. 1983. Environments, People and Health. *Annual Review of Public Health* 4:335–59.

National Center for Health Statistics. 1986a. Advance Report of Final Mortality Statistics, 1984. *Monthly Vital Statistics Report* 35(6, Suppl. 2). Hyattsville, Md.

———. 1986b. Advance Report of Final Marriage Statistics, 1983. *Monthly Vital Statistics Report* 35(1, Suppl.). Hyattsville, Md.

Noelker, L.S., and S.W. Poulshock. 1982. *The Effects on Families of Caring for Impaired Elderly in Residences.* Final Report to the Administration on Aging. Cleveland: Benjamin Rose Institute.

O'Rand, A.M., and J.C. Henretta. 1982. Midlife Work History and the Retirement Income of Older Single and Married Women. In *Women's Retirement,* ed. M. Szinovacz. Beverly Hills: Sage Publications.

Rosenmayr, L. 1977. The Family: A Source of Hope for the Elderly. In *Family, Bureaucracy and the Elderly,* eds. E. Shanas and M. Sussman, 132–157. Durham, N.C.: Duke University Press.

Schaefer, C., J.C. Coyne, and R.S. Lazarus. 1981. The Health-related Functions of Social Support. *Journal of Behavioral Medicine* 4:381–406.

Schorr, A. 1980. "*. . . Thy Father and Thy Mother . . .*" A Second Look at Filial Responsibility and Family Policy. Social Security Administration pub. no. 13–11953. Baltimore, Md.

Soldo, B., and K. Manton. 1984. Health Status and Service Needs of the Oldest Old: Current Patterns and Future Trends. *Milbank Memorial Fund Quarterly/Health and Society* 63:286–319.

Struyk, R.J. and H.M. Katsura. 1987. Aging at Home: How the Elderly Adjust Their Housing Without Moving. *Journal of Housing for the Elderly* 4(2):1–192.

Tillson, D. (Ed.) 1989. *Aging in Place.* Chicago: Scott Foresman.

Tissue, T., and J.L. McCoy. 1981. Income and Living Arrangements among Poor Aged Singles. *Social Security Bulletin* 44(4):3–13.

Troll, L.E. 1971. The Family of Later Life: A Decade Review. *Journal of Marriage and the Family* 33:263–90.

Turner, R.J. 1981. Social Support as a Contingency in Psychological Well-Being. *Journal of Health and Social Behavior* 22:357–67.

U.S. Bureau of the Census. 1975. *Historical Statistics of the United States, Colonial Times to 1970, Bicentennial Edition, Parts 1 and 2.* Washington.

Williams, A.W., J.E. Ware, and C.A. Donald. 1981. A Model of Mental Health, Life Events, and Social Supports Applicable to General Populations. *Journal of Health and Social Behavior 22:324–36.*

15

The Black Oldest Old: Health, Functioning, and Informal Support

ROSE C. GIBSON and JAMES S. JACKSON

Blacks constitute the most rapidly growing portion of the oldest old population (Siegel and Taeuber 1986; Taeuber and Rosenwaike, Chapter 2, this volume). Little is known about very old blacks, except that compared with whites of the same age, their number is growing more rapidly; they are more likely to live in families with limited economic resources and more likely to be in poor physical and functional health, yet less likely to be institutionalized. The rapid growth of this group, combined with their tendency to live with families that can ill afford to keep them economically, make their levels of health, functioning, and quality of family support matters of high national concern. These issues shape the long-term care needs of the black oldest old. The purpose of this chapter is to describe the health, functioning, and informal supports of the black oldest old and to recommend new directions for research on this population.

Mortality rates after age 80 are lower for blacks than for whites. Whereas white men at age 80 in 1981 could expect 6.7 years more of life and white women 8.8, black men could expect 8.8 years and black women 11.5 (U.S. Department of Health and Human Services 1983). Blacks account for 12 percent of the total population, 7 percent of those aged 85 and over, and 14 to 21 percent of those aged 100 and over (90 percent confidence intervals). From 9 to 27 percent of these black centenarians are aged 105 and over, in contrast to only 4 to 10 percent of white centenarians (U.S. Bureau of the Census 1987). There are also race differences in the sex ratio after age 100. For blacks aged 100 and over, there are 84 men per 100 women, but for whites, only 37 men per 100 women.

Despite this disproportionate growth of the black oldest old, the white oldest old are more likely to be institutionalized. Although whites aged 65 to 74 are slightly less likely than blacks of that age to be in nursing and personal-care homes, whites aged 75 to 84 are about one and one-half times more likely to be institutionalized. However, at age 85 and over, whites are almost twice as likely to be institutionalized (U.S. Department of Health and Human Services 1988), with the ratio increasing to about four times as likely for whites as blacks after age 100 (U.S. Bureau of the Census 1987). What might these increasingly large race disparities in institutionalization in successively older age groups mean?

1. Could there be differences in health and functioning between the black and white older age cohorts?
2. Might the poverty of older blacks increase with age?
3. Do special values of the black family in caring for the very old at home militate against institutionalization? Or might aspects of black family and social support uniquely meet their needs, thereby sustaining the old and disabled in the community?

DIFFERENCES IN HEALTH AND FUNCTIONING

Data from the 1984 Supplement on Aging of the National Health Interview Survey (SOA–NHIS) indicate that the physical health and functioning of community-dwelling blacks aged 65 and over is generally poorer than that of their white age-mates (Table 15–1). However, although the numbers are very small, blacks aged 85 and over are not clearly in poorer health than their white age-mates on two of three measures of health and functioning: number of chronic conditions and level of difficulty with activities of daily living (ADL). Blacks and whites aged 85 and over are about equally likely to have three or more chronic health conditions and a great deal of difficulty with ADLs. It is also interesting that the associations between age and number of chronic conditions, and between age and overall health status, are significant for whites but not for blacks. This suggests a more linear relationship for whites than for blacks between age and these two measures of health status. These findings raise the question of whether very old blacks are living in the community in disproportionate numbers because a larger number are fairly healthy and functionally able. However, only limited insight into the disproportionate institutionalization of the age-race groups is provided by these data because, as Table 15–1 indicates, the 1984 SOA–NHIS contains small numbers of blacks aged 85 and over.

INCREASED POVERTY IN OLDER BLACKS

Blacks aged 65 and over are nearly three times as likely as their white counterparts to live in families with incomes less than $5,000 a year (U.S. Bureau of the Census 1987). Poverty has been the most frequently cited reason for the lower rates of institutionalization of older blacks. However, there is not much evidence that proportions of older blacks living in poverty, increase in a strictly linear fashion in successively older age groups. For example, the official poverty rates in 1979 for black women aged 65 to 69, 70 to 74, 75 to 79, and 80 to 84 were, respectively, 35.7, 32.9, 37.8, and 32.5 (Danziger 1989). There were too few black men to support poverty calculations in the very oldest age groups. Although poverty figures illustrate large disparities between older blacks and whites, they tend not to support the idea that increasing proportions of blacks living in poverty in successively older age groups are the reason for increasing race disparities in institutionalization.

Table 15–1 Measures of Health and Functioning by Age and Race from the 1984 Supplement on Aging of the National Health Interview Survey (n = 11,345[a])

	65–74		75–79		80–84		85 and Over	
	Black (n = 553)	White (n = 6441)	Black (n = 166)	White (n = 2123)	Black (n = 87)	White (n = 1164)	Black (n = 47)	White (n = 768)
*Number of chronic conditions***[b]								
None	15.9 (88)	21.6 (1394)	19.7 (31)	18.9 (398)	16.3 (14)	15.1 (173)	8.1 (3)	16.8 (130)
One	28.2 (157)	30.8 (1986)	27.3 (45)	29.0 (618)	20.4 (19)	26.4 (310)	29.0 (13)	27.7 (210)
Two	25.5 (158)	24.2 (1550)	27.6 (48)	26.3 (560)	34.8 (31)	25.7 (297)	30.6 (16)	24.1 (187)
Three or more	27.4 (150)	23.3 (1511)	25.5 (42)	25.8 (547)	28.5 (23)	32.8 (384)	32.3 (15)	31.4 (241)
*Level of difficulty with ADL***[c]								
None, very little	53.8 (268)	72.8 (4272)	49.8 (75)	61.4 (1184)	22.1 (15)	46.6 (480)	28.1 (12)	30.9 (209)
Some	12.9 (67)	9.9 (581)	14.6 (21)	12.6 (249)	14.0 (9)	12.6 (133)	11.2 (5)	12.7 (87)
A lot	28.1 (137)	13.4 (802)	28.3 (42)	18.7 (365)	44.1 (31)	27.8 (289)	37.5 (16)	34.5 (238)
A great deal	5.3 (27)	3.9 (228)	7.4 (11)	7.2 (139)	19.8 (13)	12.9 (134)	23.2 (11)	21.9 (154)
*Overall health status***[b]								
Excellent	8.1 (45)	16.9 (1075)	14.4 (22)	16.1 (340)	5.3 (5)	15.2 (179)	8.3 (4)	15.1 (118)
Very good	18.5 (101)	20.8 (1320)	15.1 (26)	20.4 (434)	16.9 (16)	21.0 (246)	16.6 (8)	20.7 (154)
Good	22.5 (124)	32.8 (103)	26.0 (42)	33.7 (705)	21.8 (18)	28.8 (328)	27.4 (13)	29.0 (221)
Fair	30.0 (165)	20.3 (1319)	27.6 (46)	19.6 (418)	30.0 (25)	20.6 (231)	26.6 (12)	22.1 (174)
Poor	20.9 (115)	9.3 (603)	16.9 (26)	10.1 (215)	26.0 (22)	14.4 (164)	21.2 (10)	13.1 (98)

Note: Percentages are followed by *N*s in parentheses. Weighted data. Numbers in table are total sample *N*s. Chi squares were computed on black and white samples of equal size.

[a] Excludes all except blacks and whites.
[b] Significant for whites only.
[c] Significant for both black and whites.
** Chi square level of significance ≤ .01
*** Chi square level of significance ≤ .001

VALUES, FAMILY, AND SOCIAL SUPPORT

Research suggests that the social and family support of blacks have special characteristics that aid in adaptation to old age (Chatters, Taylor, and Jackson 1985; Jackson 1988). These characteristics include a system of beneficial reciprocities (Stack 1974), a broader base of helpers, and a virtuosity of substituting helpers one for another (Gibson 1982, 1986a,b,c; Gibson and Jackson 1987). Very little is known, however, about the social and family support systems of the black oldest old that might facilitate community living.

First, drawing on two studies of black Americans, we describe the health and functioning of the black oldest old (individuals aged 80 and over) by comparing them with the black young-old (aged 65 to 74) and old-old (aged 75 to 79). Next, we discuss race-by-age differences in health and functioning, and then proceed to describe the family and social supports of the black oldest old. The data for our analyses are drawn from two national samples, the National Survey of Black Americans (NSBA) (Jackson, Tucker, and Gurin 1987) and the Three Generation Black Family Study (TGBFS) (Jackson and Hatchett 1986).

These two samples are particularly appropriate for our purpose because they contain good measures of health, functioning, and social support; provide larger numbers of older blacks than most social surveys, which permits subdivision into the age categories of interest. The studies also are based on an instrument designed to be culturally relevant for the black population. These are carefully collected sources of information on the non-institutionalized black elderly population; and by virtue of special sampling procedures, the data sets produce findings that are representative of the black oldest old from the high-rises of New York City to the most rural areas of the South. Sampling procedures, instruments, and the rationale for combining the two samples for analysis are discussed in the Technical Appendix. In view of the small numbers in the very oldest age groups; self-reports rather than more objective reports of health; inadequacies of cross-sectional data in separating the effects of time of measurement, cohort, and aging; and social survey rather than epidemiological data, obvious caution should be exercised in interpreting the findings. Social characteristics of the 734 black men and women aged 65 to 101 in the effective sample are presented in Table 15–2.

CHARACTERISTICS OF THE BLACK OLDEST OLD

As indicated in Table 15–2, compared with the old old (aged 75 to 79) and the young old (aged 65 to 74), the oldest old (aged 80 and over) are more likely to have fewer than 9 years of school and to live in the South and in rural areas. A large proportion of the oldest old have helpers available: more than 70 percent do not live alone, more than 80 percent have living children, and over one-third live with these children. This availability of helpers alone could be a reason for the black oldest old's lower rates of institutionalization.

Proportions of older blacks with family incomes under $5,000 do not increase

Table 15–2 The Black Elderly Study Sample: Percentages Comparing the Black Young, Old, and Oldest Old from the NSBA–TGBFS ($n = 734$)

Variable	Age (percent)		
	65–74 ($n = 462$)	75–79 ($n = 142$)	80+ ($n = 130$)
Gender			
Men	33.1	36.6	35.4
Women	66.9	63.4	64.6
Family Income in Dollars per Year			
Less than 5,000	44.6	43.4	40.9
5,000–9,999	18.6	18.0	15.9
10,000–19,999	10.6	7.5	6.8
20,000 or more	5.2	2.6	9.1
Not ascertained	20.9	28.5	27.3
Education (number of grades completed)			
0–8	68.6	72.3	79.8
9–11	16.4	11.3	10.1
12	8.6	7.8	8.5
More than 12	6.4	8.5	1.6
Lifetime Occupation (men)			
Professional, managerial, sales, clerical	13.9	6.3	22.5
Craftspersons, operatives	46.5	29.2	35.0
Laborers, farmers, farm workers	25.7	35.4	30.0
Service	13.9	29.2	12.5
Lifetime occupation (women)			
Professional, managerial, sales, clerical	9.5	9.7	7.1
Craftspersons, operatives	15.2	9.7	15.4
Laborers, farmers, farm workers	4.9	11.1	13.5
Service	70.4	69.4	63.5
Region			
Northeast	12.3	12.7	6.2
North central	15.8	19.0	17.7
South	68.2	63.4	73.1
West	3.7	4.9	3.1
Area of Residence [a]*			
Large urban	37.8	50.0	36.0
Small urban	35.2	24.2	22.0
Rural	27.0	25.8	42.0
Marital Status**			
Married	42.2	31.2	20.8
Never married, divorced, separated	13.2	10.6	5.4
Widowed	44.6	58.2	73.8
Number of Living Children			
None (never had or deceased)	16.3	17.3	17.2
One	13.9	14.4	11.7
Two or more	69.8	68.3	71.1
Where Children Live [b]*			
In respondent's house	27.7	18.2	34.0
Outside respondent's house	72.3	81.8	66.0

Table 15–5   (Continued)

	Age (%)		
Variable	65–74 ($n = 462$)	75–79 ($n = 142$)	80+ ($n = 130$)
Residents in Respondent's House by Relationship[b]			
Respondent alone	29.1	38.5	28.2
Respondent and spouse	22.2	25.6	14.1
Respondent and other Nuclear Family[c] Combinations	15.7	14.1	24.4
Respondent, Extended and Augmented Family[d] Combinations	33.0	21.8	33.3

Note: Totals do not equal 100 percent due to rounding.

[a] Three-generation study respondents were not asked the question.

[b] Cross section study respondents were not asked the question.

[c] For example, respondent, spouse, and children; or respondent, no spouse, and children.

[d] For example, respondent, other relatives, or nonrelatives.

*Chi square level of significance ≤.05.

**Chi square level of significance ≤.001.

from the youngest to the oldest age group. And the oldest old are more likely, not less likely, to have incomes over $20,000. This finding is consistent with Danziger's census data, cited earlier, in which the poverty rate was lower, not higher, for black women aged 80 to 84 than for those aged 75 to 79. Thus, neither the census nor the NSBA data support increasing poverty in successively older age groups of blacks as a reason for increasing race disparities in rates of institutionalization.

Quite unexpectedly, the middle group, the old old, were more likely than the young old to live alone, a condition that might be related to the old old's better health and functioning compared with that of the young old (as we discuss later). This condition might also be a factor in the larger race disparities in institutionalization in the older than the younger group. We should bear in mind, however, that the age differences found in this sample of community-living blacks could also reflect differential selection bias due to the different rates of institutionalization in the age groups.

HEALTH AND FUNCTIONING

We turn now to ways in which the black young old, old old, and oldest old differ in health and functioning. Although age differences were significant only for number of activities of daily living problems (ADLs), trends in the remaining four variables were suggestive. As Table 15–3 indicates (and as would be expected), the oldest old seemed to be doing more poorly than the two younger groups on four of five measures of health and functioning. They were the most likely to have four or more chronic conditions, very serious health problems, difficulty with three or more ADLs, and to be greatly limited in the amount of work or activities they could do. Against

Table 15–3 Physical Health and Functioning Percentages Comparing the Young, Old, and Oldest Old from the NSBA–TGBFS (n = 734)

Variable	65–74 (n = 462)	75–79 (n = 142)	80 + (n = 130)
Number of Chronic Conditions			
0	13.4	14.1	13.1
1	23.4	20.4	14.6
2–3	44.4	50.0	47.7
4 or more	18.8	15.5	24.6
Satisfaction with Health[a]			
Very satisfied	52.6	53.6	62.0
Somewhat satisfied	32.4	27.9	26.4
Somewhat dissatisfied/very dissatisfied	15.0	18.6	11.6
Self-rated Health[a]			
Very best of health	46.3	50.0	36.1
Health problems, but not very serious	38.1	29.4	37.5
Very serious health problems	15.6	20.6	26.4
Number of Activities of Daily Living (ADL) Problems[b]*			
None	42.2	38.8	23.8
1–2	36.6	35.0	40.0
3–7	21.1	26.3	36.3
Extent of Physical Functional Limitation			
Not limited at all or limited very little	50.9	53.5	40.8
Limited some	23.2	21.8	24.6
Limited "a great deal"	26.0	24.6	34.6

[a] Three-generation telephone respondents excluded from percentage base.

[b] Cross section respondents are excluded from percentage base.

*Chi square level of significance ≤ .05.

expectations, however, the old old (aged 75 to 79) were slightly better off than the young old on three of the measures. They were less likely to have four or more chronic conditions, more likely to be in the best of health, and more likely not to be limited, or to be limited very little. Satisfaction with health and number of ADL problems were exceptions: proportions with three of more ADL problems increased significantly in successively older age groups (but, interestingly, not among those with one or two ADL problems), and the 75- to 79-year-olds were more, not less, likely to be dissatisfied with their health.

Several facts are notable. First, both the SOA–NHIS and the NSBA data suggest that the associations between age and number of chronic conditions, age and overall health status, and age and functional status are linear among whites but nonlinear among blacks. It is also interesting to note, from Table 15–3, that nearly equal proportions in each age group of blacks from the NSBA had no chronic conditions and fully 40 percent of the oldest old were not limited at all, or were limited very little in their activities. Thus, nonlinearities of relationships between age and certain measures of health tentatively identify three age groups of older blacks in regard to health and functioning: two sicker disabled groups—one young (aged 65 to 74) and one very old (aged 80 and over)—sandwiching a healthier and more able group (aged 75 to 79). The somewhat better general health and functioning of the 75- to 79-year-olds compared with the 65- to 74-year-olds might also account for the greater race disparity in rates of institutionalization in the older group.

Our findings on age, health, and functioning of older blacks nicely fit Rowe and Kahn's (1987) concept of "successful" versus "usual" aging. Usual agers are "normal" agers, in that they exhibit typical age-linked physiologic losses. Successful agers, on the other hand, do not resemble the mean of their age group on age-linked measures of health. Rowe and Kahn suggest that extrinsic factors such as lifestyle, diet, and social support distinguish the usual and successful agers: beneficial health habits and adequate social support are more prevalent among successful agers. Within this framework, the 75- to 79-year-olds in our sample, because their health characteristics are unlike the typical black elderly (ages 65 and over), might be considered successful agers with different distributions or risk factors for aging and disease. We move now to ways in which the three age groups of blacks identified in the NSBA data, compared with whites on health and functioning.

RACE, AGE, HEALTH, AND FUNCTIONING

Persistent trends across eight national and regional data sources and across a variety of objective and subjective measures of health and functioning substantiated the age-related variations in health and functioning found in the NSBA–TGBFS data. The trends also identified a fourth group of relatively healthy and able very old blacks aged approximately 85 and over. Table 15–4 presents information on the eight data sources and summarizes the main findings. In general, the pattern that emerged was alternating age groups of sick and healthy blacks: a 65- to 74-year-old group that was sicker and more disabled than a 75- to 79-year-old group and an 80- to 84-year-old group that was sicker and more disabled than an older group aged 85 and over (approximate age breaks). Even more interesting was that race differentials in health and functioning were not equal across these four age groups. Although age for age better health and functioning prevailed among whites, black–white disparities were greatest in comparisons involving the two black sick-disabled and least in comparisons involving the two healthier-able groups—the healthier black groups more closely resembled their white counterparts.

When logit regressions were performed on the NSBA–TGBFS data, we found the same age effects (the probability of disability was lower in alternate age groups of blacks) lower for those aged 75 to 79 than for the younger group aged 65 to 74; and lower for those 85 and over than for the group aged 80 to 84 (findings are not tabulated). Thus, both our bivariate and multivariate findings in the NSBA data were consistent with findings across the other eight data sources in Table 15–4 and fuel the argument for alternating age groups of the more robust and sick among older black Americans.

The age–race differences in health and functioning are compelling because they provide some limited support for the presence of adverse mortality selection processes: a morbid but young subgroup of blacks may die out rather rapidly, leaving an older, highly select group of black survivors among whom mortality rates are not nearly as high (Manton, Patrick, and Johnson 1987). This hypothesis, in fact, is supported by Manton and Soldo's (1985) longitudinal sample in which an older group of blacks had fewer explicit pathological changes over time than did a younger group, which succumbed to death rather rapidly from time 1 to time 2 of measurement.

What else might these black–white differentials in health and functioning in the four age groups mean? They could be cohort differences that reflect, within each of the race–age cohorts, differing distributions of risk factors for aging, health, and functioning. We might ask here what was more favorable in the histories of blacks born around the turn of the century in terms of environmental exposures, health habits, quality of health care and social support, stress, distress, and other personal resources. The race–age differentials in health and functioning could also account for the more rapid growth of the proportion of blacks than whites in certain older age groups and the differential rates of institutionalization of the race–age groups.

Although these race-by-age trends in health and functioning found across the eight sources of data are highly suggestive, they are by no means conclusive. Some limitations result from small sample sizes at the very old ages, inconsistent age categories across the data sources, and descriptive rather than multivariate procedures of analysis in several instances. Also, race or age-cohort differences, or both, might exist in the structure and measurement of self-reported health. Andersen, Mullner, and Cornelius (1987), in fact, demonstrate that black–white disparities in health vary according to data source and specific measure of health. Blacks apparently report their health and functioning more accurately in global-subjective measures than in measures requiring specific recall of particular symptoms. Applied to our findings, the age–race differentials found for self-reports of satisfaction with health, self-ratings of health, and global assessments of functional limitation may be more valid than differentials for number of diagnoses of chronic illness and specific problems with activities of daily living.

Within our framework of inadequate social support as a risk factor for institutionalization, it would be useful at this point to examine the differential distribution of social support in each of the four age groups of blacks identified earlier. Small numbers of individuals aged 85 and over in our data sets, however, preclude this kind of meaningful comparison, and limit our analyses to comparisons of the age groups 65 to 74, 75 to 79, and 80 and over.

In the next section, we examine whether the social supports of these three age groups are commensurate with their differing levels of health and physical functioning, providing some additional insight into their different rates of institutionalization.

INFORMAL SUPPORT AND EXCHANGES WITH ADULT CHILDREN

Returning to the NSBA data, Table 15–5 indicates that the black informal network responds more to the young old and oldest old (those aged 65 to 74 and 80 and over), whose health and functioning is poorer, than to those aged 75 to 79, who are healthier and functioning better. This provides some limited support for the idea that the race gap in institutionalization is wider among the oldest old than among an immediately younger group because of a special adequacy of the oldest old's informal support networks. The social-support findings provide less insight, however, into

Table 15–4 Race–Age Differentials in Health and Functioning: Summary of Findings from Eight Studies

Data source	Investigators	Health and functioning measures examined	Black age and health status groups identified	Age groups—largest race differentials	Age groups—smallest race differentials	Method of analysis
DLSA	Manton and Soldo (1985)	Blood pressure Infarction Ischemia Hypertension Cardiovascular Self-assessed health	74.8 (S)[a] 83.2 (H)	[b]	[b]	Grade of membership
1984 NHIS published tables	Gibson and Jackson (1988)	No. persons with no activity limitation due to chronic conditions No. chronic conditions/1000 (diabetes, heart disease, hypertension, cerebrovascular disease)	65–69 (S) 70 and over (H) 65–74 (S) 75 and over (H)	65–69 65–74	70 and over 75 and over	Percentage point difference
GAHSP	Manton, Patrick, and Johnson (1987)	Diabetes, heart problems, ADLs[d]; dementia; psychological and behavioral problems, acute medical problems, cancer, stroke, neurological disorders, hip fractures, medical treatments, bedfastness, service use, nursing home admission	65–74 (S) 75–79 (H)[c] 80–84 (S) 90 and over (H)	[b]	[b]	Grade of membership
NHIS	Manton, Patrick, and Johnson (1987)	Hypertension, diabetes, circulatory diseases	65–69 (S) 70 and over (H)	65–69	70 and over	Black–white relative risks

1984 SOA, NHIS	Gibson and Jackson (1988)	ADLs, no. chronic conditions, self-assessed health	65–74 (S) 75–79 (H) 80–84 85 and over	65–74 80–84	75–79 85 and over	Percentage point difference
NLTCS	Manton, Patrick, and Johnson (1987)	ADLs, IADLs[e]	65–74 (S) 75–84 (H) 85 and over	65–74	75–84 85+	Black–white percentage ratios
NHEPESE	Foley et al. (1987)	ADLs (unable to bathe/walk) No. chronic conditions (hypertension, cancer, diabetes, heart disease, stroke), diastolic and systolic blood pressure, gross mobility (heavy housework, climb stairs, walk ½ mile), self-assessed health	65–69 (S) 70–74 (S) 75–79 (H)	65–74	75–79	Percentge point difference
ACL	Gibson and Jackson (1987)	ADLs, number chronic conditions, extent limitation, self-assessed health, satisfaction with health	65–74[f] 75–79[f] 80–84 (S) 85 and over (H)	65–74 80–84	75–79	Percentage point difference

Note: DLSA = Duke Longitudinal Study of Aging: NHIS = National Health Interview Survey; GAHSP = Georgia Adult Health Services Program; SOA, NHIS = Supplement on Aging of the National Health Interview Survey; NLTCS = National Longterm Care Survey; NHEPESE = New Haven, Established Populations for Epidemiologic Studies of the Elderly; ACL = American's Changing Lives; S = Sick; H = Healthier.

[a] Average age of each group.

[b] No race comparisons made.

[c] Ages predominating in the group.

[d] Activities of Daily Living.

[e] Instrumental Activities of Daily Living.

[f] Not clearly sicker or healthier.

Table 15–5 Informal Support and Exchanges with Adult Children: Percentages
Comparing the Young, Old, and Oldest Old from the NSBA–TGBFS ($n = 734$)

	Age (%)		
Variable	65–74 ($n = 462$)	75–79 ($n = 142$)	80+ ($n = 130$)
Availability of helpers			
Geographical Proximity of Most Immediate Family Members*			
No immediate family	16.1	24.8	18.3
In same household, neighborhood, city	36.8	29.9	34.9
In same county; or state	21.4	12.4	23.0
Outside of state	25.8	32.8	23.8
Number of Neighbors Know Well Enough to Visit*			
Have no neighbors, or know none well	3.9	14.5	8.0
A few	48.3	43.5	40.0
Many, some	47.8	41.9	52.0
Number of Friends with whom to Discuss Problems			
Many, some	27.5	20.7	27.3
A few/none	72.5	79.3	72.7
Have Best or Close Friend?			
Have best friend	58.5	60.4	58.6
No best friend, but someone close	28.1	23.7	24.2
No best friend, no one close	13.4	15.8	17.2
Who on this List Would Give Help if Ill?[g]			
Nuclear family member	77.5	70.5	73.3
Other family member	17.5	21.0	16.8
Nonrelative	5.0	8.6	9.9
Rely More on Family or Friends?			
Relatives	48.0	41.1	44.5
Friends	18.0	24.8	18.8
Both	33.3	34.0	35.9
Neither, no one	.7	.0	.8
Frequency of contact/help			
Family Help[a]			
Very often, often, sometimes	70.7	70.8	74.6
Never	29.3	29.2	25.4
Church Member Help[b]			
Often	27.8	18.9	31.0
Sometimes	27.3	33.7	33.3
Hardly ever, never	44.9	47.4	35.6
Family Contact			
At least once/week	60.6	61.3	55.5
At least once/month	26.2	25.2	25.5
A few times/year; hardly ever; never	13.2	13.5	19.1
Friend Contact*			
At least once/week	70.1	62.5	55.5
At least once/month	16.5	20.5	20.0
A few times/year; hardly ever; never	13.5	17.0	24.5
Type of help			
From family[c]			
Emotional	33.9	35.8	27.9
Instrumental	66.1	64.2	72.1

Variable	Age (percent)		
	65–74 ($n=462$)	75–79 ($n=142$)	80+ ($n=130$)
From Church Members[d]			
Emotional	26.0	30.0	25.4
Instrumental	16.1	10.0	7.3
Prayer	57.8	60.0	67.3
From Close Friend[e]			
Emotional	63.0	70.9	64.6
Instrumental	37.0	29.1	35.4
Exchanges with adult children			
R Helps Children[f]			
Very often	37.1	28.6	31.0
Fairly often	13.3	10.7	13.1
Not too often	31.8	36.9	31.0
Never	17.8	23.8	25.0
Type of Help R Gives Children[f]			
Emotional	29.3	32.2	29.0
Instrumental (goods/services)	11.8	20.3	17.7
Financial	29.7	27.1	33.9
Other (such as care of adult child's family members)	29.3	20.3	19.4
R Helps Children More or Less Often[f] or the Same as in the Past			
More	10.1	8.1	8.7
Less	43.3	39.4	52.2
Same	46.6	52.5	39.1
Children Help R More or Less Often, or the Same as in the Past[f]			
More	22.0	30.6	37.6
Less	21.3	17.3	11.8
Same	56.7	52.0	50.5

Note: R = respondent.

[a] Those whose families never help; respondents who never needed help are excluded from the percentage base.

[b] Those who never needed help; those who have not attended church since age 18 are excluded from the percentage base.

[c] Excluded from percentage base: Family never helped; never needed help.

[d] Have not attended church since age 18; attended less than once a year; hardly ever or never receive help; never needed help are excluded from the percentage base.

[e] No close friends; friend does nothing; telephone respondents are excluded from the percentage base.

[f] Those without children; cross-sectional respondents are excluded from the percentage base.

[g] Multiple mentions are possible.

*Chi-square level of signficance $\leq .05$.

why the race disparity in institutionalization is smallest among the youngest group of elderly (aged 65 to 74), other than the fact that blacks aged 65 to 74 are sicker and more disabled than an immediately older group.

Blacks aged 65 to 74 and 80 and over tended to have more helpers than did those aged 75 to 79. Family members were more likely to be geographically close, there was more reliance upon relatives, larger numbers of neighbors and friends were available, and fellow church members helped frequently. The young old and oldest old were also more likely to receive instrumental support from family members and close friends. Because frequency of contact and help did not seem to be associated with the differential health and functioning of the three age groups, the response of the black informal network to poor health and diminished functioning may lie more in the variety of helpers available and the quality of help than in its frequency. This is consistent with Antonucci's (1985) premise that affective aspects of social support are more beneficial to the health and well-being of the recipient than structural ones.

When compared with the two younger groups, the oldest old were as likely or more likely to have a number of neighbors and friends, a close or best friend, and family members upon whom to rely in times of illness. The oldest old seemed, however, to have more varied sources of help and to reach beyond family members for assistance. For example, they were slightly more likely than younger groups to say they rely on *both* family and friends, and to receive frequent help from church members (Chatters, Taylor, and Jackson 1985). These findings, although cross-sectional, parallel the longitudinal findings of Gibson (1982), which indicate that blacks compared with whites, as they age, do not limit help-seeking to single family members, but rather exhibit a certain virtuosity in substituting one type of informal helper for another as spouses and children are lost. The phenomenon, although more prevalent among blacks than whites, is not unique to blacks (Antonucci 1985; Cantor 1979; Litwak 1986).

Exchanges with adult children appear to be influenced more by advancing age than by poor health and functioning. Percentages who never help their children, who have given less help to their children than in the past, and whose children have given more help to them all increase among the oldest old. Overall, the black informal network seems to respond to the sick and disabled and the very old by broadening the range of helpers who offer the type of help needed most and by shifting the reciprocity ratio of help to the very old from their adult children, responses that might ease the community living of older and disabled blacks. More research is needed on these aspects of informal support as risk factors for the institutionalization of the black oldest old.

SUMMARY AND CONCLUSIONS

The purpose of this chapter was to describe the health, functioning, and informal support of the noninstitutionalized black oldest old. Our concern was that despite rapid growth in their numbers, as well as their poorer health and functioning, the group was much less likely than white age-mates to be institutionalized. NSBA data sets provided the opportunity to examine the health, functioning, and social support of older blacks using culturally relevant measures from the largest social-survey samples of older black Americans to date. By disaggregating their data into finer age categories, and by examining other sources of health data on blacks and whites, our findings add substantially to what is already known about the health and functioning of older blacks.

We found some evidence of a racial morbidity crossover, or at least some inflections of the data, at about age 75 that might account for race differentials in institutionalization in the older age groups. Four age groups of older blacks were identified across eight diverse data sources differing, in unexpected ways, from each other and from their white age-mates in health and functioning. There were alternating groups of the sick and healthy, possibly meaning that the healthier group aged 75 to 79 are the survivors of high death rates among blacks aged 65 to 74; the sicker group aged 80 to 84 reflects the development of chronic illnesses, resulting in higher death rates at those ages; and the healthy group 85 and over are the survivors of this second mortality sweep. The selection cycle might continue on in this fashion, creating alternate groups of robust and morbid elderly blacks. These are compelling findings because, coupled with the longevity edge of blacks that increases after age 80, as reported by Taeuber and Rosenwaike (in Chapter 2, this volume), they could explain the more rapid growth in the number of very old blacks and thus provide some limited support for adverse mortality selection explanations of the racial mortality crossover (Manton 1982; Manton and Soldo 1985; Wing et al. 1985).

The crossover refers to the fact that up to about age 80, whites can expect to live longer than blacks; but after that age, blacks can expect to live longer than whites. An artifactual explanation of the racial mortality crossover has been most prevalent: older blacks misrepresent their age to the extent that they are younger than they say they are at the time of death. Recently, however, examination of data from tightly controlled closed-cohort studies (Wing et al. 1985) presents important evidence that the crossover is a valid and replicable phenomenon (Manton et al. 1987). Nam, Weatherby, and Ockay (1978) similarly find that the crossover effect obtains:

1. When life expectancy at each age is substituted for age-specific death rates;
2. For every decennial year back to 1900 (Ewbank [1987], however, suggests that the mortality data of blacks are largely unreliable before 1933);
3. In cohort as well as in period data; and
4. In comparisons of racial or ethnic groups in other parts of the world.

Some allow that these are cohort effects and that as environmental exposures and resources equalize for the races in the United States, greater proportions of blacks will survive to later ages, the effects of selection will disappear, and the crossover will advance to later ages and eventually disappear (Jackson 1981; Jackson 1985; Manton, Patrick, and Johnson 1987). Thus, in addition to biological factors, social and environmental factors are believed associated with these selection processes (Nam, Weatherby, and Ockay 1978).

Several other speculations appear in the literature as possible explanations of the crossover:

1. Blacks at advanced ages are a more biologically select group: those who survived despite inadequate medical care earlier in life (Manton 1982; Nam, Weatherby, and Ockay 1978).
2. Aging is retarded in some way among blacks at advanced ages: race differences in biological aging (Manton 1982).
3. Blacks are especially insulated in some way at more advanced ages against the leading killer diseases of old age: heart disease, cancer, stroke, and generalized arteriosclerosis (Manton 1982).
4. Social and psychological factors have a different impact on the mortality of blacks and whites at older ages (Jones 1980).
5. Despite the highly suspect validity of age reporting among the long-lived pop-

ulations of Equador, the Soviet Union, and Turkey (Medvedev 1974), there are similarities between those longevous and the black oldest old in the United States (Jones 1980).

Our findings also shed some limited light on the unequal rates of institutionalization of blacks and whites in specific age groups. The largest race disparities in health and functioning were in the age group in which blacks are more likely than whites to be institutionalized (ages 65 to 74); the smallest were in the age group in which blacks are least likely to be institutionalized (ages 85 and over). It is interesting that, across several data sources, blacks aged 85 and over were no worse off than comparably aged whites on two conditions related to institutionalization—number of chronic-illness diagnoses and extent of difficulties with ADLs. Thus, the increasing race disparity in institutionalization could be due to a decreasing disparity in health and functioning in the very old age groups.

On the other hand, it is possible that unequal rates of institutionalization in certain race–age cohorts are determinants rather than consequences of differential levels of health and functioning in the four black and white age groups of community dwellers. If that were the case, however, given the fact that the race disparity in institutionalization steadily increases in successively older age groups, morbidity and disability should increase accordingly in these successively older age groups of community-dwelling blacks and decrease steadily in comparable groups of whites. This should result overall in greater race differences in health and functioning at ages 85 and older, and smaller differences at the younger ages—65 to 74. The reverse, however, was true. Larger differences in health and functioning were found across eight independent data sources in comparisons of blacks and whites aged 65 to 74, and smaller differences were found between blacks and whites aged 85 and over. Race-by-age differentials in health and functioning appear to be causes rather than effects of the disproportionate institutionalization of the races.

Our findings suggest that a variety of helpers and shifting reciprocities with adult children facilitate the community living of the black oldest old. New research might productively focus on these aspects of informal support as risk factors for aging, disease, and institutionalization, especially as their distributions differ in the four race–age cohorts identified in this research.

Some limitations of the present study were insufficient numbers in the very oldest age groups, a lack of objective measures of health and functioning, and difficulties in isolating the effects on health and functioning that were due to class, cohort, time of measurement, and the aging process itself. These limitations should be addressed by longitudinal studies that include ample numbers of very old blacks and whites, and objective as well as subjective measures of health and functioning. The black oldest old should be disaggregated into finer age categories for analysis because, as our findings indicate, the failure to do so obscures important countervailing health and functioning trends among the subgroups. This requires new and larger samples of very old blacks. Because the black oldest old are rare elements in the population, special screening and sampling procedures will be needed to identify and locate them. These strategies could build upon those developed by Jackson and his colleagues to identify and locate blacks in predominantly white areas (Jackson and Hatchett 1986) and those developed by Gibson and Herzog (1984) to generate supplemental samples of older blacks from existing samples.

In addition to longitudinal studies and class-by-race comparisons, it is important to examine the differing validities of current measures of health and functioning for the black and white oldest old. It could be the case that black–white disparities are due in part to differences in the structure and measurement of the health construct.

In light of our findings, how might future cohorts of the black oldest old be different? If current rates of growth in the oldest age groups of blacks continue, undoubtedly the cohort will be larger. If adverse mortality-selection processes are operant, the age–race differentials in health and functioning identified among the age cohorts today should persist among future cohorts. Theoretically, new cohorts of the black oldest old should be healthier. We must exercise caution, however, in projecting better health and functioning for these new cohorts. Despite increases in the quantity of health care for older blacks brought about by the introduction of Medicare and Medicaid, improvements in the quality of that care are not as apparent.

Although the analyses in this chapter suggest that family and other social supports aid in maintaining the black oldest old in the community, several growing trends could considerably alter the size, composition, availability, and quality of this family support for future cohorts of the black oldest old. Continuing high rates of unemployment among black youth and adults (resulting in reduced resources available for retirement over the long term), increases in black families headed by women, and dwindling resources of the black community could stretch immediate and extended black families to their economic and psychological limits, decreasing the number of oldest old who could be cared for in the community. Furthermore, the more rapid growth of the black compared with the white oldest old, and the higher fertility rate of black compared with white women, may create more of a dilemma for black than white families of the future in caring simultaneously for their very young and very old. The morbid younger group of black elderly identified in this research can only add to this burden.

These economic, health-care, and mortality selection process factors need to be examined in tandem with the distribution of risk factors for aging, disease, and institutionalization. The analysis of these factors within a single study that focuses on both community and institutionalized populations, following individuals as they move from one setting to another, is a research imperative. For it is the interrelatedness of such factors that will determine the long-term care needs of the black oldest old of tomorrow—a growing but poorly understood group.

TECHNICAL APPENDIX
THE BLACK OLDEST OLD—HEALTH, FUNCTIONING, AND INFORMAL SUPPORT

The National Survey of Black Americans and the Three-Generation Family Study are samples based on a common frame. Because the items and question formats used in the present research were identical, we combined the two studies to yield a larger sample of older blacks for analysis.

The National Survey of Black Americans (NSBA)

The NSBA cross-sectional sample is a multistage probability sample of the black population consisting of 2,107 respondents aged 18 to 101 (Jackson, Tucker, and Gurin 1987). The sampling design was based on the 1970 census, and each black American residing in an individual household in the continental United States had an equal chance of being selected. The sample design is similar to that of most national surveys, but has unique features of primary area selection and stratification to make it responsive to the distribution of the black population. Eligibility for selection into this household sample was based on citizenship and noninstitutionalized living in the continental United States. Reflecting the nature of the distribution of the black population, more than half (44) of the 76 primary areas used for final selection of households were located in the South. Two methods of screening were developed to guarantee inclusion of blacks meeting the selection criteria in both high- and low-density areas. The sample had a 69 percent response rate, and all face-to-face interviewing was conducted from 1979 to 1980 by black interviewers trained through the Survey Research Center of the University of Michigan's Institute for Social Research.

The questionnaire used in the NSBA was developed especially for use with the black population. Two years of pretesting and refinement preceded actual use in the field. The instrument contained both open- and closed-ended items and took, on average, 2 hours and 20 minutes to administer. Although our present concerns are physical health and functioning, mental health, neighborhood life, family, social support, and demographic sections, the questionnaire also includes the broad areas of work, retirement, racial and self-identity, and political participation. Jackson (in press) provides a detailed description of the NSBA methods and sample.

The Three-Generation Family Study

The cross-sectional NSBA served as the parent study for the Three-Generation Family Study. When respondents in the cross-sectional survey had living family members from at least two other generations, interviews were attempted with one randomly selected representative from each of these generations. The cross-sectional respondent was reinterviewed with a form of the three-generation instrument. Multiplicity sampling was adapted to generate the new national probability samples from the original national cross-sectional sample. For descriptions of multiplicity sampling see, for example, Frankel and Frankel (1977) and Sirkin (1970). For adaptations of multiplicity sampling for use in generating a supplemental sample of black elderly, see Gibson and Herzog (1984). Having a defined set of inclusion–exclusion rules, and having established specific probabilities of selection for each of the three-generation respondents, the Family Network Sampling Procedure generated a nationally distributed sample of three-generation families. Jackson and Hatchett (1986) contains a detailed description of these methods. Data on the adult children of the black oldest old were drawn from this three-generation sample.

Acknowledgments—This chapter was written while James S. Jackson held a National Research Council/Ford Foundation Senior Postdoctoral Fellowship at Ecole des Hautes Etudes en Sciences Sociales, Group d'Etudes et de Recherches sur la Science, Paris, France. We gratefully acknowledge the support of grants AG03553 and AG05561 from the National Institute of Aging. We wish to thank Toni Antonucci for her helpful comments on the first draft of this chapter; Letha Chadiha and Linda Shepard for their help with the analyses; and Sally Oswald and Karin Clissold for help with the tables.

REFERENCES

Andersen, R.M., R.M. Mullner, and L.J. Cornelius. 1987. Black-White Differences in Health Status: Methods or Substance? *The Milbank Quarterly* 65(Suppl. 1):72–99.

Antonucci, T.C. 1985. Personal Characteristics, Social Networks, and Social Behavior. In *Handbook of Aging and the Social Sciences,* 2nd ed., eds. R.H. Binstock and E. Shanas, 94–128. New York: Van Nostrand Rheinhold.

Cantor, M.H. 1979. Neighbors and Friends: An Overlooked Resource in the Informal Support System. *Research on Aging* 1:434–63.

Chatters, L.M., R.J. Taylor, and J.S. Jackson. 1985. Size and Composition of the Informal Helper Networks of Elderly Blacks. *Journal of Gerontology* 40(2):605–14.

Danziger, S. 1989. (Unpublished.) Calculations from the 1980 Census Computer Tapes.

Ewbank, D.C. 1987. History of Black Mortality and Health before 1940. *The Milbank Quarterly* 65 (Suppl. 1):100–28.

Foley, D.J., L.F. Berkman, L.C. Branch, M.E. Farmer, and R.B. Wallace. 1987. Physical Functioning. In *Established Population for Epidemiological Studies of the Elderly,* eds. J. Huntley, D. Brock, A. Ostfeld, J. Tayler, and R. Wallace, 56–94. National Institutes of Health pub. no. 86-2443. Bethesda, Md: National Institute on Aging.

Frankel, M.R., and L.R. Frankel. 1977. Some Recent Developments in Sample Survey Design. *Journal of Marketing Research* 14:280–93.

Gibson, R.C. 1982. Blacks at Middle and Late Life: Resources and Coping. *Annals of the American Academy of Political and Social Science* 464:79–90.

———. 1986a. *Blacks in an Aging Society.* New York: Carnegie Corporation.

———. 1986b. Blacks in an Aging Society. *Daedalus* 115(1):349–71.

———. 1986c. Outlook for the Black Family. In *Our Aging Society: Paradox or Promise?,* eds. A. Pifer and L. Bronte, 181–97. New York: Norton.

Gibson, R.C., and A.R. Herzog. 1984. Rare Element Telephone Screening (RETS): A Procedure for Augmenting the Number of Black Elderly in National Samples. *Gerontologist* 24:477–82.

Gibson, R.C., and J.S. Jackson. 1987. Health, Functioning, and Informational Support Among the Black Elderly. *The Milbank Quarterly* 65(Suppl. 2):421–54.

Jackson, J.J. 1981. Urban Black Americans. In *Ethnicity and Medical Care,* ed. A. Harwood, 37–129. Cambridge, Mass.: Harvard University Press.

———. 1985. Race, National Origin, Ethnicity, and Aging. In *Handbook of Aging and the Social Sciences,* eds. R.H. Binstock and E. Shanas, 264–91. New York: Van Nostrand Rheinhold.

Jackson, J.S. 1988. Growing Old in Black America: Research on Aging Black Populations. In *The Black American Elderly: Research on Physical and Psychosocial Health,* ed. J.S. Jackson, 3–16. New York: Springer.

———. in press. The Program for Research on Black Americans. In *Advances in Black Psychology,* ed. R. Jones. Richmond, Calif: Cobb and Henry.

Jackson, J.S., and S.J. Hatchett. 1986. Intergenerational Research: Methodological Considerations. In *Intergenerational Relations*, eds. N. Datan and H.W. Reese, 51–76. Hillsdale, N.J.: Erlbaum.

Jackson, J.S., M.B. Tucker, and G. Gurin. 1987. *The National Survey of Black Americans.* Ann Arbor, Mich.: Institute for Social Research, University of Michigan. ICPSR no. 8512.

Jones, G. 1980. Black Longevity after Age 80: A Real or Actuarial Phenomenon? Ohio: Bowling Green University. (Unpublished.)

Litwak, E. 1986. *Helping the Elderly.* New York: Guilford Press.

Manton, K.G. 1982. Temporal and Age Variation of United States Black/White Cause-specific Mortality Differentials: A Study of the Recent Changes in the Relative Health Status of the United States Black Population. *Gerontologist* 22(2):170–79.

Manton, K.G., C.H. Patrick, and K.W. Johnson. 1987. Health Differentials between Blacks and Whites: Recent Trends in Mortality and Morbidity. *Milbank Memorial Fund Quarterly* 65(Suppl. 1):129–99.

Manton, K.G., and B.J. Soldo. 1985. Dynamics of Health Changes in the Oldest Old: New Perspectives and Evidence. *Milbank Memorial Fund Quarterly/Health and Society* 63(2):206–85.

Medvedev, Z. 1974. Caucasus and Altay Longevity. *The Gerontologist* 14:381–87.

Nam, C.B., N.L. Weatherby, and K.A. Ockay. 1978. Causes of Death Which Contribute to the Mortality Crossover Effect. *Social Biology* 25(4):306–14.

National Center for Health Statistics. 1984. *National Health Interview Survey: Supplement on Aging* (NHIS–SOA). Washington: Department of Health and Human Services.

———. 1987. D.A. Dawson and P.F. Adams: Current Estimates from the National Health Interview Survey, United States, 1986. *Vital and Health Statistics,* series 10, no. 164, DHHS pub. no. (PHS) 87–1592. Washington.

Rowe, J.W., and R.L. Kahn. 1987. Human Aging: Usual and Successful. *Science* 237:143–49.

Siegel, J.S., and C.M. Taeuber. 1986. Demographic Perspectives on the Long-Lived Society. *Daedalus* 115:77–118.

Sirken, M.G. 1970. Household Surveys with Multiplicity. *Journal of the American Statistical Association* 65:257–66.

Stack, C. 1974. *All Our Kin.* New York: Harper & Row.

U.S. Bureau of the Census. 1987. America's Centenarians. *Current Population Reports,* series P-23, no. 153. Data from the 1980 Census. Washington.

U.S. Department of Health and Human Services. 1983. *Health: United States, 1982.* DHHS pub. no. (PHS) 83-1232. Washington.

———. 1988. *Health: United States, 1987.* DHHS pub. no. (PHS) 88-1232. Washington.

Wing, S., K.G. Manton, E. Stallard, C.G. Hanes, and H.A. Tyroler. 1985. The Black/White Mortality Crossover: Investigation in a Community-based Study. *Journal of Gerontology* 40:78–94.

16

The Robust Oldest Old: Optimistic Perspectives for Increasing Healthy Life Expectancy

RICHARD M. SUZMAN, TAMARA HARRIS, EVAN C. HADLEY,
MARY GRACE KOVAR, and RICHARD WEINDRUCH

Images of the oldest old are predominantly of disability and frailty. The policy implications of the projected rapid growth of the oldest-old population have seemed unremittingly pessimistic. This reflects the expensive burden of chronic disability which in the oldest-old population often requires the everyday help of another person. Given the costs of this long-term care (LTC), research initially concentrated on describing both the levels of morbidity and disability that require everyday care and the trajectory of decline in functional ability. When the estimates of the burden of disability within the current oldest-old population generated by this research were combined with Bureau of the Census projections on the size of the oldest-old population, policy makers came to the seemingly inescapable conclusion that we must prepare for a dramatic and costly expansion of the long-term-care system.

An alarming possibility is that the mortality assumptions used by the Bureau of the Census may be far too conservative, and that the oldest-old population may grow more rapidly than even the highest projections (Guralnik, Yanagishita, and Schneider 1988; Manton and Stallard, forthcoming). These much higher projections could jeopardize the initiation of a national long-term-care insurance program. However, these concerns often assume that the disability of very old persons is fixed.

Disability and frailty represent one of the last conceptual barriers in the gerontological or geriatric tradition. Until recently, aging research has involved unraveling disease processes from "normal aging" in areas other than disability and frailty. For example, the concept of "normal" old-age senility has been replaced by specific diagnoses of dementia that occur against a background of apparently benign changes in cognitive function in old age. Research funding is naturally concentrated in areas where the problems appear to be soluble. In the case of the oldest old, an unrealistically hopeless perception encourages an unhealthy therapeutic nihilism and discourages research efforts. Unfortunately, these negative views do not take into account the probability that disability and frailty, like other aging processes, are far more dynamic than was originally suspected. From an examination of the heterogeneity within the oldest-old population, we can infer that the projected increases in service demand could be lowered by modifying disability among the very old.

HETEROGENEITY OF THE OLDEST OLD

Until recently, there has been little recognition of the heterogeneous nature of disability among the oldest-old population. Rather, the focus has been on those with the heaviest burden of morbidity and disability or on the fewer than one-fourth who are institutionalized. Little attention has been devoted to the robust oldest old who remain independent. Yet 57 percent of *all* the oldest old living in the community experience little or no difficulty in going about their everyday activities without *any* personal assistance. Forty-three percent are able to remain in the community with some help from another person in meeting the needs of everyday life.

Still less attention has been devoted to those who report retention or recovery of function. As research progresses, however, we develop better descriptions of the dynamics of the older population's functional status. Much early work was derived from cross-sectional studies not well suited to estimating the numbers undergoing changes in functional status. However, as we will show in this chapter, data from newer longitudinal studies now suggest that functional change in the oldest old does not consist of only continuous decrements. In fact, substantial portions of the population may stabilize after a decline. Others may even recover function through remission or effective treatment of the underlying medical condition, or through adaptation or intervention to overcome the disability caused by impairment. Because of limitations imposed by small sample sizes and unfamiliarity with multiple increment-decrement life-table methodology, many demographic estimates of healthy life expectancy did not represent the fraction who regained independence (Katz et al. 1983). Only recently has this error been rectified (Manton and Stallard 1990b; Manton, Woodbury, and Stallard 1990; Rogers, Rogers, and Branch 1989; Rogers, Rogers, and Belanger 1989).

Even given the gains in descriptive epidemiology of disability, little is understood about the details of the compensatory mechanisms that individuals employ to help them remain independent despite their impairments. Such information is critical in determining whether adoption of these mechanisms for persons with similar impairments could greatly increase the proportion of the oldest old who remain independent.

The identification of risk factors for disability is limited because epidemiological studies and surveys often included age ceilings or had insufficient numbers of the very old. For example, the National Health and Nutrition Examination Surveys I and II (NHANES) held the age ceiling at 74. Early plans for the current NHANES III would have excluded those aged 85 and over, although the final survey design focuses special attention on the determinants of physical functioning in the oldest old.

Many epidemiological studies and clinical trials omitted those aged 65 (or 75) and over in part because of the high prevalence of multiple conditions, or comorbidities, that make the conduct of the trial or interpretation of the results more difficult. But the impact and success of interventions in the presence of other complicating conditions are precisely what are of most interest for the oldest old. Perhaps many earlier studies did not collect the epidemiological data needed to initiate a disability prevention program among the oldest old because of both the inherent difficulties and a pessimistic attitude about the probability of effective intervention. In turn, perhaps the failure to gather systematic data on the oldest-old population encouraged an attitude of interventionist nihilism.

EVIDENCE FOR OPTIMISM

Recently, researchers focusing on "successful aging" (Rowe and Kahn 1987) have proposed more optimistic views. They suggest the possibility of identifying the environmental, social, and physiological modifiers of biological aging, which may be amenable to preventive strategies even among the oldest old. Although few studies describe the oldest old who have retained or recovered robust levels of functioning, there are grounds for optimism deriving from other avenues of gerontological research.

What are the grounds for optimism? Health-service research is revealing that a relatively large percentage of those in old age remain low-cost users of medical services; the small percentage that accounts for a large fraction of expenditures generally incurs these costs in the last year of life, a period that is expensive at any age (Scitovsky 1988). Studies of disability and healthy aging have identified modifiable risk factors from middle age that are associated with health and physical well-being among the oldest old (Benfante, Reed, and Brody 1985; Guralnik and Kaplan 1989), suggesting the possibility of interventions well before very old age. Prospective studies of medical interventions using available technologies have shown that it is possible to reduce disability and to slow deterioration in physical ability in the very old (Applegate et al. 1987, 1990).

National data show that a surprisingly large percentage of the oldest old not only require no personal assistance on a daily level but also are physically robust. Further, over a 2-year period, many retain their robustness and a smaller number, who are initially nonrobust, are apparently able to recover their robustness.

THE EMPIRICAL EVIDENCE

This chapter uses data drawn primarily from analyses of the national Longitudinal Study of Aging (Harris et al. 1989) to consider the potential for increasing healthy life expectancy among the very old: those aged 80 and over (the study's sample size does not permit the age category of 85 and over to be used for the study of this issue). The data are used to answer two questions:

1. What proportion of those aged 80 and over in the community are physically robust and, over a 2-year time period, what fraction *sustain* robustness, what fraction of the nonrobust *regain* robustness, and what fraction *lose* robustness?
2. What are the correlates of maintained or regained robustness that might be candidates for prevention, treatment, or rehabilitation?

Although available data do not permit detailed analysis of the physiological factors or therapeutic interventions that might account for the observed recovery of function, we will review examples of interventions that could underlie the observed improvement or could be instituted in order to boost the percentage who do recover function. We also present illustrations of interventions and approaches to reducing frailty and its disabling consequences in the very old that are currently under development.

Evidence from the Longitudinal Study of Aging

The data on robustness in this chapter are drawn from 1,791 white persons aged 80 or older in 1984 who participated in the Supplement on Aging (SOA) and who, at follow-up in 1986, either participated in the Longitudinal Study of Aging (LSOA) reinterview or were known to be institutionalized, or to have died. For a description of the LSOA, see Chapters 5 and 14, this volume. This sample included 1,214 women and 577 men. It is likely that a significant percentage of those not located in 1986 had died and will be identified in future matches to the National Death Index.

Robustness was defined at baseline (and follow-up) as no difficulty in: walking one-quarter of a mile; stooping, crouching, or kneeling; lifting 10 pounds; or walking up 10 steps without resting. These measures were chosen because they have been used to assess ability to work (Nagi 1976) and because of their relation to large motor-function skills that underlie many of the activities of daily living (ADLs) and instrumental activities of daily living (IADLs) that people must perform to live independently. Only individuals with no difficulty on all four measures were considered robust.

In 1984, 33 percent of surveyed whites aged 80 or older (44 percent of the men and 28 percent of the women) were robust (Figure 16–1). Sixty-seven percent had no difficulty lifting 10 pounds, 57 percent had no difficulty walking up 10 steps, 49 percent had no difficulty walking one-quarter of a mile, and 47 percent had no difficulty stooping, crouching, or kneeling. The order of difficulty for each of the measures was similar for men and women, although women had more difficulty on each item.

Although this group appeared robust and functionally fit, it is also important to know if they were healthier than the nonrobust. One crude indicator is utilization of health services. About three-quarters of the robust group had no hospitalizations and fewer than six doctor visits in the 12 months prior to baseline interview, compared with slightly more than one-half of the nonrobust comparison group (Figure 16–2). Ten percent of the comparison group had two or more hospitalizations compared with only 2 percent of the robust group.

The suggestion that the robust were healthier was supported by consideration of morbidity and mortality risks over the 2-year follow-up period. Participants in the baseline survey were divided into five functional categories; the robust (no impairments of ADL, IADL, or the higher-level Nagi functional measures cited above) were used as the reference group for risk calculation. The nonrobust group was at least twice as likely as the robust one to have died over the follow-up period. Persons at every other functional level, including those with impairments only of the robustness measures, were more likely to die within the 2-year period. Thus, those who

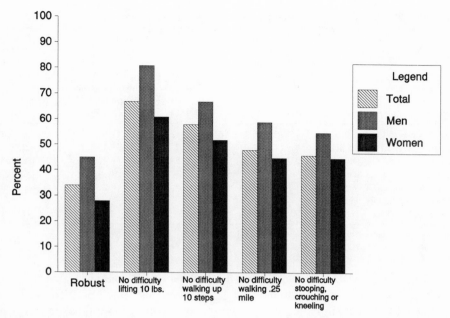

Figure 16–1   Robustness in men and women at age 80. (Source: Harris et al. 1989)

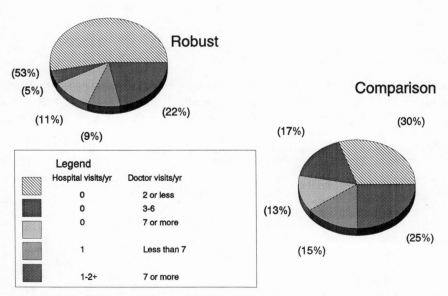

Figure 16–2   Robustness and reported medical utilization. (Source: NCHS, Supplement on Aging 1984)

Table 16–1 Morbidity and Mortality Risks by Level of Function

		Among survivors		
Status at baseline*	Death ($n = 338$)	Any nursing-home admission ($n = 152$)	Two or more hospitalizations in prior year ($n = 150$)	Six or more physician visits in prior year ($n = 368$)
Receive help with ADL	4.4 (3.2, 6.1)	6.7 (3.8, 12.8)	3.3 (1.9, 5.5)	2.3 (1.6, 3.4)
Difficulty with ADL—no help	1.9 (1.3, 2.7)	3.7 (2.0, 7.4)	2.0 (1.1, 3.4)	1.3 (0.9, 1.9)
Any difficulty with IADL	2.2 (1.4, 3.3)	2.8 (1.4, 5.6)	2.5 (1.4, 4.5)	1.6 (1.0, 2.3)
Not robust, but no difficulty with ADL or IADL	1.5 (1.0, 2.2)	2.2 (1.1, 4.1)	2.1 (1.2, 3.5)	1.3 (0.9, 1.9)
Robust—no difficulty with ADL or IADL	1.0	1.0	1.0	1.0

*Adjusted for age and sex (95 percent confidence intervals).
Source: Harris et al. (1989).

needed help with ADLs (the most seriously disabled of the nonrobust groups) were more than four times as likely to have died. The nonrobust were also more likely to be admitted to a nursing home or to be hospitalized two or more times in the year prior to reinterview (Table 16–1).

Of 1,453 persons alive at follow-up, 25 percent were robust; this was 33 percent of the men and 22 percent of the women. After 2 years, about half the women and 40 percent of the men who were robust at baseline continued to meet criteria for robustness at follow-up (Table 16–2). Eleven percent of the women and 7 percent of the men in the disabled comparison group met criteria for robustness at follow-up. Thus, although the general direction of change was toward a diminution of function, a significant fraction retained their robustness, with a smaller fraction recovering some function.

Evidence from Comparable Studies

Other studies of the oldest old have found similar patterns even among those who had higher-level impairments. A prospective study (Branch et al. 1984; Branch and Ku 1989) of functional status in a Massachusetts panel ($N = 97$ aged 85 and over)

Table 16–2 Change in Robustness from Baseline to Follow-up

		Status at follow-up (%)		
Status at baseline	N	Robust	Other	Dead
Men				
Robust	251	42	43	15
Comparison	326	11	57	32
Women				
Robust	343	50	43	7
Comparison	871	7	74	19
Total	1,791	368	1,085	338

Source: Harris et al. (1989).

found that over a 15-month period, 55 to 58 percent of those aged 85 and over maintained functional independence, as measured by standard ADL scales. Of those aged 85 and over who were initially functionally dependent, between 4.3 and 9.5 percent (depending upon the scale used) returned to independence. Over a longer period, from year 1.25 to year 6, the percentage who maintained their functional state dropped to between 27 and 17 percent. Only a negligible fraction of those who were functionally dependent after the first 15 months returned to independence by year 6. However, given that life expectancy at age 85 is about 6 years, 15 months is, relatively speaking, long-term improvement.

Data from a much larger study, the 1982–1984 National Long Term Care Survey (NLTCS) (Manton 1988a, b), which included 2,704 persons aged 85 and over, found that 48.8 percent of males and 46.5 percent of females aged 85 and over who were not disabled in 1982 retained ADL and IADL independence between 1982 and 1984. Meaningful numbers of the total sample aged 65 and over showed a 2-year improvement in functioning, even at high initial levels of impairment. Improvement also occurred for those aged 85 and over, but recovery to a fully nondisabled state was limited to 2 percent.

Given the different methodologies used by these three studies (i.e., the LSOA, the Massachusetts Panel, and the NLTCS), including the definitions of functional endpoints and age cut points, it is difficult to make exact comparisons. On the other hand, the consistency in direction of the results of the three studies increases confidence that the LSOA results represent real stability and recovery of function rather than just measurement effects.

A number of factors could have influenced the estimates of change and stability. Many with chronic illness and impairment do not perceive themselves as being disabled; adaptation to physical decrements could result in a redefinition of one's own functioning. Depressed mood and motivation probably also influence self-reported disability. The changeover from in-person face-to-face interviews in the SOA to telephone interviews in the LSOA could also have affected the results. New methodologies (e.g., actual measurement of physical performance and improved questionnaire design) are being developed to improve future longitudinal studies of physical functioning (see Applegate et al. 1990). Until these methodologies are applied in order to reduce measurement error, the magnitude of the estimates must remain uncertain. However, concerns about their accuracy must be tempered by the fact that, on average, self-reported disability shows remarkable predictive validity for "hard," well-defined endpoints like medical-care usage, institutionalization, and mortality (Manton 1988a, b, 1989).

In summary, it seems likely that a nontrivial fraction of the 2-year survivors aged 80 and over are able to sustain their functional independence and robustness. Moreover, a lesser, but still meaningful proportion of those initially disabled do manage to improve functional status over a 1- or 2-year period, although the exact fraction that returns to robustness or functional independence at age 85 and over is more uncertain.

What are the Factors for Maintaining Robustness?

Within the LSOA, were any factors from the baseline survey associated with continued robustness in the oldest old over the 2-year follow-up period? Factors examined included those associated with morbidity or mortality in old age: chronic diseases such as arthritis; cardiovascular disease (report of stroke, heart attack, angina, or heart condition) and hypertension; vision or hearing problems; difficulty chewing; body mass index: sex, age, education; and a measure of social isolation.

In multivariate models (Table 16–3), the correlates of maintained robustness included never having had cardiovascular disease, no arthritic complaints in the year prior to the baseline interview, and a moderate body mass index. Lack of hypertension was also associated with retained robustness. Other variables associated with maintained robustness included younger age, male gender, and higher educational status. These factors are also consistent with findings on robustness from younger populations (Benfant, Reed, and Brody 1985; Guralnik and Kaplan 1989; Pinsky, Leaverton, and Stokes 1987). Education as a factor is of particular interest because there is evidence that older persons of higher education tend to use more preventive services. Because future cohorts of the oldest old will have dramatically higher levels of education (see Chapter 3 by Preston in this volume), and because the repertoire of preventive and early intervention options is increasing, future cohorts of the oldest old may be significantly more robust.

Table 16–3 Correlates of Continued Robustness at Follow-up

Variable	Relative odds (95% confidence intervals) ($N=513$)
Age 80 vs. age 90	2.0 (1.1, 3.6)
Male vs. female	3.2 (1.2, 8.6)
Education (years completed)	
0–6	1.0
7–8	2.2 (1.2, 4.0)
9–12	2.1 (1.2, 3.8)
13+	2.4 (1.2, 4.7)
Social contact—men	0.7 (0.4, 1.4)
Social contact—women	1.7 (0.8, 3.6)
No vision problems	1.1 (0.6, 2.1)
No hearing problems—men	0.6 (0.4, 1.2)
No hearing problems—women	1.5 (0.9, 2.5)
No difficulty chewing	1.3 (0.8, 2.4)
Never had hypertension	1.5 (1.0, 2.1)
Never had cardiovascular disease	2.1 (1.2, 3.7)
Never had arthritis	1.9 (1.2, 2.7)
Body mass index	
<25th percentile	1.8 (1.0, 3.2)
25th–49th percentile	1.7 (1.0, 2.9)
50th–74th percentile	2.1 (1.2, 3.6)
>75th percentile	1.0

Source: Harris et al. (1989).

To what extent might medical and surgical procedures be associated with sustaining (or regaining) robustness between the LSOA baseline and 2-year follow-up? At the current stage of research, little is known about this, but future analyses of Medicare data now linked to both the LSOA and NLTCS might reveal the impact of procedures such as effective control of hypertension, lens removal, and hip replacement on the transition to or from disability, discussed above. Unfortunately, Medicare's statistical system is not able to capture a number of other important (although probably still rare) practices such as geriatric assessment and case management, non-reimbursable rehabilitation therapies, and in-home fall-prevention efforts for linkage to the national longitudinal surveys of disability.

In conclusion, the data support the view that factors such as cardiovascular disease, hypertension, arthritis, body weight, and education are associated with the onset of new disability in old age. These factors could provide the basis for preventive and intervention strategies to maintain health and perhaps also to recover function.

THE ROLE OF THERAPEUTIC INTERVENTIONS

Thus far, we have found evidence from three descriptive population-based studies that a sizable proportion of very old persons are either free of disability or are able to cope with it free of personal assistance or, alternatively, are able to demonstrate stabilization or recovery of function over time. We have also identified factors that could serve as the basis for prevention and intervention programs for older persons. The population-based research has not yet been able to explore the role of specific interventions in retaining or recovering robustness. Additional analyses will be possible from the national population-based longitudinal studies when more waves are added, when linked administrative data are analyzed, and when data from the NLTCS on substituting mechanical aids and housing adaptations for expensive personal help are more fully analyzed. However, we may be close to the limitations of the current large survey-based disability studies, which are relatively poor in risk-factor assessment and do not measure such promising new, but rare, clinical practices as geriatric assessment. A wide array of interventions are currently undergoing development and testing, and we must turn to the clinical-trials literature to provide examples of potential therapeutic interventions that could increase healthy life expectancy in the oldest old.

In general, there is little direct information on the *efficacy* (i.e., the impact of the intervention under ideal and well-controlled "laboratory" conditions, often with complex cases excluded) or *effectiveness* (i.e., when the intervention is more widely implemented under everyday general clinical conditions) of specific interventions for the oldest old. The reason for this dearth of knowledge is that, until very recently, the oldest old have rarely been targeted for preventive efforts and have been usually excluded from many therapeutic and rehabilitation trials (or have been included in insufficient numbers to allow for separate analyses). We must therefore extrapolate from studies of the very old that do not include separate breakdowns on the oldest old. However, given the many existing differences from the younger old (e.g., lower education, higher levels of poverty, more extensive widowhood, and comorbidity), outcomes from studies on younger groups may not be fully generalizable to the oldest old.

It should also be noted that to the extent that it is feasible to define appropriate or optimal treatment for the oldest old, in most areas insufficient epidemiological data exist to estimate the extent to which the oldest old actually receive this care. Thus, although there has been much debate in the literature on expensive over-treatment, data are sparse for the oldest old on the prevalence of treatable medical conditions with probable good outcomes that go untreated. No comprehensive review is attempted of this area. Rather, to illustrate that effective interventions do exist, we give just two main examples. The first, cataract surgery, a well-established, high-volume procedure among the oldest old, appears to lead to important secondary and tertiary gains in functioning. The second, a more general orientation in practice that is effective but generally underutilized, is geriatric assessment and rehabilitation.

Cataract Surgery

Surgical procedures are among the better-studied interventions. Aggregate annual data on the leading surgical procedures on those aged 85 and over reveal the leading surgical procedures to be cataract removal, fracture reduction, pacemaker insertion, hip replacement and arthroplasty, and prostatectomy (Moien and Liu 1987). There are a number of reports on how well the very old tolerate anesthesia for these and other procedures in the absence of complicating conditions. However, less is known about the impact of these procedures on disability-free (i.e., active) life expectancy for those aged 85 and over. Although evidence for some surgical procedures shows that they may lead to significantly improved functional status, procedures like reduction of hip fractures are associated with considerable morbidity and mortality (Magaziner et al. 1989, 1990).

Cataract surgery, on the other hand, has been tested for efficacy in improving functional capacity in older persons. Cataracts are responsible for a sizable fraction of visual impairments in older persons. One study (Applegate et al. 1987) evaluated the impact of cataract surgery with lens implantation on 293 elderly patients over age 70 (mean age 77 years, with a range of 70 to 95 years) from two ophthalmology practices. Surgery improved visual acuity, including binocular vision, at both 4 and 12 months after surgery when rated by ophthalmic tests and by patients themselves. Significant secondary and tertiary gains were also evident. Scores on the ADL scale improved significantly, though modestly, at 4 months after surgery. Self-ratings of vision-dependent activities such as newspaper reading and driving were also improved at 4 and 12 months. At 12 months the improvement in ADL functional capacity was no longer significantly different from presurgery levels, although, because there was no control group, the analysis does not take into account the general downward trend in functional status that often occurs at advanced ages. Moreover, the ADL scores 1 year after surgery showed a striking decline in a smaller subgroup, which worsened or showed no improvement in vision.

Improvements in objective measures such as mental status measures and timed manual performance scores were even more remarkable. Although visual impairments are known to be a factor in accidental falls, the study does not report on whether visual improvements led to a reduction in falls.

Geriatric Assessment and Rehabilitation

Medical rehabilitation, a field highly germane to interventions to reduce geriatric frailty, has traditionally emphasized the treatment of younger individuals with acute or chronic disabilities and not the chronic disabilities afflicting many older persons. Rehabilitation professionals have developed techniques that hold great potential for counteracting frailty. Numerous reports describe effective assessment and rehabilitation procedures that should be, but are not, used widely within the general elderly population (Ory and Williams 1989). For example, geriatric assessment and case management are reported to lead to improved function, decreased institutionalization, and a reduction in mortality (Rubenstein et al. 1984). Geriatric assessment has emerged as a new tool for the prevention of disability and a model intervention strategy to interrupt the decline in functional assessment (National Institutes of Health 1987).

For example, a new randomized controlled trial of a geriatric assessment unit in a community rehabilitation hospital provides evidence that such a unit can improve the physical function of elderly hospitalized patients with moderate illness and functional impairment (Applegate et al. 1990). Patients who had been referred to a geriatric assessment unit were selected for randomization into a geriatric assessment unit or control group. The referred patients were recovering from acute medical or surgical illnesses and were at risk of nursing-home placement, with loss of independence in one or more ADLs and a potentially reversible impairment. About 44 percent of the patients referred were randomized into the trial. Those accepted had an average age of about 79 (range, 61 to 100). Common diagnoses included hip and other fractures and circulatory disorders. In the geriatric assessment unit, an interdisciplinary team evaluated the medical, social, and psychological functioning of the study patients soon after admission and provided specific treatment, rehabilitation, or both. Patients receiving rehabilitative care had to meet the Medicare requirement of having a degree of impairment needing therapy three times daily. After reaching their rehabilitative goal or stability, the patients were discharged.

In contrast, the control group received the usual care provided by their physicians, as well as a wide range of additional care that included for some, home health care and rehabilitation services in special units.

At 6 months after randomization, the group assigned to the geriatric assessment unit showed significantly more improvement in a number of ADLs, although these differences disappeared after one year. Lower-risk patients improved more than higher-risk patients. At one year, the control-patient survivors were likely to be institutionalized. However, because this study did not include specialized follow-up care in a geriatric clinic, it did not test the limit of current rehabilitation technology. For example, there is some optimism that relatively brief cognitive interventions can improve performance in the area of fluid intelligence in older persons (Baltes and Lindenberger 1988; Willis 1987).

Numerous social experiments to reduce institutionalization have been proposed, although outcomes of actual studies have been mixed, especially in terms of costs (Kemper 1988). Experiments to improve functional level in nursing homes have also been carried out. For example, urinary incontinence, which has a substantial prevalence rate within the elderly nursing home population, can be reduced by behavioral training (Burns et al. 1990; Schnelle et al. 1989), with possibly some potential cost savings (Hu 1989).

INTERVENTIONS UNDER DEVELOPMENT

Cataract surgery and rehabilitation are examples of interventions that are used at late stages in the disease process. What about interventions that are preventive or can be instituted at much earlier stages? Based on findings from the LSOA, further control of cardiovascular disease, hypertension, and arthritis could lead to gains in the reduction of disability among the oldest old. In conditions such as osteoporosis, simply delaying the onset of a disease by about 5 years could have a profound effect on the disability caused by the disease in very late life (Brody 1985; Riley and Bond 1983).

Deficits related to frailty include diminished skeletal-muscle strength, bone strength, cardiopulmonary fitness, gait speed, and postural stability. Also prominent are limitations in joint range of motion and musculoskeletal flexibility. The etiology of these conditions is typically complex, arising from a combination of age, disease, and disuse-associated factors. Psychological factors, including depression, lack of social facilitation, or phobic and self-protective constriction of activity, motivation, grit or resiliency, and redefinition of physical capacity, sometimes play important roles in the etiological chain.

One study (Tinetti, Speechley, and Ginter 1988) found that the aggregate accumulation or simple count of many of these conditions associated with frailty predicted the risk of falling better than did specific single conditions. Reducing the accumulation of these conditions could lead to a reduction in falls and resultant fractures. Research on comorbidity is at too early a stage to reveal if the impact of the conditions underlying physical frailty is simply additive or if multiplicative interactions exist. If, as it seems plausible to conjecture, some conditions potentiate each other or cause complications for treatment, reductions in a few could have even greater positive effects.

Although definitive evidence is lacking, a few recent small-scale studies, reviewed below, do seem to indicate that some deficits associated with physical frailty are preventable or reversible. The following sections provide a few examples of drug, exercise, and nutritional interventions that are being developed to ameliorate two important conditions underlying physical frailty: improved muscle strength and bone strength. No comprehensive review is attempted, and the examples are only meant to illustrate a few of the potential interventions.

Increasing Muscle and Bone Strength

Exercise regimens have been found to improve strength and mobility in older persons (Vallbona and Baker 1984). Other studies suggest that exercise programs may retard the rate of age-related bone loss and increase cardiac fitness in older adults (Smith, Smith, and Gilligan 1988). A recent study of very old (average age, 90 years) nursing-home residents indicates that 8 weeks of leg-strength training markedly improved their limited walking ability, both in speed and in distance (Fiatarone et al. 1990). The improvement was associated with doubled leg-muscle strength and significantly increased muscle size. This is the first time that the benefits of strengthening exercises have been demonstrated in very old persons. Because lower-limb weakness appears to predispose to falls (Whipple, Wolfson, and Amerman 1987), this type of intervention may reduce the risk of falling. Such results do not, of course, imply that all exercise programs will significantly improve functional status. For example, one community-based exercise program for older persons produced less than significant improvements in performance or functional status (Thompson 1988). Careful evaluation of the effectiveness of each intervention, is needed.

Nutritional factors have also been shown to have potential for increasing muscle mass and functional capacity in older persons (Meredith 1990). Most of this research has focused on the younger old (i.e., 60 to 75-year-old people without serious functional impairments).

Treatment with genetically engineered growth hormone administered for 6 months in a randomized clinical trial of 21 men (aged 61 to 81) who initially had low levels of growth hormone apparently produced impressive changes (Rudman et al. 1990), including a 15 percent decrease in body fat, a 9 percent increase in lean body mass, and increased skin thickness. It is likely that this increase in lean body mass was largely due to increased muscle mass, although this was not reported. Similarly, although it is likely that muscle strength was increased, this was also not reported. Whether these results can be generalized to other subgroups is not yet known, nor are the potential long-term side effects.

Rapidly growing attention to osteoporosis has increased interest in prevention or therapy for older persons. A variety of promising approaches including calcium supplementation, estrogens, calcitonin and other hormones, bisphosphonates such as etidronate, other drugs, and exercise (Reginster et al. 1987; Smith, Reddan, and Smith 1981; Watts et al. 1990) are currently under investigation. Again, relatively little is known about the efficacy of interventions in the oldest old because most data are derived from young-old populations. More attention has been devoted to effects on vertebral, rather than hip fractures. There are almost no data from controlled trials on the efficacy of interventions to prevent hip fractures, the most severe consequence of osteoporosis in the oldest old. Epidemiological data suggest that estrogens protect against hip fractures, but again, these data are derived from persons under age 75 (Weiss et al. 1980; Williams et al. 1982). The benefits of potential therapies for men, among whom osteoporosis is quite prevalent above the age of 85, are practically unstudied.

RESEARCH NEEDED

The total burden of morbidity for the oldest old is a simple function of the age-specific disability rate multiplied by the number in the age group. Over a decade ago, Gruenberg (1977) warned of the "failures of success"—when episodes of highly disabling chronic conditions are extended by effective treatment of their fatal complications. There is little evidence to suggest that the increase in life expectancy over the last two decades has been accompanied by a commensurate increase in disability-free life expectancy (e.g., Crimmins 1987; Crimmins, Saito, and Ingegneri 1989; Tu

1990; Verbrugge 1984). Especially for women, much of the available evidence suggests the opposite.

Given the projections of the total burden of disability among the oldest old (Manton and Stallard 1990b), it is clear that we must begin systematically to evaluate the efficacy, effectiveness, and efficiency (cost benefit) of preventive, rehabilitative, and therapeutic interventions geared to the oldest old and those who will become the oldest old. The development of a successful comprehensive intervention strategy will require multilevel approaches that include (1) population-based epidemiological and medical demographic studies that chart and explain the heterogeneity of trajectories of change and stability of robustness and functional dependency in the community, and (2) clinical studies of specific medical, behavioral, or environmental interventions.

The descriptions in this chapter of subgroups, such as those who are robust, those who are able to stabilize successfully after experiencing a decline, and those who are able to regain function and independence, are relatively crude first approximations. Future descriptions should include richer detail of the risk factors, processes, sequences, and interventions. The knowledge base must include information on both current and earlier modifiable risk factors.

Manton and Suzman, in Chapter 5, detail the evolution in the ability of the national data system to describe functional change in the oldest old. Data currently being collected will provide added information. By the end of 1991, four waves of the LSOA and three waves of the NLTCS will be available and linked with Medicare data. The National Health and Nutritional Examination Survey III, which is currently in the field, includes those over age 74. The proposed follow-ups of NHANES III (and the extension of the NHANES I follow-up) will in time provide additional information on risk factors for functional capacity of the oldest old, although the numbers will be small. The intramural epidemiology program of the National Institute on Aging is about to launch a community-based study of some of the mechanisms underlying disability in women.

We suggest in this chapter that analyses of the maintenance and the regaining of robustness will soon reach the resolving power of national surveys like the LSOA and the NLTCS. The next generation (or future waves) of the LSOA and NLTCS will need to include more detailed descriptions of the processes by which function is maintained or regained.

In order to illuminate these processes, shorter measurement intervals are needed (at least for subsamples) than 2-year periods. Study populations have to be large enough to allow analysis of the heterogeneity of the oldest-old population subgroups. Studies need to use both performance and self-report measures and to include information on psychological adjustments to disability. Motivational and other poorly understood psychosocial factors are likely to play important roles in translating results based on limited study subjects into effective standard practice. There should be a constant interplay among national population-based demographic and epidemiological descriptive studies, which permit more complete analyses of heterogeneity and community-level studies with a more detailed focus. As interventions move from the more ideal conditions of clinical trials with strong exclusion criteria into everyday practice the prevalence and effectiveness of the interventions in the real world need to be monitored and evaluated in representative epidemiological and demographic studies.

While interventions adaptable to the oldest-old are already being developed in clinical trials and evaluations, more targeted efforts to develop interventions for the frail older population are underway. For example, a 1988 "Workshop on Reducing Frailty and Fall-Related Injuries in Older Persons" presented the state of current knowledge on these subjects (Weindruch, Ory, and Hadley 1990). The following recommendations emerged:

1. Conduct initial studies to test the efficacy of different intervention approaches.
2. Encourage interventions in populations that have low, intermediate, or high functional impairment, matching the intervention to the appropriate target population so that the population is likely to respond to the intervention.
3. Emphasize functional capacities, injury risk, and health behaviors as critical outcome measures.
4. Evaluate factors that affect compliance with the interventions.

This research initiative has resulted in collaborative studies of a number of biomedical, behavioral, and environmental interventions.

Clinical trials that seek to include appreciable numbers of the oldest old must face the issue of how to deal with the serious problem of the high prevalence of comorbidity. Although clinical trials often exclude those (frequently the 85-and-over group) with serious comorbid problems, doing so for the oldest old would result in greatly diminished generalizability. The growing European movement away from what some consider overcontrol in random clinical trials has special significance for the oldest old. In order to run randomized clinical trials on the oldest old, it may be necessary to accept trials that are relatively small in size and to include individuals with substantial levels of comorbidity. Meta-analytic techniques could be used to integrate results from such studies and to assess the best combination of interventions to increase active life expectancy for the oldest old.

CONCLUSION

A critical factor in moderating the impact of the growth of the population aged 85 and over will be the degree to which there will be a compression or expansion of the duration of disability at later ages. The existence of a subgroup of the community of oldest old who are robust and active, or who improve in functional status over a 2-year time period, is a cause for optimism. Many of the factors that influence the maintenance or recovery of robustness appear susceptible to interventions. It is unclear how well successful clinical trials of carefully selected study populations can be translated into everyday practice in the community population, and how cost effective potential interventions will be. However, increasing the percentage of the oldest old who are able to maintain or regain robustness over a 2-year period by 10 to 20 percent appears to be a realistic and significant goal for this decade.

REFERENCES

Applegate, W.B., S.T. Miller, J.T. Elam, J.M. Freeman, T.O. Wood, and T.C. Gettlefinger. 1987. Impact of Cataract Surgery with Lens Implantation on Vision and Physical Function in Elderly Patients. *Journal of the American Medical Association* 257:1064–66.

Applegate, W.B., S.T. Miller, M.J. Graney, J.T. Elam, R. Burns, and D.E. Akins. 1990. A Randomized, Controlled Trial of a Geriatric Assessment Unit in a Community Rehabilitation Hospital. *New England Journal of Medicine* 322(22):1572–78.

Baltes, P.B., and U. Lindenberger. 1988. On the Range of Cognitive Plasticity in Old Age as a Function of Experience: 15 Years of Intervention Research. *Behavior Therapy* 19:283–300.

Benfante, R., D. Reed, and J. Brody. 1985. Biological and Social Predictors of Health in an Aging Cohort. *Journal of Chronic Disease* 38:385–95.

Branch, L.G., S. Katz, K. Kniepmann, and J. Papsidero. 1984. A Prospective Study of Functional Status among Community Elderly. *American Journal of Public Health* 74(3):266–68.

Branch, L.G., and L. Ku. 1989. Transition Probabilities to Dependency, Institutionalization, and Death among the Elderly Over a Decade. *Journal of Aging and Health* 1(3):370–408.

Brody, J.A. 1985. Prospects for an Aging Population. *Nature* 315(6):463–66.

Burns, P.A., K. Pranikoff, T. Nochajski, P. De Sotelle, and M.K. Harwood. 1990. Treatment of Stress Incontinence with Pelvic Floor Exercises and Biofeedback. *Journal of the American Geriatrics Society* 38:341–44.

Crimmins, E.M. 1987. Evidence on the Compression of Morbidity. *Gerontologica Perspecta* 1:45–49.

Crimmins, E.M., Y. Saito, and D. Ingegneri. 1989. Changes in Life Expectancy and Disability-Free Life Expectancy in the United States. *Population Development Review* 15:235–67.

Fiatarone, M.A., E.C. Marks, C.N. Meredith, L.A. Lipsitz, and W.J. Evans. 1990. High Intensity Strength Training in Nonagenarians; Effects on Skeletal Muscle. *Journal of the American Medical Association* 263:3029–34.

Fitti, J., and M.G. Kovar. 1988. *The 1984 Supplement on Aging. Vital and Health Statistics,* series 1, no. 21. Washington: National Center for Health Statistics.

Gruenberg, E.M. 1977. The Failures of Success. *Milbank Memorial Fund Quarterly*/Health and Society 55(1):3–24.

Guralnik, J.M., M. Yanagishita, and E.L. Schneider. 1988. Projecting the Older Population of the United States: Lessons from the Past and Prospects for the Future. *Milbank Quarterly* 66(2):283–308.

Guralnik, J.M., and G.A. Kaplan. 1989. Predictors of Healthy Aging: Prospective Evidence from the Alameda County Study. *American Journal of Public Health* 79(6):703–8.

Harris, T., M.G. Kovar, R. Suzman, J.C. Kleinman, and J.J. Feldman. 1989. Longitudinal Study of Physical Ability in the Oldest Old. *American Journal of Public Health* 79(6):698–702.

Hu, T.W., et al. 1989. Cost-effectiveness of Training Incontinent Elderly in Nursing Homes. *Health Services Research* 25:455–77.

Katz, S., L.G. Branch, M.H. Branson, J.A. Papsidero, J.C. Beck, and D.S. Greer. 1983. Active Life Expectancy. *New England Journal of Medicine* 309:1218–24.

Kemper, P. 1988. The Evaluation of the National Long Term Care Demonstration. *Health Services Research* 23:161–74.

Magaziner, J., E.M. Simonsick, T.M. Kashner, J.R. Hebel, and J.E. Kenzora. 1989. Survival Experience of Aged Hip Fracture Patients. *American Journal of Public Health* 79(3):274–78.

Magaziner, J., E.M. Simonsick, T.M. Kashner, J.R. Hebel, and J.E. Kenzora. 1990. Predictors of Functional Recovery One Year Following Hospital Discharge for Hip Fracture: A Prospective Study. *Journal of Gerontology* 45(3):101–7.

Manton, K.G. 1988a. A Longitudinal Study of Functional Change and Mortality in the United States. *Journal of Gerontology* 43(5):153–61.

———. 1988b. Planning Long-Term Care for Heterogeneous Older Populations. *Annual Review of Gerontology and Geriatrics* (vol. ed., G.L. Maddox and M.P. Lawton) 8:217–55.

———. 1989. Epidemiological, Demographic, and Social Correlates of Disability Among the Elderly. *Milbank Quarterly* 67(Suppl. 1); 13–58.

Manton, K.G., and E. Stallard. 1991. Cross-sectional Estimates of Active Life Expectancy for the U.S. Elderly and Oldest-Old Populations. *Journal of Gerontology* 48(Suppl.):170–82.

Manton, K.G., M.A. Woodbury, and E. Stallard. 1991. Statistical and Measurement Issues in Assessing the Welfare Status of Aged Individuals and Populations. *Journal of Econometrics* (Forthcoming.)

Meredith, C.N. 1991. The Role of Nutrition in the Prevention and Treatment of Frailty in Older Persons. In *Reducing Frailty and Falls in Older Persons,* eds. R. Weindruch, E.C. Hadley, and M.G. Ory, 219–35. Springfield, Ill.: Charles C Thomas.

Moien, M., and B.M. Liu. 1987. Use of Health Care: Care in Short-Stay Hospitals. In *Health Statistics on Older Persons—United States, 1986,* eds. R. Havlik and B.M. Liu. Hyattsville, Md.: National Center for Health Statistics.

Nagi, S.Z. 1976. Epidemiology of Disability among Adults in the United States. *Milbank Memorial Fund Quarterly/Health and Society* 54:439–68.

National Institutes of Health. 1987. Geriatric Assessment Methods for Clinical Decision Making. *Consensus Development Conference Statement.* Bethesda, Md.: U.S. Department of Health and Human Services.

Ory, M.G., and T. Franklin Williams. 1989. Rehabilitation: Small Goals, Sustained Interventions. *Annals of the American Academy of Political and Social Science* 503:60–71.

Pinsky, J., P. Leaverton, and J. Stokes. 1987. Predictors of Good Function: The Framingham Study. *Journal of Chronic Diseases* 40(1):1595–675.

Reginster J.Y., D. Denis, A. Albert, R. Deroisy, M.P. Lecart, M.A. Fontaine, P. Lambelin, and P. Franchimont. 1987. One-Year Controlled Randomised Trial of Prevention of Early Premenopausal Bone Loss by Intranasal Calcitonin. *Lancet* 2:1481–83.

Riley, M.W., and K. Bond. 1983. Beyond Ageism: Postponing the Onset of Disability. In *Aging in Society: Selected Reviews of Recent Research,* eds. M.W. Riley, B.B. Hess, and K. Bond, 243–52. Hillsdale, N.J.: Erlbaum.

Rogers, R.G., A. Rogers, and A. Belanger. 1989. Active Life Expectancy among the Elderly in the United States: Multistate Life-table Estimates and Population Projections. *Milbank Quarterly* 67(3–4):370–411.

Rogers, A.R., R.G. Rogers, and L.G. Branch. 1989. A Multistate Analysis of Active Life Expectancy. *Public Health Reports* 104:222–25.

Rowe, J., and R. Kahn. 1987. Human Aging: Usual and Successful. *Science* 237:143–49.

Rubenstein, L.Z., K.R. Josephson, G.D. Wieland, P.A. English, J.A. Sayre, and R.L. Kane. 1984. Effectiveness of a Geriatric Assessment Unit: A Randomized Clinical Trial. *New England Journal of Medicine* 311:1664–70.

Rudman, D., A.G. Feller, H.S. Nagraj, et al. 1990. Effects of Human Growth Hormone in Men Over 60 Years Old. *New England Journal of Medicine* 323:1–6.

Scitovsky, A.A. 1988. Medical Care in the Last Twelve Months of Life: The Relation between Age, Functional Status, and Medical Care Expenditures. *Milbank Quarterly* 66(4):640–60.

Schnelle, J.F., B. Traughber, V.A. Sowell, D.R. Newman, C.O. Petrilli, and M. Ory. 1989. Prompted Voiding Treatment of Urinary Incontinence in Nursing Home Patients: A Behavioral Management Approach for Nursing Home Staff. *Journal of the American Geriatrics Society* 37:1051–57.

Smith, E.L., Jr., W. Reddan, and P.E. Smith. 1981. Physical Activity and Calcium Modalities for Bone Mineral Increase in Aged Women. *Medical Science in Sports and Exercise* 13:60–64.

Smith, E.L., P.E. Smith, and C. Gilligan. 1988. Diet, Exercise and Chronic Disease Patterns in Older Adults. *Nutrition Reviews* 46:52–61.

Thompson, R.F., D.M. Crist, M. Marsh, and M. Rosenthal. 1988. Effects of Physical Exercise for Elderly Patients with Physical Impairments. *Journal of the American Geriatric Society* 36:130–35.

Tinetti, M.E., M. Speechley, and S.F. Ginter. 1988. Risk Factors for Falls Among Elderly Persons Living in the Community. *New England Journal of Medicine* 319(26):1701–7.

Tu E. Jow-Ching. 1990. Life Expectancy in Various States of Health, New York State 1980 and 1990. Paper presented at the Annual Meeting of the Population Association of America, Toronto, May.

Vallbona, C., and S.B. Baker. 1984. Physical Fitness Prospects in the Elderly. *Archives of Physical Medicine and Rehabilitation* 65:194–200.

Verbrugge, L.A. 1984. Longer Life but Worsening Health? Trends in Health and Mortality of Middle-aged and Older Persons. *Milbank Memorial Fund Quarterly/Health and Society* 62(3):475–519.

Watts, N.B., S.T. Harris, H.K. Genant, R.D. Wasnich, P.D. Miller, R.D. Jackson, A.A. Licata, P. Ross, G.C. Woodson, M.J. Yanover, W.J. Mysiw, L. Kohse, M.B. Rao, P. Steiger, B. Richmon, and C.H. Chesnut. 1990. Intermittent Cyclical Etidronate Treatment of Postmenopausal Osteoporosis. *The New England Journal of Medicine* 323(2):73–79.

Weindruch, R., M. Ory, and E.C. Hadley. 1990. *Reducing Frailty-Related Injuries in Older Persons*. Springfield, Ill.: Charles C Thomas.

Weiss, N.S., C.L. Ure, J.H. Ballard, A.R. Williams, and J.R. Daling. 1980. Decreased Risk of Fractures of the Hip and Lower Forearm with Postmenopausal Use of Estrogen. *New England Journal of Medicine* 303(21):1195–98.

Whipple, R.H., L.I. Wolfson, and P.M. Amerman. 1987. The Relationship of Knee and Ankle Weakness to Falls in Nursing Home Residents: An Isokinetic Study. *Journal of the American Geriatrics Society* 35:13–20.

Williams, A.R., N.S. Weiss, C.L. Ure, J.S. Ballard, and J.R. Daling. 1982. Effect of Weight, Smoking, and Estrogen Use on the Risk of Hip and Forearm Fractures in Postmenopausal Women. *Obstetrical Gynocology* 60(6):695–99.

Willis, S.L. 1987. Cognitive Training and Everyday Competence. In *Annual Review of Gerontology and Geriatrics*, ed. K.W. Schaie, 159–88. New York: Springer.

17

Making It Last: Economic Resources of the Oldest Old

G. LAWRENCE ATKINS

Congress increasingly is considering proposals to shift more of Medicare costs to the elderly themselves. Public policy proposals aimed at shifting costs to elderly beneficiaries, such as the ill-fated Medicare Catastrophic Coverage Act of 1988, have often ignored age variations in the economic resources of the elderly. The oldest old are treated just like the newly retired, regardless of differences that may exist in their ability to bear these costs. Yet, as the oldest old population grows in size and prominence, public policy will need to become more sensitive to their unique conditions. This chapter addresses the question of whether the economic resources of the oldest old are sufficiently different to justify more age-specific public policy.

POLICY QUESTIONS

The question of whether the oldest old have the resources to pay a greater share of their health costs late in life or deserve special treatment leads us directly to two empirical questions. The first is whether the oldest old as a group have fewer economic resources than younger elderly age groups. This chapter will initially review the relative cash incomes and poverty rates of the young and old elderly. It will later go beyond cash income to assess the relative assets, in-kind benefits, tax burdens, and consumption patterns of the young and old elderly and tie these together into an overall assessment of relative economic well-being.

The second question is whether these differences can be expected to continue in the future. Are they related to the aging process, and thus a phenomenon for all cohorts that reach very old age, or are they related to events influencing only today's group of the very old? This is a more difficult question to answer.

Theory suggests that people plan to consume their lifetime savings in old age, and thus inevitably have the fewest resources in very old age. According to the life-

Author's note: Data from the year 1984 are used throughout this chapter. More recent data are available from some sources but not all, and I have chosen to maintain 1984 data throughout for consistency. More recent data would show higher nominal income and asset levels, but would not substantially change the patterns analyzed in this chapter or the conclusions I have drawn from this analysis.

cycle hypothesis of savings, individuals accumulate assets during their working lives to finance steady levels of consumption for the remainder of their expected life spans (Modigliani and Brumberg 1954). Following this theory, the elderly should be expected to spend down their assets in retirement, leaving assets for bequests only if the expected life span has been overestimated.

Mounting empirical evidence suggests, however, that older people as a group may not consume their resources as they age. Economists have speculated that many people may either intend not to consume all of their resources in retirement, saving in part to leave bequests, or may be unwilling to consume their resources due to uncertainty about life expectancy and the cost of retirement (Davies 1981; Menchik and David 1983; Mirer 1979).

There are currently no studies that measure directly the effect of aging on the consumption of resources. This is largely because existing data are from cross-sectional studies that enable us to compare older and younger groups of the elderly, but not to follow a group as it ages. The data and conclusions presented here should be considered suggestive and not definitive. Greatly expanded sample sizes and more explicit data are needed to assess reliably the economic status of the oldest of the older Americans.

INCOME OF THE OLDEST OLD

Strictly on the basis of annual cash income, today's generation of the oldest old has substantially fewer resources than today's young elderly. Not only is the median income of aged units in the oldest age group substantially lower than the median for younger groups, but also there is a much greater concentration of the oldest old in the lowest income ranges.

The median family cash income of the oldest cohort (aged 80 and older) is less than three-quarters that of the youngest cohort (aged 65 to 69). Tabulations from the March 1985 Current Population Survey (CPS) show that in 1984 the median cash income of couples aged 80 and older was $13,190 compared with $19,500 for couples aged 65 to 69, and the median family income of single persons aged 80 and older was $5,940 compared with $7,510 for persons aged 65 to 69 (see Table 17–1).

The oldest old are also much more heavily concentrated in low income ranges than are the young elderly. The clearest indicator of this difference is the poverty

Table 17–1 Median Total Money Income (in dollars) of Aged Units by Age Group

Marital status and sex	Age of aged units			
	65–69	70–74	75–79	80+
Married couples	19.500	17,480	15,100	13,190
Unmarried persons	7,510	7,100	6,660	5,940
Men	8,190	8,050	7,040	6,710
Women	7,340	6,910	6,530	5,850

Source: Grad (1985, table 12).

Table 17-2 Percentage of Older Persons by Ratio of Family Income to Poverty Level, by Age Group

Ratio of income to poverty level (%)	Age of person			
	65–69	70–74	75–79	80+
<100	9	10	13	17
100–124	6	8	9	12
125–149	6	8	9	9
Total <150	21	26	31	38

Source: Grad (1985, unpublished tabulations).

rate. Persons aged 80 and older are nearly twice as likely to be poor or near poor as those aged 65 to 69. In 1984, 17 percent of persons aged 80 and older had incomes below the poverty level, compared with only 9 percent of persons aged 65 to 69. Another 21 percent of the oldest old had incomes that were between one and one half times the poverty level compared with only 12 percent of the youngest group (see Table 17–2).

That there is a higher concentration of the oldest old at low income levels is also apparent from a comparison of the income distribution curves for younger and older groups. Figure 17–1 reveals a high concentration of the population aged 80 and older in the income range of $3,000 to $7,000, while the population aged 65 to 69 is fairly evenly distributed across the income range from $3,000 to $20,000 (Grad 1985).

Why is there such a substantial difference in the incomes of the older and younger cohorts? Two alternative hypotheses are plausible. The first is that income declines with age. The second is that the younger cohorts have earned better retirement income benefits than their predecessors. Of course, cross-sectional data provide no basis for drawing definitive conclusions on either point. However, some clues are worth noting.

Some evidence is consistent with the view that income declines with age. A study by Duncan, Hill, and Rodgers (1985) of changes in economic status over time, using longitudinal data from the University of Michigan's Panel Study of Income Dynamics (PSID), indicates that the average economic well-being of older persons declines steadily once they retire. This study shows that an improvement in the economic status of the elderly as a group between 1968 and 1982 was largely due to the fact that new generations of retirees were reaching retirement with more resources. Retired individuals, on average, experienced deterioration in their economic status as they aged (Duncan, Hill, and Rodgers 1985).

Two factors seem to contribute significantly to a decline in economic status associated with aging: change in marital status and change in sources of income. Of the two, the change in marital status appears to be more important.

The marital characteristics of the younger and older cohorts of the elderly are substantially different. Most people reach age 65 with a spouse and lose their spouse as they grow older. Most of the surviving spouses are women because women as a group have longer life expectancies.

Most of the difference between the income distributions of the oldest old and the youngest old can be attributed to the greater concentration of single persons in the

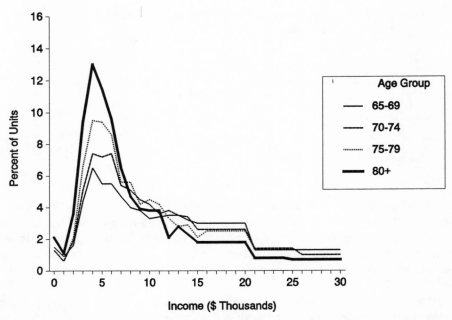

Figure 17–1   Distribution of income by age, all aged units, 1984. (Source: Grad 1985)

oldest-old population. Single elderly persons[1] in each of the age groups have similarly shaped income distributions: they are heavily concentrated in low income ranges, with a sharply peaked distribution (see Figure 17–2). The income distribution for all persons in the oldest age group has a shape that is similar to those of the distributions for single persons in the various age groups (see Figure 17–1). By contrast, the income distributions for elderly couples of all ages are much flatter. Again, there is relatively little difference in the shape of the income distribution for couples in the various age groups (see Figure 17–3). The income distribution for all persons in the youngest age group has a shape more like the general shape for elderly couples (see Figure 17–1).

The great difference between the shapes of the single elderly and elderly couple income distributions, and the similarity of the distributions of various age groups within each category, suggest that marital status has more of an effect on the shape of the income distribution than does age. Thus marital status change, particularly due to the death of a spouse, is an important factor contributing to age cohort differences among the elderly.

The effect of the death of a spouse on income is suggested by comparisons of the median incomes of different groups. The median incomes of older women of different ages but the same marital status are fairly similar. Unmarried women aged 80 and older have four-fifths as much income on average as unmarried women aged 65 to 69 (see Table 17–1). At the same time, the difference in incomes for women with different marital statuses is substantial. Widowed older women have a median income ($6,440) only one-third that of older couples ($17,250) (see Table 17–3).

[1] The word "persons" is used throughout this section, rather than the more technically precise term "units," with the understanding that income has actually been measured for single and couple units, not persons.

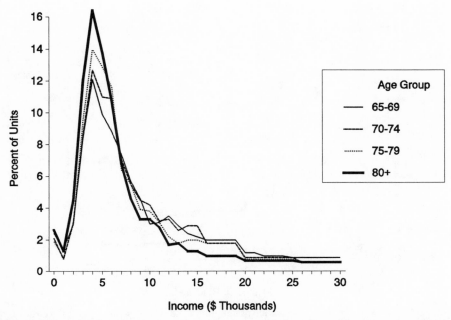

Figure 17–2 Distribution of income by age, aged nonmarried persons, 1984. (Source: Grad 1985)

There are a number of ways in which the death of a spouse can precipitate a substantial loss of income, particularly for women who have not earned retirement benefits on the basis of their own work histories. For one, a surviving dependent spouse receives only two-thirds the Social Security benefits previously received by the couple. In addition, in the absence of joint-and-survivor benefits, pension annuities received by a retired worker are forfeited upon that worker's death. Although joint-and-survivor benefits are gradually becoming more common, they are rare among current retirees, particularly among older cohorts. Finally, the death of a working older spouse will result in a loss of earned income.

Table 17–3 Median Total Money Income of Aged Units by Marital Status

Marital status	Median income (in dollars)
Married couples	17,250
Single persons	
Men	
Widowed	7,900
Divorced	6,980
Never married	6,620
Women	
Widowed	6,440
Divorced	6,750
Never married	8,490

Source: Grad (1985, table 13).

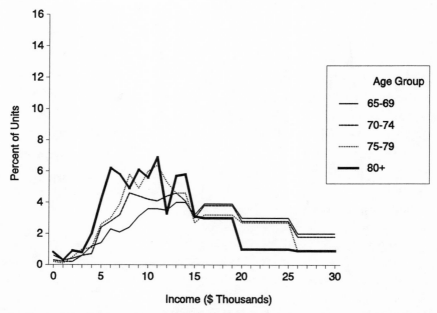

Figure 17–3   Distribution of income by age, aged married couples, 1984. (Source: Grad 1985)

Duncan, Hill, and Rodgers' study of longitudinal data from the PSID affirmed the importance of living arrangements to the economic well-being of the elderly. Using various measures of economic well-being over three separate time periods, the authors found that at least two-thirds of the gap in economic well-being between elderly men and women would be eliminated if the chances of an older woman being in a husband–wife family were the same as those of an older man (Duncan, Hill, and Rodgers 1985).

The relationship between the death of a spouse and loss of income is further supported by an analysis of longitudinal data from the Retirement History Survey (Holden, Burkhauser, and Myers 1986). This study found poverty rates among a group of elderly widowed women to be twice as high as before they became widows. The study further concluded that poverty is not always a permanent status for women impoverished by widowhood. It was found that the incomes of over 80 percent of the widows who became poor during the survey rose above the poverty level within 3 years of their entry into poverty, and only 50 percent of these later reentered poverty. It is not clear how significant a phenomenon the impoverishment and emergence from poverty of elderly widows is, because the study did not measure the size of the income adjustment that moved people across the poverty threshold.

Widowhood by itself, however, is not a complete explanation for lower incomes among the older age cohorts. Those who have survived as couples into the oldest ages also have lower average incomes ($13,190) than couples now entering the youngest cohorts of the elderly ($19,500) (see Table 17–1). The difference in the amount of income received by various age groups also appears to be associated with a change in the composition of income. Older cohorts are more dependent on Social Security and asset income than are younger cohorts (see Figure 17–4). Earnings, in particular,

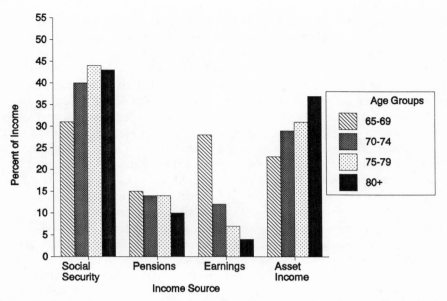

Figure 17–4   Income sources of aged units by age group, 1984. (Source: Grad 1985)

disappear as a major source of income in the older cohorts. Although the group aged 65 to 69 earns 28 percent of its total income, the group aged 80 and older earns only 4 percent of its income. Social Security takes the place of earnings, providing 43 percent of the total income to the cohort aged 80 and older, compared with only 31 percent of the total income received by the group aged 65 to 69 (see Table 17–4). However, Social Security, pensions, and asset income do not fully replace lost earnings. In addition, average benefit levels from each of those sources are lower for the oldest group than for the youngest. Social Security benefits, for example, average $5,070 for beneficiaries aged 80 and older, compared with $6,010 for those aged 65 to 69, many of whom receive reduced benefits because they still work (Grad 1985).

The decline in the median income of couples may also be attributable to erosion in the value of benefits as people age. Although some pension plans provide ad hoc

Table 17–4   Percentage of Aggregate Income of Aged Units, by Income Source and Age Group

	Age of aged unit			
Source of income	65–69	70–74	75–79	80+
Social security	31	40	44	43
Private pension	7	6	6	4
Public pension	8	8	8	6
Earnings	28	12	7	4
Asset income	23	29	31	37
Public assistance	1	1	1	2
Other	3	3	3	3
Total	100	100	100	100

Source: Grad (1985, table 46).

inflation adjustments, most pension benefits are less than fully indexed and lose real value with each passing year. A benefit first paid at age 65 in a period of low annual inflation (5 percent), and never adjusted, would be worth only 38 percent of its initial value by the time the retiree reaches age 85. In addition, if individuals draw down their assets in retirement, their income from assets will also decline. Thus, an increasing reliance on retirement and asset income and the declining role of earnings in the incomes of older cohorts may account, in part, for the lower income levels.

Although it seems plausible that aging itself causes some erosion in income, a credible alternative hypothesis may be that younger cohorts today are entering retirement with greater resources than older cohorts did more than 20 years ago. The first generation to spend a full working career covered by Social Security reached retirement age in the 1980s. This new cohort of retirees has also benefited from the growth of private pension coverage in the 1950s and 1960s, and from the post–World War II boom in real wages and disposable income. By comparison, those who are today aged 80 or older reached retirement age in the late 1950s or early 1960s, with relatively short periods of Social Security and pension coverage to their credit.

As the Social Security program and private pension plans have matured, each succeeding wave of retiring workers has received higher average benefits than the previous wave. For example, the average real Social Security benefit paid to a worker retiring at age 65 increased in constant 1984 dollars from $3,607 in 1967 to $5,485 in 1984 (U.S. Department of Health and Human Services 1985, table 36). In addition to the growth in retirement benefits, asset income has increased substantially, causing an overall increase in the share of total income from assets. The median asset income for those 65 and older increased in constant 1984 dollars from $934 in 1967 to $2,100 in 1984 (Bixby et al. 1975; Grad 1985). As a result, the share of aggregate income to aged units from assets rose from 15 percent to 28 percent over the same period (Grad 1985; Upp 1983). Some of the growth in income from assets is the result of higher current yields from financial markets in recent years. It is also possible, however, that the entrance of new generations of workers into retirement with larger amounts of personal savings than previous generations has also contributed to this effect.

The relative income of future generations of the oldest old will depend upon the extent to which this pattern of growth in retirement benefits of succeeding generations continues and the extent to which "aging effects" erode income after retirement. If future generations can be expected to have higher real incomes at retirement and if the aging effect is relatively weak, then future cohorts of the oldest old may have relatively more income in relation to younger cohorts than today's oldest group. On the other hand, if future benefit levels do not grow in real terms or if the aging effect is substantial, then the oldest old will continue to have relatively low incomes into the future.

One plausible view of the future is that the relative increase in retirement benefits we have seen in recent decades will not continue over the long run. For a short time, there may be a continued increase in retirement income of the oldest cohorts as cohorts of new retirees with greater initial benefits continue to pass into the oldest age groups. In the long run, the real growth in retirement benefits may level off for several reasons. First, because future cohorts of retirees have full wage histories covered by public and private pensions, initial benefits should generally be fixed in relation to preretirement wages. Second, for succeeding generations of retirees at the beginning of the next century, Social Security benefits paid at any specific age will actually start to decline due to the scheduled increase in Social Security's retirement age. Third, Social Security and pension coverage of workers is not likely to continue to expand in the future. Social Security coverage is now nearly universal. Pension coverage, which grew rapidly with coverage of the manufacturing work force in the 1950s and 1960s, has actually declined slightly in recent years due to the decline in manufacturing jobs and the growth in the less well covered service sector. Fourth, real wage losses in recent years may slow the growth in average wage histories of coming generations of retirees. These trends imply that there could be a leveling off or even a decline in the relative incomes of future generations of the elderly.

Any decline in real future benefits is likely to be moderated to some extent by labor force and benefit changes, which may raise future benefit levels for some groups of workers. The pension and Social Security benefits of women retiring in the future with more continuous labor-force attachment than previously retired generations will be more directly related to their own earnings and thus should be somewhat higher. In addition, pension reforms, enacted in the 1984 Retirement Equity Act or the 1986 Tax Reform Act to increase pension receipt and improve benefits for divorced and widowed women, and lower-income and mobile workers, may redistribute pension income within future cohorts of retirees from couples to surviving spouses and from those with large pensions to those with small pensions. These changes should result in a broader income distribution and higher average income for those who survive into the oldest age groups.

The incomes of future generations of the oldest old will be affected by a combination of benefits earned over their working lives and events during retirement that affect their income levels. Significant improvements in benefit levels or changes to protect the incomes of the elderly from inflation, marital-status changes, or other events would reduce the vulnerability of the oldest old.

ASSETS

Although income may decline with age, life-cycle theory suggests that assets are converted to make up the loss and maintain level consumption after retirement, leaving those who live to the oldest ages with few remaining assets. Empirical evidence, however, suggests that older people may actually retain or increase their assets. Even if the elderly delay converting their assets to income, they still receive economic benefit in the form of "service flows" from the use of housing they own and live in, automobiles, and other accumulated durable goods (Danzinger et al. 1983).

Information on the assets of the very old is, unfortunately, limited. Nonetheless, data from more recent surveys have helped to provide a clearer picture than was available from earlier studies. Past studies usually imputed wealth from reported asset income and rarely measured it directly. In addition, most surveys of income were thought to substantially undercount asset income, either because the questions did not clearly specify all forms of asset income or because respondents were hesitant to report certain types of asset income, particularly nontaxable types. Data from the more recent Survey of Income and Program Participation (SIPP) are an improvement over traditional asset data in that they have a low nonresponse rate on questions about types of assets. However, nonresponse on amount of assets remains a problem, and assets of the upper end of the income distribution are undercounted.

SIPP is also an improvement over previous cross-sectional studies in that it uses panels of respondents to collect information over short periods of time. The time periods are too short, however, to help answer the questions of whether and when the elderly spend down their assets as they age. The SIPP data are also limited in that they measure the assets of households, which in the case of elderly households could actually be owned by younger household members. Thus, it is possible, particularly in the case of the oldest old, who are most likely to live with their children, that the asset holdings of the elderly are overstated. With these caveats in mind, however, some interesting patterns are suggested by these and other available data.

The overwhelming majority of the elderly hold assets primarily in the form of home equity. Nearly 75 percent of persons aged 65 and older own their own homes, and more than 80 percent of these own their homes "free and clear" (U.S. Bureau of the Census 1983, 1984). Home ownership is widespread among elderly of almost all income levels and living arrangements (Struyk and Soldo 1980).

The most substantial asset of most elderly persons is their home equity. Bruce Jacobs has determined, from tabulations of the 1983 Annual Housing Survey, that nearly half (46 percent) of all elderly homeowners had net home equity in excess of $50,000. Many of these "house rich" elderly are actually "cash poor." Nearly one-quarter (23 percent) of the poor elderly homeowners had at least $50,000 in home equity. Jacobs contends that this disparity between income and net worth is either a result of the recent dramatic appreciation in the value of real estate that the elderly bought cheaply or a result of declines in income at the onset of retirement or widowhood. In either case, if this home equity could be converted to annuities, he suggests, single older persons, on average, could raise their incomes by 25 percent and married older couples could raise their income by 10 percent.

Although the oldest age group has, on average, the smallest amount of home equity, this group would benefit most from home-equity conversion by receiving larger monthly payments over a shorter life expectancy. Jacobs estimates that reverse mortgage payments could provide the majority (61 percent) of homeowners aged 80 and older with $3,000 a year or more in added income. By comparison, only 11 percent of the homeowners aged 65 to 69 could receive equivalent reverse mortgage payments (see Table 17–5) (Jacobs 1986). Mobility and trading down of housing to free up assets is thought to be relatively infrequent among the elderly, however. One recent study indicates that rather than reducing the equity in their homes, the elderly appear to accumulate more home equity as they age. Even among those who would benefit most from conversion—those with low incomes and relatively high home equity—there is little evidence that older persons convert these assets (Merrill 1984).

Financial assets are neither as widespread nor as evenly distributed as home equity. Although some elderly persons have accumulated substantial financial assets, many have accumulated few or no assets by the time they reach retirement. Nearly one-fourth of SIPP respondents aged 65 and older reported no income of any type from interest-earning financial assets. Of those who did report assets other than home equity, 33 percent owned less than $10,000 total, whereas only 15 percent owned $100,000 or more (see Table 17–6) (U.S. Bureau of the Census 1986a).

Table 17–5 Percentage of Homeowners by Size of Yearly Reverse Mortgage Payments and Age

Yearly payments (in dollars)	Age of homeowner			
	65–69	70–74	75–79	80+
Less than 1,000	39	30	19	11
1,000–1,999	36	32	27	15
2,000–2,999	14	21	23	13
3,000–4,999	8	13	19	30
5,000 or more	3	4	12	31
Total	100	100	100	100

Source: Jacobs (1986).

The oldest old have significantly lower median net worth than the younger elderly. The median nonhousing net worth for persons aged 80 and older ($13,425) is only two-thirds as great as the median ($20,000) for persons aged 75 to 79 (see Table 17–7 and Figure 17–5). The oldest age group also has a higher percentage of persons with few or no assets than the younger elderly age groups. Over 42 percent of those aged 80 and older had assets of less than $10,000, compared with 35 percent of those aged 75 to 79 (see Table 17–7) (U.S. Bureau of the Census 1986b).

The fact that, at a given time, all elderly age groups but the oldest have similar net worths may suggest that people continue to accumulate assets after retirement until they reach the oldest age group and are forced to begin consuming them. It is conceivable that the elderly reserve their assets in anticipation of inadequate incomes and substantial health-care costs later in life.

OTHER RESOURCES

The economic status of the elderly as a group is also influenced by the value of in-kind benefits they receive and by the effect of tax payments on their net incomes. These effects are discussed here for the entire group over age 65 because there is little information on unique effects for the oldest old.

Noncash benefits provided by the government or by employers improve an indi-

Table 17–6 Percentage of Households by Net Worth (less home equity) and Age of Head

Net worth (in dollars)	Age group			
	65–69	70–74	75–79	80+
Less than 5,000	29.3	31.2	31.9	34.3
5–25,000	23.6	25.6	22.5	25.6
25–50,000	16.0	15.3	12.9	13.9
50–100,000	15.7	15.7	20.0	15.0
100,000+	15.4	12.2	12.7	11.2
Total	100.0	100.0	100.0	100.0

Source: U.S. Bureau of the Census (1986b).

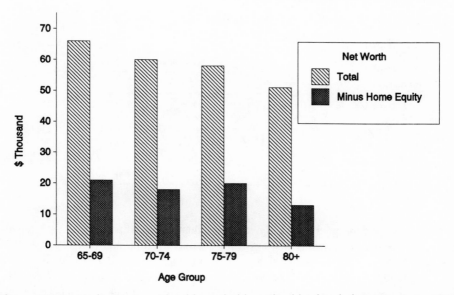

Figure 17–5 Median net worth of households with older heads by age group, 1984. (Source: U.S. Bureau of the Census. 1986a)

vidual's economic status by reducing the demand on cash income to purchase similar goods and services. Thus, they act as a substitute for cash income. The elderly as a group, because a large proportion of them no longer work, rely heavily on government-provided noncash benefits. The most significant benefit is Medicare hospital insurance, provided without regard to income to over 95 percent of the elderly. Only about one-fifth of the elderly receive Medicaid, energy assistance, food stamps, subsidized housing, or other means-tested benefits aimed at improving the economic status of those with the lowest cash incomes (U.S. Senate 1984, 330). Most of those who receive in-kind benefits other than health insurance receive only one of these benefits. Only 4 percent of the elderly receive more than one nonhealth benefit (U.S. Dept of Health and Human Services 1986b, 19).

Tax payments, on the other hand, reduce the economic resources of the elderly. Actually, the federal tax burden on the elderly is relatively light due to four special

Table 17–7 Median Net Worth of Elderly by Age Group

Net worth	Age group			
	65–69	70–74	75–79	80 +
Total net worth				
Median	$65,568	$59,885	$57,756	$50,939
Percent with zero	3.1	4.0	4.2	4.1
Net worth (less home equity)				
Median	$20,942	$18,399	$20,000	$13,425
Percent with zero	4.3	4.9	5.2	6.0

Source: U.S. Bureau of the Census (1986b).

tax provisions that enable them to receive tax-free income or pay reduced taxes. Specifically, the elderly have benefited from:

1. Exclusion from taxable income of Social Security, railroad retirement, and veterans' pension benefits—although the Social Security and railroad retirement exclusions were limited by legislation enacted in 1983;
2. Additional personal exemption for elderly taxpayers—although the additional exemption was eliminated with the increase in the personal exemption for all taxpayers beginning in 1987;
3. Special elderly tax credit, targeted to relatively low-income taxpayers; and
4. One-time exclusion of capital gains from home sales after age 55.

Additionally, older persons without earnings from work no longer pay the Social Security payroll tax. Just over half of all older Americans actually pay federal income taxes. In 1984, only 16 million persons aged 65 or older—57 percent of the elderly population—filed federal income tax returns with any reported taxable income (U.S. Department of Treasury 1986).

The effects of state and local taxes on the elderly are less clear. In many states, older taxpayers benefit from special state income tax exemptions or exclusions of retirement income that often parallel federal income-tax provisions. On the other hand, older persons pay their full share of state sales taxes and, in many cases, pay full property taxes. The property tax is often the most burdensome for older home-owners because of the appreciation of the market value of their homes. In many states and municipalities, this burden is ameliorated for low-income elderly by special "homestead exemptions" and "circuit-breakers" designed to protect them from high property taxes relative to their income.

Tax payments should take up a smaller portion of income for older age groups than for the younger elderly because the older groups depend less upon taxable earnings and depend more on nontaxable retirement benefits. Recent data from the 1983–1984 Consumer Expenditure Survey supports this conclusion for younger elder age cohorts. It does not, however, for the oldest old (see Table 17–8). The average percentage of income paid in taxes by persons aged 80 and older—roughly 9.1 percent of income—is the highest percentage of all aged cohorts. Although this result is surprising, it may reflect a greater reliance on taxable asset income and capital gains from the conversions of assets to income. It is also possible, however, that this result is not significant given the small sample sizes.

Although the effects of taxes and in-kind benefits on resources offset each other, they do not necessarily affect the same elderly individuals. In fact, it is likely that the group receiving most of the means-tested benefits pay little in income taxes, if they file returns at all. Thus, the combined effect of taxes and in-kind benefits most likely improves the economic status of those with the lowest incomes and reduces the economic status of those with the highest incomes. The question is whether the combination of taxes and in-kind benefits offsets the lower cash incomes of the oldest old and whether these factors give equal advantage to all age groups among the elderly.

In a broad context, it remains to be seen whether, as the elderly age, lose spouses, and suffer declines in income, their other resources enable them to maintain level

Table 17–8   Average Consumer Expenditures by Age Group

Variable	Age group			
	65–69	70–74	75–79	80+
Income pretax (dollars)	17,550	15,579	12,257	10,632
Tax payments (dollars)	1,346	699	610	967
Total expenditures (dollars)	16,586	14,462	11,559	9,516
Persons per unit	2.0	1.8	1.6	1.5
Average expenditures (in dollars)				
Food	2,930	2,595	2,034	1,736
Shelter	2,515	2,266	1,957	1,817
Utilities	1,620	1,563	1,281	1,242
Clothing	793	608	412	247
Transportation	3,361	2,533	1,504	1,020
Health care	1,224	1,503	1,458	1,277
Other	4,143	3,394	2,913	2,177
Percentage of total expenditures				
Food	17.7	17.9	17.6	18.2
Shelter	15.2	15.7	16.9	19.1
Utilities	9.8	10.8	11.1	13.1
Clothing	4.8	4.2	3.6	2.6
Transportation	20.3	17.5	13.0	10.7
Health care	7.4	10.4	12.6	13.4
Other	25.0	23.5	25.2	22.9
Total	100.0	100.0	100.0	100.0

Source: U.S. Department of Labor (1986b).

consumption in old age. A review of data on consumer expenditures by the old and young elderly may shed some light on this question.

CONSUMER EXPENDITURES

Evidence from the Consumer Expenditure Surveys suggests that today's oldest cohort of the elderly purchases fewer goods and services than younger cohorts, with the significant exception of health care (U.S. Department of Labor, 1986a, b). Reported consumption is not a full measure of the standard of living for older persons, because a larger portion of their overall consumption is not paid for with cash but is derived from the service value of assets. For consumption that is purchased with cash, the major differences in the spending patterns of older and younger elderly cohorts seem to be related to the lower levels of income, smaller households, and different needs of the oldest households.

Expenditures by the oldest households are constrained by significantly lower household income. As a result, the oldest households buy less of everything (except health care) than younger elderly households. Average spending by the oldest units in 1984 was $9,516, compared with $17,550 for the youngest elderly units (see Table 17–8).

Although the smaller size of older households may account for some of the difference in expenditure levels, older households still spend less on a per-person basis than younger households. To some extent, older households may need to buy less overall and to buy a different mix of products because they are smaller households. The oldest units in the Consumer Expenditure Survey have an average of only 1.5 persons, compared with 2.0 persons in units headed by persons aged 65 to 69. Even adjusting for unit size, however, the oldest units still spend considerably less than the youngest. The oldest units actually spend nearly $2,000 less per person than the youngest elderly units ($6,344 per person for units aged 80 and older, compared with $8,293 per person for units aged 65 to 69). Because older households are smaller, they are also devoting a larger share of their budget to costs that vary little with household size—such as housing and utilities. At the same time, older households spend a fixed or smaller share of their budget on costs that can vary with household size—such as food and clothing.

Health care is the only category of spending on which the oldest old actually spend as much in cash—and a much greater share of their budget—as younger groups of the elderly. Consumer units in which the principal person was aged 80 or older spent, on average, about as much out of pocket for health care in 1984 ($1,277) as units with a principal person aged 65 to 69 ($1,224). Because the total budget for older households was smaller, health costs were a much more significant part of the budget of the oldest old than of the youngest old. Overall, households with a principal person aged 80 or older spent 13.4 percent of their budget on health care, compared with only 7.4 percent for households with a principal person aged 65 to 69 (see Figure 17–6).

This statistical picture of the health-care spending of the oldest old may under-

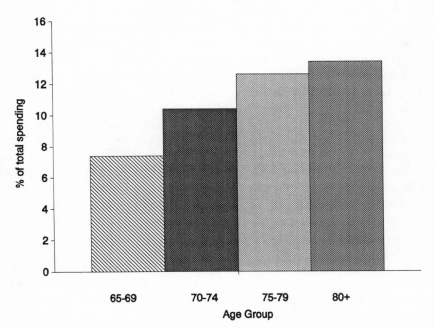

Figure 17–6 Health care expenses as a percentage of total spending of older persons by age group, 1983–84. (Source: U.S. Department of Labor 1986b)

state their actual health-care spending because it does not include those elderly already in nursing homes, consuming most of their resources to pay for care, and "spending down" to Medicaid eligibility. The cost of a nursing-home stay, which ranges between $12,000 and $50,000 a year, is easily the most significant and financially destructive expense for the oldest old. Although Medicaid plays a major role in paying for nursing-home care—covering 40 percent of those discharged from nursing homes—many older persons pay for nursing-home care themselves, sometimes spending down their resources to become eligible for Medicaid. Recent estimates reveal that about 10 percent of those discharged on Medicaid spent down during their stay, while 36 percent of all those discharged were private pay at both the beginning and the end of their stay (Spence and Wiener 1989).

The tremendous amounts spent on nursing-home care are not measured in the Consumer Expenditure Survey because this survey, like most of the others referenced in this chapter, collects data only from the noninstitutionalized population. At any one time, 20 percent of the oldest old—those aged 85 and older—are permanent or long-term residents of nursing homes, and thus are excluded from any of the measurements of economic well-being (U.S. Senate 1986a, 233). These are the elderly who are the sickest and pay the most for health care. Excluding this group from the survey minimizes health-care costs and the effect of these costs on the assets and resources of the oldest old.

CONCLUSIONS

This generation of the oldest old has, in total, substantially fewer resources than younger elderly cohorts to meet the health-care expenses that loom large in their budgets. Will this difference in economic resources between the old and young elderly continue for future generations of retirees because of economic changes associated with the aging process itself, or is this difference merely a cohort or historical effect? If the latter is true, can we expect future generations entering into the oldest ages to be better prepared for the higher health costs they will encounter?

Crude evidence suggests that the elderly do deplete their resources as they grow older. Without longitudinal data, there can be no definitive statement on this subject. Cross-sectional data, however, do seem to indicate that loss of a spouse can be associated with a great reduction in income. In addition, the oldest cohorts no longer have employment earnings and have lower real benefit levels than younger cohorts. The oldest old have the lowest relative pension benefits, in part because pension benefits tend not to be fully indexed for inflation. Finally, the oldest old have substantially lower net worth than younger groups, which, in combination with the similarity in net worth among other elderly age groups, suggests that there may be some tendency to convert and consume assets at the oldest ages.

Although it is reasonable to assume that some of the difference in resources between today's young and old elderly is due to the loss or devaluation of income with age, it is also reasonable to assume that some of the difference is the result of better-prepared generations reaching retirement. If succeeding waves of retirees continue to retire with better resources, the disparity in income between the young and old elderly will continue. If future generations reach retirement no better prepared than their predecessors, then some of the disparity may well diminish over time.

What capacity, then, do the old elderly appear to have for greater cost sharing in their health and long-term care expenses? Medicare already imposes considerable cost sharing on the elderly through premiums, deductibles, coinsurance, and excess charges. Cost sharing does not vary with the income of the elderly, and so the poor and the old elderly, who do not have coverage under gap-filling health plans, pay a higher percentage of their health cost out of pocket than other elderly beneficiaries. Surprisingly, only one-fourth of elderly poor Medicare enrollees are covered by Medicaid for these costs (U.S. Senate 1984, 384). With rapidly rising health-care costs, spending by the elderly for health care is also rising and consuming an increasing share of their income. Already, people aged 65 and older pay about 25 percent of their medical bills (including about 50 percent of their long-term-care bills) directly out of pocket. This expense is estimated to consume about 15 percent of per capita income, up from 12 percent in 1977 (U.S. Senate 1986b, 79–80). Without any changes in public policy, it is likely that health care will become an increasing financial burden for the elderly in the near future.

Medical and long-term-care costs for the oldest old are the highest of any of the elderly, and yet the oldest old appear to have the fewest economic resources by all measures. Additional cost sharing of any kind would greatly increase the already substantial financial burden of health costs for the oldest old. If beneficiaries are to pay more of the costs, the choice of cost-sharing measures would greatly affect the relative distribution of resources among the young and oldest old.

Cost sharing related to utilization would impose the greatest burden on the oldest old, because their use of medical and long-term-care services is greatest. For example, modifications to raise Medicare deductibles and copayments, lower the Medicare lifetime-payment cap, or establish experience-rated premiums would substantially increase the exposure of the oldest old to health-care expenses and shift more of the health-care costs from the younger to the oldest old.

Cost sharing allocated on a per capita basis, such as a premium increase, would not be as burdensome to the oldest old as utilization-based measures. Still, fixed-dollar increases would raise the percentage of the household budget spent on health care by a greater amount for the oldest old than for the younger elderly. Proposals to limit catastrophic expenses for the elderly by enabling them to gain the protection of an annual cap on out-of-pocket health care expenses would protect the oldest old from utilization-based increases in health-care costs. At the same time, however, the fixed premium and indexed dollar limit on annual out-of-pocket costs would consume a larger proportion of the incomes of the oldest old than of the younger elderly (U.S. Department of Health and Human Services 1986a).

Of all approaches, use of means-tested or age-adjusted payments would allocate the smallest share of cost to the oldest old. Proposals for income-related premiums or for advance funding of health or long-term-care insurance would have a more equitable effect on the budgets of older persons of different ages. A recent proposal to raise the age of eligibility for Medicare from age 65 to 67 would similarly have protected the oldest old. However, the increase in age of eligibility would substantially increase the exposure of some of the younger elderly to health-care costs.

Already facing unpredictable and potentially catastrophic risks of medical expenses, older persons may well be reluctant to consume their financial assets and convert their home equity too rapidly as they age. Nevertheless, the resources they retain to their oldest ages provide only a limited and nonliquid reserve against unanticipated expenses. Most of the oldest old have their assets in home equity, which is not easily converted to income when medical bills are due. Many of those with more liquid assets appear to have quite limited amounts. Thus, the consequence of a public policy that inadvertently places the greatest burden on the oldest old could well be self-defeating, eventually forcing an even greater reliance by this age group on publicly financed health care.

REFERENCES

Bixby, L.E., S. Grad, W.W. Kolodrubetz, P. Lauriat, and J. Murray. 1975. *Demographic and Economic Characteristics of the Aged: 1968 Social Security Survey.* DHHS research report no. 45. Washington: Social Security Administration, Office of Research and Statistics.

Danzinger, S., J. van der Gaag, E. Smolensky, and M.K. Taussig. 1983. Implications of the Relative Economic Status of the Elderly for Transfer Policy. In *Retirement and Economic Behavior,* eds. H. Aaron and G. Burtless, 175–96. Washington: Brookings Institution.

Davies, J.B. 1981. Uncertain Lifetime, Consumption, and Dissaving in Retirement. *Journal of Political Economy* 89:561–77.

Duncan, G.J., M. Hill, and W. Rodgers. 1985. The Changing Economic Status of the Young and Old. Paper prepared for the National Academy of Science Workshop on Demographic Change and the Well-Being of Dependents, September 5–7, Woods Hole, Mass.

Grad, S. 1985. *Income of the Population 55 and Over, 1984.* DHHS pub. no. 13–11871. Washington: Social Security Administration.

Holden, K.C., R.V. Burkhauser, and D.A. Myers. 1986. Income Transitions at Older Stages of Life: The Dynamics of Poverty. *The Gerontologist* 26:292–97.

Jacobs, B. 1986. The National Potential of Home Equity Conversion. *The Gerontologist* 26:496–504.

Menchik, P.L., and M. David. 1983. Income Distribution, Lifetime Savings, and Bequests. *American Economic Review* 73:672–90.

Merrill, S. 1984. Home Equity and the Elderly. In *Retirement and Economic Behavior,* eds. H. Aaron and G. Burtless, 197–227. Washington: Brookings Institution.

Mirer, T.W. 1979. The Wealth–Age Relation among the Aged. *American Economic Review* 69:435–43.

Modigliani, F., and R. Brumberg. 1954. Utility Analysis and the Consumption Function: An Interpretation of Cross-Section Data. In *Post-Keynesian Economics,* ed. K. Kurihara, 388–436. New Brunswick, N.J.: Rutgers University Press.

Spence, D., and Wiener, J. 1989. *Estimating the Extent of Medicaid Spending in Nursing Homes.* Draft report of The Brookings Institute, August 11, 1989.

Struyk, R.J., and B.J. Soldo. 1980. *Improving the Elderly's Housing.* Cambridge, Mass.: Ballinger.

Upp, M. 1983. Relative Importance of Various Income Sources of the Aged, 1980. *Social Security Bulletin* 46:3–10.

U.S. Bureau of the Census. 1983. *Residential Finance.* U.S. Census of Housing, HC80-5. Washington.

————. 1984. *Annual Housing Survey: 1983*. Current Housing Reports, series H-150-83. Washington.

————. 1986a. *Household Wealth and Asset Ownership: 1984. Data from the Survey of Income and Program Participation*. Washington, D.C.

————. 1986b. Tabulations from the Survey of Income and Program Participation, Wave 4. Washington. (Unpublished.)

————. 1985. *Social Security Bulletin, Annual Statistical Supplement, 1984–85*. Washington.

U.S. Department of Health and Human Services. 1986a. *Catastrophic Illness Expenses. A report to the President. Washington.*

U.S. Department of Health and Human Services, Social Security Administration. 1986b. *Income and Resources of the Population 65 and Over. A Chartbook*. Washington.

U.S. Department of Labor. 1986a. Consumer Expenditure Survey Results from 1984: *News.* Washington: Bureau of Labor Statistics.

————. 1986b. Tabulations from the 1983–84 Consumer Expenditure Surveys. Washington. (Unpublished.)

U.S. Department of Treasury, Internal Revenue Service. 1986. *Individual Income Tax Returns, 1984*. Washington.

U.S. Senate. Special Committee on Aging. 1984. *Developments in Aging, 1983*. Vol. 1. Washington.

————. 1986a. *Developments in Aging, 1985*. Vol. 1 Washington.

————. 1986b. *Developments in Aging, 1985*. Vol. 3. Washington.

VI
SOCIAL AND MEDICAL POLICY TOWARD THE OLDEST OLD

18

Sharing Increasing Costs on Declining Income: The Visible Dilemma of the Invisible Aged

BARBARA BOYLE TORREY

Today the federal government provides an estimated $50 billion in benefits and services to the 6 million people who are very old (80 years of age and over). These are more benefits than are given for all of the nonaged poor; it is also twice what is spent today for total veterans benefits or unemployment benefits in the United States. As the size of this age group grows disproportionately to the rest of the aged, their total benefits will increase faster than for any other beneficiary group.

Even though the very old are one of the most important federal beneficiary groups today, little information about their specific income benefits and economic resources is known. The federal government considers the aged a single beneficiary group of people 65 years of age and over, and data collectors consider them a single cohort. As a result the very old are virtually invisible to policy makers, program managers, and the public.

Before World War II, people 65 years of age and over were a very small beneficiary and cohort group, and therefore, summary statistics on the aged were appropriate. However, since World War II the number of people 65 years of age and over has more than doubled, and life expectancy at age 65 years has increased 23 percent. Consequently, today the aged are not only the largest single group of federal beneficiaries, they are also more diverse economically than the nonaged. Our information about them, however, has lagged behind their growing importance. While health statistics have recognized the importance of information about specific groups among the aged, the information about nonhealth federal benefits for the aged usually aggregates information about the elderly. And economic data about them are almost always provided for the aged as a whole rather than for age groups among the elderly. Yet, when the federal benefits and economic data for the aged are disaggregated, they describe a situation that is much more complex than the summary statistics suggest.

This chapter describes how the federal costs for the aged increase with age and

Originally published in the Milbank Memorial Fund Quarterly/*Health and Society*, Vol. 63, No. 2, 1985, pp. 377–94.

how the costs for the very old are estimated to grow disproportionately in the future. It then briefly describes recent proposals to share some of the costs of federal benefits and the effects of such proposals given the distribution of income and assets among the aged. And finally, it discusses the problems of sharing the costs for the very old between generations.

THE FEDERAL COSTS OF THE VERY OLD

The major federal benefits of the aged increase significantly as they age. As shown in Table 18–1, major federal benefits for the person who is 80 years of age and over are an estimated 16 percent more than for the person who is recently aged (65 to 69 years of age). This is the net result of larger medical and long-term care benefits offset by smaller Social Security benefits for the very old than for the newly aged.

The estimation of these federal benefits for the aged by age group in 1984 is an aggregation of what information exists about the age distribution of Medicare, Social Security, and long-term-care benefits. These estimates of federal benefits aggregate all benefits for those 80 years of age and over because that was the oldest age group used in the Medicare history sample in 1978 from which the Medicare information is derived. Because of the lack of federal data by age, the estimated aggregate and per capita federal benefits provided aged beneficiaries are more illustrative than definitive. However, estimates suggest how important it is to understand better what happens to federal benefits, both as beneficiaries age and as succeeding cohorts of the aged age.

The Medicare benefit estimates for each age group in Table 18–1 are from the Medicare history sample of 1978. They were adjusted by the medical consumer price index (CPI) to approximate the benefits in 1984 dollars. As can be seen in Table 18–1, people aged 80 and over receive, on average, 77 percent more Medicare benefits than the younger old. Eighty-three percent of the increase in Medicare benefits between the young and old elderly is because of the increase in hospital insurance (HI)

Table 18–1 Major Federal Benefits for the Aged in 1984

		Per capita benefits (in dollars)					
Age of beneficiary	Population[a] (in thousands)	Medicare[b]			Social Security[c] (OASI)	Federal cost of long-term care (LTC)[d]	Total OASI, HI, SMI, and LTC
		HI	SMI	Subtotal			
65–69	9,095	885	517	1,402	5,689	60	7,151
70–74	7,501	995	559	1,554	5,568	60	7,182
75–79	5,409	1,238	592	1,830	5,425	262	7,517
80 years and older	5,980	1,781	704	2,485	4,972	864	8,321

[a]U.S. Bureau of the Census, 1984.

[b]Medicare history sample: average Medicare reimbursement for 1978 converted to 1984 dollars.

[c]*Social Security Bulletin. Annual Statistical Supplement* (1983). 1982 benefits adjusted by increase in CPI to estimate 1984 benefits.

[d]The federal per capita cost of long-term care is based on the probability of needing the care and age-specific costs, as described in U.S. Public Health Service (1983).

benefits; the supplementary medical insurance (SMI) benefit, which pays some of the outpatient health costs, increases relatively little as a person ages.

Social Security estimates of benefits by age are for specific categories of beneficiaries. The estimates shown in Table 18–1 are for average benefits for retirees, who are the largest group of aged Social Security beneficiaries. The per capita benefits, however, are somewhat higher than the average benefits for other Social Security beneficiaries, who include dependents and survivors. Average Social Security benefits for the very old retirees are 13 percent less, relative to the newly retired. In general, the newly retired have a higher real wage history than older retirees. Because the wage history is the basis of the calculation of the primary Social Security annuity, the higher wage histories of the newly old result in higher benefits than those received by the very old.

The federal benefits that increase the most as a person ages are those for long-term care. These estimates are also the most speculative because the calculation of total federal long-term care benefits are based on a number of assumptions. The long-term-care estimates in Table 18–1 include benefits provided primarily by Medicaid and the Veterans Administration. They do not include the long-term-care benefits that are provided by Medicare because those benefits have already been included in the estimates of Medicare benefits by age group. They also do not include the long-term-care benefits provided by the states through matching Medicaid payments for the aged. However, the state Medicaid benefits for long-term care are substantial and should be included in any study that goes beyond the focus of this chapter on federal benefits.

The estimated federal long-term-care costs are distributed among the aged by the 1983 probability that each age group was in a long-term care facility. Rough estimates of the annual per capita federal cost of long-term care not covered by Medicare in 1984 range from $60 for every person aged 65 to 74 to $864 for each person aged 80 and over. Although these numbers are not large on a per capita basis because most aged never use long-term care, the costs for the average 5 percent of the aged who annually actually require long-term care are, of course, considerably larger than the per capita numbers shown in Table 18–1.

Federal health and long-term-care benefits increase 129 percent between the youngest and oldest cohorts of the elderly. However, this increase is substantially offset by the decrease in the per capita Social Security benefits between the two cohorts. When the estimated per capita benefits for Medicare, Social Security, and long-term care are added together by age group, the total per capital benefit for the very old is only 16 percent higher than the benefit for the newly retired in 1984. This difference in the per capita benefits between the young aged and the very old is quite modest. When that difference is multiplied by the difference in the future rate of growth between the different age groups, however, the fiscal implications become more serious.

Between 1984 and the year 2000 the total number of aged is expected to increase 25 percent. The ratio of the aged to the potential work force, which is a measure of the aged-dependency burden, is likely to increase only 12 percent. These aggregate numbers, however, mask the aging of the aged cohort themselves and, therefore, tend to underestimate the potential size of future federal benefits.

By the year 2000 the group aged 65 to 69 will be virtually the same size as it is today, compared with a 66 percent increase in people 80 years of age and older. This growth of the group aged 80 and older, combined with their somewhat larger per capita benefits, will increase the total cost for this group rapidly. The aging of the aged population, however, will not increase health costs proportionately. Much of the increase in health costs for the older age groups can be attributed to the high cost of dying in the United States. If the life expectancy of the aged increases in the future as now projected, dying will occur at later ages than today (U.S. Bureau of the Census 1984). Therefore, the high costs of dying in the future will occur in older cohorts than it does today (Fuchs 1984). Utilization of health services at younger ages may also decline (Manton 1982).

Simply to illustrate the potential importance of the future growth in the very old federal beneficiaries, however, cost estimates are presented in Table 18–2 that assume that the real per capita costs of the major federal benefits remain the same in the future for the age cohorts of beneficiaries. These estimates probably overestimate future health costs for the reasons stated above. They also probably underestimate total federal costs because they do not include a number of other federal benefits for the aged such as civil service and military retirement, supplementary security income, and food stamps as disaggregated age-specific data are not readily available for these benefits. However, we do know that virtually all of the aged receive federal benefits of some kind. Therefore, the estimates in Table 18–2 assume that all of the aged in each age cohort receive the average per capita benefits presented in Table 18–1 even though we know that some receive considerably more and others less. This assumption, however, allows us to begin estimating how the aging of federal aged beneficiaries will affect federal benefits in the future. These estimates will be improved considerably when better program data become available and when better estimates can be made of health costs for future aged cohorts.

If we assume that the average real per capita federal benefits remain the same, then by 1995 the federal government will be paying $23 billion more (in 1984 dollars) than in 1984, solely because of the increase in the number of people aged 80 and older.[1] By 2000 it will be $33 billion more than in 1984 as shown in Table 18–2. The 66 percent real increase in estimated federal benefits provided to people aged 80 and older in the next 15 years is twice the increase for any other subgroup of the aged population. By the year 2000, total benefits for the very old will be larger than any other subgroup of the aged or, for that matter, the general population.

These population projections assume that mortality-rate improvements will continue in the future, but not as rapidly as in the last 15 years (U.S. Bureau of the Census 1984). If mortality-rate improvements do continue as rapidly as in the last 15 years, there will be 700,000 more people aged 80 and older in the year 2000 than are presently estimated. This would then increase the estimates of total federal benefits for this group 7 percent more than is suggested in Table 18–2.

The estimates of major federal benefits by age groups in the future are not definitive because the data are inadequate for precise estimates. But the changes in the magnitudes of the total benefit and the benefits by cohorts are suggestive of how the

---

[1] Estimates of major federal benefits disaggregated by age cohorts among the aged after 1984 are not available. Therefore 1984 is used as the base year in the projections.

Table 18–2 Effects of Population Changes Alone on Major Federal Benefits for the Aged, by Age Groups for 1984, 1990, 1995, and 2000[a] (population in thousands; benefits in billions of 1984 dollars)

	1984		1990		1995		2000	
Age group	Popu-lation	Total benefits	Popu-lation	Total benefits	Popu-lation	Total benefits	Popu-lation	Total benefits
65–69	9,095	65.0	9,996	71.5	9,736	69.6	9,096	65.0
70–74	7,501	53.9	8,039	57.7	8,767	63.0	8,581	61.6
75–79	5,409	40.7	6,260	47.1	6,640	49.9	7,295	54.8
80 years and older	5,980	49.8	7,402	61.6	8,745	72.8	9,949	82.8
Total	27,985	209.4	31,697	237.9	33,888	253.3	34,921	264.2

[a] Assumes 1984 average annual per capita Social Security, Medicare, and long-term-care benefits.

aging of the aged will affect federal programs. These projections reinforce the results of other projections that federal health benefits for the aged in particular are likely to increase substantially in the future. All of the projections raise issues about how the costs for these future benefits should be paid. One of the most important issues is whether the beneficiaries should share part of the costs of their future benefits.

COST-CONTROL PROPOSALS

The Medicare program is estimated to begin running large deficits within the next 10 years, according to program actuaries and analysts (Palmer and Torrey 1984). These deficits will be largely the result of the increase in the number of the aged, the aging of the aged population, and the increase in medical costs as a person ages. Some proposals to reduce or eliminate the pending deficits focus on constraining the cost of medical care, the income of the providers, or the provision of services. Other proposals suggest new kinds of insurance coverage, such as for long-term care. Still other proposals focus on sharing the federal costs more directly with the beneficiaries, their families, or their estates. These latter cost-sharing proposals raise the issues of what economic resources the aged and their families have and how well they could, in fact, share their costs. More specifically, these proposals raise the issues of whether the aged who have the most costs are those who have the individual or family resources to share them.

Proposals to share Medicare costs with the beneficiaries do so by proposing to increase their deductible, coinsurance, or premiums. These proposals are not only expected to decrease federal outlays as private out-of-pocket costs for the aged increase, but also to increase the incentives of the aged to use Medicare benefits more efficiently. Several of these cost-sharing proposals include means-test provisions so that the aged who could not afford the increased costs would not have to bear them (Davis and Rowland 1984; Meyer 1984). However, in order to understand how these proposals would affect the aged, we must know not only the distribution of costs among the aged, but also the distribution of their income.

THE INCOME OF THE VERY OLD

A number of studies suggest that the income of the aged on average is, at least on a per capita basis, comparable to the income of the nonaged (Danziger et al. 1984; Hurd and Shoven 1985). Because the aged, however, represent people spanning 35 years in age, a single income average does not adequately describe their heterogeneity. Although good data exist on the income of the aged in general, most cross-sectional surveys such as the Current Population Survey or the Survey of Income Program Participation do not have sample sizes that are statistically reliable for the very old. And longitudinal surveys such as the Retirement History Survey have not yet followed a significant number of the retired into very old age. The 1980 decennial census is as yet the only published source of statistically reliable information available on the income of the very old. The census contains extensive data for age cohorts within the aged and for the institutionalized population. People who are institutionalized for whatever reason—sickness, mental disorders, or convenience—are usually ignored by other surveys because of the sampling and measurement problems.

The decennial census is, of course, a cross-sectional survey; therefore, the economic behavior of a single cohort over time cannot be determined from it. Also, for all age groups, income data from the census are generally biased downward. It is probable that the data on the elderly are more biased than data for the younger population because the elderly tend to underreport their money income considerably more than the nonaged (Radnor 1981). The underreporting of income is the result of both underestimating the amount of income received and underreporting whether the income is received at all. If underreporting is directly related to age among the aged, then it may mean that the differences in income among the young and the older aged are somewhat less than the census data shown in Table 18–3 suggest. Despite these problems with the decennial census, the data are adequate for discussing the ability of the very old today to share their increasing medical costs.

As shown in Table 18–3, the average income of people aged 85 and older is 36 percent less than the income of people aged 65 to 69. This difference is largely the result of lower earned income as labor-force participation drops 74 percent between the two cohorts and the lower average Social Security benefits of older retirees. Table 18–3 also records a comparison of the age-specific income of different groups among the aged, such as unmarried men and women and couples. Some of these groups overlap, of course; the disaggregation of the average income, however, suggests which groups among the aged are most important in determining the income trends among the cohorts.

Aged men in general and couples in particular experience the biggest difference in income from ages 65 to 69 years to 85 years and older; these are the two groups that were most likely to be in the labor force in the cohort aged 65 to 69 and, therefore, experience a greater decline in income as they age and leave the labor force. The smallest income difference is among the poor aged. Because the level of poverty benefits is the same regardless of age, the poor may appear to be more homogeneous across aged cohorts than the nonpoor aged.

The income of the institutionalized is actually larger for the oldest cohorts relative

Table 18–3 1980 Average Income of the Aged

| Category of aged | All ages | Years | | | | | Percentage difference in average total income between ages 65–69 and 85 + |
		65–69 years	70–74 years	75–79 years	80–84 years	85 +	
Population (in thousands)	25,517	8,784	6,816	4,789	2,930	2,197	—
Average income:							
Total aged	7,505	8,621	7,534	6,923	6,381	5,540	−36%
Aged men	10,245	11,993	10,029	8,986	8,256	7,212	−40
Aged women	5,535	5,756	5,631	5,557	5,339	4,748	−18
Aged couples	15,476	17,458	15,018	13,676	12,810	11,723	−33
Unmarried men	7,545	8,641	7,605	7,183	6,865	6,338	−27
Unmarried women	6,123	7,023	6,462	5,996	5,536	4,803	−32
Poor couples	5,702	5,697	5,736	5,712	5,669	5,596	−02
Poor unmarried men	3,722	4,147	3,679	3,519	3,509	3,405	−09
Poor unmarried women	2,672	2,720	2,723	2,683	2,628	2,513	−08
Institutionalized	3,563	3,464	3,484	3,647	3,701	3,493	+01

Source: U.S. Bureau of the Census, The 1980 Decennial Census, unpublished tabulations from the 5 percent public use microdata sample.

to the newly old cohorts. This suggests that the people in institutions who are very old may have a considerably different economic history than the institutionalized aged who are younger. It also may be the result of measurement and response problems because many of the institutionalized do not receive their income directly, and, therefore, may not accurately estimate the level of income that is provided for them.

When the differences in medical costs by age groups among the aged are compared with the differences in income among the same age groups, the dilemma of sharing Medicare costs becomes clearer. As income declines 36 percent between ages 65 to 69 years and at 85 years and older, Medicare costs increase 77 percent between ages 65 to 69 years and at 80 years and older. In 1984 people 80 years of age and older received an estimated $2,845 in benefits from Medicare, which is almost one-third of the average income they received. If, for example, new cost-sharing provisions required 20 percent of present Medicare benefits to be paid by the beneficiary, it would result in an average $500 a year increase in cost for the very old and a $3 billion savings to the federal government because of their cost sharing. It would, however, decrease the income of the very old by 8 percent. If the cost sharing was income-tested, then much less than the $3 billion would be saved by the federal government because the very old as a group have so little income.

The distribution of income among the aged and the role public transfers have played in modifying the distribution are important issues not addressed in this chapter. This chapter also does not discuss the dramatic drop in poverty rates among the aged in the last 20 years, largely due to the growth in public income and in-kind benefits. However, these topics are fully discussed by G. Lawrence Atkins (Chapter 17, this volume).

ASSETS OF THE VERY OLD

Ironically, the very old, who have the highest health costs, may have considerably more assets than income. The Medicaid program, which provides most of the federal long-term-care benefits to the aged, recently recognized this possibility by allowing states to attach a lien to the estates of the aged who receive long-term-care benefits from Medicaid. When the beneficiaries die, their estates can then be used to defray the costs of their long-term care. In order to address the issue of assets, however, we need to know more than we do now about the distribution of assets among the aged.

Although the very old are one of the most important federal beneficiary groups, almost nothing is known about the distribution of their assets or how they spend them. The life-cycle hypothesis suggests that people will save enough while they are working so that they can maintain their consumption after retirement by dissaving (Modigliani 1980). In other words, people will build up their assets during their working years, and then, when they retire and their income declines, spend their savings. Before the recent tax reforms there was also a strong incentive to give wealth to heirs while still alive to avoid the estate taxes. Unfortunately, whether the aged do dissave for whatever reason cannot be determined yet because of insufficient data.

There are two sources of information on the assets of the aged: the 1979 Survey of Income and Program Participation (SIPP) and the Retirement History Survey (RHS). A third source of information is the Federal Reserve Board's Survey of Consumer Finances. All three surveys, however, do not adequately sample the very old, and therefore, no significant data exist on the assets of this group.

Recent analysis of SIPP data has made the first attempt to show assets by different cohorts of the aged. The SIPP data have the same underreporting problems described for the 1980 decennial census. There are substantial nonresponses to asset-value questions, and financial assets appear to have the highest percentage of underreporting (Radnor 1984). Nevertheless, all respondents said they had some form of assets, which is a higher response than in the Retirement History Survey.

As shown in Table 18–4, the same percentage of people 75 years of age and older have assets as those 65 years of age and older. The net worth of the assets, however, is 22 percent more for the group aged 65 and older than for the older subgroup. More than half of the difference can be explained by the difference in home equity and durable goods. Financial assets are actually slightly higher for the older cohort of aged than for all those aged 65 years of age and older.

Recent studies based on the longitudinal Retirement History Survey (RHS) avoid the problems of interpreting cross-sectional data and provide insights into how a

Table 18–4 Average Amounts of Assets, and Percentage Holding Each Type of Asset, 1979[a]

Type of asset	Age of householder (years)	
	Total, 65 +	Total, 75 +
Average amounts		
Net Worth	79,390	65,030
Wealth	79,930	65,530
Home equity	25,110	19,480
Financial assets	28,020	28,610
Liquid	8,020	7,560
Nonliquid	20,000	21,040
Business equity	5,660	3,400
Other assets	14,090	8,640
Durable goods	7,060	5,410
Unsecured debt	540	500
Percentage holding each asset		
Net Worth	100%	100%
Wealth	99	100
Home equity	66	59
Financial assets	95	96
Liquid	95	96
Nonliquid	36	31
Business equity	4	3
Other assets	18	16
Durable goods	98	99
Unsecured debt	39	28

[a] All estimates are preliminary. Dollar amounts are rounded to the nearest $10.

Source: 1979 Survey of Income and Program Participation: Second and Fifth Waves. As presented in a paper titled The Wealth and Income of Aged Households by Daniel B. Radner, presented at the American Statistical Association meeting, Philadelphia, August 1984.

single cohort of newly aged people behave over time. Burtless and Moffitt (1984) found that the real wealth of the RHS respondents declined somewhat between 1969 and 1979 even though real home equity grew. Friedman's (1982) study of a subset of the same data base suggests that the aged reduced their consumption in the first 6 years after retirement and continued to save, but then dissaved afterward. Using the same data, Hammermesh (1983) confirms the reduction in consumption in the early years of retirement, and Merrill (1984) confirms the growth in home equity over time.

But the RHS, which is the basis for these studies, is describing the economic behavior of a cohort as they approach and enter retirement. The initial RHS interviews were made in 1969 of 11,000 respondents who were between the ages of 58 and 63. By 1979 these respondents were between 68 and 73 years of age; therefore, the assets of a cohort as it becomes very old has yet to be described.

Although the SIPP and RHS clues are useful, none of them is definitive enough yet to conclude how many assets the very old have and what they do with their assets. Both studies, however, suggest that the aged may have substantial assets. One recent proposal was to have the final Medicare contribution paid after a beneficiary's death (Long and Smeeding 1984). The contribution could be made from a limited portion of the decedent's estate to pay for the Medicare benefits received that were in excess of previous contributions to the program. The final payment would have to be limited to a fraction of the estate after both spouses die. Because estates of the aged may be considerable, the proposal would provide significant revenue without reducing the economic security of the beneficiaries while they are alive. The reduction of the estate, however, would affect the heirs directly, although it could be argued that the negative income effects of such a proposal on the heirs would be partially offset by a slower rise in their social insurance taxes than would be necessary without an estate contribution.

Historically, the families of the aged, not the federal government, have been expected to bear the major burden of their support. In 1965, the federal government paid for only 15 percent of the health care of the aged (Fisher 1980). With the advent of Medicare benefits, the burden of support for elderly parents was increasingly shared with the federal government, which today provides approximately half of the medical benefits of the aged. A final Medicare contribution from the decedents' estates, in effect, would be a contribution from the heirs that would begin to return some of the responsibility of health costs of the aged to the families. Again, however, if the effects of the proposal are examined with respect to the very old in particular, instead of the aged in general, the issues become somewhat more complex.

INTERGENERATIONAL COST SHARING

The age of the children of the elderly will, in part, determine how feasible it is for them to increase their future responsibilities for their parents either through direct contributions or estate contributions. The children of the younger aged are, in general, 20 to 35 years younger than their parents and, therefore, are in the middle of their working years, near the peak of their earning power. While they also have financial responsibilities for children and mortgages, they, in general, are likely to have substantial resources. The children of the very old, however, are themselves either aged or approaching retirement, when their income is expected to decrease significantly. As Table 18–5 records, the median age of the children of women who are 85 years of age in 1985 is 59 years. And this median age of the children stays remarkably constant for 85-year-old women until the mothers of the baby boom, who had their children at early ages, retire.

The children of the very old are, in general, considerably older than the children of the newly old. As a consequence, the ability of the children of the very old to share the increasing costs of their parents may differ significantly from the ability of the children of the younger aged. Much more needs to be learned about how much the children of the very old today do provide in financial and housing support to their parents relative to the children of the newly old. And these differences will be important to address in any proposals for intergenerational cost sharing.

CONCLUSION

Since 1960 considerable federal resources have shifted from children to the aged (Preston 1984). This shift paralleled the change in the relative size of each group. This reallocation of resources is likely to be repeated among the aged themselves in the next 15 years. As the very old become the largest group among the aged, more resources are likely to be used by them than by other age groups.

Already, the federal per capita cost of the very old is demonstrably larger than for the rest of the aged, and the increase of these costs relative to other benefits to the aged is inevitable. Little attention, however, has focused on the needs and resources of the very old. They are almost invisible economically because they are statistically small.

The aged as a group are very diverse, not only as federal beneficiaries but also as economic units. However, the limited economic and beneficiary statistics we have been using to describe the aged have helped to mask the diversity among them.

Table 18–5 Median Age of the Children of 85-year-old Women[a]

Year in which mother is 85 years of age	Year in which mother was born	Age of mother after having half her children	Median age of child when mother is 85 years of age
1980	1895	26.7	58
1985	1900	26.1	59
1990	1905	25.9	59
1995	1910	26.8	58
2000	1915	27.4	58
2005	1920	27.2	58
2010	1925	26.7	58
2015	1930	25.8	59
2020	1935	24.7	60

[a]These estimates assume similar mortality rates of mothers and nonmothers and of children regardless of their cohort.

Source: Fertility Tables for Birth Cohorts by Color, U.S. 1916–73, *Vital Statistics of the U.S.*, Vol. 1, *Natality.*

Longitudinal surveys, such as the RHS, allow us to estimate not only income and assets at one point in time for different groups among the aged, but even more important, to see also how people behave economically as they age. Even though each cohort may age differently, the insights from such a survey would be invaluable.

Even a series of cross-sectional surveys would be helpful in determining the present distribution of economic resources among the subgroups of the aged. Reliable surveys, however, require considerably larger sample sizes for the very old than are now used, and increasing sample sizes costs money. Yet, until we have more disaggregated data, we will continue to treat the aged as a homogenous group. And the very old will continue to be statistical ghosts who leave only a few clues to their benefits, needs, and economic resources.

Note. The views and opinions expressed in this chapter are those of the author and do not necessarily reflect the position of the U.S. Bureau of the Census.

REFERENCES

Burtless, G., and R. Moffitt. 1984. The Effect of Social Security on Labor Supply of the Aged. In *Retirement and Economic Behavior*, ed. H. Aaron and G. Burtless, 135–74. Washington: Brooking Institution.

Danziger, S., J. van der Gaag, E. Smolensky, and M. Taussig. 1984. Income Transfers and the Economic Status of the Elderly. In *Retirement and Economic Behavior*, ed. H. Aaron and G. Burtless, 175–93. Washington: Brookings Institution.

Davis, K., and D. Rowland. 1984. Medicare Financing Reform: A New Medicare Premium. *Milbank Memorial Fund Quarterly/Health and Society* 62(2):300–16.

Fisher, C. 1980. Difference by Age Groups in Health Care Spending. *Health Care Financing Review* 1(4):65–90.

Friedman, J. 1982. Asset Accumulation and Depletion among the Elderly. Paper presented at the Brookings Institution Conference on Retirement and Aging, Washington, March.

Fuchs, V. 1984. Though Much Is Taken: Reflections on Aging, Health, and Medical Care. *Milbank Memorial Fund Quarterly/Health and Society* 62(2):143–66.

Hammermesh, D. 1983. Consumption During Retirement: The Missing Link in the Life Cycle. Working paper no. 930. Cambridge, Mass.: National Bureau of Economic Research.

Hurd, M.O., and J.B. Shoven. 1985. The Economic Status of the Elderly: 1969–79. In *Horizontal Equity, Uncertainty, and Measures of Well-being*, ed. T.M. Smeeding and M.H. David, 125–77. Chicago: National Bureau of Economic Research and University of Chicago Press.

Long, S.H., and T.M. Smeeding. 1984. Alternative Medicare Financing Sources. *Milbank Memorial Fund Quarterly/Health and Society* 62(2):325–48.

Manton, K.G. 1982. Changing Concepts of Morbidity and Mortality in the Elderly Population. *Milbank Memorial Fund Quarterly/Health and Society* 60(2):183–244.

Merrill, S. 1984. Home Equity and the Elderly. In *Retirement and Economic Behavior*, ed. H. Aaron and G. Burtless, 197–227. Washington: Brookings Institution.

Meyer, J.A. 1984. Comment on "Medicare Financing Reform: A New Medicare Premium." *Milbank Memorial Fund Quarterly/Health and Society* 62(2):317–24.

Modigliani, F. 1980. The Life-Cycle Hypothesis of Saving Twenty Years Later. In *The Collected Papers of Franco Modigliani*, vol. 2, pp. 41–75. Cambridge: MIT Press.

Palmer, J.L., and B.B. Torrey. 1984. Health Care Financing and Pension Programs. In *Federal Budget Policy in the 1980's,* ed. G.B. Mills and J.L. Palmer, 121–56. Washington: Urban Institute Press.

Preston, S. 1984. Children and the Elderly: Divergent Paths for America's Dependents. *Demography* 21(4):453–57.

Radnor, D. 1981. Adjusted Estimates of the Size Distribution of Family Money Income for 1972. Working paper no. 24. Washington: Office of Research and Statistics, Social Security Administration.

————. 1984. The Wealth and Income of Aged Households. Paper presented at the American Statistical Association meetings, August.

U.S. Bureau of the Census. 1984. Projections of the Population of the United States, by Age, Sex, and Race. *Current Population Reports,* series P-25, no. 952. Washington.

U.S. Public Health Service. 1983. *Health: United States: 1983.* DHHS pub. no. (PHS) 84–1232. Washington.

19

The Oldest Old and "Intergenerational Equity"

ROBERT H. BINSTOCK

In 1984 the National Institute on Aging launched a major research initiative focused on the oldest old, persons aged 85 years and older (U.S. Department of Health and Human Services 1984). The initiative has proven to be a timely measure for better understanding the implications of population aging because it has generated valuable studies of a swiftly growing group in which the prevalence of chronic illnesses and disabilities is very high compared with that of other age groups within the older population.

This focus on the oldest old, however, is highly susceptible to familiar mechanisms of distortion that may generate unwarranted stereotypes of persons in this older age range. In turn, such stereotypes may exacerbate the implications of contemporary issues of so-called intergenerational equity, in some instances with pernicious implications for older persons and our society in general.

This chapter analyzes the emergence of issues of intergenerational equity, showing that they are spuriously constructed on the basis of inaccurate old-age stereotypes, superficial reasoning, and unrealistic extrapolations from existing public policies. It suggests how stereotypes of the oldest old may fit into the scenarios framed by these issues. Further, it illustrates how artificial issues of intergenerational equity—such as "justice between age groups" in the allocation of health care—divert our attention from seeking more useful alternative issues to confront in dealing with our domestic social-policy dilemmas.

THE PUBLIC POLICY CONTEXT

Studies of the oldest old are emerging in a climate of American politics and public discourse that is increasingly hostile to older persons in general. As we begin the 1990s, public resources are perceived as scarce. The need to "reduce the deficit" is a rhetorical mainstay of domestic politics. "Containing health care costs" is widely considered to be one of the major problems of our day.

Population aging is commonly perceived as worsening each of these problems, and others as well. Many issues of domestic policy portray "the aged" as in conflict with other groups of Americans or as a growing and unsustainable burden that will undermine our national well-being. How did this political hostility to older persons develop?

Compassionate Ageism and the "Old-Age Welfare State"

From the Social Security Act of 1935 through the 1970s, American policies toward older persons have been adopted and amended in substantially different social, economic, and political contexts. Interpretations of the original goals of such policies vary widely (Achenbaum 1983; Campion 1984; Cohen 1985b; David 1985; Derthick 1979; Graebner 1980; Harris 1966; Holtzman 1963; Marmor 1970).

Regardless of the original intent of various policies toward aging, by the late 1960s and early 1970s a common theme was taking shape: Through the cumulative impact of many disparate legislative actions, American society had adopted and financed a number of age-categorical benefit programs and tax and price subsidies for which eligibility is not determined by need. Through Social Security, Medicare, the Older Americans Act, and a variety of other measures, older persons were exempted from the screenings that are customarily applied to other Americans in order to determine whether they are worthy of public help.

This theme was strengthened as a number of old-age-based interest groups articulated compassionate stereotypes of older persons (Binstock 1972; Pratt 1976). These advocates for the aged told us repeatedly that the elderly are poor, frail, socially dependent, objects of discrimination, and, above all, *deserving* (Kalish 1979).

Through this compassionate ageism—the attribution of the same characteristics, status, and just deserts to the elderly—advocates managed to artificially homogenize, package, label, and market a heterogeneous group of older persons as "the aged" (Binstock 1983). However, ageism, in contrast with racism, has provided many benefits to older persons (Kutza 1981).

During the 1960s and 1970s, almost any issue or problem affecting older persons that could be identified by advocates for the aging became a governmental responsibility: nutritional, supportive, and leisure services; housing; home repair; energy assistance; transportation; employment assistance and protection; special mental-health programs; a separate National Institute on Aging; and on, and on, and on (Estes 1979).

By the late 1970s, if not earlier, American society had learned the catechism of compassionate ageism very well and had expressed it through a variety of governmental programs and objectives that constituted an "old age welfare state" (Myles 1983). Although proposals for universal national health insurance were rejected for example, national health insurance for the elderly was established through Medicare (Marmor 1970).

Because older persons came to be stereotyped as the "deserving poor," programs for the aged have not been subject to the disdain and stigmatization attached to other welfare programs in American political culture. In truth, of course, any of the "deserving" needs for collective assistance that have been symbolized by compassionate old-age stereotypes can be found among persons of all ages. Yet, the great bulk of our social-welfare and health expenditures is for benefits to the aged.

The Emergence of the Aged as Scapegoat

Since 1978, however, the long-standing compassionate stereotypes of older persons have been undergoing an extraordinary reversal (Binstock 1983). Older persons have come to be portrayed as one of the more flourishing and powerful groups in American society and have been attacked as a burdensome responsibility. These new stereotypes, devoid of compassion, are:

1. The aged are relatively well off—not poor, but in great economic shape.
2. The aged are a potent political force because there are so many of them and they all vote in their self-interest; this "senior power" explains why more than one-quarter of the annual federal budget is spent on benefits to the aged.
3. Because of demographic changes, the aged are becoming more numerous and politically powerful, and will claim even more benefits and substantially larger proportions of the federal budget. They are already costing too much, and in the future will pose an unsustainable burden for the American economy.

Even as the earlier compassionate stereotypes of older persons were partially unwarranted, so are these current stereotypes. They are generated by applying simplistic assumptions and aggregate statistics to a group called "the aged" in order to gloss over complexities. If one chooses to compare changes in the median or average income of all older persons with changes in the income of other groups, one can conclude that the aged are relatively well off and ignore millions of older persons who are in dire economic circumstances (Smeeding 1990). If one wishes to ignore abundant evidence to the contrary (Hudson and Strate 1985; Jacobs 1990), one can assume that the votes of older persons are determined by issues, and one particular issue above all others, which they will respond to with self-interest, and that their self-interests will be common. If one pretends that outlays for Medicare, Old Age Insurance, and other policies are mechanistically determined by demographics rather than by legislative and administrative decisions, one can conclude that benefits to the aged constitute an unsustainable burden for the American economy. Certainly, the enactment of the Medicare Catastrophic Coverage Act of 1988 and its speedy repeal in 1989 (Findlay 1989; Tolchin 1989b) should remind us that extrapolation from existing policies and institutional arrangements is a poor mode of prediction.

The new stereotypes of older persons began to appear in the late 1970s during a so-called crisis in the cash flow of the Social Security system, within the larger context of a depressed economy during President Carter's administration (Estes 1983). Although this cash-flow problem may have been an immediate precipitating factor, two more fundamental elements seem to account prominently for the reversal of stereotypes.

One element was a tremendous growth in the amount of federal funds expended on benefits to the aging, which journalists (Samuelson 1978) and academicians (Hudson 1978) began to notice and publicize in the late 1970s. By 1982 an economist in the U.S. Office of Management and Budget (Torrey 1982) had reframed the classical tradeoff metaphor of political economy from "guns versus butter" to "guns versus canes." By the late 1980s, the proportion of the annual federal budget being spent on benefits to the aging had remained at about 26 percent for more than a decade

(U.S. Senate 1988) and had been widely recognized as one of the few large expenditure categories in the federal budget (along with national defense and interest on the national debt).

Another element in the reversal of old-age stereotypes was dramatic improvement in the aggregate status of older Americans, in large measure due to the impact of federal benefit programs. Social Security, for example, helped to reduce the proportion of elderly persons in poverty from about 35 percent three decades ago (Clark 1990) to 12.8 percent today (U.S. Senate 1988). Journalists can now accurately depict older persons, in the aggregate, as "more prosperous than the general population" (Tolchin 1988).

Regardless of specific causes, the reversal of stereotypes continued throughout the 1980s to the point where the new stereotypes can now be readily observed in popular culture. Typical of contemporary depictions of older persons was a "cover story" in *Time* Magazine entitled "Grays on the Go" (Gibbs 1988). It was filled with pictures of senior surfers, swingers, and softball players. Older persons were pictured as America's new elite—healthy, wealthy, powerful, and "staging history's biggest retirement party."

A dominant theme in such portrayals of older persons is that their selfishness is ruining the nation. *The New Republic* highlighted this motif early in 1988 with a cover displaying "Greedy Geezers." The table of contents "teaser" for the story that followed (Fairlie (1988) announced, "The real me generation isn't the yuppies, it's America's growing ranks of prosperous elderly." Or, as a *New York Times* "Op-Ed" article was headlined: "Elderly, Affluent—and Selfish" (Longman 1989).

In serious forums of public discourse these new stereotypes have bolstered the use of the aged as a scapegoat for an impressive list of American problems. As social psychologist Gordon Allport observed in his classic work on the *ABC's of Scapegoating:* "An issue seems nicely simplified if we blame a group or class of people rather than the complex course of social and historical forces" (1959, 13–14).

Advocates for children and demographer Samuel Preston (1984) have blamed the political power of the elderly for the plight of youngsters who have inadequate nutrition, health care, and education and lack supportive family environments. Former Secretary of Commerce Peter Peterson (1987) has suggested that a prerequisite for the United States to regain its stature as a first-class power in the world economy is a sharp reduction in programs benefiting older Americans.

A ludicrous manifestation of this trend took place in 1989 when a distinguished "executive panel" of American leaders convened by the Ford Foundation designated older persons to be the only group of citizens responsible for financing a broad range of social programs for persons of all ages, including infants. In a report on *The Common Good: Social Welfare and the American Future,* the panel recommended a series of policies costing a total of $29 billion. And how did the panel propose that this $29 billion be financed? Solely by taxing the Social Security benefits of older persons (Ford Foundation 1989, 81).

Perhaps the most serious scapegoating of the aged—in terms of the vulnerability of older persons, the oldest old, and, maybe, of all persons in our society—has been in the area of health care. A widespread concern about high rates of inflation in health-care costs has been refocused in the past few years from health-care providers, suppliers, administrators, and insurers—the parties that are responsible for setting the prices of care—to the elderly patients for whom health care is provided and who pay for more than 40 percent of their aggregate care (U.S. House of Representatives 1989, 8).

Americans aged 65 and older, about 12 percent of our population, account for one-third of the nation's annual health-care expenditures, over $175 billion in 1988 (U.S. House of Representatives 1989, 4). Because the elderly population is growing, absolutely and proportionately, health-care costs for older persons have been depicted as an unsustainable burden, or as ethicist Daniel Callahan has put it, "a great fiscal black hole" that will absorb an unlimited amount of our national resources (1987, 17). Indeed, because of concerns for health-care costs of the old, in 1984 the then Governor of Colorado, Richard Lamm, was widely reported to have pronounced that terminally ill old people have a "duty to die and get out of the way" (Slater 1984).

Americans for Intergenerational Equity (AGE)

Parallel to this emergence of the aged as scapegoat for a number of societal problems have been the activities of a new organization, Americans for Generational Equity (AGE). Established to propound issues of "intergenerational equity," it appears to have solid financial backing from the corporate sector as well as political support from selected members of congress (Quadagno 1989). From its Washington office it publishes and disseminates *The Generational Journal*.

Established in 1985, AGE defines itself as "a non-partisan non-profit coalition . . . dedicated to forging a coalition among all generations to protect the future of young Americans"; and its "central mission is to promote greater public understanding of the trends arising from the aging of the U.S. population of the United States and to foster increased public support for policies that will serve the economic interests of all Americans in the next century" (*Generational Journal* 1989).

Each year AGE organizes conferences focused on themes suggesting that public expenditures on older persons are wasteful and should be reallocated to younger age groups. For example, at a conference entitled "Medicare and the Baby Boom Generation," one of the organization's prominent board members espoused the view that "In the interest of doing the greatest good for the greatest number, some forms of medical intervention should be denied, as a matter of government policy, to elderly or terminally-ill patients" (Lamm 1987, 77).

Central to AGE's credo is the proposition that the large aggregate of public transfers of income and other benefits to today's cohorts of older persons, financed through burdensome taxes on the contemporary labor force, are unlikely to be available in the future as old-age benefits (e.g., Social Security and Medicare) when the present cohort of workers becomes elderly retirees (Longman 1987). Moreover, AGE contrasts the relatively prosperous circumstances of the elderly with those of other groups such as disadvantaged children and an estimated 37 million Americans who lack health insurance. Every indication suggests that this organization will likely persist in adding to the rhetoric that pits the young and the middle-aged against the old, as exemplified by the title of one of AGE's recent conferences: "Children at Risk: Who Will Support Our Aging Society?"

Some members of Congress, like Senator David Duhrenberger of Minnesota, are among the founding members of Americans for Generational Equity, and they have recruited former Governor Lamm, demographer Preston, biomedical ethicist Callahan, and others of like mind to their organization. But they have yet to inject into legislative proposals their view that inequities represented by programs benefiting the aging should be redressed through drastic policy changes. So far they have confined their efforts to conferences, speeches, and publications.

Nonetheless, AGE's basic approach—framing public policy questions as issues of intergenerational conflict—seems to reflect and/or to have captured successfully the mind set of the media and of powerful members of Congress. For example, as the Medicare Catastrophic Act of 1988 was repealed in November 1989, Congressman Dan Rostenkowski, Chairman of the House Ways and Means Committee, observed: "One of the most unhappy results of our ongoing budget gridlock has been an uneven contest between the very young and the very old." He said that "the sad story of the 1980s" was that "the old have gotten more while the young have gotten less" (Tolchin 1989b).

THE OLDEST OLD AND "INTERGENERATIONAL EQUITY"

The oldest old are receiving attention at a time when issues of intergenerational equity have become axioms of public rhetoric. In this context it is more than possible that the subgroup of persons aged 85 and over will become subject to stereotyping on the basis of multiple old-age categories. "The oldest old," in contrast with "the aging," could well become a common label for extreme conditions of frailty, disease, disability, and social dependency among the elderly.

A notable precedent in such a stratification of old-age stereotypes took place in the 1980s through, ironically, a distortion of Bernice Neugarten's (1974) effort to break down age-based stereotypes. It became a widespread practice to label persons 65 to 74 years of age as the "young old" and to perceive all persons in this age group as healthy and capable of earning income. If retired, they were seen as a rich reservoir of resources to be drawn upon for providing unpaid social and health services and fulfilling a variety of other community roles (Kieffer 1986). In contrast, persons aged 75 and older became commonly termed the "old old" and tended to be saddled with the traditional compassionate stereotypes of older persons as poor and frail.

These age-stratified conventions that developed in the 1980s staked out—in effect—a high ground in the politics of compassionate ageism. They served politically to legitimate marginal changes in the traditional ages used for old-age categorical policies, without the need to confront the basic issue of whether it makes sense to continue policies that utilize old-age categories, rather than need, for determining eligibility (Neugarten 1982). For example, due to the Social Security Reform Act of 1983, the age of initial eligibility for full Old Age Insurance benefits is scheduled to rise gradually from age 65 to 67 early in the next century. Furthermore, many suggestions have been made for moving the age of Medicare eligibility up to age 67, 70, or even 75. In short, a multiplication of strata for old-age stereotypes has made it easier politically to effect minor changes in the ages that are used as very crude markers in public policies for approximating those among the elderly who may need collective assistance of one kind or another.

Today the label "oldest old" may breed a new level in the stratification of old-age stereotypes. In turn, stereotypes of the oldest old may shape political issues and policy choices. Such stereotypes may be inaccurate, based on misinformation and misconceptions. But, nonetheless, they may have important consequences for how America copes with the challenges of population aging.

The term "intergenerational equity" has already become a sweeping conventional label for describing trade-offs in health and social-welfare allocations. In turn, it has spawned a series of metaphors to describe dilemmas in particular sectors of American life: a perceived need for new principles by which to allocate acute health-care resources; challenges of providing adequate long-term care for the elderly; macroeconomic burdens of supporting a large, dependent older population; and "the inevitability" of political conflict between a powerful bloc of self-interested seniors and the rest of us.

It is easy enough to envision how a stereotyped oldest-old group might fit into the scenarios framed by these issues. In some scenarios the casting of roles for the oldest old may be relatively benign, but in others it may be extremely pernicious.

Justice Between Age Groups

"Justice between age groups" (Daniels 1983) has become a metaphor for concerns that ever-increasing health care costs in the United States will bring about far more rationing of acute health care than we have thus far experienced informally (Blank 1988). Such concerns appeared well founded in 1989 as Alameda County, California, and the state of Oregon became the first governments in this country to begin a process of explicitly rationing health care among patients in their jurisdictions who are paid for by Medicaid, the federal-state health insurance program for "the medically indigent" (Garland 1989; Gross 1989). Both governments ranked medical procedures, with descriptions of age categories and sex, as well as health-care need.

There is no inherent reason, of course, why issues of justice in allocating health-care resources need to be framed on the basis of age. One can frame tradeoffs just as easily within age groups or without regard to age. In fact, health-care resources—like most other goods and services in the United States—have long been allocated on the basis of social class and ability to pay (Churchill 1987). Many procedures—even relatively low-cost ones, such as immunization—are not readily available to persons of low economic and social status (Hiatt 1987).

Nonetheless, old age came sharply into focus as a prime target for stepped-up acute-care rationing in the past decade. In a 1983 speech, economist Alan Greenspan, now chairman of the Federal Reserve Board, stated that 30 percent of Medicare is annually expended on 5 to 6 percent of Medicare eligibles who die within the year. He pointedly considered whether it is worth it. (Schulte 1983). Richard Lamm says that he was misquoted in 1984 when he was reported as urging older persons to die in order to make room for the young (Slater 1984), but he has been delivering the same message repeatedly since then, in only somewhat more delicately worded fashion (e.g., Lamm 1987, 1989a).

During the last half of the 1980s, this focus spread to a number of forums. Philosophers generated principles of equity to undergird "justice between age groups" in the provision of health care (e.g., Daniels 1988) rather than, for instance, justice between rich and poor. Conferences and books explicitly addressed the issue of "Should Health Care Be Rationed By Age?" (e.g., Smeeding et al. 1987), and biomedical ethicists turned to examining the economics of terminal illness (Veatch 1988) and "assisted suicide" in old age (Battin 1987).

In the context of this ongoing dialogue on old-age-based health-care rationing, the swiftly increasing oldest-old population may well develop as the leading symbol for "runaway" health costs. Persons aged 85 and older, for instance, stand out— even among elderly persons—as high users of health-care resources.

For instance, persons aged 85 and older presently use days of care in "short-stay" (as opposed to chronic disease) hospitals in the United States at a rate that is 123 percent higher than that of those aged 65 to 74 and 83 percent higher than that of those aged 75 to 84 (National Center for Health Statistics 1987). Similarly, about 1 percent of Americans aged 65 to 74 years are in nursing homes, compared with 6 percent of persons 75 to 84 years of age and 22 percent of persons aged 85 and older (Hing 1987). The greater numbers of persons who will be in the oldest-old category, combined with their current high rates of health care use, lead to projections that Medicare costs for the oldest old may increase sixfold by the year 2040, as estimated in constant, inflation-adjusted dollars (Schneider and Guralnik 1990).

Even in the mid-1980s, as issues of health-care costs and allocations began to be framed as tradeoffs between age groups, it did "not take much imagination to envision that a stereotyped group termed the 'oldest old' will be assembled in the front row of the trading block" (Binstock 1985, 433). And indeed, they have been by ethicist Daniel Callahan, who is willing to transcend the bounds of traditional Judeo-Christian morality (Post 1991) regarding the sanctity of human life.

In a book entitled *Setting Limits: Medical Goals in an Aging Society,* Callahan proposes that life-saving health care should be officially forbidden to all American citizens who are of an advanced age category. He depicts the elderly as "a new social threat" and a "demographic, economic, and medical avalanche . . . that could ultimately (and perhaps already) do great harm" (1987, 20). Callahan's remedy for this threat is to use "age as a specific criterion for the allocation and limitation of health care" (23), by denying life-extending health care—as a matter of public policy—to persons who are aged in their "late 70s or early 80s" and/or have "lived out a natural life span" (171).

Although Callahan's arguments are seriously flawed (Binstock and Kahana 1988), his proposal received a great deal of national attention. It was reviewed in national magazines, *The New York Times, The Washington Post, The Wall Street Journal,* and almost every relevant professional and scholarly journal and newsletter. Callahan himself was and continues to be invited to present and/or debate his proposal in a number of public forums throughout the country, and he has reiterated his viewpoint in a recent book (Callahan 1990). It appears that his proposal to forbid lifesaving care to the oldest among us has come to be rather firmly embedded in public discourse concerning health-care policies in the United States.

Such proposals are likely to persist, albeit with refinements. And they will probably stay focused on very old persons because of preoccupations with financing and outlays for the Medicare program, the biggest single source of payment for health care in America (Health Care Financing Administration 1987). Moreover, Medicare, widely perceived as the "health program for the elderly," is a prime target for cost-containment reforms because its approaches to paying for care affect the financial incentives of a very high percentage of American hospitals, nursing homes, physicians, and other health-care providers and suppliers.

Long-term Care

"Long-term care" has become a metaphor for health care and social supports for chronically ill and disabled elderly persons. But long-term care, and the costs of providing it, are issues very pertinent to persons of all ages. Consider, for example, that in the United States the number of severely disabled adults aged 18 to 64 who live outside institutions is more than twice the total of all chronically ill and severely disabled persons aged 65 and older who reside in nursing homes and elsewhere (Gornick et al. 1985, 22–23).

Here again the issue is framed myopically to emphasize the enormous economic, social, and familial burdens of caring for the needs of older persons, without granting comparable public attention to the implications of such needs and burdens generated within other population groups. To the extent that attention is given to such needs within younger populations, however, rehabilitation—whether focused on the goals of compensation for, or restoration of lost functional capacities—receives a reasonable amount of attention. However, only a few (for example, Brody 1984–1985; Williams 1984) have given attention to rehabilitation as a dimension of treatment for the chronically disabled elderly, even with the modest goal of *maintenance* of existing functional capacities.

Stereotyping of the oldest old would likely reinforce current tendencies to perceive the challenges of chronic illness and disabilities in terms of care, *without rehabilitation,* for elderly residual human entities as their functional capacities gradually erode or precipitously decline just before death. Indeed, this perspective has already been propounded by philosophers (e.g., Daniels 1988) and ethicists (e.g., Callahan 1987). They view long-term care as a hospicelike palliative measure, as relatively inexpensive, and as a desirable public-funding alternative to (what they incorrectly perceive as) more costly health-care measures that can preserve, improve, or at least maintain the quality of an older individual's life.

Certain philosophical and ethical proponents of funding long-term care (rather than acute care and functionally oriented rehabilitation) for the very old believe that persons of advanced aged should philosophically accept that they are near the end of their "natural life course." Their emphasis not only consigns the oldest old to the social role of dying, but also keeps in limbo the far greater number of functionally disabled persons of all ages who, along with their families, have been struggling to get help through public policy for many years.

Some years ago, the president of the American Coalition of Citizens with Disabilities expressed the hope that a coalition of the organized constituencies of older persons and the disabled might become a powerful force in American politics (Rubenfeld 1986). However, there has been no sign of such a movement since then. Indeed, a case study of the politics involved in a long-term care bill in California (Torres-Gil and Pynoos 1986) suggests that stereotyping has led organized groups of the aged and disabled to compete with each other rather than to form an effective coalition.

Increasing Dependency Ratios

"Increasing dependency ratios," conventionally expressed as the size of the retired population relative to the working population, has become a metaphor for anxieties about the economic burdens of population aging. This construct grossly distorts the issues involved because it is largely an artifact of an existing policy, Social Security, that finances benefits to retirees through a tax based on the paychecks of workers. It does not capture the range of major elements that determine whether a society is economically capable of supporting dependents within it.

The most fundamental problem with this construct lies in using the number or proportion of workers in a society in order to assess the productive capacity of the economy. Productive capacity is a function of a variety of factors—including capital, natural resources, balance of trade, and technological innovation—as well as number of workers. Hence, issues involving productive capacity and number of workers should be expressed in terms of "productivity per worker" in order to take account of an appropriately full range of macroeconomic variables (Committee on an Aging Society 1986; Habib 1990).

More specific flaws in common usage of dependency ratios express the ubiquitous impact of ageism in the framing of issues. Age categories are used to estimate the numbers of workers and retirees—rather than actual and projected labor-force participation rates—even though the two approaches can yield substantially different results. In addition, the focus on retirees as the "dependent population" ignores the fact that many retired older persons are economically independent. It also ignores children and unemployed adults of any age who are economically dependent; for instance, research has indicated that a decline in "youth dependency" during the decades ahead may well moderate or even dominate the economic significance of projected increases in "elderly dependency" (Crown 1985; Habib 1990).

Nevertheless, discussions of increasing dependency ratios have generated several assumptions that may be unwarranted: First, we will need a far greater number of workers in the decades ahead than is projected from current age norms for entering and retiring from the labor force. Second, older persons who retire in the context of contemporary policies, many of whom engage in unpaid productive activities (Committee on an Aging Society 1986), will want to and be able to work for pay in the future if incentives to retire and the ages associated with them are marginally adjusted. Third, it is assumed that there will be employer demand for such workers.

Even though these assumptions may be unwarranted, policies pursuant to them would probably be bolstered by a stereotyped oldest-old population. The more that the ages of 85 and over are equated with frailty, disability, and social dependency, the easier it will be to perceive all persons at younger ages—in their seventies and below—as capable of and *obligated* to earn their own livings. Stereotypical distinctions between the oldest old and the rest of the aging population could therefore politically facilitate policy measures that attempt to turn dependent older persons into productive workers.

Such policies might also be based upon misperceptions regarding incentives and disincentives that influence the decisions of older workers regarding work and retirement. For example, it is commonly proposed that the ages of eligibility for Social Security retirement benefits be moved up, beyond the minor increases that will be phased in gradually in the next century. Yet, we know today that two-thirds of current Social Security beneficiaries choose to retire early, before age 65, even though it means that they receive reduced benefits; we also know that poor health and the availability of private-pension income are powerful influences in the decision to retire early (Quinn and Burkhauser 1990; Schulz 1988, especially Chapter 3).

The Political Power of the Aged

"The political power of the aged" is still another metaphor frequently used to misframe issues in terms of age-group conflicts (e.g., Chakravarty and Weisman 1988). Although older persons have constituted 16.7 to 21 percent of those who voted in national elections during the 1980s (U.S. Senate 1988, 11), election exit polls have demonstrated repeatedly that the votes of older persons are distributed among candidates in about the same proportions as the votes of other age groups of citizens (*New York Times*/ CBS News Poll 1980, 1982, 1984, 1986, 1988). Even in the context of a state or local referendum that presents a specific issue, rather than candidates, for balloting—such as propositions to cap local property taxes or to finance public schools—old age is not a statistically significant variable associated with the distribution of votes (Chomitz 1987).

These data should not be surprising because there is no sound reason to expect that a cohort of persons would suddenly become homogenized in self-interests and political behavior when it reaches the old-age category (Simon 1985). Diversity among older persons may be at least as great with respect to political attitudes and behavior as it is in relation to economic, social, and other characteristics (Hudson and Strate 1985).

Moreover, the scholarly literature indicates that organized demands of older persons have had little to do with the enactment and amendment of the major old-age policies such as Social Security and Medicare. Rather, such actions have been largely attributable to the initiatives of public officials in the White House, Congress, and the bureaucracy who have focused on their own agendas for social and economic policy (Cohen 1985a; Derthick 1979; Hudson and Strate 1985; Jacobs 1990; Light 1985).

The Medicare Catastrophic Coverage Act of 1988 was the latest example of such a policy enacted through the initiatives of public elites, rather than in response to interest groups (see Iglehart 1989). Its demise in 1989 "was a stunning defeat for the American Association of Retired Persons, which had . . . fought repeal" (Tolchin 1989a, 3). By all accounts, a relatively small, unrepresentative proportion of comparatively well-off older persons, who were upset by having to pay a new progressively scaled surtax, were able to cow their congressional representatives into repealing it. As Representative Pete Stark, an author of the repealed legislation put it, "We are being stampeded by a small group to deny benefits to everyone else"; and Representative Dan Rostenkowski added, "Because we in this Congress can't take the heat from the wealthy few, all principles are abandoned" (Tolchin 1989b, 1).

At present, the old-age interest organizations seem to be functioning as what political scientist Heclo (1984) terms an "anti-redistributive veto force" in American politics. Even in this so-called veto role, however, the force of old-age interests appears to be relatively weak.

A number of public policy decisions that are conventionally perceived as adverse to the self-interests of older persons proved to be politically feasible in the 1980s through changes in Medicare, Social Security, and other programs. Medicare deductibles, co-payments, and Part B premiums have increased continuously. Old Age Insurance (OAI) benefits have become subject to taxation. The legislated formula for cost-of-living-adjustments (COLAs) to OAI benefits has been rendered less generous. The Omnibus Reconciliation Act of 1981 narrowed five benefit and eligibility provisions of Social Security, which had a directly adverse effect on OAI recipients. The Tax Reform Act of 1986 eliminated the extra personal exemption that all persons 65 years of age and older had been receiving in filing their federal income-tax returns. Most recently, the politics of enacting and repealing of the Catastrophic Coverage Act clearly illustrated that older persons are not a homogeneous group, either politically or in terms of self-interests.

Despite these facts, the image of so-called senior power persists because it serves certain purposes. It is used by journalists as a tabloid symbol to simplify the complexities of politics. It is marketed by the leaders of old-age-based organizations who have many incentives to inflate the size of the constituency for which they speak, even if they need to homogenize it artificially in order to do so. It is attacked by those who would like to see greater resources allocated to their causes and who depict the selfishness of the aged as the root of many problems (Longman 1987).

What might happen if a stereotyped focus on the oldest old were to become an added ingredient in the senior power caricature of the American political process? One children's advocate has already proposed that parents receive an "extra vote" for each of their children who are under the voting age of 18 in order to combat older voters (Carballo 1981). Alternatively, why not treat the very old like children? Someone may soon revive and update Douglas Stewart's (1970) proposal that all persons be "disfranchised . . . at retirement or age 70, whichever is earlier," a proposal made because its author was disgusted by his perception that the aged were responsible for the election of Ronald Reagan as Governor of California. In comparison with age 70, age 85 would be an easy target for disfranchisement.

TRANSCENDING INTERGENERATIONAL EQUITY: PERSPECTIVES ON OLD-AGE–BASED HEALTH-CARE RATIONING

These examples of current metaphors in the politics of health and social welfare allocations may be sufficient to illustrate that issues are being framed in terms of conflicts between age groups; that these issues are frequently constructed from spurious and unwarranted assumptions; and that the emergence of the oldest old within these scenarios tends to exacerbate the implications of the issues that have been framed.

The lesson to be drawn from this is *not* that research on the oldest old should cease or be muted. Indeed, multidimensional knowledge about persons who are in their late eighties and older will be essential for coping with the challenges posed by population aging. It is important to note, however, that the issues of intergenerational equity—although arbitrary and flawed—have focused the social-policy agenda and diverted attention from other ways of viewing tradeoffs and options available to us that may be more accurate and propitious.

The lesson *is* that any description of the axis upon which equity is to be judged tends to circumscribe the major options available for rendering justice. If we can perceive issues that express equity in ways other than intergenerational tradeoffs (Heclo 1988; Kingson, Hirshorn, and Cornman 1986; Neugarten and Neugarten 1986; Wisensale 1988), those alternative issues may generate a series of new practical choices for public and private institutional arrangements in the decades ahead. It is not within the scope of this discussion to set forth a blueprint for such arrangements. But it is feasible to illustrate the principle by briefly considering some of the ways in which issues of health-resources allocation, presently expressed in terms of old-age-based rationing proposals, can be viewed in other terms.

Many contemporary discussions about old-age-based rationing are laden with misperceptions of what is actually happening in the world of health care for elderly Americans. Physicians are viewed as blindly pursuing a "heroic model" of medicine (see Cassel and Neugarten 1991) in which no cost or form of intervention will be spared in attempting to extend the lives of persons who are already near the end of their natural life course. These expenditures and interventions are seen as largely futile and wasteful, especially when applied to the very old. And their elimination, through one means or another, is perceived as an important measure for reducing health-care costs, particularly because of the swiftly increasing size of the oldest-old population.

But the decision processes through which physicians actually decide whether and how to treat elderly patients are not widely known. The benefits such patients receive from treatments are not understood, either in comparison with younger patients or in terms of cost effectiveness for society. Frequently quoted statistics concerning health-care costs are often unexamined with respect to their significance.

The Myth of Overly Aggressive, High-Technology Care for the Elderly

A central theme in most current discussions of whether American society should deny or limit health care to older persons is that costly, high-technology medicine is used too frequently and wastefully in treating elderly patients (e.g., Callahan 1987; Daniels 1988; U.S. Congress 1987). For some years the press has provided dramatic accounts of organ transplants and other forms of surgery on persons in their seventies, eighties, and nineties (e.g., Koenig 1986), as well as reports of legal issues involving the extended ordeals of older patients who linger on the edge of death in hospitals, sustained only by mechanical breathing ventilators or nutrition obtained intravenously or through tube feeding (e.g., Kleiman 1985).

However, the popular conception that elderly persons are frequently subject to "Faustian technologies" of intensive care (Lamm 1989a, 6) against their wishes is wrong (Schwartz and Reilly 1986). The majority of the funds expended on health care for the aged in the United States are not for dramatic technological interventions or even for hospitals. In 1988 nursing homes accounted for 21 percent of health expenditures on older persons, yet only a negligible proportion of elderly nursing-home patients receive life-sustaining technologies (U.S. Congress 1987, 12). A wide range of nonhospital and nonphysician health services—such as prescription drugs, dental care, home health care, vision and hearing aids, and medical equipment and supplies—totaled 16 percent of expenditures, and outpatient and inpatient physician fees were 22 percent. The remaining 41 percent was for payments to hospitals (U.S. House of Representatives 1989, 21).

Studies in both the United States (Scitovsky 1984) and Canada (Roos, Montgomery, and Roos 1987) indicate that aggressive acute-care medical interventions are comparable across adult age groups in the last years of life, although elderly persons are far more likely to incur expenses for nursing homes and home-care services. In fact, a study of several hundred older persons who died within a 12-month period indicates that severely impaired geriatric patients who received only supportive care—and little of it from hospitals and physicians—averaged only slightly fewer expenses for the year (amounting to about 8 percent less) than the most expensive decedents, who were treated aggressively with high-technology measures (Scitovsky 1988).

Old age, as a single factor or independent variable, is a poor predictor of whether a medical intervention will be "wasted," even for highly technical and aggressive medical interventions (see Jahnigen and Binstock 1991). Moreover, experience with advanced medical technologies—such as those used in renal dialysis, liver transplantation, and heart transplantation—shows that those older patients who are selected for such procedures unquestionably benefit from them, sometimes more than younger patients (Evans 1991). In certain cases, even transplantations are the most cost effective mode of treatment. For example, kidney-transplant recipients whose new organs function satisfactorily incur far lower treatment expenses than dialysis patients (Evans et al. 1987; Evans, Manninen, and Thompson 1989).

At the same time, the caricature of contemporary physicians as Don Quixotes who will tilt at "death as an enemy," regardless of cost and prognosis, misses the mark badly. Transplantation specialists, for example, take great care to select older candidates for surgery who have outstanding prospects for survival and benefit (Evans 1991). Furthermore, it is clear that physicians generally recognize the futility of many interventions for older persons, depending on disease and level of function (Gillick 1988; La Puma et al. 1988; Miles and Ryder 1985; Scitovsky 1988; Youngner et al. 1985).

Can We Save Money on Elderly Patients Who Die Within the Year?

Even if health-care treatment of older persons is not wasteful or overly aggressive, it is not always successful. Alan Greenspan's 1983 pronouncement (Schulte 1983) that a high proportion of Medicare expenditures is accounted for by a small proportion of Medicare enrollees who die within the year was basically correct. About 6 percent of Medicare enrollees who die within a year account for about 28 percent of Medicare's annual expenditures (Lubitz and Prihoda 1984). In 1987, when the total Medicare expenditure was $81 billion (Letsch, Levit, and Waldo 1988), this would mean that about $22.6 billion in Medicare funds was used to reimburse health care for about 6 percent of Medicare eligibles who died.

Suppose it were possible, both clinically and ethically, to identify prospectively those Medicare patients who were going to die within the year, and whose treatment would be *comparatively costly,* to choose not to undertake aggressive treatment of them, and thereby to save unnecessary health care costs? How much would be saved in terms of Medicare resources and the nation's annual health expenditures? To the extent that it is possible to estimate, not very much.

The best available nationwide study (Lubitz and Prihoda 1984) found that in 1978 only 3 percent of Medicare-eligible decedents had reimbursements of $20,000 or more, and they accounted for 3.5 percent of total Medicare expenditures that year. This $20,000 or more per capita figure for the high cost of Medicare decedents would undoubtedly be much larger today because health-care costs have increased substantially in the ensuing years (U.S. House of Representatives 1989, 10).

Placing these findings in the context of a more recent year, the 3.5 percent of Medicare spent on high-cost decedents in 1978 would have yielded a total of $2.84 billion for 1987. To be sure, changing medical practices such as the introduction of high-cost technologies and low-cost hospice programs may have had the net effect of increasing or decreasing the percentage of Medicare spent on high-cost decedents since 1978. Even an increase of 1 or 2 percent, however, would not substantially change the general picture.

In the context of 1987, when national health-care expenditures were over $500 billion and Medicare expenditures were $81 billion, saving an estimated $2.84 billion seems negligible. If there is some sort of health-care-cost crisis in the United States, saving such an amount in itself would hardly make a dent in the overall situation. Nonetheless, some analysts and professionals may feel it is important to conserve such health-care resources that do not prove beneficial. Can it be done? Apparently not.

Even if our nation were firmly resolved, as a matter of public policy, to eliminate all wasteful and unnecessary health-care expenditures, and even if it was ethically palatable to do so, would it be possible to eliminate such "waste" by not treating Medicare patients who are likely to be expensive decedents? Only, apparently, if we are willing not to treat costly patients who will recover—to throw away those high-cost patients who would survive into the same "wastebasket" as costly decedents. The study by Lubitz and Prihoda (1984) found about the same numbers of survivors and decedents in the high-cost patient category and about the same amount of aggregate expenditures on them. Of 49,000 Medicare enrollees in the high-cost category, 25,000 survived and 24,000 died.

Prospective distinctions between high-cost survivors and decedents are usually problematic, especially in cases that are likely to involve high costs (Scitovsky 1984). In short, even for those who may feel that it was not worth it in 1987 to spend $2.84 billion—*or six-tenths of 1 percent of a national total of $500.3 billion*—on high-cost Medicare decedents, there is no practical way to operationalize a policy that would save such funds without deliberately cutting off successful treatment for an equal number of likely survivors as well.

Is More Health Care Rationing Necessary?

Much of the public discourse about health-care rationing has been explicitly undergirded by concerns about rising health-care costs. These concerns flared up in the 1980s as a "cost-containment" fever that shows no sign of subsiding. From 1980 to

1988 consumer health-care costs rose at an annual average rate of about 12 percent (U.S. House of Representatives 1989, 11). By 1987 the nation's annual health-care expenditure had exceeded $500 billion and was more than 11 percent of the gross national product (GNP) (Letsch, Levit, and Waldo 1988).

During the first three quarters of this century, the providers of health care, rather than those who paid for it, were largely able to control the prices and mechanisms for allocating health care resources (Starr 1983). However, at the outset of the 1980s the governmental and corporate entities that pay for an overwhelming proportion of American health care began attempting to limit their financial obligations (Thurow 1985). California, Massachusetts, and several other states enacted statutes—at the behest of insurance companies and large corporate employers—to curb hospital costs (Kinzer 1983). In 1983 the federal government limited Medicare reimbursements to hospitals by implementing a prospective payment system through which the size of payments were fixed in accordance with a "diagnosis-related group" (DRG) classification for each Medicare inpatient, rather than the length of hospital stay and the services received by the patient (Latta and Helbing 1988). By the end of the decade, executives of major corporations were breaking a long-standing taboo by announcing their support for the notion of national health insurance, as a means of cutting their firms' costs for employee health-insurance premiums, and redistributing the expense to taxpayers in general (e.g., Freudenheim 1989a, b).

Health Care Costs: How Much Is "Too Much"?

As this cost-containment milieu has developed, it has been accompanied by a chorus of opinions that we are spending "too much" of our national resources on health care (e.g., Lamm 1989a). Health-policy analysts who want us to curb our national health-care investment feel that larger health-care expenditures will have adverse consequences for American economic competitiveness, government budgets, and a variety of other social and economic responsibilities (e.g., Mechanic 1985).

Although health care cost containment is a reasonable political objective, it is not supported by any "iron law" of economics. Advocates of cost containment warn, rhetorically, that we cannot sustain increasing health care expenditures. But no one has yet articulated the inevitable dire consequences that would ensue for our nation if such costs continue to increase and if we exceed a specific percentage of GNP in our annual health-care expenditures. It is not at all clear, for instance that escalating health-care costs hurt the global position of the American economy. Despite present laments about the economic decline of the United States, our share of the world's GNP has held constant at 23 percent since the mid-1970s (Nye 1990), a period during which our health care costs increased annually at a rate ranging from two to three times our general rate of inflation.

An arbitrary but commonly used, frame of reference for arguing that the United States spends too much is comparison with other countries. We spend far more of our national wealth on health care than does any other developed nation. For instance, the proportion of U.S. resources allocated to health expenditures is 74 percent greater than that of the United Kingdom and 27 percent greater than that of Canada (Waldo, Levit, and Lazenby 1986).

On the other hand, Americans might not be satisfied with the levels of care generally available in these other nations. The quality of health care provided by the smaller proportions of national wealth spent on it in the United Kingdom, Canada, and elsewhere has been increasingly questioned by both indigenous and foreign observers of those systems (for the United Kingdom, see Aaron and Schwartz, 1984; Grimes 1987; Smith 1989; for Canada, see Barber 1989; Iglehart 1986; Walker 1989). British Prime Minister Margaret Thatcher proposed a reorganization of the British health system in response to such complaints about quality of care, but her proposal was premised on the level of expenditures that currently existed. Reportedly, the British Medical Association viewed the new plan as one that would engender a competition of "the health of the patient versus the cost of the treatment" (Whitney 1989).

As such comparisons indicate, there are no universal or scientific criteria for determining what is too much for a nation to spend on health care. The proportion of our national wealth that we can or ought to invest in health care (as opposed to other purposes) is not a technical issue but, of course, a value judgment that will be resolved through politics.

Costs and Scarcity Are Separate Issues

Regardless of competing value judgments as to the appropriate amount of GNP to spend on health care, cost containment appears to have become an end in itself in the United States. However, anxieties that excalating costs must lead to acute health-care rationing on a scale far greater than ever before, through public policy, may be unfounded. As Moody (1991) has observed, situations that justify "rationing," as opposed to allocation, are characterized by both a *scarcity* of supply and a widely shared sense of *crisis*.

Although there may be a sense of crisis about costs, health-care resources are actually expanding (Gornick et al. 1985; Letsch, Levit, and Ward 1988). The concern about containing health care costs has generated changes in the sources and mechanisms of payment for health care. One consequence of these changes is fierce competition among health-care providers. For providers who are winning in the competition, resources are plentiful. For the providers who are losing, particularly those primarily dependent on public insurance reimbursement, resources are scarce; and it is for their customers—patients dependent upon public insurance—and for the 37 million Americans without any insurance that resources are scarce and for whom informal rationing takes place.

If we can put aside our preoccupation with Medicare and its age-category principle, perhaps we will see that it is the capacity of patients to pay for charges—out of pocket or through third-party reimbursements—that has a great deal to do with the allocation of care. It is not a scarcity of health resources that poses a problem, but an unwillingness and/or incapacity of our political system to allocate them through some means other than economic and social stratification.

"Justice between rich and poor" may be a better metaphor than "justice between age groups" for the dilemmas of equity we might confront in the allocation or rationing of acute care. With the issue framed on this axis, the specific policy options we might generate and consider would be rather different from those we are contemplating now, and would more likely reflect the true trade-offs that do take place in the allocation of health-care resources.

As many qualified observers have pointed out (e.g., Schwartz and Aaron 1985), there is no inherent reason why 11, 12, 13 percent, or more of our GNP cannot be expended on health care. After two decades of socialization to the rights or entitlements provided through Medicare and Medicaid, it could well be that Americans—reassured that they are not paying for waste and excess profits—will not want to impose a ceiling on health-care expenditures and/or will not be willing to acquiesce in rationing practices that such a ceiling might impose (Aaron and Schwartz 1984). After all, as Abel-Smith (1985) has noted, among the industrialized nations in the world, the United States is "the odd man out" in its approaches to the regulation, delivery mechanisms, and financing of health care.

Walzer (1983) has argued that notions of justice throughout history have varied not only among cultures and political systems, but also among distinct spheres of activities and relationships within any given culture or political system. Nothing requires us to devise or accept separate spheres of justice within the health-care arena, either spheres separating age groups or spheres separating the relatively wealthy from the relatively poor. We may prefer to delineate the health-care arena as a single sphere of justice within which no such distinctions are made. Uwe Reinhardt (1986, 29) explains the choice very clearly: "If the American public, and the politicians who represent it, really cared about the nation's indigent, they ought to be able to exploit the emerging surplus of health care resources to the advantage of the poor."

CONCLUSION

This discussion of perspectives on old-age-based health-care rationing represents but one example of how contemporary dilemmas can be perceived in terms that express neither compassionate and dispassionate ageism nor conflicts between age groups. Whether such perceptions are more accurate or even more propitious ways to frame issues is certainly open to debate. They have been offered to illustrate that preoccupations with stereotypes, conventional wisdom, and existing policies and institutional arrangements can divert us from seeking alternative ways to anticipate and deal with the implications of population aging and other societal challenges.

Even as we generate valuable knowledge about the oldest-old population to inform our choices for the future, it is especially important that we examine the principles of equity implicit in the choices that we frame. If we allow our thinking to be confined by an agenda of intergenerational equity issues, and by our current policies and the principles that they have come to reflect, we may very well find ourselves engaged in policy debates on issues of age-group conflict that are far worse than those we have experienced to date: trading off the value of one human life against another as a matter of official policy.

Ultimately, the principles of equity that we use to describe our choices will be far more important than data and policy analyses for shaping the quality of life and the nature of justice in our society, and for the oldest old among us.

REFERENCES

Aaron, H.J., and W.B. Schwartz. 1984. *The Painful Prescription: Rationing Hospital Care.* Washington: Brookings Institution.

Abel-Smith, B. 1985. Who Is the Odd Man Out?: The Experience of Western Europe in Containing the Costs of Health Care. *Milbank Memorial Fund Quarterly/Health and Society* 63(1):1–17.

Achenbaum, W.A. 1983. *Shades of Gray: Old Age, American Values, and Federal Policies Since 1920.* Boston: Little, Brown.

Allport, G.W. 1959. *ABC's of Scapegoating.* New York: Anti-Defamation League of B'nai B'rith.

Barber, J. 1989. Sick to Death: Caught Between Rising Costs and More Restraints, Hospitals Are Cutting Services. *Maclean's* (February 13):32–35.

Battin, M.P. 1987. Choosing the Time to Die: The Ethics and Economics of Suicide in Old Age. In *Ethical Dimensions of Geriatric Care,* ed. S. Spicker, 161–189. Dordrect, Holland: Reidel.

Binstock, R.H. 1972. Interest-group Liberalism and the Politics of Aging. *The Gerontologist* 12:265–80.

———. 1983. The Aged as Scapegoat. *The Gerontologist* 23:136–43.

———. 1985. The Oldest-Old: A Fresh Perspective or Compassionate Ageism Revisited? *Milbank Memorial Fund Quarterly/Health and Society* 63:420–51.

Binstock, R.H., and J. Kahana. 1988. An Essay on *Setting Limits: Medical Goals in an Aging Society,* by D. Callahan. *The Gerontologist* 28:424–26.

Blank, R.H. 1988. *Rationing Medicine.* New York: Columbia University Press.

Brody, S.J. 1984–1985. Merging Rehabilitation and Aging Policies and Programs: Past, Present, and Future. *Rehabilitation World* 8(4):6–9, 42–44.

Callahan, D. 1987. *Setting Limits: Medical Goals in an Aging Society.* New York: Simon and Schuster.

———. 1990. *What Kind of Life: The Limits of Medical Progress.* New York: Simon and Schuster.

Campion, F.D. 1984. *The AMA and U.S. Health Policy Since 1940.* Chicago: Chicago Review Press.

Carballo, M. 1981. Extra Votes for Parents? *The Boston Globe* (December 17):35.

Cassel, C.K., and B.L. Neugarten. 1991. The Goals of Medicine in an Aging Society. In *Too Old for Health Care?: Controversies in Medicine, Law, Economics, and Ethics,* eds. R.H. Binstock and S.G. Post, 75–91. Baltimore, Md: Johns Hopkins University Press.

Chakravarty, S.N., and K. Weisman. 1988. Consuming Our Children? *Forbes* 142:222–32.

Chomitz, K.M. 1987. Demographic Influences on Local Public Education Expenditures: A Review of Econometric Evidence. In *Demographic Change and the Well-Being of Children and the Elderly,* eds. Committee on Population, Commission on Behavioral and Social Sciences Education, National Research Council, 45–53. Washington: National Academy Press.

Churchill, L.R. 1987. *Rationing Health Care in America: Perceptions and Principles of Justice.* Notre Dame, Ind.: University of Notre Dame Press.

Clark, R.L. 1990. Income Maintenance Policies in the United States. In *Handbook of Aging and the Social Sciences,* 3rd ed., eds. R.H. Binstock and L.K. George, 382–97. San Diego, Calif.: Academic Press.

Cohen, W.J. 1985a. Securing Social Security. *New Leader* 66:5–8.

———. 1985b. Reflections on the Enactment of Medicare and Medicaid. *Health Care Financing Review* (Annual Supplement):3–11.

Committee on an Aging Society, Institute of Medicine and National Research Council. 1986. *America's Aging: Productive Roles in an Older Society.* Washington: National Academy Press.

Crown, W. 1985. Some Thoughts on Reformulating the Dependency Ratio. *The Gerontologist* 25:166–71.

Daniels, N. 1983. Justice between Age Groups: Am I My Parents' Keeper? *Milbank Memorial Fund Quarterly/Health and Society* 61(3):489–522.

———. 1988. *Am I My Parents' Keeper? An Essay On Justice Between the Young and the Old.* New York: Oxford University Press.

David, S.I. 1985. *With Dignity, the Search For Medicare and Medicaid.* Westport, Conn.: Greenwood Press.

Derthick, M. 1979. *Policymaking For Social Security.* Washington: Brookings Institution.

Estes, C.L. 1979. *The Aging Enterprise.* San Francisco: Jossey-Bass.

———. 1983. Social Security: The Social Construction of a Crisis. *Milbank Memorial Fund Quarterly/Health and Society,* 61:445–61.

Evans, R.W. 1991. Advanced Medical Technology and Elderly People. In *Too Old for Health Care? Controversies in Medicine, Law, Economics, and Ethics,* eds. R.H. Binstock and S.G. Post, 44–74. Baltimore, Md.: Johns Hopkins University Press.

Evans, R.W., D.L. Manninen, L.P. Garrison, Jr., and L.G. Hart. 1987. *Special Report: Findings from the National Kidney Dialysis and Kidney Transplantation Study.* Baltimore, Md.: Health Care Financing Administration (HCFA pub. no. 03230).

Evans, R.W., D.L. Manninen, and C. Thompson. 1989. *A Cost and Outcome Analysis of Kidney Transplantation: The Implications of Initial Immunosuppressive Protocol and Diabetes.* Seattle, Wash.: Battelle Human Affairs Research Centers.

Fairlie, H. 1988. Talkin' 'bout My Generation. *The New Republic* 198(13):19–22.

Findlay, S. 1989. The Short Life of Catastrophic Care. *U.S. News and World Report* (December 11):72–73.

Ford Foundation. Project on Social Welfare and the American Future, Executive Panel. 1989. *The Common Good: Social Welfare and the American Future.* New York: Ford Foundation.

Freudenheim, M. 1989a. A Health-Care Taboo Is Broken. *The New York Times* (May 8):23.

———. 1989b. Calling for a Bigger U.S. Health Role. *The New York Times* (May 30):29.

Garland, S.B. 1989. Health Care for All or an Excuse for Cutbacks? *Business Week* (June 26):68.

Generational Journal 1989. Untitled statement of organizational purpose and tax status of Americans for Generational Equity. 1(4):104.

Gibbs, N.R. 1988. Grays on the Go. *Time,* 131(8):66–75.

Gillick, M. 1988. Limiting Medical Care: Physicians' Beliefs, Physicians' Behavior. *Journal of the American Geriatric Society* 36:747–52.

Gornick, M., J.N. Greenberg, P.W. Eggers, and A. Dobson. 1985. Twenty Years of Medicare and Medicaid: Covered Populations, Use of Benefits, and Program Expenditures. *Health Care Financing Review* (Suppl.):13–59.

Graebner, W. 1980. *A History of Retirement: The Meanings and Functions of an American Institution, 1885–1978.* New Haven, Conn.: Yale University Press.

Grimes, D.D. 1987. Rationing Health Care. *Lancet* 1 (8533):615–16.

Gross, J. 1989. What Medical Care the Poor Can Have: Lists Are Drawn Up. *The New York Times* (March 27):1.

Habib, J. 1990. The Economy and the Aged. In *Handbook of Aging and the Social Sciences,* 3rd ed., eds. R.H. Binstock and L.K. George, 328–45. San Diego, Calif.: Academic Press.

Harris, R. 1966. *A Sacred Trust.* New York: American Library.

Health Care Financing Administration. 1987. National Health Expenditures, 1986–2000. *Health Care Financing Review* 8(4):1–36.

Heclo, H. 1984. The Political Foundations of Anti-Poverty Policy. Paper prepared for the IRP conference, *Poverty and Policy: Retrospect and Prospects,* 6–8. Madison, Wis.: Institute for Research on Poverty.

————. 1988. Generational Politics. In *The Vulnerable,* eds. J.L. Palmer, T. Smeeding, and B.B. Torrey, 381–411. Washington: Urban Institute Press.

Hiatt, H.H. 1987. *America's Health in the Balance: Choice or Change?* New York: Harper & Row.

Hing, E. 1987. *Use of Nursing Homes by the Elderly: Preliminary Data from the 1985 National Nursing Home Survey, Advance Data No. 135.* Hyattsville, Md.: National Center for Health Statistics, May 14.

Holtzman, A. 1963. *The Townsend Movement: A Political Study.* New York: Bookman.

Hudson, R.B. 1978. The "Graying" of the Federal Budget and Its Consequences for Old Age Policy. *The Gerontologist* 18:428–40.

Hudson, R.B., and J. Strate. 1985. Aging and Political Systems. In *Handbook of Aging and the Social Sciences,* 2nd ed., eds. R.H. Binstock and E. Shanas, 554–85. New York: Van Nostrand Reinhold.

Iglehart, J.K. 1986. Canada's Health Care System. *New England Journal of Medicine* 313:202–8, 778–84, 1623–28.

Iglehart, J.K. 1989. Medicare's New Benefits: "Catastrophic" Health Insurance. *New England Journal of Medicine* 320:329–36.

Jacobs, B. 1990. Aging in Politics. In *Handbook of Aging and the Social Sciences,* 3rd ed., eds. R.H. Binstock and L.K. George, 349–61. San Diego, Calif.: Academic Press.

Jahnigen, D.W., and R.H. Binstock. 1991. Economic and Clinical Realities: Health Care for Elderly People. In *Too Old for Health Care?: Controversies in Medicine, Law, Economics and Ethics,* eds. R.H. Binstock and S.G. Post, 13–43. Baltimore, Md.: Johns Hopkins University Press.

Kalish, R.A. 1979. The New Ageism and the Failure Models: A Polemic. *The Gerontologist* 19:398–407.

Kieffer, J.A. 1986. The Older Volunteer Resource. In *America's Aging: Productive Roles in an Older Society,* eds. Committee on an Aging Society, Institute of Medicine and National Research Council, 51–72. Washington: National Academy Press.

Kingson, E.R., B.A. Hirshorn, and J.M. Cornman. 1986. *Ties That Bind: The Interdependence of Generations.* Washington: Seven Locks Press.

Kinzer, D.M. 1983. Massachusetts and California—Two Kinds of Cost Control. *New England Journal of Medicine* 308:838–41.

Kleiman, D. 1985. Death and the Court. *The New York Times* (January 19):9.

Koenig, R. 1986. As Liver Transplants Grow More Common, Ethical Issues Multiply: By Operating on the Elderly, Thomas Starzl Steps Up Patient Selection Debate. *Wall Street Journal* (October 14):1.

Kutza, E.A. 1981. *The Benefits of Old Age.* Chicago: University of Chicago Press.

La Puma, J., M. Silverstein, C. Stocking, D. Roland, and M. Siegler. 1988. Life-Sustaining Treatment: A Prospective Study of Patients with DNR Orders in a Teaching Hospital. *Archives of Internal Medicine* 148:2193–98.

Lamm, R.D. 1987. A Debate: Medicare in 2020. *In Medicare Reform and the Baby Boom Generation,* edited proceedings of the second annual conference of Americans for Generational Equity, April 30–May 1, 77–88. Washington: Americans for Generational Equity.

————. 1989a. Columbus and Copernicus: New Wine in Old Wineskins. *Mount Sinai Journal of Medicine* 56(1):1–10.

————. 1989b. Saving a Few, Sacrificing Many—At Great Cost. *The New York Times* (August 8):23.

Latta, V.V., and C. Helbing. 1988. Medicare: Short-Stay Hospital Services, by Leading Diagnosis-Related-Groups, 1983–1985. *Health Care Financing Review* 10(2):79–107.

Letsch, S.W., K.R. Levit, and R. Waldo. 1988. National Health Expenditures, 1987. *Health Care Financing Review* 10(2):109–22.

Light, P. 1985. *Artful Work: The Politics of Social Security Reform.* New York: Random House.

Longman, P. 1987. *Born to Pay: The New Politics of Aging in America.* Boston: Houghton Mifflin.

———. 1989. Elderly, Affluent—and Selfish. *The New York Times* (October 10):27.

Lubitz, J., and R. Prihoda. 1984. The Use and Costs of Medicare Services in the Last Two Years of Life. *Health Care Financing Review* 5(3):117–31.

Marmor, T.R. 1970. *The Politics of Medicare.* London: Routledge & Kegan Paul.

Mechanic, D. 1985. Cost Containment and the Quality of Medical Care: Rationing Strategies in an Era of Constrained Resources. *Milbank Memorial Fund Quarterly/Health and Society* 63:453–57.

Miles, S., and Ryder, M. 1985. Limited-Treatment Policies in Long-Term Care Facilities. *Journal of the American Geriatric Society* 33:707.

Moody, H.R. 1991. Allocation, Yes: Age-Based Rationing, No. In *Too Old For Health Care?: Controversies in Medicine, Law, Economics, and Ethics,* eds. R.H. Binstock and S.G. Post, 180–203. Baltimore, Md.: Johns Hopkins University Press.

Myles, J.F. 1983. Conflict, Crisis, and the Future of Old Age Security. *Milbank Memorial Fund Quarterly/Health and Society* 61:462–72.

National Center for Health Statistics. 1987. Utilization of Short-Stay Hospitals, United States, 1985, Annual Summary. *Vital and Health Statistics,* series 13, no. 91. Washington: U.S. Department of Health and Human Services.

Neugarten, B.L. 1974. Age Groups in American Society and the Rise of the Young Old. *Annals of the American Academy of Political and Social Science* 415:187–98.

———. 1982. *Age or Need?.* Beverly Hills, Calif.: Sage.

Neugarten, B.L., and D.A. Neugarten. 1986. Age in the Aging Society. *Daedalus* 115(1):31–49.

New York Times/CBS News Poll. 1980. How Different Groups Voted for President. *The New York Times* (November 9):28.

———. 1982. Party Choices of Voters, 1982 vs. 1978. *The New York Times* (November 8):B11.

———. 1984. Portrait of the Electorate. *The New York Times* (November 8):A19.

———. 1986. Portrait of the Electorate: The Vote for House of Representatives. *The New York Times* (November 6):15Y.

———. 1988. Portrait of the Electorate. *The New York Times* (November 10):18Y.

Nye, J.S., Jr. 1990. The Misleading Metaphor of Decline. *The Atlantic Monthly* 265:86–94.

Peterson, P. 1987. The Morning After. *The Atlantic* 260(4):43–69.

Post, S.G. 1991. Justice and the Elderly: Judeo-Christian Perspectives. In *Too Old For Health Care?: Controversies in Medicine, Law, Economics, and Ethics,* eds. R.H. Binstock and S.G. Post, 120–37. Baltimore, Md.: Johns Hopkins University Press.

Pratt, H.J. 1976. *The Gray Lobby.* Chicago: University of Chicago Press.

Preston, S.H. 1984. Children and the Elderly in the U.S. *Scientific American* 251(6):44–49.

Quadagno, J. 1989. Generational Equity and the Politics of the Welfare State. *Politics and Society* 17(3):353–76.

Quinn, J.F., and R.V. Burkhauser. 1990. Work and Retirement. In *Handbook of Aging and the Social Sciences,* 3rd ed., eds. R.H. Binstock and L.K. George, 307–27. San Diego, Calif.: Academic Press.

Reinhardt, U. 1986. Letter of June 9, 1986, to Arnold S. Relman. *Health Affairs* 5(2):28–31.

Roos, N.P., P. Montgomery, and L.L. Roos. 1987. Health Care Utilization in the Years Prior to Death. *Milbank Memorial Fund Quarterly/Health and Society* 65:231–54.

Samuelson, R.J. 1978. Aging America: Who Will Shoulder the Growing Burden? *National Journal* 10:1712–17.

Schneider, E.L., and J.M. Guralnik. 1990. The Aging of America: Impact on Health Care Costs. *Journal of the American Medical Association* 263:2335–46.

Schulte J. 1983. Terminal Patients Deplete Medicare, Greenspan Says. *Dallas Morning News* (April 26):1.

Schulz, J.H. 1988. *The Economics of Aging,* 4th ed. Dover, Mass.: Auburn House.

Schwartz, D., and P. Reilly. 1986. The Choice Not to be Resuscitated. *Journal of the American Geriatric Society* 34:807–11.

Schwartz, W.B., and H.J. Aaron. 1985. Health Care Costs: The Social Tradeoffs. *Issues in Science and Technology* 1(2):39–46.

Scitovsky, A.A. 1984. "The High Cost of Dying": What Do the Data Show? *Milbank Memorial Fund Quarterly/Health and Society* 62:591–608.

———. 1988. Medical Care in the Last Twelve Months of Life: The Relation between Age, Functional Status, and Medical Care Expenditures. *Milbank Memorial Fund Quarterly/Health and Society* 66:640–60.

Simon, H.A. 1985. Human Nature in Politics: The Dialogue of Psychology with Political Science. *American Political Science Review* 79:293–304.

Slater, W. 1984. Latest Lamm Remark Angers the Elderly. *Arizona Daily Star* (March 29):1.

Smeeding, T.M. 1990. Economic Status of the Elderly. In *Handbook of Aging and the Social Sciences,* 3rd ed., eds. R.H. Binstock and L.K. George, 362–81. San Diego, Calif.: Academic Press.

Smeeding, T.M., M.P. Battin, L.P. Francis, and B.M. Landesman, eds. 1987. *Should Medical Care Be Rationed by Age?* Totowa, N.J.: Rowman & Littlefield.

Smith, T. 1989. BMA rejects NHS Review But . . . Doctors Must Develop Coherent Alternative. *British Medical Journal* 298:1405–6.

Starr, P. 1983. *The Social Transformation of American Medicine.* New York: Basic Books.

Stewart, D.J. 1970. Disfranchise the Old: The Lesson of California. *The New Republic* 163(8–9):20–22.

Thurow, L.C. 1985. Medicine versus Economics. *New England Journal of Medicine* 313:611–14.

Tolchin, M. 1988. New Health Insurance Plan Provokes Outcry Over Costs. *The New York Times* (November 2):1.

———. 1989a. House Acts to Kill '88 Medicare Plan of Extra Benefits. *The New York Times* (October 5):1.

———. 1989b. Lawmakers Tell the Elderly: "Next Year" on Health Care. *The New York Times* (November 23):10Y.

Torrey, B.B. 1982. Guns vs. Canes: The Fiscal Implications of an Aging Population. *American Economics Association Papers and Proceedings* 72:309–13.

U.S. Congress. Office of Technology Assessment. 1987. *Life-Sustaining Technologies and the Elderly.* Washington.

U.S. House of Representatives. Select Committee on Aging. 1989. *Health Care Costs For America's Elderly, 1977–88.* Washington.

———. 1988. *Developments In Aging: 1987—Volume I.* Washington.

Veatch, R. 1988. Justice and the Economics of Terminal Illness. *Hastings Center Report* 18(4):34–40.

Waldo, D., K. Levit, and H. Lazenby. 1986. National Health Expenditures, 1985. *Health Care Financing Review* 8(1):1–21.

Walker, M.A. 1989. From Canada: A Different Viewpoint. *Health Marketing Quarterly* (First Quarter):11–13.

Walzer, M. 1983. *Spheres of Justice*. New York: Basic Books.

Whitney, C.R. 1989. Thatcher's New Health Plan: An Outcry Rises on All Sides. *The New York Times* (June 26):1.

Williams. T.F. (Ed.) 1984. *Rehabilitation and the Aging*. New York: Raven Press.

Wisensale, S.M. 1988. Generational Equity and Intergenerational Policies. *The Gerontologist* 28:773–78.

Youngner, S., W. Lewandowski, D. McClish, B. Juknialis, C. Coulton, and E. Bartlett. 1985. Do Not Resuscitate Orders: Incidence and Implications in a Medical Intensive Care Unit. *Journal of the American Medical Association* 253:54–57.

Author Index

Italic numbers refer to chapter references.

Subject Index

familial-aged, 28
flaws in common usage of, 403
increasing, 403–4
Developed countries, total population and
percentage in elderly age categories
(1965–2025), 60–63
Developing countries, total population and
percentage in elderly age categories
(1965–2025), 61, 63
Diabetes, 76, 194
age-specific conditional probabilities of
having, 222–23
underlying cause (UC) and total mention
(TM) mortality rates for, 167, 169,
170–73
Diagnosis related groups (DRGs), 91, 211,
409
Differential tolerance of threshold
hypothesis, 237
Digestive tract, diseases of, 186–87, 191–92
Disability, 9–11, 218–32
epidemiology of, 268–82
cognitive disability, 278–79
development of new sources of data,
268–79
physical disability, 271–74
vision and hearing problems, 274–78
gender and prevalence of, 219, 268–82
health service use and, 232–34
institutional population, 229–32
in life-table models, 218–20
morbidity and, 220–21
prevalence of selected chronic diseases
and of condition-related, 209, 210
projections of, in community, 221–29
reductions in rate of, 11
self-reported, 347
"turnover" of disabled persons, 9–10
Diseases
chronic, 165, 209–11
major transition from infectious to chronic
degenerative (1960–1980), 75
See also Death, causes of; *specific
diseases*
Divorced oldest old, 70
Duhrenberger, David, 398
Duke Longitudinal Study of Aging, 212,
214–15, 216, 226
Dying, costs of, 384

Early Breast Cancer Trialists' Collaborative
Group, 118
Eastern Europe, total population and
percentage in elderly age categories
(1965–2025), 61, 63

Economic resources of oldest old, 359–77
assets, 367–69, 372, 388–90
consumer expenditures and, 372–74
impact of events of youth on eventual, 48
income. *See* Income
noncash benefits, 369–70, 371
policy questions regarding, 359–60
tax payments and, 370–72
Educational attainment, 41–43, 50–54
Alzheimer's disease prevalence and, 287,
288, 290, 294–95
maintenance of robustness and, 348
mortality differentials by, 51–54
of older blacks, 325
of oldest-old persons living in institutions,
33
projected distribution of, among oldest
old, 51, 52
Efficacy and effectiveness of therapeutic
interventions, 349
Elderly, oldest old as percentage of all the,
66–67
in U.S., 58–59, 66, 67
Eligibility for Medicaid, "spending down"
to, 374
Embarrassment of the elderly, gaining access
and, 124–25
Emotional burden of interviews, 129–31
Emotional responses, problem of provoking,
126
Emphysema, 222–23
Employer pensions, 80–81
Endorsement, data collection and, 142–43
Endowments among classes, shifting
distribution of innate, 53–54
England. *See* United Kingdom
Environment, social. *See* Social environment
EPESE. *See* Established Populations for
Epidemiological Studies of the
Elderly (EPESE) program
Epidemiological Study of Heart Disease in
Framingham, Massachusetts, 272
"Epidemiological transition," theory of, 244
Equity, home, 368, 369
Equity, intergenerational. *See*
Intergenerational equity
Error, sources of
proxy reporters as, 146
in surveys of the elderly, 135–39
Eskimo oldest old, 27, 39, 40
Established Populations for Epidemiological
Studies of the Elderly (EPESE)
program, 89–90, 93, 111, 115, 268–
79
Alzheimer's disease study, 285, 286–96
cognitive disability in, 278–79